PSYCHOLOGY AND WORK

Psychology and Work is a new textbook for introductory Industrial and Organizational (I/O) Psychology classes. Written by award-winning I/O professors with expertise in I/O Psychology and teaching this course, the book is organized into three main sections. It first includes an overview of the history of I/O Psychology and a chapter on research methods, subsequently covers the core principles of Industrial Psychology, and then discusses the key areas of Organizational Psychology.

The book contains numerous features that highlight key concepts and their relevance to students:

- Learning goals direct students to the main objectives of each chapter
- What Does This Mean for You? and Workplace Application boxes address the implications of the material for students
- Case studies with accompanying questions illustrate how concepts are relevant in real-world practice
- Reading lists and Your Turn... questions provide further discussion
- Keywords defined in the margins help students grasp important concepts
- Sections discussing global and current issues give students a sense of what's happening in the I/O psychology field

The book also has extensive online resources such as interactive features, quizzes, PowerPoint slides, and an instructor's manual. Accompanied by a dynamic design and a strong set of pedagogical tools, *Psychology and Work* presents all-new content and relevant coverage for the I/O psychology course.

Donald M. Truxillo is Professor of Industrial/Organizational Psychology at Portland State University.

Talya N. Bauer is the Cameron Professor of Management and Affiliated Psychology Faculty Member at Portland State University.

Berrin Erdogan is Professor of Management and Affiliated Psychology Faculty Member at Portland State University.

PSYCHOLOGY AND WORK

Perspectives on Industrial and
Organizational Psychology

Donald M. Truxillo
Talya N. Bauer
Berrin Erdogan

Routledge
Taylor & Francis Group

NEW YORK AND LONDON

First published 2016
by Routledge
711 Third Avenue, New York, NY 10017

and by Routledge
27 Church Road, Hove, East Sussex BN3 2FA

Routledge is an imprint of the Taylor & Francis Group, an informa business

Library of Congress Cataloguing in Publication Data
Truxillo, Donald M.
Psychology and work : perspectives on industrial and organizational psychology /
Donald M. Truxillo, Talya N. Bauer, Berrin Erdogan.
    pages   cm
1. Psychology, Industrial.   2. Organizational behavior.   3. Organizational
sociology.   4. Work–Psychological aspects.   I. Bauer, Talya.   II. Erdogan, Berrin.
III. Title.
HF5548.8.T746   2015
158.7–dc23   2015012691

ISBN: 978-1-84872-507-2 (hbk)
ISBN: 978-1-84872-508-9 (pbk)
ISBN: 978-1-315-88204-8 (ebk)

Typeset in Whitney
by Out of House Publishing

For Chip
-DT

For Horst
-TB

For Emre
-BE

CONTENTS

PREFACE

We are proud to present this new I/O psychology textbook, *Psychology and Work: Perspectives on Industrial and Organizational Psychology*. This was definitely a labor of love: All three of us are dedicated teachers. And we are all passionate about the field of Industrial/Organizational (I/O) psychology, or psychology applied to the workplace. How could we not be? I/O psychology is devoted to the place where most adults spend the majority of their waking hours. We are especially excited about giving students their first exposure to this vibrant and growing discipline: According to the US Department of Labor Statistics, "I/O psychologist" is currently the fastest growing job in the US (http://www.bls.gov/emp/ep_table_103.htm).

We set out to create a book that would reflect our enthusiasm for the field as well as our love of both teaching and researching the many important issues involved in I/O psychology. We wanted to translate and share the best and most recent of I/O psychology's evidence-based knowledge for students so they would have the opportunity to become as excited and passionate about the importance and usefulness of I/O psychology as we are! Of course, we covered the primary areas of I/O psychology, giving students a broad survey of the course content. However, with over 60 years of combined teaching experience among the three of us, we also wanted to bring what we have seen work in the classroom to the forefront. We wanted to create a book that would be a great resource by being both engaging *and* informative for students. We also wanted to it to be a useful tool for instructors to bring the topic to life for students ranging from those who have little work experience to those with a great deal of it. In light of this, our book has a number of distinguishing features to make it useful and accessible for both students and instructors:

For Students

- A clear statement of learning goals at the beginning of each chapter.

After studying this chapter, you should be able to:
- describe the primary areas of research and practice in industrial and organizational (I/O) psychology
- describe the contexts and organizations in which I/O psychologists work, as well as the training that I/O psychologists receive
- list the primary professional organizations to which I/O psychologists belong
- describe historical eras that have affected I/O psychology (e.g., World War I era, Civil Rights era) and various phases in the history of I/O psychology

Learning goals for this chapter

- Clear workplace examples to illustrate key concepts throughout the book.

Workplace Application

The Use of Big Data in Organizational Research

The term "big data" has been getting a lot of attention in the popular press over the last few years. Although the definition of big data varies even among experts, it generally refers to the analysis of massive datasets that includes the data of thousands or even millions of people. In fact, these datasets are so big that they may be difficult to analyze using standard data analysis tools. Data sources might include the analysis of data within an organization, data across organizations (e.g., healthcare companies), or internet activity. The hope is that the analysis of big data will lead to better decisions, on a broad range of topics such as finance, consumer products, marketing, and healthcare.

- Colorful photos and graphics in every chapter.
- Review questions at the end of each chapter focused on the application of course material.

YOUR TURN ... WHAT DO YOU THiNK?

1. A friend of yours has decided to pursue a graduate degree in I/O psychology. What advice would you give him or her in considering graduate training and for making a strong application?

2. Consider the career that you are planning to pursue after you finish college or graduate school. How do you think that technological advances may change this job over your career? What kinds of research questions could I/O psychologists carry out to address these changes and to support workers through these changes?

3. A friend learns that you are taking a class on I/O psychology. She wonders if this is about counseling workers about their problems. Can you explain to her what I/O psychology is actually about?

4. Consider the different eras of I/O psychology and related fields that were described in the chapter (Scientific Management/World War I, Human Relations, World War II, Civil Rights). What do you think it would be like to be a low-level factory employee in each of these eras? Describe what your experience would be like in each of them.

5. Which of the current issues identified in the chapter do you think will have the greatest impact during your career?

- Contemporary case studies at the end of each chapter highlighting how I/O psychology theories and concepts matter to both organizations and employees including:
  - a diverse set of organizations including Amazon, the Consumer Financial Protection Bureau, Costco, Google, Nissan, Wegmans, and Yum! Brands
  - professions such as teaching and nursing
  - issues such as job satisfaction, test security, and training for supervisors to help them be more supportive.

CASE STUDY: The Job Satisfaction Survey

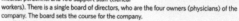

Enrique Mora was recently hired as the assistant HR manager of a mid-sized medical services company, Tabular Medical. Tabular has approximately 300 employees in 10 offices spread across New York and New Jersey. Their focus is family practice. There are approximately 80 physicians, with about 100 other medical personnel and 100 support staff (clerical workers). There is a single board of directors, who are the four owners (physicians) of the company. The board sets the course for the company.

Tabular has been quite successful in its 20 years of business, growing from a single medical practice to its present size. Throughout its history, Tabular has prided itself on having a strong team spirit and has attributed their success to each office maintaining its own independence and good collegiality.

- Interactive figures and tables (available on the companion website) to help show critical processes.

"See website for interactive material"

Interactive: Eras of industrial and organizational psychology.

1870–1900	1900–1920s	1927–1940	1941–1945	1946–1963	1964–present	2000–present
Early Years and World War I		Human Relations era begins	World War II and Post-War		Civil Rights era	High-Tech HR
Training of Munsterberg and Cattell by Wundt	1913: Munsterberg's Industrial Psychology text published in English	1927: Beginning of the Hawthorne Studies	1945: SIOP Founded as APA Div. 14	Post-WWII	1964: US Civil Rights Act	Beginning of online and high-tech delivery of HR functions
	1917: Army Alpha and Army Beta exam (Scott & Bingham) and *Journal of Applied Psychology* established by APA	Beginnings of organizational psychology			1978: *Uniform Guidelines on Employee Selection Procedures* (see Chapter 7)	
	1905-1920: Scientific Management				1990: Americans with Disabilities Act	
	1915: Lillian Gilbreth receives first I/O Ph.D. in US					

- Legal issues sections to demonstrate the intersection of I/O psychology with implications of law.
- The impact of cross-cultural and international issues on I/O psychology – critical in today's global economy.
- Discussions of current issues and controversies, particularly focused on the impact of the new technology and the dynamic nature of the workplace.

- "What does this mean for you?" sections at the end of each chapter that illustrate how chapter material can be applied to individual students in or entering the workplace.

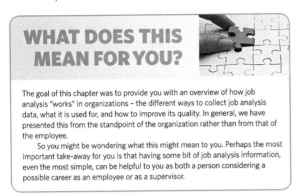

WHAT DOES THIS MEAN FOR YOU?

The goal of this chapter was to provide you with an overview of how job analysis "works" in organizations – the different ways to collect job analysis data, what it is used for, and how to improve its quality. In general, we have presented this from the standpoint of the organization rather than from that of the employee.

So you might be wondering what this might mean to you. Perhaps the most important take-away for you is that having some bit of job analysis information, even the most simple, can be helpful to you as both a person considering a possible career as an employee or as a supervisor.

- A range of format options, including hardcover, paperback, and electronic versions.

For Instructors

- Vibrant, well-designed PowerPoint slides for every chapter to accompany and support the textbook.
- Video clips, both embedded as links in the PowerPoint slides and available in the "Instructor Area" of our companion website.
- A truly high-quality test bank developed by Ph.D.s in I/O psychology which includes multiple-choice, true/false, and essay questions.
- Carefully designed instructional materials to help support pedagogy and class discussions.
- Interviews with leaders in I/O psychology explaining the application of course concepts, available on the companion website.

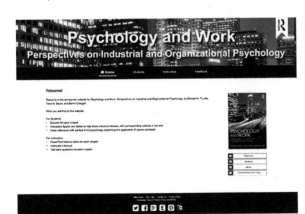

As you might guess, we are very proud of this textbook, and frankly, we've had a great time working on it. We hope that you will enjoy studying I/O psychology as much as we do!

Special Thanks

We thank Anne Duffy, who approached us with her vision to write an I/O psychology textbook which leveraged technology and embedded it into the book and its supporting materials. We also thank Darcy Bullock and Lauren Verity for their support in bringing this book to fruition.

Special thanks are given to David Caughlin and Frankie Guros for their fantastic work on the instructor materials, and Ty Marbut for his incredible job with the video and audio work on the companion website. We would not have such a fine result without you.

We thank our departments for the collegial environment they provide every day. We also thank our students at Portland State University for teaching us so much, and especially thank students Brittany Bradford, Grant Brady, Addison Brothers, and Didem Karpuzcu for their help and feedback on early drafts of chapters from the book. And finally, last but not least, we would like to thank the many anonymous reviewers who provided such helpful, insightful, and actionable feedback on earlier drafts of this text.

And last, but not least, we give special thanks to all the I/O psychologists who agreed to give their time to share their stories, insights, and expertise in our Video Interviews series. These can all be viewed on the Companion Website for this textbook and interviewees include a great wealth of experience in both the science and practice of I/O psychology.

- Tammy Allen
- Jose Cortina
- Alicia Grandey
- Steve Hunt
- Ruth Kanfer
- Eden King
- Kurt Kraiger
- Jeff McHenry
- Julie Olson-Buchanan
- Mark Poteet
- Ann Marie Ryan
- Eduardo Salas
- Evan Sinar
- Enrique Washington
- Brian Welle

ABOUT THE AUTHORS

Donald M. Truxillo (Ph.D., Louisiana State University) is Professor of Psychology at Portland State University. His research examines issues related to applicant reactions, age differences at work, and occupational health and safety. He has published over 70 peer-reviewed journal articles and book chapters. He served as Associate Editor for the *Journal of Management* and is currently an Associate Editor at *Work, Aging and Retirement*. His research has been supported by grants from the Society for Human Resource Management (SHRM) Foundation and the National Institute for Occupational Safety and Health (NIOSH). Since 2010 he has served on the Doctoral School Committee at the University of Trento, Italy. He has also been a Visiting Scholar at the University of Zurich (Switzerland), University of Valencia (Spain), ISCTE Business School (Lisbon, Portugal), and University of Palermo (Italy). He is a Fellow of the Society for Industrial and Organizational Psychology (SIOP), the American Psychological Association, the Association for Psychological Science, and the International Association for Applied Psychology. In 2013 he received a Fulbright Scholarship to work at the University of Trento (Italy). He is the recipient of SIOP's 2012 Distinguished Service Contributions Award. He currently serves as Treasurer for the Alliance for Organizational Psychology.

Talya N. Bauer (Ph.D., Purdue University) is the Cameron Professor of Management and Affiliated Professor of Psychology at Portland State University. She is an award-winning teacher and researcher and recipient of the SIOP Distinguished Teaching Award. She conducts research about relationships at work including recruitment, applicant reactions to selection, onboarding, and leadership. Her work has been supported by grants from both the SHRM and SIOP Foundations and has been published in research outlets such as the *Academy of Management Journal*, *Academy of Management Learning & Education*, *Journal of Applied Psychology*, *Journal of Management*, and *Personnel Psychology*. She has worked with dozens of government, Fortune 1000, and start-up organizations and has been a Visiting Scholar in France, Spain, and at Google Headquarters. She has served in elected positions including the HRM Executive Committee of the Academy of Management and as Member-at-Large for SIOP. She currently serves as an Associate Editor for the *Journal of Applied Psychology* (and is the former Editor of the *Journal of Management*). Her work has been discussed in the *New York Times, Business Week, Wall Street Journal, Harvard Business Review, USA Today,* and on NPR's *All Things Considered.* She is a Fellow of SIOP, the American Psychological Association, and the Association for Psychological Science.

Berrin Erdogan (Ph.D., University of Illinois at Chicago) is Express Employment Professionals Professor of Management and Affiliated Professor of Psychology at Portland State University. She conducts studies exploring factors that lead to engagement, well-being, effectiveness, and retention in the workplace, with a focus on manager–employee relationships and under-employment. These studies have taken place in a variety of industries including manufacturing, clothing and food retail, banking, healthcare, education, and information technology in the USA, Turkey, India, China, France, and Vietnam. Her work has appeared in journals including the *Academy of Management Journal, Journal of Applied Psychology, Journal of Management,* and *Personnel Psychology* and has been discussed in media outlets including the *New York Times, Harvard Business Review,* and the *Oregonian.* Dr. Erdogan has been a Visiting Scholar in Koç University (Istanbul, Turkey), the ALBA Business School at the American College of Greece, and the University of Valencia (Spain). In addition to serving on numerous editorial boards, she currently serves as an Associate Editor for *Personnel Psychology,* has served as an Associate Editor for the *European Journal of Work and Organizational Psychology,* and is the Co-Editor of the forthcoming *Oxford Handbook of Leader–Member Exchange.* She is a Fellow of SIOP.

PART I
BACKGROUND

Chapter 1

INDUSTRIAL AND ORGANIZATIONAL PSYCHOLOGY
The Profession and its History

I/O psychologists work to understand and influence how people behave in the workplace – the place where most adults in industrialized societies spend a significant part of their lives. This chapter will describe I/O psychology as a profession as well as its history.

After studying this chapter, you should be able to:

- describe the primary areas of research and practice in industrial and organizational (I/O) psychology

- describe the contexts and organizations in which I/O psychologists work, as well as the training that I/O psychologists receive

- list the primary professional organizations to which I/O psychologists belong

- describe historical eras that have affected I/O psychology (e.g., World War I era, Civil Rights era) and various phases in the history of I/O psychology

- identify key legal and global issues surrounding I/O psychology

- describe current issues and controversies around I/O psychology.

Learning goals for this chapter

Introduction

You are probably reading this book because you are taking a college course. One reason that many people attend college is to prepare for the workplace or for a specific profession. But consider this: Once a person begins their career, the workplace is where they will spend the greatest part of their waking hours until they retire. That being the case, wouldn't it be good to understand how people behave at work, what explains their work performance, how they feel about it, and how it can affect their nonwork lives?

I/O psychology:
A specialization in psychology focused on the application of psychological principles to understanding people in the workplace.

This is the goal of industrial and organizational psychology (I/O psychology). Specifically, **I/O psychology**, also called "the psychology of work," is a specialization focused on the application of psychological principles to understanding people in this important context, the workplace. As you will see in this book, this includes a range of issues, from how best to find a good fit between a person and a job through hiring procedures, how to train and evaluate employees, what motivates people at work, and what makes them happy with their work. It also examines how work affects people in their nonwork lives, and what employers can do to keep workers healthy, productive, and satisfied with their jobs. In short, I/O psychology involves the application of psychological principles to the workplace. In other words, if you want to understand what makes people happy and productive in their jobs, this is the book for you.

In this introductory chapter, we will examine the range of issues studied by I/O psychologists. We will also discuss I/O psychology as a profession both in the US and around the world, including the types of contexts where I/O psychologists typically work. We will discuss the historical factors that have shaped the field and the development of I/O psychology over the years. We conclude this chapter by describing some of the factors that drive I/O research and practice today.

The Major Areas of I/O Psychology: Industrial and Organizational

As you can tell by the name, industrial and organizational psychology involves two areas of study, historically separate but both focused on the psychology of work. Traditionally, *industrial psychology* in North America focuses on human resource procedures in the workplace which are guided by psychological principles. Traditionally, this includes the areas of job analysis, personnel selection, performance appraisal, and training. For example, I/O psychologists who study selection are interested in topics such as psychological testing and measurement, and those who study training are interested in the cognitive and motivational processes that can be used to enhance employee learning. *Organizational psychology* focuses more

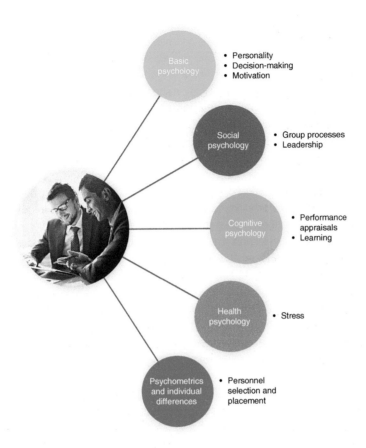

Figure 1.1 I/O psychology is a truly interdisciplinary field, with heavy influences from other branches of psychology.

on the "human side" of the worker, including topics such as work motivation, leadership, teams, job satisfaction, and work-life balance. In this sense, organizational psychology is more like the field of organizational behavior in business schools, but again, with a more decidedly psychological focus.

Industrial psychology and organizational psychology merged many decades ago, such that there is no longer a separate "industrial" or "organizational" psychology. This is because a dichotomy between the two areas is neither accurate nor useful. Both are concerned with the psychology of work, and any separation of the two is a bit artificial. But more importantly, concepts from both industrial and organizational psychology inform one another. For example, if you were trying to hire the best salesperson for your company, you could rely on the best research from "industrial" psychology in terms of how to conduct a structured interview (Chapter 6). But you would also want to consider what we know about motivation from "organizational" psychology in trying to predict what will motivate that salesperson to take the job offer and do a good job. In short, it's best to think of I/O psychology as the application of psychology to the workplace – keeping workers productive, engaged, happy, and healthy.

I/O psychology is a truly interdisciplinary branch of applied psychology. It blends theories, concepts, and principles borrowed from different parts of psychology, and you will recognize these influences throughout the book. For example, the discussion of motivation, personality traits, and personnel selection has been influenced by research in to psychometrics and individual differences, and decision-making has been influenced by the field of basic psychology. Our understanding of group processes, leadership, and communication shows the influence of social psychology. Cognitive psychology left its mark in topics ranging from training to performance appraisals, and health psychology has been influential in our understanding of stress and its impact on the worker. (See Figure 1.1.)

I/O psychologists use scientific principles to analyze and answer questions that have implications for worker health, well-being and effectiveness. Large organizations such as the FBI and NASA, and multinational corporations such as Google, Amazon, Nestlé, and Starbucks, as well as public sector, military, and not-for-profit and smaller organizations around the world, apply core I/O psychology principles to design employee selection, training, and promotion programs, while keeping employees safe and engaged at work.

It is important to remember that I/O psychology as a field aims to benefit both the organization *and* the worker. In other words, I/O psychologists are interested in helping organizations place the right worker into the right position, which would result in greater productivity and retention for the organization. But in addition, many I/O psychologists work to improve employees' work lives, including more positive job attitudes and health outcomes for employees.

I/O Psychology Professional Organizations

Society for Industrial and Organizational Psychology (SIOP): The primary professional organization to which most I/O psychologists in the US and Canada belong.

The primary professional organization to which most I/O psychologists in the US and Canada belong is the Society for Industrial and Organizational Psychology (SIOP) (http://www.siop.org/). SIOP was established in 1945 as Division 14 of the American Psychological Association (APA). As of 2014, SIOP had a total membership of approximately 8,288, of whom 43 percent were student affiliates. In addition, SIOP has over 400 international affiliates from outside of the US and Canada (L. Nader, personal communication, June 3, 2014). (See Figure 1.2.) Although SIOP is Division 14 of APA, many members of SIOP choose membership in the Association for Psychological Science (APS). SIOP works to promote the scientific study of I/O psychology to help both organizations and workers.

SIOP supports I/O psychologists in a number of ways, including through publications, its annual conference, and promotion and advocacy for the profession. SIOP publishes the professional journal, *The Industrial-Organizational Psychologist* (*TIP*), which keeps SIOP members up-to-date on current professional issues (e.g., employment laws), as well as a journal of current research and practice topics and controversies in the field, *Industrial and Organizational Psychology: Perspectives on Science and Practice.* SIOP's annual conference, which attracts upwards of 4,000 people each year, is considered one of the premier conferences to learn the latest

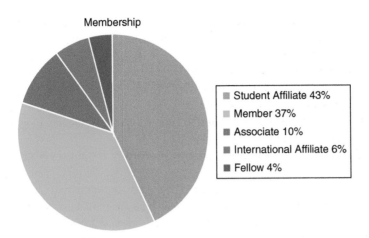

Membership

- ■ Student Affiliate 43%
- ■ Member 37%
- ■ Associate 10%
- ■ International Affiliate 6%
- ■ Fellow 4%

Figure 1.2 Membership breakdown of the Society for Industrial and Organizational Psychology (SIOP).

in what's happening in I/O psychology research and practice. In addition, SIOP promotes I/O psychology in several ways, such as by providing information and resources for undergraduates and graduate students interested in I/O psychology; and white papers that provide guidance to policy-makers and managers about the most up-to-date science on topics from hiring employees to helping with employee stress. In fact, all three of the authors of this book have written SIOP white papers (Bauer, McCarthy, Anderson, Truxillo, & Salgado, 2012; Searle, Erdogan, Peiró, & Klehe, 2014). Many of these resources are available on the SIOP web page. Further, SIOP also advocates for I/O psychology to increase the visibility and usefulness of our science to lawmakers and to the public at large. Students who are interested can join SIOP for a nominal fee.

In addition to SIOP, there are numerous local (city-level) I/O organizations within the US and Canada. (Table 1.1 presents a non-exhaustive list of these local I/O psychology organizations.) Many of these local organizations hold local meetings and have regular presentations to learn more about the most current science and practice in I/O. If you live in a community that has an I/O psychology organization, you can check out their activities to learn more about I/O.

In addition, there are many I/O-focused professional organizations around the world. In many parts of the world, such as Europe, the field is referred to as "work and organizational psychology". One of the largest I/O organizations is the European Association of Work and Organizational Psychology (EAWOP) (http://www.eawop.org/). EAWOP is made up of 25 organizations from different countries across Europe (e.g., Germany, Italy, the United Kingdom). As of 2015, EAWOP publishes two journals, the *European Journal of Work and Organizational Psychology* and *Organizational Psychology Review*. EAWOP's conference is held every two years in a different European country. Further, EAWOP promotes Small Group Meetings on specific research topics. Past topics included personnel selection, employment for workers with disabilities, and the aging workforce.

Further, there is Division 1 of the International Association for Applied Psychology (IAAP Div. 1, Work and Organizational Psychology), which publishes the journal *Applied Psychology: An International Review*. IAAP is one of the oldest professional associations for psychologists, dating back to 1920. Its conference (ICAP) is

Work and organizational psychology: Term used in many parts of the world, such as Europe, referring to the field of I/O psychology.

European Association of Work and Organizational Psychology (EAWOP): One of the largest I/O organizations, EAWOP consists of 25 constituent organizations from different European countries.

Table 1.1 Some local I/O organizations across the US

ASAP (Atlanta Society of Applied Psychology)
www.linkedin.com/groups/Atlanta-Society-Applied-Psychology-3430710/about

BAAP (Bay Area Applied Psychologists)
www.linkedin.com/groups?home=&gid=2523213

CIOP (Chicago I/O Psychologists, formerly GCAIOP)
www.ciop.net

DAIOP (Dallas Area I-O Psychologists)
www.linkedin.com/groups/DAIOP-Dallas-Area-Industrial-Organizational-2624489/about

ECAP (Erie Canal Applied Psychology Network; Upstate New York)
http://ecapnetwork.syr.edu/

GIOP (Gateway I/O Psychologists; St. Louis)
www.gatewayio.org

HAIOP (Houston Area Industrial and Organizational Psychologists)
www.haiop.org

HODN (Kansas City area)
www.supertoolbox.com/od/

KCAPS (Kansas City Applied Psychology Society)
http://kcaps.org

MAIOP (Michigan Association of I-O Psychologists)
www.maiop.org

METRO (Metropolitan New York Association for Applied Psychology)
www.MetroAppPsych.com/

MPPAW (Minnesota Professionals for Psychology Applied to Work)
www.mppaw.org

NCIOP (North Carolina Industrial and Organizational Psychologists)
http://iopsychology.chass.ncsu.edu/ncio/

NESAP (New England Society for Applied Psychology)
www.NESAP.org

NYSPA IOP Division (New York State Psychological Association's Industrial, Organizational & Personnel)
www.NYSPA.ORG

PIOPA (Portland Industrial & Organizational Psychology Association)
www.linkedin.com/groups/PIOPA-Portland-Industrial-Organizational-Psychology-3458218/about

PSAIOP (Puget Sound Association of I-O Psychologists)

SDIOP (San Diego Industrial and Organizational Professionals)
www.SDIOP.org

Table 1.2 Examples of professional organizations in I/O psychology around the world

Australian Psychological Society: Organisational Psychology

British Psychological Society: Division of Occupational Psychology

Canadian Society for Industrial and Organizational Psychology

Division of Industrial Psychology, Chinese Psychological Society

European Association of Work and Organizational Psychology

Global Organization for Humanitarian Work Psychology

International Association for Applied Psychology Division 1 (IAAP Div. 1, Work and Organizational Psychology)

Society for Industrial and Organisational Psychology of South Africa

Society for Industrial and Organizational Psychology (SIOP)

held every four years, and past conferences have taken place in Singapore, Greece, Australia, and France. Recently, SIOP, EAWOP, and IAAP agreed to form the Alliance for Organizational Psychology (AOP), to be a worldwide alliance to increase communication among I/O professional organizations and increase visibility of I/O psychology around the world (http://allianceorgpsych.org/).

In addition to organizations that are specifically focused on I/O psychology, many I/O psychologists, particularly academics, belong to the Academy of Management (AoM). AoM has a number of divisions that are of interest to I/O psychologists, such as the Organizational Behavior division, the Human Resources division, and the Gender and Diversity division. Another division of potential interest to I/O psychologists is the Research Methods group. AoM also publishes a number of journals that are important to I/O researchers such as *Academy of Management Journal* and *Academy of Management Review*. Table 1.2 shows a non-exhaustive list of I/O psychology professional organizations around the world.

Training in I/O Psychology

One of the issues that you may be wondering about is how I/O psychologists are trained. In other words, what sort of degree do they need? Important to all areas of I/O is the training in terms of an advanced degree. Generally, to be considered a psychologist, one has to obtain doctoral training (such as a Ph.D. or Psy.D.) in I/O psychology or a related field. Further, SIOP has created recommendations for the doctoral training of I/O psychologists. These include a total of 25 areas, ranging from selection, training, and job analysis, to motivation, leadership, and employee stress – all topics that you will see covered in later chapters in this book. Doctoral training in the US and Canada generally requires at least four years of training beyond the

Table 1.3 Some key areas of training in I/O psychology

History of I/O Psychology

Research Methods and Statistics

Individual Differences

Job Analysis and Compensation

Theories of Job Performance

Recruitment and Selection

Performance Appraisal and Feedback

Employee Training

Employee Motivation

Leadership in Organizations

Groups and Teams

Job Attitudes

Employee Stress, Safety, and Health

Organizational Theory and Organizational Development

Organizational Consulting

Ethical and Legal Issues

Source: Adapted from SIOP, 1999, 1994.

bachelor's degree, including coursework, research, a master's thesis and dissertation, and a challenging set of comprehensive exams. People who want to focus more on practice than on conducting research often earn a master's degree in I/O psychology, and SIOP has provided detailed guidelines for master's training as well (SIOP, 1994). A summary of SIOP's recommendations for training for Ph.D.s and masters is given in Table 1.3. Those with an undergraduate degree in psychology may work in fields such as Human Resources Management, but having at least a master's degree in I/O is necessary for I/O psychology jobs. According to the National Center for O*NET Development (2012), 48 percent of I/O psychologists held a doctoral degree, 47 percent held a master's degree, and 5 percent had completed post doctoral training.

Generally, good opportunities are available for I/O psychologists with either Ph.D. or master's degrees. In organizational settings and consulting firms in the US and Canada, the pay may be higher for I/O psychologists with doctoral degrees. However, this is a key difference between the US and Canada compared with European countries: In Europe, most people who plan to work in organizational settings acquire master's degrees, with the Ph.D. being purely a research degree and usually only pursued by people interested in university jobs.

So what does it take to get into a graduate program (Ph.D. or master's) in I/O psychology? In the US and Canada, there are several criteria that are used in admitting students to graduate programs. First, of course, is grade point average: If you're interested in graduate school, don't let your GPA slide (including your statistics and research methods classes). Second, most graduate programs require high scores on the Graduate Record Examinations (GRE). Our advice is never to wait until the last minute to take your GREs, and to do all you can to prepare for them, since they will be weighted heavily in graduate school admission. Third, especially for the Ph.D., get some research experience while pursuing your undergraduate degree. This is essential for most graduate programs, so that you have a "preview" of what the job of graduate student will be like. Fourth, consider that strong letters of reference, especially from professors able to speak to your specific academic and research skills, are essential. We have worked with many undergraduate students over the years who have gone on to have successful academic and industry-based careers after completing their Ph.D. degrees. Because they worked with us in our research lab, it was relatively easy to write strong letters of recommendations for them and their suitability for graduate school. Finally, remember to carefully check out the graduate programs that would be the best fit for you. Graduate school admissions are a competitive process – remember that I/O psychology is a growing profession – so be sure to apply for more than one school. A list of graduate I/O programs is available on the SIOP website (http://www.siop.org/ioprograms.aspx).

Other I/O professional organizations outside of the US and Canada also provide guidelines for the training of I/O psychologists. One of the challenges in Europe is assuring some consistency in the training of work psychologists across a wide range of European countries. To achieve this goal, the European Certificate in Psychology (or **EuroPsy**) was established to assure some comparability of training across countries and be sure that psychologists can practice work psychology in different European countries (EAWOP, 2014). EuroPsy is meant to provide a standard for evaluating the professional training of psychologists in Europe, providing a subspecialty in work and organizational psychology.

EuroPsy: The European Certificate of Psychology provides a standard for evaluating the professional training of psychologists in Europe, providing a subspecialty in work and organizational psychology.

The Scientist-Practitioner Model

One of the central tenets of I/O psychology as stipulated by SIOP's training guidelines (SIOP, 1999) is the **scientist-practitioner model**. This sounds like what it is, namely, that a strong I/O psychologist should be both a scientist engaged in research and an active practitioner. There are several implications of the scientist-practitioner approach. First, this means that I/O psychologists who focus primarily on research, such as on the development of theory and empirical research to test it, also consider the applicability to field settings – where it is going to be used. In other words, it is important for I/O researchers – for example, professors conducting research at universities – to consider the applicability of their research to work organizations. Second, many I/O psychologists focus primarily on the application of I/O principles, theory, and research in actual work organizations. In doing so, it is important for them to keep up with current research so that they can apply robust theories and practices that have been tested and shown to be valid. In other words, practitioners need to be sure that they are recommending organizational

Scientist-practitioner model: A central tenet of I/O psychology stating that a strong I/O psychologist will be both a scientist/researcher as well as a strong practitioner.

practices that are based in strong research. In addition, the scientist-practitioner model suggests that I/O psychologists engage in both the creation of I/O research and its application in organizational settings (SIOP, 1999).

The scientist-practitioner model challenges I/O psychologists to consider not only strong theories that have been rigorously tested with strong research, but the applicability of this research to work organizations. The scientist-practitioner model also challenges I/O psychologists to be sure that they make practice recommendations for organizations that are based on strong research findings. Of course, each I/O psychologist – whether working in an academic setting or working in an actual organization – focuses on science and practice to varying degrees, but the goal is to blend the two whenever possible. In short, the model suggests that to be effective researchers, practitioners, and teachers of I/O psychology, I/O psychologists need to understand how to do good research and the challenges of applying research to the workplace.

Where Do I/O Psychologists Work?

I/O psychologists work in a broad range of contexts. (See Figure 1.3.) Many I/O psychologists work in academic settings. Their typical responsibilities include conducting research, training graduate students, teaching undergraduate and graduate classes, and engaging in internal and external service work. In addition to Departments of Psychology, many I/O professors work in Business Schools, usually in Departments of Management. This is because many of the principles of I/O psychology are applied to business contexts. In fact, today over half of I/O psychology professors work in Schools of Business (L. Nader, personal communication, June 3, 2014). This is an issue that continues to provoke discussion among I/O psychologists about the direction of the field, the training of future I/O psychologists, and their identity (i.e., whether they are more psychology or business scholars, Aguinis, Bradley, & Brodersen, 2014).

But as you might expect, I/O psychology is very much an applied field of psychology, and a large number of I/O psychologists work in non-academic settings. In fact, it may surprise you to learn that as of February 2014, I/O psychology is the fastest-growing occupation in the US in terms of percentage growth according to the Bureau of Labor Statistics (2014). One can categorize these non-academic settings in which I/O psychologists work in the following way. First, some I/O psychology practitioners work for individual companies and corporations. Typically, they work in corporate headquarters (often as part of the human resources function), conducting research and applying I/O principles to improve organizational functioning. Examples of their work are wide-ranging in nature and include conducting employee surveys and analyzing the results, developing selection systems to hire the best talent, designing training programs to help workers maximize their productivity, and developing interventions to reduce employee stress. Second, government agencies, especially at the federal level in the US, employ I/O psychologists to support their human resource functions. Relatedly, military organizations have historically

Figure 1.3 Areas of practice for I/O psychologists.

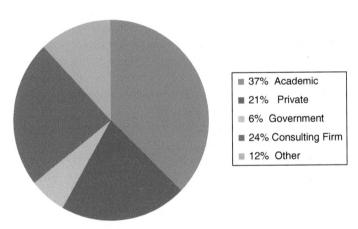

- ■ 37% Academic
- ■ 21% Private
- ■ 6% Government
- ■ 24% Consulting Firm
- ■ 12% Other

Figure 1.4 Employment sectors for SIOP membership by percentages. *Source:* L. Nader, personal communication, June 4, 2014.

employed I/O psychologists to select the best people, match them to the appropriate position, and train them most effectively.

However, if an organization does not have the resources of a large corporation it may not invest in hiring an I/O psychologist on a permanent basis. How do those organizations typically get the help of I/O psychologists? To address this issue, there has been a large growth in I/O consulting firms, either large firms of dozens of I/O psychologists, or much smaller firms of only a few individuals. They provide their services as needed to organizations that are unable to hire I/O psychologists on a full-time basis. For example, they might help a smaller company design a program for selecting employees, or give input on how to support employees in terms of their work-life balance. Or they might step in to help a larger corporation when a large project needs to be completed and a lot of I/O talent is needed at one time. Figure 1.4

shows the breakdown of the types of organizations where I/O psychologists work by percentages.

Subspecialties in I/O Psychology

Looking over SIOP's areas of training for I/O psychologists (again, see Table 1.3) is important for another reason: It is a good way for you to see the specific subspecialties that I/O psychologists are able to focus on. While most I/O psychologists have some training in all of these areas, they will tend to focus their research and practice on only a few of them. In other words, an I/O psychologist might focus primarily on selection and training issues, or on employee health and stress. To use your authors as examples, one of us focuses primarily on personnel selection, employee safety, and the aging workforce; another of us studies leadership and new employee socialization; and another of us studies leadership, performance appraisals, and new employee overqualification. But keep in mind that to be most effective, an I/O psychologist will not work only within his or her own narrow interests, but rather bring their broad knowledge of the field to bear on the research or practice issue they are working on. For example, an I/O psychologist who is focused on employee training could also use the research on motivation to design a training program that will motivate learners and thus increase the effectiveness of the program.

 "See website for interactive material"

Interactive: What I/O psychologists do.

Communicating I/O Psychology Research Findings: Journals and Conferences

We have spent a good bit of this chapter discussing the types of research I/O psychologists do, and arguing that workplace practices should be based on rigorous research. We will also spend a good bit of time in this book discussing I/O research findings. This raises the question of how I/O psychologists keep up with the latest research. Perhaps the most important way for them to do that is through I/O psychology journals. A list of some of the top journals in the field is shown in Table 1.4. The articles in these journals are "peer reviewed" – that is, other experts in I/O psychology review these articles for their rigor and their contribution to research and practice, so that the articles that appear in the journals are some of the best current science. Generally these journals either include articles focused on empirical research or on reviews that summarize the research.

Besides academic journals, I/O psychologists also present their research at professional conferences. These would include the annual SIOP conference and Academy of Management conference, the biennial EAWOP Congress, and the ICAP Congress

Table 1.4 Examples of highly respected academic journals related to I/O psychology

Academy of Management Journal

Academy of Management Review

Administrative Science Quarterly

Applied Psychology: An International Review

European Journal of Work and Organizational Psychology

Group & Organization Management

Human Performance

Human Relations

Industrial and Organizational Psychology: Perspectives on Science and Practice

International Journal of Selection and Assessment

Journal of Applied Psychology

Journal of Business and Psychology

Journal of Management

Journal of Occupational and Organizational Psychology

Journal of Occupational Health Psychology

Journal of Organizational Behavior

Journal of Vocational Behavior

Leadership Quarterly

Organizational Behavior and Human Decision Processes

Organizational Psychology Review

Organizational Research Methods

Personnel Psychology

every four years. The papers presented at these conferences are peer-reviewed, albeit not with the same rigor of peer review as for a journal, and this allows I/O psychologists to learn what some of the most current research is on a given topic.

In addition to peer-reviewed, scientific journals, it is possible to read about I/O research findings in practice-oriented journals such as *Academy of Management Perspectives*, *Harvard Business Review*, and *Sloan Management Review*. These publications tend to translate scientific research findings for both an I/O and a non-I/O practitioner audience. Articles in these types of outlets will be based on scientific findings, but will include less technical detail. Finally, there are a number of trade journals targeting consumers of I/O research as an audience. These journals include *HR Magazine*, *People Management*, *HR Focus*, and *T+D*. Trade journals often showcase specific I/O-related activities of companies, or else they discuss industry trends and information about new products or techniques that are of interest. These trade publications tend not to be peer-reviewed, and are not necessarily committed to communicating scientifically validated findings.

A Brief History of I/O Psychology

I/O psychology has roots in psychology going back at least a century. However, it is sometimes difficult to say just when a certain period of history began, or when the major eras or "shifts" in thinking occurred. Moreover, it is difficult to trace when certain developments were taking place in the US versus other parts of the world (Vinchur, 2008). In fact, research and application of I/O psychology principles were taking place around the world: Some of the earliest I/O researchers were trained in Europe but later moved to the US for the greater part of their career. And while much of the early history of I/O is sometimes thought to be quintessentially American with its use of psychology in selection, similar research was taking place in other parts of the world as well (Salgado, 2001). In this section, we will describe some of the key "threads" of I/O psychology. Note that the interested reader should look to more detailed discussion of the history of I/O psychology (e.g., Koppes, 2007; Landy, 1997).

The reader may be wondering why one would need to know the history of I/O psychology. First, understanding the roots of I/O psychology is necessary to understanding the nature of I/O psychology as a profession, including its goals and focus. For example, some of the early researchers in industrial psychology were focused on individual differences, and within industrial psychology today there is still a strong focus on using individual differences in making hiring decisions. Second, the profession has changed quite a bit in the last 100 years, and seeing where it has been can help to explain where it might be headed at this point. For example, within the field of personnel selection, much of the work for the twentieth century had been in the US and focused on Western culture. Although this research is likely to continue, leaders in the field have pointed out that this is changing as the world of work becomes increasingly globalized (Ryan & Ployhart, 2014). Third, understanding what research has been studied in the past can help us to see where to go next. If an issue has already been studied, there may be no reason to look at it again; or this understanding of the past can help us to come at the problem from a different angle. For example, research on leadership has gone through a number of phases over the last 100 years, starting with a focus on what traits (e.g., height, gender) make a person a great leader. Although this trait approach to leadership fell out of favor long ago, it is now being revived but with a new twist – which personality traits may lead to a person's success in certain situations.

Early Years and World War I

Early Psychologists and the Study of Work

Some authors trace the beginnings of I/O psychology to psychologists trained in Wilhelm Wundt's lab in Germany. At that time, German researchers were leading the way in psychology just as artists in France were leaders in the arts; and just as an artist in the nineteenth century might go to study in France to learn the techniques of Impressionism, researchers interested in psychology would study in Germany to learn the newest research techniques (Landy, 1997). In particular, two psychologists, Hugo Munsterberg and James McKeen Cattell, trained for many years under Wundt and eventually came to America, and there initiated some of the earliest work in the field of I/O (Landy, 1997). Munsterberg, a German, came to Harvard University, and he went on to tie individual differences in people to work performance. He also wrote the first I/O psychology textbook in German (in 1912), which was later published in English in 1913. Cattell, an American psychologist, settled at Columbia University for most of his career. Cattell was one of the first to recognize the role that individual differences can play in behavior, and that behavior is not solely a function of the environment. Moreover, Cattell went on to found the Psychological Corporation in 1921, a major publisher of tests in the US for generations (although now absorbed by larger test publishing houses). In short,

Hugo Munsterberg

James McKeen Cattell

both of these psychologists were focused on the application of psychology in the workplace, particularly the role that individual differences play in human behavior.

Meanwhile, another American, Walter Dill Scott, had also trained in Wundt's lab, and returned to the US, working at Northwestern University for much of his career. Scott's fame in industrial circles came with the publication of a series of essays on the application of psychology to industrial settings. Given that his focus in these early publications was less on theory and research and primarily on application, his work was particularly accessible to business leaders; for that reason, Scott can be credited with making industrial psychology visible to the general public (Landy, 1997). Another psychologist, Walter Bingham, had studied individual differences, such as in the testing of students for college admissions and for placing them into appropriate disciplines.

When the US entered World War I in 1917, the US military had to quickly deal with over 1 million recruits and how to process and place them. At this point, Scott and Bingham were able to contribute to the selection and placement of personnel. Specifically, they adapted an existing cognitive ability test, the Stanford-Binet, to a format that could be used to test large numbers of individuals at one time. There were two versions of the test, the **Army Alpha**, the version of the test for recruits who could read, and the **Army Beta**, the version for recruits who were illiterate. These two tests did much to promote the use of testing in personnel selection – a major component of I/O psychology today, which we will discuss in Chapters 6 and 7.

It is important to note that several themes began to take root during these early years of industrial psychology in the US – and at that time, it was all industrial psychology, not organizational psychology – due to several societal and scientific influences (Vinchur, 2008; Zickar & Gibby, 2007). These were an emphasis on productivity and efficiency, which are issues of interest primarily to management rather than to workers; an emphasis on quantification and statistics; a focus on personnel selection as a key aspect of the field; and a tension between science and practice.

Army Alpha: The version of the Stanford-Binet adapted during World War I for use with large numbers of army recruits who were able to read.

Army Beta: The version of the Stanford-Binet adapted during World War I for use with large numbers of army recruits who were illiterate.

Frederick Taylor is widely considered the "father" of Scientific Management.

Scientific Management

Although not specifically a part of I/O psychology, the early work in Scientific Management, founded by Frederick Taylor (the "father" of Scientific Management) runs parallel to much of the work in the early years of I/O (Koppes & Pickren, 2007; Vinchur, 2008). As originally described by Taylor, Scientific Management was meant to use logical, scientific principles in the management of organizations. At the time, large corporations were just beginning to develop. Up until that time, organizations had been managed through "common sense" and very informal procedures. For example, if you were hiring a steel worker, you might just hire a relative or a friend-of-a-friend rather than taking a systematic approach. Moreover, work did not always have standardized procedures. Taylor proposed a break with this approach, promoting that management should choose the "best man" (using his term) for the job, and that the role of management was to decide the "one best way" to do the job. While this may have been a significant improvement over past approaches, in general Scientific Management took a rather pessimistic view of human nature, in that workers were assumed not to know the best way to do their jobs (management had to tell them) and that people were primarily motivated by money. But the approach of taking a scientific, systematic approach to managing people fit with the general feeling of the early twentieth century that science could be applied to the management of people – similar to industrial psychology.

In addition to Taylor, two other people are important to the field of Scientific Management and to I/O psychology. These were the couple Frank and Lillian Gilbreth (Koppes, 1997). Perhaps the Gilbreths are best known for the book that two of their children wrote about them called *Cheaper by the Dozen*, so named because of the Gilbreths' 12 children. (There have also been two movies based on this book.) Frank was a building contractor and management engineer who was focused on efficiency. The Gilbreths were some of the first to apply the then new technology of motion pictures to do time-and-motion studies to help study the most efficient ways to do work by eliminating unnecessary motions. With specific reference to

Scientific Management: Developed in the early part of the twentieth century, an approach meant to use logical, scientific principles in the management of organizations and that runs parallel to much of the work in the early years of I/O psychology.

Frederick Taylor: The "father" of Scientific Management, he proposed a break from the simple "common sense" approach to management. Proposed management should choose the "best man" for a job and the "one best way" for doing a job.

Frank and Lillian Gilbreth: A couple important in the field of scientific management and to I/O psychology, they focused on improving efficiency in the workplace.

Lillian Gilbreth is often considered to be the first person in the U.S. to earn a Ph.D. in industrial psychology.

I/O psychology, Lillian Gilbreth is often cited as the first person to receive a Ph.D. in industrial psychology (and she did this while she was parenting 12 children) from Brown University in 1915. Although Frank died at the age of 55, Lillian went on to a long career in consulting and academics.

Human Relations Era (1927–1940s)

Human Relations:
A movement that touted the effects of considering workers' feelings and attitudes on performance.

Perhaps in reaction to the focus on efficiency used by the proponents of Scientific Management, the **Human Relations** movement touted the importance of considering the effects of workers' feelings and attitudes on performance. The Human Relations movement is said by many to have begun at the Hawthorne Works of Western Electric (which made telephone equipment) in Cicero, Illinois. The original study was really a "scientific management" type of study, examining the optimal level of light for worker efficiency (Roethlisberger & Dickson, 1939). As the researchers increased the lighting, worker productivity increased. But much to their surprise, worker productivity continued to increase even as the researchers lowered the lighting levels. The researchers concluded that the effects were due to the workers wanting to please the researchers (dubbed the **"Hawthorne effect"**, a term still used in psychological research, describing a situation where research participants behave in certain ways because they know that they are in a study), and that productivity could be affected by the feelings of workers. This began a series of studies at the Hawthorne plant. For example, the bank wiring observation room study examined how workers behaved in groups. This study concluded that worker behavior is determined not only by company rules. For example, cliques within a work group develop informal norms about issues such as how quickly they should work, and workers can pressure each other to enforce these norms. This is not a surprising idea today, but it was something that had generally been ignored by Scientific Management and other management scholars. The Hawthorne studies have been criticized through the years for being based on very small sample sizes and for a focus on management's goals rather than those of the workers (e.g., Highhouse, 2007; Sonnenfeld, 1985). However, this focus on worker attitudes and group processes is said to have formed a basis for today's organizational psychology.

Hawthorne effect:
When participants in psychological research behave in certain ways because they know that they are in a study.

World War II (1941–1945)

At the start of World War II, I/O psychology was again called upon to assist in the selection of enlistees, including some of the original developments in the use of biographical data in selection (see Chapter 6). In addition, I/O psychologists made a number of contributions to the training of US army personnel. They also provided recommendations for the redesign of airplane cockpits to be standardized and consistent, so that pilots could easily go from one plane to another without needing to re-learn the instrumentation.

Civil Rights Era (1964–Present)

Perhaps one of the greatest shifts in the practice of I/O psychology, having a substantial influence on research as well, was the passage of the 1964 *Civil Rights Act* in the US. This act put fairness of hiring practices front and center. Prior to that time, a company could use a selection procedure or test without paying attention to whether it adversely affected certain ethnic groups. The Civil Rights Act, however, challenged organizations to ensure that they used fair selection procedures that were also defensible in court (issues we will focus on in Chapter 7). In addition, this civil rights legislation, and other legislation that followed, has awakened organizations not only to the importance of assuring that their hiring procedures are fair and valid, but also to the broader concepts of managing diversity in organizations and on teams.

High-Tech HR Era (2000–present)

Since about the year 2000, we have seen profound changes in the delivery of typical HR functions within organizations, and these changes are happening more and more quickly. Whereas at one time job applications were submitted on paper, today the norm is for job applications to be submitted electronically. Similarly, whereas job applicants used to report to an organization's HR department to take the required tests for a job and then wait weeks to see if they passed, today these tests are often administered online and scored immediately. Many forms of employee training are no longer tethered to a live trainer, but are regularly delivered via the Internet to locations around the world. And the era of "big data" now allows a range of performance measures to be gathered about thousands of employees and used to conduct research on how to predict which employees have the greatest potential. This era of high-tech HR continues to unfold rapidly: Perhaps the most interesting issue for the field of I/O psychology is that this new technology is developing more quickly than the I/O research, so that we are not sure which technological developments are helpful, and which ones may actually provide incorrect information. A case in point is the use of social networking sites to screen employees, an organizational practice that raises legal challenges but has also been called into question in terms of its usefulness (Van Iddekinge, Lanavich, Roth, & Junco, 2013). In short, while these changes to technology have allowed for more efficient HR practices, they are also expected to keep I/O psychologists busy examining how best to use technology to remain within legal and ethical guidelines and to provide the best value to organizations and workers.

Interactive: Eras of industrial and organizational psychology.

"See website for interactive material"

1870–1900	1900–1920s	1927–1940	1941–1945	1946–1963	1964–present	2000–present
Early Years and World War I		Human Relations era begins	World War II and Post-War		Civil Rights era	High-Tech HR
Training of Munsterberg and Cattell by Wundt	1913: Munsterberg's Industrial Psychology text published in English	1927: Beginning of the Hawthorne Studies	1945: SIOP Founded as APA Div. 14	Post-WWII	1964: US Civil Rights Act	Beginning of online and high-tech delivery of HR functions
	1917: Army Alpha and Army Beta exam (Scott & Bingham) and *Journal of Applied Psychology* established by APA	Beginnings of organizational psychology			1978: *Uniform Guidelines on Employee Selection Procedures* (see Chapter 7)	
	1905-1920: Scientific Management				1990: Americans with Disabilities Act	
	1915: Lillian Gilbreth receives first I/O Ph.D. in US					

Figure 1.5 The eras of industrial and organizational psychology.

Workplace Application

The Use of Big Data in Organizational Research

The term "big data" has been getting a lot of attention in the popular press over the last few years. Although the definition of big data varies even among experts, it generally refers to the analysis of massive datasets that includes the data of thousands or even millions of people. In fact, these datasets are so big that they may be difficult to analyze using standard data analysis tools. Data sources might include the analysis of data within an organization, data across organizations (e.g., healthcare companies), or internet activity. The hope is that the analysis of big data will lead to better decisions, on a broad range of topics such as finance, consumer products, marketing, and healthcare.

Some of the current challenges with the use of big data are determining which types of employee data are acceptable to use and what types of research studies are acceptable from an ethics standpoint (Goel, 2014). For instance, Facebook conducted an experiment in 2012 on how emotions spread through a large population of users. Specifically, Facebook intentionally altered the number of positive and negative items in people's newsfeeds to see if it would affect the types of Facebook posts that people made. The ethics of these types of studies have been called into question.

Not surprisingly, big data is a hot topic in workplace research as well. Although the mining of data in organizational settings is only in its infancy, it is an issue that is drawing interest from many employers in the hopes that it can help them better understand workers' attitudes, motivation, and performance. The use of big data touches on many areas of organizational research, as we discuss in several chapters in this book.

Sources: Dutcher, 2014; Goel, 2014; Lohr, 2014.

LEGAL ISSUES

As we have already mentioned, legal issues affect a number of areas of practice within I/O psychology. In the US, most of these issues originate in civil rights legislation, specifically in the area of personnel selection (see Chapters 6 and 7). In addition, civil rights laws also apply to many other areas that we will cover in this text, such as compensation, training, and occupational health. We will touch on these in the legal issues sections of each chapter.

GLOBAL IMPLICATIONS

Because of an increasingly globalized world – with an increasingly globalized workforce – global issues have become critical to both research and practice in I/O psychology. For that reason, throughout this book, we will call out the global implications for the topics covered in each chapter. Here we touch on two important issues related to globalization for I/O psychology as a whole.

Multinational Organizations

With increased globalization, there has been an increase in multinational organizations. This has led to people working with others across international boundaries in ways that were unheard of in the last century. Such interaction among people from different backgrounds has led to a need to understand how such cross-cultural interaction affects teams and organizations. Different cultures have different norms for appropriate workplace behaviors, an issue that we will discuss further in Chapter 14. In addition, teams now need to work with little face-to-face interaction and in different time zones. Multinational organizations, with their integration of people from very different backgrounds, have also challenged I/O psychologists to understand issues such as how to deliver training across large, geographically dispersed organizations, how to develop hiring practices that are both legal and valid across cultures, and how to understand culture's effects on issues such as leadership and work motivation. In short, multinational companies will continue to increase in importance and challenge I/O psychologists to address new questions to enhance individual, team, and organizational effectiveness. For this reason, throughout this book we discuss the issues associated with applying I/O concepts in different countries and cultures.

International Practice

For most of the history of I/O psychology, I/O psychologists have been trained and have practiced within a single country. But because of the rise in multinational

One of the major changes in the workforce is the development of international teams. This requires that team members integrate with people from different backgrounds, and often work remotely and in different time zones. I/O psychologists will need to address issues associated with these teams in their research.

organizations, I/O psychologists need to be prepared to work across a wide range of different countries and cultures. As noted earlier in this chapter, EuroPsy was established to address this issue by assuring some comparability of training across countries and ensure that psychologists can practice work psychology in different European countries (EAWOP, 2014). In addition, I/O psychology training has begun to explicitly address how to provide I/O psychologists with an understanding of how to work in different countries and cultures (Griffith, Foster Thompson, & Armon, 2014). As just one example, the Erasmus Mundus Master's program in work and organizational psychology (Martinez-Tur, Peiró, & Rodriguez, 2014) provides graduate training from eight universities across six countries (Brazil, Canada, France, Italy, Spain, and Portugal). It thus provides students with educational and practical experiences across a variety of countries.

CURRENT ISSUES AND CONTROVERSIES

Today, there are a number of issues that are shaping the types of problems addressed by I/O psychologists in organizations. These issues are also shaping the research issues that are addressed in the I/O literature. Many of these are issues that are continuing to unfold and are shaping people's relationship with their work (see Figure 1.6).

Changes in the Nature of Work

The last decades have seen significant changes in the way that work is done, and the coming decades are expected to hold further changes. As examples, increased automation is decreasing the need for many low-skills jobs, while at the same time there has been an increase in the need for customer service and technical jobs. These changes require that workers develop new skills just to keep up and for countries and societies to keep their workforces competitive (Aguinis & Kraiger, 2009). I/O psychology can provide significant input on how to develop workers' skills so as to keep organizations and societies productive and keep workers engaged, satisfied, and healthy. Further, the increased use of **telework** (or working from a remote location away from a standard office or work site) challenges I/O

Telework: Working from a remote location away from a standard office or work site.

Changes in the Nature of Work

 Diversity Management

 Aging, Age-Diverse Workforce

 Humanitarian Work Psychology

 Occupational Health Psychology

 I/O as a Growing Field

Figure 1.6 Forces shaping the research and practice in industrial and organizational psychology.

It is becoming increasingly common to engage in "tele-work" or working from locations outside of the traditional office. This change provides a number of research questions for I/O psychologists, such as how workers can maintain workplace relationships when they are located physically away from other team members.

More work organizations are realizing the importance of taking diversity issues seriously. Recently, MGM Resorts received an award for its diversity efforts (Market Watch, 2014).

psychologists to better understand how telework alters workplace relationships. For instance, a recent study (Gajendran & Harrison, 2007) found that large amounts of telework improved employees work–life balance issues but had a negative effect on their relationships at work.

Diversity Management

Today's workforce is becoming increasingly diverse in terms of race, gender, ethnicity, age, and sexual orientation. The question is not whether the twenty-first-century workplace will be diverse – that's a certainty. Rather, the question is how an organization can effectively manage the diversity of its workforce through its practices around recruitment and selection (e.g., Avery, 2003), training (e.g., Kalinoski, 2013), socialization and mentoring (e.g., Ragins, 2011), leadership (Nishii & Mayer, 2009; Roberson & Park, 2007), and teams (e.g., Van Knippenberg & Schippers, 2007). This includes valuing diversity and inclusion (Ferdman, 2014; Shore et al., 2011) by creating an environment where people from different backgrounds can feel safe to be their authentic selves and promoting a culture at all organizational levels that values and supports people from different backgrounds. As you can see, diversity management is not achieved through any one organizational practice. For that reason, we will interweave issues of diversity management throughout this book, demonstrating specific I/O psychology research on diversity in various areas.

Aging, Age-Diverse Workforce

Trends in most industrialized societies show that the workforce is aging, with people working beyond traditional retirement ages (Eurostat, 2013; Toossi, 2007, 2012). Part of this is because of recent economic challenges, and also because many retirement systems at the national level are raising retirement ages because people are living longer and cannot be supported financially through long retirements. This "graying" of the workforce provides a number of psychological challenges to the workplace. For example, workers of diverse ages are working side-by-side as never before (Truxillo, Cadiz, & Rineer, 2014), and organizations are now needing to find ways to keep workers motivated throughout their careers (Kanfer, Beier, & Ackerman, 2013). Moreover, organizations need to find ways to support the differential needs of older and younger people, for example, through providing different types of training for them (Wolfson, Kavanaugh, & Kraiger, 2014). And such increases in age diversity will focus more attention on potential discrimination against people of different age groups – both younger and older (e.g., Finkelstein, Burke, & Raju, 1995; Posthuma & Campion, 2009). We will focus on age diversity as a specific issue in Chapter 12.

Humanitarian Work Psychology

For much of its history, I/O psychology has focused on improvements in worker attitudes and performance, largely with the focus on serving the needs of organizations. (This is perhaps especially true in the US.) Recently, there has been a move to increase the scope of I/O psychology to include more humanitarian interests. One of these ways is a recent interest in **humanitarian work psychology** (Olson-Buchanan, Koppes Bryan, & Foster Thompson, 2013), which focuses on using organizational psychology to improve the welfare of people not only in relatively wealthy industrialized countries but low-income nations as well.

Humanitarian work psychology: Focuses on using organizational psychology to improve the welfare of people, not only in relatively wealthy industrialized countries, but in low-income nations as well.

Workplace Application

Humanitarian Work Psychology

Humanitarian work psychology (HWP), which focuses on the application of organizational psychology to issues such as poverty reduction and other humanitarian work around the globe (Berry et al., 2011), has attracted growing interest in recent

years from I/O psychologists and their professional organizations. The activities of humanitarian work psychologists could range from supporting relief workers to more direct involvement in humanitarian efforts. Examples of HWP projects to date include helping to select humanitarian workers operating in disaster zones as well as developing systems to support and train these workers as they carry out their difficult tasks (Berry et al., 2011). SIOP has also recently gained non-governmental organization (NGO) status at the United Nations so as to be better positioned to advise the United Nations on key issues such as poverty eradication (Scott, 2012). Moreover, a recent book published in SIOP's Frontiers series (Olson-Buchanan, Koppes Bryan, & Foster Thompson, 2013) focuses on the work being done in this arena.

Sources: Berry et al., 2011; Olson-Buchanan et al., 2013; Scott, 2012.

Occupational Health Psychology

A field related to I/O psychology is **occupational health psychology** (OHP). OHP focuses on a range of topics to benefit workers in terms of their health, well-being, and safety. This includes an examination of ways to reduce worker stress and improve work–life balance. OHP involves not only I/O psychology concepts, but

Occupational health psychology (OHP): A field related to I/O psychology that focuses on a range of topics to benefit workers in terms of their health, well-being, and safety.

concepts from fields such as clinical and counseling psychology as well. We will discuss a number of OHP topics in Chapter 12.

I/O Is a Growing Field

Obviously given all the value that I/O psychologists can provide to individuals, organizations, and society, it should not be surprising that they are in high demand. However, as we have mentioned, I/O psychology is the fastest-growing occupation in the US in terms of percentage growth according to the Bureau of Labor Statistics (2014). In fact, outside of mental health specialties such as clinical psychology, there are more I/O psychology graduate applicants than in any other area of psychology (Boutelle, 2014). I/O psychology is a vibrant field, with increased need for our services to organizations. According to SIOP's 2012 salary survey (Khanna, Medsker, & Ginter, 2013), the median income for master's-level I/Os was upwards of $80,000 per year, while that of Ph.D.s was upwards of $100,000.

WHAT DOES THIS MEAN TO YOU?

In this chapter, we have covered a number of issues that are relevant to employees, supervisors, and managers.

First, I/O psychology provides insights into a number issues of interest to workers. For example, perhaps you'd like to understand what motivates you at work. Chapter 9 will discuss a number of motivation theories. These theories may help you to understand what you find most rewarding about work. This could help you not only to manage your time most effectively, but also help you understand the types of organization where you want to work – and which may not be the best fit for you. This text may also help you to figure out what employers are looking for when they hire people (Chapters 6 and 7), and the types of training you might need.

In addition, even if you are not currently supervising others, you very likely will be some day, so the material in this book may help you to understand people who report to you. Often, workers who appear unmotivated are simply responding to the supervision they are receiving. Supervising others isn't easy, and I/O psychology should help you to figure out how you might change your leadership style to be most effective with others (Chapter 10).

Although only a few of you may be managers, you will see how best to manage and support employees to increase the effectiveness of individuals and organizations. Too often, managers forget that people are their greatest resource. That being the case, I/O psychology can provide guidance for how to attract, support, develop, and retain the best talent.

Conclusion

I/O psychology is a well-established field, with over 100 years of history. There are thousands of I/O psychology practitioners and researchers worldwide, at both the master's and Ph.D. levels. Applying psychology to the field of work, I/O works to benefit both organizations and employees by improving outcomes such as performance, well-being, and satisfaction. I/O psychology is also well prepared to answer important questions about the evolving nature of work, and as such, is expected to be one of the most high-growth fields over the next decade. In the coming chapters, you'll glimpse the many ways in which I/O psychology can improve organizational decisions and the working conditions of employees.

YOUR TURN ...

1. A friend of yours has decided to pursue a graduate degree in I/O psychology. What advice would you give him or her in considering graduate training and for making a strong application?

2. Consider the career that you are planning to pursue after you finish college or graduate school. How do you think that technological advances may change this job over your career? What kinds of research questions could I/O psychologists carry out to address these changes and to support workers through these changes?

3. A friend learns that you are taking a class on I/O psychology. She wonders if this is about counseling workers about their problems. Can you explain to her what I/O psychology is actually about?

4. Consider the different eras of I/O psychology and related fields that were described in the chapter (Scientific Management/World War I, Human Relations, World War II, Civil Rights). What do you think it would be like to be a low-level factory employee in each of these eras? Describe what your experience would be like in each of them.

5. Which of the current issues identified in the chapter do you think will have the greatest impact during your career?

Additional Reading

Dipboye, R. L., & Colella, A. (Eds.). (2008). *Discrimination at work: The psychological and organizational bases.* New York: Psychology Press.

Griffith, R. L., Foster Thompson, L., & Armon, B. K. (Eds.). (2014). *Internationalizing the curriculum in organizational psychology.* New York: Springer.

Koppes, L. L. (Ed., 2007). *Historical perspectives in industrial and organizational psychology.* Mahwah, NJ: Lawrence Erlbaum Associates.

Olson-Buchanan, J., Foster Thompson, L., & Koppes Bryan, L. (Eds.). (2013). *Using industrial-organizational psychology for the greater good: Helping those who help others.* New York: Routledge.

Vinchur, A. J., & Koppes, L. L. (2011). A historical survey of research and practice in industrial and organizational psychology. In S. Zedeck (Ed.), *APA handbook of industrial and organizational psychology, Vol 1: Building and developing the organization.* APA Handbooks in Psychology (pp. 3–36). Washington, DC: American Psychological Association.

Warr, P. (2007). Some historical developments in I-O psychology outside the United States. In L. Koppes (Ed.), *Historical perspectives in industrial and organizational psychology* (pp. 81–107). Mahwah, NJ: Lawrence Erlbaum Associates.

References

Aguinis, H., & Kraiger, K. (2009). Benefits of training and development for individuals and teams, organizations, and society. *Annual Review of Psychology, 60,* 451–474.

Aguinis, H., Bradley, K. J., & Brodersen, A. (2014). Industrial-organizational psychologists in business schools: Brain drain or eye opener? *Industrial and Organizational Psychology: Perspectives on Science and Practice, 7,* 284–303.

Avery, D. R. (2003). Reactions to diversity in recruitment advertising - are differences black and white? *Journal of Applied Psychology, 88,* 672–679.

Bauer, T. N., McCarthy, J., Anderson, N., Truxillo, D. M., & Salgado, J. (2012). *What we know about applicant reactions: Research summary and best practices.* SIOP White Paper series. Bowling Green, OH: Society for Industrial and Organizational Psychology.

Berry, M. O. N., Reichman, W., Klobas, J., MacLachlan, M., Hui, H. C., & Carr, S. C. (2011). Humanitarian work psychology: The contributions of organizational psychology to poverty reduction. *Journal of Economic Psychology, 32,* 240–247.

Boutelle, C. (2014). Industrial-organizational psychology tops list of fastest growing occupations. Retrieved May 23, 2014 from https://www.siop.org/article_view.aspx?article=1219#.

Bureau of Labor Statistics. (2014). *Fastest growing occupations.* Retrieved May 23, 2014 from http://www.bls.gov/ooh/fastest-growing.htm.

Dutcher, J. (2014). What is big data? Datascience@berkeley blog. September 3, 2014. Retrieved February 18, 2015 from http://datascience.berkeley.edu/what-is-big-data/.

European Association of Work and Organizational Psychology. (n.d.). EuroPsy background. Retrieved May 21, 2014 from http://eawop.org/europsy-background.

Eurostat. (2013). Employment statistics. European Commission. Retrieved May 23, 2014 from http://epp.eurostat.ec.europa.eu/statistics_explained/index.php/Employment_statistics.

Ferdman, B. M. (2014). The practice of inclusion in diverse organizations. In B. M. Ferdman & B. R. Deane (Eds.), *Diversity at work: The practice of inclusion* (pp. 3–54). San Francisco: John Wiley & Sons.

Finkelstein, L. M., Burke, M. J., & Raju, N. S. (1995). Age discrimination in simulated employment contexts: An integrative analysis. *Journal of Applied Psychology, 80,* 652–663.

Gajendran, R. S., & Harrison, D. A. (2007). The good, the bad, and the unknown about telecommuting: Meta-analysis of psychological mediators and individual consequences. *Journal of Applied Psychology, 92,* 1524–1541.

Goel, V. (2014). As data overflows online, researchers grapple with ethics. *New York Times,* August 12, 2014. Retrieved August 13, 2014 from http://www.nytimes.com/2014/08/13/technology/the-boon-of-online-data-puts-social-science-in-a-quandary.html.

Griffith, R. L., Foster Thompson, L., & Armon, B. K. (Eds., 2014). *Internationalizing the curriculum in organizational psychology.* New York: Springer.

Highhouse, S. (2007). Applications of organizational psychology: Learning through failure or failure to learn? In L. Koppes (Ed.), *Historical perspectives in industrial and organizational psychology* (pp. 331–352). Mahwah, NJ: Lawrence Erlbaum Associates.

Kalinoski, Z. T., Steele-Johnson, D., Peyton, E. J., Leas, K. A., Steinke, J., & Bowling, N. A. (2013). A meta-analytic evaluation of diversity training outcomes. *Journal of Organizational Behavior, 34,* 1076–1104.

Kanfer, R., Beier, M. E., & Ackerman, P. L. (2013). Goals and motivation related to work in later adulthood: An organizing framework. *European Journal of Work and Organizational Psychology, 22,* 253–264.

Khanna, C., Medsker, G. J., & Ginter, R. (2013). *2012 income and employment survey results for the Society for Industrial and Organizational Psychology.* Bowling Green, OH: Society for Industrial and Organizational Psychology. Retrieved May 12, 2015 from http://www.siop.org/2012SIOPIncomeSurvey.pdf.

Koppes, L. L. (1997). American female pioneers of industrial and organizational psychology during the early years. *Journal of Applied Psychology, 82,* 500–515.

Koppes, L.L. (Ed.). (2007). *Historical perspectives in industrial and organizational psychology.* Mahwah, NJ: Lawrence Erlbaum Associates.

Koppes, L. L., & Pickren, W. (2007). Industrial and organizational psychology: An evolving science and practice. *Historical perspectives in industrial and organizational psychology* (pp. 3–35). Mahwah, NJ: Lawrence Erlbaum Associates.

Landy, F. J. (1997). Early influences on the development of industrial and organizational psychology. *Journal of Applied Psychology, 82,* 467–477.

Lohr, S. (2014). In big data, shepherding comes first. December 14, 2014. Retrieved February 18, 2014 from http://www.nytimes.com/2014/12/15/technology/in-big-data-shepherding-comes-first-.html.

Market Watch. (2014). MGM Resorts named among nation's top companies for diversity by DiversityInc. Retrieved May 23, 2014 from http://www.market-watch.com/story/mgm-resorts-named-among-nations-top-companies-for-diversity-by-diversityinc-2014-04-25.

Martinez-Tur, Vicente, Peiró, J. M., & Rodriguez, I. (2014). Teaching and learning work, organizational, and personnel psychology internationally: The Erasmus Mundus Program. In R. L. Griffith, L. Foster Thompson, & B. K. Armon (Eds.), *Internationalizing the curriculum in organizational psychology* (pp. 105-125). New York: Springer.

National Center for O*NET Development. (2012). Summary report for 19-3032.00 - industrial-organizational psychologists. Retrieved June 3, 2014 from http://www.onetonline.org/link/summary/19-3032.00.

Nishii, L. H., & Mayer, D. M. (2009). Do inclusive leaders help to reduce turnover in diverse groups? The moderating role of leader–member exchange in the diversity to turnover relationship. *Journal of Applied Psychology, 94,* 1412-1426.

Olson-Buchanan, J., Foster Thompson, L., & Koppes Bryan, L. (Eds.). (2013). *Using industrial-organizational psychology for the greater good: Helping those who help others.* New York: Routledge.

Posthuma, R. A., & Campion, M. A. (2009). Age stereotypes in the workplace: Common stereotypes, moderators, and future research directions. *Journal of Management, 35,* 158-188.

Ragins, B. R. (2011). Diversity and workplace mentoring relationships: A review and positive social capital approach. In T. D. Allen & L. T. Eby (Eds.), *The Blackwell handbook of mentoring: A multiple perspectives approach* (pp. 281-300). Malden, MA: John Wiley & Sons.

Roberson, Q. M., & Park, H. J. (2007). Examining the link between diversity and firm performance: The effects of diversity reputation and leader racial diversity. *Group & Organization Management, 32,* 548-568.

Roethlisberger, F. J., & Dickson, W. J. (1939). *Management and the worker.* Cambridge, MA: Harvard University Press.

Ryan, A. M., & Ployhart, R. E. (2014). A century of selection. *Annual Review of Psychology, 65,* 693-717.

Salgado, J. F. (2001). Some landmarks of 100 years of scientific personnel selection at the beginning of the new century. *International Journal of Selection and Assessment, 9,* 3-8.

Scott, J. C. (2012). SIOP and the United Nations. *Industrial Psychologist, 50,* 137-138. Retrieved August 14, 2014 from http://www.siop.org/tip/oct12/22UN.aspx.

Searle, R., Erdogan, B., Peiró, J. M., & Kleke, U. K. (2014). *What we know about youth unemployment: Research summary and best practices.* SIOP White Paper series. Bowling Green, OH: Society for Industrial and Organizational Psychology.

Shore, L. M., Randel, A. E., Chung, B. G., Dean, M. A., Ehrhart, K. H., & Singh, G. (2011). Inclusion and diversity in work groups: A review and model for future research. *Journal of Management, 37,* 1262-1289.

Society for Industrial and Organizational Psychology, Inc. (1994). *Guidelines for education and training at the master's level in industrial-organizational psychology.* Arlington Heights, IL: Author. Retrieved May 21, 2014 from http://www.siop.org/guidelines.aspx.

Society for Industrial and Organizational Psychology, Inc. (1999). *Guidelines for education and training at the doctoral level in industrial/organizational psychology.* Bowling Green, OH: Author. Retrieved May 21, 2014 from http://www.siop.org/PhDGuidelines98.aspx.

Sonnenfeld, J. A. (1985). Shedding light on the Hawthorne studies. *Journal of Organizational Behavior, 6,* 111–130.

Toossi, M. (2007). Labor force projections 2016: More workers in their golden years. *Monthly Labor Review, 130,* 33–52.

Toossi, M. (2012). Labor force projections to 2020: A more slowly growing workforce. *Monthly Labor Review, 135,* 43–64.

Truxillo, D. M., Cadiz, D. M., & Rineer, J. R. (2014). The aging workforce: Implications for human resource management research and practice. In S. Jackson (Ed.), *Business and management.* Oxford handbooks online. DOI: 10.1093/oxfordhb/9780199935406.013.004

Van Iddekinge, C. H., Lanivich, S. E., Roth, P. L., & Junco, E. (2013). Social media for selection? Validity and adverse impact potential for a Facebook-based assessment. *Journal of Management.* DOI: 0149206313515524

Van Knippenberg, D., & Schippers, M. C. (2007). Work group diversity. *Annual Review of Psychology, 58,* 515–541.

Vinchur, A. J. (2008). Early industrial psychology: A very brief and highly selective history. *Sociology Compass, 2,* 122–138.

Wolfson, N.E., Cavanagh, T.M., & Kraiger, K. (2014). Older adults and technology-based instruction: Optimizing learning outcomes and transfer. *Academy of Management Learning & Education, 13,* 26–44.

Zickar, M. J., & Gibby, R. E. (2007). Four persistent themes throughout the history of IO psychology in the United States. In L. Koppes (Ed.), *Historical perspectives in industrial and organizational psychology* (pp. 61–80). Mahwah, NJ: Lawrence Erlbaum Associates.

Chapter 2

RESEARCH METHODS

Research methods are the cornerstone of I/O psychology.

After studying this chapter, you should be able to:

- describe the relationship between research and theory

- describe basic research concepts and the research designs and methods commonly used in I/O research

- understand the uses of common statistics used to analyze data

- describe the ways for estimating the reliability of a psychological measure

- describe the typical ways to operationalize measurement validity

- discuss some of the core ethical issues faced by I/O psychologists in their research, as well as global implications, and current issues and controversies.

Learning goals for this chapter

Introduction

Students are major consumers of the research results that are presented in classes. Specifically, if you are pursuing a psychology degree or have taken a number of psychology classes, you have undoubtedly studied the results of psychological research studies. You have also been presented with some of the basic ideas regarding research methodology.

I/O psychology continues to grow as a research field. Each year the number of research journals grows, indicating that the volume of academic research continues to increase. But I/O psychology research is not just something done by college professors: it is also carried out by I/O practitioners in organizations. As we noted in Chapter 1, I/O psychology has continued to expand as a profession, and more and more organizations are utilizing the services of I/O psychologists. Moreover, at the time of this writing, the US Department of Labor predicts that I/O psychologists have the highest level of growth, at least in terms of a percentage increase, of any career (Bureau of Labor Statistics, 2014; see Chapter 1). This means that more and more applied research is being done within organizations, and that decisions about employees are being made based on this research. This includes a wide range of topics that are important to workers, such as training, work–life balance programs, and hiring and promotion decisions.

In other words, I/O psychology research is not just an academic pursuit. It is also a very real, important factor affecting the work lives of millions of employees around the world. Our point is that anyone planning to work in the coming decades should have a basic understanding of I/O research methods because the results of I/O research are probably going to affect them.

In this chapter, we present an overview of the issues involved in conducting I/O psychology research. Our goal is not to make you research experts after reading just this one chapter, or to burden you with the technical details of statistical analyses – although the need for expertise in research and statistical analysis will continue to grow in the twenty-first century. Rather, we want to present you with enough background to be able to understand the types of research conducted by I/O psychologists in both academic and applied settings so you become a more informed consumer of such research. With that in mind, we begin by presenting an overview of the research process, followed by a few of the key concepts in designing a research study. We next provide examples of some of the research designs commonly used by I/O psychologists and the basic statistical "tools" that are used to answer different research questions. We conclude with a discussion of measurement issues and ethics.

Theory, Research, and the Research Process

If you were to read a research paper from a top-tier I/O psychology journal, you would likely notice two things. First, there is a lot of space devoted to the methodology used as well as the results that were found (often including statistical tests). In other words, a large portion of the article will be about how the actual research study was conducted and what was found statistically. But you might also notice a second element: That the article begins with a description of past research and the theory that underlies it, and it concludes with a discussion of the implications of the study results for future research, practice, and theory. Let's go through the reasons why journal articles use this structure of (1) reviewing past theory and research, (2) describing the study methods and results, and then (3) concluding with implications for practice, theory, and future research.

Relationship between Theory and Research

Theory: A description of the relationship among variables and how they influence each other in order to explain a particular phenomenon.

Although there are exceptions, good research is based on a good **theory**. A theory is a description of the relationships among variables and how these variables influence each other in order to explain a particular phenomenon. Theory is very important to both research and practice because it provides some guidance as to how to understand a phenomenon and where to begin in studying and understanding it. For example, if you wanted to study how fair treatment might affect workers' health, you would not need to begin to study this "from scratch"; rather there has been considerable research on the effects of fair treatment (organizational justice theory) in the past (Colquitt, Conlon, Wesson, Porter, & Ng, 2001), and even considerable work on how unfair treatment can negatively impact worker health (Robbins, Ford, & Tetrick, 2012). Your job as a researcher would be to conduct a study that picks up where previous research left off and carry the ball further down the field, in order to support the current theory or show how the

Figure 2.1 Theory, research, and practice inform each other, and build upon each other.

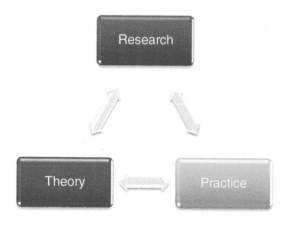

theory might need to be tweaked a bit. This study would be **empirical research**, or research that is based on direct or indirect observations. It is often done to see if the theory stands up when tested.

Empirical research: Research based on direct or indirect observations. It is often done to see if a theory stands up when tested.

Once the study is done, the researcher should interpret the results in order to clarify the theory and to guide what future studies should do. This is important, because clarifying the theory so that it better describes the phenomenon can help future researchers as well as organizational applications. In short, theory informs research, and research, in turn, informs theory. And, as we discussed in Chapter 1, according to the scientist-practitioner model, both theory and research inform practice, and issues that arise in practice set the agenda for future research. Figure 2.1 describes this complex set of interrelations.

Over time a series of studies can substantially develop and further elaborate theories in order to better understand and explain a phenomenon. An example from I/O psychology would be organizational justice theory, which is a well-established theory to explain people's feelings about their treatment by and relationship with their organization. Organizational justice theory explains how workers experience fair treatment at work and the effects of this fair treatment on their attitudes and behaviors. Organizational justice theory's roots are in equity theory (for more detail on this, please see Chapter 9), which was developed in the early 1960s by Adams (1965). Equity theory focused on how the perceived fairness of the outcomes a person receives relative to the outcome received by other people affects motivation and behavior. And at the beginning, equity theory was mostly applied to the fairness of the pay that people received relative to others. Moreover, equity theory focused on the fairness of outcomes, namely, what a person received.

Although equity theory was supported by the early research, it also evolved over the years as researchers conducted more empirical studies on it and used the results to add to the theory. The theory became broader and included other aspects of fairness of the outcomes a person gets, and the theory evolved into what's now called organizational justice theory. This was due to empirical research being done to qualify the theory. For example, researchers discovered that although the fairness of outcomes definitely mattered to people, the *processes* used to get to the outcomes mattered as well. In other words, it wasn't just the pay decision (e.g., a raise) a person received, but the process the company used to make the pay decisions that mattered as well. Later still, researchers realized that, in addition to the fairness of outcomes and processes, people were also concerned with the fairness of *interpersonal treatment* they received. In other words, it wasn't just the outcome you received or the process used to give you that outcome, but also that you were treated with respect. And what's more, researchers found out that organizational justice theory could be applied to more than just pay situations: It could be applied to any number of issues such as the fairness of promotions, treatment by the boss, selection procedures used to assess job applicants, and the general respect with which coworkers are treated by their bosses. We also now know that people's perceptions of fair treatment affect a number of important outcomes such as their job attitudes, performance, and even health.

Workplace Application

Buffering the Effects of Organizational Injustice

As we mention in the text, unjust situations can have negative consequences for employees. For instance, a recent meta-analysis (Robbins, 2012) found that perceived injustice is related not only to measures of employee stress and burnout, but also to measures of employee mental health and physical health.

But other research has shown that fair treatment by supervisors can sometimes reduce the negative effects of unjust outcomes received by employees. In one classic field study about the impact of organizational justice on sleep (Greenberg, 2006), nurses who experienced a salary reduction showed increased insomnia as a result of the unfair outcome. However, nurses whose supervisors were trained about how to be more interpersonally fair experienced less insomnia than nurses whose supervisors were not – and these effects lasted for six months after the interpersonal fairness training. In short, the better interpersonal treatment from supervisors appeared to mitigate some of the negative sleep effects caused by the salary reduction.

The development of organizational justice theory to where it is today demonstrates three important points about theories in organizational research. First, it shows how theories can develop over time to describe a phenomenon in greater detail and with greater accuracy. In this case, we have learned that fair treatment is more than simply the outcomes an employee receives, but also includes the way the process is decided and the respect a person is treated with in the organization. Second, it demonstrates one of the key benefits of a theory, namely, that a good theory can explain a phenomenon (in this case, perceptions of fairness) over a range of very different contexts: In this instance, not just pay decisions but other kinds of organizational decisions as well. In this sense, a good theory can be super-useful to aiding our understanding, in that it can be used to explain a number of different phenomena. In fact, there's a famous quotation from psychologist Kurt Lewin that says, "There is nothing so practical as a good theory." And third, a robust theory such as organizational justice theory, in combination with the strong support from empirical research, is extremely valuable to practice. (Remember what we said in Chapter 1 about how research and practice are intertwined in the scientist-practitioner model?) In other words, based on organizational justice theory, we now know what organizations should consider when making decisions if they want to have a positive impact on workers' attitudes and behavior. Specifically, organizations should be sure not only to give people a fair outcome, but also be sure to use a fair and transparent process and treat workers with respect, because all three aspects of fairness are important to people.

At this point it would also be good to discuss two fundamentally different approaches to doing research. **Deductive** approaches are where we start with

Deductive approach: A research approach that begins with a theory and sets out to test hypotheses based on this theory.

Inductive Approach	Deductive Approach
The inductive approach starts with observing a phenomenon and then develops theory to explain it. "Big data" is an example of an inductive approach.	The deductive approach starts off with a theory that needs to be tested. Much of the research in the top psychology journals these days takes a deductive approach, but that wasn't always the case.

Figure 2.2
Inductive and deductive research approaches.

a strong theory and then set out to test hypotheses based on this theory. The example of organizational justice theory described above is closer to a deductive approach because the theory is the starting point; but it includes inductive elements, because empirical research was used to make changes to the theory. However, research can go in the other direction: **Inductive** approaches to research begin with observing a phenomenon and then developing a theory to explain it. For example, a company might use "big data" (see Chapter 1) to explain employee satisfaction. In this case, there may be no theory that is guiding the research; rather the researcher is open to many possible factors that could explain why employees are satisfied with their jobs. In short, both deductive and inductive research approaches advance theory, which can lead to better organizational practices.

Inductive approach: A research approach that begins with observing a phenomenon and then developing a theory to explain it.

Basic Research Concepts: Independent and Dependent Variables

Now that we have explained the nature of research and how it informs theory and practice, we will cover some key concepts for understanding empirical research. We will also discuss the specific terms that are used in different types of I/O psychology research.

The first of these concepts is the **independent variable** (also known as an IV). The independent variable is the variable that is manipulated by the researcher to see *how it affects* participants. For example, you might provide a stress-reduction intervention to employees to see if it has positive effects on the health of employees. In this case, the intervention is the independent variable. In this example, you would have two levels (or conditions) within the independent variable: the intervention condition and the control condition that receives no intervention. Second

Independent variable (IV): The variable that is manipulated by the researcher to see its effects on a given dependent variable.

Dependent variable (DV): The variable that is affected by the independent variable.

is the **dependent variable** (also known as a DV). The dependent variable is what is *affected by* the independent variable. In this example where we're interested in the effects of a workplace intervention on employee health, health would be the dependent variable, perhaps measured by taking employees' blood pressure over time.

However, as you will see, many I/O psychology studies do not involve actual experiments, but rather include the examination of the existing relationships between variables such as employee personality and outcomes like job perform-ance. In this case, we would not technically have an independent variable, because a variable like personality cannot be manipulated. As one example, a researcher might examine the effects of job satisfaction on job performance. Because job satisfaction cannot be directly controlled or manipulated by the researcher, it is not an IV. And if there is no IV, there is technically no DV either. In these sorts of situations, we tend to use different terms for these variables. For example, job satisfaction might be described as an *"antecedent"* of job performance, and job performance might be referred to as an *"outcome"*. Or, in the case of using per-sonality to predict job performance, personality would typically be referred to as a *"predictor"*, while job performance in personnel selection research is typically called a *"criterion variable"*.

Research Designs

In this section we will discuss more of the "nuts and bolts" of specific types of studies in organizations. These include true experiments that are common in many fields of psychology, plus others that are more suited to the applied, prac-tical issues examined by I/O psychologists.

True Experiments

Experiment: A type of study which includes random assignment to experimental conditions and contains at least one experimental group that receives the manipulation of the IV, and a control group that does not receive the IV and is used for comparison.

Experimental group: The group that receives the manipulation of the IV.

Control group: The group that does not receive the IV and is used for comparison.

Random assignment: Participants are randomly assigned to the experimental or control group.

Confound variable: A variable that covaries with the IV and whose effects on the dependent variable are not easily disentangled from the IV.

The classic type of study done in many areas of psychology is the **experiment**. To be a true experiment, a study must have some key features. First, it should involve the use of an **experimental group** that receives the manipulation, and a **control group** that does not receive it and is used for comparison. For example, in a study regarding the effects of goal-setting on training performance, a researcher might train a group of participants; one group (the experimental group) is provided with goals, whereas the control group is not. In this example, the provision of goals is the IV. Second, true experiments involve the use of **ran-dom assignment** of participants to experimental and control groups so that we can consider the experimental and control groups to be equivalent. Consider an example where random assignment does not happen: What if the members of the experimental group were all men, but the members of the control group were all women? If this were the case, the researcher would not be able to dis-entangle the effects of goal-setting from the effects of gender. In this example, gender would be considered a **confound variable**, that is, a variable that covar-ies with the independent variable and whose effects on the dependent variable

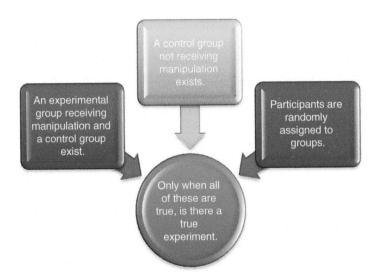

Figure 2.3 Is it a true experiment?

are not easily disentangled from the independent variable. However, random assignment allows for the control of confound variables and any other extraneous variables – other variables that might affect the dependent variable – by assuring that the levels of the extraneous variables are evenly distributed across the experimental and control conditions. For example, by randomly assigning participants to conditions, we would hope that workers with more and less job tenure would be evenly distributed across the two groups, so that job tenure would not be a confound variable.

Field Experiments

Of course, there is the possibility of carrying out true **field experiments** in actual organizational settings. That is, an organization may actually work with researchers to randomly assign their employees to experimental and control conditions. For example, if a researcher was studying an intervention to reduce employee stress, half of the company's employees would be randomly assigned to receive the stress reduction intervention, and the other half would be randomly assigned to the control condition. This sort of true experiment is quite valuable, because it provides a "gold standard" for evaluating the effects of a workplace policy or intervention: If differences are found in only the experimental group, we can conclude that it was due to the treatment.

On the other hand, such true field experiments are not very common for several reasons. First, true field experiments are more difficult to carry out, and thus require a good bit of work on the part of the researcher. The researcher would have to find an organization whose characteristics are a good fit for the question that they are studying, and they have to find an organization that trusts the researchers enough to be willing to work with them. Second, true experiments require an organization that is willing and able to assign workers to different conditions. For example, supervisors may be unwilling to give randomly chosen employees a health improvement intervention while leaving other employees out,

Field experiments:
When an experimental design is used in an organizational setting. This usually means when an organization allows researchers to randomly assign employees to experimental and control conditions.

for reasons of fairness and morale. Third, certain manipulations might be unethical or illegal in organizational contexts. For example, the authors of this book study the topic of "applicant reactions" (see Chapter 6), or the effects of how the treatment of job applicants affects their job attitudes and behavior. But a true experiment – where actual job applicants for the same job are randomly assigned to different conditions in which they are treated differently – might not be legal in a real-world setting.

Laboratory Experiments

Laboratory experiments: A type of experiment that in psychology often involves the use of undergraduate students or online samples.

Given some of the challenges of doing field experiments, another option is to do **laboratory experiments**. In psychology, these typically involve college students, or, more recently, the use of online samples such as Amazon Mechanical Turk™ (an online source where participants are paid small amounts for their participation in a variety of research tasks and/or survey completion; see "Current Issues and Controversies"). Depending on the topic, a great deal can be learned from such student studies. Sometimes a laboratory experiment using students may allow for an initial test of the effects of an IV in a setting that is far less costly than it would be in a field setting. For example, if you were interested in the effects of workplace redesign on employee productivity, it would be cheaper and easier to do this in a small student study first to see if it worked before completely redesigning a company's workplace. Thus, in I/O psychology research, many experimental studies that you see published use undergraduate students as participants.

Generalizable: How well the results from a study using one population transfer to another (e.g., the results from a study of college undergraduates to working professionals).

However, although research on undergraduates provides a lot of useful information, there can be a problem with this type of research as well. Most notably, the results may not be **generalizable** (or transferrable) to actual work settings because the students may be quite different from the working population, and the experimental context can be quite different from what an actual employee would face. For example, students may be younger than the working population, they may not be employed, and they are reacting to an artificial situation, not a work situation. Nevertheless, such laboratory experiments provide samples easily, and they provide a great deal of experimental control (e.g., ease of random assignment) to the researcher.

Quasi-Experimental Designs

As noted, true experimental designs can be difficult in actual work organizations. Yet conducting research in an organizational setting is important to knowing whether your results actually hold up in the workplace. As a solution, some field research uses what is known as a quasi-experimental ("almost" experimental) design approach. This design is close to a true experiment, but may be missing one aspect such as random assignment to conditions. As an example, employees in one division of the company (e.g., Northeastern states) might receive a health promotion intervention, while employees in other parts of the company (Midwest) would be in the control group. This quasi-experimental design does not have all of the advantages of random assignment, but it can be far more practical in a field setting. The use of quasi-experiments is discussed in greater detail in

Chapter 8 in the context of training evaluation because training was one of the first I/O research areas to use quasi-experimental designs. For now, it is important just to know that there is this additional, practical research design that can be used in organizational settings.

Other Designs Used in Organizational Research

Many of the issues studied by I/O psychologists are not easily studied as field experiments because they may involve examining the effects of stable employee characteristics such as personality. For these reasons, much of the field research in I/O psychology relies a good deal on **correlational studies** where the focus is on looking at the relationships among variables. Correlational studies have a lot of advantages, the most important of which is that they can be done in organizations using samples of actual working people. Moreover, they typically involve practical and relatively inexpensive forms of data collection such as surveys. For example, a researcher may be interested in examining the relationship between employee adaptability (a stable characteristic) and their advancement in the company. Adaptability cannot be manipulated as in an experiment, but the relationship between adaptability and advancement can be examined.

Correlational studies: Studies where there is no definite IV or DV; these studies look at the relationships among the variables.

Challenges with Correlational Studies

As you might guess, correlational studies also come with their own challenges. One is that with correlational studies it can sometimes be difficult to determine **causality**, or determining the direction of relationships between variables. Here are two very different examples: In the first example, a researcher is interested in the relationship between neuroticism (a personality trait) and job satisfaction. In this case, we can assume that because neuroticism is a fairly stable personality trait that remains stable in adulthood, that neuroticism is likely to affect job satisfaction, and not the other way around. (Although we admit that one could build a case for low satisfaction causing neurotic responses on a questionnaire.) As a second example, what about the relationship between job satisfaction and job performance? Both job satisfaction and job performance are fairly dynamic variables (i.e., they can change a lot within a person, even day to day), and so while job satisfaction could be thought of as affecting performance, job performance could also affect job satisfaction (i.e., some people could be satisfied with their work because of the positive outcomes they get from performing well on the job). In this second example, determining the direction of the relationship between job satisfaction and performance - which causes which - is a challenge.

Causality: Determining which variable is affecting the other variable.

Another issue, particularly with correlational studies where there is only one survey, is the concern about inflated relationships. That is, by giving a single survey on a single occasion to a group of employees, many of the relationships between the variables will be inflated because of factors like the employees' mood or some other factor going on that day that affects all of the variables on the survey. For example, let's go back to the study above on the relationship between neuroticism and job satisfaction. An employee who is having a very good day would be less likely to give neurotic responses to the neuroticism items, and also to indicate satisfaction with their job; an employee who has just had a nasty encounter with a customer might tend to give more neurotic responses to the neuroticism items and also to indicate lower satisfaction. In both cases, positive and negative, the responses to the neuroticism items – which should be fairly stable – have been distorted and could show a stronger relationship with job satisfaction than they actually should because of circumstances on the day of the survey.

Addressing Causality and Inflated Relationships in Correlational Studies

Other than using an experimental design – perhaps one of the best ways to show causality and reduce inflated relationships – what are some of the solutions to address these issues with correlational studies? One of the factors that is necessary to show that one variable causes another is **temporal ordering**, or the order of two variables in the data collection. Although temporal ordering is not sufficient to show causality, it is a first step. As for ways to reduce inflated relationships between variables, first, separating the measurement of different variables so that they are measured at different times decreases the likelihood of inflated relationships due to mood or other chance factors. Second, another solution for reducing inflated relationships is to use multiple sources of data, for example, from supervisors or company records. Using the example above, job performance might be obtained from supervisor ratings or company records, and a rating of the personality factor of neuroticism might be rated by coworkers.

Temporal ordering: When two variables are placed in a particular order that helps with their interpretation, e.g., the predictor placed first and the outcome placed second. (Temporal ordering alone, however, is not sufficient to explain causality.)

Which Research Designs Are Best?

So which of these approaches to research design is best – laboratory experiments, field experiments, quasi-experiments, or correlational studies? As you might guess, the answer is that each of these approaches has its strengths and weaknesses, and some combination of these study designs is probably best. Further, it very much depends on the phenomenon you are trying to study. For example, if you want to know the relationship between a stable personality variable and employee attitudes, it probably does not make much sense to use an experiment where it would be impossible to manipulate personality. On the other hand, if you want to examine how job applicants might perceive a particular hiring policy, you might want to first do a laboratory study with some students to see how it goes before implementing it in a real work setting. In short, to be most confident in your results regarding a research question, you need to choose the right research method, and if possible, use multiple methods also known as the "triangulation" of results.

Data Collection Methods

I/O psychologists also use a number of different methods to collect data. The prevalent norm in I/O research has been to focus on quantitative data collection methods as opposed to qualitative methods (i.e., methods not involving statistical

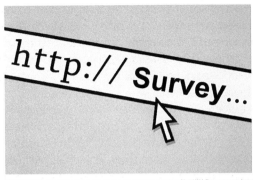

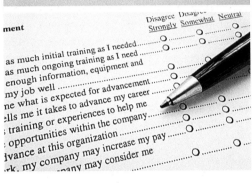

Surveys (both online and paper-and-pencil versions) are the method that I/O psychology researchers use most often.

calculations). However, this appears to be changing, with a greater appreciation of qualitative methods in understanding behavior in organizations and their importance in the triangulation of results.

Survey methods, in which people report their responses on a paper or online questionnaire, are perhaps the most frequently used methods in I/O research. The survey approach generally uses pre-established survey items or scales that have been shown by past research to have good reliability and validity. The advantage of survey methods is that they allow a researcher to collect a large amount of data from many participants relatively easily. For this reason, because they provide large samples of participants, surveys provide data that can be analyzed using a wide range of statistical techniques. However, because surveys may sometimes fail to ask all of the questions relevant to a phenomenon, they may not provide the richest data available, that is, detailed data about the individual and his or her experiences that the researcher hadn't considered. On the other hand, qualitative data sources such as interviews with employees, focus groups, and **observational methods** (where employees are observed doing their work) can provide this rich data, giving numerous insights that might not emerge from conducting a survey. This includes a range of issues that affect the way employees do their jobs and feel about their jobs. Further, with a bit of additional work on the part of the researcher, data from interviews and observations can often be coded so that statistical analyses can be done on them. The downside to interviews and observations is that they are relatively time-consuming, and large numbers of employees cannot be sampled all at once with these methods, as they could be with a survey. However, even researchers who focus primarily on survey research spend some of their time doing interviews and observations to better understand the organization and the phenomena involved.

Survey methods: One of the most commonly used research methods, where people report their responses on a paper or online questionnaire.

Observational methods: Observing employees while they are working; this can provide insights that might not emerge from a survey.

For example, as we will see in Chapter 3, job analysis methods involve multiple sources of data – interviews, observations, and surveys – to better understand what the job involves. In addition, I/O psychologists use other data collection methods, as we will see in later chapters of this book. For example, tests that measure individual differences such as skills, personality, or cognitive ability are frequently used to make personnel selection decisions and to do research on selection.

Finally, another source of data for researchers can come from **archival sources**, or datasets that have already been collected by others and are made available for analysis. Researchers may get archival datasets from an organization that is willing to share their data or from other researchers. In addition, archival datasets are collected through government-sponsored survey projects, and they can provide very large datasets that sample an entire population very well (e.g., workers, retirees). These archival datasets are available in the US as well as in many European countries; some archival datasets even sample the entire European Union. Although archival datasets can sometimes be very useful for researchers, they do have some drawbacks. Most notable is that archival datasets were rarely collected with an individual researcher's research questions in mind, and for that reason, archival datasets may not include all of the variables needed for a given research project.

Statistics

Statistical analysis is a central part of most I/O research. Statistical analyses allow the researcher to determine whether the results are just a matter of chance, or whether they are a systematic effect due to the phenomenon being studied. The purpose of this section is not to cover the details of statistical analyses, or how one might actually calculate a number of specific statistics. Rather, we want to show you the purpose of different statistical analyses. In that sense, we treat these different types of statistics as tools that can be used by the researchers to examine the results of a study.

Basic Statistical Concepts

Before we get into the more detailed aspects of statistical analyses, it's important to review some basic statistical concepts. We will begin by examining statistics that indicate central tendency. The first of these is one that you're probably familiar with, the **mean**, or the average. If a company wanted to know what the average job satisfaction is among their employees, they could do a satisfaction survey and simply calculate the average. Let's say the job satisfaction among a group of nine employees was as follows on a five-point scale.

Mean: A statistic measuring the central tendency, also referred to as the average. The mean is calculated by taking the sum of the scores and dividing it by the number of scores.

Employee responses:

5, 5, 4, 4, 3, 3, 1, 1, 1

In this case, the mean would be:

$$\frac{5 + 5 + 4 + 4 + 3 + 3 + 1 + 1 + 1}{9} = 3$$

Second is the **median**, or the central score in a group of scores or distribution of scores. The median would be 3, because 3 is the middle number in the list of nine scores. Finally, the **mode**, or most frequently occurring number in the group of scores, is 1.

In addition to central tendency, there are statistics that reflect the spread of scores. One of these is the **range**, or the highest minus the lowest score. In this case, the scores given are from 1 to 5, so the range is 4. In addition there is the **standard deviation**, which expresses the variability of scores around the mean as the average deviation from the mean. The same list of numbers is shown in Table 2.1, demonstrating how the standard deviation can be calculated.

Table 2.1 Example calculation of a mean and standard deviation

Score	Minus the Mean (3)	Squared
5.00	2	4
5.00	2	4
4.00	1	1
4.00	1	1
3.00	0	0
3.00	0	0
1.00	−2	4
1.00	−2	4
1.00	−2	4
Total = 27		Total = 22
Mean = 3		22/(9 − 1) = 2.75
		$\sqrt{2.75}$ = 1.66

We would total the numbers in the final column (22), divide by n−1 (in this case 9 − 1 = 8), which equals 2.75, and take the square root. In this case, the standard deviation would be 1.66. So with this group of scores, the mean is 3, and the standard deviation is 1.66.

Now that we have gone over these basic statistics that can be used to describe datasets, it's time to talk about some of the statistics that allow us to test hypotheses based on our samples. These statistics, which should be seen as "tools" for answering different types of research questions, are summarized in Figure 2.4. These statistical tests allow us to see if the relationship between variables or if the differences between groups are statically significant. **Statistical significance** means that the results of a study appear to be "real" and are not just due to chance. The norm among most researchers for statistical significance is that there is less than a 5 percent chance that the results are simply due to chance.

Figure 2.4
Common
statistics and
what they are
used for.

	Statistic	Purpose
X?Y	Correlation	To determine the degree of **relationship between two variables, X and Y,** and whether this relationship is statistically significant. This includes both the magnitude and direction of the relationship. The squared correlation expresses the percent of variance explained in one variable by the other.
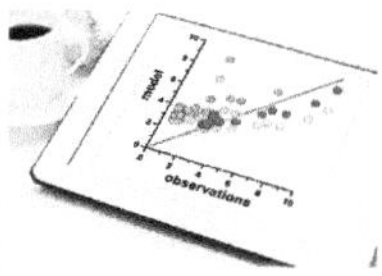	Linear regression	To determine the degree of relationship between two variables, X and Y, and whether this relationship is statistically significant. **It describes the "best fit" line** that describes that relationship by means of an equation. This equation also allows you to calculate a "predicted score" on the Y variable from a given X variable.
	t-test	To determine whether the difference between **two means** is statistically significant. This can be for **two groups** (e.g., an experimental and control group), or two means of the same group at different times (e.g., the mean of one group before an intervention compared with its mean after an intervention).
	Analysis of variance (ANOVA)	To determine whether the difference among **three or more means** is statistically significant.
	Meta-analysis	To statistically summarize the results of a group of studies.

Correlation: A Test of the Relationship between Variables

Correlation: Indicates the magnitude of the relationship between two variables as well as the direction of that relationship, on a scale of −1.0 to 1.0.

The first of these statistics is **correlation**, which indicates the magnitude of the relationship between two variables, X and Y, as well as the direction of that relationship, on a scale of −1.00 to 1.00. Values closer to −1.00 or 1.00 indicate a stronger relationship. Here we give a few examples.

Suppose you are interested in examining the relationship between job satisfaction and job performance in a sample of 100 employees. You end up with a scatter plot as shown in Figure 2.5, where job satisfaction is on the X-axis, and performance is on the Y-axis.

Note that this scatter plot by itself does not really tell you how strong the relationship is, that is, the degree to which variability in job satisfaction relates to the

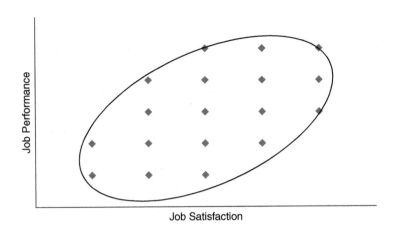

Figure 2.5 Simple scatter plot of relationship between job satisfaction and performance.

variability in job performance. However, let's say that you calculate the correlation coefficient (using software such as SPSS or Excel) and you come up with a correlation of $r = .30$. This suggests that higher job satisfaction scores tend to be related to higher scores in job performance. There is no way to tell if one causes the other, or if some variable affects them both – only that they coincide.

Also, consider that the squared correlation describes the *percentage of variance in one variable accounted for by the other* (sometimes referred to as the "coefficient of determination"). In this case, job satisfaction accounts for 9 percent of the variance in job performance. But again, we can't assume causality.

One last example: let's say you're trying to choose between two tests to see which is a better predictor of job performance. Here are the correlations with job performance for the two tests:

Test A: $r = .30$
Test B: $r = -.40$.

Which of these is the better predictor of job performance? In this case, the better predictor of job performance is Test B, because if you square both correlations, Test B accounts for 16 percent of the variance, while Test A accounts for 9 percent of the variance.

Linear Regression: Predicting One Score from Another

Correlations are one of the most frequently used statistics in psychological research, but they definitely have their limitations. Specifically, while you can tell the *degree* of relationship between two variables, you can't try to estimate or predict a person's score on the Y measure from their score on X. For example, in the example above with job satisfaction and performance, even if you know that a given person's job satisfaction score is 4, you can't predict what their level of performance will be.

That's where **linear regression** comes in. The use of linear regression produces an equation that describes the best fitting line for expressing the relationship between two variables. Let's consider the data shown above for the relationship between job satisfaction and performance. The graph in Figure 2.6 also indicates a "best fit" line to that particular set of data that expresses the relationship between the two variables.

Linear regression: Used to determine the degree of relationship between two variables, X and Y, and whether this relationship is statistically significant. It also describes the best-fit line that describes the relationship in terms of an equation. This also allows one to calculate a predicted score on the Y variable from a given X variable.

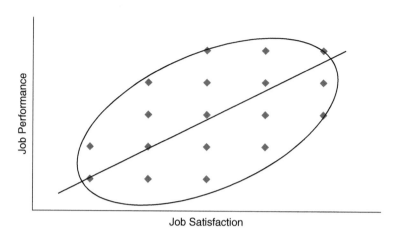

Figure 2.6 Best-fit regression line explaining the relationship between job satisfaction and performance.

The line is expressed in terms of:

Y = bx + a.

Here, Y is the predicted job performance score, b is the relative weight of the predictor (slope of the line), x is the job satisfaction score, and a is the y-intercept or constant. (Note that while you can calculate a regression equation by hand, this is beyond the scope of this book, and such statistics are typically calculated by means of statistical software these days.) So let's say that the regression equation for predicting job performance from job satisfaction was:

Y = 2x + 3.

If a new employee, Marcia, had a job satisfaction level of 4, we would predict that her job performance level would be 11.

There is one important caveat here. In our example, 11 would be Marcia's *predicted* score, but we don't know for sure what her actual job performance score would be. In other words, 11 is our best guess, but depending on the strength of the relationship between job satisfaction and performance, her actual job performance score could be quite different. (In fact, there is a standard deviation around the predicted score, depending on how strong the correlation is between X and Y.)

In summary, linear regression allows us not only to know the degree of relationship between two variables, but also to express this relationship in terms of a line. Moreover, a linear regression equation allows us to use this line to estimate what a person's score would be on the Y variable based on their score on the X variable. And one more thing: Regression also allows us to predict a Y value from *multiple* X scores. For example, one might use measures of both "job satisfaction" (X_1) and "engagement" (X_2) to predict job performance (Y).

Differences between Two Means: T-Tests

As we discussed earlier in this chapter, sometimes a researcher can have two groups – an experimental and control group, for instance – that he or she wants to

Table 2.2 T-test example

Control Group	Trained Group (Classroom Training)
56.00	70.00
57.00	65.00
53.00	68.00
44.00	70.00
67.00	82.00
50.00	59.00
70.00	72.00
45.00	68.00
78.00	80.00
60.00	60.00
Mean = 58.00	Mean = 69.40

compare to see if they are similar or different. For example, perhaps the researcher wants to examine the effects of a classroom-based training program designed to improve employee job knowledge. She compares the job knowledge (as measured on a test) of a group of trained employees with that of a control group that has not received any training. A statistic she could use to compare the mean of two groups is the **t-test**. For example, let's say that the job knowledge test scores of the two groups are shown in Table 2.2.

Clearly, the mean for the trained group scores is higher than the mean in the control group, suggesting that the training was effective. But is this a statistically significant difference? Running a t-test can tell you that. In this case, by calculating a t-test using statistical software, the researcher found that the t-value was 2.7, which with a sample size of 20 is statistically significant. This suggests that those in the trained group were higher than the control in terms of job knowledge, and that this difference was big enough that it wasn't just due to chance.

Keep in mind that the t-test can be used not only to compare two different groups of people, but also the same group of people at different times. For example, you might have a group of 10 employees, and you put them all through a training program, and then compare their scores before training with their scores after training. You would again use a t-test (although with a different formula) because you would be comparing two means.

T-test: Used to determine whether the difference between two means is statistically significant. This can be for two groups (e.g., an experimental and control group), or two means of the same group at different times (e.g., the mean of one group before an intervention compared with its mean after an intervention).

Differences between Three or More Means: ANOVA

Frequently, studies require that you compare the means of more than two groups. In this case, the statistic of choice is Analysis of Variance or **ANOVA**. ANOVA calculates a statistic (called an *F*-test) which tells you whether the differences among three or more groups are statistically significant. Let's stick with the same training example. Let's say that instead of having only a group trained in the classroom, the

Analysis of Variance (ANOVA): Used to compare the means of more than two groups. ANOVA calculates an *F*-ratio that tells you whether the differences among three or more groups are statistically significant.

Table 2.3 ANOVA example

Control Group	Trained Group (Class-room Training)	Trained Group (Online Training)
56.00	70.00	68.00
57.00	65.00	65.00
53.00	68.00	68.00
44.00	70.00	70.00
67.00	82.00	83.00
50.00	59.00	59.00
70.00	72.00	77.00
45.00	68.00	68.00
78.00	80.00	82.00
60.00	60.00	56.00
Mean = 58.00	Mean = 69.40	Mean = 69.60

researcher wants to also examine the effectiveness of an online training program compared to the classroom training and the control group. The results that he finds are shown in Table 2.3.

In this case, the researcher runs an ANOVA and finds that there are statistically significant differences between the groups. The researcher would then follow up with t-tests to see where those differences are. In this case, both of the trained groups scored better than the control, but the differences between the two trained groups are not statistically significant. In other words, the two types of training appear to be equally effective, and both are more effective than no training at all.

Summarizing the Findings of Multiple Studies: Meta-Analysis

Meta-analysis:
A statistical analysis of a group of studies by researchers so that conclusions might be drawn about a particular phenomenon.

As in most areas of science, I/O psychology accumulates a body of knowledge on a particular topic. But even after many studies have been conducted, it can be hard to conclude what the actual findings are. Some studies might show a weak, non-significant relationship between variables, while others might show that the relationship is robust. How do we interpret findings like this? In addition to a careful reading and review of the various studies – an important step in any research area – it is also possible to summarize research findings across many studies. This statistical analysis is called **meta-analysis**. Pioneered in I/O psychology by Frank Schmidt and John Hunter (e.g., Schmidt & Hunter, 1981), meta-analysis allows for a statistical analysis of a group of studies by researchers so that conclusions might be drawn about a particular phenomenon – perhaps the relationship between two variables or the effects of a particular type of workplace intervention. It takes into account a number of statistical issues about the studies, such as their sample sizes. For example, the reason that some studies might not show a strong relationship between two variables is that those studies used samples that were too small. By analyzing the results of multiple studies, meta-analysis is able to take the sample size into account, resulting in more precise estimates and making sense of inconsistent findings. Further, meta-analytic studies also allow you to see if different results in different studies might be due to other variables (referred to as "moderators"). For example, it might be that the relationship between two variables differs by whether the sample is workers in one industry versus another or whether studies were conducted in the lab or the field. Meta-analysis allows you to look at other factors such as these. As you can see, meta-analysis is a powerful tool for understanding a body of research, and thus it has become indispensable not only in I/O psychology, but also in many areas of research such as medicine (DerSimonian & Laird, 1986).

 "See website for interactive material"

Interactive: Knowing which statistic to use to answer a particular research question.

Workplace Application

How a Meta-Analysis Changed HR Practice

For many years, I/O psychologists considered personality tests to be of low value for making hiring decisions. This was because much of the research on personality tests for selection was focused on tests of abnormal personality. However, a landmark meta-analysis by Barrick and Mount (1991) found that personality tests of normal adult personality can predict job performance. This meta-analysis led to a dramatic change in HR practice, where today personality tests are part of the hiring process for many jobs, and some work is even focused on measuring personality using gaming technology (Lohr, 2013).

Measurement of Variables

Now that we have discussed some of the issues involved in research, including the design of studies and an overview of key statistics, we next spend some time on the concept of psychometrics, that is, the measurement of psychological variables. Let's go back to our sample where we wanted to examine the relationship between job satisfaction and job performance. How do you know whether you have good measures or not? In other words, whether or not you find the relationship between satisfaction and performance, you cannot know how to interpret your findings unless you know that you have actually got strong measures of satisfaction and performance. What kind of measures will you use – for example, a test completed by each participant or a rating scale completed by their coworkers? How do you know if your two measures (i.e., of satisfaction and performance) are actually measuring what they are supposed to measure? Answering these questions involves deciding what kind of scales you want to use to measure the main study variables. Plus, you should be confident that the measures really are dependable and measure what they are supposed to measure.

These issues around the measurement of variables in research are very important to psychological research, including I/O psychology. In fact, as you will see in Chapter 7, there are even professional and legal (in the US) guidelines about how to develop measures that are used for making selection systems. Let's look at some of the measurement issues, starting with the type of scale. Then we'll move on to the super-important issues of showing that our measures actually are good, that is, the concepts of reliability and validity. Our discussion of measurement is based on "true score theory" (e.g., Lord & Novick, 1968), which is the most commonly used approach to measurement in psychological research.

Types of Measurement Scales

The first choice is to consider what type of measurement scale to use. Here's an example from a work organization. Let's say that a manager is interested in assessing the performance of her employees. She might simply rank the employees from best to worst. This might be fine, but the problem with this approach is that it doesn't really say whether the employees are performing well or not. Alternatively, she might rate them on a scale of 1 to 5, with 5 being excellent and 1 being poor. This would allow her to consider not only who is performing better than whom, but also to see how the employees are doing in absolute terms. This can also be important for providing employees with feedback. Let's consider the situation of one of her employees, Chris. Put yourself in Chris's place. Chris might be told that he is not doing as well as Maya, but is doing better than Jaime. That doesn't really tell him whether he is doing well or poorly – he may not even know Jaime and Maya. But if he is given a more meaningful rating, say, a 4 out of 5, that tells him a lot more about how he is performing. This example shows the difference between a **relative** scale, which indicates only a person's level on a variable relative to other people, versus an **absolute** scale, which also indicates a person's level on a variable in specific terms. (These scales will be discussed in more depth in Chapter 5.)

Another way to think about different measures is along a continuum with four points: nominal, ordinal, interval, and ratio. A **nominal** scale simply classifies a person into a category. An example would be a scale that classifies a person as male or female or by ethnicity. This is certainly good information to have, but categorical variables are limited in terms of the statistics that can be performed on them. Next is **ordinal** variables, which indicate where someone falls on a scale relative to others. This is the relative scale we discussed earlier. Statistically, this scale is more enriched than simply a nominal scale, but it is not sufficient for most research purposes. **Interval** scales, on the other hand, have meaningful differences between them, such that the difference between a 1 and a 2 is the same as the difference between a 2 and a 3, a 3 and 4, and so on. Most psychological variables are measured on interval scales (or else they are assumed to do so), and these are the types of scales that are best analyzed using the main statistics we have described - t-tests, correlations,

Relative scale: Indicates a person's level on a variable relative to other people.

Absolute scale: Indicates a person's level on a variable in specific terms.

Nominal scale: Classifies a person into a category such as male/female.

Ordinal scale: Indicates the place someone falls on a scale relative to others. However, this does not provide a meaningful difference between positions on the scale.

Interval scales: Have meaningful difference between positions on the scale, such that the difference between a 1 and 2 is the same as the difference between a 2 and a 3.

ANOVAs, or regressions. Finally, we can also use **ratio** scales, which are assumed to have an absolute zero, but that is not as common with most psychological measures. For instance, it is highly unlikely that a person would be classified as having "zero" conscientiousness or intelligence. Rather, ratio types of measures would include age or income – where it is in fact possible for the measure to be zero.

Once you know what type of scale you are using, it's also important to know that the measures you are using really are dependably measuring something that you care about. This is where the key concepts of reliability and validity come into the decision-making process.

Ratio scales: Are assumed to have an absolute zero, as well as a meaningful difference between positions on the scale.

Reliability: Dependability or Consistency of Measurement

One of the first things a researcher wants to be sure about when using psychological measures in their research is that the measures are reliable. **Reliability** refers to the dependability of a measure, or its consistency in measuring people relative to others in a group. A quick example: Let's say you are measuring the conscientiousness of a group of employees. You would assume that your conscientiousness measure assesses a stable variable, like most personality variables. Let's assume that your conscientiousness measure is on a scale of 1 to 10, and you have been able to administer your conscientiousness measure on two occasions, one week apart. In looking over the conscientiousness scores for the group, you notice that people's scores change a lot: For instance, you notice that one of the employees, Carmela, scores a 9 one week and a 2 the next week. You also notice that another employee, Virgil, scores a 3 one week and a 10 the next. If you got these kinds of results, you would be correct in worrying about the quality of this measure, because it does not give consistent measures of the employees. In fact, the test seems to be giving you random numbers rather than any kind of consistent measurement.

This then is at the heart of reliability, namely, whether a measure gives you consistent and dependable measures of something. Why is this so important? Reliability has an inverse relationship with measurement error. (See Figure 2.7.) That is, the more unreliable a measure is, the higher it is in measurement error or error variance. In the example above, this would suggest that differences in test scores are mostly due to random error, or giving you random numbers – not very helpful in differentiating among individuals. Rather, for reliable measures, people should give consistent responses each time they complete a measure. Further, the measure should be consistent in its ordering of a group of individuals: For example, a personality test should be consistent in terms of who gets the highest and lowest scores among a group of individuals.

How do you know how reliable the test is? Reliability is measured on a scale of 0 (not reliable, pure measurement error) to 1 (perfect reliability, no measurement error). Note that in the real world, few, if any, psychological measures have perfect reliability. But our goal is to get the reliability as high as possible by developing good measures. In addition, you can't really know "the reliability" of a measure – all you can do is come up with these sorts of estimates of it. Let's look at the different approaches researchers can take to estimating the reliability of a measure. As you will see, none of these estimates of reliability is perfect, and in deciding which way to

Reliability: Refers to the dependability of a measure, or its consistency in measurement.

Figure 2.7
The inverse relationship between reliability and error variance.

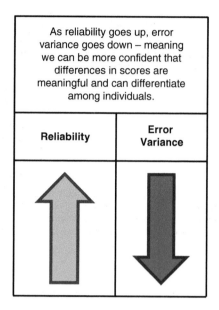

As reliability goes up, error variance goes down – meaning we can be more confident that differences in scores are meaningful and can differentiate among individuals.

Reliability	Error Variance

estimate reliability, researchers usually need to consider the type of test and sample, as well as practical issues such as the availability of the sample. A summary of the different reliability estimates described in this chapter is given in Figure 2.8.

Test–Retest Reliability

Test-retest reliability: Where a test is given to a group of people twice in order to see how stable their scores are by correlating their test scores.

The first way of estimating the reliability of a measure, referred to as **test-retest reliability**, is to administer it to a group of people and see how stable their scores are. For example, a researcher might give the measure of conscientiousness to a group of workers one week, and then give it to them again a week later. The test-retest reliability estimate would be the correlation between the scores from the two administrations. Let's give an example. In Table 2.4, we show the hypothetical test data for a group of 15 employees who have taken a conscientiousness test one week apart. To calculate the test-retest reliability, we would simply correlate their test scores from the first week with their scores on the second week. The result in this case is a correlation of .95, which is the test-retest reliability for this test.

There are a couple of caveats with the test-retest approach. First, you do not want to give the two tests too close together. If you do, people may remember what they put the first time and just put the same answers again. This would cause the correlation between the two administrations to be very high and give you an over-estimate of the reliability. On the other hand, you do not want to administer the measures too far apart, either. Here's an example of how that could create problems. Let's say you want to know the reliability of a test of 3rd grade reading, and you give the test to some schoolchildren in the fall and then later in the spring. You would probably get an underestimate of the reliability: The kids probably change over that period of time, and so their scores six months apart would be very different, and you would end up with a low reliability estimate. But those changes would be real and would not really be indicating low reliability. One key issue with test-retest, then, is to be sure that you have chosen the right length of time between

Reliability Estimate	What It Involves	Points to Consider
Test–Retest Test A Time 1 Test A Time 2	Administer the test or measure to a group of people on **two occasions.** Correlate scores from the two occasions.	• Participants may not come back for the second administration. • Participants may remember what they put on the first administration and give an overestimate of reliability. • Time interval between two test administrations must not be too long or people may change (maturation effects) and give an underestimate of the reliability.
Parallel Forms Test Form A Test Form B	Administer two, parallel forms of the measure to a group of people on a **single occasion.** Correlate the scores obtained from the two measures.	• Difficult to develop two different measures. • Participants may become fatigued.
Internal Consistency		
• Split Halves Test A Odds Test A Evens	Administer the measure to a group of people on a single occasion. Correlate their scores on the two halves of the test (e.g., odd-numbered items and even-numbered items).	• Gives a reliability estimate of a test that is only half as long (under-estimate), so must correct using Spearman-Brown correction. • May not be suitable for measures that assess multiple constructs.
• Coefficient Alpha Test A Intercorrelation	Administer the measure to a group of people on a single occasion. Calculate intercorrelations of the items.	• Not suitable for measures that assess multiple constructs.
Interrater Rater A Rater B	Used when two people rate a series of job candidates (e.g., in a hiring interview) or employees. Calculate the correlation between Rater A's scores and Rater B's scores.	• To help enhance reliability, raters should be trained on what to look for in their ratings.

Figure 2.8
Summary of reliability estimates.

the two administrations of the measure. One additional challenge with test–retest reliability is that you may lose some people between the two administrations, or people may simply refuse to participate in your study a second time. That is where other ways of estimating test reliability might come in handy instead.

Parallel Forms Reliability

Let's say you don't want to be bothered to test people on two occasions, or there is no way to get participants to come in twice to take a test or measure. An alternative way is to give participants two parallel forms of the test or measure. This

Parallel forms reliability: Where two forms of a test are given to the same people at the same time and the scores on both measures are correlated to provide a reliability estimate.

Table 2.4 Test scores for a group of 15 employees

Test Taker	Test Score at Time 1	Test Score at Time 2
Stephanie	12	14
Jermaine	14	14
Kim	11	12
Luis	12	11
Larry	4	3
Vernon	6	8
Kelly	2	1
Yusef	15	15
Theresa	11	10
Millicent	8	9
Nancy	3	5
Martha	3	3
LaRue	16	14
Mark	14	11
Silvia	6	7

Note: Time 1 and Time 2 are the test scores for each employee on two occasions, one week apart.

is a common practice for many test publishers, who have different forms or versions of the test available in order to preserve test security. Parallel forms is quite straightforward: Instead of having people take the same test twice on separate occasions, you would have them take the two versions of the test one time. So, going back to the example, you might have two versions of the conscientiousness measure and your employees take Form A and Form B of the conscientiousness test, both on the same day. The reliability estimate would be the correlation between their scores on Form A and Form B. The employees don't need to come back again, so in this regard, it's an easy way to estimate reliability.

So what are the drawbacks? First, making two parallel versions of a test is a lot of work – twice the work. In other words, parallel forms are usually used to estimate reliability when there is the need for multiple versions of a test; you would not make a second version just to use it to calculate reliability. Second, it can be very difficult to develop truly parallel forms of a test. In other words, try as you might, the tests are never completely parallel, so they may underestimate the reliability. Third – and this is important – even though participants don't need to come back for a second test administration, they do have to sit through two versions of the test or measure. They may become fatigued towards the end and lose motivation to do their best on the assessment.

Internal Consistency Estimates

Internal consistency reliability estimates are just what they sound like: They assume that the test or measure assesses one thing, and thus if they are reliable, the test will be internally consistent and thus the items should be intercorrelated, or that each respondent answered each of the items similarly. There are two common ways to do this.

The first approach is **split-halves** reliability, in which the two halves of the test, usually the odd-numbered and even-numbered items, are treated as two small tests and then correlated with each other. In this sense, split-halves is like parallel forms: It assumes that the two halves of the test are just two smaller tests administered at the same time. Further, split-halves is convenient – it takes only one test administration, and you need only one version of the test. One caveat, however: The reliability from simply correlating the scores on the odd- versus even-numbered items gives a slight underestimate of the reliability. This is because a short test will always have lower reliability than a longer test. In other words, if you have a 100-item test, and correlate its two halves, you've actually calculated the reliability of a 50-item test. For this reason, we use the Spearman-Brown formula to slightly correct (increase) the reliability estimate.

A second type of internal consistency is one you may have seen in journal articles, and it is called **coefficient alpha**. Alpha is an index of the intercorrelation among scale items, or the average of all possible split-halves. Alpha is very commonly used these days because it is calculated by most statistical software used in the social sciences. However, because alpha is based on the assumption that the test measures only one dimension, it is not appropriate in situations where a test measures more than one construct. An example would be where a test of "scholastic achievement" measures mathematical ability and verbal ability. Calculating an alpha reliability for the whole test under those conditions would be inappropriate, because the test actually measures two subdimensions. A detailed discussion of the uses – and misuses – of alpha is given in Cortina (1993).

Interrater Reliability

So far we have talked about ways to calculate reliability for tests or scales. But there are other measures commonly used in I/O psychology where two or more people evaluate individuals. An example would be the structured interview (see Chapter 6), where two interviewers would rate a series of job candidates. In that case, you can also use **interrater reliability** to estimate the reliability of a test, where the ratings of one rater are correlated with the ratings of another rater. Let's give an example. Suppose you have 20 applicants applying for the job of software engineer. Two senior engineers together interview these 20 applicants, and their ratings are shown in Table 2.5. If you simply correlated the ratings for Interviewer 1 with Interviewer 2, the correlation is .73. This, then, is the interrater reliability estimate for these interview scores.

Some Final Words About Reliability

We would like to make a few points before leaving the concept of reliability. First, there are other ways to calculate reliability, but here we have given you some of the

Internal consistency estimates: Measures of reliability that assume the test or measure assesses one thing, and thus if reliable, the test will be internally consistent and the items should be intercorrelated.

Split-halves reliability: An internal consistency estimate in which two halves of the test (e.g., odd-numbered and even-numbered items) are treated as two small tests and measures how consistent the scores are between the two tests.

Coefficient alpha: An index of the intercorrelation among scale items, or the average of all possible spilt-halves reliability estimates.

Interrater reliability: Where ratings of one rater are correlated with the ratings of another rater.

Table 2.5 Ratings of 20 job applicants for a software engineer's job by two interviewers

Job Applicant	Ratings for Interviewer 1	Ratings for Interviewer 2
Tom	5	3
Karen	4	3
Bernard	1	2
Abdul	5	4
Maria	4	5
Cecily	3	2
Howard	2	2
Ramon	4	3
Antonio	4	5
Jiang	3	3
Darrell	2	1
Camille	2	2
Manuela	5	5
Alice	4	5
Ana	4	4
Vanessa	3	2
Brian	4	3
Tamara	5	4
Lincoln	4	4
Bill	4	4

most common types. Second, one question you may have throughout this discussion is "How much reliability is enough?" There is no definite way to answer that, and there has been a bit of controversy on this topic (Lance, Butts, & Michels, 2006). Some researchers would say that for measures used in most I/O research, a reliability of .70 is a minimum (Nunnally, 1978). On the other hand, that can vary by what the measure is used for. For example, the reliability of measures used in making hiring decisions are recommended to be at least .85 (Gatewood, Feild, & Barrick, 2011). In any case, more reliability is always better because that means less error variance.

Third, one of the reasons that reliability is so important is because it is a necessary condition for validity: If a test is not reliable, it cannot be valid. Consider our example of a conscientiousness test: If you found that the test was not reliable, in other words, that it was all error variance, how could the test possibly be valid in terms of measuring a specific construct? For that reason, we want to have measures that are as reliable as possible to ensure that they can be valid. We discuss the concept of validity next.

Validity: What a Scale Is Actually Measuring

Once you have shown that a measure is reliable, the next issue is to show that it is valid. **Validity** is the extent to which the measure is actually measuring what it is supposed to measure. Think of it this way: Reliability indicates that a measure is measuring *something* consistently, but we don't know what that "something" is. For example, you might have a scale that consistently says you weigh 20 pounds. It is reliable because it consistently gives this weight every time you step on the scale. However, as an adult, it is highly unlikely that you actually weigh 20 pounds. Validity takes the next step and shows *what* the measure is measuring – in this case, your true weight.

There are a number of different ways to show that a scale or test is valid. Here we will describe the three most common ways to demonstrate validity – content, construct, and criterion-related validity – because this is a straightforward way to explain the validation process to people who are not experts in psychometrics. However, as other authors have pointed out (Landy, 1986), we really should think of "validity" as a single concept, not three; there are many ways to accumulate evidence that a test is measuring what it is supposed to measure. For those interested in additional information about the validation of psychological measures, a particularly accepted source in I/O psychology research is Hinkin (1998), which describes the steps involved in accumulating validity evidence. In addition, note that in Chapter 7 we go into further detail regarding validity within the context of personnel selection, particularly in the legal sense, including legal guidelines such as the *Uniform Guidelines on Employee Selection Procedures* (1978) and SIOP's *Principles for the Validation and Use of Employee Selection Procedures* (2003). In any case, here we describe three common ways of accumulating validity evidence which, taken together, can demonstrate the test's validity.

Content validity is really more of a process, showing that the measure was developed in a way that sampled the domain of interest. For example, if you were developing a test of conscientiousness, you might ask experts in personality psychology to provide you with item content for a test of conscientiousness. Or as another example, if you wanted to develop a content-valid test of college algebra, you might refer to algebra textbooks and consult with college algebra instructors in developing your items for the test. In short, content validity involves relatively little in terms of statistical analysis, but is heavy on *documenting* that the test actually samples a domain that you want to measure.

By contrast, **criterion-related validity** involves the empirical demonstration that the test predicts a criterion or outcome that you care about, usually as demonstrated through a correlation between the test and the criterion. Let's give a simple example. Suppose that you were trying to predict employee turnover within a company. Given that this is a sales job, you have some evidence from the company that the people who are leaving are more introverted than others. Your goal, then, is to see whether introversion is a predictor of turnover in the company. You give the measure of introversion to 400 new hires and then correlate the test scores with whether the person has left the company six months later. You find that introversion is in fact correlated .32 with turnover, a statistically

Validity: The extent to which the measure is actually measuring what it is supposed to measure.

Content validity: A process demonstrating a measure was developed in a way that sampled the domain of interest. This process involves documenting that the test actually samples the desired domain.

Criterion-related validity: Involves the empirical demonstration that the test predicts a criterion or outcome that you care about. This is commonly done by correlating the test and the criterion.

Figure 2.9 Construct validity subsumes other types of validity evidence. Multiple methods of accumulating validity evidence lead to better understanding the construct measured.

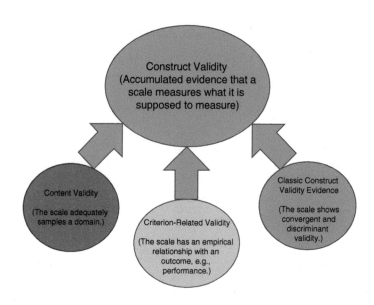

significant relationship. This would then be evidence that the introversion test has some criterion-related validity, because it does in fact predict turnover; and .32, the correlation between the introversion measure and the important criterion you are trying to predict, would be referred to as the **validity coefficient**. Note that there are different types of criterion-related validity designs – where the data are collected at one time point (*concurrent validity study*) and where the data are collected at two time points (*predictive validity study*) – which are discussed in greater detail in Chapter 7.

A third, very important approach to validity is **construct validity**, or the accumulation of evidence that the measure really is measuring what it is supposed to measure. We say construct validity is important because the accumulated evidence from construct validity studies is at the heart of showing just what it is that a test or scale measures; in other words, construct validity is at the heart of validity. Let's slow down and give some examples of different types of construct validity evidence.

First are the concepts of convergent and discriminant validity. **Convergent validity** is the degree to which a measure correlates with other measures with which it should have a relationship. Going back to our example of the college algebra test, if you found that it correlated with other measures of algebra, and perhaps to a lesser extent with measures of "geometry" and "trigonometry", that would be great convergent validity evidence. By contrast, **discriminant validity** (sometimes also called "divergent validity") is the degree to which the measure does *not* show a relationship with things it should not relate to. For example, you would not expect your algebra test to correlate with a measure of "verbal fluency". In that sense, a low correlation between algebra test scores and verbal fluency scores would indicate high discriminant validity (in other words, you want a discriminant validity coefficient to be low). In fact, if you found that your algebra test did show a strong relationship with a verbal fluency test, it would set off some alarms that it was not really a pure measure of algebra skills but also contained a strong verbal

Validity coefficient: The coefficient calculated between the test and the criterion, commonly a correlation between the two variables.

Construct validity: The accumulation of evidence that the measure really is measuring what it is supposed to measure.

Convergent validity: The degree to which a measure correlates with measures it should have a relationship with.

Discriminant (divergent) validity: Sometimes called divergent validity, it is the degree to which the measure does not show a relationship with things it should not be related to.

component as well. A final point to consider with construct validity is that it in many ways overarches or subsumes the others. For example, what if you also found that your test of conscientiousness was related to job performance ratings of dependability from supervisors? Under some circumstances, people might consider this as criterion-related validity because it is showing the relationship between the measure and an important outcome, job performance. On the other hand, this is also pretty good evidence that the test is measuring what it is supposed to measure - it is in fact correlated with another measure of dependability taken from the job. Our point here is that there are not three "types" of validity, but many different types of evidence that a measure is valid, and that in many ways, construct validity is the overarching method for accumulating validity evidence because of its focus on the accumulation of validity evidence from multiple studies.

Workplace Application

Legal and Ethical Issues around Test Validation

How to go about validating a test may seem to be a purely academic subject, but nothing could be further from the truth. In fact, as we'll see in Chapter 7, the procedures for validating tests used to make hiring decisions are stipulated not only by professional guidelines (such as SIOP's *Principles for the Validation and Use of Personnel Selection Procedures*, 2003), but also by federal court cases and guidelines (*Uniform Guidelines on Employee Selection Procedures*, 1978). In fact, failing to comply with validation guidelines can result in costly lawsuits and bad publicity for the organization.

Ethical Issues

Throughout the research process, it is important to consider the ethical treatment of research participants. This includes issues like providing participants with informed consent before they agree to participate in the study so that they can know what the study will require before they begin. Participation in the study must be completely voluntary: For I/O research conducted in organizations, this includes participants being informed that their participation is completely voluntary, and that their participation or lack of participation will not have negative effects. In addition, some I/O studies include anonymity of participants so that it will not be possible to identify who participated in the study or their responses. Similarly, rather than completely removing all identifying information, some studies may simply require that the researcher keep participants' study responses confidential. These basic principles behind research ethics - voluntary, informed consent - are

Institutional Review Board (IRB): A board or group of people who govern the research process at an institution.

important to keep in mind. Most universities have an **institutional review board** (IRB), which governs the research process at that institution. Some organizations such as Microsoft have even taken steps to create their own internal procedures to ensure that research is done in an appropriate manner (Goel, 2014).

For I/O psychologists working in non-academic settings, a number of ethical dilemmas may present themselves. One of the things that makes the ethics issue particularly challenging is that ethical issues can take so many forms in organizations because of the diversity of issues that I/O psychologists are involved in: For example, selection, occupational safety and health, and training all present very different ethical issues. Lowman (e.g., Lowman, 2006, 2012) provides a discussion of the ethical issues related to I/O psychology, including case studies on a range of issues relevant to I/O.

Given these challenges, I/O psychologists should look to guidance from professional organizations. The American Psychological Association provides a detailed ethical code (2010) which includes a number of principles such as justice and integrity. It also addresses issues that are relevant to I/O, such as balancing organizational demands with ethical principles, working only within areas of competence, avoiding harm, and conflicts of interest. Further, the Academy of Management provides its own code of ethics (2006), including guidelines for treatment of research participants, students, and employees, as well as managers and people within the community.

GLOBAL IMPLICATIONS

Although we point out research issues that relate to the chapter in question throughout this text, here we note a few general issues that can arise in doing cross-cultural research in organizations (Truxillo & Fraccaroli, 2014). First, when comparing findings across countries, it is important to know whether the survey measures are equivalent. For example, if a researcher were measuring job satisfaction in the US and in Colombia, it would be important to know that the job satisfaction items had been carefully developed so that the English and Spanish items were measuring the same thing. One way to do this is through a process called translation and back-translation (Brislin, 1970). In the example here (see Figure 2.10), if beginning with a measure of job satisfaction that is originally in English, the job satisfaction items would be translated into Spanish, and then back-translated by a different person back into English. The original English items would then be compared to the back-translated English items to see if they were equivalent. If so, we would know that the Spanish and English items had the same semantic meaning. A second, more fundamental issue with doing cross-cultural research is whether concepts that exist in one culture even exist in another. For example, many personality frameworks were developed in Western cultures, and they may not even be relevant in some cultures. In other words, researchers should be careful when doing research in other cultures that they are not overly biased by their own cultural background.

Figure 2.10 Simple example of translation and back-translation. Because the original and the final English item have the same meaning as the original, the process was successful, and the new Spanish item can be used.

CURRENT ISSUES AND CONTROVERSIES

In recent years, new methodological opportunities and questions have arisen in I/O psychology with new advances in statistics, computing capabilities, and online technology. The first of these is the very recent introduction of using online samples such as Amazon Mechanical Turk™ (mTurk) into I/O research. Online samples can provide an inexpensive way to pilot research questions that might be too costly to pilot in field settings, and also provide a useful way to test out survey scales. Although these online samples have been challenged as being artificial, one could make a similar argument about using unemployed college sophomores to examine workplace issues – a sample that has been used for quite some time. Further, although there are concerns about the quality of mTurk data (e.g., that those who do online surveys are careless), there are ways to check the quality of datasets, and some studies have shown that mTurk samples can provide robust results (Buhrmester, Kwang, & Gosling, 2011). In any case, the appropriateness of using such online samples is not a settled issue within the research community.

A second issue is the increasing use of sophisticated statistical computing approaches to analyze HR data (Lohr, 2013). This may lead to new discoveries about how to manage people – such as which worker behaviors are predictive of turnover. On the other hand, understanding how to interpret these findings in ways that are meaningful and generalizable to other settings may be a challenge. We have already touched on this use of "big data" in organizational research in Chapter 1, and it is also relevant to many of the chapters of this text.

Third, researchers are beginning to challenge some of the traditional approaches to research used by I/O psychologists. This may be due to the highly quantitative research approach I/O psychologists have taken in much of their work. Specifically, some scholars have raised concerns that the traditional approach to I/O research is to examine the relationship among variables, viewing the participant solely in terms of the variables identified in the study (Weiss & Rupp, 2011). This approach misses the point that participants are more complex than a sum of variables – they are complete individuals – and thus I/O psychologists should do more to consider the "whole person" rather than just a group of variables.

A fourth issue is a growing interest in I/O psychology in intervention research, that is, what employers can actually do to improve the attitudes, well-being, health, and performance of workers. Such intervention work can be challenging as it involves coordination (and trust) between researchers and the organizations where such intervention studies can be carried out. However, a number of recent studies (e.g., Hammer, Kossek, Anger, Bodner, & Zimmerman, 2011; Morgan, Walker, Hebl, & King, 2013) point to the value of examining the effectiveness of workplace interventions and the underlying processes that may explain their effectiveness.

WHAT DOES THIS MEAN TO YOU?

We have covered a number of topics that are relevant to research in I/O psychology. However, research design and data analysis are also relevant to anyone who must consume the results of research every day. More and more, that's all of us. What are some issues you should be aware of?

First, one study (especially in the social sciences) usually can't prove something definitively. Studies may use small samples, or they may be done only on limited populations, which makes it difficult to know whether the results will generalize to other groups. For instance, the results of a small-sample medical study where data are collected in only one country may not generalize to another country, where there may be differences in diet and exposures and even genetic differences in the populations. In most fields, multiple studies are required to draw definite conclusions.

Second, it is possible for researchers to present the results of studies in ways that can be misleading. For example, if a new product claimed that "70 percent of doctors surveyed said that this product is effective," it would imply that the medical profession is behind the product. But just which physicians were surveyed? Was the sample all of the physicians in the US, or those chosen to participate in the survey who were already using the product? Our point is that it is possible to easily mislead with the way that study results are presented, and it's always good to be a little bit skeptical – and ask a few questions – when you hear about the results of a study.

Third, one issue that we have mentioned in our discussion of statistics is statistical significance, for example, the results of a t-test, ANOVA, or correlation. As we've noted, statistical significance means that the results of a study are not simply due to chance – the norm among most researchers is that there is a less than 5 percent chance that the results are not at random. But statistical significance is not necessarily the same as **practical significance** or whether a result is meaningful and important. For example, if a manager in a company hears that a particular employee training program had a statistically significant effect on employee job knowledge, that might get her attention. But if she then heard that employees' knowledge went from 75/100 to 75.5/100, and the training cost $10,000 per employee, it would suggest that the results may not be of practical significance. In short, keep in mind that while statistical significance is important, it does not mean that the results are practical and meaningful.

In short, research can be quite valuable to you as a consumer, but care in interpreting the results – and asking a few questions – can be helpful.

Conclusion

Practical significance: Whether a result is meaningful or important in a real-world application.

In this chapter, we have discussed some of the key research issues in I/O psychology, from the development of research questions and theory, to research design, statistics, and measurement. Although it may seem that we have covered a large number of issues (which we have), we should also point out that this is just the "tip of the iceberg" – there are more elaborate research designs and statistical techniques that you'll encounter in reading the current I/O journals. However, this chapter should give you the basic building blocks for understanding how research in the field progresses and the challenges and decisions faced in I/O psychology research.

YOUR TURN... WHAT DO YOU THiNK?

1. What do you think is the value of a theory for (a) advancing science and (b) addressing problems in organizations? Consider both the relationship between research and theory, and also that between science and practice (Chapter 1).
2. You work in a research laboratory focused on figuring out the relationship between employees' perceptions of their coworkers and employees' health. What research design(s) would you consider? What would be the advantages and disadvantages of each? What types of data collection techniques would you use, and why?

3. A colleague of yours wants to develop a measure of "undergraduate student stress". Assuming that she can develop a reliable measure, how might you suggest that she go about showing the validity of the measure? (Consider all types of validity evidence.)

4. As noted in the chapter, I/O researchers often collect data using undergraduate students to answer certain types of research questions. What are the advantages and disadvantages of using these kinds of datasets for I/O research? How would they compare with using employees from a single company? Give an example of a case where you think that using undergraduate students might be appropriate.

5. Describe the type of statistical analysis you would use for each of these research questions:

a. What is the relationship between employee conscientiousness and work engagement?

b. What is the effect of a workplace stress-reduction program? You want to compare the mean stress levels of employees in the experimental and control conditions.

c. What is the effect of two workplace stress reduction programs and a control condition?

Additional Reading

Chan, D. (2011). Advances in analytical strategies. In S. Zedeck (Ed.), *APA handbook of industrial and organizational psychology, Vol 1: Building and developing the organization* (pp. 85–113). Washington, DC: American Psychological Association.

Greenberg, J. (2006). Losing sleep over organizational injustice: Attenuating insomniac reactions to underpayment inequity with supervisory training in interactional justice. *Journal of Applied Psychology, 91,* 58–69.

Guion, R. M. (2011). *Assessment, measurement, and prediction for personnel decisions.* New York: Routledge.

Landy, F. J. (1986). Stamp collecting versus science: Validation as hypothesis testing. *American Psychologist, 41,* 1183–1192.

Lefkowitz, J. (2003). *Ethics and values in industrial-organizational psychology.* London: Psychology Press.

Stone-Romero, E. F. (2011). Research strategies in industrial and organizational psychology: Nonexperimental, quasi-experimental, and randomized experimental research in special purpose and nonspecial purpose settings. In S. Zedeck (Ed.), *APA handbook of industrial and organizational psychology, Vol 1: Building and developing the organization* (pp. 37–72). Washington, DC: American Psychological Association.

CASE STUDY: The Job Satisfaction Survey

Enrique Mora was recently hired as the assistant HR manager of a mid-sized medical services company, Tabular Medical. Tabular has approximately 300 employees in 10 offices spread across New York and New Jersey. Their focus is family practice. There are approximately 80 physicians, with about 100 other medical personnel and 100 support staff (clerical workers). There is a single board of directors, who are the four owners (physicians) of the company. The board sets the course for the company.

Tabular has been quite successful in its 20 years of business, growing from a single medical practice to its present size. Throughout its history, Tabular has prided itself on having a strong team spirit and has attributed their success to each office maintaining its own independence and good collegiality.

Enrique was hired as part of the growth of the company: The organization had grown a bit too large for a single HR manager and staff, and the assistant HR manager position was created to take on special projects that the manager could not handle on her own.

As one of his projects, Enrique has been asked to conduct the company's first employee satisfaction survey. Specifically, the board has told Enrique that they want to see how satisfied employees are with the company, their work, and their coworkers so that they can bring the company to the next level.

Enrique has never conducted a survey before, but Tabular has agreed to provide him with an assistant for this job as well as with online survey software he might need to carry out the project.

Questions

1. How might Enrique go about developing items for the survey? What are some ways he could determine the survey's quality (reliability and validity)?

2. The board would like to use the survey to answer the following questions. For each question, state what statistical analysis you would recommend:

   a. What is the degree to which employee pay is related to job satisfaction?

   b. Is there a difference in satisfaction between the offices in New York and in New Jersey?

   c. Are there differences in levels of satisfaction across the 10 offices?

3. What are the ethical issues that are important for Enrique to keep in mind in this situation? Consider research ethics as well as ethics related to organizational practice.

4. One of the results of the survey is that one of the offices has lower job satisfaction than the others. Enrique is contacted by the manager of that office to learn more about the problem. Specifically, she wants to know which employees are "part of the problem." How should Enrique respond to this request?

References

Academy of Management. (2006). *Academy of Management code of ethics.* Retrieved August 12, 2014 from http://aom.org/uploadedFiles/About_AOM/Governance/AOM_Code_of_Ethics.pdf.

Adams, J. S. (1965). Inequity in social exchange. *Advances in Experimental Social Psychology, 2,* 267–299.

American Psychological Association. (2010). *Ethical principles of psychologists and code of conduct.* Retrieved August 12, 2014 from http://www.apa.org/ethics/code/principles.pdf.

Barrick, M. R., & Mount, M. K. (1991). The big five personality dimensions and job performance: A meta-analysis. *Personnel Psychology, 44,* 1–26.

Buhrmester, M., Kwang, T., & Gosling, S. D. (2011). Amazon's Mechanical Turk: A new source of inexpensive, yet high-quality, data? *Perspectives on Psychological Science, 6,* 3–5.

Bureau of Labor Statistics. (2014). *Fastest growing occupations.* Retrieved May 23, 2014 from http://www.bls.gov/ooh/fastest-growing.htm.

Brislin, R. W. (1970). Back-translation for cross-cultural research. *Journal of Cross-Cultural Psychology, 1,* 185–216.

Colquitt, J. A., Conlon, D. E., Wesson, M. J., Porter, C., & Ng, K. Y. (2001). Justice at the millennium: A meta-analytic review of 25 years of organizational justice research. *Journal of Applied Psychology, 86,* 425–445.

Cortina, J. M. (1993). What is coefficient alpha? An examination of theory and applications. *Journal of Applied Psychology, 78,* 98–104.

DerSimonian, R., & Laird, N. (1986). Meta-analysis in clinical trials. *Controlled Clinical Trials, 7,* 177–188.

Gatewood, R., Feild, H., & Barrick, M. (2011). *Human resource selection.* Mason, OH: Cengage Learning.

Greenberg, J. (2006). Losing sleep over organizational injustice: Attenuating insomniac reactions to underpayment inequity with supervisory training in interactional justice. *Journal of Applied Psychology, 91,* 58–69.

Goel, V. (2014). As data overflows online, researchers grapple with ethics. *New York Times,* August 12, 2014. Retrieved August 13, 2014 from http://www.nytimes.com/2014/08/13/technology/the-boon-of-online-data-puts-social-science-in-a-quandary.html.

Hammer, L. B., Kossek, E. E., Anger, W. K., Bodner, T., & Zimmerman, K. L. (2011). Clarifying work-family intervention processes: The roles of work-family conflict and family-supportive supervisor behaviors. *Journal of Applied Psychology, 96,* 134–150.

Hinkin, T. R. (1998). A brief tutorial on the development of measures for use in survey questions. *Organizational Research Methods, 1,* 104–121.

Lance, C. E., Butts, M. M., & Michels, L. C. (2006). The sources of four commonly reported cutoff criteria: What did they really say? *Organizational Research Methods, 9,* 202–220.

Landy, F. J. (1986). Stamp collecting versus science: Validation as hypothesis testing. *American Psychologist, 41,* 1183–1192.

Lohr, S. (2013). Big data, trying to build better workers. *New York Times,* April 20, 2013. Retrieved August 10, 2014 from http://www.nytimes.com/2013/04/21/technology/big-data-trying-to-build-better-workers.html?pagewanted=all.

Lord, F. M., & Novick, M. R. (1968). *Statistical theories of mental test scores.* Reading, MA: Addison-Wesley.

Lowman, R. L. (2006). *The ethical practice of psychology in organizations.* Washington, DC: American Psychological Association.

Lowman, R. L. (2012). The scientist-practitioner consulting psychologist. *Consulting Psychology Journal: Practice and Research, 64,* 151–156.

Morgan, W. B., Walker, S. S., Hebl, M. M. R., & King, E. B. (2013). A field experiment: Reducing interpersonal discrimination toward pregnant job applicants. *Journal of Applied Psychology, 98,* 799–809.

Nunnally, J. C. (1978). *Psychometric theory* (2nd ed.). New York: McGraw Hill.

Robbins, J.M., Ford, M.T., & Tetrick, L.E. (2012). Perceived unfairness and employee health: A meta-analytic integration. *Journal of Applied Psychology, 97,* 235–272.

Schmidt, F. L., & Hunter, J. E. (1981). Employment testing: Old theories and new research findings. *American Psychologist, 36,* 1128–1137.

Society for Industrial and Organizational Psychology (SIOP). (2003). *Principles for the validation and use of personnel selection procedures* (4th ed.). Bowling Green, OH: Author.

Truxillo, D. M., & Fraccaroli, F. (2014). The science of a global organizational psychology: Differing approaches and assumptions. In R. L. Griffith, L. Foster Thompson, & B. K. Armon (Eds.), *Internationalizing the curriculum in organizational psychology* (pp. 41–55). New York: Springer.

Uniform Guidelines on Employee Selection Procedures. (1978). *Federal Register, 43,* 38290–38315.

Weiss, H. M., & Rupp, D. E. (2011). Experiencing work: An essay on a person-centric work psychology. *Industrial and Organizational Psychology: Perspectives on Science and Practice, 4,* 83–97.

PART II
INDUSTRIAL PSYCHOLOGY

Chapter 3
JOB ANALYSIS

Job analysis is a necessary first step before recruiting, hiring, training employees and evaluating their performance.

After studying this chapter, you should be able to:

- describe the primary purposes for conducting a job analysis and what job analysis is used for within organizations
- list the primary methods for collecting job analysis data and the advantages and disadvantages of each
- describe the steps that need to be completed in preparing for a job analysis, such as reviewing sources of job analysis data, preparing subject matter experts, and how to manage the job analysis as an organizational process
- describe some of the main approaches to job analysis such as task-KSA analysis, PAQ, and critical incidents technique
- describe the different sources of job analysis data
- describe what is meant by competency modeling and what it is used for within organizations

**Learning goals
for this chapter**

- describe the purpose of job evaluation and what it is used for, as well as the issue of comparable worth
- identify key legal and global issues surrounding job analysis
- describe the current issues and controversies around job analysis.

Introduction

As we have discussed in Chapters 1 and 2, much of I/O psychology involves selecting employees, training them, and evaluating their performance. But before we undertake any of these efforts, it's important to know what the job requirements are. For instance, let's say you are working for a cable sales company and were asked to recruit for new customer service employees and develop procedures for hiring them. You would have a number of questions before getting started. For example, what are the tasks and responsibilities for the customer service job? What knowledge, skills, abilities, and other characteristics (KSAOs) does a person need to be able to take on the job tasks and responsibilities? And what are the critical issues that a customer service employee might face on the job?

Job analysis: The systematic process which helps you identify the job tasks and responsibilities, KSAOs, and critical incidents faced on the job.

This is where you would turn to a **job analysis,** the systematic process which helps you identify the job tasks and responsibilities, KSAOs, and critical incidents faced on the job. In this chapter, we will give an overview of how job analysis data are used in organizations, as well as how to conduct good job analyses. We will describe some of the commonly used job analysis methods as well as the related concepts of competency modeling and job evaluation. And we hope you'll get a chance to see just how interesting it can be to do a job analysis – you get to learn about jobs that you may have always wondered about.

How Are Job Analysis Data Used?

Given what we've described above, it is no surprise that job analysis has been described as the basis of other HR functions (Morgesen & Dierdorff, 2011). In other words, a good job analysis forms the basis for a lot of the functions I/O psychologists and HR professionals are concerned with. (See Figure 3.1.) Let's discuss the most important of these.

Jobs differ in the tasks involved and the knowledge, skills, abilities, and other characteristics (KSAOs) a person needs to perform them. Job analysis identifies these tasks and KSAOs.

First, the job analysis can become the basis for **job descriptions** and **job specifications.** You might be wondering what the differences are between job analyses, job descriptions, and job specifications. A job analysis usually implies a deep analytical process that is used to describe the job and what a person needs in order to perform the job. A good job analysis can allow a person who is relatively unfamiliar with a job to have a solid understanding of it. A detailed job analysis, for example, might describe hundreds of tasks. In contrast, a job description is a simpler document that can be provided to employees so that they understand their main responsibilities, and is perhaps only a page or two long. Similarly, job specifications give a relatively brief overview of the characteristics needed to do a job, rather than a lengthy list, including the minimum qualifications. In any case, the job analysis can be used to create these job descriptions and job specifications.

Second, if an organization is planning to hire new employees, they need a job analysis to understand what **qualifications** (skills, experience) are required to do the job. Moreover, to be able to select the best employees, the organization will want to build up a large pool of qualified applicants to choose from through recruitment. (We will discuss issues around recruitment in greater detail in Chapter 7.) The job analysis can provide important information about the job before starting to try to **recruit** the best people, that is, to increase your applicant pool. Consider how much easier it would be to write a job ad or posting for a job if you had detailed information about what the job entails. Alternatively, consider how difficult it is to try to write a good job posting to attract good applicants if you had little information about the job. In addition, a job analysis is necessary to choose and develop **valid selection procedures**, such as tests and interviews, used to hire employees. (We will discuss these issues in Chapter 6 and 7.) For example, if you wanted to develop good, job-related interview questions to select the best customer service workers, a detailed job analysis would help you to do so. In fact, in the US, legally defensible selection systems should be based on a job analysis (*Uniform Guidelines on Employee*

Job description: An overview of a job, typically one to two pages outlining what the job entails.

Job specifications: A brief overview of the requirements for doing the job, including the minimum qualifications necessary to do a job.

Qualifications: The skills and experience required to do a job.

Recruitment: A method for increasing your applicant pool in an attempt to find the best people for the job.

Valid selection procedures: Methods, such as tests and interviews, which can be used in order to assist in hiring the best applicant for a job.

Figure 3.1 The relationship between job analysis and other HR functions.

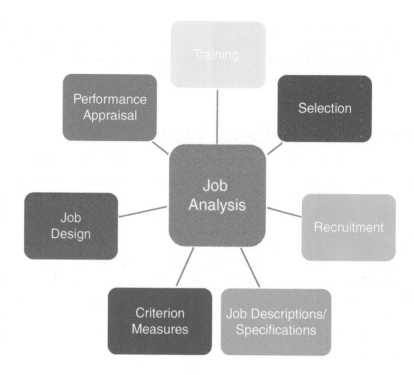

Criterion measures:
Tools used to evaluate job performance.

Performance appraisals:
An evaluation used by supervisors to evaluate employees' performance.

Training: A key part in developing employees.

Job design: A systematic analysis of the organization of work, which often includes job analysis to identify the best way to allocate various tasks and responsibilities among different jobs.

Job evaluation:
A particular type of job analysis, used to determine the relative value that jobs have within an organization.

Selection Procedures, 1978). Further, SIOP's *Principles for the Validation and Use of Selection Procedures* (2003; discussed in greater detail in Chapter 7) note that job analysis is a necessary part of developing a good selection system in most situations.

At the same time, job analysis data are necessary to develop strong **criterion measures**, that is, measures of job performance (see Chapter 4). For example, the job analysis might help you to determine what a satisfactory level of performance would be for the customer service specialists, such as the number of customers they help on a given day. Similarly, the **performance appraisals** (see Chapter 5) wherein supervisors or others evaluate employees' performance should be based on a job analysis. In fact, some research has shown that performance appraisals that are based on job analysis may be a key part of making performance appraisals less susceptible to legal challenges (Feild & Holley, 1982).

As we will see in Chapter 8, **training** employees is a key part to organizations remaining competitive. As we will also see, job analysis is a critical part of a thorough training needs assessment. Consider it this way: How effective can someone be at training employees if they do not know the knowledge, skills, and abilities that a person needs to do the job? This would be bad for the organization but also bad for the person doing the job as he or she would struggle to do well without the necessary personal resources to do a good job.

There are at least two more areas of I/O psychology practice that rely on job analysis. First, **job design**, or a systematic analysis of the organization of work, often includes job analysis to identify the best way to allocate various tasks and responsibilities among different jobs. Finally, one particular type of job analysis, referred to as **job evaluation**, is also used to determine the relative value or pay that jobs have in an organization. Although it is generally the focus of specialists in compensation (pay) issues, we will discuss some of the basic principles behind job evaluation. In summary, as you can see from this brief overview, job analysis is necessary for carrying out many of the processes we will discuss in this book.

Some Job Analysis Terminology

Before explaining the different ways that you can do a job analysis, let's begin with some vocabulary. First, a task is a basic element that can be used to describe a job. Together, a large set of tasks makes up the job. Often, tasks are stated in terms of an *action verb*, *object*, and *purpose* (although sometimes tasks can be quite long and elaborate). An example of a task for the customer service job would be "Answers (action verb) telephone calls (object) to resolve customers' issues and concerns (purpose)." Often tasks may be grouped into functional categories, or groups of tasks that serve a similar purpose. (These groups of tasks are sometimes said to be grouped into larger "responsibilities".) For example, the following tasks might all be grouped into the functional category of "Responding to customer complaints":

- answers telephone calls to resolve customers' issues and concerns
- writes e-mails to address customers' inquiries
- engages in chat sessions with customers to answer their specific concerns about products and services.

Another commonly used term in job analysis is knowledge, skills, and abilities (KSAs). Whereas tasks are used to describe the job, KSAs are used to describe the characteristics the employee needs to do the job. It can be difficult to differentiate between knowledge, skill, and ability, but typically, knowledge is generally something that someone can learn, as in from a book. An example might be "knowledge of company rules and procedures". A skill is something that they can learn how to do, such as "ability to handle customer complaints"; and an ability is something more long-lasting or innate that the person brings with them to the job, such as "mechanical skill" (Cascio & Aguinis, 2011; Gatewood, Feild, & Barrick, 2011; Morgeson & Dierdorff, 2011). There are two important things to note. First, rather than trying to differentiate between knowledge, skills, and abilities, it may be easier just to think of them, collectively, as what a person needs to do the job tasks. Second, many I/O psychologists use the term "KSAOs," meaning knowledge, skills, abilities, and other characteristics (including, for instance, personality) (Cascio & Aguinis; Morgeson & Dierdorff), although the two terms, KSA and KSAO, are frequently used interchangeably.

Another important term that is used frequently in job analysis is subject matter expert (typically called an "SME"). An SME is an expert about the job in question, that is, the person from whom we get the job analysis information.

Task: A basic element that can be used to describe a job. Together, a large set of tasks makes up a job.

Functional categories: A group of tasks that serve a similar purpose. These groups of tasks are sometimes said to be grouped into larger "responsibilities".

Knowledge, Skills, and Abilities (KSAs): Used to describe the characteristics an employee needs to do the job. Knowledge is generally something that someone can learn, for example from a book. A skill is something that you can learn how to do, such as handle a customer complaint properly. An ability is more innate, and something that the person brings with them to the job, such as a mechanical skill.

Subject matter expert (SME): A job expert with a great deal of knowledge about and/or experience of the job, these are the people from whom we get the job analysis information. Typically an incumbent or supervisor.

Incumbent: The person doing a given job, the person most familiar with the job. These people are sometimes consulted as subject matter experts.

Supervisors: Those overseeing job incumbents; for job analysis purposes supervisors as SMEs may have a better idea of how a given job fits into the overall organization.

Job analyst: The person conducting a job analysis, this person is usually an I/O psychologist or HR specialist.

In the field of job analysis this is usually the person doing the job (**incumbents**) and their **supervisors.** Incumbents and supervisors each can provide important information about the job. Incumbents, of course, actually do the job, and thus they are the most familiar with the job. On the other hand, supervisors of the job in question may have a better idea of how the job fits into the overall organization. Together, these incumbents and supervisors can provide complementary information about the job. A final term is the **job analyst**, or the person conducting the job analysis. This is typically an I/O psychologist; an HR specialist who works at the organization or who was hired from outside the organization; or it may be someone from the organization's human resources department.

Getting Started: What Are Some Sources of Job Analysis Data to Use as a Starting Point?

Let's say that you have been tasked with doing a job analysis for the customer service workers in your company. How might you get started with doing a job analysis? This is where you need to think about the different ways you have available to collect job analysis data, and there are quite a few (Brannick, Levine, & Morgeson, 2007; Gatewood et al., 2011; Morgeson & Dierdorff, 2011).

Existing Job Analysis Data

First, one source of job analysis data is to look at old job analyses. In other words, if the company has already done a job analysis, there would be no reason to start from scratch. Instead, you might use the old job analysis as a starting point. Clearly, your organization has decided to do a job analysis, so we will assume that the job analysis needs to be updated. But the existing job analysis can give you a good place to start.

Similarly, you might be able to get a job analysis for a similar job from another organization. Although this is not very common in the private sector because of the competition between organizations, it is more common in the public sector. For example, if you worked for a city government and had to do a job analysis for the job of firefighter, you might go to a city of similar size and with similar types of buildings and layout and ask if they have an existing job analysis available. This was a common practice when one of the authors of this book worked in a city government. Because city governments are not in competition with each other, they are often willing to share these types of information with each other.

Government Sources

Dictionary of Occupational Titles (DOT): Published by the US government in paper form, this contains short job descriptions of nearly every job. The last edition was published in 1991.

Other sources of job analysis information are published by the US government. The first of these, the ***Dictionary of Occupational Titles*** or *DOT*, has been around since

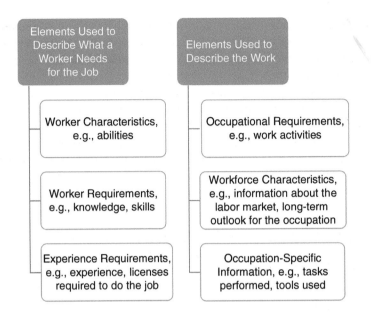

Figure 3.2
Summary of the content model of the O*NET database.
Source: http://www.onetcenter.org/content.html.

the 1930s. During the Great Depression, the Roosevelt Administration wanted to support businesses by helping to provide job analysis information. That is when the *DOT* was developed. It eventually grew to the size of two large telephone books and contained thousands of short job descriptions. The *DOT* contains just about every job you can imagine, from secretary to leather tanner. One important thing to keep in mind: The *DOT* listings are not job analyses in themselves; what a secretary does at one company could be quite different from what secretaries do at another. However, the *DOT* provides a reasonably generic start to doing a job analysis. The most recent version of the *DOT* was published in 1991.

One of the challenges with the *DOT* was that it came only in paper form and did not change as new information was learned about jobs. It was also hard to update and did not provide additional information that might be available about jobs. To solve this, the US Department of Labor developed the **Occupational Information Network** or O*NET (Peterson et al., 2001), an online job analysis database which is available for free online (http://www.onetonline.org/). If you go to the O*NET website and type in a job title that is of interest to you, you will find considerable information about the job. The types of data about each job in the O*NET database are shown in Figure 3.2. The O*NET database describes worker characteristics and requirements (which includes the KSAs), the experience needed for the job, the type of work activities, and the occupation-specific information such as tasks. Thus, it describes both characteristics of the job and what a worker needs to be able to do the job. Getting back to our customer service example, if you type "customer service" into the O*NET database, you will see that there is a job called "customer service representative" which is the closest match to your job. The key here is to find the job that seems aligned with the job you want to analyze. One of the things that may be very interesting to you as a student is the *workforce characteristics information*, which provides information about what the outlook is expected to be for the job.

Occupational Information Network (O*NET):
An online database developed by the US Department of Labor. The database contains job analyses from various job titles, and provides considerable information on work characteristics and requirements, as well as the experience needed for the job.

A few points about O*NET. First, you may be wondering how this information "magically" gets into the O*NET database. The data are collected via surveys from employees around the US who are in these particular occupations. In other words, O*NET provides information about what the average employee does in this occupation. But this raises a second point. Although O*NET is far more detailed than the *DOT*, it still does not tell you what a particular job is like in *your* organization. That is, detailed though the O*NET information is, simply looking at an O*NET listing does not tell you what a particular job is like in your organization. However, O*NET gives you a place to start in understanding factors related to conducting a job analysis in your organization.

Job Analysis Data Collection Methods

Once you've looked at different existing sources for job analysis information such as old job analyses and O*NET, it's time to think about how you might actually collect job analysis data in your organization. There are a number of ways to do this (Brannick et al., 2007; Gatewood et al., 2011; Morgeson & Dierdorff, 2011), and no one method is best – each provides useful information for doing the job analysis.

Observations: One of the most basic ways to learn about a job, observations are done by watching incumbents and SMEs doing their job.

One of the most basic ways to learn about a job is through observations of SMEs doing the work. This is especially useful for times when the job is fairly technical and the job analyst cannot completely understand all of the technical terms that might come up in an interview. As an example, one of the authors of this book did a number of job analyses related to firefighting. Without actually observing people doing the job and demonstrating the use of the equipment, it would be difficult to understand what actually takes place on the job. A related type of observational job analysis method is referred to as a "ride-along", which is a common job analysis method when much of the work is done in the field, such as in police work. Again, riding along with patrol officers may be necessary to thoroughly understand the details of police procedures.

Job analysis interview: When a job analyst asks SMEs questions about job responsibilities, tasks performed, critical incidents faced, and what KSAOs, experience, and qualifications are needed to effectively perform the job.

Perhaps one of the most common job analysis data collection methods is the job analysis interview. With this method, the job analyst meets with SMEs to ask questions about the job, such as what are the typical responsibilities and tasks performed on the job, what KSAs are needed for a person to do the job effectively, critical incidents faced on the job, and what types of qualifications and experience a person needs to be effective on the job (see Figure 3.3). One question is whether it is better to do interviews individually or with groups of two or more SMEs. In fact,

Focus groups: When a job analyst gathers groups of SMEs and asks structured sets of questions regarding their jobs.

some job analysts use focus groups in which groups of SMEs are asked structured sets of questions about their jobs. Each of these methods yields something slightly different: The group interview might allow SMEs to build off each other in trying to describe the job, but group interviews may cause SMEs not to say certain things in front of each other, or to tailor what they say to the other SMEs in the group. Consider doing a job analysis for the job of police officer, where you are interviewing an officer and his or her supervisor. The power difference between different ranks in

Job Analysis Interview Questions
1. What are the major responsibilities of the position?
2. For each responsibility, what critical tasks are performed?
3. Describe a typical day in the job.
4. What materials are used?
5. What equipment is used (e.g., computer, specialized equipment)?
6. What forms must be completed? (obtain them)
7. What documents, manuals, etc. are used? (obtain if possible)
8. What is the working environment? (e.g., indoors/outdoors; desk/mobile; etc.)
9. What are the physical demands?
10. What kinds of hours or shifts?
11. For each task and responsibility described earlier (Question 2), ask:
    What KNOWLEDGE must a person have for the job? (expert, working)
    What SKILLS? (e.g., typing; physical abilities)
    What ABILITIES? (e.g., spatial relations; supervision; oral and written communication)
    What OTHER CHARACTERISTICS? (e.g., personality traits)
12. To whom does the person report?
13. How much contact do they have with their supervisor?
14. With whom would they interact? (e.g., the public, other employees)
15. Whom would they supervise (if any), and if so, how many?
16. What are some critical work incidents faced?
    What are some examples of ideal and poor behaviors for this position?
    What are some typical decisions made by a person in this position?
17. What rules, regulations, laws, standards, etc. must be used by a person in this position? (obtain them)
18. What qualifications (education, training, certification, experience, etc.) do you think that a minimally qualified applicant would need to possess?

Figure 3.3 A list of possible job analysis questions to be used with incumbent or supervisor SMEs.

a police department might be such that the officer would only agree with his boss, rather than coming up with his or her own description of the job.

Interviews for job analyses provide rich information about the job. However, what do you do if you are in a large organization that may have thousands of employees in a single position? It would be difficult to interview all of these employees. This is why a number of organizations use **job analysis surveys**, in which large numbers of employees complete questionnaires about the job. As we will see, many job analysis approaches, such as task-KSA analysis and the PAQ (which we will describe shortly), rely a good bit on surveys. The main thing in conducting job analysis surveys of large numbers of employees is to be sure that the survey adequately samples employees in the job in terms of demographics such as gender and ethnicity, and that it adequately samples employees from different work shifts and geographical areas of the company (Gatewood et al., 2011).

Job analysis survey: A questionnaire given to a large number of employees about the job in order to conduct the job analysis.

Given these different choices in job analysis methods, which is best? The answer is that some combination of these methods may be the best, as each has unique advantages and disadvantages. Morgeson and Campion (1997) identify and describe a number of different types of bias that may affect the quality of different job analysis methods. These biases include a range of issues, from impression management (such as wanting to look like a diligent worker in front of others) to cognitive overload (when a job analysis method is too long or tiring for the SME). Different job analysis methods seem to be susceptible to different levels of these biases. For example, task questionnaires which may be very long (see discussion later in this chapter) are particularly susceptible to cognitive overload. Perhaps the best advice here is to be cognizant of the different biases and challenges associated with each job analysis data collection method and try to reduce them as much as possible (Sanchez & Levine, 2012). Another bit of advice may be to use multiple methods for data collection.

Preparing SMEs for the Job Analysis

Suppose you are working in a company as a sales person. One day you hear from your boss that someone from HR wants to come to interview you about "what you do on your job." Without additional information than that, how would you feel about this visit from someone in HR? This might be a very frightening thing to hear, as you might think that the company is concerned about your performance. Or let's say that one day you are asked to complete a survey about your job, without any explanation as to what the survey is for. How would it feel not to know why people are asking you all of these questions about your job?

Although job analysis may seem like a very straightforward process from the job analyst's perspective – simply learning more about the job so they can develop selection procedures or training – this needs to be clearly communicated to employees. SMEs may feel threatened by the job analysis if they don't understand what it is for. Or they may not take the process seriously (e.g., they might be careless when filling out surveys) if they don't realize that this process will affect who is hired into the organization. Perhaps even worse, without any explanation, employees may begin to draw their own conclusions about what the job analysis results will be used for – and they may conclude that the job analysis is for some "sinister" reason. Under these conditions, it may affect morale, or employees may even try to sabotage the job analysis process. Our point here is that explaining the purpose of the job analysis to SMEs can be critical to making the job analysis process a success. Further, SMEs should feel that they had the opportunity to participate in the job analysis and that everyone's opinion was heard. If all employees are not chosen to participate in the job analysis – and it is commonplace for them not to be when there are large numbers of SMEs – there should be some explanation as to how SMEs were chosen for participation. Finally, it is important to let SMEs know the kinds of things you will be asking them about – their jobs, what a person needs to do the job – well in advance of any actual job analysis meeting. This gives the SMEs time to think about what their job involves so that they are prepared to give complete information to the job analyst. Moreover, letting the SME know that the job analysis is simply to get information from them will make them less likely to inflate their job responsibilities.

Job Analysis Frameworks

Next we will discuss some examples of different approaches or frameworks for collecting job analysis information. Each of these frameworks takes a slightly different approach, such as focusing more on the job elements (e.g., tasks) versus focusing more on the person elements (e.g., KSAOs). As a result, each of these

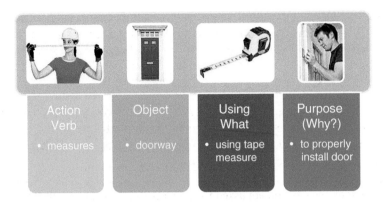

Figure 3.4 The structure of a task statement.

methods results in a different kind of job analysis data, and thus each method is more appropriate depending on what you are doing the job analysis for (e.g., developing a selection test, developing a training program). Note that each also requires a different amount of resources.

Here we present only a few of the most important examples of job analysis methods such that the reader will have a basic idea of the range of different approaches you can take to doing a job analysis. If you want to know more about the details of a particular job analysis method, or would like to know about other job analysis possibilities, we direct you towards classic treatments of job analysis methods, including the details of how to actually conduct one (Brannick et al., 2007; Cascio & Aguinis, 2011; Gatewood et al., 2011).

Work-Oriented Job Analysis Methods

Some job analysis methods are classified as "work-oriented" in that the primary unit of analysis is the characteristics of the job. Although there are several of these methods (Brannick et al., 2007), we will focus primarily on just a couple of common examples.

Task-KSA Analysis

Task-KSA analysis involves generating the list of critical job tasks involved in a given job. The list of tasks can be used to generate the KSAOs needed to do the job, and which are clearly linked to the job. Task analysis in its own right has been around for many years (Brannick et al., 2007). Although KSAOs can be deduced from the list of tasks, the explicit integration of KSAs into the task analysis process is also common (Gatewood et al., 2011), as we will describe here.

In its simplest form, task-KSA analysis would involve generating a list of critical tasks and the KSAOs needed to do them through observations by the job analyst and SME interviews. Tasks are generally expressed in this form:

ACTION VERB_OBJECT_HOW; USING WHAT EQUIPMENT_PURPOSE

For example, as shown in Figure 3.4, for the job of carpenter, a task might be:

"Measures (action verb) doorway (object) using tape measure (how) to properly install door (purpose)."

Work-oriented job analysis method: A job analysis method in which the primary unit of analysis is the characteristics of the job.

Task-KSA analysis: Involves generating a list of critical job tasks, and the KSAOs needed to do them, through observations and SME interviews.

Workplace Application

Task Analysis in the Workplace

Task analysis is essential for the development of training programs. Honda of America Manufacturing, when they decided to rely exclusively on internal sourcing of technicians, completed a task analysis. Top performing expert employees described the tasks of a technician. These tasks were prioritized, and then the company developed training programs around top-rated tasks. This is a classic example of how tasks determined from a job analysis can be used as the basis for an HR function such as training.

Source: Anonymous, 2013.

For task-KSA analysis, throughout the job analysis interview, the focus would be on what the critical tasks are, and what KSAOs are needed to do these tasks, documenting in the interviews that the KSAOs really are linked to the tasks. The interview material is then documented by the job analyst into a list of tasks and KSAOs for the job. If there are only a few SMEs available, the process often stops here (Brannick et al., 2007).

However, if there are larger numbers of SMEs, it can become cumbersome to interview all of them. At the same time, these larger numbers provide the opportunity to further examine and document that the list of tasks and KSAOs really are critical to the job and that the tasks and KSAs are linked to each other. We will describe here an example of a task-KSA analysis survey process for the job of professor.

Task Criticality Survey

Criticality: How important a task is to job performance, typically in terms of importance to the job or relative time spent on the job.

In this survey, a sample of SMEs is asked to rate each task identified by the job analysts from the interviews. The SMEs rate the tasks in terms of **criticality**, or how critical the tasks are to job performance, most typically in terms of importance to the job or relative time spent on the job. (There are other criticality measures sometimes used in task analysis, such as whether the task needs to be performed the first day on the job.) Note that these task surveys can be quite long, commonly over 100 tasks. That means that the SMEs would have to make a lot of ratings, sometimes leading to fatigue and decreased motivation on the part of SMEs (which we will discuss later in the chapter). Figure 3.5 provides a hypothetical criticality rating survey for the tasks associated with the job of college professor.

At this point you may be wondering just what you do with this criticality data that has been collected from the SMEs. The answer is that you want to be sure that all of the tasks you have identified (1) really are critical to the job and (2) that the SMEs generally are in agreement on their ratings (Gatewood et al., 2011). To do this, you perform some simple statistics on the ratings. First, you calculate a mean SME rating for each task to see if the ratings are high enough, and you calculate a standard deviation (SD) to see if the SMEs are in agreement. If the SMEs are in disagreement

JOB TASKS	A. How important is this task for the job of professor? (circle one)	B. How much time is spent on this task relative to others? (circle one)
1. Develops course syllabus for students.	1 2 3 4 5	1 2 3 4 5
2. Writes notes on course materials to support student learning.	1 2 3 4 5	1 2 3 4 5
3. Writes test items to assess student knowledge.	1 2 3 4 5	1 2 3 4 5
4. Meets with students as needed to explain course assignments.	1 2 3 4 5	1 2 3 4 5
5. Grades exams to assess student learning and provide feedback to students.	1 2 3 4 5	1 2 3 4 5
6. Meets with teaching assistants who can help support student learning to provide input on mentoring of undergraduates.	1 2 3 4 5	1 2 3 4 5
7. Completes paperwork regarding research grants.	1 2 3 4 5	1 2 3 4 5
8. Encourages class discussions regarding the material.	1 2 3 4 5	1 2 3 4 5
9. Generates new knowledge via own research.	1 2 3 4 5	1 2 3 4 5
...		
...		
88. Keeps desk and office tidy to facilitate work with students.	1 2 3 4 5	1 2 3 4 5
89. Attends faculty meetings to engage in department governance.	1 2 3 4 5	1 2 3 4 5

Please rate each task on the following scales:

A. How important is this task for the job of professor?
5 – Very important
4 – Important
3 – Moderately important
2 – Slightly important
1 – Not important

B. How much time is spent on this task relative to others?
5 – Much more
4 – More
3 – Moderately More
2 – Slightly more
1 – None at all

Figure 3.5 A hypothetical task criticality rating form (in this case, importance and time spent ratings) for the job of college professor.

about the ratings of a task, it will show up in a high standard deviation. The job analyst usually determines in advance the mean and SD that will be required to retain a task. Any task with a low mean – say, below 4.00 on a 5-point scale – is tossed out. Similarly, any task where there is a high SD – say, above 1.00 – is tossed out.

Figure 3.6
Hypothetical
statistical analysis
(means and stand-
ard deviations) for
the task importance
ratings for job of
college professor,
obtained from 50
professors.

Means and Standard Deviations for the Importance Ratings of Each Job Task		
JOB TASKS	MEAN (1–5 scale)	Standard Deviation
1. Develops course syllabus for students.	4.5	0.9
2. Writes notes on course materials to support student learning.	4.9	0.2
3. Writes test items to assess student knowledge.	4.8	0.32
4. Meets with students as needed to explain course assignments.	4.3	0.44
5. Grades exams to assess student learning and provide feedback to students.	4.5	0.67
6. Meets with teaching assistants who can help support student learning to provide input on mentoring of undergraduates.	4.4	0.82
7. Completes paperwork regarding research grants.	4.8	1.41
8. Encourages class discussions regarding the material.	4.3	.76
9. Generates new knowledge via own research.	4.8	.22
...		
...		
...		
88. Keeps desk and office tidy to facilitate work with students.	3.4	0.91
89. Attends faculty meetings to engage in department governance.	4.1	0.89

Let's look at some hypothetical data collected from 50 professors, shown in Figure 3.6. Figure 3.6 shows the mean importance ratings for each task as well as the standard deviation. Keeping in mind we want the mean importance rating to be greater than 4 and the SD to be less than 1.00, two tasks stand out as problematic. Task 7, "Completes paperwork regarding research grants," has a high mean, but the SD is high (over 1.00), showing that the SMEs are in disagreement about its importance. Similarly, Task 88, "Keeps desk and office tidy to facilitate work with students," has a low mean (less than 4.00), showing that the professors don't think it is important. For these reasons, we will drop these two tasks from the job analysis,

KSAO	How important is this KSAO for the job of professor? (circle one)	How much time is spent on using this KSAO relative to others? (circle one)	To what degree does possessing this KSAO differentiate good from poor performance? (circle one)
A. Knowledge of course content	1 2 3 4 5	1 2 3 4 5	1 2 3 4 5
B. Knowledge of teaching and pedagogy	1 2 3 4 5	1 2 3 4 5	1 2 3 4 5
C. Knowledge of university rules and policies about grading	1 2 3 4 5	1 2 3 4 5	1 2 3 4 5
...			
...			
G. Knowledge of university administrative policies	1 2 3 4 5	1 2 3 4 5	1 2 3 4 5
H. Interpersonal skills	1 2 3 4 5	1 2 3 4 5	1 2 3 4 5

Figure 3.7
A hypothetical KSA criticality rating form for the job of college professor.

and you won't be seeing them in later discussions. What you are left with, then, is a list of tasks that a large number of SMEs have rated as critical to the job.

KSA Criticality

The KSAOs that have been identified in earlier stages of the job analysis are the employee characteristics that are needed to do the tasks. How do you then assess the criticality of KSAs that have been identified in earlier stages of the job analysis? It is really quite similar to the way we treat the tasks – through another criticality survey. Figure 3.7 shows an example of a hypothetical KSA survey for the job of college professor. In this case, we have given three ratings of KSA criticality. Note that the data from the KSA criticality survey would be analyzed in the same way as the task survey. Again, you would want to retain the KSAs that have been given high mean criticality ratings by SMEs and low SDs. What you are left with, then, is a list of KSAs that a large number of SMEs have rated as critical to the job.

Task-KSA Linkage Survey

Now that you have your list of critical tasks and critical KSAOs, you must be done, right? Well, almost. One last step that is typically carried out is what is called a **task-KSA linkage survey**, in which SMEs document the degree to which the KSAOs really are needed to do the tasks (Gatewood et al., 2011). We show an example of such a survey in Figure 3.8. For each task-critical job task, a new group of SMEs is asked to rate how important each KSAO is for each task. In the end, you want all KSAs to be linked to at least one critical job task. This documents yet further that the KSAOs really are needed to do the critical job task, and you can be confident that these are the key KSAOs. Any KSAOs that are not linked by the SMEs to a job task are discarded. A summary of the task-KSA process is shown in Figure 3.9.

Task-KSA linkage survey:
A step in the task-KSA analysis in which SMEs document the degree to which the KSAOs really are needed to do the tasks.

Summary of Task-KSA Analysis

As you can see, task-KSA analysis provides rich job analysis data, including a description of hundreds of tasks on the job and the KSAOs needed to do them,

Figure 3.8 A hypothetical task-KSA linkage rating form for the job of college professor.

Instructions: How important is each KSA across the top for performing the task in the left-hand column? Please use the following scale:
5 – Essential
4 – Very important
3 – Important
2 – Moderately important
1 – Not important

JOB TASKS	A. Knowledge of course content	B. Knowledge of teaching and pedagogy	C. Knowledge of university rules and policies about grading	......	G. Knowledge of university administrative policies	H. Interpersonal skills
1. Develops course syllabus for students.	1 2 3 4 5	1 2 3 4 5	1 2 3 4 5		1 2 3 4 5	1 2 3 4 5
2. Writes notes on course materials to support student learning.	1 2 3 4 5	1 2 3 4 5	1 2 3 4 5		1 2 3 4 5	1 2 3 4 5
3. Writes test items to assess student knowledge.	1 2 3 4 5	1 2 3 4 5	1 2 3 4 5		1 2 3 4 5	1 2 3 4 5
4. Meets with students as needed to explain course assignments.	1 2 3 4 5	1 2 3 4 5	1 2 3 4 5		1 2 3 4 5	1 2 3 4 5
5. Grades exams to assess student learning and provide feedback to students.	1 2 3 4 5	1 2 3 4 5	1 2 3 4 5		1 2 3 4 5	1 2 3 4 5
6. Meets with teaching assistants who can help support student learning to provide input on mentoring of undergraduates.	1 2 3 4 5	1 2 3 4 5	1 2 3 4 5		1 2 3 4 5	1 2 3 4 5
...						
...						
...						
89. Attends faculty meetings to engage in department governance.	1 2 3 4 5	1 2 3 4 5	1 2 3 4 5		1 2 3 4 5	1 2 3 4 5

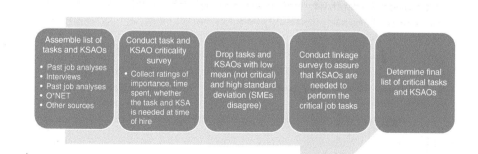

Figure 3.9 Summary of a task-KSA process.

Table 3.1 Some critical incidents for the job of customer service worker

Incident	Example of Positive Response	Example of Negative Response
A customer calls in angry because a product they ordered is defective. They yell at the customer service worker.	The customer service worker stays calm, tries to show concern for the customer, and tries to find a way to solve the problem. In the end, the customer is satisfied with the transaction and thanks the customer service worker.	The customer service worker loses their cool and responds rudely to the customer. As a result, the customer becomes more upset and asks to speak to their supervisor.
A customer wants to exchange an item that was purchased on sale. But they want a credit for the item as if it were a full-priced item. They argue that the item is no longer on sale so they should be able to get the full price.	The customer service worker explains the company's policy. They explain that they can only credit the customer for the amount that they paid for the item while it is on sale. They also help the customer decide what replacement item they would like. The customer leaves the transaction satisfied with their new purchase.	The customer service worker agrees to give the customer a full price credit even though the customer had not paid full price. They do this to appease the customer and make them go away. The company thus loses money.

including robust documentation for the criticality of the tasks and KSAOs and how they link up. This sort of job analysis is great if you are developing a personnel selection test based on content validity (see Chapter 2 and Chapter 7) where you need to carefully sample what the job is. This can also provide a rich source of job analysis information for developing training. On the downside, task-KSA analysis is very time-consuming, requiring that the job analyst develop a custom set of tasks and KSAOs for each job. One way to think of task-KSA analysis is to say that it provides in-depth information about a single job. For this reason, it is more commonly used when it is worthwhile, that is, when you need detailed information about a single job that might have hundreds of positions in it, as in when analyzing jobs such as for a police officer or firefighter. On the other hand, there are simpler ways to approach job analysis, which are less time-consuming and allow you to compare across jobs. We will describe these in the coming sections.

Other Work-Oriented Job Analysis Methods

Another commonly used work-oriented method of job analysis is the **critical incidents technique** (Flanagan, 1954), which is focused on documenting examples of critical situations faced by job incumbents, examples of good and poor ways to handle them, and the results. The critical incidents technique can generate rich information that can be used in a number of ways, for instance, to develop

Critical incidents technique:
A worker-oriented method of job analysis focused on documenting examples of critical situations faced by job incumbents, such as examples of good and poor ways to handle them, and the results.

Consider the range of critical incidents that are faced by customer service personnel. There are a number of decisions to be made, and emotions can run high, so handling the situation correctly or poorly can lead to quite different results – for the company, the customer, and the employee.

performance appraisal forms such as behaviorally anchored rating scales or BARS (see Chapter 5), developing work-related scenarios for training, or writing interview and test questions for selection. We show some examples of critical incidents for the job of customer service worker in Table 3.1. Note that each example includes an important incident faced by employees, and positive and negative responses by the employee and the consequences. How do you collect critical incidents from SMEs? During the job analysis interview, SMEs are asked to think about some critical situations faced on the job, and to note examples of poor and good responses that they have seen employees take to those incidents. (See Figure 3.3; question 16 is an example of an interview question used to generate critical incidents.)

Worker-Oriented Methods

Worker-oriented job analysis approaches:
Methods of job analysis that focus on the characteristics of the employee; examples of this are the position analysis questionnaire (PAQ) and competency modeling.

Position Analysis Questionnaire (PAQ):
A standardized, pre-written job analysis questionnaire containing 195 items. The items describe a broad range of jobs, and are an alternative to the more time-consuming method of developing a task-KSA analysis.

In contrast to work-oriented methods of job analysis, **worker-oriented job analysis approaches** focus on characteristics of the employee. We will discuss two examples of these methods.

Position Analysis Questionnaire

The **Position Analysis Questionnaire** (PAQ) is an off-the-shelf (pre-written, standardized) job analysis method based on a survey of 195 items (McCormick, Jeanneret, & Mecham, 1972). These items are written to describe a broad range of jobs. As opposed to the lengthy development process involved in task-KSA analysis, the PAQ process involves the completion of a survey which is then scored online. Because the PAQ has been around since the 1960s, there is a large accompanying database including hundreds of thousands of entries. This means that when the survey is scored, the I/O psychologist can receive not only the profile of the job, but also recommendations for the types of assessments that might be used to hire people into this job. For example, the PAQ database might recommend that for a particular job you use a test of clerical ability for hiring employees. This does not mean that you can simply start using a clerical ability test to hire workers, but it does mean you might research such tests for your job to see if they actually are valid predictors of job performance (see Chapter 7). In addition, the PAQ database can provide guidance for the point values of jobs relative to one another to help in developing a pay plan in the organization (see the section on job evaluation later in this chapter).

What are the advantages and disadvantages of the PAQ? If one needs a fairly simple job analysis completed, the PAQ is much easier than other methods in that it is pre-made ("off-the-shelf") and does not require creating extensive lists of tasks or KSAOs from scratch. Further, if you want to compare jobs, the PAQ is a good choice: Whereas task-KSA analysis allows for detailed analysis of only one or two jobs, the PAQ is good for comparing jobs in order to look for differences. Moreover, the PAQ database can even provide some information about the relative value of jobs for making pay decisions. (See the section on job evaluation later in this chapter.) One should be aware of the potential disadvantages, though. The PAQ does not provide great detail about jobs, such as you might get with other job analysis methods. Rather, it uses the 195 generic descriptors to describe the job. Second, the PAQ requires a fairly high reading level (college level), such that you can't simply hand it to SMEs to be completed, but that the job analyst must complete the PAQ survey after interviewing SMEs. But if the need is to get a general idea about a job's requirements or to compare jobs, the PAQ can be a practical choice (Brannick et al., 2007; Gatewood et al., 2011).

Competency Modeling

Over the last couple of decades, the popularity of **competency modeling** has grown in many organizations (e.g., Schippmann et al., 2000). Related to job analysis, competency modeling involves describing the general characteristics needed in jobs in an organization, especially within a series of jobs or across a range of jobs. What is interesting about competency modeling, though, is that it often includes some information about the values of the organization and its mission. This is quite different from standard job analysis methods: Whereas job analysis usually examines individual jobs and the human requirements for them, competency modeling also includes the flavor of the goals and values of the organization (Cascio & Aguinis, 2011; Sanchez & Levine, 2009; Shippmann et al., 2000). For example, if an organization values its customers, these sorts of values would be expressed in the competency model, across all jobs in the organization. In short, competency models provide similar information to job analyses regarding the human requirements for a job, but they also include more about the organizational context and culture. Recent discussions of competency modeling and job analysis note that although competency modeling and job analysis are quite similar, the two processes may complement each other when used together in organizational practice (Sanchez & Levine, 2009). For example, Campion et al. (2011) point out that, compared to standard job analysis, competency models tend to focus on top performance rather than just average performance; focus on how the competencies vary across different organizational levels; and tend to be directly linked to business strategies.

Other Job Analysis Methods

There are a number of other systems for conducting job analyses. Although we only touch on these briefly, they have a long history of application, and we point the interested reader to other sources to learn more about them (e.g., Brannick et al., 2007). **Functional job analysis** (FJA; e.g., Fine, 1988) focuses on the fact that all jobs require that workers need to deal with people, data, and things, and that the job

Competency modeling: A method of job analysis that involves describing the general characteristics needed in jobs in a company, especially within a series of jobs or across a range of jobs. This often includes the company values or mission statement.

Functional job analysis: Focuses on the purpose or functions of the job as opposed to the actual tasks being performed.

tasks can be specified to include who performs the task, what action is performed, what the result is, what tools or equipment are used, and what procedures and instructions are followed. Although FJA provides some excellent detail about the job, it does require a good bit of work on the part of a well-trained job analyst. Another established job analysis method is the job element method (JEM; Primoff, 1975). The JEM is a worker-oriented job analysis method designed to specify the worker characteristics needed to do a job. After these elements are identified, they are then specified further into subelements. For example, for the job of barista, an element might be "ability to make coffee drinks", while the subelements might be "finding out what the customer wants", "estimating the heat of coffee and milk", and "understanding the equipment". Note that JEM is much more focused on describing worker characteristics but to a large degree skips over the explicit definition of job tasks. For that reason, it may be less suitable in situations where you want to know a lot of detail about what is actually done on the job.

Workplace Application

The Society for Human Resource Management's HR Competency Model

The Society for Human Resource Management (SHRM) has been a leader for HR professionals around the world. Recently, SHRM has undertaken to develop a competency model for the HR profession. The processes involved were impressive, including initial input from over 1,000 HR professionals from around the world, followed by a survey of over 32,000 respondents. The result was a robust model containing nine competencies required for effectiveness in HR. It is also interesting to note that the model was developed through input from I/O psychologists, specifically, the Society for Industrial and Organizational Psychology (SIOP) Taskforce on Competency Modeling (http://www.shrm.org/HRCompetencies/Pages/FAQs.aspx).

Source: Society for Human Resource Management, 2014.

"See website for interactive material"

Interactive: Choosing a job analysis method.

Assessing and Assuring the Quality of Job Analysis Data

One question that you might have is how accurate job analysis data are. The good news is that because job analyses are based on the judgments of SMEs – experts

1. Develops course syllabus for students.
2. Writes notes on course materials.
3. Writes test items to assess student knowledge.
4. **Encapsulates rigorous metallurgical characters.**
5. Meets with students as needed to explain course assignments.
6. Grades exams to provide feedback to students.
7. Meets with teaching assistants who can help support student learning.
8. **Changes hand towels in campus restrooms.**
9. Attends faculty meetings.
10. Encourages class discussions regarding the material.

Note: Items 4 & 8 are bogus items.

Figure 3.10 Sample job tasks for the job of college professor, including carelessness items.

on the job in question – one can argue that job analysis data do, at least to some extent, have content validity. (See Chapter 2.) However, the quality of job analysis data should be of some concern because job analysis data come from the subjective judgments of SMEs. Moreover, we don't have any objective measures to tie job analysis data to. So how do we know whether job analysis data are accurate? There are several ways to try to estimate how accurate job analysis data are. There are also some studies that can give us hope that job analysis is fairly accurate.

Reliability of Job Analysis Data

As we've said, there is no standard to compare job analysis data to, so trying to assess their validity against some criterion or standard is difficult. However, recall from Chapter 2 that reliability is a necessary condition to show validity. This being the case, how can we show the reliability of job analysis data? Typically, this is done through some demonstration of interrater reliability or agreement. In other words, if the SMEs are generally in agreement in their ratings on a job analysis survey, this is a good sign that the data are reliable, and at least holds promise that they are valid as well.

Detecting and Removing SMEs Who Are Providing Poor Ratings

Remember when we discussed task/KSA analysis, that we noted how long some task surveys can be, and how tiring they can be for SMEs? One concern with job analysis surveys, then, is to see whether SMEs are paying attention, or are showing signs of boredom, fatigue, or carelessness. This has led to the development of **carelessness indices** (e.g., Green & Stutzman, 1986) to detect whether SMEs are paying attention. The **carelessness index** consists of bogus job analysis items, scattered throughout the survey, that are either nonsensical or have nothing to do with the job. If an SME endorses too many of these items as being a part of his job, it suggests that he/she isn't paying attention, and that his/her data should be removed from further analysis. Consider the tasks that are in Figure 3.10 that describe some of the job tasks for a college professor. (We have seen some of these tasks earlier in the chapter.) In this case, Item 4 (which is nonsense) and Item 8 (which is not part of a professor's job) are the carelessness items. If an SME endorses these items, which are clearly not part of the professor's job, the SME should be considered for removal.

Carelessness index: A method for detecting whether SMEs are paying attention. These consist of bogus or nonsensical questions throughout a survey, which if endorsed, indicate that the SME is being careless.

Who Are the Best SMEs?

A good bit of thought should go into how to choose SMEs for participation in the job analysis. In other words, how do you choose SMEs in order to end up with the most successful job analysis process? There are a number of issues to consider here, such as SME demographics in terms of gender and ethnicity, the level of experience of the SMEs, and whether to choose some of the top performers in the organization. Let's go through each of those issues.

With regard to gender and ethnicity, it is important that the SME sample is representative of the demographic makeup in the organization and applicant pool. This is for at least two reasons. First, the US courts have indicated that SME samples used for job analysis should represent the makeup of the organization. Second, it is important to be inclusive of all groups in the organization. For example, let's say you were doing a job analysis for police sergeants, but asked mostly the male sergeants to participate in the job analysis. Such an approach could lead to the female sergeants being shut out of the process and having no voice. Further, if the stated purpose of the job analysis was to develop tests for promoting officers to sergeant and training them, it could cause concerns that the promotional test and training was "biased in favor of men" and lead to significant feelings of resentment. One final issue regarding gender and ethnicity is whether men and women and people of different ethnicities actually provide different types of job analysis data. The answer is "generally no." Research shows that people give relatively similar job analysis data regardless of their gender or ethnic background, or that the differences are fairly small (Landy & Vasey, 1991). In addition, recent reviews of the job analysis literature suggest that any such demographic differences may be besides the point, and that instead of examining the effects of SMEs' demographic characteristics, we should be looking at more substantive factors like the effects of SMEs' social or professional identities (Sanchez & Levine, 2012).

What about the experience levels of SMEs? In other words, will a person on the job for one year provide different job analysis data than a person with 10 years of experience? Let's consider an example of a firefighter. Would you be concerned that a firefighter who has been on the job for 10 years provides different types of job analysis information from one who has been in the job for two years? This is a fairly "thorny" question. One could argue that a newer firefighter would have the standard tasks uppermost in their mind, but on the other hand they might not have learned all of the tricks to be most effective on the job. In contrast, a more experienced firefighter could know all of the "tricks of the trade", but might also be less able to articulate all aspects of their work because they are "second nature". This is an interesting phenomenon that we have found in doing job analysis interviews. Sometimes when experienced employees are asked to describe the main tasks they do on their job, they will not mention some fairly obvious tasks. When they are questioned about why they have skipped these important tasks, they'll reply, "Well of course I do that – it's so obvious I forgot to mention it." In any case, the research shows that people of different experience levels may give different types of job analysis data (e.g., Sanchez, Prager, Wilson, & Viswesvaran, 1998; Tross & Maurer, 2000), and thus sampling SMEs of differing experience levels can affect the job analysis results (Sanchez & Levine, 2012)

With regard to choosing your top performers in the organization to participate in the job analysis, it is obvious that these need to be considered to provide legitimacy for the job analysis. Going back to our example of choosing police sergeants as

SMEs for a job analysis, what if by chance you chose only those sergeants who were known not to be good supervisors, or who had had some disciplinary problems? How would this affect the credibility of your job analysis process? As you can imagine, under those conditions the job analysis might not have much credibility among the police officers, and anything you developed from it might be considered flawed. That in itself suggests that you should be cognizant of who the most respected SMEs are in an organization and be sure to include them in your job analysis. On the other hand, does the level of SME skill or performance have much effect on job analysis results? While there is some research that shows that it might (e.g., Sanchez et al., 1998), SMEs' job performance has not been consistently shown to affect their job analysis results (Conley & Sackett, 1987; Wexley & Silverman, 1978).

Finally, given that the SMEs are often job incumbents, just how good are the data obtained? Dierdorff and Wilson (2003) found in a meta-analysis that the job analysis information from incumbents may be less reliable than the information obtained from job analysts or technical experts. Although this may be concerning, other authors have pointed out that lower reliability in job analysis results (i.e., disagreement among raters) may merely indicate that the job is done differently by different employees with the same job title (Sanchez & Levine, 2012).

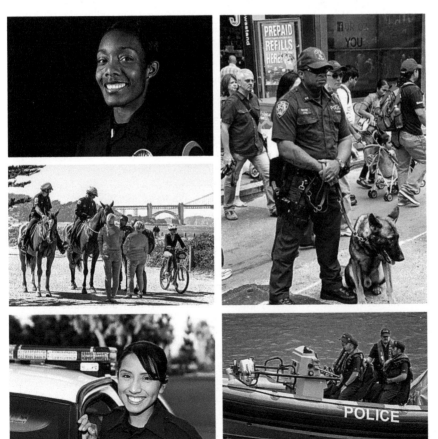

Why would it be important to consider different viewpoints in doing a job analysis for police officers?

What about Tasks versus KSAs?

One question that has come up in the job analysis literature is what types of job analysis data are more susceptible to judgment errors. The way that this has played out in the literature is comparing data collected from tasks versus KSAs in terms of their quality. Here's the reason that researchers suspect that there may be some differences between the quality of data obtained from tasks ratings versus KSA ratings. For one thing, tasks are more concrete in the mind of the SMEs, whereas KSAs are more abstract. Let's explain this a little bit more. Tasks are definite behaviors that SMEs may do all day long, and watch their colleagues' performance many times. On the other hand, KSAs are not actual behaviors of people, but are the characteristics a person needs to do the job. They are not easily observable, but require inferences on the part of SMEs. As an actual example, let's get back to our police sergeant example. When comparing the task of "Completes required reports and paperwork regarding police officers" with the associated KSA of "Knowledge of government personnel policies" the task is something the sergeant does quite frequently and observes her colleagues doing quite frequently. On the other hand, the KSA is not something that can be easily observed but must be inferred by an SME. This notion has in fact been supported by some research. Dierdorff and Morgeson (2009) found that KSA ratings showed lower reliability than task ratings. Similarly, Morgesen, Delaney-Klinger, Mayfield, Ferrera, and Campion (2004) found that KSA ratings were more likely to be inflated than tasks ratings. In considering these findings, we would not suggest that analysts should focus on task statements rather than KSAOs in doing job analyses. Indeed, KSAOs are very important to understanding what the personal characteristics are that a person must possess to do the job, and thus are very important to I/O psychologists. Rather, these findings just suggest that we should be especially careful in developing KSAO statements and in interpreting data based on them.

Training SMEs

So far in this section we have talked about ways to assess whether job analysis data are good, how to identify careless SMEs, and how to choose SMEs so that you have a representative sample. We've also talked about the fact that different types of job analysis data (e.g., task ratings) may lead to more reliable data than others (e.g., KSA ratings). One last issue is how we might help SMEs to make good ratings. Some of these are obvious and are standard practice in job analysis: For example, we should do all that we can to remove the cognitive load from SMEs and give them sufficient time to complete their job analysis forms; this might involve asking SMEs to attend a job analysis session during work hours rather than just sending them a job analysis form to complete. (Just sending SMEs job analysis questionnaires to complete often leads to low response rates because the job analysis questionnaires may not be a lot of fun to complete and so the SME never gets around to completing it.) We might also provide some incentive for SMEs who complete their surveys. In addition, some research has examined the possibility of training SMEs to improve job analysis quality. For example, Aguinis, Mazurkiewicz, and Heggestad (2009) examined the possibility that SMEs could be trained to improve the quality of their job analysis data. They found that providing SMEs with training reduced the correlation between SMEs' personality characteristics and the ratings SMEs gave for a job's personality requirements.

Job Evaluation: Job Analysis Informing Pay Structures

We have spent the bulk of this chapter discussing some of the primary types of job analysis methods that are used by I/O psychologists. These job analyses are typically used for developing criteria and other measures to assess performance (Chapter 4), performance appraisal systems (Chapter 5), personnel selection procedures (Chapters 6 and 7), and training programs (Chapter 8) – the types of issues that most I/O psychologists are involved in. However, there is another HR function that is important in most organizations: compensation and pay. Generally, the issue of **compensation** involves setting the pay levels within an organization. We present here a particular type of job analysis that is used in developing compensation systems, namely, job evaluation (Brannick et al., 2007), or determining the relative value of jobs within the organization ("who makes more than whom").

When considering pay, a key point is to make sure that the pay system is fair to employees. As we will see in Chapter 9, fairness is an important factor in the way that employees interpret their relationship with their organization. For this reason, compensation systems need to assure that pay systems are administered in a way that is fair to employees, such that an employee's pay is fair relative to other employees in the organization (internal equity) as well as to others in the external labor market (external equity). In fact, pay fairness was one of the original applications of a major motivation theory, equity theory (see Chapter 9).

Thus, a key goal of job evaluation is to assure **internal equity**, that is, fairness of relative pay values within the organization. The actual pay levels of jobs are then largely determined by outside market forces, or **external equity**. Here we present an overview of how job evaluation works. Note that it is just an overview, and interested readers should know that many business schools devote entire courses to the issue of determining pay.

Internal Equity

One of the key issues involved in doing job evaluation is assessing the relative value of jobs in the organization. For example, we know that if salespersons receive a certain level of pay, it is assumed that their supervisors will make more given their supervisory responsibilities. But how much more? Thinking more broadly to other jobs, how much relative value would customer service specialists, truck drivers, and secretaries bring to the company relative to the sales people?

This is where job evaluation can come in. Although there are many ways to conduct a job evaluation, a common approach is to assess the relative value of each job in the organization in terms of points. The number of points given to each job in the organization is determined based on pre-determined criteria, often referred

Compensation: Involves setting pay levels within an organization.

Internal equity: A key goal of job evaluation, the intention of internal equity is to assure fairness of relative pay values within the organization.

External equity: Assessment of fair compensation in relation to market conditions for a particular job. This is important for attracting and retaining the best talent for each position.

Figure 3.11 Point values as determined for four hypothetical jobs within an organization.

Figure 3.11 Point values as determined for four hypothetical jobs within an organization.

to as compensable factors. One of these compensable factors might include the working conditions. Tough working conditions normally command more pay. For example, a firefighter's job is paid more relative to some others because of the dangerous and rough working conditions. A second compensable factor often used is the experience or knowledge required of the job, with greater experience and knowledge requirements commanding more pay. For example, a research scientist would get more pay relative to some other employees because of the technical knowledge they are required to have. And a third compensable factor is the level of responsibility: Jobs with a lot of responsibility get paid more than those with less responsibility. For example, a manager supervising a dozen employees would get paid more than a worker with no supervisory responsibilities.

Consider Figure 3.11, which shows the relative number of points that has been given to a number of jobs in a fictitious organization. Based on the compensable factors, the managers have 952 points, the engineers 750 points, the secretaries 350 points, and the truck drivers 325 points. Thus we can assume that the managers should make approximately three times as much as the secretaries and truck drivers, and the secretaries and truck drivers should make about half as much as the engineers.

External Equity

At this point, we only know the relative values of the jobs in terms of points, not in terms of what they should be paid. A next step would be to assess external equity relative to the market conditions for those particular jobs. This can be done through salary surveys of the market. These salary surveys might be conducted by the organization, obtained from government data, or purchased from a consulting firm. The salary survey allows you to see what the value of a job is on the market. Maintaining this external equity with the job market is important for attracting the best talent, as well as for retaining the best employees. Also, it may be that the company does not have the resources to do salary surveys for all of the different types of jobs in its organizational structure. Instead, organizations often only do surveys for their most essential jobs (often called benchmark jobs), and the pay for the other jobs is extrapolated. In the example above, if the salary survey showed that engineers were paid about $150,000 per year, we could extrapolate that managers should make approximately $200,000.

Other Considerations

Keep in mind, though, that although this all sounds quite logical, sometimes it's not as simple as calculating the point values of jobs relative to each other and plugging in the dollar values from the salary surveys. A number of other issues may need to be considered. Perhaps the most important of these is that the market rates for jobs may not match the relative values of the jobs as determined through the job evaluation. For example, because of the market value that engineers might have, you could end up with a situation where the salary surveys would indicate that the engineers are paid more than a supervisor at the next level above them. As another example, you might find that the external market is paying secretaries less than truck drivers. This means that the organization will have to find some way to reconcile the value of the jobs as determined by the job evaluation with the external market forces.

Comparable Worth

The earlier example of secretaries and truck drivers also raises the issue of **comparable worth**, most commonly discussed in terms of gender differences in jobs. Comparable worth as a legal issue points out that many traditionally female jobs (in this case, secretaries) are often paid less than traditionally male jobs (in this case, truck drivers) that have been shown through the job evaluation to be worth the same to the organization. In this example, even though secretaries were found to have slightly greater value to the job, the market might suggest that they should get paid less. Note that the comparable worth issue is different from the fact that women and men within the same profession (e.g., male and female college professors) might get paid differently. This would be a simple matter of equal pay for the same work, an issue for many professions, from stockbrokers (Madden, 2012) to movie stars (De Pater, Judge, & Scott, 2014). Rather, comparable worth focuses on pay differences for different jobs that are traditionally associated with men (truck driver) versus those associated with women (secretary). Although the issue of comparable worth gained some traction in the 1980s, it has to some extent died down because the courts have generally come down on the side of organizations needing to use market forces to set pay (Killingsworth, 2002). Moreover, there is today greater fluidity in the opportunities open to men and women in different jobs: Women and men have far greater opportunity in terms of which jobs are available to them than at any other point in history.

Comparable worth: Commonly discussed in terms of gender differences. Points to differences in pay for typically male versus typically female jobs based on job evaluation and market value.

LEGAL ISSUES

Perhaps the most clear legal issue with regard to job analyses is that they must be done as part of the validation of a selection system (see Chapters 6 and 7). For example, according to the *Uniform Guidelines on Employee Selection Procedures*, selection systems in the US should be based on a job analysis in order to be legally defensible. Moreover, a job analysis needs to be detailed enough to give you the specific information that you will need to develop selection procedures (e.g., Brannick et al., 2007; Thompson & Thompson, 1982). For example, the job analysis used for developing personnel selection tests must be reported in writing, the procedure used to do the job analysis must be clearly described, and a wide variety of sources should be used in the analysis.

GLOBAL IMPLICATIONS

Given the recent growth in global organizations, we see a number of implications for job analysis. First is the issue of what a particular job title means in one country versus another. Although job titles may be the same in different countries, the responsibilities may be quite different: This may be due to cultural differences, or due to the fact that global organizations may be the result of the merger of different organizations. Whatever the reason, one challenge, then, is to assure that a company's job titles mean the same thing in different parts of the world. Second, the use of competency modeling, which is so highly dependent on the culture and values of the organization, seems particularly susceptible to cultural differences from one part of a company to another, creating some headaches in its implementation. On the other hand, because competency modeling focuses on showing how the organization's goals and values are reflected in the job, competency modeling may be especially useful in helping to transmit the organization's goals and values across different parts of the company, including in different parts of the world. Although the job analysis literature has done little to tackle issues related to multinational organizations, the time seems ripe to do so.

CURRENT ISSUES AND CONTROVERSIES

Although job analysis has been an integral part of I/O psychology for many years, there are some new issues beginning to emerge within the field. Many of these new issues have to do with the fact that job analysis practices have not changed over the years, while workplace practices and the field of I/O have changed quite a bit. While we don't see this as an end to job analysis, it does mean that a number of approaches to job analysis may change in the coming decades. We provide several such examples below.

First, as we describe throughout this book, the ability of large employers to collect data in the workplace has changed through the years. This has included a detailed monitoring of what employees do at work. While this raises a number of issues, both positive (e.g., ability to know what workers are actually doing) and negative (e.g., decreased privacy), it also means that job analysis data can be collected in new ways. As we have noted throughout this chapter, job analysis data collection has generally been considered a subjective process. But with the ability to know what employees are actually doing at work, job analysis may be able to include more objective information, not just the subjective judgments of SMEs. This is a fairly large shift from the way that organizations have traditionally done job analysis.

Second, many of our approaches to job analysis have been around for decades, when jobs were more finite and changed very slowly. Today, jobs can change quickly and be much more fluid. For that reason, there has been a movement towards using the term "**work analysis**", which implies the fact that clear-cut, specific "jobs" are not always easily analyzed in today's workforce (Sanchez & Levine, 2012). As noted by some authors (Morgeson & Dierdorff, 2011), rather than just thinking about single jobs with tasks that do not change much over time, we should be thinking more broadly of work roles. This acknowledges that the work that individuals do in organizations changes over time and that workers do not work in isolation but are integrated into large teams and contexts.

Work analysis: The term acknowledging that jobs are quickly changing and more fluid in today's market.

Moreover, interest in job analysis research seems to be falling off in many of the top I/O psychology journals (Morgeson & Dierdorff, 2011). However, in their review of the job analysis literature, Sanchez and Levine (2012) point out that this decreased interest is not because job analysis is unimportant, but because job analysis is not usually an end itself; rather, job analyses are usually done in support of other more "important" I/O functions such as personnel selection or training. In other words, some I/O psychologists may not see job analysis as that important because it is only one part of a larger HR process. However, Sanchez and Levine (2012) argue that doing a job analysis is clearly a psychological process, requiring judgments by SMEs about what they do on the job and what characteristics a person needs to carry out the job. In short, job analysis is still a very important part of any organizational human resources system, although its focus and approach may change over the coming years as job environments become more dynamic and fluid.

Third, there are already a number of new approaches to job analysis on the scene. One of these is **cognitive task analysis** (Brannick et al., 2007), which goes beyond traditional task analysis by focusing specifically on the cognitive processes involved in doing the job. In other words, rather than just focusing on what a person does (e.g., "prepare coffee drinks"), this would be a focus on the cognitive processes involved (e.g., "calculate the heat of steamed milk," "remain aware of own emotions under stress.") Such cognitive task analysis is time-consuming and expensive, but may be worthwhile for understanding high-risk, critical jobs. Further, there is an increased interest in explicitly assessing elements of jobs and additional worker characteristics, such as personality traits required for the job.

Cognitive task analysis: A newer approach to job analysis, this goes beyond traditional task analysis by focusing specifically on the cognitive processes involved in doing the job.

(Raymark, Schmit, & Guion, 1997), perhaps because of increased interest in the effects of personality on worker performance over the last two decades (Barrick & Mount, 1991). Although we only provide these two examples, we anticipate changes in the types of information that can be collected through job analyses in the coming years.

Due to its critical and stressful nature, the job of air traffic controller would seem like a good candidate for cognitive task analysis.

WHAT DOES THIS MEAN FOR YOU?

The goal of this chapter was to provide you with an overview of how job analysis "works" in organizations – the different ways to collect job analysis data, what it is used for, and how to improve its quality. In general, we have presented this from the standpoint of the organization rather than from that of the employee.

So you might be wondering what this might mean to you. Perhaps the most important take-away for you is that having some bit of job analysis information, even the most simple, can be helpful to you as both a person considering a possible career as an employee or as a supervisor.

For you as a student considering possible careers, it's important for you to understand what your chosen career involves. What are the working conditions? What skills and personality characteristics are needed? With whom would you work? These are the types of questions that you should be asking yourself. (Of course pay is important, but a job that pays well but is a bad fit for you is a difficult situation to find yourself in.) You have a great, free source of job analysis information available to you (http://www.onetonline.org/). But in addition, it's useful to speak to someone in the job or even shadow them to learn more about what you're getting into. What you're looking for is a job that's a good fit for you.

From the standpoint of an employee, it's important to realize that most large organizations should have some bit of job analysis data, even if it is just a simple job description. This is important for you to be aware of, as it will help you to understand just what is expected of you. Of course, sometimes job analyses and job descriptions may not exist; or if they do, they may be outdated (and thus not entirely accurate) given the speed with which jobs may change. For you as an employee, though, it is important to be aware of what the written expectations are for your job. If you find that your job description does not seem entirely accurate, you might (politely) suggest to your supervisor or to HR that it may be time to update the document the organization keeps about the job. On rare occasions, employees may find that they are working so far outside of what their job description is that their current position should be reclassified. This may even mean that you need to receive a pay raise.

From the standpoint of the supervisor, being aware of what is actually in your employees' job description is essential. If you are a supervisor, you should be cautious not to make demands on employees that go beyond their current job descriptions. Second, knowing what the job requirements are can be essential to you as a supervisor as you strive to hire and develop your team, as well as to provide them with feedback. Again, if job descriptions and job analyses seem out of date, it may be time to bring this to the attention of the human resources department.

Conclusion

In this chapter, we have illustrated the importance of job analysis to a number of issues of interest to I/O psychologists such as selection, performance appraisal, and training. There are a number of ways to collect job analysis data, and a number of systems for framing the issue of job analysis, including more work-oriented and more worker-oriented approaches. Each of these approaches has a number of advantages and disadvantages depending on what it is that you will use the job analysis data for. At the same time, the research and practice on job analysis have identified a number of ways to improve job analysis data. The future of job analysis (or "work analysis") is expected to evolve in the coming years as the nature of work continues to change in radical ways.

YOUR TURN...

WHAT DO YOU THINK?

1. A friend of yours has been asked to do a job analysis for the salespeople in his company. He tells you he plans to do the job analysis simply by downloading the "retail salespersons" listing from the O*NET website because he says "the data are from thousands of people, so it's good enough for our company." How might you advise him to use the O*NET data?

2. Consider doing a job analysis for a job for which you are an SME, the job of student. What would it be like to do a job analysis for the job of student? Whom would you ask to be your SMEs (besides yourself)? On your own or in groups, list what you consider to be the primary, critical tasks performed by a student, as well as the critical KSAs. Also list some critical incidents faced by university students, including both positive and negative examples.

3. Your boss has tasked you with hiring a new team member for your group, which is charged with developing new video games. Specifically, this new person, who is replacing someone who has received a better job offer elsewhere, will take on coordinating the team's activities and managing individual projects for your team. Your boss wants you to use an interview that will assess the skills a person would need to do the job. Which approach to job analysis would you take and why? (Note there is no single correct answer to this question.)

4. As you know, the world of work is changing quickly. In fact, we described a number of these changes in Chapter 1. How do you think that these changes would affect job analysis? Explain your answer.

5. Given the usefulness of O*NET as a resource for conducting job analysis, check out the website (http://www.onetonline.org/). Try typing in a few job titles that might be of interest to you and take a look at the job requirements. Which of these seem to be the best fit for you based on the O*NET data?

6. As we discussed in this chapter, some types of job analysis questionnaires (e.g., task questionnaires) can be quite long and require a good bit of time on the part of the SME to complete. They also require a good bit of dedication. What are some ways that job analysts might make these surveys, which need to be fairly long, easier on the SMEs who must complete them (and thus improve the quality of the data)? Consider ways to increase the motivation of the SME and also ways to decrease the cognitive load on them.

Additional Reading

Brannick, M. T., Levine, E. L., & Morgeson, F. P. (2007). *Job and work analysis: Methods, research, and applications for human resource management*. Thousand Oaks, CA: Sage.

Cascio, W. F., & Aguinis, H. (2011). *Applied psychology in human resource management* (7th ed.). Upper Saddle River, NJ: Prentice Hall.

Gatewood, R., Feild, H., & Barrick, M. (2011). *Human resource selection*. Mason, OH: Cengage Learning.

Harvey, R. J. (1991). Job analysis. In M. D. Dunnette & L. M. Hough (Eds.), *Handbook of industrial and organizational psychology, Vol. 2* (2nd ed.) (pp. 71–163). Palo Alto, CA: Consulting Psychologists Press.

Morgeson, F. P., & Dierdorff, E. C. (2011). Work analysis: From technique to theory. In S. Zedeck (Ed.), *APA handbook of industrial and organizational psychology, Vol. 2* (pp. 3–41). Washington, DC: American Psychological Association.

Sanchez, J. I., & Levine, E. L. (2012). The rise and fall of job analysis and the rise of work analysis. *Annual Review of Psychology, 63,* 397–425.

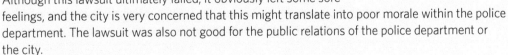

CASE STUDY: Job Analysis Quality, Job Analysis Politics

Carol Hernandez is an I/O psychologist who has been hired by the City of Trent (a Midwestern city of approximately 400,000 people) to develop selection procedures for hiring new police officers. In the past, the Trent HR department developed its own tests in-house. However, historically, there have been high tensions in the police department, and this is manifested by the fact that controversy always seemed to follow the hiring procedures. For example, a few years ago the City of Trent and its police department were sued by one of the two police unions for using unfair hiring procedures that did not result in hiring enough women and minority officers. Although this lawsuit ultimately failed, it obviously left some sore feelings, and the city is very concerned that this might translate into poor morale within the police department. The lawsuit was also not good for the public relations of the police department or the city.

Carol realizes that her first step is to conduct a job analysis. Because of the way she wants to approach the development of the tests, she knows that she has to get as much detailed information as possible about the police officer's job and what a person needs to do the job. However, she knows that one of the unions is already saying in the media that they are concerned that the process will be biased in favor of members of the other union, which is primarily white and male. Carol needs to get together a plan that will lead to her collecting high-quality job analysis data while also reducing some of the negative feelings in the department – or at least not making them worse.

Questions

1. Given Carol's goals, what job analysis method(s) do you recommend that she use, and why?

2. How might Carol address some of the concerns in the police unions that there is a bias towards certain groups or others? Specifically, how might she handle the job analysis in a way that lessens the unions' concerns?

3. Let's say Carol is asked to sit down and explain to union leaders about the effects of different background variables on job analysis data. Develop a series of "talking points" for her as she discusses these issues.

References

Aguinis, H., Mazurkiewicz, M. D., & Heggestad, E. D. (2009). Using web-based frame-of-reference training to decrease biases in personality-based job analysis: An experimental field study. *Personnel Psychology, 62*, 405–438.

Anonymous. (2013, March). Honda finds DACUM valuable for training. *T+D*, 80.

Barrick, M. R., & Mount, M. K. (1991). The big five personality dimensions and job performance: A meta-analysis. *Personnel Psychology, 44*, 1–26.

Brannick, M. T., Levine, E. L., & Morgeson, F. P. (2007). *Job and work analysis: Methods, research, and applications for human resource management.* Thousand Oaks, CA: Sage.

Cascio, W. F., & Aguinis, H. (2011). *Applied psychology in human resource management* (7th ed.). Upper Saddle River, NJ: Prentice Hall.

Campion, M. A., Fink, A. A., Ruggeberg, B. J., Carr, L., Phillips, G. M., & Odman, R. B. (2011). Doing competencies well: Best practices in competency modeling. *Personnel Psychology, 64*, 225–262.

Conley, P. R., & Sackett, P. R. (1987). Effects of using high- versus low-performing job incumbents as sources of job-analysis information. *Journal of Applied Psychology, 72*, 434–437.

De Pater, I. E., Judge, T. A., & Scott, B. A. (2014). Age, gender, and compensation: A study of Hollywood movie stars. *Journal of Management Inquiry, 23*, 407–420.

Dierdorff, E. C., & Morgeson, F. P. (2009). Effects of descriptor specificity and observability on incumbent work analysis ratings. *Personnel Psychology, 62*, 601–628.

Dierdorff, E. C., & Wilson, M. A. (2003). A meta-analysis of job analysis reliability. *Journal of Applied Psychology, 88*, 635–646.

Feild, H. S., & Holley, W. H. (1982). The relationship of performance appraisal system characteristics to verdicts in selected employment discrimination cases. *Academy of Management Journal, 25*, 392–406.

Fine, S. (1988). Functional job analysis. In S. Gael (Ed.), *The job analysis handbook for business, industry and government* (pp. 1019–1035). New York: Wiley.

Flanagan, J.C. (1954). The critical incident technique. *Psychological Bulletin, 51*, 327–358.

Gatewood, R., Feild, H., & Barrick, M. (2011). *Human resource selection*. Mason, OH: Cengage Learning.

Green, S. B., & Stutzman, T. (1986). An evaluation of methods to select respondents to structured job-analysis questionnaires. *Personnel Psychology, 39*, 543–564.

Harvey, R. J. (1991). Job analysis. In M. D. Dunnette & L. M. Hough (Eds.), *Handbook of industrial and organizational psychology, Vol. 2* (2nd ed.) (pp. 71–163). Palo Alto, CA: Consulting Psychologists Press.

Killingsworth, M. R. (2002). Comparable worth and pay equity: Recent developments in the United States. *Canadian Public Policy/Analyse de Politiques, 28*, S171–S186.

Landy, F. J., & Vasey, J. (1991). Job analysis: The composition of SME samples. *Personnel Psychology, 44*, 27–50.

Lindell, M. K., Clause, C. S., Brandt, C. J., & Landis, R. S. (1998). Relationship between organizational context and job analysis task ratings. *Journal of Applied Psychology, 83*, 769–776.

Madden, J. F. (2012). Performance-support bias and the gender pay gap among stockbrokers. *Gender and Society, 26*, 488–518.

McCormick, E.J., Jeanneret, P.R., & Mecham, R.C. (1972). A study of job characteristics and job dimensions as based on the position analysis questionnaire (PAQ). *Journal of Applied Psychology, 56*, 347–368.

Morgeson, F. P., & Campion, M. A. (1997). Social and cognitive sources of potential inaccuracy in job analysis. *Journal of Applied Psychology, 82*, 627–655.

Morgeson, F. P., Delaney-Klinger, K., Mayfield, M. S., Ferrera, P., & Campion, M. A. (2004). Self-presentation processes in job analysis: A field experiment investigating inflation in abilities, tasks, and competencies. *Journal of Applied Psychology, 89*, 674–686.

Morgeson, F. P., & Dierdorff, E. C. (2011). Work analysis: From technique to theory. In S. Zedeck (Ed.), *APA handbook of industrial and organizational psychology, Vol. 2* (pp. 3–41). Washington, DC: American Psychological Association.

Peterson, N. G., Mumford, M. D., Borman, W. C., Jeanneret, P. R., Fleishman, E. A., Levin, K. Y., …, & Dye, D. M. (2001). Understanding work using the Occupational Information Network (O* NET): Implications for practice and research. *Personnel Psychology, 54*, 451–492.

Primoff, E. S. (1975). *How to prepare and conduct job element examinations*. Washington, DC: US Civil Service Commission. Retrieved February 14, 2015 from http://babel.hathitrust.org/cgi/pt?id=uiug.30112011740708;view=1up;seq=11.

Raymark, P. H., Schmit, M. J., & Guion, R. M. (1997). Identifying potentially useful personality constructs for employee selection. *Personnel Psychology, 50*, 723–736.

Sanchez, J. I., Levine, E. L. (2009). What is (or should be) the difference between competency modeling and traditional job analysis? *Human Resource Management Review, 19*, 53–63.

Sanchez, J. I., & Levine, E. L. (2012). The rise and fall of job analysis and the rise of work analysis. *Annual Review of Psychology, 63,* 397–425.

Sanchez, J. I., Prager, I., Wilson, A., & Viswesvaran, C. (1998). Understanding within-job title variance in job-analytic ratings. *Journal of Business and Psychology, 12,* 407–419.

Shippmann, J. S., Ash, R. A., Battista, M., Carr, L., Eyde, L. D., Hesketh, B., & Sanchez, J. I. (2000). The practice of competency modeling. *Personnel Psychology, 53,* 703–740.

Society for Human Resource Management. (2014). *HR competencies FAQ.* Retrieved June 8, 2014 from http://www.shrm.org/HRCompetencies/Pages/FAQs.aspx.

Society for Industrial and Organizational Psychology (SIOP). (2003). *Principles for the validation and use of personnel selection procedures* (4th ed.). Bowling Green, OH: Author.

Thompson, D. E., & Thompson, T. A. (1982). Court standards for job analysis in test validation. *Personnel Psychology, 35,* 865–874.

Tross, S. A., & Maurer, T. J. (2000). The relationship between SME job experience and job analysis ratings: Finding with and without statistical controls. *Journal of Business and Psychology, 15,* 97–110.

Uniform Guidelines on Employee Selection Procedures. (1978). *Federal Register, 43,* 38290–38315.

Wexley, K. N., & Silverman, S. B. (1978). An examination of differences between managerial effectiveness and response patterns on a structured job analysis questionnaire. *Journal of Applied Psychology, 63,* 646–649.

Chapter 4
CRITERION MEASURES

I/O psychologists must assess the performance of employees in order to evaluate the quality of selection and training programs. This chapter will discuss some of the available options for measuring employee performance.

After studying this chapter, you should be able to:

Learning goals for this chapter

- define what is meant by the term "criteria" and what criteria are used for in I/O psychology
- describe what is meant by "actual" versus "conceptual" criteria
- list the characteristics that good criteria should have
- differentiate between task performance and contextual performance
- describe the difference between multiple and composite criteria and when each should be used
- list and define some of the most important performance outcomes examined by I/O psychologists and the challenges with measuring them
- differentiate between subjective and objective criteria and the advantages and disadvantages of each

- identify key legal and global issues surrounding the use of criteria in organizations
- describe the current issues and controversies in the use of criterion measures.

Introduction

As you will see in the coming chapters, I/O psychologists develop, administer, and research a number of organizational interventions and processes to make organizations more productive. These could include, for example, developing selection procedures (e.g., tests, interviews) used to hire new employees; developing training programs to increase the knowledge, skills, and abilities of existing employees; or administering safety interventions to reduce workplace accidents and injuries. However, in today's results-driven organizations, it's important to show that these interventions actually are effective, such that selection procedures result in hiring more competent new employees, that training leads to increased worker knowledge and performance, or that safety practices lead to improved safety outcomes.

Criteria: Outcome variables – such as measures of job performance – that can be used to demonstrate the performance or effectiveness of an employee or group of employees. Criteria are used to show whether employee outcomes such as work behavior have improved as a result of a personnel selection measure, a training system, or some other workforce intervention.

That's where **criteria** (singular, "criterion") come in (Guion, 2011). Criteria are outcome variables – such as measures of job performance – that capture the performance or effectiveness of an employee or group of employees; these criteria are used to show the effectiveness of HR functions such as selection and training. Specifically, criteria can show whether employee outcomes – such as attitudes, behavior, knowledge, or competence – have improved as a result of a personnel selection test, a training system, or some other workforce intervention. For example, if an I/O psychologist can show that job applicants who get a high score on a selection test actually perform better on the job after they are hired, that shows that the selection test should be used in hiring applicants. (As we mention in Chapter 2, this is also the basis for establishing the criterion-related validity of a test.) If we can show that employees who were trained using a new online training system perform better on the job than those who were not trained, this suggests that the training program is worth keeping and administering to other employees. Or if the new safety program leads to a decrease in on-site accidents and injuries, this would suggest that the safety program is worth the investment.

As you can see, criteria are essential to showing the value of many of the programs I/O psychologists develop and administer. And for that reason, it's important for I/O psychologists to have high-quality criterion or work performance measures available to them to evaluate the effectiveness of the systems, processes, and programs that they put into place. But this is a challenge as well, because developing good performance criteria is not easy. For example, one of the most commonly used criteria for validating selection tests comes in the form of supervisor performance ratings. However, as we'll see in Chapter 5, supervisor ratings are susceptible to errors and biases – and are also time-consuming. To the degree that performance ratings contain errors, it is more difficult to use them to evaluate the effectiveness of selection and training programs.

In this chapter, we will review these and other major challenges in developing good performance measures and how to overcome these challenges. We will also discuss some of the different types of criterion measures (e.g., supervisor ratings; objective performance measures) and the advantages and disadvantages of each. Finally, we will discuss the most important dimensions of work performance (e.g., core task performance, contextual performance) that I/O psychology researchers and practitioners have identified through the years.

Workplace Application

Measuring CEO Performance

Many large organizations tie CEO compensation, such as pay, bonuses, and stock options, to CEO performance. One major challenge, though, is to measure CEO performance. For instance, it is common to assess CEO performance in terms of financial performance (e.g., stock price), that is, the short-term benefit for the stockholders. However, there are a number of other measures that might also be considered in assessing a CEO's performance – but often are not – such as product quality, workplace safety, development of future talent in the company, and litigation that has happened on the CEO's watch. Another issue is whether the CEO focuses on long-term results rather than focusing on short-term profits. For example, Jeff Bezos of Amazon was recently listed at the top of a list of CEOs whose performance was in line with their organization's long-term performance.

Sources: Harvard Business Review, 2014; Stanford Graduate School of Business, Center for Leadership Development and Research, 2013.

Conceptual versus Actual Criteria

One way to think about measuring job performance is to think about the ideas of conceptual criteria and actual criteria. In this section, we will define each of these terms and discuss challenges with conceptual and actual criteria in organizational settings.

Conceptual Criteria: Definition and Challenges

A **conceptual criterion** is not something you can actually measure directly. Rather, it is just that – a concept – an abstract idea of the "essence" of a job. In other words, if you wanted to capture what makes up the job, what KSAOs would go into it, and what job behaviors would be included, if these could be perfectly measured? Of course, you could get some of this from doing a job analysis – in fact, that's the best place to go – but you can never fully capture what the essence of the job is.

Conceptual criterion: An abstract idea of the "essence" of a job. It cannot be measured directly.

For example, if we were to do a job analysis for the job of barista, we would be able to identify the primary tasks involved in the job, as well as most of the KSAOs that a person needs to do the job. But even if a job analysis is done carefully, it would probably be lacking some details about the barista's job, and it might also include some tasks that some but not all baristas do. Or, another problem might be that our job analysts were not able to accurately describe in writing all that a barista does. In other words, our definition of the conceptual criterion is usually not perfect.

Actual Criteria: Definition and Challenges

Actual criterion: The performance measure or measures (e.g., performance ratings, sales figures) you will actually use to try to capture the conceptual criterion. All actual criteria have some degree of unreliability and measurement error.

The second major idea is that of the **actual criterion**, the measure or measures you will actually use to try to capture the conceptual criterion. These are the measures that you will use to measure individual employees' performance. One thing to keep in mind is that *all actual criterion measures are flawed in some way because they have some degree of error*. As we noted in Chapter 2, most measures used in psychology have some degree of unreliability and error, and the same is true for measures of job performance used in organizations. Going back to our barista example, supervisor performance ratings would give us some information about how well an individual barista is performing, but it is impossible to eliminate all of the biases and inaccuracies inherent when one person rates another. What about using more objective measures of performance instead, such as the number of drinks produced by a barista each hour? Even these are not perfect, because conditions in the work environment, such as differences in the equipment or in the support received from colleagues, may vary. In other words, even objective criteria may not be able to capture all of the nuances of the particular situation that the employee is working in (Austin & Villanova, 1992). For example, research has consistently shown that employee safety behaviors are a function not only of the characteristics of individual employees, but also of the safety "climate" of the work site (the support for safety in the employee's social environment at work; Christian, Bradley, Wallace, & Burke, 2009). In other words, employee safe behaviors and accidents are a function of both the employee and the social environment that the employee is working in. In addition, employees' work performance may be affected by the physical environment such as equipment. So, an individual employee's performance is a function not only of that employee's KSAOs and motivation, but also the social environment, such as climate, and the physical environment, such as tools and equipment.

Safety performance is a function not only of the individual employee but of the social and physical work environment as well. One example is a safety culture that supports the use of the proper protective equipment.

As another example of problems with actual criterion measures, let's say you decided to use number of customer complaints as a measure of job performance for customer service workers. That could certainly be useful information, but it will probably be flawed in some ways. For example, perhaps the supervisor always gives the most difficult customers to the best employee in the group, because he or she is good at handling difficult people. That employee would clearly provide a valuable service to the company, but that employee might also have a large number of customer complaints because they are always assigned the most difficult customers. Or, there is also the possibility of simple random error in the measure of performance: One employee may, by chance, have gotten a large number of difficult customers and therefore gotten more complaints – but they might be a good customer service worker.

The Criterion Problem

In short, in measuring job performance, we have defined two major problems. First, we can never be sure that we have accurately and completely specified the job to determine the conceptual criterion. Second, we must use actual criterion measures, such as performance ratings or objective performance measures, which all contain some error. And herein lies the **criterion problem**, or the difficulty of completely and accurately capturing job performance with the actual criterion measures. The criterion problem – being able to know that we have accurately identified all parts of the conceptual criterion through the job analysis, and that our actual criterion measures are without error – is a perennial challenge in I/O psychology (Guion, 2011; Ryan & Ployhart, 2014).

Choosing Good Actual Criterion Measures

The Venn diagram in Figure 4.1 illustrates the challenge of the conceptual criterion: It shows that there is only some degree of overlap between the conceptual and actual criterion. Our goal is to make that overlap as great as possible. This diagram implies that we want to increase the overlap between the conceptual and actual criterion as much as possible.

This Venn diagram also illustrates another way to think about the relationship between the conceptual and actual criterion. In choosing actual criteria to be used to measure employees' performance, we want to consider three important issues: (1) criterion deficiency, (2) criterion contamination, and (3) relevance of the actual criterion (see Figure 4.2). **Criterion deficiency** is the degree to which the actual criterion fails to overlap with the conceptual criterion. For example, a car rental company may try to measure the job of customer service assistant by using customer complaints as an actual criterion. Customer complaints may be a good measure, but if it leaves out other important parts of the job such as the number of customer calls each employee processes, there would be some deficiency. **Criterion contamination** is when an actual criterion includes something that it should not, leading to error. For example, a paper mill might use supervisor ratings of employees as an actual criterion to measure the performance of its workers, but to the extent that the ratings are affected by supervisor bias, there is contamination of the ratings. **Criterion relevance** is the degree to which the actual criterion overlaps with the

Criterion problem: The difficulty of capturing the conceptual criterion with the actual criterion measures. This is because the job analysis does not completely define the conceptual criterion, plus the actual criterion measures are unreliable and contain some measurement error.

Criterion deficiency: The degree to which the actual criterion fails to overlap with the conceptual criterion.

Criterion contamination: When an actual criterion measure includes something that it should not (e.g., bias), leading to error.

Criterion relevance: The degree to which the actual criterion overlaps with the conceptual criterion.

Figure 4.1 Overlap between the conceptual and actual criterion.

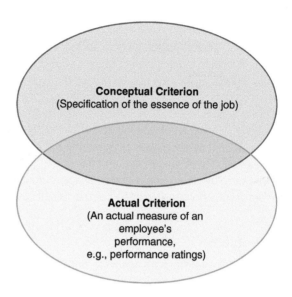

Conceptual Criterion
(Specification of the essence of the job)

Actual Criterion
(An actual measure of an employee's performance, e.g., performance ratings)

Figure 4.2 Criterion contamination, deficiency, and relevance.

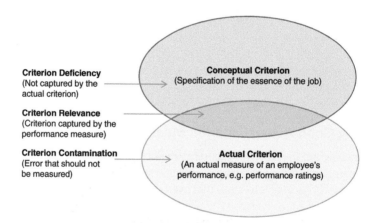

Criterion Deficiency
(Not captured by the actual criterion)

Criterion Relevance
(Criterion captured by the performance measure)

Criterion Contamination
(Error that should not be measured)

Conceptual Criterion
(Specification of the essence of the job)

Actual Criterion
(An actual measure of an employee's performance, e.g. performance ratings)

conceptual criterion. Criterion relevance can be increased (improved) by reducing criterion deficiency and contamination as much as possible.

One additional important recommendation for choosing actual criterion measures is to *choose actual criteria that overlap as much as possible with the conceptual criterion, but not with each other,* that is, are not redundant with each other. This is like the criteria in the Venn diagram in Figure 4.3. This would allow you to capture much of the conceptual criterion. In the situation shown in Figure 4.4, however, the actual criteria are almost entirely redundant with each other and do not capture very much of the conceptual criterion. In other words, you would be taking the time and money to measure three aspects of job performance, when in fact they are redundant with each other. Rather, the goal is to

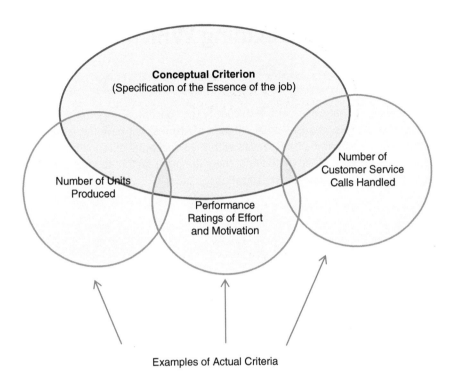

Examples of Actual Criteria

Figure 4.3 The use of many actual criteria to capture more of the conceptual criterion.

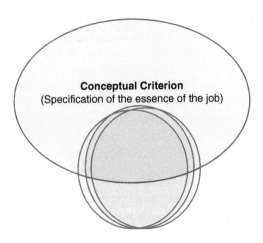

Figure 4.4 Multiple actual criterion measures that are redundant with each other and thus explain relatively little unique variance in the conceptual criterion.

choose criteria that are not redundant with each other but explain as much variance as possible in the criterion.

Interactive: Using the overlap of conceptual and actual criteria to increase criterion relevance and reduce contamination/error.

"See website for interactive material"

Issues When Deciding Which Criterion Measures to Use

So far we've said that it's important to specify the conceptual criterion accurately through job analysis, choose actual criterion measures that have the least error, and choose actual criteria that overlap with the conceptual criterion but are not redundant with each other. In addition, there are other factors to consider when choosing criterion measures in organizations.

Changes in Job Performance over Time

Dynamic criteria: The concept that performance for an individual employee may change over time.

First is the concept of **dynamic criteria** and change in performance over time (Alessandri, Borgogni, & Truxillo, 2015; Deadrick & Madigan, 1990; Guion, 2011). That is, performance for an individual may change over time, for example, shortly after they are hired in comparison with after they have been on the job for quite some time. Thus, it's important to decide what your time-frame should be for the measurement of the criterion and this largely depends on the goals of your particular research question. For instance, if a company hired workers for only six months at a time, they might decide to hire workers using selection tests that predict employee performance during their first six months on the job. However, if they are interested in long-term performance, they might want to use a selection test that predicts employee performance over a longer period of time.

Typical versus Maximum Performance

Typical performance: The job performance that an employee usually exhibits.

Maximum performance: The performance that an employee is capable of carrying out.

A second issue is to be sure whether you want to measure employees' **typical performance**, the job performance they usually exhibit, or **maximum performance**, the performance they are capable of carrying out (e.g., Beier & Ackerman, 2012; Sackett, Zedeck, & Fogli, 1988). Sackett et al. found that employees' typical performance and maximum performance are not strongly correlated. Later research examining the performance of managers (Marcus, Goffin, Johnston, & Rothstein, 2007) confirmed that typical and maximum performance are distinct and have different antecedents. For instance, maximum performance may be best predicted by cognitive ability, and typical performance may be best predicted by personality (see Chapter 6). This distinction between typical and maximum performance can be important in organizational research. For example, if you were to examine the effectiveness of a training program by measuring the training's effect on an employee's maximum performance, you might not be able to tell whether the training program affected employees' typical performance day to day.

Other Characteristics of Good Criteria

As we've discussed so far, like any measure used in psychological research, criteria should be reliable. As we discussed in Chapter 2, reliability implies that a measure is low in measurement error, which also allows for increased validity. Put differently, if a criterion measure is not reliable, it won't be able to detect differences among employees. For instance, it could make a good selection test look as if it isn't predicting performance, or it could make an effective training program look as if it didn't work.

There are other factors to consider as well when choosing among actual criteria to measure in organizational settings (Gatewood, Feild, & Barrick, 2011). First, criteria need to be able to detect differences among employees. For example, as we will see in Chapter 5, if an organization had a performance rating system that used a 1-5 rating scale, but all employees received a 5, the performance ratings would not be useful (unless, of course, all employees really were outstanding – which is highly unlikely!). Second, criteria should be accepted by employees and supervisors. If they are not, the use of the criteria will likely be resisted by employees and supervisors, and may even be sabotaged by them. For example, if an organization decided to use its supervisor performance rating system to make layoff decisions, and this possibility had not been explained to supervisors when they made their ratings, supervisors and employees might resent it, and supervisors might in the future provide inaccurate, useless ratings. Third, it is important to be able to collect criterion data in an organizational setting without too much cost or disruption. Of course, if organizational budgets were unlimited, it would be possible to measure performance through a number of methods that would provide great data. As an extreme example, all worker performance might be video-recorded over a period of months and then rated by trained, independent raters. While this method might provide some good data, it would be prohibitively expensive, and thus would not be practical.

Multiple versus Composite Criteria

One of the major questions in using criteria is deciding whether to keep each criterion measure separate, or to combine the criteria together into a composite (Cascio & Aguinis, 2011; Gatewood et al., 2011). As an example, consider a situation in which you are trying to measure the job performance of computer programmers. Let's say that you have three different measures of their performance – how quickly they can write computer code, how much code they can write (e.g., how many lines per day), and how well they work with other programmers on their team. Now that you have these three performance measures, you have a choice: Should you average these three measures of job performance together (criterion composite), or should you look at each of the measures separately (multiple criteria)? A criterion composite (or **composite criterion**) is the combination of multiple criteria, added or averaged together, or else weighted (usually based on job analysis) and then combined. In contrast, the use of **multiple criteria** involves treating each criterion measure separately in analysis. Each approach could be acceptable, depending on what the goals of the study are (Cascio & Aguinis, 2011; Schmidt & Kaplan, 1971). If your goal is to see what the "bottom line" is – for example, whether a training program worked or not – the composite is the way to go. This could be useful if you need to present the results of your training program to decision-makers in the organization.

Let's give another specific example related to the customer service job we discussed earlier in this chapter. Figure 4.5 shows an example for a customer service job. Assume that the reason you have collected the criterion measures is to evaluate an employee training program. Recall that the organization has done a good job

Composite criterion (or criterion composite): A combination of multiple criteria, added or averaged together, used to show the "bottom line" work performance. For example, one could see whether a training program helps an employee's behavior overall.

Multiple criteria: Treating each criterion measure separately in an analysis. For example, one could see whether a training program helps customer service behavior, safety behavior, and other behaviors of employees.

Figure 4.5
Example of a composite criterion and multiple, separate criteria for a customer service job.

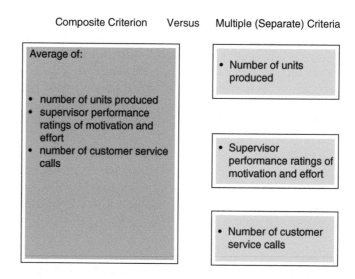

coming up with three actual criterion measures based on a detailed job analysis and discussions with SMEs: number of units produced; supervisor performance ratings of motivation and effort; and number of customer service calls. When you go to evaluate the training program, should you look to see if the training changed the overall composite, or should you examine change in the individual, separate criteria? Figure 4.6 shows the training evaluation results (pre-training and post-training) for the three separate, multiple criteria as dotted lines, while the composite (average) criterion is the solid red line. (And see also Table 4.1.)

Based on Figure 4.6, we can see that the training generally did work – overall employee performance, based on the composite criterion, is higher after the

Figure 4.6 Using multiple versus composite criteria: graph for training evaluation example.

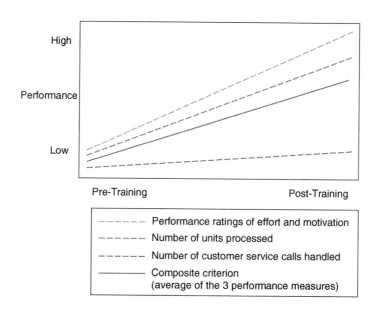

Table 4.1 Using multiple versus composite criteria: data for training evaluation example

Criterion Measure	Pre-Training (1–5 Scale)	Post-Training (1–5 Scale)
Performance ratings of effort and motivation	1.5	4.5
Number of units processed	1.4	4
Number of customer service calls handled	1.2	2
Composite (average)	1.37	3.5

training than it was before the training. However, notice that looking at the composite criterion gives only part of the story: It is masking the fact that there were some fairly substantial differences in terms of the degree to which the training affected each of the individual criteria. Specifically, although performance ratings and units produced seemed to go up quite a bit after training, the number of customer service calls handled didn't change much at all. So one could say that the training had a strong effect on the first two criteria but nearly no effect on the third one. This is very important information for organizational researchers to have, because it suggests that the training may need to be revised so that it can also address the number of calls handled.

Here's a second example related to the topic of selection test validation (see Figure 4.7). In this example, we are looking at the relationship between a test and

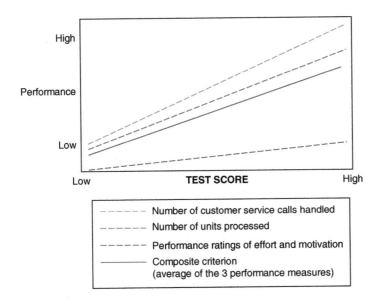

Figure 4.7 Using multiple versus composite criteria: test validation example.

job performance expressed as a regression line. (We have covered this briefly in Chapter 2 but will cover the use of regression in selection test validation in greater detail in Chapter 6.) In this case, we can see that the test does a good, "bottom line" job of predicting the composite criterion of job performance. Basically, the test "works" and is valid for predicting job performance. That's great news. However, a little closer inspection of the figure shows that although the test predicts two of the criterion measures well, it doesn't do a very good job of predicting performance ratings of motivation and effort. In other words, the organization may want to consider revising the test (e.g., adding additional questions) or adding other tests to the test battery so that they can predict employee performance ratings of motivation and effort as well.

In summary, then, there is no "correct" approach as to whether one should use separate, multiple criteria or an overall criterion composite. Using a composite makes sense for getting a bottom-line understanding and may be especially useful for communicating with non-researchers like company top management, but keeping multiple, separate criteria would be important for getting a deeper understanding of what is going on and certainly is better for organizational research purposes.

 "See website for interactive material"

Interactive: Using multiple versus composite criteria.

Models of Job Performance

Task performance (or core task performance): The core tasks that make up a particular job, typically shown in a job description.

Contextual performance: Behaviors that support the social environment in the workplace.

Organizational citizenship behaviors (OCBs): Behaviors focused on helping individual coworkers and helping to support the organization.

As we have stated previously, one of the best ways to determine the dimensions of a job performance criterion is to look at the job analysis. This will give you a lot of guidance about what the specific job performance dimensions are for that particular job. But I/O psychologists have also tried to consider which job performance dimensions might be common to all jobs. One of the models that has dominated over the last 20 years is the division of job performance into **task performance** (or core task performance) and **contextual performance** (Borman & Motowidlo, 1993; Motowidlo & Van Scotter, 1994). Task performance includes the core tasks that make up a particular job, and that varies for different jobs. For instance, the core task performance for a barista would involve making coffee, for a computer programmer it would be writing code, and for a customer service worker task performance behaviors might include working with customers to solve problems and providing information about company products. In contrast, contextual performance involves behaviors that support the social environment in the workplace, and according to Borman and Motowidlo (1997), those contextual performance behaviors are fairly similar across jobs. We provide some examples of contextual performance in Table 4.2. For example, contextual performance would include helping team members complete their tasks, following rules, or staying late to help on a project. As you can see, contextual performance involves a good bit of being a good organizational citizen, or what we call **organizational citizenship behaviors** (OCBs), that is, behaviors focused on helping individual coworkers and helping to support the organization (which will be discussed in more detail in Chapter 11).

Can You Have Too Much Contextual Performance?

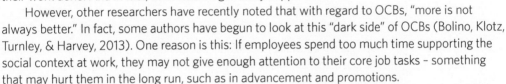

Implied in our discussion of task and contextual performance is that both of them are good. In other words, it's good for employees to do their core job tasks well, and it's also good for them to support the work context and be a good organizational citizen so that the group can get their work done. And in fact, the research generally supports this.

However, other researchers have recently noted that with regard to OCBs, "more is not always better." In fact, some authors have begun to look at this "dark side" of OCBs (Bolino, Klotz, Turnley, & Harvey, 2013). One reason is this: If employees spend too much time supporting the social context at work, they may not give enough attention to their core job tasks – something that may hurt them in the long run, such as in advancement and promotions.

For example, in a study by Bergeron and colleagues (Bergeron, Shipp, Rosen, & Furst, 2013), the effects of task and contextual performance on career advancement were examined among employees at a professional services firm. The authors found that employees who spent more time on OCBs tended to spend less time on task performance. But which was more important to advancement? In this case, it was task performance, not OCBs. In fact, employees who spent more time on OCBs had fewer salary increases and advanced less quickly than employees who spent less time on OCBs.

This research doesn't suggest that employees shouldn't participate in OCBs or that OCBs will always lead to negative outcomes for employees. However, it does suggest that as a field we may need to examine the effects of OCBs on the organization, the team, and the individual in greater detail, and not always assume that more OCBs are always better.

There are other frameworks for looking at the dimensions of job performance as well, perhaps the most influential of which is that by John Campbell (e.g., Campbell, McCloy, Oppler, & Sager, 1993). Campbell argues that most jobs can be described using the following eight dimensions, which can also be used to describe most jobs in the *Dictionary of Occupational Titles* and in O*NET (see Chapter 3). These eight dimensions are as follows:

- *Job-specific task proficiency*, comparable to task performance.
- *Non-job-specific task proficiency*, which includes tasks that are not core but required for the job. An example might be an organization that requires safety behaviors of all employees.
- *Written and oral communication task proficiency*.
- *Demonstrating effort, in particular*, demonstrated consistency in effort day to day.
- *Maintaining personal discipline*, such as following the rules of the organization.
- *Facilitating peer and team performance*, including helping and supporting coworkers.

Table 4.2 Borman and Motowidlo's Taxonomy of Contextual Performance

Persisting with enthusiasm and extra effort as necessary to complete own task activities successfully

Volunteering to carry out task activities that are not formally part of own job

Helping and cooperating with others

Following organizational rules and procedures

Endorsing, supporting, and defending organizational objectives

Source: Based on Borman & Motowidlo, 1997.

- *Supervision/leadership*, or including influencing the behavior of subordinates.
- *Management/administration*, different from direct supervision and leadership, which is focused on the use of resources and setting goals for the work unit.

The model has been supported across a number of studies in the military (e.g., Campbell, McHenry, & Wise, 1990), although like so much in our field, research on it continues.

Counterproductive work behavior (CWB): Work behaviors such as theft, derailment of others, and abusive leadership.

In addition, there are a number of additional dimensions of job performance that have gained attention in recent years. One of these is **counterproductive work behavior** (CWB) such as theft, derailment of others, abusive leadership, and high levels of organizational politicking (Dalal, 2005; O'Boyle, Forsyth, Banks, & McDaniel, 2012; Penney & Spector, 2005). CWBs are not simply the opposite of OCBs, but as you might suspect, the two are negatively correlated (−.32; Dalal, 2005). Another type of job performance that has received attention in the literature, perhaps because of the rapidly changing work environment in the twenty-first century, is **adaptive behavior** (Pulakos, Arad, Donovan, & Plamondon, 2000). Adaptive behavior has to do with how well an employee adapts to the task and social environments, includes factors such as adapting to work stress, solving problems creatively, handling emergencies, and cultural and interpersonal adaptability. The full list of dimensions of adaptability according to Pulakos et al.'s taxonomy are given in Table 4.3.

Adaptive behavior: Includes factors such as adjusting to new social and tasks environments. It includes adapting to work stress, solving problems creatively, handling emergencies, and cultural and interpersonal adaptability.

Creative performance: Involves problem-finding, flexibility, originality, and evaluation of ideas.

A third type of job performance that has been identified as important to the performance domain, especially for certain types of jobs, is **creative performance** (e.g., Davis, 2009), which involves dimensions such as finding problems, ideation (flexibility and originality), and evaluation of ideas. Example creativity behaviors would include taking risks in generating new ideas and identifying opportunities (Tierney, Farmer, & Graen, 1999). Although there has been a good deal of interest in these additional job performance behaviors, there has still not been a lot of empirical research on these other types of job behaviors in terms of their use as criterion measures (Ryan & Ployhart, 2014), and thus much more needs to be done.

Table 4.3 Pulakos et al.'s dimensions of adaptive behavior

Dimension	Example
Handling emergencies in crisis situations	Making quick decisions based on clear thinking
Handling work stress	Not overreacting to unexpected situations
Solving problems creatively	Developing creative solutions from unrelated information
Dealing with uncertain and unpredictable work situations	Changing course in response to unpredictable or unexpected events and circumstances
Learning work tasks, technologies, and procedures	Showing enthusiasm for learning new things
Demonstrating interpersonal adaptability	Being flexible when interacting with other people
Demonstrating cultural adaptability	Interacting with different values, customs, and cultures
Demonstrating physically oriented adaptability	Adjusting to challenging environments

Source: Based on Pulakos et al., 2000.

Many organizations have begun to assess and reward creative performance. General Electric assesses employees' "capacity to take risks in championing ideas, learn from the experience and drive improvement" (*New York Times*, 2012).

What Are Some Types of Actual Criterion Measures?

Objective measures: Performance measures not based on the judgment of others, such as number of sales (for a sales job) or number of units produced (for jobs that can be quantified).

Subjective measures: Performance measures based on the judgment of another person such as supervisor performance ratings.

There are quite a few different types of criterion measures that are typically available in organizations, and we have already discussed these a little in this chapter. Let's dig into these a bit more.

As we've mentioned, researchers might consider using **objective measures** of performance such as number of sales (for a sales job) or number of units produced (for jobs that can be quantified). Or, researchers might choose **subjective measures** of performance (measures based on the judgment of another person) such as supervisor performance ratings, which are perhaps the most commonly used job performance measures in terms of test validation. Which of these types of measures is best? You guessed it – there is no simple answer to that question.

While objective measures might sound good (after all, they're objective, and that seems like a good and fair thing, right?), they are not without their flaws. Let's go through some of the most commonly used objective job performance measures and the problems that may arise with them.

- Sales figures: Sales figures are certainly a good way to judge the performance of salespeople. They are, after all, what largely determines the organization's profitability. But not all sales figures are the same. Tamara may sell $40,000 worth of large computer equipment per month, and Sam sells only $30,000 worth. But what if Tamara inherited a client list from a friend who recently quit the company? Sam may be an outstanding salesperson, but you can't really tell just by his sales figures. Similarly, Javier and Caroline may both work in retail clothing sales where Caroline sells more clothing in dollars than Javier. But if Javier's store is a less busy one in a less wealthy part of town, it's hard to tell from these sales figures which of them is the better employee.
- Units produced: Again, units produced (for example, in a factory setting) can be an excellent way to assess performance. And let's say that Emile makes 10 units per day, while Renee makes 8. But if Emile works in a factory that is more modern than where Renee works, that could affect their productivity.
- Absenteeism: Unexcused absences, or employees calling in sick to work when they are actually not sick, can be an important loss for organizations. And certainly organizations should do their best to measure this outcome and try to prevent it, and even see if they can use tests during the hiring process to predict this problem (e.g., integrity tests; see Chapter 6). Plus unexcused absences can leave other employees having to do additional work. On the other hand, it can be very difficult to know whether absences are excused or not. Certainly, organizations should not penalize employees for using sick days when they are actually ill. This can lead to another problem called "**presenteeism**", where a worker comes to work sick, perhaps because they thought that the boss expected them to. Besides, it is possible for the very best employee to take an occasional day off (unexcused) but to be such a great employee in other ways that it doesn't matter to the organization: the employee provides

Presenteeism: A situation in which a worker comes to work sick, perhaps because they thought that the boss expected them to do so.

Although simple sales figures can be a great way to evaluate the effectiveness of an organization's salesforce, they also may also fail to capture some important aspects of the job.

excellent value anyway. In other words, absenteeism is an important outcome for organizations to consider, but the situation is much more complex than simply whether or not an employee shows up to work.

- Tardiness: Similarly, for certain types of jobs tardiness is problematic. One can't have an emergency medical person who is an hour late for their shift, possibly leaving people in danger. But again, tardiness may not be that import-ant for certain jobs. At one time, one of the authors worked for an adminis-trator who was late most of the time: She often did not arrive at work on time, and she was often late for meetings with her subordinates. On the other hand, she was considered one of the most hard working and dedicated – and effective – people in the agency, and she managed to accomplish a lot for the agency under adverse conditions. Certainly her tardiness was not a strength, and it probably wasn't a great example for her employees, but her remarkable effectiveness in all other aspects of her job far outweighed this one issue.

- Turnover: Turnover may be one of the greatest expenses in many organiz-ations, especially when the organization has invested a lot in the training and development of employees. (Note that we will discuss turnover a bit more when we discuss job attitudes in Chapter 11.) And organizations can do a lot to reduce turnover through selection, training, and treatment of employees – all issues of interest to I/O psychologists. As an example, organizations often use selection procedures that predict the likelihood that an employee will turn over in the next year. For instance, they might ask job applicants about the number of jobs they have held over the last five years to predict how long they are likely to stay with the company (see biodata, Chapter 6). However, measuring turnover can be difficult and can mean dif-ferent things: When a person quits, it is sometimes hard to know why they quit, or it may not be well documented by the organization. Consider these two examples: A top-performing employee may quit because they got a better job elsewhere, or a poor-performing employee may quit because they know they are going to be fired. These are very different circumstances, and unless the cause of turnover can be measured accurately, simply knowing that an employee quit may not be very helpful information.

- Customer complaints/commendations: Again, these can be important for an organization to collect, but you guessed it – like all criterion measures, they are not perfect. A particular employee may get an excess number of complaints or compliments strictly by chance. Plus, customer complaints may be due to organizational reasons outside of the employee's control. For example, a restaurant server may get customer complaints, but it may be because the restaurant is understaffed.

- Theft: Employee theft is a negative performance measure that is of importance to many organizations, especially retailers. However, the measurement of employee theft is a tricky business – and not always accurate. For example, how much theft actually goes undetected? Organizations sometimes measure "shrinkage" or the degree to which organizational materials, inventory, or supplies disappear. However, it would be incorrect to assume that all missing materials are necessarily stolen, and it is often difficult to tie missing material to any particular employee.

Besides these objective performance measures, we can also choose from a number of subjective measures as well such as performance ratings by supervisors. We will talk about these measures more in Chapter 5. But as we've already said, performance ratings by supervisors also include rating errors and biases, and as such are not perfect.

So what is the best way to deal with the fact that there is no best way to measure performance? The best strategy is to use multiple types of job performance measures that can complement each other in terms of strengths and weaknesses. For example, objective measures may compensate for some of the biases inherent in subjective performance ratings. And subjective ratings may compensate for some of the factors that are not captured by objective ratings; using the example above, a supervisor may know that Sam is a better salesperson than Tamara – even if Tamara has better sales figures – and take that into account in giving their performance ratings. In short, as we've said, there is no one best way to measure performance. But being aware of the limitations of various performance measures, and choosing performance measures that complement each other, is a good start.

LEGAL ISSUES

There are legal issues that can arise in the use of job performance measures in organizations. For example, if job performance measures are used to make personnel decisions (e.g., promotion decisions), they can be subject to the same legal guidelines as personnel selection methods (see Chapter 7). This would especially be an issue if the performance measures were shown to be biased against certain legally protected groups and could not be demonstrated to be job-related. Thus, organizations should be careful to ensure that any criterion measures that might affect employees are carefully documented.

GLOBAL IMPLICATIONS

With the increase in multinational corporations (MNCs), one challenging issue is how to measure performance across multiple countries and cultures. It would certainly be useful to have one comprehensive way to measure employee performance across the organization: It would allow managers to know the strengths and weaknesses of different parts of the organization, and to understand the level of different types of human capital across the organization. This could also be helpful in finding out which parts of the organization may need some improvement either through training or through hiring practices.

The challenge, of course, is comparability across countries and cultures. National culture can have significant effects on performance management systems (DeNisi & Smith, 2014) and thus on the measurement of job performance. However, the research thus far on the management of performance within global organizations is scant (Cascio, 2006; Maley & Moeller, 2014). But we do know that performance management across cultures can be affected by a range of issues such as language and perceived importance of different performance dimensions. For example, the very purpose of evaluating an employee's performance can vary significantly from country to country (Cascio, 2006). Although the field has begun to identify the factors that may affect the measurement of performance within an MNC, more is needed on how to address them.

CURRENT ISSUES AND CONTROVERSIES

There are a number of current research and practice issues in the area of defining and measuring criteria. First, there are many additional criteria than have been described in past models of performance, and only recently have they been explicitly identified and named. One of these that we have already mentioned is adaptive behavior (e.g., Pulakos et al., 2000), which is the ability of employees to adjust to new social and task environments. Adaptive behavior is especially important because jobs can change quickly today, and also because technology is becoming more and more a part of jobs, with requirements for technological savvy and sophistication. Thus, while adaptive behaviors are relatively recent additions as criteria in I/O psychology, they are important because they are a part of more and more jobs in today's world. Because it is such a new topic, the empirical research on adaptive behavior at work has been relatively scant despite its importance to twenty-first-century organizations (Ryan & Ployhart, 2014). However, we are starting to fill these gaps. One meta-analytic study (Huang, Ryan, Zabel, & Palmer, 2014) has identified ambition and emotional stability as personality variables that are related to adaptive performance. Further, another challenge is that there is currently disagreement among researchers about what adaptive behavior is (Baard, Rench, & Kozlowski, 2014).

Today's workplace with jobs that change quickly may require higher levels of adaptable behavior from employees. This is why organizations are interested in selecting and developing adaptable employees. For example, Cisco Systems developed knowledge-sharing systems and started "Cisco University" and coaching programs to increase employee adaptability (Lane, 2013).

Second is a move to examine criteria not just at the individual level, but at the unit or organization level as well. For example, in the past, when I/O psychologists have looked at the effects of training programs on performance, we have tended to consider their effects on the performance of individual employees. But given the need to show the value of what I/O psychologists do in organizations, it may be worthwhile to move beyond this approach and also consider whether a selection procedure or training program improves the overall productivity of work units and organizations as a whole, or even entire countries and societies (Aguinis & Kraiger, 2009). Although relatively few studies have taken this approach (e.g., Van Iddekinge et al., 2009), there seems to be a push among researchers to consider performance at these higher levels (Ryan & Ployhart, 2014).

Further, there is a growing interest in the concept of "big data" (see Chapter 1), or the use of very large datasets of multiple measures in the assessment of work performance (e.g., Peck, 2013). Such datasets would go beyond traditional performance measures such as supervisor ratings and sales figures to detailed analyses of factors such as numbers of face-to-face meetings and other more minute behaviors (such as keystrokes) that can now be measured in the workplace. These datasets might also allow for more complex models to predict which employees should be promoted into other jobs. We expect to see their increased use in the coming decades, although challenges remain in terms of obtaining high-quality work data about employees to use in big-data analytics.

Finally, perhaps the greatest challenge in the coming decades is the identification of job performance criteria in jobs that are constantly evolving: As we pointed out in Chapter 3, the practice of job analysis may have to change because a single "job" does not necessarily exist: Jobs are constantly evolving, such that employees may have a broad set of changing responsibilities, and work may require a broad range of skills (Sanchez & Levine, 2012). By the same token, identifying which performance dimensions we should be measuring will become a greater challenge in the coming decades as the idea of static, unchanging jobs becomes less common.

With the advent of "big data", the assessment of work performance (or "people analytics") is moving into a new era. Big data analytics are used not only in large corporations such as Intel and Google, but at smaller companies like McKeen Foods, the makers of Little Debbie snack cakes (Peck, 2013).

WHAT DOES THIS MEAN TO YOU?

Throughout this chapter, we have considered measures of job performance primarily from the organization's perspective. Specifically, we have considered how job performance measures can be used by organizations to evaluate the effectiveness of HR programs such as selection systems and training programs. But what does this mean for the employee?

Perhaps the most important point is that organizations measure performance in many ways. By this we mean two things.

First, organizations measure performance in terms of many different dimensions. They consider factors such as core task performance, but also factors such as contextual performance and safety performance. For you, this means that performance in your job is not just one thing, but rather it is multi-dimensional. Each employee brings different strengths to the workplace. It is good for you to keep this in mind as an employee, and to think about your strengths, and also which dimensions of performance matter most to your organization and to your boss. And if you are a supervisor, you might want to consider that different employees make different contributions to the workforce and to the team.

Second, we mean that organizations can use different measurement media to assess performance. This could mean supervisor ratings, or objective measures such as sales data. Each adds to the picture, but each also has its limitations. As an employee, it's good to reflect on the ways in which your organization measures performance, and also to consider which of these the organization considers most important.

Conclusion

Identifying and measuring the range of behaviors that are performed on various jobs is a key issue for organizations, as these provide the basis for important metrics used to evaluate employee effectiveness. In addition, however, criteria are used not only to evaluate individuals, but to evaluate the effectiveness of organizational functions and programs such as recruitment and selection systems, training programs, and other interventions. In short, it's important to get criteria right: If they are not, it can lead to poor organizational decisions in terms of human capital.

YOUR TURN...

1. Consider the job of police officer in your town. How would you decide what the conceptual criterion is for this job? What types of actual criteria would you use to measure performance, and what are the advantages and disadvantages of each of these actual criteria?

2. What do you think about the idea of using "big data" to evaluate employee performance? What types of measures do you think that organizations should use? Which measures would it be fair or not fair for an organization to use? Explain your answers.

3. A friend of yours is working at a department store that has started to focus entirely on sales volume in dollars to assess employee performance. Do you think that this is fair? Is it a good way to measure the performance of its salespeople? Explain your answer.

4. You're supervising a group of computer programmers. Consuela is absolutely the best in your group – she writes the most code, she makes very few mistakes, and she helps her coworkers. In fact, her coworkers seem to value her contributions to the group. However, several times a month she's late for work. How would you deal with this issue?

Additional Reading

Borman, W. C., & Smith, T. N. (2012). The use of objective measures as criteria in I/O psychology. In N. Schmitt (Ed.), *The Oxford handbook of personnel assessment and selection* (pp. 532–542). New York: Oxford University Press.

Cascio, W. F., & Aguinis, H. (2011). *Applied psychology in human resource management* (7th ed.). Upper Saddle River, NJ: Prentice Hall.

Drasgow, F., & Schmitt, N. (2002). *Measuring and analyzing behavior in organizations: Advances in measurement and data analysis.* San Francisco, CA: Jossey-Bass.

Gatewood, R., Feild, H., & Barrick, M. (2011). *Human resource selection.* Mason, OH: Cengage Learning.

Guion, R. M. (2011). *Assessment, measurement, and prediction for personnel decisions.* New York: Routledge.

Van Iddekinge, C. H., & Ployhart, R. E. (2008). Developments in the criterion-related validation of selection procedures: A critical review and recommendations for practice. *Personnel Psychology, 61*, 871–925.

Woehr, D. J., & Rock, S. (2012). Supervisory performance ratings. In N. Schmitt (Ed.), *The Oxford handbook of personnel assessment and selection* (pp. 517–531). New York: Oxford University Press.

CASE STUDY: Measuring Schoolteacher Performance through Value-Added Measurement

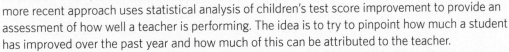

Over the last few decades, there has been much public discussion of how to measure teacher effectiveness. Some schools rely on students' test scores, others rely on classroom observations. One more recent approach uses statistical analysis of children's test score improvement to provide an assessment of how well a teacher is performing. The idea is to try to pinpoint how much a student has improved over the past year and how much of this can be attributed to the teacher.

The method, called value-added measurement, works like this: Based on a student's past performance history, a model is calculated to predict how well the student should be performing in the current year. It also ties the student's performance to individual teachers and subjects to see whether the student is doing better or worse than would be expected from past years, and whether that change can be attributed to the teacher. If the student does much better than expected, the teacher gets a high rating. If the student does worse, though, the teacher gets a low grade.

As might be expected, there are some differences of opinion about this measure of teacher performance. While some argue that this approach to assessing teacher performance is fair because it looks to tie student gains to individual performance and who their teachers were during that time, others note that the approach does not take into account what teachers are actually doing in the classroom. However, still others point out that value-added measurement can provide one additional bit of information to see how well teachers are performing.

Questions

1. How would you classify value-added measurement; specifically, is it a subjective or objective measure? What do you see as its weaknesses, and what other types of

measures of teacher performance might compensate for these weaknesses?

2. What KSAOs are being assessed by value-added measurement? Is it primarily a

measure of task performance, contextual performance, or both?

3. One analysis found that the wealthiest school districts are three times more likely to have teachers with high value-added scores than poor districts. What are the contextual factors that may have caused this? Does it mean that value-added measurement is unfair?

4. Consider the multiple stakeholders in this case: Parents and students, teachers, and administrators. What do you think would be the viewpoint of each of these stakeholders concerning value-added measurement?

5. If you were in the position of assessing teacher performance, what measures would you use? Describe the strengths and weaknesses of each of these sources of data.

Sources: Hanushek & Rivkin, 2010; Lieaszkovszky, 2013; Loeb, Soland, & Fox, 2014.

References

Aguinis, H., & Kraiger, K. (2009). Benefits of training and development for individuals and teams, organizations, and society. *Annual Review of Psychology, 60,* 451–474.

Alessandri, G., Borgogni, L., & Truxillo, D. M. (2015). Tracking job performance trajectories over time: A six-year longitudinal study. *European Journal of Work and Organizational Psychology, 24,* 560–577.

Austin, J. T., & Villanova, P. (1992). The criterion problem: 1917–1992. *Journal of Applied Psychology, 77,* 836–874.

Baard, S. K., Rench, T. A., & Kozlowski, S. W. (2014). Performance adaptation: A theoretical integration and review. *Journal of Management, 40,* 48–99.

Beier, M. E., & Ackerman, P. L. (2012). Time in personnel selection. In N. Schmitt (Ed.), *Oxford handbook of personnel assessment and selection* (pp. 721–739). New York: Oxford University Press.

Bergeron, D. M., Shipp, A. J., Rosen, B., & Furst, S. A. (2013). Organizational citizenship behavior and career outcomes: The cost of being a good citizen. *Journal of Management, 39,* 958–984.

Bolino, M. C., Klotz, A. C., Turnley, W. H., & Harvey, J. (2013). Exploring the dark side of organizational citizenship behavior. *Journal of Organizational Behavior, 34,* 542–559.

Borman, W. C., & Motowidlo, S. J. (1993). Expanding the criterion domain to include elements of contextual performance. In N. Schmitt & W. C. Borman (Eds.), *Personnel selection in organizations,* pp. 71–98. San Francisco, CA: Jossey-Bass.

Borman, W. C., & Motowidlo, S. J. (1997). Task performance and contextual performance: The meaning for personnel selection research. *Human Performance, 10,* 99–109.

Campbell, J. P., McCloy, R.A., Oppler, S. H., & Sager, C. E. (1993). A theory of performance. In N. Schmitt & W. C. Borman (Eds.), *Personnel selection in organizations* (pp. 35–70). San Francisco, CA: Jossey-Bass.

Campbell, J. P., McHenry, J. J., & Wise, L. L. (1990). Modeling job performance in a population of jobs. *Personnel Psychology, 43,* 313–333.

Cascio, W. S. (2006). Global performance management systems. In G. K. Stahl, and I. Bjorkman (Eds.), *Handbook of research in international human resource management* (pp. 176–196). Northampton, MA: Edward Elgar.

Cascio, W. F., & Aguinis, H. (2011). *Applied psychology in human resource management* (7th ed.). Upper Saddle River, NJ: Prentice Hall.

Christian, M. S., Bradley, J. C., Wallace, J. C., & Burke, M. J. (2009). Workplace safety: A meta-analysis of the roles of person and situation factors. *Journal of Applied Psychology, 94,* 1103–1127.

Dalal, R. S. (2005). A meta-analysis of the relationship between organizational citizenship behavior and counterproductive work behavior. *Journal of Applied Psychology, 90,* 1241–1255.

Davis, M. A. (2009). Understanding the relationship between mood and creativity: A meta-analysis. *Organizational Behavior and Human Decision Processes, 108,* 25–38.

Deadrick, D. L., & Madigan, R. M. (1990). Dynamic criteria revisited: A longitudinal study of performance stability and predictive validity. *Personnel Psychology, 43,* 717–744.

DeNisi, A., & Smith, C. E. (2014). Performance appraisal, performance management, and firm-level performance: A review and a proposed model. *Academy of Management Annals, 8,* 127–179.

Gatewood, R., Feild, H., & Barrick, M. (2011). *Human resource selection.* Mason, OH: Cengage Learning.

Guion, R. M. (2011). *Assessment, measurement, and prediction for personnel decisions.* New York: Routledge.

Hanushek, E. A., & Rivkin, S. G. (2010). Generalizations about using value-added measures of teacher quality. *American Economic Review, 100,* 267–271.

Harvard Business Review. (2014, November). The best-performing CEOs in the world. Retrieved February 28, 2015 from https://hbr.org/2014/11/the-best-performing-ceos-in-the-world.

Huang, J. L., Ryan, A. M., Zabel, K. L., & Palmer, A. (2014). Personality and adaptive performance at work: A meta-analytic investigation. *Journal of Applied Psychology, 99,* 162–179.

Lane, G. (2013, August). Culturally aligned. *Industrial Engineer,* 49–53.

Lieaszkovszky, I. (2013). Grading the teachers: Measuring teacher performance through student growth. *NPR.* Retrieved February 8, 2015 from http://stateimpact.npr. org/ohio/2013/ 06/17/ grading-the-teachers- measuring-teacher-performance-through- student-growth/.

Loeb, S., Soland, J., & Fox, L. (2014). Is a good teacher a good teacher for all? Comparing value-added of teachers with their English learners and non-English learners. *Educational Evaluation and Policy Analysis, 36,* 457–475.

Maley, J. F., & Moeller, M. (2014). Global performance management systems: The role of trust as perceived by country managers. *Journal of Business Research, 67,* 2803–2810.

Marcus, B., Goffin, R. D., Johnston, N. G., & Rothstein, M. G. (2007). Personality and cognitive ability as predictors of typical and maximum managerial performance. *Human Performance, 20,* 275–285.

Motowidlo, S. J., & Van Scotter, J. R. (1994). Evidence that task performance should be distinguished from contextual performance. *Journal of Applied Psychology, 79,* 475–480.

O'Boyle, E. H., Forsyth, D. R., Banks, G. C., & McDaniel, M. A. (2012). A meta-analysis of the dark triad and work behavior: A social exchange perspective. *Journal of Applied Psychology, 97,* 557–579.

Peck, D. (2013, December). They're watching you at work. *Atlantic Monthly.* Retrieved March 7, 2014 from http://www.theatlantic.com/magazine/archive/2013/12/theyre-watching-you-at-work/354681/.

Penney, L. M., & Spector, P. E. (2005). Job stress, incivility, and counterproductive work behavior (CWB): The moderating role of negative affectivity. *Journal of Organizational Behavior, 26,* 777–796

Pulakos, E. D., Arad, S., Donovan, M. A., & Plamondon, K. E. (2000). Adaptability in the workplace: Development of a taxonomy of adaptive performance. *Journal of Applied Psychology, 85,* 612–624.

Ryan, A. M., & Ployhart, R. E. (2014). A century of selection. *Annual Review of Psychology, 65,* 693–717.

Sackett, P. R., Zedeck, S., & Fogli, L. (1988). Relations between measures of typical and maximum job performance. *Journal of Applied Psychology, 73,* 482–486.

Sanchez, J. I., & Levine, E. L. (2012). The rise and fall of job analysis and the future of work analysis. *Annual Review of Psychology, 63,* 397–425.

Schmidt, F. L., & Kaplan, L. B. (1971). Composite vs. multiple criteria: A review and resolution of the controversy. *Personnel Psychology, 24,* 419–434.

Stanford Graduate School of Business, Center for Leadership Development and Research. (2013). *2013 CEO performance evaluation survey.* Retrieved February 12, 2015 from http://www.gsb.stanford.edu/sites/default/files/documents/2013_CEO_Performance_Evaluation_Survey%20Results.pdf.

Tierney, P., Farmer, S. M., & Graen, G. B. (1999). An examination of leadership and employee creativity: The relevance of traits and relationships. *Personnel Psychology, 52,* 591–620.

Van Iddekinge, C. H., Ferris, G. R., Perrewé, P. L., Perryman, A. A., Blass, F. R., & Heetderks, T. D. (2009). Effects of selection and training on unit-level performance over time: A latent growth modeling approach. *Journal of Applied Psychology, 94,* 829–843.

Chapter 5

PERFORMANCE APPRAISAL
Measurement and Management of Performance

Performance appraisal refers to the assessment of performance for the purposes of performance management. In this chapter, you will learn how organizations evaluate performance of employees.

After studying this chapter, you should be able to:

- describe the reasons why organizations typically develop performance appraisal systems
- identify ways in which performance can be assessed, and the strengths and limitations of different approaches
- list the characteristics of an effective performance appraisal system
- explain potential rater errors in performance appraisals and ways to deal with them
- understand the effects of the performance appraisal context on the fairness and objectivity of performance ratings

Learning goals for this chapter

- learn how to conduct a performance appraisal interview
- uncover steps that can be taken in appraisal system design and application in order to deal with common problems with performance appraisals.

Introduction

In organizations, measuring performance is an important step in managing performance. In Chapters 6 and 7, we will discuss the importance of having valid selection systems that predict who will be strong performers on the job. To develop effective selection procedures, we need to have good measures of performance. Similarly, in Chapter 8, we will see that when we train individuals we are interested in increasing their performance level. Good performance measures will allow us to see if the training leads to increased performance. When rewarding and motivating employees, as covered in Chapter 9, we are often interested in having a clear tie between pay and performance. But all of these examples beg the fundamental question of how we measure performance.

Performance measurement may seem relatively simple until you start thinking about it at a deeper level. Consider the job of a retail sales associate who greets customers enthusiastically once they walk into the store, answers all questions fully, and helps customers find the right product. Was this person's performance high? *Maybe.* But how would the organization actually measure the performance of the sales associate, given that the transaction occurred between the sales associate and the customer? Assuming that customer service is the only dimension we are interested in measuring, we would need a way to document a given service level. As we saw in Chapter 4, looking at sales figures alone could be misleading because factors such as store location will influence these figures. Plus, the person with the best sales figures may simply be the quickest person to reach the customer while neglecting other important aspects of their job, such as shelving the products or processing returned items. We can try to measure customer service performance from the customer's perspective through surveys, but then we would need to motivate customers to fill out these surveys – and assume that the customers can rate employees accurately. How about if managers observe customer service performance of the employee as it occurs? You may envision some problems with this approach as well: When managers are watching, employees may be on their best behavior, or close observation may cause stress for the employee, affecting performance.

As you can see, there are many issues that prevent performance measurement in organizations from being straightforward or easy. In fact, these problems and others may explain the negative reactions to performance appraisals from raters and ratees. A study by People IQ of 45,000 employees and managers showed that only 13 percent of employees found their company's performance appraisal system useful, and 88 percent reported thinking that performance appraisals damage the reputation of their company's HR department (People IQ Study, 2005). At the same time, a well-designed performance appraisal system may shape employee commitment to the organization. In fact, past research shows that changes in a performance appraisal system to make it more acceptable to employees increase trust in management (Mayer & Davis, 1999).

In a perfect world, performance would be measured easily because there would be objective, unbiased metrics of key dimensions of performance. (For more on the problems with objective measures, refer back to Chapter 4.) In reality, performance measurement involves human beings evaluating each other's performance on subjective criteria. The challenges of performance appraisal do not reduce the importance of measurement of performance, though. Organizations need to measure performance to manage it. In this chapter, we will start with more technical issues involved in designing a performance appraisal system, providing you with a general understanding of the tradeoffs and challenges in system design. Then, we will also discuss how raters use these systems, and how to increase the effectiveness of these systems through system design and rater training, focusing particularly on the social context of performance appraisals.

What Is Performance Appraisal?

Performance appraisal is defined as the measurement of employee performance based on pre-established criteria, and communication of this information to the employee. Whereas in Chapter 4 we discussed a number of ways to measure performance, performance appraisal is a specific, subjective method of performance measurement, typically from the viewpoint of an employee's supervisor.

In a typical performance appraisal implementation, I/O and HR professionals design the performance appraisal system. The more effective systems tend to be designed with the involvement and participation of future users of the system, including raters and ratees (usually supervisors and employees, who are also SMEs). Once the system is in place, a rater, usually the immediate supervisor, observes the performance of the employee during the appraisal period and gives frequent feedback as well as coaches the employee as needed. When it is time for the appraisal, the rater evaluates the ratee's performance in the past year, past six months, or quarter, using the previously determined rating form. Then, the rater meets with the employee to conduct an interview in which the level of performance is discussed with the employee, and an action plan is created for potential ways to improve performance. In other words, performance appraisal entails elements of system design, observation of performance, rating of the employee's performance, and communication.

Note that performance appraisal is simply one component of a performance management system. For organizations that do performance appraisals, it is an important event during the year, but it is not by any means the only time the employee should be given feedback. The most successful organizations make feedback for employees a frequent event; the manager checks in with the employee regularly, and feedback is given as it is needed.

Performance appraisal:
Measurement of employee performance based on pre-established criteria, and communication of this information to the employee.

Figure 5.1 Basic stages of a performance appraisal system.

1. Performance appraisal system is designed, with user involvement.

2. Rater observes performance during the year

3. Rater gives informal feedback to employee regularly during the year along with coaching

4. Rater completes the appraisal form when it is time for the appraisal

5. Rater and ratee discuss the appraisal feedback in a meeting, concluding with an action plan

6. Rater and ratee follow their action plan

"See website for interactive material"

The Dual Nature of Performance Appraisals in Organizations

In order to design and implement performance appraisal systems effectively, we need to understand their dual nature: Performance appraisal can be thought of as a cognitive process and a social/relational process. The idea of performance appraisal as simply a cognitive process was very popular prior to the 1990s (Ilgen, Barnes-Farrell, & McKellin, 1993). According to this idea, you may think of performance appraisal as a measurement problem. The rater's challenge is to observe performance of a ratee as it occurs, store this information in their memory, and recall it when it is time to assess performance. There are numerous influences over the observation-storage-retrieval stages of information processing. Therefore, it is important to understand systematic tendencies in human capacity to observe, and biases that prevent raters from achieving accuracy (DeNisi, Cafferty, & Meglino, 1984), and design systems accordingly. We will discuss some of these issues later in the chapter.

Later research started adopting the perspective that performance appraisal is also a social/relational process (Levy & Williams, 2004; Murphy & Cleveland, 1995). This perspective recognizes that performance appraisal occurs within the context of an existing relationship between a manager and an employee. Raters have goals beyond rating performance objectively: They are interested in preserving the relationship they have with the ratee, appearing as competent managers to those higher up, motivating employees reporting to them, and minimizing their own discomfort. They observe employee performance as part of an ongoing relationship, and as a result, rater and ratee behaviors during the appraisal depend on the organization's culture, overall relationship quality, and the level of trust in the rater and the organization (Erdogan, 2002). In other words, while we try to *enable* raters to rate accurately and objectively by designing reliable and valid instruments, we need to also *motivate* them to take the appraisal seriously and use it effectively. This dual nature of performance appraisals is important to keep in mind when learning how to design appraisal systems because both are important when preparing raters and ratees to take part in these systems.

What Are the Main Purposes of a Performance Appraisal System?

Performance appraisal is an important element of talent management systems. In organizations, performance is measured for many reasons. In fact, one of the first things organizations need to decide when designing performance appraisal systems is to determine *why* they need a performance appraisal system. This is because there are different types of systems, ranging from a simple essay where a manager writes about strengths, limitations, and areas of improvement of an employee, to more structured forms where managers rank all their employees from strongest to weakest. If the purpose of conducting an appraisal is primarily to give employees feedback and develop future effectiveness, probably an essay form would suffice. But if the primary reason is to decide to whom to give future promotions and pay raises, then knowing where employees stand compared to each other is important. In other words, the reasons for conducting appraisals will drive some of the design decisions.

Performance appraisals are basically used for four broad categories of reasons: First, appraisals are conducted to develop future performance (**developmental reasons**). Developmental reasons include identifying and remedying performance problems and development opportunities. By using performance

Developmental reasons:
Appraisals conducted with the primary purpose of developing future performance.

appraisals, organizations give employees feedback about where they stand and how they can improve. This information can be used to decide who will attend specific training programs, as well as to coach employees to deal with problematic issues. It is assumed that one way to change employee behavior is to give employees feedback about how they are currently performing. Therefore, giving employees feedback is an important objective of performance appraisal systems.

Administrative reasons: Appraisals conducted to make decisions on past performance, such as pay or promotions.

Second, appraisals are used to make decisions based on past performance (**administrative reasons**). For example, one way organizations tie pay to performance is to distribute merit pay or bonuses to high-performing employees as identified by a performance appraisal system. Decisions such as who will be terminated or who will receive a promotion will also be based on performance appraisal results.

Research purposes: Appraisals conducted to validate a selection battery or validating and assessing the effectiveness of a training program.

Third, performance appraisals can be done for **research purposes**. In Chapters 4 and 7, we discuss how to validate selection systems by correlating scores in a selection battery to performance scores, and such validation necessitates the existence of a performance measure (criterion), which is often performance appraisal scores. Similar evaluation of training programs can be done using appraisal results as well (Chapter 8). Studies have shown that whether the appraisal is done for administrative, developmental, or research purposes influences the ratings given by raters. A review of 22 studies on performance appraisal purpose suggested that ratings are typically higher when the purpose of the appraisal is administrative (tied to pay and promotions) as opposed to when the appraisal is purely developmental or when the appraisal is conducted for research purposes (Jawahar & Williams, 1997). There is also evidence that administrative ratings tend to be less accurate than ratings done for research (Dobbins, Cardy, & Truxillo, 1988). So, if the purpose is to validate selection systems or assess the effectiveness of a training program, collecting performance information after instructing raters that the ratings are for research purposes will yield more accurate results than relying on the appraisal ratings conducted for administrative reasons.

Legal reasons: Conducting appraisals for the purpose of legal documentation.

Finally, performance appraisals are also conducted for **legal reasons**. Appraisals are an essential defense for organizations faced with an employment discrimination claim. For example, when Chevron Phillips Chemical fired an administrative assistant experiencing chronic fatigue syndrome, the US Equal Employment Opportunity Commission (EEOC) sued the company for failing to comply with the Americans with Disabilities Act (ADA). In defense of their termination decision, the company needed to demonstrate that the employee was not performing the essential job functions effectively and this was the reason for the termination. However, the performance appraisal results conducted only a few weeks before the employee was fired showed satisfactory performance, which resulted in a court decision in favor of the employee (HR Focus, 2013b). Businesses often need to show their compliance with employment law by showing that unfavorable decisions against a particular employee (such as termination, demotion, or being passed over for a promotion or pay raise) were due to performance and not due to a discriminatory reason. Therefore, having an objective, systematic, and reliable performance appraisal system is a business necessity, at least for companies operating in the US.

Characteristics of an Effective Performance Appraisal System

How do we know whether the performance appraisal system in place is effective? There are a few criteria to assess the effectiveness of an appraisal

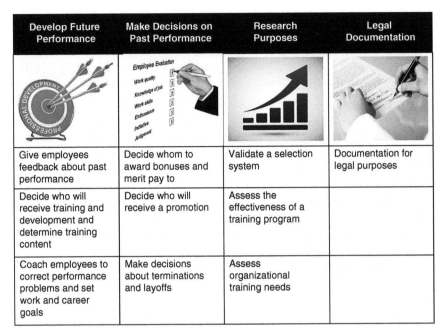

Develop Future Performance	Make Decisions on Past Performance	Research Purposes	Legal Documentation
Give employees feedback about past performance	Decide whom to award bonuses and merit pay to	Validate a selection system	Documentation for legal purposes
Decide who will receive training and development and determine training content	Decide who will receive a promotion	Assess the effectiveness of a training program	
Coach employees to correct performance problems and set work and career goals	Make decisions about terminations and layoffs	Assess organizational training needs	

Figure 5.2
Common uses of performance appraisals.

 "See website for interactive material"

system which include strategic fit, content validity, accuracy, fairness, and practicality.

Strategic Fit

The performance appraisal system in place should be aligned with an organization's strategy. Each organization expects employees to contribute to its mission in different ways. For example, Walmart expects its employees to engage in cost savings, to be efficient, to be accurate, and to be quick in what they do. Nike expects its employees to be innovative and team-oriented. As a result, the performance appraisal system should do a good job measuring these dimensions. If the behaviors desired of employees are not contained in the appraisal form and instead the form focuses on completely different behaviors, the organization will not know whether employees are displaying the desired behaviors, and will not be able to directly recognize and reward these behaviors. Thus, organizations need to ensure that whatever behaviors the organization cares about and relies on for accomplishing its mission are actually included in the form.

Content Validity

We discussed the concept of content validity in Chapter 2 and will go into greater detail about it in Chapter 7. Just as some selection procedures are shown to be content valid, a performance appraisal system needs to cover the job domain. This means that the performance appraisal should be neither contaminated nor deficient (see Chapter 4). For example, imagine that you are interested in evaluating the performance of an administrative support employee. The appraisal form would typically include factors such as consistently meeting deadlines, and showing up to work on time. If an important aspect of the job (such as completing projects

Strategically Aligning Appraisals at Zappos

In its early days, performance appraisals at Zappos consisted of rating employees on criteria such as being punctual and meeting deadlines. The online shoe and apparel retailer, which prides itself with its revolutionary customer service, abandoned this system in favor of one that better fits with its strategy. Now, managers evaluate employees on factors such as how frequently they display "wow" levels of service and humility (Pyrillis, 2011).

Further, Zappos is an organization that prides itself on its unique culture emphasizing camaraderie, employee engagement, fun, and putting customers first. Because they view their organizational culture as their greatest asset, they utilize their performance appraisals as a way of safeguarding their corporate culture. About half of a performance appraisal for each employee captures the degree to which employees embody the 10 core Zappos values (Frauenheim, 2009).

accurately and without errors) is not included as part of the performance appraisal, the system is considered to be deficient. If factors that are not part of the job (such as whether the employee has a great sense of humor and has an advanced sense of fashion) are included, the system is considered to be contaminated. Each of these issues is problematic, as this would mean that important aspects of the job are not being measured and instead irrelevant factors are being tracked. How can an organization ensure that the system in place is content valid? The starting point of designing a performance appraisal system is the job analysis (Chapter 3) and job description.

Accuracy

A key criterion is the degree to which the appraisal is accurate, or reflects the true level of the employee's performance. When an appraisal score is higher or lower than what is warranted by the employee's level of effectiveness, the system loses its effectiveness. When appraisals are inaccurate, the systems dependent on appraisals will also suffer. For example, when assessing the effectiveness of a selection system or a training program, the assumption is that performance scores are accurate reflections of employee performance. For example, if scores on an employee selection test do not correlate with employee performance, the inference we make is that the selection test is not valid. However, an alternative explanation could be rater inaccuracy: when raters give everyone very similar scores, correlations with selection test scores will be weak. Therefore, inaccurate scores will not only harm employee morale, but also reduce the usefulness of other systems that depend on performance appraisals. We will review reasons for inaccurate scores (rater errors) later in this chapter.

Ratee Reactions: Perceived Fairness and Usefulness

Perhaps the ultimate test of any appraisal system is ratee reactions and how they feel about it. In fact, even the best-designed appraisal system can alienate employees and damage their relationship with their manager and the company if employees do not perceive the appraisal system and their own rating as fair. A fair performance appraisal follows due process. This means that these systems give employees adequate notice (letting employees know what criteria will be used to evaluate them), fair hearing (explaining to employees why they were rated a particular way), and judgment based on evidence (performance criteria are used impartially and consistently to evaluate all employees). Research shows that performance appraisals meeting these three criteria are regarded as more useful and acceptable even when employees receive low scores (Taylor, Tracy, Renard, Harrison, & Carroll, 1995). Performance appraisals that allow employees to participate in the process instead of being passive listeners are usually perceived as more fair (Levy & Williams, 2004).

Whether ratees find the performance feedback they receive accurate and useful is of critical importance. Feedback improves performance only if recipients of feedback perceive it as useful and accurate, and think that changing behavior is actually possible (Smither, London, & Reilly, 2005). Unfortunately, providing feedback perceived as useful is not necessarily easy or straightforward, because how useful ratees find the performance appraisal system to be is directly correlated with how high their ratings are (Brett & Atwater, 2001). Research also shows that feedback that is perceived as useful is delivered in a tactful and considerate manner, and by a rater perceived as credible (Steelman & Rutkowski, 2004).

Negative ratee reactions to performance appraisals are the biggest challenge in appraisal effectiveness. Unfortunately, negative attitudes about appraisals are pervasive worldwide. In a recent staff survey, the National Health Service (NHS) of the UK, one of the largest employers in the world with over 1.7 million employees, found that only 39 percent of those who went through the appraisal process thought it was well structured (Picker Institute Europe, 2013).

Practicality

Performance appraisals need to be perceived as practical and easy to use. Today, many organizations have flat structures where each manager is responsible for supervising and evaluating a large number of employees. Plus, performance appraisals often are conducted at a single time point in the entire organization, which means the raters will typically need to evaluate the performance of all employees reporting to them at once. If the performance appraisal form is too long, complicated, and difficult to understand, raters will not be motivated to be accurate in their ratings.

Design and Measurement Considerations in Performance Appraisals

Designers of a performance appraisal system will need to make a number of decisions among alternatives:

* How should performance be defined?
* Should the appraisal focus on each employee's performance one at a time or ask raters to compare ratees to each other?
* What type of a rating scale should be used?
* Who should be the rater?

Each of these is an important design choice, and there is probably no perfect method. When making these choices, system designers will have multiple considerations. First, the chosen method should have good psychometric properties. Decades of research have examined the effectiveness of different performance appraisal formats for rater accuracy, trying to identify rating methods that are less susceptible to rater cognitive biases. Second, user reactions are important: some methods receive more favorable reactions from raters and ratees, are perceived as more practical, and increase the rater's motivation to fully participate in the appraisal system. Cost of the method matters, too: Some methods are more complicated to develop and require significant time investments from system designers. Other methods (such as those requiring multiple raters) require significant time investments on the part of system users.

In this section, we will critically review key measurement considerations in appraisal system design. When reviewing each decision, we need to remember the two properties of the performance appraisal. First, performance is not an objective reality. Thus, raters will ultimately need to observe, interpret, recall, and rate employees in a relatively bias-free manner. This requires adopting a cognitive approach to appraisals and designing systems leading to accurate judgments (DeNisi et al., 1984). Second, performance appraisals do not occur in a laboratory setting and instead are conducted within an existing relationship between raters and ratees, with purposes that go beyond accurately rating the employee, in a context where raters are not necessarily motivated to rate objectively. Therefore, the appraisal design will need to consider the social and organizational context of appraisals (Levy & Williams, 2004).

What Should Be Measured? Trait, Behavior, and Outcome Appraisals

As we discussed in Chapter 4, an important decision that needs to be made is how to define performance. For example, what exactly is the performance of a crew member at McDonalds? Should we measure their friendliness and knowledge about food preparation procedures? Should we measure how frequently they smile at the customer and greet them by name? Or should we measure the satisfaction level of their customers with the service quality they received? In other words, should the appraisal focus on traits, behaviors, or outcomes?

Trait appraisals focus on measuring employee knowledge, skills, abilities, and other characteristics. Example traits may include reliability, honesty, punctuality, or friendliness. Traits are expected to influence job behaviors. However, there are a number of potential problems relating to the use of trait appraisals (Murphy & Cleveland, 1995). First, trait appraisals tend to focus on the person, rather than performance. Traits are not easily observable, whereas performance is. Trait appraisals also tend to focus on factors that are harder to change and more intrinsic to the person. Therefore, they have limited usefulness for feedback purposes. As you might imagine, explaining to someone "they should be more reliable" communicates limited information about what the problem is and why it needs to change. Worse, because it targets the person rather than performance, it is likely to result in more defensiveness on the part of ratees, reducing the sense of fairness. Finally, trait appraisals tend to increase common rating biases and errors. Because traits tend to be vague and less objective, raters tend to interpret traits differently, resulting in less consistency across different raters.

Behavioral appraisals measure the frequency with which specific observable work behaviors occur. Example behaviors may be the frequency with which the employee greets the customers in a friendly manner, asks questions to understand their needs and then provides appropriate recommendations, and addresses each customer with their name at the register. A behavioral appraisal gives more specific feedback to the ratee and points out which behaviors the employee should display more of. At the same time, these forms are more time-consuming to develop, because they require a careful analysis of the behaviors desired of high performers. (See Chapter 3 on job analysis.) Another downside of behavioral appraisals is the assumption that there is only one way of being a high performer. Because behaviors

Trait appraisals: Appraisals which focus on measuring employee knowledge, skills, and abilities such as reliability, honesty, punctuality, or friendliness.

Behavioral appraisals: Appraisals that measure the frequency with which specific observable work behaviors occur.

How should a movie theater measure the performance of employees at the concession stand? Their product knowledge and friendliness (traits), the frequency with which they complete orders accurately (behaviors), or the number of combo packages sold (outcomes)?

are very specific, sometimes the expected behavior may not fit the specific situation and may reduce the effectiveness of the employee. As a case in point, in the United States, many retail stores expect cashiers to read the name of the customer from the receipt or credit card and then address the customer by their name, and this could be a criterion in a behavioral appraisal. Depending on the ease with which the customer's name may be pronounced, this behavior may create an awkward customer service interaction, instead of improving customer service!

Outcome appraisals:
Appraisals which focus on quantitative metrics such as sales figures, number of units produced, or number of mistakes.

Outcome appraisals focus on quantitative metrics such as sales figures, number of units produced, or the level of absenteeism. You may remember that we covered objective measures of performance in Chapter 4. Objective metrics focus on quantifiable aspects of performance and therefore are perceived as fair when the metrics capture the most important elements of the job. These metrics are also less subject to many of the rating errors (to be discussed later in this chapter). Despite their advantages, however, metric-based appraisals have their own set of limitations as described in Chapter 4. First, these appraisals tend to be less under the control of employees. For example, it is clear that greeting customers by name or promptly answering customer questions are within the employee's control. However, sales figures are affected by factors such as store location, proximity of competitors, general state of the economy, and quality of the product, which are outside the influence of the employee. Second, outcome-based appraisals may not cover all important aspects of the job. Sales performance may be an important aspect of a sales associate's performance, but other, equally important aspects such as helping coworkers, or keeping the store presentable, may not be covered by it, and if the organization is overemphasizing metrics, the store may have difficulty finding employees to stock the shelves. Finally, metrics may create ethical dilemmas. For example, when physician performance measurement includes patient satisfaction ratings, the intent of the system is to motivate doctors to focus on patient satisfaction. But what if patients are demanding inappropriate treatment, such as asking for an antibiotic for a viral infection? Achieving patient satisfaction may be at odds with doing the right thing.

Outcome-based appraisals are often combined with goal-setting between the employee and their supervisor. In addition to reviewing past performance, future goals may be set. We will provide a comprehensive overview of goal-setting in Chapter 9 when we discuss motivation. For now, let's just say that goal-setting is an effective planning and motivational tool and is a good way of translating company objectives into individual objectives.

This discussion illustrates that each approach to conceptualizing employee performance has its associated set of limitations. So which approach should we take? First, most agree that a trait approach is undesirable because traits are not easily observable or measured. One way of dealing with the limitations of behavioral and outcome methods might be to combine them, as we suggested in Chapter 4, so that their strengths and limitations would compensate for each other. Of course, there are situations where outcomes or behaviors will be more appropriate. For example, sometimes outcome measures are not available. On the other hand, when there are many different ways of being successful, specifying behaviors expected from all employees may be less useful and limit employee initiative. These conditions may make outcome appraisals more appropriate. And when outcomes are not within the employee's control, or when we can specify behaviors that all employees are expected to demonstrate, behaviors may be preferable.

Absolute and Relative Rating Scales

Imagine you are taking a test. Which method of grading would be more acceptable and fair? One alternative is to compare your level of performance to clear and objective performance standards such that your performance score is higher if you are exceeding the performance standards, and lower if you fail to reach these standards. This is actually how most tests are: Your knowledge is assessed using a specific test of the content of the class, and the greater the number of correct answers, the higher will be your grade. These are **absolute appraisals**, which compare performance to pre-established criteria. In these appraisals, theoretically the entire class can get an A, if all students know all the answers. Or, all students can theoretically get an F if no one gets the questions right! In other words, one student's score is independent of the scores of other students. In an organizational setting, if the organization is asking raters to evaluate cashiers by asking raters questions about whether the cashiers follow proper procedures in completing transactions, the cashier will be rated highly to the extent to which they follow procedures, and all cashiers who follow the correct procedures will be rated highly.

Absolute appraisals: Appraisals that compare one's performance to pre-established criteria.

In contrast, **relative appraisals** involve comparing performance to other ratees' performance. In an exam, this could mean that the instructor would grade strictly on a curve. They could pick the best 20 percent of test scores and give them an A, the next best 30 percent could receive a B, the next 30 percent could receive a C, with the remainder failing the exam. In this method, students are compared to each other. There are a fixed number of students who can score as the highest performers, and there is a predetermined number who will fail the test.

Relative appraisals: Appraisals that compare one's performance to other ratees' performance.

As a student, we can guess which one you would prefer! In organizations, the situation is not very different, with employees perceiving absolute systems as fairer than relative appraisals (Roch, Sternburgh, & Caputo, 2007). In addition, relative systems of appraisals don't really say how well an employee is doing, just how well they are doing compared to other employees. Yet some organizations still use relative appraisals. Relative appraisals offer some distinct advantages over absolute appraisals. For example, as we will discuss later in this chapter, one challenge of performance appraisals in general is that they tend to be inflated. If all employees are given the rating "exceeds expectations," the appraisal becomes less useful for making decisions about whom to reward, promote, or terminate. To tackle this challenge, some organizations require raters to rank their employees, or at least follow a forced distribution, limiting the number of employees who can be placed into the highest performer category. At the same time, relative appraisals have significant problems. One problem is that they are legally less defensible. When Ford, Goodyear, and Capital One implemented relative appraisals, they were all challenged for ranking older workers disproportionately low (Osborne & McCann, 2004). Further, relative rankings tend to be perceived as less fair than absolute ratings (Roch et al., 2007).

There are a number of different types of absolute appraisal rating formats: They include graphic rating scales, behaviorally anchored rating scales (BARS), behavioral

Figure 5.3
Types of relative
and absolute
appraisals.

Absolute Appraisals

- Graphic rating scale
- Behaviorally anchored rating scale (BARS)
- Behavioral observation scale
- Essay appraisal form

Relative Appraisals

- Straight ranking
- Forced distribution

observation scales, and critical incident diaries. Relative appraisals include straight ranking and forced distribution. Each of these will now be discussed briefly.

Graphic rating scale:
A scale that lists traits and behaviors, where raters assess ratees on a scale consisting of a continuum.

Graphic Rating Scale

This type of absolute appraisal scale lists traits and behaviors, and raters assess ratees on each dimension using a scale consisting of a continuum. Ratings could be on a scale ranging between "needs significant improvements" to "exceeds expectations" and the scale could have 3, 4, 5, 7, or even 10 points. These scales tend to be convenient and practical. One challenge is to ensure that each dimension is very clearly defined, because vague traits or behaviors would lead to more rating errors. The numerical ratings inherent in graphic rating scales create the illusion that scales are objective and someone rated as a 5 by one rater is superior to someone rated as a 3 by another rater. It is important to remember that ultimately these scales involve subjective judgment of raters.

Behaviorally anchored rating scale (BARS):
A performance appraisal format that identifies the most important aspects of a job and includes behavioral descriptions of high, average, and low levels of performance for each aspect.

Behaviorally Anchored Rating Scale (BARS)

Another type of absolute appraisal, **BARS**, consists of identifying the most important aspects of a job, and then specifying indicators of high, average, and low levels of that particular dimension. The rating scale includes specific descriptions of what high, average, and low levels of performance look like. This method involves designing a specific rating scale for key positions within the company, using the critical incident method. BARS is developed using input from managers, subject matter experts, and job incumbents. First, the panel of experts determines the core job dimensions. Then, for each dimension, the panel is asked to identify high, medium, and low levels of performance incidents. Next, an independent set of experts goes over the performance incidents generated by the panel to see how well each incidence matches the job dimension in question. Ultimately, example behaviors representing each point on the scale are determined.

The advantage of BARS is that because specific levels of exemplary and poor performance are defined, these specific behaviors will be useful in training employees and to use as benchmarks. Further, because the scale is behavioral and utilizes input from a large number of individuals, it tends to result in higher levels of

Demonstrates knowledge of assigned work		
(A) Above expectations	(B) Meets expectations	(C) Below expectations

Overall performance of the employee

Exceptional	Highly successful	Successful	Inconsistent	Unsatisfactory

Expresses ideas clearly

Outstanding	Good	Needs improvement	Not applicable

Figure 5.4 Sample graphic rating scales.

involvement by raters and ratees in the design process, which means its chances of being accepted by users of the system is higher. In fact, this seems to be the main advantage of BARS: Those who are involved in the system design process had more favorable perceptions about the performance appraisal in general (Silverman & Wexley, 1984). At the same time, developing these scales tends to be cumbersome, and identifying different levels of a particular performance dimension tends to be challenging even for subject matter experts. Despite the careful way it is constructed

DIMENSION: Knowledge of Students		Example Behaviors and Point Values
Very high performance	5	5 This instructor learns every student's name and something personal about them early in the term, and always uses this information to draw students into class conversations.
High performance	4	4.1 This instructor learns many student names and something personal about most of them, and often uses this information to draw students into class conversations.
Neither high nor low performance	3	3 This instructor learns some student names and something personal about some students, and sometimes uses this information to draw students into class conversations.
Poor performance	2	2.3 This instructor learns a few student names and infrequently uses this information to draw students into class conversations.
Very poor performance	1	1.2 This instructor learns no student names and uses no personal information to draw students into class conversations.

Figure 5.5 Sample of a BARS scale for one performance dimension of college professor. The example behaviors and their values are determined during the BARS development process by SMEs.

Figure 5.6 Behavioral observation scale for a lecturer.

Question	Never	Seldom	Sometimes	Usually	Always
Course content follows the syllabus.					
Class begins and ends on time.					
Course content evolves to incorporate relevant news items of the day as they occur.					
Instructor invites student participation.					

and its psychometric advantages, BARS tends to be disliked by raters and ratees and therefore is a less desired method of appraisal compared to graphic rating scales and Behavioral Observation Scales (BOS) (Tziner & Kopelman, 2002).

Behavioral Observation Scale (BOS)

Behavioral observation scale (BOS): A hybrid of BARS and graphic rating scale, this appraisal format asks raters to describe the frequency with which each behavior takes place.

BOS is a hybrid of graphic rating scales and BARS. Specifically, BARS asks raters to think back on the ratee's performance and consider whether the ratee actually demonstrated a particular behavior, or could be expected to demonstrate the described behavior. Instead, the BOS describes a particular behavior exemplifying high levels of performance at a particular dimension, and the rater is asked to report the *frequency* with which a particular behavior occurs. Similar to BARS, the specific behaviors exemplifying different dimensions of performance are arrived at through the critical incident method. BOS tends to share many of the advantages of BARS in that it is behavioral and is therefore useful to ratees in showing which behaviors are expected of them. Research has shown that this method is superior to BARS because it results in lower levels of rating inflation and greater agreement among raters (Landy & Farr, 1980).

In summary, graphic rating scales, BARS, and BOS are rating methods that have received a lot of research attention to examine their psychometric properties. It seems that what makes a rating method effective is the level of care and attention put into developing it, overlap with job content, the degree of user involvement, and rater training. In other words, rather than the specific method of assessment being used, how the system is arrived at may be more important (Landy & Farr, 1980).

Essay Appraisal Form

Essay appraisal form: An appraisal form whose primary purpose is to give feedback and is in the form of an essay.

The final type of absolute appraisal scale we will discuss is the **essay appraisal form**. The appraisal form may take the form of an essay especially when the primary purpose of the appraisal is to give feedback to employees. In this style of appraisal, the rater types in short answers to a small number of questions. The employee is not necessarily rated on a numerical scale, and the purpose of the form is to simply document the examples of high and low levels of performance to serve as the basis for the appraisal interview. The form may be combined with a brief numerical scale if the organization is interested in using the form to distribute rewards as well. Sample questions may include "Please summarize the impact of this employee on the team during the past six months, using examples." Particularly for knowledge workers, where each person is performing a unique job that is different from their coworkers', this style of evaluation may be a simple, straightforward method of conducting a performance appraisal. The key downside is that these forms are not intended to make comparisons across employees, as they will contain unique information for each worker. Further, the quality of the appraisal will depend on the observation and essay-writing skills of the rater.

Straight Ranking

This method of relative appraisal asks raters to rank people they are rating from strongest to weakest performer. Depending on how many people will be rated, **straight ranking** may be straightforward or mentally exhausting. In addition to the difficulty of ranking a large number of ratees, this method forces raters to differentiate even when the employees that are being rated do not differ meaningfully from each other in their performance level. Furthermore, this method assumes that the difference between a ranking of ratees ranked 1 and 2 is equal to the difference between employees ranked 5 and 6. In reality, employees 1–5 may be demonstrating similar levels of high performance whereas employee 6 may be a very poor performer. Ranking employees disguises these distinctions. Finally, this approach yields results that are hard to compare across different groups in the organization. Imagine a team consisting of star employees, and another team consisting of relative newcomers. The bottom-ranked employee of the first team may be vastly superior in performance compared to the top-ranked employee of the second team, but these differences are ignored in the straight-ranking method. Despite downsides, the straight-ranking method is useful for decision-making purposes, primarily because it forces raters to differentiate and identify their top-performing employees.

Straight ranking: A type of relative appraisal where the rater ranks each employee from strongest to weakest in performance.

Forced Distribution

This method of relative appraisal asks the rater to place employees into different categories such as excellent, very good, average, and needs improvement. Further, raters are required to differentiate so that only a specific percentage of employees can be placed in each category. For example, General Electric (GE) uses an appraisal system where 15 percent of employees can be placed in the top category, 75 percent in the middle category with the requirement to place 10 percent of employees in the bottom category. Sometimes referred to as "stack ranking" or "rank and yank" systems, these often result in employees in the bottom category being let go (Kwoh, 2012). The main advantage of this method is again to make raters differentiate among employees. Further, defenders of these systems highlight that it is kinder and more fair to eliminate poor performers early on in their careers as opposed to waiting until later when it would be harder for employees to find jobs (Olson, 2013). Criticisms of forced distribution include the argument that it destroys teamwork and, like ranking, forces raters to differentiate even when performance levels of ratees may not be meaningfully different. In other words, a supervisor may have a team of star performers but would be asked to rate some of them low, possibly leading to their termination – not good for either the employee or the company! On the other

Forced distribution: A relative appraisal format where there are restrictions on what percentage of employees can be placed in the top, middle, and bottom categories.

Stack ranking systems attract much criticism due to negative employee reactions and perceived unfairness. In 2013, Microsoft eliminated this much-derided practice while Yahoo! adopted it for the first time (Brustein, 2013).

hand, another manager with all low performers would rank their employees, with some receiving high ratings despite low performance. Our point here is that in addition to some of the fairness issues associated with ranking systems, they may not even provide accurate data.

As you can see, there are different advantages and disadvantages of relative and absolute appraisals. It seems that their low levels of acceptance among employees are a key limitation of relative appraisals. However, one of the key criticisms of absolute systems is the lack of differentiation. If managers are objectively rating employees and differentiating among employees, absolute systems would meet the needs of organizations. However, if the organization realizes that lack of differentiation is a problem and raters are using the top rating category so generously as to deem it useless, then providing a suggested distribution (without using it as a quota) and encouraging and training raters to differentiate may lead to the same result. Where possible, including objective performance metrics will be another way of addressing this concern.

Who Should Be the Rater?

Managers

Managers (direct supervisors of employees) are typically the ones who collect and deliver the performance feedback to the employee. Today, relying on a single manager is becoming less common, and in Fortune 500 companies it is more typical to use multi-rater systems (Ghorpade, 2000). Even when multiple raters are used, the manager of the employee remains the primary rater, and the person who gathers and interprets performance information from other raters.

There are downsides to relying only on managers: Often, employees perform their jobs under conditions and in locations remote from their managers. For example, pharmaceutical sales representatives will spend the greater part of their work day in the field, visiting hospitals and clinics as opposed to interacting with their managers. When managers don't have opportunities to observe employees, rating accuracy will suffer (Heneman & Wexley, 1983). Further, employees will feel that being rated by someone who rarely interacts with them is unfair (Greenberg, 1986). When managers have limited opportunities to directly observe the ratee, the manager will have to gather additional information, and this may indicate that a multi-rater system is more appropriate. It is advisable that the primary rater is the person with sufficient opportunities to observe the employee.

Peer Appraisals

Gathering feedback from one's coworkers in addition to the manager is one way of improving the quality of feedback, as peers can observe ratees on different occasions and they are more numerous than a single supervisor. Particularly when teamwork is of importance, assessing how the employee contributes to the team will necessitate peer opinions. This seems like a great idea, right? In fact, a review of the research on peer feedback suggests clear benefits. First, peer appraisals provide valid and relevant information that is not necessarily captured by manager ratings (Conway, Lombardo, & Sanders, 2001). Further, it is usually useful to ratees to know what their colleagues think about their performance.

However, this source of feedback is not without its downsides. Someone will need to collect information from peers, make sense of that information, and provide feedback using that information while maintaining confidentiality of the source when necessary. This introduces some administrative burden and may be time-consuming. Further, just like supervisors, peers bring their own biases to the appraisal. There is some evidence that when peers like the ratee, they give high ratings, whereas dislike for the ratee results in harsh ratings (Taggar & Brown, 2006). The degree of friendship or rivalry among peers may influence the quality and tone of the feedback.

Customers

For employees performing customer service, customers may be a relevant source of performance information. Customers do not necessarily mean external customers and clients. For employees performing support functions such as employees working in human resources or information technology, the quality of service they provide in their interactions with other departments' employees may be an important performance metric. Using customer feedback as part of performance assessments will also serve as an indicator that the organization cares about customer service. At the same time, this method has its own downsides: First, it is often cumbersome to collect customer satisfaction information. This necessitates reaching out to customers and motivating them to give feedback. Unfortunately, negative feedback may be easier to collect compared to positive, which may demoralize employees. Second, unlike peers or supervisors, customers are not required to justify their ratings and they are typically anonymous. Research from laboratory and field experiments have shown that customer ratings may suffer from gender and race biases (Hekman et al., 2010). Therefore, overreliance on customer ratings without verifying the information is probably not a good idea.

Customers as a Source of Feedback

Feedback from customers is an important source of information for retail employees. Customer feedback may come in many forms: anonymous comments from customers, the number and content of customer complaints or compliments received, or even the return rate of existing customers provide valuable feedback. Fred Meyer stores increased its customer satisfaction ratings from 68 percent to 84 percent in three years, in response to changes in associate behavior thanks to "secret shopper" feedback (Klepacki, 2012).

Secret shoppers (sometimes referred to as mystery shoppers) are hired by the organization to visit specified locations posing as customers. After their visit, they complete a questionnaire about their visit, reporting on the behavior of employees they interacted with, the look and feel of the store, speed of service, or any other issue the hiring organization is curious about. One of the key advantages of secret shoppers hired by the organization as a source of feedback is that it communicates to employees that connecting with and interacting with customers is more important than tasks that are less interactive, such as cleaning and organizing. In today's competitive grocery market with low profit margins, customer service provides a competitive advantage to stores, and employees approaching, greeting, and interacting with customers may achieve high-quality customer service more readily.

Subordinates

For ratees in leadership roles, how their direct reports view them is an important aspect of their effectiveness on the job. This approach will reveal strengths and limitations of the ratee in leadership, and feedback derived from subordinates may be used to coach and train the managers. At the same time, this information is challenging to collect, and subordinates may be less than forthcoming when sharing the perceived limitations of their boss, fearing that this information may be identifiable and may damage their relationship with their manager. Research found that employees felt more comfortable giving upward feedback if the answers were kept anonymous, and rated their managers more highly if their responses were identifiable (Antonioni, 1994). In groups where the identity of the employees can be kept confidential, such as within large groups, incorporating feedback from subordinates may be useful. Another challenge associated with upward feedback is that, similar to peer ratings, upward ratings reflect how much subordinates like their manager (Antonioni & Park, 2001).

Self-Appraisal

It may surprise you that in addition to others they interact with, ratees themselves may provide useful input to the performance appraisal. You may suspect that self-appraisals will be uniformly positive. This is actually not always the case (Somers & Birnbaum, 1991), but organizations do not use self-appraisals to distribute rewards or in other decision-making. Instead, self-appraisal is used to ensure that ratees have input into the process. Self-appraisal ensures that the ratee thinks about his/her past performance, considers areas for improvement, and comes to the appraisal meeting prepared. Further, self-assessment could be useful for managers to have before they complete their own evaluations because this may help raters remember some key accomplishments of the employee that they may have forgotten about. Finally, self-assessment may be a good way of ensuring that the ratee takes an active role in the appraisal process and may generate more positive reactions to the appraisal because the ability to express oneself during the appraisal is positively related to appraisal satisfaction (Korsgaard & Roberson, 1995).

At the same time, self-appraisals that directly pit employee and manager ratings against each other may be problematic, as the discrepancy between self- and other ratings results in negative reactions toward the appraisal. In other words, those who have an inflated sense of their performance (and therefore those who need feedback the most) are least receptive to it (Brett & Atwater, 2001). One way to incorporate self-appraisals into the appraisal system is to invite employees to answer more general questions about their past and future performance, and ask ratees to justify their self ratings.

360-Degree Feedback

Given that different rating sources have their own unique advantages and downsides, a common method of appraisal is to use a **360-degree appraisal** ("360") where data are collected from multiple raters at all levels. The use of 360-degree appraisals is widespread among Fortune 500 companies, along with government institutions, and this method is regarded as particularly useful for increasing the quality of feedback employees receive. It is advantageous in performance appraisal systems because it incorporates the viewpoints of multiple raters, who are expected to provide their unique perspectives on the performance of the employee. Ideally, 360 appraisal should result in more useful feedback being provided to the employee, and each rater rating only performance dimensions they are familiar with.

360-degree appraisal: A performance appraisal system where data are collected from multiple raters at all levels, including managers, peers, subordinates, and customers.

However, despite their frequent use, 360 appraisals have numerous downsides. First, self-other rating discrepancies are associated with more negative reactions toward the appraisal feedback (Brett & Atwater, 2001). Further, experts suggest that many aspects of 360 appraisals make them less useful for feedback purposes. For example, DeNisi and Kluger (2000) suggested that the presence of both self- and other ratings in these systems moves the focus away from performance and makes them more "self-focused," which reduces the usefulness of this method for feedback purposes. 360 appraisals are administratively more cumbersome, as the information from multiple sources needs to be collated and interpreted. Thankfully, the recent advances in performance management software from companies such as SuccessFactors (acquired by SAP), Halogen, and Rypple (acquired by Salesforce. com) help streamline the process, but still coordination and collation can be a challenge. Finally, ratee acceptance of 360 feedback depends on how positive the feedback is (Facteau, Facteau, Schoel, Russell, & Poteet, 1998), which again casts doubt on the usefulness of 360 systems.

So, who should be the rater? It seems that this question is less straightforward than one might expect. The right answer will need to take into account the nature of the job and organization, and the opportunities of each rating source to observe the performance of the employee. The acceptability of feedback to employees is important to motivate employees to change and improve their performance, so source credibility also matters. Recall also that whether the appraisal is conducted for developmental or administrative purposes will matter. As a result, when using multiple rater systems, the feedback provided may be more objective and useful if such feedback is provided for developmental reasons and raters are provided with this information as well.

Conducting the Performance Appraisal

Once the performance appraisal form is designed, the system in place will be periodically (typically semi-annually, annually, or quarterly) used to evaluate employee performance. The success of the appraisal system will partially depend on its design features, such as whether traits, behaviors, or outcomes are being rated, whether the organization is using a multi-rater system as opposed to relying on a single rater, and whether the system was designed with adequate input from users at all levels to ensure their buy-in. At the same time, effective use of the appraisal will also depend on the rater's motivation and ability to use the system effectively, and therefore will be ultimately in the hands of the system users.

During the performance appraisal period, the rater will need to do the following:

- observe and record performance during the appraisal period;
- provide frequent and timely feedback to the employee during the appraisal period, along with coaching;
- when it is time to actually conduct the performance appraisal, use the designed form to rate the employee;
- communicate the performance rating to the employee in a meeting.

Each of these stages is an important element of the performance appraisal process and will be reviewed in this section.

Observation and Recording of Performance

An important responsibility of managers is to observe and monitor employee performance during the appraisal period. Observation should be the basis of the rating given to the employee; otherwise performance ratings will be a function of personal feelings and biases as opposed to actual incidents of effective or ineffective behaviors. Observation and monitoring of performance should consist of an adequate sampling of behavior over time. For example, when managing call-center employees, the manager may decide to listen to six recorded conversations, randomly selected over the past six months. It is not necessary, and would in fact be impossible, to listen to every single recorded conversation, and it would probably not be fair to listen to six conversations from a single week. (What if the employee was overly stressed that week?)

Observation may be personal and direct, such as watching the employees as they interact with customers. The advantage is that this method allows the rater to pay attention to the situational cues, and better make sense of the reasons for high or low performance. However, having the manager there to observe may interfere with performance itself. Particularly if the employee is not an expert, knowing that they are being evaluated can hurt their performance (Henchy & Glass, 1968). When direct observation is not possible or may harm performance, the rater may collect information by sampling work performance, talking to others who interact with the employee, or viewing recordings of performance.

Even though they are advised to recognize the importance of adequate observation of performance in order to arrive at accurate and fair ratings, raters are not necessarily unbiased samplers of performance. For example, a rater will seek more information when an observed incident is thought to be caused by the situation, whereas they will stop observing and commit their observation to memory if the performance incident is thought to be caused by the ratee's personality and other stable characteristics. Moreover, prior beliefs about the ratee will interfere with which information is paid attention to, is encoded into memory, and remembered later (DeNisi et al., 1984).

In addition to observing performance, the rater will benefit from recording the performance incidents. Human memory is notoriously inaccurate, and recording information about job performance as it occurs during the appraisal period may be useful for dealing with rating errors, as will be reviewed shortly.

An important current development in observing and recording of performance is the use of **electronic performance monitoring** systems. These systems utilize technology such as video cameras, recording of employee–customer conversations, or recording keyboard strokes on a computer to observe, review, and act on employee performance in a continuous fashion. How do these systems affect performance appraisals and eventual performance? There is evidence that when an electronic monitoring system is first introduced, it negatively affects performance of some employees because it creates anxiety about being watched (Watson et al., 2013). Once these systems are in place employees become accustomed to them, and the effects on performance are typically positive (Bhave, 2014; Carroll, 2008). These systems introduce concerns about privacy and lack of autonomy at work, but because they measure performance continuously and impartially, they have some advantages over relying on the observations of a human being (Stanton, 2000). Ultimately, the effects of these systems will depend on whether they violate employee trust in the organization, erode the sense of autonomy at work, and whether they are perceived as fair by employees.

Electronic performance monitoring: Systems that utilize technology such as video cameras, recording of employee–customer interactions, or recording keyboard strokes to observe, review, and act on employee performance in a continuous fashion.

Feedback and Coaching throughout the Year

Why should the rater observe the employee? Yes, this information is important for performance appraisal purposes, but more importantly, it is the job of a manager

Coaching: Training and development of a person to achieve professional goals.

to be aware of the performance of each employee reporting to them in order to provide feedback, help, and support during the term. Therefore, as the rater is observing performance, feedback should be provided in a timely fashion, along with **coaching**. Coaching refers to the training and development of a person to achieve professional goals. Research shows that when feedback is followed by coaching focused on self-awareness and behavioral management, the results in terms of satisfaction and commitment are more positive (Luthans & Peterson, 2003). Further, the ability of performance appraisal feedback to improve performance was enhanced when the employee was provided with regular feedback throughout the performance period (Kuvaas, 2011).

As we noted earlier, performance appraisal is merely one piece of the overall process of performance management, and it is the manager's job to manage the performance of employees on a day-to-day basis. However, it is quite easy for managers and employees to miss each other during a work day, and not make time to interact. A commonly used tool to ensure that managers check in with employees on a routine basis is to schedule a regular **one-on-one meeting**. These short and regular sessions (such as 30 minutes every two weeks) ensure that the manager is always ready to support the employee, give guidance and feedback, and help solve problems (Tate, 2013).

One-on-one meeting: A short, regularly scheduled meeting between the manager and employee for coaching and regular connecting.

Rating of the Employee: Errors and Biases

Unless the organization is using objective metrics such as sales performance or number of calls completed (which have their own limitations), performance appraisal usually involves observing the performance of an employee over a period of time and then recalling that information when it is time to assess performance. It is inherently a subjective system, and even when raters have every intention to be objective, oftentimes they rate performance in a way that does not match the "real" performance of the employee. To complicate the matter even more, it would be naïve to expect that managers are always interested in rating employees objectively and accurately. While past research in performance appraisals tended to assume that raters are interested in being objective and the challenge is to identify psychometrically sound measures, current researchers recognize that raters differ in their motivation to be accurate (Levy & Williams, 2004; Longenecker, Sims, & Gioia, 1987). Managers may have other personal agendas and motives when assessing performance. For example, they may be too generous in their ratings because they want to avoid confronting a poor performer. In other words, the rating errors to be discussed in this section may be intentional or unintentional. Being aware of the nature of a potential error is important so that precautions can be taken against it. For unconscious errors, the problem resides in limitations of human information-processing capabilities. Therefore, the solutions tend to take the form of designing appraisal forms and systems that help raters observe and store information more accurately, and training raters to avoid common rater errors (DeNisi et al., 1984). When rating errors are intentional, such methods will be less useful, and instead organizations will need to find ways of motivating their raters to rate accurately, such as training and supporting raters in how to give performance feedback, because rater discomfort with communicating negative feedback may make them avoid difficult confrontations.

Range Restriction Errors

A key concern is the potential for range restriction in appraisals, or using only a limited portion of the rating scale. Giving all employees a very high rating is referred to as **leniency error** whereas giving all employees low ratings is referred to as **strictness** (or severity). Of course, ratings may alternatively be in the middle, which we refer to as **central tendency error**. Ultimately, all of these are problematic because the rater is using only part of the rating scale. These errors may be intentional or unintentional. Raters may be too lenient because of their own personality traits such as high agreeableness and low conscientiousness (Bernardin, Cooke, & Villanova, 2000) or vagueness of appraisal criteria, or they may be too lenient because they are feeling reluctant to deliver negative feedback (Villanova, Bernardin, Dahmus, & Sims, 1993). Other reasons raters are lenient include the desire to look like effective managers ("my employees are great"), the desire to get a larger share of rewards for their employees, and even wanting to promote a problem employee out of their department (Spence & Keeping, 2011). Regardless of the reason, range restriction errors prevent accurate feedback from being shared with employees, result in unfair reward distribution in the organization (if some managers are lenient and others are not, employees reporting to lenient managers may unfairly get a higher share of rewards and bonuses), and reduce the utility of appraisals for legal documentation.

Contrast Error

Even when an organization is using absolute ratings rather than relative ranking systems, managers naturally compare employees to each other. A person's performance may appear higher or lower than it actually is, due to its contrast with other employees within the work group. For example, let's say Mary is an excellent employee working in a team of star employees. Mary may be rated average if she is compared to coworkers, even though her performance exceeds expectations. Instead, the boss should rate the employees in terms of their absolute performance, not how they perform compared to other team members.

Halo Effect

A rater's overall impression of a ratee may drive the entire assessment of the employee, regardless of what questions are being asked. This impression is often derived from one dimension of performance affecting the ratings of all performance dimensions. For example, if a rater feels that Tom is an excellent salesperson, then regardless of what other dimensions of Tom's performance are being assessed, Tom may be rated in the excellent category. Essentially this renders the performance appraisal form useless, because the fine-tuned, specific questions that were included in the form in the hopes that the employee would receive specific feedback will be answered in a uniform way. This is also problematic if the performance appraisal form consists of specific and independent performance dimensions that are not necessarily correlated with each other.

Leniency error: A type of distribution error in which the rater gives all ratees a very high rating without distinguishing among them.

Strictness: A type of distribution error in which the rater gives all ratees a low rating without distinguishing among them.

Central tendency error: A type of distribution error in which the rater gives all ratees a medium rating without distinguishing among them.

Contrast error: A rater error where a person is rated higher or lower than warranted because the person's performance is higher or lower than their peers'.

Halo effect: A rating error where the ratee's overall impression in the eyes of the rater drives the performance score, regardless of the questions being asked.

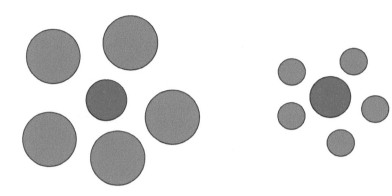

Figure 5.7
Which employee designated by the red circle will be rated higher?

Similarity and Liking

Similarity and liking: A rating error where the ratee is evaluated higher than warranted because the rater likes the ratee or because the rater feels that the ratee is similar to the rater.

Psychologists have long shown that similarity breeds attraction. This is true for friendships, but it is also true in manager–employee relationships, such that employees viewed as more similar to the manager end up developing a higher-quality relationship with their manager (Liden, Wayne, & Stilwell, 1993). Further, when managers have a high-quality relationship with an employee, they rate the performance of that employee at high levels regardless of objective performance metrics (Duarte, Goodson, & Klich, 1994). As a result, a threat to the validity of appraisals is interpersonal similarity and liking that exists in the relationship. Given that performance appraisals take place within the context of an existing relationship, it is natural that the relationship quality will affect the assessment of the employee. It is also important to remember that if liking is related to performance appraisal scores, this does not necessarily mean that the manager is biased: researchers note that liking may be a consequence of performance, as opposed to being a bias (DeNisi & Peters, 1996). Yet we should be aware of the possibility that at least in some cases, liking may play a biasing role, which would result in performance appraisal being perceived as an unfair, political process. We also know that liking has a stronger influence over ratings when traits and subjective measures, as opposed to more objective measures of performance, are used (Robbins & DeNisi, 1998).

Recency Error

Recency error: A rater error where events that occurred in the recent past have undue influence over the performance appraisal compared to events that occurred in the more distant past.

Performance appraisals tend to be semi-annual or annual events. It is possible to have them more often, but typically they occur at long intervals. This means that raters may forget what happened at the beginning of the evaluation period by the time they are facing the performance appraisal form. This is problematic, because performance appraisal should be an accurate reflection of the entire assessment period, rather than the last few weeks. Instead, positive and negative events that occur just before the assessment may have an undue influence over the rating.

Techniques to Minimize the Effects of Appraisal Errors

There are many methods that can be used to minimize the effects of rating errors, to ensure that performance appraisals are consistent, fair, and motivate employees to perform better. Here are some that have been shown to be useful.

Training

Studies have shown that simply explaining rating errors and making raters aware of them does not necessarily eliminate these errors. **Rater error training** is a type of training familiarizing raters with different types of rating errors in the hopes that they would avoid committing these errors. Interestingly, this type of training actually results in less observational accuracy and greater levels of leniency (Woehr & Huffcutt, 1994). This may be because making raters aware of rater errors and asking them to avoid the errors can lead the rater to overcompensate and thus decrease accuracy. ("Barry seems good on every dimension. I must be committing halo error. I'll rate him down on some dimensions to be more accurate.") Instead, perhaps a better type of training program involves training raters on how to rate. This type of training is labeled **frame-of-reference training**. Raters watch videos of employees performing, or read scenarios of employees displaying particular behaviors. They are asked to rate each person based on the information given them. Then, they are told what the "correct" rating is, as defined by experts and higher-level managers. The idea is to teach raters the meaning of each performance dimension, what type of information to pay attention to, and what type of information to ignore. Frame-of-reference training shows raters how to use the system, and also helps develop a common reference point in the minds of raters, so that different raters observing the same person achieve higher agreement in their ratings. This method would help deal with some unintentional rating errors, such as leniency, central tendency, and harshness bias, as well as halo error, and has been shown to improve rating accuracy (Woehr & Huffcutt, 1994). This also helps all raters to share the same rating schema or frame of reference. This is important when comparing the ratings of employees who are being rated by different supervisors.

Raters may also be trained in system characteristics. **Performance appraisal system training** teaches employees the specific features of the appraisal system as it is designed in that organization as well as how to communicate with ratees during a performance appraisal meeting, how to be a better listener, and how to communicate negative feedback in a way that will result in behavioral change. This type of training could involve mock interviews and role playing, followed by feedback to raters about their feedback giving style. The purpose of this type of training is to make raters more comfortable and efficacious in giving feedback, and as a result this method may be a good way of dealing with intentional rating errors, such as leniency error when leniency is being caused by feeling uncomfortable rating employees negatively to avoid a confrontation.

Calibration Meetings

Not a type of rater training *per se*, this method is a rater reliability session, where a group of raters come together to review each other's ratings and explain the rationale for their own ratings. This meeting is conducted before the actual ratings are communicated to the ratees, as a last step. The purpose of this meeting is to keep raters accountable to each other and make ratings from different managers more comparable (Pulakos & O'Leary, 2011). For example, some supervisors may see that they are evaluating their employees much more leniently than others, which

Rater error training: A type of training familiarizing raters with different types of rating errors in the hope that raters will avoid committing these errors.

Frame of reference training: A type of rater training teaching raters the meaning of each performance dimension and level, showing raters how to rate.

Performance appraisal system training: This training program educates raters about the features of the appraisal system, as well as teaches raters how to give feedback and communicate more effectively during the appraisal process.

Calibration meeting: A rater reliability session where raters come together to discuss the ratings they gave to the employees they are rating, defending and justifying their particular ratings.

may help them correct the ratings to make them more comparable to each other. This method is not without its downsides. It is a time-consuming method, and further, managers may now justify a lower than expected rating to an employee by blaming the calibration meeting. Finally, a manager's ability to speak up and justify the ratings will depend on their personality, and some managers may push back objections of their peers while others may go along with the group, with significant consequences for employees. At the same time, if used correctly, calibration meetings may result in better-thought-out, more defensible appraisals, and once managers have a good grasp of the norms of how to rate, the need for calibration may go away. This method may be useful in dealing with both unintentional, cognitive errors, and intentional errors that occur during the appraisal process.

Diary keeping: A method where the rater keeps records of important performance incidents.

Diary Keeping

Problems such as recency error occur because human memory is fallible, and it is challenging for raters to remember all of what happened during the appraisal period. One method of dealing with this is to keep performance logs. As raters record instances of high and low performance, there will be more documentation of important performance incidents, and the actual appraisal will be a better reflection of important occurrences of the appraisal period. Of course, the success of this method will depend on the rater's persistence in recording performance information, which may be hard to do due to the time pressures that managers face. Interestingly, diary keeping does not necessarily reduce the effects of liking on performance ratings. In fact, when raters keep a performance diary for employees, there tends to be a stronger relationship between liking and ratings (DeNisi & Peters, 1996). Why? It could be that when they keep diaries, raters are more likely to note positive events for employees they like, and negative events for employees they dislike. At the same time, DeNisi and Peters (1996) also showed that diary keeping improves rater reactions to the performance appraisal system, probably because diary keeping improves recall and therefore makes rating easier.

Using Objective Appraisals

Many appraisal errors occur because of limitations in observation and recall, and the potentially political nature of appraisals. Using objective metrics will help deal with some of these. When results, as opposed to traits and behaviors, are being measured, there is less room for human error. As noted in Chapter 4, objective appraisals are not a panacea, and they may result in omission of important aspects of an employee's contributions in favor of what is easy to measure. At the same time, using metrics in combination with behaviors may result in reducing some of the biases inherent in the appraisal system.

Using Multiple Raters

Another way of ensuring that appraisals capture more than one person's biases is to introduce multiple rating systems such as 360-degree feedback, or, where appropriate, having more than one supervisor rate an employee's performance. This method may increase perceived fairness of the appraisal system by limiting the effects of many of the unintentional errors, and prevents one person's perceptions from dominating the entire assessment.

Using Forced Distribution

We noted that relative appraisals are not perceived as fair and come with a large set of problems, mainly relating to ratee reactions. At the same time, if the organization's performance appraisal system is losing its usefulness due to lack of differentiation among ratees, then one way of ensuring that raters vary their ratings is to give them a suggested distribution of scores. This method will signal to raters that they are expected to differentiate among ratees, and also communicate that the highest category is truly reserved for exceptional performers, rather than those simply doing a good job. It is important to use this method carefully, and to present the categories in the form of suggested ways for how each category should be used, as opposed to strictly enforcing them and forcing raters to differentiate between identical performers. However, forced distribution or ranking are sometimes necessary, such as when layoff decisions must be made.

Increasing Accountability

Perhaps one of the most challenging aspects of a performance appraisal is to ensure that raters take it seriously and complete their ratings carefully, fairly, and honestly. If raters are not motivated and are not serious about using the performance appraisal system the way it is intended, it may waste everyone's time, and may be a systematic and negative influence over employee fairness perceptions. Therefore, organizations may get better results out of their performance appraisal systems by keeping their managers accountable for being effective raters. For example, General Electric includes the ability to evaluate employees effectively as one criterion of manager effectiveness. In other words, a manager's ability to get a good evaluation depends on their effectiveness in conducting a fair appraisal.

Workplace Application

Performance Management without Appraisals at Netflix

It is important to emphasize function over form in performance appraisals. In fact, performance management does not require the presence of a formal performance appraisal system. Netflix, the online DVD rental and video-streaming company with over 2,000 employees, built a performance culture without actually conducting annual formal performance reviews. They use an informal 360-degree appraisal system where employees report what their colleagues should stop, start, and continue doing. In addition, performance conversations are a critical part of a manager's work (McCord, 2014). Performance management requires documenting performance, giving employees frequent feedback about their performance, and reinforcing high performance while dealing with performance problems. Netflix is an example of a company that meets these goals without using annual performance appraisals.

Conducting the Performance Appraisal Meeting

An essential element of the performance appraisal process is a meeting in which the manager and the employee get together to review the employee's effectiveness and areas for improvement, concluding with an action plan. At the end of the feedback meeting, it is hoped that the ratees will have a clear understanding of their strengths and limitations, be motivated, and feel capable of improving their performance. Despite its promise to improve effectiveness, and despite its intuitive appeal, feedback has a mixed record in I/O research in terms of its effectiveness in creating behavioral change. In fact, Kluger and DeNisi's (1996) review of the literature on feedback and performance improvements suggested that feedback actually reduces performance when it switches attention from the task to the self, and when it threatens self-esteem. Therefore, how feedback is given is much more important than whether feedback is given.

Conditions Enabling High-Quality Feedback

Feedback context: The conditions under which feedback is delivered; includes factors such as the relationship quality between employees and managers, team cohesiveness, organizational culture.

When learning how to give feedback, you should remember the importance of the feedback context. **Feedback context** refers to the conditions under which feedback is delivered, and includes factors such as the relationship quality between employees and managers, team cohesiveness, and organizational culture. To begin with, the appraisal process including the feedback meeting occurs within the context of an ongoing relationship between the rater and ratee. Unlike an employee selection meeting where the interviewer and interviewee are meeting for the first time, the quality of the feedback and ratee reactions will be shaped by how much trust exists in the relationship. In fact, manager–employee relationship quality is a key predictor of perceived fairness as well as reactions toward the appraisal system (Elicker, Levy, & Hall, 2006; Erdogan, 2002). You might think that if the feedback being given is true, objective, and well intentioned, it should not matter who is delivering the feedback. Yet, the identity of the deliverer makes a big difference. If the ratee does not trust the rater, the ratee will be skeptical about the feedback received, and the feedback is less likely to motivate the employee to change behavior. Further, the quality of the feedback environment will make a difference. If the organizational culture emphasizes continuous improvement of performance, frequently giving each other feedback and then changing one's behavior based on feedback, then reactions to feedback during performance appraisal will be more positive, and such feedback will have greater chances of improving performance (Levy & Williams, 2004). In supportive feedback cultures, managers understand the importance of delivering feedback, and upper managers engage in role modeling for lower-level managers by seeking feedback publicly, and then making changes based on feedback (Dahling & O'Malley, 2011).

What to Do before the Meeting

The performance appraisal meeting is a critical event that may motivate or demoralize the ratee. Therefore, raters would benefit from preparing for this event adequately. Things to do before the meeting include completing the performance appraisal form carefully and asking the ratee to complete the self-appraisal form. The rater is also responsible for scheduling a time and place for the meeting location where an in-depth conversation can take place in privacy. Because this is an important meeting for the employee, raters may even benefit from practicing how to discuss the key elements of the appraisal.

What to Do during the Meeting

In the appraisal meeting, the employee and the manager are expected to contribute to the discussion so that the conversation is not one-sided. Mark Murphy, the CEO of the consulting company Leadership IQ, describes this as having an "adult to adult" rather than a "parent to child" conversation (HR Focus, 2013a). It may be beneficial to limit the number of topics being discussed. Instead of discussing 10 areas of improvement, focusing on the most important two or three areas might be more fruitful. During the meeting, the manager will need to recognize positive aspects of performance by giving specific praise. For example, "you are very creative" is less impactful praise compared to "The web pages you design are a great combination of function and appearance. Both clients and team members rate them highly." In other words, effective feedback, even when positive, should be specific and behavioral.

When discussing negative aspects of performance, the discussion may follow the structure below. Again, it is important to remember that what is being discussed and criticized is not the person, but the specific behavior. Focusing on character traits of the employee is likely to disengage the ratee and may result in rejection of the feedback. In other words, the focus should be on performance.

- *What is the problem to be corrected?* ("I noticed that you do not always submit time sheets on time").
- *How frequently does this problem occur?* ("In the past two months, there were three instances in which time sheets were not submitted by the deadline").
- *Why is this a problem?* How does it affect others in the company, team members, or the employee's effectiveness at work? ("When timesheets are not submitted by the deadline, we cannot bill our clients, which affects the credibility of the entire team in the eyes of our clients").
- *How should the problem be solved?* ("Let's brainstorm some ways in which we can solve this problem. How can I help? Are there structural changes we can make to help facilitate that?")

"Your evaluation is based on the
next 30 seconds. Go!"

Sandwich technique: A method of delivering feedback; starting with more positive pieces of feedback, followed by areas for improvement, ending the meeting on a positive note with an action plan.

One method of delivering feedback, known as the **sandwich technique**, involves starting with more positive pieces of feedback, followed by areas for improvement, ending the meeting on a positive note with an action plan. This method is a useful heuristic, reminding raters that the meeting should not start with, or be dominated by, negative information, due to the potentially damaging effects of criticism. Research on moods suggests that when people are experiencing positive moods, their ability to handle negative information goes up, which might mean that discussing areas for improvement after recognizing the proud moments of the employee may allow them to build cognitive resources first (Bouskila-Yam & Kluger, 2011). At the same time, this method should be used with caution, because it may be used to "hide" the areas of improvement between positive information and comments, effectively resulting in the ratee not understanding and disregarding criticisms and areas for improvement. Instead, it is important to ensure that strengths of the employee are given plenty of specific praise, areas for improvement are discussed fully, and a specific action plan, consisting of specific and concrete goals set for the employee, is developed.

Action plan: Setting goals for the near future regarding what the employee and the manager will do to improve the employee's effectiveness.

An **action plan**, or setting goals for the near future regarding what the employee and the manager will do to improve the employee's effectiveness, is a key aspect of any appraisal. Performance appraisal is only one piece of performance management, and simply documenting level of performance, giving the employee feedback, and making reward decisions will not necessarily result in changes in performance. Often, the manager will need to provide specific support to help the employee. The employee may need to take part in additional training and coaching. Therefore, unless there is a specific action plan with follow-up, the usefulness of appraisals will be limited.

Looking at it from the ratee's perspective, receiving negative feedback is likely to be an emotional event. The criticism may feel unfair, or may threaten the employee's self-identity, which could result in anger, sadness, and frustration. Retaining control of emotions is important to prevent damage to the relationship and to ensure that the employee can make the best use of feedback. For a ratee, being defensive and arguing are unlikely to result in positive outcomes, but asking clarifying questions and asking for time to think about the feedback may be helpful. When receiving feedback, remember that feedback is one person's opinion of your performance, so there is likely to be some truth in it, but you are less likely to process it effectively when emotions are high.

LEGAL ISSUES

One major concern is legal issues in performance appraisal. To the extent that performance appraisals are used to make employment decisions (e.g., for promotions), they are covered by the *Uniform Guidelines*, discussed in greater detail in Chapter 7. In other words, if an organization is using a performance appraisal system to terminate an employee or to decide who is going to be promoted, they may need to defend the system from a legal standpoint. Interestingly, a study by Feild and Holley (1982) examined court cases involving performance appraisals (where the company was being sued by an employee) and which performance appraisal characteristics resulted in a positive verdict for the company. Best practices related to the company being able to defend itself were as you would expect – for example, that the appraisal was based on a job analysis, provided written instructions to raters, and used performance appraisal methods based on observable behaviors.

GLOBAL IMPLICATIONS

Performance appraisal is a system that has Western origins. Even though these systems are in use around the world, some of the underlying assumptions reflect individualistic and egalitarian origins. For example, performance appraisal assumes that performance is under the control of employees and that managers are interested in and are capable of influencing an employee's performance. It assumes a relatively egalitarian relationship where employees can engage in two-way communication with their managers, and may express their viewpoints. Multi-rater systems such as 360 assume that employees can give professional and objective feedback to their colleagues or even supervisors. In fact, research shows that many of these assumptions do not hold in all countries (Fletcher, 2001). One recent study compiling data from 21 countries showed that multi-rater systems were more acceptable in individualistic, egalitarian, and future-oriented cultures such as the United States, Australia, and Denmark (Peretz & Fried, 2012). Moreover, the degree to which performance appraisal practices in the organization matched national culture norms predicted lower levels of absenteeism and turnover in the same study. Therefore, organizations will need to ensure that the type of system they use fits with local norms and expectations.

CURRENT ISSUES AND CONTROVERSIES

One of the significant developments in the past decade has been the quick pace with which information technology has advanced and now pervades all aspects of organizational life. A direct consequence of this has been advances in electronic monitoring of employees. On the one hand, such systems resulted in an increase in the amount of objective data available to employees. This means that employees can often see how well they are doing with more precision (Fletcher, 2001). At the same time, this might mean overuse of results-based appraisals compared to more behavioral systems. As you may recall from the earlier discussion, results are not always the best way to measure performance, and overreliance on performance metrics may have unintended consequences, including neglect of performance dimensions more difficult to capture, fatigue and alienation as a result of constant monitoring, and creation of a "results at all costs" mentality.

Second, a big challenge for performance appraisal is the widespread dissatisfaction with annual performance appraisal processes in general. In fact, books with titles such as "Abolishing Performance Appraisals" are gaining traction. In other words, given that performance appraisals have limited usefulness as feedback tools (because they are typically once-a-year occurrences) and may damage relationships when used inappropriately, some practitioners are calling for an end for this practice. At the same time, companies still need tools to document performance and tie pay and other opportunities to performance. In other words, while in theory getting rid of appraisals may solve one problem, it creates others. So, we are seeing experimentation with different formats and different ways of conducting appraisals, such as essay-type appraisals where the assessment is simply a short essay facilitating the performance conversation. While the performance appraisal tools available may not completely meet the needs of contemporary organizations, the need is still there. Scholars are proposing that instead of being overly focused on which form to use and trying to design error-free systems, organizations should treat appraisals as simply one component of performance management systems, and the focus should be on rater motivation to give feedback and ratee motivation to receive feedback (DeNisi & Sonesh, 2011).

Finally, the field of psychology is seeing some developments in the form of positive psychology, which challenges some of the fundamentals of appraisals. Typical appraisals are based on a "deficit model" where weaknesses are identified and improved. Instead, positive psychology proposes that a "strengths-based" approach would be more effective. Based on this view, organizations should focus on employee strengths, build them even further, and give employees opportunities to use these strengths. Any limitations of the employee can be resolved by assigning these tasks to others (Bouskila-Yam & Kluger, 2011). It remains to be seen whether this approach to appraisals will gain traction.

WHAT DOES THIS MEAN TO YOU?

This chapter shows that organizations are interested in assessing the performance levels of their employees and give them feedback in order to make administrative decisions about their employees as well as develop their talent. This chapter was written from the perspective of those who make design decisions about the appraisal system and those who rate employees. Your future job may involve either of these roles. But what does this mean to you as an employee?

First, you may be asked to play the role of a rater for your coworkers, managers, or yourself. This is an opportunity to improve the effectiveness of those around you. However, you should remind yourselves of the cognitive limitations of raters. What are you basing your rating on? Is this based on a prevalent behavior? Or is your overall liking or disliking of the person shading your judgment? Can you provide behavioral examples of what you observed? If you feel the temptation to protect your friends and those you like from negative feedback, you may need to remind yourself that it is not kind to withhold information that may help them improve their performance. When employees find out about their limitations mid-career, it is often harder for them to find a better-fitting job or unlearn bad habits. You may think of constructive and developmental feedback as a gift you are giving your colleagues.

Second, the ability to receive feedback in addition to give feedback is a skill that will serve your career well. Again, remember that good feedback is a gift, and the feedback giver usually has to take a risk in communicating bad news. Reacting to feedback negatively by being defensive on the spot, arguing with the feedback giver at that moment, and losing control of your emotions will likely reduce the amount of feedback you receive in the future; it also deprives you of an opportunity to improve your skills. Even when you believe that someone's observation of your behavior is misguided and inaccurate, ask yourself: Why does this person think this about me? Feedback is simply one person's perception, but what are you doing to create that perception? There may be valuable take-aways in even the most seemingly inaccurate feedback you receive.

Third, remember that the fairness of an appraisal usually depends on relationship quality between managers and employees. So a good way of improving the quality of the feedback you receive will be to invest in a high-quality professional relationship with your manager. One way of doing this is to seek feedback yourself, without waiting for the big event. Seeking feedback shows that you care about improving, and also that you care about that person's opinion, so it could be a relationship builder in addition to reducing anxiety experienced in the appraisal.

Conclusion

Assessment of performance is important for its management. In this chapter, we discussed many issues organizations need to decide when designing a performance appraisal system. The most effective systems are perceived as fair and useful, fit the company strategy, have high content validity, and are practical. Each decision made about the appraisal system involves tradeoffs and there does not seem to be one best system that would fit organizations of all types. Recent thinking on this subject treats performance appraisal less as an objective measurement instrument, and more as a system where effectiveness depends on rater motivation to rate objectively, the overall quality of the relationship between managers and employees, and a performance feedback culture that emphasizes high performance and immediate, constructive feedback.

YOUR TURN...

1. If you visit your local book store or the library, the management section will likely contain some books about "ready-made performance appraisals" you can start implementing in your organization, and "performance appraisal phrases" that give you pre-packaged ways of expressing common performance problems and concerns managers may encounter. Explain what you think about these tools in terms of how useful they are to organizations interested in developing an internal appraisal system, or to managers interested in giving high-quality feedback to employees.

2. Several informal surveys by consulting companies indicate that managers tend to have negative reactions to their organization's performance appraisal system, noting that they are not very useful, and they are stressful. What could be the source of negative manager reactions to performance appraisals? How can organizations resolve these concerns and secure managers' buy-in?

3. A performance appraisal meeting is usually about the employee's performance. However, performance appraisal results are also typically tied to employee bonuses or pay raises. Do you think raises and bonuses should be a part of the performance appraisal interview? Why or why not?

4. Imagine that you are working for a fitness center. What would be different ways of evaluating performance of employees? Develop trait, behavior, and outcome-based criteria to assess performance.

Additional Reading

Aguinis, H. (2013). *Performance management.* Boston, MA: Pearson Education.

Cardy, R. L., & Leonard, B. (2011). *Performance management: Concepts, skills, and exercises.* Armonk, NY: M. E. Sharpe.

Fletcher, C. (2008). *Appraisal, feedback, and development: Making performance review work.* Abingdon, England: Routledge.

Murphy, K. R., & Cleveland, J. (1995). *Understanding performance appraisal: Social, organizational, and goal-based perspectives.* Thousand Oaks, CA: Sage.

Pulakos, E. D. (2009). *Performance management: A new approach for driving business results.* Singapore: Wiley-Blackwell.

Smither, J. W., & London, M. (2009). *Performance management: Putting research into action.* Society for Industrial and Organizational Psychology, The professional practice series. San Francisco, CA: Jossey-Bass.

CASE STUDY: Trouble with Performance Appraisals at CFPB

Consumer Financial
Protection Bureau

The Consumer Financial Protection Bureau (CFPB) is an independent government agency charged with preventing discrimination in consumer finance. For example, the agency tries to protect consumers from being charged discriminatory dealer markups when buying a car, by comparing how much members of different demographic groups pay in interest rates.

In a strange twist of fate, this employer of 1,300 full-time employees found itself the target of allegations of discrimination, based on a similar type of analysis – this time involving a comparison of performance appraisal ratings of different groups of employees.

This young organization (established in 2011) has been using a performance appraisal system that is quite common: managers rate employees on core organizational competencies such as collaboration and communication, as well as job-specific competencies and accomplishment of objectives. Employees are rated on a scale ranging between 1 = unacceptable and 5 = role model, with higher ratings expected to be the exception, rather than the norm. Each rating was to be completed by the immediate supervisor of the employee, and then reviewed by a higher-level manager. Higher-level managers had access to narratives written by lower-level managers, as well as information about the distribution of ratings in their division. Other features included a formal grievance process for the appraisal, and a separate process for reporting discriminatory treatment. As a downside, managers did not receive training on the system. The appraisal results were directly tied to employee bonuses, as well as to merit pay; thus they had serious consequences for employees.

Attesting to the lack of popularity of performance appraisal systems in many organizations, employee reactions to this performance appraisal approach were not positive. A 2013 survey revealed that less than half of the agency employees were satisfied with promotion and pay raises, and fewer than three in five employees agreed with their performance appraisal and thought that they understood how to improve their ratings in the future.

Where this story became newsworthy was when the auditing firm, Deloitte, was commissioned to conduct an audit of the organization's internal diversity practices, which then became public in an *American Banker* article. The audit revealed a lack of a fairness climate in general within the organization, a lack of commitment to diversity, and a sense of disengagement and low morale among employees. Further, analyses revealed a number of statistical differences among different groups with respect to appraisal ratings. For example, white employees were more likely to be rated in the top performer category compared to nonwhite employees. There were also statistical differences between ratings of employees younger and older than 40

(3.94 vs. 3.78), union status (3.79 for unionized employees and 4.04 for non-union employees) headquarter vs. field employees (3.95 for headquarter employees versus 3.63 for field), and tenure (3.69 for less than a year, 3.92 for employees with more than a year).

Faced with accusations that the appraisal system was discriminatory, the agency announced that it was abolishing its performance appraisal system. All employees would now be compensated retroactively to eliminate the effects of the appraisal system – the agency would pay all employees the difference between their actual rating and the top score, essentially giving everyone the top score retroactively, costing the organization more than $5 million. While this case is being written, the agency announced that it would move to a simple pass/fail system. According to the president of the National Treasury Employees Union, the agency and the union would now work toward building a system that gives employees more voice, focuses on performance improvement and career development, and is less subjective.

Questions

1. If you had not seen the results of the Deloitte report, what would have been your thoughts about the characteristics of the appraisal system?

2. After reviewing the internal audit findings, do you see sufficient evidence that CFPB is using a problematic performance appraisal system? What additional information would be helpful for you to make this judgment?

3. Do you agree that CFPB needs a brand-new appraisal system? If you were consulting for this organization, what would you do in order to solve the problems associated with the current appraisal system?

4. How do you think the employees will react to the solution that all employees be given top scores retroactively? Do you feel that this is a satisfactory solution to the problem? What else could the agency have done? How do you think this decision will affect the agency culture and morale, as well as employees' sense of fairness and motivation?

5. What are your thoughts about the agency's plans to design a new system that will be less subjective and give less power to managers? What would such a system look like?

Source: http://www.consumerfinance.gov/.
Sources: This case is partially based on information included in CFPB, 2014; Moore, 2014; Pollock, 2014; Rubin, 2014; Witkowski, 2014a, 2014b.

References

Antonioni, D. (1994). The effects of feedback accountability on upward appraisal ratings. *Personnel Psychology, 47,* 349–356.

Antonioni, D., & Park, H. (2001). The relationship between rater affect and three sources of 360-degree feedback ratings. *Journal of Management, 27,* 479–495.

Bernardin, H. J., Cooke, D. K., & Villanova, P. (2000). Conscientiousness and agreeableness as predictors of rating leniency. *Journal of Applied Psychology, 85,* 232.

Bhave, D. P. (2014). The invisible eye? Electronic performance monitoring and employee job performance. *Personnel Psychology, 67,* 605–635.

Bouskila-Yam, O., & Kluger, A. N. (2011). Strength-based performance appraisal and goal-setting. *Human Resource Management Review, 21,* 137-147.

Brett, J. F., & Atwater, L. E. (2001). 360° feedback: Accuracy, reactions, and perceptions of usefulness. *Journal of Applied Psychology, 86,* 930-942.

Brustein, J. (2013, November 12). Yahoo's latest HR disaster: Ranking workers on a curve. *Bloomberg Business Week.* Retrieved May 4, 2014, from http://www.businessweek.com/articles/2013-11-12/yahoos-latest-hr-disaster-ranking-workers-on-a-curve.

Carroll, W. R. (2008). The effects of electronic performance monitoring on performance outcomes: A review and meta-analysis. *Employee Rights & Employment Policy Journal, 12,* 29-47.

Consumer Financial Protection Bureau (CFPB). (2014, May). Fiscal year 2013 performance management analysis: Snapshot of findings. Retrieved June 16, 2014, from http://www.federalnewsradio.com/pdfs/cfpb_performance_appraisals.pdf.

Conway, J. M., Lombardo, K., & Sanders, K. C. (2001). A meta-analysis of incremental validity and nomological networks for subordinate and peer rating. *Human Performance, 14,* 267-303.

Dahling, J. J., & O'Malley, A. L. (2011). Supportive feedback environments can mend broken performance management systems. *Industrial and Organizational Psychology, 4,* 201-203.

DeNisi, A. S., Cafferty, T. P., & Meglino, B. M. (1984). A cognitive view of the performance appraisal process: A model and research propositions. *Organizational Behavior and Human Performance, 33,* 360-396.

DeNisi, A. S., & Kluger, A. N. (2000). Feedback effectiveness: Can 360-degree appraisals be improved? *Academy of Management Executive, 14*(1), 129-139.

DeNisi, A. S., & Peters, L. H. (1996). Organization of information in memory and the performance appraisal process: Evidence from the field. *Journal of Applied Psychology, 81,* 717-737.

DeNisi, A. S., & Sonesh, S. (2011). The appraisal and management of performance at work. In S. Zedeck (Ed.), *APA handbook of industrial and organizational psychology, Vol. 2* (pp. 255-279). Washington, DC: American Psychological Association.

Dobbins, G. H., Cardy, R. L., & Truxillo, D. M. (1988). The effects of purpose of appraisal and individual differences in stereotypes of women on sex differences in performance ratings: A laboratory and field study. *Journal of Applied Psychology, 73,* 551-558.

Duarte, N. T., Goodson, J. R., & Klich, N. R. (1994). Effects of dyadic quality and duration on performance appraisal. *Academy of Management Journal, 37,* 499-521.

Elicker, J. D., Levy, P. E., & Hall, R. J. (2006). The role of leader–member exchange in the performance appraisal process. *Journal of Management, 32,* 531-551.

Erdogan, B. (2002). Antecedents and consequences of justice perceptions in performance appraisals. *Human Resource Management Review, 12,* 555-578.

Facteau, C. L., Facteau, J. D., Schoel, L. C., Russell, J. E. A., & Poteet, M. L. (1998). Reactions of leaders to 360-degree feedback from subordinates and peers. *Leadership Quarterly, 9,* 427-448.

Feild, H. S., & Holley, W. H. (1982). The relationship of performance appraisal system characteristics to verdicts in selected employment discrimination cases. *Academy of Management Journal, 25,* 392–406.

Fletcher, C. (2001). Performance appraisal and management: The developing research agenda. *Journal of Occupational and Organizational Psychology, 74,* 473–487.

Frauenheim, E. (2009). Jungle survival. *Workforce Management, 88*(10). 1018–1023.

Frauenheim, E. (2011). Study: Stocks sizzle when staff goals set, but some skeptical. *Workforce Management, 90*(7), 6.

Ghorpade, J. (2000). Managing five paradoxes of 360-degree feedback. *Academy of Management Executive, 14*(1), 140–150.

Greenberg, J. (1986). Determinants of perceived fairness of performance evaluation. *Journal of Applied Psychology, 71,* 340–342.

Hekman, D. R., Aquino, K., Owens, B. P., Mitchell, T. R., Schilpzand, P., & Leavitt, K. (2010). An examination of whether and how racial and gender biases influence customer satisfaction. *Academy of Management Journal, 53,* 238–264.

Henchy, T., & Glass, D. C. (1968). Evaluation apprehension and the social facilitation of dominant and subordinate responses. *Journal of Personality and Social Psychology, 10,* 446–454.

Heneman, R. L., & Wexley, K. N. (1983). The effects of time delay in rating and amount of information observed on performance rating accuracy. *Academy of Management Journal, 26,* 677–686.

HR Focus. (2013a, June). For better reviews, discuss money first, avoid "compliment sandwiches." *HR Focus,* 8–9.

HR Focus. (2013b, November). Job descriptions, performance reviews can make or break ADA case. *HR Focus,* 8–9.

Ilgen, D. R., Barnes-Farrell, J. L., & McKellin, D. B. (1993). Performance appraisal process research in the 1980s: What has it contributed to appraisals in use? *Organizational Behavior and Human Decision Processes, 54,* 321–368.

Ilgen, D. R., & Feldman, J. M. (1983). Performance appraisal: A process focus. In B. M. Staw (Ed.), *Research in organizational behavior, Vol. 2* (pp. 141–197). Greenwich, CT: JAI Press.

Jawahar, I. M., & Williams, C. R. (1997). Where all the children are above average: The performance appraisal purpose effect. *Personnel Psychology, 50,* 905–925.

Klepacki, L. (2012) Focus on: Mystery Shopping: Retailers using data to improve customer service. *Chain Store Age,* November 27. Retrieved June 16, 2014, from http://chainstoreage.com/article/focus-mystery-shopping.

Kluger, A. N., & DeNisi, A. (1996). The effects of feedback interventions on performance: A historical review, a meta-analysis, and a preliminary feedback intervention theory. *Psychological Bulletin, 119,* 254–284.

Korsgaard, M. A., & Roberson, L. (1995). Procedural justice in performance evaluation: The role of instrumental and non-instrumental voice in performance appraisal discussions. *Journal of Management, 21,* 657–669.

Kuvaas, B. (2011). The interactive role of performance appraisal reactions and regular feedback. *Journal of Managerial Psychology, 26,* 123–137.

Kwoh, L. (2012). "Rank and yank" retains vocal fans. *Wall Street Journal – Eastern Edition, 259,* January 31, 24.

Landy, F. J., & Farr, J. L. (1980). Performance rating. *Psychological Bulletin, 87,* 72–107.

Levy, P. E., & Williams, J. R. (2004). The social context of performance appraisal: A review and framework for the future. *Journal of Management, 30,* 881–905.

Liden, R. C., Wayne, S. J., & Stilwell, D. (1993). A longitudinal study on the early development of leader–member exchanges. *Journal of Applied Psychology, 78,* 662–674.

Longenecker, C. O., Sims, H. P., & Gioia, D. A. (1987). Behind the mask: The politics of employee appraisal. *Academy of Management Executive, 1*(3), 183–193.

Luthans, F., & Peterson, S. J. (2003). 360-degree feedback with systematic coaching: Empirical analysis suggests a winning combination. *Human Resource Management, 42,* 243–256.

Mayer, R. C., & Davis, J. H. (1999). The effect of the performance appraisal system on trust for management: A field quasi-experiment. *Journal of Applied Psychology, 84,* 123–136.

McCord, P. (2014, January–February). How Netflix reinvented HR. *Harvard Business Review,* 71–76.

Moore, J. (2014). CFPB, union go back to the drawing board on performance ratings. *Federal News Radio,* May 30.

Murphy, K. R., & Cleveland, J. (1995). *Understanding performance appraisal: Social, organizational, and goal-based perspectives.* Thousand Oaks, CA: Sage.

Olson, E. G. (2013). Microsoft, GE, and the futility of ranking employees. *Fortune,* November 19.

Osborne, T., & McCann, L. A. (2004). Forced ranking and age-related employment discrimination. *Human Rights Magazine, 31,* 6.

People IQ Study. (2005). Performance appraisals are damaging HR's reputation. *PRWeb,* March 16. Retrieved June 16, 2014, from http://www.prweb.com/releases/2005/03/prweb218518.htm.

Peretz, H., & Fried, Y. (2012). National cultures, performance appraisal practices, and organizational absenteeism and turnover: A study across 21 countries. *Journal of Applied Psychology, 97,* 448–459.

Picker Institute Europe. (2013). *Staff survey 2013.* Retrieved June 16, 2014, from http://www.nhsstaffsurveys.com/Page/1010/Home/Staff-Survey-2013/.

Pollock, R. (2014). CFPB misses diversity mark, outside consultant says. *Washington Examiner,* May 22. Retrieved June 16, 2014 from http://washingtonexaminer.com/cfpb-misses-diversity-mark-outside-consultant-says/article/2548746.

Pulakos, E. D., & O'Leary, R. S. (2011). Why is performance management broken? *Industrial and Organizational Psychology, 4,* 146–164.

Pyrillis, R. (2011). The reviews are in. *Workforce Management, 90*(5), 20–22, 24–25.

Robbins, T. L., & DeNisi, A. S. (1998). Mood vs. interpersonal affect: Identifying process and rating distortions in performance appraisal. *Journal of Business and Psychology, 12,* 313–325.

Roch, S. G., Sternburgh, A. M., & Caputo, P. M. (2007). Absolute vs relative performance rating formats: Implications for fairness and organizational justice. *International Journal of Selection and Assessment, 15,* 302–316.

Rubin, R. L. (2014). When "disparate impact" bites back: Is the Consumer Financial Protection Bureau guilty of the same discrimination it polices in the lending world? *Wall Street Journal,* March 9.

Silverman, S. B., & Wexley, K. N. (1984). Reaction of employees to performance appraisal interviews as a function of their participation in rating scale development. *Personnel Psychology, 37,* 703–710.

Smither, J. W., London, M., & Reilly, R. R. (2005). Does performance improve following multisource feedback? A theoretical model, meta-analysis, and review of empirical findings. *Personnel Psychology, 58,* 33–66.

Somers, M. J., & Birnbaum, D. (1991). Assessing self-appraisal of job performance as an evaluation device: Are the poor results a function of method or methodology? *Human Relations, 44,* 1081–1091.

Spence, J. R., & Keeping, L. (2011). Conscious rating distortion in performance appraisal: A review, commentary, and proposed framework for research. *Human Resource Management Review, 21,* 85–95.

Stanton, J. M. (2000). Reactions to employee performance monitoring: Framework, review, and research directions. *Human Performance, 13,* 85–113.

Steelman, L. A., & Rutkowski, K. A. (2004). Moderators of employee reactions to negative feedback. *Journal of Managerial Psychology, 19,* 6–18.

Taggar, S., & Brown, T. C. (2006). Interpersonal affect and peer rating bias in teams. *Small Group Research, 37,* 86–111.

Tate, C. (2013, December). Make SPACE for coaching. *T+D,* 62–63.

Taylor, M. S., Tracy, K. B., Renard, M. K., Harrison, J. K., & Carroll, S. J. (1995). Due process in performance appraisal: A quasi-experiment in procedural justice. *Administrative Science Quarterly, 40,* 495–523.

Tziner, A., & Kopelman, R. E. (2002). Is there a preferred performance rating format? A non-psychometric perspective. *Applied Psychology, 51,* 479–503.

Valle, M., & Bozeman, D. P. (2002). Interrater agreement on employees' job performance: Review and directions. *Psychological Reports, 90,* 975–985.

Villanova, P., Bernardin, H. J., Dahmus, S. A., & Sims, R. L. (1993). Rater leniency and performance appraisal discomfort. *Educational and Psychological Measurement, 53,* 789–799.

Watson, A. M., Behrend, T. S., Thompson, L. F., Rudolph, J. V., Whelan, T. J., & Gissel, A. L. (2013). When big brother is watching: Goal orientation shapes reactions to electronic monitoring during online training. *Journal of Applied Psychology, 98,* 642–657.

Witkowski, R. (2014a). Hensarling probes CFPB on employee complaints, evaluations. *American Banker, 179* (F310).

Witkowski, R. (2014b). CFPB moved slowly to fix evaluation disparities: Lawmakers. *American Banker, 179* (F320).

Woehr, D. J., & Huffcutt, A. I. (1994). Rater training for performance appraisal: A quantitative review. *Journal of Occupational and Organizational Psychology, 67,* 189–205.

Chapter 6

PERSONNEL SELECTION
Tests and Other Selection Procedures

Personnel selection is an important way for organizations to build a competitive workforce, and it is one of the largest areas of I/O practice. In this chapter, you'll learn some of the key predictors used by organizations to select their employees.

After studying this chapter, you should be able to:

- describe the major formats for predictors used in personnel selection
- identify the different personnel selection tests – tests of cognitive abilities, personality, and integrity – discussed in this chapter, including their relative validity, adverse impact, and other practical issues associated with their use
- identify the different types of selection interviews, including their relative validity, adverse impact, and other practical issues associated with their use
- identify the issues associated with the use of work samples, assessment centers, and situational judgment tests

Learning goals for this chapter

- describe the different types of personal history measures (e.g., biodata) and their validity
- identify other measures sometimes used in selection such as physical ability tests and credit history
- identify key legal and global issues surrounding personnel selection, tests, and selection procedures
- describe the current issues and controversies around personnel selection, tests, and selection procedures.

Introduction

If you have ever applied for a job, you have probably taken some sort of personnel selection test or participated in a selection procedure in order to get hired. You may have wondered who developed the procedure and whether it is actually useful in predicting an employee's job performance. In fact, you may have found yourself doubting whether the test could actually predict job performance at all.

As noted in Chapter 1, the systematic use of selection procedures such as tests has been around for the better part of a century, and many of these tests are highly predictive of job performance, either individually or in combination with other predictors. But it might surprise you to learn that there is also quite a bit of science behind the use of personnel selection procedures – in fact, it is probably the area of I/O psychology that has generated the most research of all. Considering that people are an organization's most important resource – their human capital – organizations can give themselves a competitive edge by using the best methods for choosing employees. However, not all employers know about this research and the resulting best practices about selection procedures, and therefore you will likely encounter some selection procedures that are not very good.

Our goal in this chapter and the next is to describe the evidence-based science behind the use of tests and other assessments among job applicants in order to predict their later job performance. You may wonder why we are taking two chapters to explain the science of personnel selection compared to the other topics covered in this book. This is for three reasons. First, personnel selection is the largest area of practice in I/O psychology. A large number of I/O psychologists work to help organizations identify and develop selection procedures to identify the best talent and to make sure they meet professional guidelines. Second are the legal implications of selection: Since the passage of the 1964 Civil Rights Act, personnel selection procedures have been held to a higher level of scrutiny than most other HR practices, and organizations spend a lot of time and resources making sure not only that their selection procedures are valid, but that they meet legal guidelines as well. Third, as we mentioned earlier in this book, a lot of selection research has been conducted since the early part of the twentieth century (Vinchur & Koppes Bryan, 2012), and because of this, selection is one of the most well-developed research areas of I/O psychology – in other words, we know quite a bit about the science of personnel selection.

We also point out that the world of personnel selection is changing rapidly – perhaps more rapidly in the last 15 years than in the last century – due to profound technological changes in the use of selection procedures in organizations (Tippins & Adler, 2011). We will point out this issue throughout both Chapters 6 and 7, and illustrate just how quickly the world of personnel selection is changing, particularly with the introduction of new technologies and analyses.

Key Terminology

Before we jump into the topic of personnel selection, it is important to point out a few key terms. We start with the term **personnel selection procedures**. This term, as well as the term "predictors", refers to a wide range of instruments that organizations can use to predict job performance. This includes not only tests of cognitive ability, personality, and other individual differences, but other types of assessments such as integrity tests, job interviews, assessment centers, and simulations. In other words, "personnel selection procedure" and "predictor" are the umbrella terms for the range of assessments used to hire people. We use the term "validity" in this chapter when describing different selection procedures. (We cover validity in greater detail in Chapters 2 and 7.) Generally this is used in referring to the validity coefficient, based on criterion-related validity. It is the degree of relationship, expressed as a correlation, that is found between the predictor and the job performance criterion (see Chapter 4). So for example, if we were to say that the validity of a selection procedure is .40, that would mean that the procedure is correlated .40 with the job performance criterion. Finally, note that a basic assumption of personnel selection is to assess individual differences – as assessed by a test or an interview, for example – to see if these individual differences can be used to predict an employee's job performance. These individual differences are generally identified through a job analysis (see Chapter 3).

Personnel selection procedures: A wide range of instruments that organizations can use to predict job performance. This includes tests and other types of assessments such as job interviews, assessment centers, and simulations.

Major changes are taking place in the world of personnel selection. For example, PepsiCo launched a mobile-optimized career site allowing applicants to apply for jobs using their mobile devices (Zielinksi, 2014).

Formats of Different Personnel Selection Procedures

Paper-and-pencil tests: Tests that are administered to job applicants in paper format.

Unproctored Internet testing: When tests are administered online so that a person might take the test at home or at some location away from a representative of the organization.

Individually administered selection procedures: Procedures administered to one applicant at a time (e.g., most interviews).

Group administered procedures: Selection procedures given to large groups of applicants at one time (e.g., many paper-and-pencil tests).

Speed tests: Tests which require the test-taker to work as quickly as possible and within a short period of time.

Power tests: Tests which let respondents go at their own pace, with no consideration for how quickly an applicant can answer the questions.

Cognitive tests: Tests measuring an applicant's general cognitive ability (general intelligence) or a specific cognitive ability (e.g., mechanical ability).

Non-cognitive tests: Tests such as personality, which tap individual differences that are not related to cognitive skills.

There are a number of formats that personnel selection procedures can take. Here we discuss the most common formats and differentiate among them. Some selection procedures have been referred to as **paper-and-pencil tests**, because they are literally tests that are administered to job applicants on paper and their responses are made using pencil so that answers may be scored easily. Many of these use a multiple-choice format. Note that, however, many tests that were traditionally administered via a paper-and-pencil format are now administered online over the Internet or at an individual computer or kiosk. In fact, when tests are administered online, so that a person might take the test at home or at some location away from a representative of the organization, this is called **unproctored Internet testing** (Tippins, 2009). We will also discuss the issues and controversies surrounding unproctored Internet testing later in the chapter.

Some selection procedures are **individually administered** such as the most common selection procedure, the employment interview. Note, however, that such individually administered selection procedures may be given live, with an interaction between the job applicant and the interviewer, or over the telephone or the Internet. In comparison, some selection procedures are **group administered** tests, given to large groups of applicants at one time (like many paper-and-pencil tests.)

It's useful to point out some additional differences between personnel selection tests. Some tests may be **speed tests**, which require the test-taker to work as quickly as possible and within a short period of time. Usually, the idea is to see how well the person can answer the questions and also how quickly they do so. For example, tests that require the test-taker to check clerical data quickly are speed tests. Typically, most applicants do not finish a speed test, the idea being that only exceptional applicants are able to do so. In contrast, **power tests** let respondents go at their own pace, with no consideration for how quickly an applicant can answer the questions. Note that this format is typical of traditional personality tests. Finally, another key term that is used to describe selection tests is whether they are **cognitive tests** or **non-cognitive tests**. Cognitive tests are just what they sound like: they measure an applicant's general cognitive ability (general intelligence, or *g* as it is sometimes referred to) or specific cognitive ability (e.g., mechanical ability). Non-cognitive tests would include tests of personality, which tap individual differences that are not related to cognitive skills.

One important issue in describing selection procedures is to differentiate between selection *methods* versus the *constructs* or KSAOs that are being measured (Arthur & Villado, 2008). For example, the job interview is a selection method. But depending on what questions are asked, different interviews measure different psychological constructs. Here we provide an example of two retail sales companies hiring people for the job of salesperson. Company A might focus their interview on job knowledge, while Company B might focus on interpersonal skills (see Figure 6.1). Both companies would be using an interview to hire, but the two interviews would be assessing different KSAOs. Our point is that while it is useful to discuss "the validity" of a particular

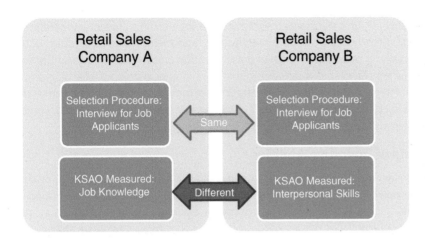

Figure 6.1
Example of two retail companies using the same selection method, but measuring different KSAOs.

selection procedure, it is also important to remember that validity may depend not only on what selection method is used, but also on what the method is measuring.

Personnel Selection Procedures

As you might have guessed, there are many different types of selection procedures that can be used to hire employees. In this section, we review the main procedures that have emerged in selection practice and the relative validity of each in terms of predicting later job performance. In addition, there are two other factors that we should mention as we discuss each selection procedure. First are the practical issues around using these various selection procedures. This might include the selection procedure's **utility** or the dollar value of using a selection procedure, which is largely determined by the procedure's validity, the cost of using it, and the benefit it provides to the organization in terms of improved performance of workers (see Chapter 7 for further discussion). Second, we will discuss one of the key factors that goes into deciding whether or not to use a selection procedure, namely, **adverse impact**. Adverse impact is the degree to which there are mean differences in the performance of different subgroups (e.g., ethnic groups, men vs. women) on a selection procedure. We will discuss this important issue in greater detail when we discuss legal and ethical issues in Chapter 7, but for now we point out that adverse impact is a major concern to most employers, and one that largely determines whether or not they are willing to use a given selection procedure, as it affects the diversity of their workforce and the likelihood of successfully defending selection procedures during potential litigation (Gatewood, Feild, & Barrick, 2011).

It is important to keep in mind that no single selection procedure is perfect at selecting employees for a given job. Rather, some combination of selection procedures (e.g., a personality test and integrity test, followed up with an interview) is typically used for hiring employees, each of which predicts some unique aspect of performance (e.g., Schmidt & Hunter 1998). For example, when hiring retail

Utility: The dollar value of using a selection procedure, which is largely determined by the procedure's validity, the cost of using it, and the benefit it provides to the organization in terms of improved performance of workers.

Adverse impact: The degree to which there are mean differences in the performance of different subgroups (e.g., ethnic groups, men vs. women) on a selection procedure.

salespeople, an organization might measure the person's product knowledge with a test, their honesty with an integrity test, and their interpersonal skills with an interview. In other words, each of these selection procedures would measure some important KSAO that is relevant to the job. Together, a group of selection procedures, referred to as a **battery of selection procedures** or **test battery**, can be used to predict job performance. We will talk in greater detail about how best to combine the results from different selection procedures in Chapter 7.

Tests of Cognitive Abilities

Battery of selection procedures (test battery): A group of selection procedures that can be used together to predict job performance.

Cognitive abilities are related to a person's ability to "perceive, process, evaluate, compare, create, understand, manipulate, or generally think about information and ideas" (Guion, 1998, p. 124). Tests of cognitive abilities have a long history in industrial psychology. This rich line of research shows that **general cognitive ability** (which psychologists consider to include reasoning, symbolic representation, and problem solving; Sternberg & Detterman, 1986) is one of the best predictors of performance across jobs. Tests of cognitive ability – both general cognitive ability (known as g) and more specific cognitive abilities, such as mechanical ability and clerical ability - are reasonably inexpensive for organizations to use. That is good news. The challenge, however, is that tests of g in particular have been shown to have adverse impact (see Chapter 7) against minority groups (Ones, Dilchert, & Viswesvaran, 2012). That is, although there is considerable overlap between different ethnic groups on tests of cognitive ability, the group mean test scores for Blacks and Hispanics tend to be lower than the mean score for Whites (with similar mean scores for White and Asian groups; Roth, Bevier, Bobko, Switzer, & Tyler, 2001). That in itself makes some employers concerned about using cognitive ability tests for making hiring decisions, for both legal reasons and for reasons of fairness and organizational diversity (Ones et al., 2012; Ryan & Powers, 2012). While this is a concern for many industrial psychologists too, there is also disagreement among I/O psychologists, with some arguing that organizations should not be so quick to dismiss an inexpensive selection tool that is also valid as a predictor of job performance. In this section we will highlight some of the key issues in the use of cognitive ability tests.

General cognitive ability: Includes reasoning, symbolic representation, and problem solving.

General Cognitive Ability (g)

In a classic paper published near the start of the twentieth century, Spearman (1904) differentiated between g and other specific abilities such as verbal and numerical reasoning. The idea is that although g and these specific abilities are separate, they are correlated, since g allows the person to develop these specific abilities depending on opportunities and interests (Ones et al., 2012). This aspect of g – its relationship with a person's knowledge acquisition both in training (e.g., Hunter, 1986) and on the job (Kuncel, Hezlet, & Ones, 2004) – is perhaps the main reason that g is such a good predictor of job performance: It allows workers to learn their job more quickly. G is also a particularly good predictor of core task performance (see Chapter 4) compared with contextual performance (Ones et al., 2012). One interesting finding is that although g is a good predictor of performance across all jobs, it is an especially good predictor of job performance for complex jobs (Schmidt & Hunter, 2004): In other words, g has an especially high correlation with job performance for complex jobs, which makes sense, given that *g* relates to a person's knowledge acquisition. This also may be because *g* is associated with a person's abilities to perform tasks, especially complex tasks (Ones et al., 2012). Moreover, similar results about *g* and job performance seem to be found outside of the US: Salgado et al. (2003) found in a meta-analysis of European studies that *g* is a consistent predictor of performance across a wide range of jobs, and that job complexity moderates the relationship between *g* and job performance. In short, numerous meta-analyses have shown that *g* is a good predictor of job performance (e.g., .51; Schmidt & Hunter, 1998), and it has been cited as one of the best predictors of job performance (Ones et al., 2012). One interesting finding is that *g* also seems to be increasing with each successive generation (Flynn, 1999).

One example of a frequently used cognitive ability test in personnel selection is the Wonderlic Personnel Test (WPT). The WPT is a 50-item test that is administered in 12 minutes, making it a convenient, quick way to assess cognitive ability. The assumption is that most candidates will not finish the test. The item types include verbal and numerical reasoning as well as spatial relations and number series. Research shows that the WPT primarily measures verbal comprehension, followed by deduction and numerical fluency (Guion 1965). The items are arranged in order of difficulty, with the easy items towards the beginning, and the difficult items towards the end. The WPT also has a long history (it was developed in the 1930s), and it therefore has extensive norms for different jobs. It is available in numerous languages (Plake & Impara, 2001).

With this good news about the validity of tests of *g* and their ease of use in personnel selection, the challenge is their adverse impact. Specifically, the mean test scores for Blacks and Hispanics are lower than for Whites. (It is also important to note that there is considerable variability within each ethnic group. There is also considerable overlap in the scores of different ethnic groups.) In any case, because of these mean differences, an overreliance on tests of *g* can lead to less diversity in organizations and fewer opportunities for some groups, and the potential for litigation if the test has not been validated (Gatewood et al., 2011). Importantly, differences between ethnic groups on actual job performance are often less than the differences on tests

Paper is to scissors as wood is to
a. knife
*b. saw
c. scissors
d. screwdriver

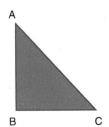

In the triangle, angles A and C are each 45 degrees. What is the size of angle B?
a. 30 degrees
b. 45 degrees
*c. 90 degrees
d. There isn't enough information.

Figure 6.2 Sample cognitive ability items. (Correct choices are indicated with an asterisk.)

of *g* (Sackett & Wilk, 1994). In other words, these ethnic differences in mean *g* test scores do not always translate into differences in job performance measures. Plus, these mean differences in tests of *g* also may reflect the fact that many of these tests focus a good bit on acquired skill (such as math and vocabulary; Schmidt, 2002).

Of course, one would never suggest using *g* as the sole predictor without, say, an interview: Cognitive ability presents only one part of the picture of how good a potential employee may be. One suggestion is that to reduce this adverse impact of *g* tests, organizations can decide to use *g* in their selection decisions in combination with other predictors that are low in adverse impact (e.g., Chernyshenko, Stark, & Drasgow, 2011; Lievens, Buyse, & Sackett, 2005) such as personality tests. Still, the adverse impact issue has certainly led many organizations to avoid the use of cognitive ability tests altogether.

Gatewood et al. (2011) provide an excellent summary surrounding the dilemma of whether to use tests of *g* in making personnel decisions, making two key points:

> The first is that the evidence shows that these tests are among the most valid of all selection tests for a large number of jobs (some selection specialists would say for all jobs). The second factor is the evidence that these tests exhibit adverse impact; that is, mean differences in test scores among demographic groups. (p. 487)

We concur with this summary of the dilemma faced by organizations considering the use of tests of *g*, which may also explain why so many organizations have chosen to use personality tests in selection because of their relatively low adverse impact. We discuss these personality tests in a following section.

Tests of Specific Cognitive Abilities

Specific cognitive ability tests: Tests that do not assess *g* but instead assess specific dimensions such as mechanical ability and/ or clerical speed and accuracy.

In addition to tests of *g*, tests of **specific cognitive abilities**, such as tests of mechanical ability and tests of clerical speed and accuracy, have also been developed for use in personnel selection. While we differentiate these tests of specific cognitive abilities from tests of *g* for simplicity's sake, we should note that they are not measuring entirely separate constructs: These measures of specific abilities generally are correlated with measures of *g*, presumably because a person's general cognitive ability allows them the capacity to develop these specific abilities (Ones et al., 2012). We provide two classic examples here. First, the *Bennett Mechanical Comprehension* test is perhaps one of the best-known tests of mechanical ability, having been around for decades (Gatewood et al., 2011). The test items provide a number of pictures of mechanical equipment such as gears, pulleys, and airplanes, and ask the respondent to answer questions about which way the pulley or gear would turn under various circumstances. (See Figure 6.3.) Tests of mechanical ability can be used for hiring people for jobs such as skilled trades, mechanics, or equipment operators.

A second example of a specific cognitive ability test is tests of clerical ability. There are a number of clerical ability tests available. The item format for most of these tests is to ask the test-taker to mark items that are different from each other. (See example in Figure 6.4.) The test-taker must quickly look at the items and report whether they are alike or different. As we mentioned earlier, most clerical ability tests are speed tests: They are timed, and the score is determined by how

If the smallest gear turns counterclockwise, which way will the largest gear turn?
*a. Counterclockwise
b. Clockwise
c. There isn't enough information provided.

Figure 6.3 Sample mechanical ability item. (Correct choice is indicated with an asterisk.)

many items the respondent completes as well as how many they get wrong. Tests of clerical ability are often used for hiring people for jobs such as office or clerical workers.

Instructions: Please put a check in the blank between the letter/number strings that are the same.

325B78	_____	325878
87t559	_____	87t559
44rt57	_____	44rt57
L521c	_____	L521e

Figure 6.4 Sample item from a clerical ability test.

Psychomotor Tests

There are also **psychomotor tests** which assess dexterity and/or coordination (Guion, 1998) and may require agility and dexterous movements of one's fingers, hands, or body. These might require that the test-taker insert pegs into boards or that they correctly use simple tools. Given the range of possible abilities assessed by these tests, it is important that the particular psychomotor skills assessed by the test match the job – in other words, it is important to do a job analysis before deciding whether to use a psychomotor test for selection, and which type of psychomotor skills are needed for the job (Guion).

Psychomotor tests: Tests which assess dexterity and/or coordination and which may require agility and dexterous movements of the fingers, hands, or body.

Personality Tests

Personality tests are one of the most frequently administered personnel selection methods today, used to select workers for a wide range of job types, from workers in large retail chains to corporate executives. Despite their popularity, it was not so long ago that I/O psychologists had largely dismissed the use of personality tests as having fairly low validity for selection (Barrick & Mount, 2012). In this section we will explain why personality assessments have become so popular over the last

20 years, which personality dimensions are the most effective predictors of job performance, how to increase the validity of personality tests, and the controversies and questions surrounding the use of personality tests in selection.

Before we begin this discussion, it is important to point out that personality itself is best viewed as a construct or system of individual differences, *not as a specific selection method or test*. In other words, we will talk about the various personality dimensions (e.g., conscientiousness, proactivity) and what the research has shown is their relationship to performance criteria. However, it is important to keep in mind that there are many personality tests available, such as the NEO (McCrae & Costa, 1987) and IPIP (Goldberg, 1999).

Background

Personality tests have been used for many years to select workers, as far back as World War I for use among army recruits (Barrick & Mount, 2012). However, many of the dominant tests since the 1940s such as the Minnesota Multiphasic Personality Inventory (MMPI) focused on clinical diagnosis and often included dimensions like "schizophrenia" or "paranoia" because they had been developed on psychiatric populations, not the normal adult population. (Note that these tests that were developed for clinical diagnosis, while generally illegal for most selection decisions today, are considered acceptable for high-risk jobs such as police officers or juvenile probation officers.) Because these personality tests were developed for a specific use (clinical diagnosis) somewhat different from uses that I/O psychologists would be most interested in (hiring employees), they were generally found to be weak predictors of job performance. In fact, at one time, the general conclusion about *all* personality tests was that they were very weak predictors of job performance. As stated by Guion and Gottier (1965), "In brief, it is difficult in the face of this summary to advocate, with a clear conscience, the use of personality measures in most situations as a basis for making employment decisions about people."

Five-Factor Model (FFM) or "Big Five" personality: A personality framework that focuses on normal adult personality and includes the five personality dimensions of openness to experience, conscientiousness, extraversion, agreeableness, and neuroticism.

Fast forward to 1991. In that year, Barrick and Mount published their groundbreaking meta-analysis on the relationship between the **Five-Factor Model** (FFM) or "Big Five" personality dimensions and job performance. Rather than focusing on abnormal personality, the FFM focuses on normal adult personality and includes the five personality dimensions of openness to experience (e.g., interested in learning; cultured), conscientiousness (e.g., achievement-oriented; detail-oriented; dependable), extraversion (e.g., sociable), agreeableness (e.g., compliant; kind), and neuroticism (e.g., anxious; easily upset) or, put positively, emotional stability (Barrick & Mount, 2012). (To help remember the names of the Big Five, think of "OCEAN". See Figure 6.5.)

Barrick and Mount (1991) found that in fact these Big Five personality dimensions are related to a number of job performance outcomes. For example, conscientiousness was the best predictor of performance across all jobs, extraversion was a good predictor of sales and management jobs, and openness to experience was a good predictor of performance in training. Table 6.1 provides some examples of Big Five items from the International Personality Item Pool (IPIP; Goldberg, 1999), one of the many tests of the Big Five that's available.

Why did the FFM catch on so quickly as an approach to selection? One factor is that although the validities of the Big Five are fairly modest (Morgeson et al., 2007), these tests are relatively inexpensive. But more important to many employers is the fact that

	Openness to Experience Includes being interested in learning and culture. A predictor of success in training.
	**Conscientiousness** Includes dimensions such as achievement-orientation, detail-orientation, and dependability. Conscientiousness is the most consistent of the Big Five in predicting performance across all jobs.
	**Extraversion** Includes being sociable, assertive, and friendly. A good predictor of performance for sales and management jobs, and also relates to training performance.
	**Agreeableness** Includes being compliant, kind, and sympathetic to others.
	**Neuroticism** Includes being anxious or easily upset. May only affect job performance if at high levels.

Figure 6.5 The "Big Five" personality dimensions.

personality tests generally show low adverse impact against protected groups (Foldes, Duehr, & Ones, 2008), especially when compared with tests of general cognitive ability. That factor alone has made personality tests very attractive to many employers.

Given this increased use of personality tests in selection, it would be good to think about why personality predicts job performance. First, personality seems to be related to most aspects of job performance, but particularly to organizational citizenship behaviors (e.g., helping coworkers; see Chapter 4) and counterproductive work behavior (e.g., arguing with others; see Chapter 4) (Ones, Dilchert, Viswesvaran, & Judge, 2007). In addition, dimensions such as conscientiousness seem to be related to work motivation, which in turn relates to job performance (Barrick, Stewart, & Piotrowski, 2002). Finally, although much of the personality research has been done in North America, research out of Europe suggests that personality measures show a similar pattern of relationships with job performance in European countries as well – an important plus for global organizations (Salgado, 1997).

The use of personality testing has grown over the last 20 years for selecting a broad range of jobs. The NFL recently had a test developed for the selection of football players, which measures a number of personality-related dimensions such as competitiveness, motivation, and learning styles (Battista, 2013; Glauber, 2014).

Table 6.1 Sample Big Five items (Goldberg, 1999)

Here are some phrases describing people's behaviors. Please use the rating scale below to describe how accurately each statement describes **you**. Describe yourself as you generally are now, not as you wish to be in the future. Describe yourself as you honestly see yourself, in relation to other people you know of the same sex as you, and roughly your same age.

Response Options

1: Very Inaccurate
2: Moderately Inaccurate
3: Neither Inaccurate nor Accurate
4: Moderately Accurate
5: Very Accurate

Extraversion

Am the life of the party.
Feel comfortable around people.
Start conversations.
Talk to a lot of different people at parties.
Don't mind being the center of attention.

Agreeableness

Am interested in people.
Sympathize with others' feelings.
Have a soft heart.
Take time out for others.
Make people feel at ease.

Conscientiousness

Am always prepared.
Pay attention to details.
Like order.
Follow a schedule.
Am exacting in my work.

Neuroticism
Get stressed out easily.
Worry about things.
Get upset easily.
Change my mood a lot.
Get irritated easily.

Openness to Experience (Intellect)
Have a rich vocabulary.
Have a vivid imagination.
Have excellent ideas.
Spend time reflecting on things.
Am full of ideas.

Source: International Personality Item Pool: A Scientific Collaboratory for the Development of Advanced Measures of Personality Traits and Other Individual Differences (http://ipip.ori.org/).

Issues Associated with the Use of Personality Tests

Over the years a number of issues have emerged in the I/O psychology research on Big Five personality that are relevant to its validity for predicting who will be the best employees. We will focus here on four of the most important issues: An "at work" frame of reference, the use of subtraits or facets of the Big Five, faking, and looking for the optimal level of personality to fit the job.

First, one of the simple ways to increase the validity of personality tests is through providing an "at work" frame of reference to test-takers, which increases the test's validity. An "at work" frame of reference means that if you simply tell test-takers to "think about how you are or behave at work," or if you add the phrase "at work" to each test item, it increases the validity of the test. For example, one study found that simply asking airline ticket-counter employees to think about how they are at work while completing a Big Five test increased the test's validity in terms of explaining job performance (Hunthausen, Truxillo, Bauer, & Hammer, 2003). One explanation why an "at work" frame of reference increases personality test validity is that people tend to behave somewhat differently in different contexts – at home, at work, and among friends. Providing a context lets test-takers know which context they should be thinking about when they respond to questions, and it also seems to better align the test questions with the criterion we want to predict, *performance at work* (Lievens, De Corte, & Schollaert, 2008). A meta-analysis confirmed this frame of reference effect (Shaffer & Postlethwaite, 2012), and it is now generally accepted that using an "at work" frame of reference increases the predictive validity of personality tests used for personnel selection.

Second, there has been an increased focus on the use of "subtraits" or facets within the Big Five, and a realization that these facets may better predict some performance criteria than the broad factors. Here is some background: Each of the broad Big Five factors is actually made up of several "subtraits". For example, the conscientiousness factor actually includes the subtraits of "achievement-striving" and "orderliness." While orderliness may certainly be important to certain types of jobs, achievement is probably more important to the prediction of

Figure 6.6 The facets of conscientiousness (Costa & McRae, 2008). Orderliness and achievement-striving are two of the facets that make up the factor of conscientiousness. Which of these two facets do you think predicts job performance for most jobs? For what kinds of jobs do you think that orderliness would be important?

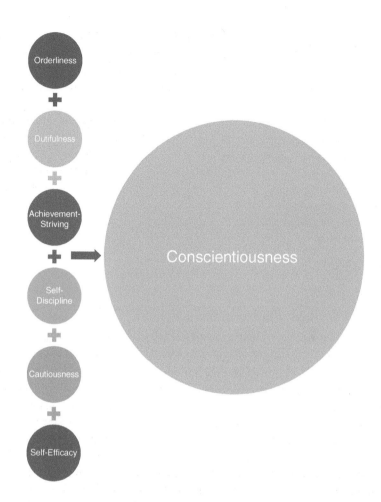

job performance in most jobs (Oswald & Hough, 2011). The point here is that researchers and practitioners are beginning to understand that greater prediction of job performance may be achieved by looking at the specific subtraits within the Big Five dimensions.

Third, one very active research area regarding the use of personality tests is a concern with applicant faking on personality tests. The idea is that some applicants may be able to fake their scores. As a results, a substantial body of research has examined ways to "catch" or control faking, including warning test-takers about faking (e.g., Fan et al., 2012; Landers, Sackett, & Tuzinski, 2011), the use of eye-track technology (where the eye movements of the test-taker can be tracked; van Hooft & Born, 2012), and the use of forced choice items (e.g., Converse et al., 2010; Heggestad, Morrison, Reeve, & McCoy, 2006), where the respondent has to choose among seemingly equally desirable alternatives. However, although faking may affect the relative scores of individual applicants (that is, how well applicants score relative to each other), the research suggests that over thousands of selection decisions in a large company, faking has minimal effects on validity (e.g., Hogan, Barrett, & Hogan, 2007). Further, it may be that applicants who fake better understand what is expected of them on the job – a good thing. Finally, Marcus (2009) proposes that the whole concept of "faking" should be reconceptualized from the applicant's perspective, namely, that the applicant is interested mostly in positive self-presentation and that this behavior on the part of applicants should not necessarily be considered a bad thing.

Fourth, some researchers have begun to question whether there is a simple linear relationship between personality and job performance. For example, we have generally assumed that conscientiousness is a good thing, and that more of it is better. But this may not be the case. More of a generally good personality trait such as conscientiousness may not always mean better performance; a person may at some point be *too* conscientious. A recent study suggests that there may be optimal levels of personality traits such as conscientiousness and that more is not always better (Carter et al., 2014).

Other Personality Constructs

In addition to the Big Five, a number of other personality traits have emerged as being of interest to selection research and practice. First is **proactive personality**. Proactive personality involves the tendency to recognize and act on opportunities in the environment (Bateman & Crant, 1993) and is an active research topic in many areas of I/O psychology. Regarding selection, proactive personality has been shown to relate to job performance. For example, Crant (1995) found that proactive personality predicted the sales performance of real estate agents. It also predicted performance over and above conscientiousness and extraversion, suggesting that proactive personality is different from these other personality traits. Another personality trait is the characteristic of **adaptability**, or a person's tendency to adjust themselves to new situations (Ployhart & Bliese, 2006) and which includes several dimensions such as learning adaptability, interpersonal adaptability, and cultural adaptability. Although adaptive behaviors have been an important performance criterion for several years (e.g., Baard, Rench, & Kozlowski, 2014; Pulakos, Arad, Donovan, & Plamondon, 2000; see Chapter 4), it has received less research as a personality trait (for an exception, see Wang, Zhan, McCune, & Truxillo, 2011), and there are relatively few studies that have tied adaptability as a personality trait to job performance (e.g., Cullen, Edwards, Casper, & Gue, 2014). Given that work in the twenty-first century will continue to change, we anticipate that adaptability will be needed by many workers, and we expect that research on adaptability as a predictor of job performance will continue to grow.

Third, a topic related to personality has been an interest among researchers and the popular press in tests focused on **emotional intelligence** (EI). EI is defined by some researchers as more of a cognitive social skill. Others have focused on EI as a non-cognitive (personality-like) trait (Joseph & Newman, 2010; Van Rooy, Viswesvaran, & Pluta, 2005). Despite EI's intuitive appeal, there has been some question as to whether EI is different from existing measures of personality and cognitive ability. Specifically, some researchers have questioned whether EI predicts job performance over and above cognitive and personality measures (Christiansen, Janovics, & Siers, 2010). One possibility is that EI is a good predictor only for jobs

Proactive personality: The tendency to recognize and act on opportunities in the environment.

Adaptability: The tendency to adjust to new situations and which includes learning adaptability, interpersonal adaptability, and cultural adaptability.

Emotional intelligence (EI): EI is defined by some researchers as more of a cognitive social skill, whereas others have focused on its non-cognitive (personality-like) properties. Used to predict social skills at work.

that require a good bit of "emotional labor" where one's true emotions and the emotions required on the job do not necessarily match (Joseph & Newman, 2010).

Fourth, Judge and colleagues (e.g., Judge, Erez, Bono, & Thoresen, 2003) have produced a series of studies developing the construct of **core self-evaluations** (CSE). CSE is made up of a combination of four traits: self-esteem, locus of control, self-efficacy, and neuroticism. CSE is described as the "bottom-line evaluations that people make of themselves" (Barrick & Mount, 2012). Judge (2009) points to evidence that CSE predicts job performance, and perhaps better than each of these individual difference variables by themselves. Finally, we point out that some researchers believe that there is actually a sixth dimension to the Big Five, which most people call "honesty/humility" and which includes sincerity, fairness, and lack of greed (Ashton & Lee, 2007). This model is referred to as the "HEXACO" model of personality (Honesty/Humility (H), Emotionality (E), Extraversion (X), Agreeableness (A), Conscientiousness (C), and Openness (O)). However, the issue of whether there actually is a sixth factor to the Big Five is far from settled.

Core self-evaluations (CSE): A combination of self-esteem, locus of control, self-efficacy, and neuroticism.

Integrity Tests

Integrity tests: Tests developed to predict a number of negative and counterproductive employee behaviors such as theft, malingering, drug use, and aggression.

Another category of selection procedures is **integrity tests**, or tests developed to predict a number of negative and counterproductive employee behaviors such as theft, malingering, drug use, and aggression. The popularity of integrity tests has grown in recent decades and stems from the outlawing of polygraph or lie detector tests in the 1980s, which up to that time had been used to predict these negative employee behaviors. Since then, the use of self-report integrity tests has increased as a method for predicting a number of negative employee behaviors.

There are two main types of integrity tests. *Overt integrity tests* directly ask the test-taker about issues like their theft, illegal drug use, or fighting. In contrast, *personality-based integrity tests* focus on predicting negative work behaviors by means of personality-type questions whose purpose may not be obvious to the test-taker. Examples of both types of items are shown in Table 6.2. From the standpoint of Big Five personality, these personality-based integrity tests are generally

Table 6.2 Examples of integrity test items

Personality-Based (Covert) Integrity Test Items

I work quickly rather than paying attention to rules and details.

I look for excitement and thrills at work.

I prefer to get along with other people [reverse scored].

Overt Integrity Test Items

I would hit someone if they insulted me.

I have used marijuana while at work.

I would call in sick if I didn't feel like coming to work that day.

a function of the Big Five personality factors of conscientiousness, agreeableness, and neuroticism (Sackett & Wanek, 1996). In addition, recall the HEXACO personality framework which has six personality factors including honesty/humility. Research has shown that the validity of overt integrity tests may be best explained by the Big Five personality framework, but the validity of personality-based integrity tests may be best explained by honesty/humility from the HEXACO framework (Marcus, Lee, & Ashton, 2007).

The literature generally does support the use of integrity tests for personnel selection. In their large meta-analytic study, Ones, Viswesvaran, and Schmidt (1993) concluded that integrity tests are good predictors of performance, with an average validity of .47 for predicting counterproductive work behaviors such as theft, absenteeism, tardiness, and violence. Moreover, meta-analyses have found that integrity tests can complement the use of cognitive tests in predicting job performance, in other words, that using a combination of cognitive tests and integrity tests together predicts job performance well, and for a range of job types (Ones et al., 1993; Schmidt & Hunter, 1998). Another study of a large dataset with over 700,000 applicants also found that integrity tests have relatively low adverse impact against ethnic minorities (Ones & Viswesvaran, 1998).

Workplace Application

The Use of Integrity Tests in Employment

The use of integrity tests in personnel selection has continued in recent decades. Integrity tests are particularly attractive to employers in certain industries such as retail sales where theft is a big problem. In addition, the validity of integrity tests is generally considered acceptable. This is especially in comparison to other personal history types of questions thought to predict counterproductive work behavior such as credit scores and

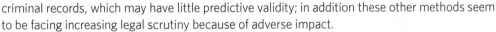

criminal records, which may have little predictive validity; in addition these other methods seem to be facing increasing legal scrutiny because of adverse impact.

The outcomes said to be predicted by integrity tests include shrinkage (lost inventory) and workers' compensation claims. For example, one published study reported a statistically significant decrease in workers' compensation claims at a large hotel chain after adoption of an integrity test as part of the hiring process (Sturman & Sherwyn, 2009).

Integrity tests are certainly not without their critics. Some people note that the test may weed out people who are not necessarily high-risk. And as noted in the text, some studies have also suggested that the validity of integrity tests may not be as high as some test publishers have reported. At the same time, integrity tests do appear to be sufficiently valid and have low adverse impact, providing additional information for employers in making hiring decisions.

Sources: Roberts, 2011; Sturman & Sherwyn, 2009.

Validating integrity tests may require some consideration of criteria that are not always measured by employers or that may not be readily available, particularly theft. (In other words, it can be difficult to detect that theft is occurring, much less to know which employees are responsible.) However, the good news is that research has shown that integrity tests are predictive of overall work performance as well. For example, Ones and Viswesvaran (2001) found that for predicting supervisory ratings of performance, the predictive validity of integrity tests was higher (.41) than that of personality tests. Moreover, reviews of the literature have consistently shown that integrity tests predict non-theft counterproductive work behavior well (Berry, Sackett, & Wiemann, 2007). Finally, there is a concern that integrity test items may be susceptible to faking and response distortion, and research continues apace on ways to detect and reduce faking on these tests (Berry et al., 2007)

Recently a meta-analysis by Van Iddekinge, Roth, Raymark, and Odle-Dusseau (2012) challenged the validity of integrity tests, noting that they predicted relatively small portions of the variance in job performance. However, Ones et al. (2012) argued that the list of studies used in the Van Iddekinge et al. paper was not sufficiently comprehensive and included measures that were not actually integrity tests; thus, Ones et al. concluded that in fact the many studies conducted thus far on integrity tests support their validity for personnel selection. In commenting on these two papers, Sackett and Schmitt (2012) concluded that integrity tests probably are sufficiently valid for predicting important outcomes, but that more research is needed.

In summary, integrity tests appear to provide a useful tool for employers, predicting not only overall job performance but also a number of negative work outcomes. Moreover, they appear to have relatively low adverse impact and appear to be considered legally defensible (Berry et al., 2007). And they have been found to be valid in countries besides the US, such as Argentina, Mexico, and South Africa (Fortmann, Leslie, & Cunningham, 2002), and in Canada and Germany (Marcus et al., 2007). More research is needed to understand differences among different types of integrity tests in terms of what they measure and for which jobs and which performance dimensions they are most valid.

Employee theft is a serious concern in the retail industry, where 1 out of 40 employees were apprehended in the largest 23 retailers in the USA (Jack L. Hayes International, 2013), with an average of over $700 lost per dishonest employee. Companies attempt to prevent this from happening by using pre-employment honesty tests, background checks, and reference checks.

Online selection interviews are becoming the norm in many organizations. Many employers have the capability for interviews to be video recorded, to be later viewed by managers on their mobile devices (Zielinski, 2014). What do you see as the advantages and disadvantages of managers watching interviews on their mobile devices?

Interviews

Undoubtedly, the interview is the most frequently used personnel selection procedure, used by both small and large employers. In fact, it is hard to imagine making a selection decision without an interview of some sort. Because the interview is so commonplace, there has been quite a bit of research on how to make interviews more predictive of performance – the field of I/O psychology has a lot of good recommendations for improving the quality of interviews. In addition, many of these recommendations can be easily adopted by even the smallest employer.

The selection interview serves many purposes besides allowing the organization to decide whether or not the applicant has the needed KSAs. The interview also allows the job applicant to learn more about the organization and whether or not the job and organization fit their needs and interests (Dipboye, Macan, & Shahani-Denning, 2012). Accordingly, the interview can also help the interviewer to "sell" the job and the organization to the applicant, as well as providing a **realistic job preview** (RJP) to the applicant about what the job is like, both good and bad. Interviews are traditionally and most commonly done face-to-face, although they can also be carried out by other means such as online and by telephone.

Keep in mind that, as we noted earlier, the interview is really a selection method, and the content of the interview can vary substantially from job to job. Basically the interview is an interpersonal interaction between a job candidate and one or more company representatives/interviewers, in which the goal is to learn whether the job applicant has the appropriate KSAs to match the job.

We will begin by discussing the different types of interviews and their relative validity. Next we'll discuss factors that can make the interview more valid and provide some examples of interview materials. Finally, we will share current research on the interview.

Unstructured vs. Structured Interviews

For many years, the available research on the selection interview was not positive. Despite the frequent use of the interview in selection, it was generally concluded that it had low predictive validity (Arvey & Campion, 1982). Part of the problem

Realistic job preview (RJP): A preview to the applicant about what the job is like, both good and bad. It can be provided in a number of ways such as through part of a job interview.

Unstructured interview: Interview that is like a casual conversation between the interviewer and the job applicant. Different applicants can be asked very different questions, and the questions are often not job-related.

Structured interview:
An interview process where job applicants are all asked the same job-related questions.

Situational interview:
A type of structured interview where applicants are asked job-related questions about hypothetical situations.

Behavioral interview:
A type of structured interview where applicants are asked job-related questions about a past experience that the applicant has had.

was that most interviews were **unstructured interviews**, or interviews that were like a casual conversation between the interviewer and the job applicant. This meant that different applicants could be asked very different questions, and that the questions were often not job-related.

However, this changed considerably with the introduction of the **structured interview**, where job applicants are all asked the same job-related questions. Two specific types of structured interview were introduced in the 1980s and have remained the dominant type of structured interview up until today. First, the **situational interview** (e.g., Latham, Saari, Purcel, & Campion, 1980) asks hypothetical, job-related questions, with all job applicants being asked the same questions. For a customer service job, a situational interview question might be, "What would you do if an angry customer called and started yelling at you about a problem they were having with the product?" The second type of structured interview, the **behavioral interview** (e.g., Janz, 1982), asks job-related questions about a past experience that the applicant has had. For the same customer service job, a behavioral interview question might be, "Think about a time that an angry customer called and started yelling at you about a problem they were having with the company. How did you handle it?" Note that the focus of the behavioral interview is past behavior, and thus it is based on the idea that the best predictor of future behavior is past behavior. We provide a number of examples of situational and behavioral interview questions in Table 6.3.

Further, research has found that situational interview and behavioral interview questions seem to measure slightly different things. In their review of the interview literature, Levashina, Hartwell, Morgeson, and Campion (2014) conclude that situational interviews seem to measure job knowledge and cognitive ability, whereas behavioral interviews seem to measure experience and some personality dimensions. In addition, although behavioral interview questions seem to have slightly higher validity than situational questions for high complexity jobs, Levashina et al. note that either or both of these interview question types might be acceptable as they really are measuring different things and could be good for different purposes.

Table 6.3 Sample situational and behavioral interview questions

Situational Interview Items	Behavioral Interview Items	Job
A customer calls who is angry about a defective product and begins yelling at you. What would you do?	Explain about a time that you had to deal with an angry customer who was yelling at you. What did you do?	Customer Service Specialist
Your team is working against a deadline to complete a project. One of your team members is not keeping up with his work and is holding back the team. What would you do?	Think of a time when you were working as a team to meet a deadline and a team member was not keeping up with his work. What did you do?	Marketing Specialist
One of your employees has a sudden drop in performance. How would you approach the problem?	Think of a time that one of your employees had a sudden drop in performance. What you did to address the problem?	Supervisor

The use of structured interviews is now standard in many companies. For example, behavioral interviews are part of Google's selection procedure (Friedman, 2014).

Moreover, perhaps the situational interview would be more appropriate in situations where the job applicants have relatively little experience. In any case, both the situational and behavioral interview are good choices in terms of validity, with higher predictive validity than the unstructured interview (e.g., .44 vs. .33; McDaniel, Whetzel, Schmidt, & Maurer, 1994).

Before we leave the topic of the unstructured interview, we need to point out that despite the consistent meta-analytic evidence that more interview structure leads to higher validity, the unstructured interview may have its uses. For example, the unstructured interview can be used to assess interpersonal skills and factors like personality (e.g., Blackman, 2002). It could also be good to see how well the applicant might fit with the group (staying within legal guidelines, of course – see Chapter 7), and also for the interviewee to ask questions about the job and the company. Further, despite the bad reputation that unstructured interviews have gotten over the years – well deserved though it might be – Dipboye et al. (2012) point out that unstructured interviews may serve a number of important roles in the selection of employees. In any case, we're doubtful that most hiring managers would be prepared to hire a prospective employee without some sort of interview to get to know them first.

Interview Structure

So we know that structured interviews – either situational or behavioral – are better predictors of job performance than unstructured interviews. But the interview can be structured in quite a few other ways. A number of authors (Campion, Palmer, & Campion, 1997; Chapman & Zweig, 2005; Williamson, Campion, Malos, Roehling, & Campion, 1997) have described the range of ways in which you can add structure to the selection interview. We discuss some of these next.

• **Use the same, job-related questions for all applicants**. This is something we have already mentioned, but there are a few key points. First, interview questions can be generated from the job analysis – from the tasks that make up the job, from the KSAs that are needed to perform the job, and from critical incidents that are generated during the job analysis process. And SMEs can either develop these questions or help the person developing the interview construct the questions. In short, you should end up with an interview that adequately samples the job, that is to say, is content valid.

Table 6.4 Sample interview rating scales

Organized by Question:

Your boss asks you to work late, but you and your friends have tickets to go to a baseball game. What would you do?

1. I'd leave and go to the game.
3. I would talk to my boss and explain that I have the tickets.
5. I would work late.

Organized by KSA:

Knowledge of company rules
1   2   3   4   5

Ability to set priorities
1   2   3   4   5

- **Develop standardized rating scales**. One of the key issues in constructing interview materials is to provide raters with standardized rating scales. Table 6.4 above provides a few examples of different types of interview rating scales. Note that some of these can be organized around the KSAs that make up the job, while others are focused on the interview questions themselves. In either case, the goal is to provide as much structure to the interviewer as possible, including examples of different points on the rating scale (e.g., Melchers, Lienhardt, Aarburg, & Kleinmann, 2011), so that raters are consistent in their evaluation of the applicants, and are consistent among themselves in making their ratings.
- **Note taking**. One typical way to standardize structured interviews is to recommend note-taking to interviewers so that they can rely on these in making their ratings and also in comparing their ratings with each other.
- **Use multiple raters**. The use of multiple raters is one way to increase the consistency and accuracy with which job applicants are rated.
- **Train raters**. One of the ways to add structure to the interview is to train raters as to how to interview. This can include the correct procedures to use for conducting the interview, providing a frame of reference to raters (e.g., Melchers et al., 2011), how to use the rating scales, and how to discuss any differences between raters. This training can also include how to avoid biases such as halo, similarity, and leniency/severity (which have been discussed in Chapter 5 with regards to performance appraisal).

As you can see, there are a number of ways to increase the structure of the interview process. Perhaps not all of these are available to a particular organization. But the more of these that can be included, the better interview validity is likely to be.

Legal Issues

Because the interview is such a commonplace selection method and involves a personal interaction, it is also important to point out some of the legal issues that

Structured interviews – either situational interviews or behavioral interviews – have become a standard part of many selection procedures. One aspect of interview structure is having multiple interviewers to help with the reliability of interviewer ratings.

may arise. First, structured interview approaches tend to lead to more positive litigation outcomes for employers; that is, the courts tend to rule in favor of organizations that use more structured interview processes (Williamson et al., 1997). Second, with regard to adverse impact, most research shows that interviews, particularly structured interviews, are relatively low in adverse impact (Moscoso, 2000), although some researchers have noted that older applicants may be treated differently in the interview (Morgeson, Reider, Campion, & Bull, 2008). In any case, the most important legal issues have to do with the questions that the interviewer may and may not ask. This includes questions regarding age, disability, citizenship, marital status, and whether the applicant has children. (See the EEOC website, http://www.eeoc.gov/laws/practices/, for a detailed discussion.) There are two important points here. First is that even if the employer does not plan to use this personal information in making a decision, it is illegal to ask a question that may cause the applicant to believe that they will face discrimination. Second, as described by the EEOC (see Chapter 7), the employer is still allowed to ask questions about whether the applicant is able to perform the key job tasks.

Current Issues

There are a number of current issues in interview research, all of which focus on understanding the interview validity. First, because the interview is a method that can be used to measure a variety of individual differences among applicants (from interpersonal skills to technical job knowledge), the interview construct validity is not clear. However, this has led to continuing research on what constructs the interview is measuring. A meta-analysis by Huffcutt, Conway, Roth, and Stone (2001) showed that interviews primarily measure personality and social skills, followed by mental ability and job knowledge and skills. Interestingly, this study also found that part of the reason for the differential validity between unstructured and structured interviews is that structured interviews measure factors that are more strongly related to the job (unstructured interviews assessing interests, education, and experience; structured interviews assessing job knowledge, organizational fit, and decision-making).

There has also been research to understand the interview more from the applicant's perspective and how this might affect interview performance. For example, research has found that interviewees who know or can figure out which dimensions are being measured by the interview questions tend to do better on those questions. Moreover, this ability among some applicants to figure out what the interview is trying to measure (e.g., Klehe, König, Richter, Kleinmann, & Melchers, 2008) can lead to higher interview scores. Another issue is how the applicant gains information about the organization, including its norms and culture, by means of the interview, and more specifically, the interviewer him or herself, and how the applicant might try to manage their impressions during the interview (Kleinmann & Klehe, 2010). Interestingly, and not surprisingly, unstructured interviews appear to be more susceptible to job applicants' impression management tactics (Barrick, Shaffer, & DeGrassi, 2009). Additional applicant-focused research has examined job applicant anxiety in the interview and understanding the various dimensions of interviewee anxiety (e.g., McCarthy & Goffin, 2004).

One last point that might be helpful to you in preparing for an interview: As pointed out by Dipboye et al. (2012), job applicants should follow a number of common-sense guidelines that help them make a good impression, and these have been supported by the research. If using a résumé, it should be clearly written. Job applicants should also wear clothes that are appropriate to the job for which they are applying, and they should be properly groomed. They should smile appropriately, make good eye contact, and show a reasonably relaxed posture.

 "See website for interactive material"

Interactive: Ways to add structure to a selection interview.

Work Samples and Related Predictors

One way that an organization can assess a job applicant's suitability for a job is to actually assess how they do the job. For that reason, when some organizations hire workers they include a probationary period during the first few weeks or months of employment: This is a time in which the organization can decide whether or not the employee is performing the job in a suitable manner. Of course, it would be even better if organizations could assess a job applicant's performance before they are hired – in other words, it would be great to get a "work sample" of the person's job performance. Some organizations do just that. Over the years, I/O psychologists have developed selection procedures that get a small sample of the applicant's job performance. These methods can be classified as classic work samples/simulations, assessment centers, and situational judgment tests.

Work Sample Tests

Work sample test: A test in which the applicant is asked to do a small portion of the job. For instance, an applicant for a mechanic's job might be required to disassemble or assemble a piece of equipment as they would do in the workplace.

Perhaps the most straightforward way to get a **work sample** is to give the employee the equipment they would use on the job and let them actually use it. For instance, an applicant for a mechanic's job might be required to disassemble or assemble a piece of equipment as they would do in the workplace. An applicant for the job of college professor might be asked to prepare and deliver a sample lecture to a group of students. Or, an applicant for a short-order cook's job might be required to actually prepare a series of meals. There are several advantages to this approach to selection. First, these work samples have clear content validity (see Chapter 7), and as such, have psychological fidelity, that is, they elicit the KSAs needed on the job (Goldstein, Zedeck, & Schneider, 1993). Moreover, meta-analysis shows that they have good criterion-related validity, correlating as much as .54 with job performance (Schmidt & Hunter, 1998). They also have good physical fidelity and actually look like the job, making them attractive to job applicants (Hausknecht et al., 2004). The downside is that it can be expensive to put applicants through work samples, as work samples can only be administered to one applicant at a time. For that reason, work samples are often administered as one of the later selection hurdles after other, cheaper selection procedures are complete. Finally, work samples should not assess job skills that applicants would be expected to learn later on the job (Gatewood et al., 2011).

Assessment Centers

Assessment centers are often described as work samples for managers. They were first used on a large scale in the US by AT&T in the 1960s, and they are used in many large organizations throughout the US and Europe today. Assessment centers put candidates for promotion to manager through a series of exercises that reflect the job. For example, the **in-box/in-basket exercise** requires that the candidate review a number of memoranda or e-mails that have been sent to him or her, determine which of these have priority, and how they would respond to them. After spending some time working on their responses, candidates would then present their answers to trained raters, experts in management or psychologists. Other exercises include the **role play**, where candidates would play out a situation that they would encounter on the job, such as a subordinate with a performance problem; or the **leaderless group discussion**, in which candidates are presented with a problem as a group, such that they can be evaluated for team work and leadership. Assessment centers can evaluate candidates on a number of managerial skills such as decision-making, leadership, prioritizing, and interpersonal skills.

Assessment centers have been around now for many years, and a good bit of research has now accumulated on them. They have a number of advantages. First, they provide a realistic context for assessing the strengths of candidates for promotion. Second, like other work samples, they are attractive to candidates because they really look like the job. Third, in addition to their obvious sampling of the job (content validity), meta-analyses have also demonstrated that they have a significant relationship with work performance (as much as .45; Arthur, Day, McNelly, & Edens, 2003). A final strength is that assessment centers can do "double duty": Organizations can use them to make a decision about whom to promote, but also they can provide rich feedback to candidates, whether or not they are promoted.

Of course, assessment centers have some challenges as well. First, as you can imagine, they are not cheap to administer: The materials need to be developed, the assessors needs to be trained and compensated, and the location needs to be rented (Lievens & de Soete, 2012). Second, there has been some recent research on the use of assessment centers and how transparent the exercise dimensions are to job applicants. It turns out that applicants who are able to correctly guess what dimensions are being assessed do better than other candidates (e.g., Kleinmann, 1993; Kleinmann et al., 2011). Finally, although the adverse impact of assessment centers is less than that of some other selection procedures, research has also shown that they may have some small amount of adverse impact as well (Whetzel, McDaniel, & Nguyen, 2008).

Assessment centers: Work samples for managers.

In-box/in-basket exercise: An assessment center exercise that requires the candidate to review a number of memoranda or e-mails that have been sent to him or her and determine which of these have priority and how they would respond to them.

Role play: An assessment center exercise where candidates play out a situation that they would encounter on the job, such as a subordinate with a performance problem.

Leaderless group discussion: An assessment center exercise in which candidates are presented with a problem as a group, such that they can be evaluated for team work and leadership.

Assessment centers are a type of work sample for management jobs. They have been used for decades to decide who will be promoted, and are popular in the US, Australia, Africa, and across Europe. Their popularity has also been increasing in Asia as well (Lievens, De Corte, & Schollaert, 2009).

Situational Judgment Tests

Considering the advantages of work samples and assessment centers, it's not surprising that many organizations are interested in these types of selection procedures. But given the cost of these assessments, how can an organization afford to use these types of selection procedures on a large scale? It is for this reason that organizations have **situational judgment tests** (SJTs), which are technically known as low-fidelity simulations. These selection procedures put the job applicant into a work-related situation and ask what he or she believes is the right action. For example, a customer service applicant might be given a situation where a customer calls to complain about product quality and asks for refund. The applicant would then be asked how they would respond to the situation. Some sample SJT items for the job of barista are presented in Figure 6.7.

Situational judgment tests (SJTs): Technically known as low-fidelity simulations. SJT questions put the job applicant into a work-related situation and ask what he or she believes is the right action.

There are multiple formats to SJTs, and they can vary as to both the stimulus and the response format (Bauer, Truxillo, Mack, & Costa, 2011). For example, the stimulus material might be in written form, or the candidate might be presented with a short video. As for the response format, SJTs can be multiple-choice or open-ended, or they can present alternatives to the candidates in written or video format.

As you might guess, SJTs are cheaper to administer than either work samples or assessment centers (after their original development costs) and are very attractive to applicants because of their realism. But are they valid predictors of work

Situational judgment tests have been used to assess the performance of medical students. One study of Belgian medical students showed that the SJT predicted their job performance several years later (Lievens & Sackett, 2012). What types of specific SJT questions do you think would be good for selecting medical students?

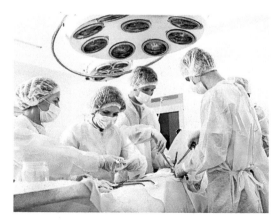

A customer complains to you that you have not correctly made the drink that she requested. What would be the best way to handle this situation?

a. Ask your boss how you should respond to her.

b. Ignore her if she is being rude.

*c. Ask her what the problem is and offer to make her another drink.

d. Ask a coworker to speak to her because you have clearly upset her.

It's suddenly very busy in the cafe. As the barista, you are having a difficult time keeping up with the many coffee drinks that you suddenly need to make, and several people are waiting for their drinks.

In addition, a line is forming at the cash register where people place their orders. Your coworker at the register asks you to help him to take orders. Which of the following would be the best way to handle this situation?

a. Stop your work making drinks to help your coworker take the orders for a while.

*b. Explain that you are having trouble keeping up making coffee drinks but offer to help when you are caught up with your work.

c. Tell your coworker you each have your job, and he just needs to do his job and you'll do yours.

d. Don't respond to your coworker at the register; you need to focus on getting your work done.

Figure 6.7 Sample SJT items for the job of barista.

performance? The evidence suggests that they are, with meta-analyses showing a good relationship between SJT dimensions and work performance (correlations with job performance from .19 to .43; Christian, Edwards, & Bradley, 2010). A compelling example is provided by a recent study by Lievens and Sackett (2012). The authors tracked Belgian medical school students from entry into medical school to the early stages of their career. They found that a video-based SJT focused on interpersonal skills predicted the candidates' internship performance seven years later, and their work performance nine years later – quite an impressive feat.

Biodata and Other Personal History Measures

One of the ways that organizations commonly assess an employee's potential fit with the job is through asking about their employment history and background. While requesting this type of information from employees is commonplace, I/O psychologists have also developed some systematic approaches to collecting and assessing such data in organizations, including biographical data and ratings of training and experience. We will also touch on the related issues of résumés and background checks.

Situational judgment tests (SJTs) are popular because they are clearly relevant to the job. SJTs have been used for personnel selection in a number of different types of jobs. Recently, the Home Care Alliance incorporated SJTs into their credentialing process for home care aides (Span, 2011).

Biodata

Biographical data or **biodata** include questions concerning an applicant's education and past work and life experience that can help decide how well the applicant can perform the job (Gatewood et al., 2011). Based on the idea that past and present behavior are the best predictors of future behavior, this method asks questions around topics like the number of jobs an applicant has held in the last five years (as a predictor of turnover) or which sports a person participated in high school (as a predictor of work in a sporting goods store). (See Table 6.5.) Note that when psychologists use the term biodata, it is also implied that some sort of detailed, empirical scoring has been used to validate the measures. Note that biodata's track record as a predictor is quite good: meta-analyses have found that biodata correlate well with job performance (correlations between .37 and .52; Hunter & Hunter, 1984; Vinchur, Schippman, Switzer, & Roth, 1998). Of course, one concern about asking about biographical items is the concern that some items can have adverse impact against women or ethnic minorities, and so this should be carefully taken into account in developing and validating these items.

There are a number of major issues involved in the use of biodata. The first of these is applicant faking (see our earlier discussion regarding personality tests). Of course, applicants should be told that any answers they provide are open to later verification by the employer. But research has also shown that asking applicants to elaborate on their answers – to provide further information and explanation for a biodata response – appears to lead to less inflated biodata responses (e.g., Levashina, Morgeson, & Campion, 2012; Schmitt & Kunce, 2002). A second issue is the best ways to develop scoring procedures for biodata items. Research has also suggested that determining the scoring key for biodata items through more empirical means (i.e., by examining biodata items' actual relationship with job performance) leads to greater validity (Cucina, Caputo, Thibodeaux, & MacLane, 2012). This also highlights the importance of doing good research in developing and validating biodata items before using them with applicants, such as basing them on job analysis, carefully considering what kinds of past experiences should lead to better performance, and thoroughly piloting biodata items (Gatewood et al., 2011).

Table 6.5 Some sample biodata items

Biodata Item	To Predict ...
How many jobs have you held in the last 5 years? (open-ended)	Employee turnover
Please list any sports that you played in school related to the job you are applying for (open-ended)	Performance in a sporting goods store
When a stranger has asked you a question, how likely are you to explain your answer to them until they understand? (1–5 rating scale)	Performance in a customer service job

Ratings of Training and Experience

Ratings of training and experience, commonly referred to as T&E forms, are commonly used in the public sector. Unlike biodata, T&E forms are not empirically scored. Rather, after asking an applicant a series of questions about their current work experience and education, they are scored by a trained rater. The questions on these forms are based on the specific job tasks and KSAs identified in a job analysis, and include questions like, "How many years of experience have you had supervising groups of five or more employees?" The validity of T&E forms can vary substantially depending on how applicants' responses are scored (McDaniel, Schmidt, & Hunter, 1988).

Résumés

Despite the fact that they are so frequently used, résumés can be a challenge for employers because of the sheer volume of résumés some employers receive. Moreover, applicants control the information that is provided on résumés, meaning that different applicants provide different types of information, making it very difficult for employers to compare applicants' résumés in a meaningful way. Despite their common use, there is little hard research on the use of résumés in selection or their validity. However, there has been an increasing use of online résumés, which include pre-formatted résumé builders asking applicants to complete specific fields about their job-related background and experience, so that the employer increases their odds of getting consistent and job-related information about all applicants (Gatewood et al., 2011).

Reference Checks

According to a poll by the Society for Human Resource Management, 76 percent of employers use some kind of reference check or background check to screen employees (SHRM, 2010). To the extent that an organization is doing background

"This is more precise than objectively reviewing resumes."

checks to simply verify information or to be sure that there are no "red flags" regarding the safety of hiring an individual, reference checks make sense. They are also important to avoid negligent hiring, or the hiring of an applicant who might, for example, hurt other people (Gatewood et al., 2011). The case for their use as an actual predictor of work performance, however, is less clear. One problem with the validity of reference checks is that job applicants tend to select their own referees based on who will be the most positive about them, avoiding people who might identify problems with their past performance.

Physical Ability Tests

Physical ability tests: Tests developed to assess dimensions like endurance or explosive strength for physically demanding jobs.

Physical ability tests are those developed to assess dimensions like endurance or explosive strength for physically demanding jobs (e.g., firefighter). Hogan (1991) noted that two broad dimensions may capture most job-related physical demands: muscular strength/endurance and physical skill in movements. The literature identifies two general approaches to testing for physical abilities (Baker & Gebhardt, 2012). The first is tests designed to measure the constructs required by the job (such as those identified by Hogan) such as the cardiovascular fitness of the applicant. The second approach is to use simulation-like exams which would have high face validity for applicants. This might require, for example, that a firefighter applicant perform some of the key tasks of the job, such as drag a dummy the size of a typical person or haul equipment up flights of stairs. An important point with this approach is to take into account whatever training applicants would receive on the job; in other words, if new hires would receive significant physical training after they are hired leading to significant improvement, it would not be appropriate to expect applicants (who are pretraining) to perform at that level. In either case, job analysis is key in assuring what the minimum requirements actually are.

One issue with some physical ability tests is adverse impact against women. One approach some organizations take to reducing such adverse impact is to offer physical training to all applicants and encourage them to take it, although the improvements in women's performance may be minimal (Courtright, McCormick, Postlethwaite, Reeves, & Mount, 2013). However, it may be impossible to eliminate adverse impact for some physical abilities tests short of redesigning the job itself to reduce its physical requirements. The EEOC cautions employers to use these tests carefully and ensure that these tests are truly job related and not arbitrary. For example, the Chicago fire department was the target of a lawsuit because the physical ability test the city used had an adverse impact on women. Even though the passing score on the test was 65 out of 100, the city used a cut-off score of 89 to select firefighters, resulting in 90 percent of male but only 19 percent of female applicants passing the test. The lawsuit ended with a settlement of almost $2 million and with the city adopting a new physical ability test (Byrne, 2013).

Other Selection Procedures

Credit History

According to a poll by the Society for Human Resource Management, nearly half of responding organizations said that they used credit history as part of their selection procedures (Rivlin, 2013). One assumption that some employers make is that

Physical ability tests may require applicants to perform some version of what they would need to do on the job – taking into account that they might be further trained after they are hired. Here an applicant for firefighter drags a fire hose while suited up in safety protective gear.

poor credit scores are associated with negative employee behaviors such as theft. However, there are concerns with using credit history for hiring decisions, especially in the recent economic downturn, during which a person's credit may have been damaged by factors outside of their control (e.g., job loss). A recent study by Bernerth, Taylor, Walker, and Whitman (2012) examined what credit history may actually be measuring and how this related to job performance, and the authors found some interesting results. First, a strong credit score was associated with high conscientiousness – but also with low agreeableness. And although credit scores were associated with some job performance dimensions, they were not associated with workplace deviance. Moreover, Bernerth et al. point out that because Blacks and Hispanics tend to have lower credit scores than Whites, the issue of adverse impact is a concern with using credit scores for hiring. Thus, organizations should carefully consider the jobs where they use credit scores in hiring and be prepared to demonstrate the validity of credit scores for their organization – and to demonstrate that measures with less adverse impact were not available.

Workplace Application

The Use of Credit Scores for Selection

A 2012 survey by the Society for Human Resource Management (SHRM) found that nearly half of responding organizations used some sort of credit check during selection. However, there are concerns about the legality and fairness of using credit scores for selection, especially during an economic downturn. As a result, at least nine US states have passed legislation to restrict the practice of using credit reports for hiring (Rivlin, 2013). For example, many people's credit scores have suffered during the economic downturn through little fault of their own. Moreover, credit scores are not necessarily a sign of workplace performance issues, as once thought

Credit Score Ratings

Credit Score	Description
760 – 849	Excellent
700 – 759	Great
660 – 699	Good
620 – 659	Average
580 – 619	Poor
below 579	Very Poor

by some employers; in fact, high credit scores may be associated with personality traits such as low agreeableness (Bernerth et al., 2012). In any case, if used for hiring, credit checks should be demonstrated to be relevant to a particular job (e.g., work in the financial industry) and should be examined for adverse impact.

Vocational Interests

Vocational interests tap into a person's preferences for certain types of work or work environments (e.g., Van Iddekinge, Putka, & Campbell, 2011). These vocational interest inventories measure dimensions such as social, artistic, and conventional. Although there has been a substantial body of research on vocational interests in the vocational counseling literature for many years (e.g., Holland, 1959), I/O psychology has generally ignored vocational interests as a selection method. One recent study suggests that these vocational interest inventories should be given another look by I/O psychologists. Using a military sample, Van Iddekinge et al. found that vocational interests were related to job performance. Vocational interests also had relatively low adverse impact – a real plus. Although more research is needed on using vocational interests in selection, this initial study illustrates that they may hold promise for making hiring decisions.

GLOBAL IMPLICATIONS

An organization's personnel selection processes may no longer take place within only one country. Multinational organizations must consider issues such as the equivalency of their assessments across different cultures and the legality of selection procedures in the different legal contexts in different countries. (See Steiner, 2012 for a thorough discussion of these issues.) Moreover, given differences in birth rates and types of education available in various countries across the globe, talent is no longer equally distributed in different countries; thus, an organization may find itself selecting employees from one country for employment in another (Ryan & Ployhart, 2014).

One key issue for the use of personnel selection procedures is that much of the selection research thus far has taken place in the US (Ryan & Ployhart, 2014). This has affected the understanding of selection procedures in two ways. First, a selection procedure that is valid in the US may not be valid in all cultures. Second, the US legal system, which we will discuss in Chapter 7, has largely influenced selection research for the last 50 years. We anticipate that the growth in multinational companies will cause selection research and practice to take a broader focus and consider legal and application issues that are relevant in other parts of the world.

CURRENT ISSUES AND CONTROVERSIES

We have already mentioned a number of current issues related to personnel selection procedures throughout the chapter, including questions about the use of integrity tests and the best ways to use personality tests. In addition, however, there are a number of current issues in personnel selection to discuss because they may mean profound changes are afoot in the practice of selection in the coming years. These include the increased use of social networking sites for applicant screening, unproctored Internet testing in selection, the emergence of global selection systems, and increased use of technology and gaming in selection. These developments have grown largely in the practice of selection without substantial research to evaluate their effectiveness, and some may pose legal questions under selection law.

First, many employers are now turning to online social networking sites for making decisions about the suitability of job candidates, but a number of questions remain (e.g., Davison, Maraist, Hamilton, & Bing, 2012; Roth, Bobko, Van Iddekinge, & Thatcher, in press). First, are such practices legal? For example, what if only some applicants have a social networking site, and checking applicant websites thus led to unequal treatment of job applicants? Or is this an invasion of privacy? Second, even if such information could be obtained legally, is it even useful? The findings of one study (Van Iddekinge, Lanivich, Roth, & Junco, in press) suggest that it is not. Van Iddekinge asked recruiters to rate the Facebook pages of college graduates, and found that the ratings were not predictive of the graduates' later job performance. They also found that the ratings tended to favor female and White applicants, leading to questions about fairness. This study calls into question whether social networking site information, if available, is even useful to selection decisions. And are job-related behaviors typically included on social networking websites? Roth et al. (2013) provide a comprehensive discussion of the use of social networking sites in selection, identifying the range of unresolved questions about the legality for selection decisions. Until these issues are resolved, we strongly recommend that employers avoid using such information about job applicants in making hiring decisions. At the same time, we recommend that job applicants carefully consider the types of information that they include about themselves online. Despite the pitfalls of using social networking sites for hiring, however, there can be value to social networking sites such as LinkedIn for recruiting job applicants (see Chapter 7.)

Second is the use of unproctored Internet testing by organizations. Despite the convenience of this testing approach for both employers and job applicants, there are some potential problems associated with it, most relating to cheating and test security (Tippins, 2015). The greatest concern is that employers may not know who is taking the exam, or whether the job applicant is receiving some assistance in taking the exam. This seems especially important for tests where there is a right or wrong answer. However, to the extent that the

Unproctored Internet tests, where the job applicant can take the exam away from the worksite and without a company proctor (e.g., at home), have become a part of many selection procedures.

selection procedure does not have an obvious correct answer – for instance, some types of non-cognitive assessments like personality tests – unproctored Internet testing may not be a problem (e.g., Beatty et al., 2011).

Third is that many new technologies have been introduced into the practice of personnel selection in the last few years. Many of these technologies have allowed the practice of selection to make enormous strides, but others have emerged with relatively little scrutiny. These include the use of games in screening employees for hiring, or simply the use of online simulations for selection. While many of these hold substantial promise, they have largely gone unexamined in terms of rigorous research (Ryan & Ployhart, 2014).

"Big data" (massive datasets) is a growing topic in many areas related to the workplace (we discussed a few of these in Chapter 4 with regard to work performance; see also Chapters 1 and 2) and personnel selection is no exception (Peck, 2013). For instance, there is interest in how the use of massive datasets of millions of people and data points – something that has only recently become available – can allow organizations to increase their predictive efficiency about workers beyond what is currently possible with existing personnel selection tests. These analyses may include a better understanding of patterns of work behavior over time that might not be possible with a standard selection test. Although the use of big data in selection may hold promise, there are challenges as well. First, to the extent that such approaches are not based in sound theories of work behavior or rationales for their effectiveness, it may be challenging to legally

There is increased interest in the use of video games in personnel selection to assess factors like how creative or easily distracted a person is. However, their value over and above traditional selection tests has yet to be determined (Rampell, 2014).

defend the use of these approaches. Moreover, we don't know how workers might feel about a "big data" approach to selection, where they may be evaluated on factors that are not known to them. Big data is a new topic with relatively little published research, and its use in the selection arena, fraught as it is with legal challenges, means it deserves more research attention.

Another technology that is seeing some increased use in selection is online games for the selection of employees (Zickar & Lake, 2011). In other words, some vendors have developed games that they claim can predict job performance, and these games may take very little time for job applicants to complete. We can imagine any number of game types that could assess certain cognitive skills or personality types, but until such selection screening games are scrutinized for their legality, validity, and the underlying constructs they assess, some caution should be taken in their use.

Finally, there has been an increase in the use of online simulations to replace previous simulations which would have been conducted in person. We can see the value of this approach to selection, and a small amount of research has begun to accumulate on such simulations (e.g., Oostrom, Bos-Broekema, Serlie, Born, & Van der Molen, 2012). Moreover, some researchers are beginning to identify which factors may differentiate live and simulated selection procedures from each other (Potosky, 2008) in terms of what they are measuring and their validity. Still, far more research is needed to understand how online simulations may differ from those administered live.

WHAT DOES THIS MEAN TO YOU?

Organizations use a number of personnel selection procedures for hiring employees. Although some of these methods are better than others, they all have the goal of deciding which candidates are the best fit for the job and for the organization. But what does this all mean to you as a potential job-seeker?

Be prepared for the fact that there is such a wide range of selection procedures that are commonly used by organizations to make selection decisions. These can be cognitive tests, personality tests and biodata, integrity tests, and interviews and assessment centers. This varies considerably by the job that you're applying for – for example, management-level jobs would tend to use more sophisticated interviews and assessment centers. And organizations can use a combination of several predictors as part of their selection process.

But across most jobs, the most commonly used selection procedure is the interview, and the structured interview is gaining popularity among employers.

That being the case, it is worthwhile to anticipate the types of interview questions you will be asked; you might think about what the job involves to anticipate what the interview questions might be.

Other advice to job-seekers is straightforward and commonsensical – and has been confirmed by the research. Résumés should be clearly written. When you go to a job interview, you should wear clothes that are appropriate to the job for which you are applying, and you should be properly groomed.

But also keep in mind that part of the selection decision rests not only with the organization, but with the applicant as well. In other words, you should be doing your best to pick up the signals about what the organization would be like as a place to work. This can come not only through your interaction with organizational members, but through the types of questions asked in interviews and your reactions on selection tests as well.

Conclusion

Organizations have a wide range of choices as to how they select their job applicants. Some organizations do a good job of this, focusing on what the research shows are the best predictors. There is quite a range of selection procedures available, each with its own set of strengths and weaknesses in terms of validity, cost, and adverse impact. They may each be suitable for different kinds of jobs and for different organizations. The key is for an employer to be sure that they are using a procedure that is valid and legally defensible, and to use procedures in a way that will provide the greatest benefit to the organization in attracting and securing the best talent. These are the issues we will address in Chapter 7.

YOUR TURN...

1   We know that tests of general cognitive ability (g) are among the best predictors of work performance – some would argue the best – and also have adverse impact against certain ethnic groups. Should organizations use these tests? If not, what are their alternatives? Give reasons for your answer, weighing the advantages and disadvantages of your recommendation.

2 Consider the job of firefighter. What sorts of personnel selection procedures would you recommend for this job? (Be specific – if you recommend personality tests, say which personality dimensions and why.) Describe how you would make your decision, starting with the job analysis.

3 You're tasked with developing an interview protocol for the job of customer service representative. What type of interview would you use? How would you develop the questions? Provide at least five interview questions.

4 We have mentioned the issue of faking with regards to personality tests and biodata items. Do you think that faking is an important issue when administering tests? Why or why not?

Additional Reading

Cascio, W. F., & Aguinis, H. (2011). *Applied psychology in human resource management* (7th ed.). Upper Saddle River, NJ: Prentice Hall.

Gatewood, R., Feild, H., & Barrick, M. (2011). *Human resource selection.* Mason, OH: Cengage Learning.

Guion, R. M. (2011). *Assessment, measurement, and prediction for personnel decisions.* New York: Routledge.

Schmitt, N. (Ed.) (2012). *The Oxford handbook of personnel selection and assessment.* New York: Oxford University Press.

Tippins, N. T., & Adler, S. (Eds.) (2011). *Technology-enhanced assessment of talent.* San Francisco, CA: Jossey-Bass.

Weekley, J. A., & Ployhart, R. E. (Eds.) (2005). *Situational judgment tests: Theory, measurement, and application.* San Francisco, CA: Jossey-Bass.

CASE STUDY: Staffing for the Growing Nursing Workforce

With the aging of the population in the US, healthcare professions are expected to grow in the coming decades (Lockard & Woolf, 2012). One profession that is expected to have large numbers of job openings in the coming years is registered nurse. This expected growth in jobs for registered nurses means that we can expect a good amount of hiring to take place in the coming decades. In other words, a number of hospitals and clinics will be looking to hire nurses that are a good fit for their organizations.

According to the O*NET (http://www.onetonline.org/link/summary/29-1141.00), the following tasks are generally required of registered nurses:

- Maintain accurate, detailed reports and records.
- Administer medications to patients and monitor patients for reactions or side effects.
- Record patients' medical information and vital signs.
- Monitor, record, and report symptoms or changes in patients' conditions.
- Consult and coordinate with healthcare team members to assess, plan, implement, or evaluate patient care plans.
- Modify patient treatment plans as indicated by patients' responses and conditions.
- Monitor all aspects of patient care, including diet and physical activity.
- Direct or supervise less skilled nursing or healthcare personnel or supervise a particular unit.
- Prepare patients for and assist with examinations or treatments.
- Instruct individuals, families, or other groups on topics such as health education, disease prevention, or childbirth and develop health improvement programs.

Also, according to O*NET registered nurses are generally licensed, and the job requires some level of college education.

Imagine you have been asked by a major hospital to develop a plan for hiring 10 new registered nurses who work on a general ward. These nurses are expected to have at least five years of work experience as a hospital ward nurse.

Questions:

1. What selection procedures do you think would be appropriate for hiring nurses for these positions? Explain why you would choose these methods. Consider their validity, practicality, and cost.
2. Are there any selection procedures that you think would be inappropriate for hiring nurses? Why?
3. Assume that an interview would be part of your selection procedure at some point. What type of interview would you choose? What would be at least two interview questions that you would ask them?
4. Which personality dimensions might be appropriate for hiring these nurses?
5. Would you consider using an integrity test for hiring? Why or why not?

Sources: Lockard & Woolf, 2012; O*NET, http://www.onetonline.org/link/summary/29-1141.00.

References

Arthur, W., Jr., & Villado, A. J. (2008). The importance of distinguishing between constructs and methods when comparing predictors in personnel selection research and practice. *Journal of Applied Psychology, 93,* 435–442.

Arthur, W., Day, E. A., McNelly, T. L., & Edens, P. S. (2003). A meta-analysis of the criterion-related validity of assessment center dimensions. *Personnel Psychology, 56,* 125–153.

Arvey, R. D., & Campion, J. E. (1982). The employment interview: A summary and review of recent research. *Personnel Psychology, 35,* 281–322.

Ashton, M. C., & Lee, K. (2007). Empirical, theoretical, and practical advantages of the HEXACO model of personality structure. *Personality and Social Psychology Review, 11,* 150–166.

Baard, S. K., Rench, T. A., & Kozlowski, S. W. (2014). Performance adaptation: A theoretical integration and review. *Journal of Management, 40,* 48–99.

Baker, T. A., & Gebhardt, D. L. (2012). The assessment of physical capabilities in the workplace. In N. Schmitt (Ed.), *The Oxford handbook of personnel assessment and selection* (pp. 274–296). New York: Oxford University Press.

Barrick, M. R., & Mount, M. K. (1991). The big five personality dimensions and job performance: A meta-analysis. *Personnel Psychology, 44,* 1–26.

Barrick, M. R., & Mount, M. K. (2012). Nature and use of personality in selection. In N. Schmitt (Ed.), *The Oxford handbook of personnel assessment and selection* (pp. 225–251). New York: Oxford University Press.

Barrick, M. R., Shaffer, J. A., & DeGrassi, S. W. (2009). What you see may not be what you get: Relationships among self-presentation tactics and ratings of interview and job performance. *Journal of Applied Psychology, 94,* 1394–1411.

Barrick, M. R., Stewart, G. L., & Piotrowski, M. (2002). Personality and job performance: Test of the mediating effects of motivation among sales representatives. *Journal of Applied Psychology, 87,* 43–51.

Bateman, T. S., & Crant, J. M. (1993). The proactive component of organizational behavior: A measure and correlates. *Journal of Organizational Behavior, 14,* 103–118.

Battista, J. (2013). N.F.L. tries new method for testing mental agility. *New York Times,* February 21. Retrieved May 12, 2015 from http://www.nytimes.com/2013/02/22/sports/football/nfl-introduces-new-way-to-test-a-players-mental-agility.html.

Bauer, T. N., Truxillo, D. M., Mack, K., & Costa, A. B. (2011). Applicant reactions to technology-based selection: What we know so far. In N. T. Tippins & S. Adler (Eds.), *Technology-enhanced assessment* (pp. 190–223). San Francisco, CA: Jossey-Bass.

Beaty, J. C., Nye, C. D., Borneman, M. J., Kantrowitz, T. M., Drasgow, F., & Grauer, E. (2011). Proctored versus unproctored Internet tests: Are unproctored noncognitive tests as predictive of job performance? *International Journal of Selection and Assessment, 19,* 1–10.

Bernerth, J. B., Taylor, S. G., Walker, H. J., & Whitman, D. S. (2012). An empirical investigation of dispositional antecedents and performance-related outcomes of credit scores. *Journal of Applied Psychology, 97,* 469–478.

Berry, C. M., Sackett, P. R., & Wiemann, S. (2007). A review of recent developments in integrity test research. *Personnel Psychology, 60,* 271–301.

Blackman, M. C. (2002). Personality judgment and the utility of the unstructured employment interview. *Basic and Applied Social Psychology, 24,* 241–250.

Byrne, J. (2013). City set to pay nearly $2 million for firefighter lawsuit. *Chicago Tribune,* September 7.

Campion, M. A., Palmer, D. K., & Campion, J. E. (1997). A review of structure in the selection interview. *Personnel Psychology, 50*, 655–702.

Carter, N. T., Dalal, D. K., Boyce, A. S., O'Connell, M. S., Kung, M. C., & Delgado, K. M. (2014). Uncovering curvilinear relationships between conscientiousness and job performance: How theoretically appropriate measurement makes an empirical difference. *Journal of Applied Psychology, 99*, 564–586.

Cascio, W. F., & Aguinis, H. (2011). *Applied psychology in human resource management* (7th ed.). Upper Saddle River, NJ: Prentice Hall.

Chapman, D. S., & Zweig, D. I. (2005). Developing a nomological network for interview structure: Antecedents and consequences of the structured selection interview. *Personnel Psychology, 58*, 673–702.

Chernyshenko, O. S., Stark, S., & Drasgow, F. (2011). Individual differences: Their measurement and validity. In N. Schmitt (Ed.), *The Oxford handbook of personnel assessment and selection* (pp. 117–151), New York: Oxford University Press.

Christian, M. S., Edwards, B. D., & Bradley, J. C. (2010). Situational judgment tests: Constructs assessed and a meta-analysis of their criterion-related validities. *Personnel Psychology, 63*, 83–117.

Christiansen, N. D., Janovics, J. E., & Siers, B. P. (2010). Emotional intelligence in selection contexts: Measurement method, criterion-related validity, and vulnerability to response distortion. *International Journal of Selection and Assessment, 18*, 87–101.

Converse, P. D., Pathak, J., Quist, J., Merbedone, M., Gotlib, T., & Kostic, E. (2010). Statement desirability ratings in forced-choice personality measure development: Implications for reducing score inflation and providing trait-level information. *Human Performance, 23*, 323–342.

Costa, P. T., & McCrae, R. R. (2008). The revised NEO personality inventory (NEO-PI-R). In G. P. Boyle, G. Matthews, & D. H. Saklofske (Eds.), *The SAGE handbook of personality theory and assessment, Vol. 2* (pp. 179–198). Thousand Oaks, CA: Sage Publications.

Courtright, S. H., McCormick, B. W., Postlethwaite, B. E., Reeves, C. J., & Mount, M. K. (2013). A meta-analysis of sex differences in physical ability: Revised estimates and strategies for reducing differences in selection contexts. *Journal of Applied Psychology, 98*, 623–641.

Crant, J. M. (1995). The Proactive Personality Scale and objective job performance among real estate agents. *Journal of Applied Psychology, 80*, 532–537.

Cucina, J. M., Caputo, P. M., Thibodeaux, H. F., & Maclane, C. N. (2012). Unlocking the key to biodata scoring: A comparison of empirical, rational, and hybrid approaches at different sample sizes. *Personnel Psychology, 65*, 385–428.

Cullen, K. L., Edwards, B. D., Casper, W. C., & Gue, K. R. (2014). Employees' adaptability and perceptions of change-related uncertainty: Implications for perceived organizational support, job satisfaction, and performance. *Journal of Business and Psychology, 29*, 269–280.

Davison, H. K., Maraist, C. C., Hamilton, R. H., & Bing, M. N. (2012). To screen or not to screen? Using the Internet for selection decisions. *Employee Responsibilities and Rights Journal, 24*, 1–21.

Dipboye, R. L., Macan, T., & Shahani-Denning, C. (2012). The selection interview from the interviewer and applicant perspectives: Can't have one without the other. In N. Schmitt (Ed.), *The Oxford handbook of personnel assessment and selection* (pp. 323–352). New York: Oxford University Press.

Fan, J., Gao, D., Carroll, S. A., Lopez, F. J., Tian, T. S., & Meng, H. (2012). Testing the efficacy of a new procedure for reducing faking on personality tests within selection contexts. *Journal of Applied Psychology, 97*, 866–880.

Flynn, J. R. (1999). Searching for justice: The discovery of IQ gains over time. *American Psychologist, 54*, 5–20.

Foldes, H. J., Duehr, E. E., & Ones, D. S. (2008). Group differences in personality: Meta-analyses comparing five US racial groups. *Personnel Psychology, 61*, 579–616.

Fortmann, K., Leslie, C., & Cunningham, M. (2002). Cross-cultural comparisons of the Reid Integrity Scale in Latin America and South Africa. *International Journal of Selection and Assessment, 10*, 98–108.

Friedman, T. (2014). How to get a job at Google. *New York Times*, February 22. Retrieved May 12, 2015, from http://www.nytimes.com/2014/02/23/opinion/sunday/friedman-how-to-get-a-job-at-google.html.

Gatewood, R., Feild, H., & Barrick, M. (2011). *Human resource selection*. Mason, OH: Cengage Learning.

Glauber, B. (2014). NFL introduces player assessment test (PAT) at combine. *Newsday*, February 24. Retrieved February 26, 2015, from http://www.newsday.com/sports/football/nfl-introduces-player-assessment-test-pat-at-combine-1.4699962.

Goldberg, L. R. (1999). A broad-bandwidth, public domain, personality inventory measuring the lower-level facets of several five-factor models. *Personality Psychology in Europe, 7*, 7–28.

Goldstein, I. L., Zedeck, S., & Schneider, B. (1993). An exploration of the job analysis-content validity process. In N. Schmitt & W. C. Borman (Eds.) *Personnel selection in organizations* (pp. 3–34). San Francisco, CA: Jossey-Bass.

Guion, R. M. (1965). *Personnel testing*. New York: McGraw-Hill.

Guion, R. M. (1998). *Assessment, measurement, and prediction for personnel decisions*. Mahwah, NJ: Lawrence Erlbaum Associates.

Guion, R. M., & Gottier, R. F. (1965). Validity of personality measures in personnel selection. *Personnel Psychology, 18*, 135–164.

Hausknecht, J. P, Day, D. V., & Thomas, S. C. (2004). Applicant reactions to selection procedures: An updated model and meta-analysis. *Personnel Psychology, 57*, 639–683.

Heggestad, E. D., Morrison, M., Reeve, C. L., & McCloy, R. A. (2006). Forced-choice assessments of personality for selection: Evaluating issues of normative assessment and faking resistance. *Journal of Applied Psychology, 91*, 9–24.

Hogan, J. (1991). Structure of physical performance in occupational tasks. *Journal of Applied Psychology, 76*, 495–507.

Hogan, J., Barrett, P., & Hogan, R. (2007). Personality measurement, faking, and employment selection. *Journal of Applied Psychology, 92*, 1270–1285.

Holland, J. L. (1959). A theory of vocational choice. *Journal of Counseling Psychology,* *6,* 35–45.

Huffcutt, A. I., Conway, J. M., Roth, P. L., & Stone, N. J. (2001). Identification and meta-analytic assessment of psychological constructs measured in employment interviews. *Journal of Applied Psychology, 86,* 897–913.

Hunter, J. E. (1986). Cognitive ability, cognitive aptitudes, job knowledge, and job performance. *Journal of Vocational Behavior, 29,* 340–362.

Hunter, J. E., & Hunter, R. F. (1984). Validity and utility of alternative predictors of job performance. *Psychological Bulletin, 96,* 72–98.

Hunthausen, J. M., Truxillo, D. M., Bauer, T. N., & Hammer, L. B. (2003). A field study of frame-of-reference effects on personality test validity. *Journal of Applied Psychology, 88,* 545–551.

Inceoglu, I., & Bartram, D. (2012). Global leadership: The myth of multicultural competency. *Industrial Organizational Psychology, 5,* 216–218.

Jack L. Hayes International Inc. (2013, June). *Twenty-fifth annual retail theft survey.* Retrieved May 12, 2015, from http://hayesinternational.com/wp-content/uploads/2013/06/SURVEY-2013-25th-Annual-Retail-Theft-Survey-Hayes-International-Thoughts-Behind-Numbers-Final.pdf.

Janz, T. (1982). Initial comparisons of patterned behavior description interviews versus unstructured interviews. *Journal of Applied Psychology, 67,* 577–580.

Joseph, D. L., & Newman, D. A. (2010). Emotional intelligence: An integrative meta-analysis and cascading model. *Journal of Applied Psychology, 95,* 54–78.

Judge, T. A. (2009). Core self-evaluations and work success. *Current Directions in Psychological Science, 18,* 58–62.

Judge, T. A., Erez, A., Bono, J. E., & Thoresen, C. J. (2003). The core self-evaluations scale: Development of a measure. *Personnel Psychology, 56,* 303–331.

Klehe, U. C., König, C. J., Richter, G. M., Kleinmann, M., & Melchers, K. G. (2008). Transparency in structured interviews: Consequences for construct and criterion-related validity. *Human Performance, 21,* 107–137.

Kleinmann, M. (1993). Are rating dimensions in assessment centers transparent for participants? Consequences for criterion and construct validity. *Journal of Applied Psychology, 78,* 988–993.

Kleinmann, M., Ingold, P. V., Lievens, F., Jansen, A., Melchers, K. G., & König, C. J. (2011). A different look at why selection procedures work: The role of candidates' ability to identify criteria. *Organizational Psychology Review, 1,* 128–146.

Kleinmann, M., & Klehe, U. C. (2010). Selling oneself: Construct and criterion-related validity of impression management in structured interviews. *Human Performance, 24,* 29–46.

Kuncel, N. R., Hezlett, S. A., & Ones, D. S. (2004). Academic performance, career potential, creativity, and job performance: Can one construct predict them all? *Journal of Personality and Social Psychology, 86,* 148–161.

Landers, R. N., Sackett, P. R., & Tuzinski, K. A. (2011). Retesting after initial failure, coaching rumors, and warnings against faking in online personality measures for selection. *Journal of Applied Psychology, 96,* 202–210.

Latham, G. P., Saari, L. M., Pursell, E. D., & Campion, M. A. (1980). The situational interview. *Journal of Applied Psychology, 65,* 422–427.

Levashina, J., Hartwell, C. J., Morgeson, F. P., & Campion, M. A. (2014). The structured employment interview: Narrative and quantitative review of the research literature. *Personnel Psychology, 67*, 241–293.

Levashina, J., Morgeson, F. P., & Campion, M. A. (2012). Tell me more: Exploring how verbal ability and item verifiability influence responses to biodata questions in a high-stakes selection context. *Personnel Psychology, 65*, 359–383.

Lievens, F., Buyse, T., & Sackett, P. R. (2005). The operational validity of a video-based situational judgment test for medical college admissions: Illustrating the importance of matching predictor and criterion construct domains. *Journal of Applied Psychology, 90*, 442–452.

Lievens, F., De Corte, W., & Schollaert, E. (2008). A closer look at the frame-of-reference effect in personality scale scores and validity. *Journal of Applied Psychology, 93*, 268–279.

Lievens, F., De Corte, W., & Schollaert, E. (2009). *Assessment centers: Overview of practice and research.* International Test Commission Website. Retrieved March 18, 2014, from http://www.intestcom.org/publications/orta/the%20assessment%20center.php.

Lievens, F., & De Soete, B. (2012). Simulations. In N. Schmitt (Ed.), *The Oxford handbook of personnel assessment and selection* (pp. 383–410). New York: Oxford University Press.

Lievens, F., & Sackett, P. R. (2012). The validity of interpersonal skills assessment via situational judgment tests for predicting academic success and job performance. *Journal of Applied Psychology, 97*, 460–468.

Lockard, C. B., & Woolf, M. (2012). Employment outlook: 2010–2012: Occupational employment projections to 2020. *Monthly Labor Review, 135*, 84–108.

Marcus, B. (2009). Faking from the applicant's perspective: A theory of self-presentation in personnel selection settings. *International Journal of Selection and Assessment, 17*, 417–430.

Marcus, B., Lee, K., & Ashton, M. C. (2007). Personality dimensions explaining relationships between integrity tests and counterproductive behavior: Big five, or one in addition? *Personnel Psychology, 60*, 1–34.

McCarthy, J., & Goffin, R. (2004). Measuring job interview anxiety: Beyond weak knees and sweaty palms. *Personnel Psychology, 57*, 607–637.

McCrae, R. R., & Costa, P. T. (1987). Validation of the five-factor model of personality across instruments and observers. *Journal of Personality and Social Psychology, 52*, 81–90.

McDaniel, M. A., Schmidt, F. L., & Hunter, J. E. (1988). A meta-analysis of the validity of methods for rating training and experience in personnel selection. *Personnel Psychology, 41*, 283–309.

McDaniel, M. A., Whetzel, D. L., Schmidt, F. L., & Maurer, S. D. (1994). The validity of employment interviews: A comprehensive review and meta-analysis. *Journal of Applied Psychology, 79*, 599–616.

McNelly, T., Ruggeberg, B. J., & Hall, C. R. (2011). Web-based management simulations: Technology-enhanced assessment for executive-level selection and development. In N. T. Tippins & S. Adler (Eds.), *Technology-enhanced assessment of talent* (pp. 253–266). San Francisco, CA: Jossey-Bass.

Melchers, K. G., Lienhardt, N., Von Aarburg, M., & Kleinmann, M. (2011). Is more structure really better? A comparison of frame-of-reference training and descriptively anchored rating scales to improve interviewers' rating quality. *Personnel Psychology, 64,* 53–87.

Morgeson, F. P., Campion, M. A., Dipboye, R. L., Hollenbeck, J. R., Murphy, K., & Schmitt, N. (2007). Reconsidering the use of personality tests in personnel selection contexts. *Personnel Psychology, 60,* 683–729.

Morgeson, F. P., Reider, M. H., Campion, M. A., & Bull, R. A. (2008). Review of research on age discrimination in the employment interview. *Journal of Business and Psychology, 22,* 223–232.

Moscoso, S. (2000). Selection interview: A review of validity evidence, adverse impact and applicant reactions. *International Journal of Selection and Assessment, 8,* 237–247.

Ones, D. S., Dilchert, S., & Viswesvaran, C. (2012). Cognitive abilities. In N. Schmitt (Ed.), *The Oxford handbook of personnel assessment and selection* (pp. 179–224). New York: Oxford University Press.

Ones, D. S., Dilchert, S., Viswesvaran, C., & Judge, T. A. (2007). In support of personality assessment in organizational settings. *Personnel Psychology, 60,* 995–1027.

Ones, D. S., & Viswesvaran, C. (1998). The effects of social desirability and faking on personality and integrity assessment for personnel selection. *Human Performance, 11,* 245–269.

Ones, D. S., & Viswesvaran, C. (2001). Integrity tests and other criterion-focused occupational personality scales (COPS) used in personnel selection. *International Journal of Selection and Assessment, 9,* 31–39.

Ones, D. S., Viswesvaran, C., & Schmidt, F. L. (1993). Comprehensive meta-analysis of integrity test validities: Findings and implications for personnel selection and theories of job performance. *Journal of Applied Psychology, 78,* 679–703.

Ones, D. S., Viswesvaran, C., & Schmidt, F. L. (2012). Integrity tests predict counterproductive work behaviors and job performance well: Comment on Van Iddekinge, Roth, Raymark, and Odle-Dusseau. *Journal of Applied Psychology, 97,* 537–542.

Oostrom, J. K., Bos-Broekema, L., Serlie, A. W., Born, M. P., & Van der Molen, H. T. (2012). A field study of pretest and posttest reactions to a paper-and-pencil and a computerized in-basket exercise. *Human Performance, 25,* 95–113.

Oswald, F. L., & Hough, L. M. (2011). Personality and its assessment in organizations: Theoretical and empirical developments. In S. Zedeck (Ed.), *APA handbook of industrial and organizational psychology, Vol 2: Selecting and developing members for the organization* (pp. 153–184). Washington, DC: American Psychological Association.

Peck, D. (2013). They're watching you at work. *Atlantic Monthly.* Retrieved March 7, 2014 from http://www.theatlantic.com/magazine/archive/2013/12/theyre-watching-you-at-work/354681/.

Plake, B. S., & Impara, J. C. (2001). *The fourteenth mental measurements yearbook.* Lincoln, NE: Buros Institute of Mental Measurements, University of Nebraska.

Ployhart, R. E., & Bliese, P. D. (2006). Individual adaptability (I-ADAPT) theory: Conceptualizing the antecedents, consequences, and measurement of individual differences in adaptability. In S. Burke, L. Pierce, & E. Salas (Eds.), *Understanding adaptability: A prerequisite for effective performance within complex environments* (pp. 3–39). St. Louis, MO: Elsevier Science.

Potosky, D. (2008). A conceptual framework for the role of the administration medium in the personnel assessment process. *Academy of Management Review, 33*, 629–648.

Pulakos, E. D., Arad, S., Donovan, M. A., & Plamondon, K. E. (2000). Adaptability in the workplace: Development of a taxonomy of adaptive performance. *Journal of Applied Psychology, 85*, 612–624.

Rampell, C. (2014). Your next job application could involve a video game. *New York Times*, January 22. Retrieved May 12, 2015 from: http://www.nytimes.com/2014/01/26/magazine/your-next-job-application-could-involve-a-video-game.html.

Reilly, R. R., & Chao, G. T. (1982). Validity and fairness of some alternative employee selection procedures. *Personnel Psychology, 35*, 1–62.

Rivlin, G. (2013,). The long shadow of bad credit in a job search. *New York Times* May 11. Retrieved March 18, 2014 from http://www.nytimes.com/2013/05/12/business/employers-pull-applicants-credit-reports.html.

Roberts, B. (2011). Your cheating heart. *HR Magazine, 56*, 54. Retrieved February 22, 2015 from http://www.shrm.org/publications/hrmagazine/editorialcontent/2011/0611/pages/0611roberts.aspx.

Roth, P. L., Bevier, C. A., Bobko, P., Switzer, F. S., & Tyler, P. (2001). Ethnic group differences in cognitive ability in employment and educational settings: A meta-analysis. *Personnel Psychology, 54*, 297–330.

Roth, P. L., Bobko, P., Van Iddekinge, C. H., & Thatcher, J. B. (in press). Social media in employment-related decisions: A research agenda for uncharted territory. *Journal of Management*, DOI: 0149206313503018

Ryan, A. M., & Ployhart, R. E. (2014). A century of selection. *Annual Review of Psychology, 65*, 693–717.

Ryan, A. M., & Powers, C. (2012). Workplace diversity. In N. Schmitt (Ed.), *The Oxford handbook of personnel assessment and selection* (pp. 814–831). New York: Oxford University Press.

Ryan, A. M., & Tippins, N. (2009). *Designing and implementing global selection systems*. Chichester, England: Wiley-Blackwell.

Sackett, P. R., & Schmitt, N. (2012). On reconciling conflicting meta-analytic findings regarding integrity test validity. *Journal of Applied Psychology, 97*, 550–556.

Sackett, P. R., & Wanek, J. E. (1996). New developments in the use of measures of honesty integrity, conscientiousness, dependability trustworthiness, and reliability for personnel selection. *Personnel Psychology, 49*, 787–829.

Sackett, P. R., & Wilk, S. L. (1994). Within-group norming and other forms of score adjustment in preemployment testing. *American Psychologist, 49*, 929–954.

Salgado, J. F. (1997). The five factor model of personality and job performance in the European community. *Journal of Applied Psychology, 82*, 30–43.

Salgado, J. F., Anderson, N., Moscoso, S., Bertua, C., De Fruyt, F., & Rolland, J. P. (2003). A meta-analytic study of general mental ability validity for different occupations in the European community. *Journal of Applied Psychology, 88,* 1068–1081.

Schmidt, F. L. (2002). The role of general cognitive ability and job performance: Why there cannot be a debate. *Human Performance, 15,* 187–210.

Schmidt, F. L., & Hunter, J. (2004). General mental ability in the world of work: Occupational attainment and job performance. *Journal of Personality and Social Psychology, 86,* 162–173.

Schmidt, F. L., & Hunter, J. E. (1981). Employment testing: Old theories and new research findings. *American Psychologist, 36,* 1128–1137.

Schmidt, F. L., & Hunter, J. E. (1998). The validity and utility of selection methods in personnel psychology: Practical and theoretical implications of 85 years of research findings. *Psychological Bulletin, 124,* 262–274.

Schmitt, N., & Kunce, C. (2002). The effects of required elaboration of answers to biodata questions. *Personnel Psychology, 55,* 569–587.

Shaffer, J. A., & Postlethwaite, B. E. (2012). A matter of context: A meta-analytic investigation of the relative validity of contextualized and no contextualized personality measures. *Personnel Psychology, 65,* 445–493.

Society for Human Resource Management. (2010). *Background checking: Conducting reference background checks, SHRM poll. Survey findings, January 22.* Retrieved May 12, 2015 from: http://www.shrm.org/Research/SurveyFindings/Articles/Pages/ConductingReferenceBackgroundChecks.aspx.

Span, P. (2011). A new credential for home care aides. *New York Times,* February 25. Retrieved March 18, 2014 from http://newoldage.blogs.nytimes.com/2011/02/25/a-new-credential-for-home-health-aides.

Spearman, C. (1904). " General Intelligence," objectively determined and measured. *American Journal of Psychology, 15,* 201–292.

Steiner, D. D. (2012). Personnel selection across the globe. In N. Schmitt (Ed.), *The Oxford handbook of personnel selection and assessment* (pp. 740–767). New York: Oxford University Press.

Sternberg, R. J., & Detterman, D. K. (1986). *What is intelligence? Contemporary viewpoints on its nature and definition.* Norwood, NJ: Ablex Publishing Corporation.

Sturman, M. C., & Sherwyn, D. (2009). The utility of integrity testing for controlling workers' compensation costs. *Cornell Hospitality Quarterly, 50,* 432–445.

Tippins, N. (2009). Internet alternatives to traditional proctored testing: Where are we now? *Industrial and Organizational Psychology, 2,* 2–10.

Tippins, N. T. (2015). Technology and assessment in selection. *Annual Review of Organizational Psychology and Organizational Behavior, 2,* 551–582.

Tippins, N. T., & Adler, S. (2011). *Technology-enhanced assessment of talent.* San Francisco, CA: Jossey-Bass.Van Hooft, E. A., & Born, M. P. (2012). Intentional response distortion on personality tests: Using eye-tracking to understand response processes when faking. *Journal of Applied Psychology, 97,* 301–316.

Van Iddekinge, C. H., Lanivich, S. E., Roth, P. L., & Junco, E. (in press). Social media for selection? Validity and adverse impact potential of a Facebook-based assessment. *Journal of Management,* DOI: 0149206313515524

Van Iddekinge, C. H., Putka, D. J., & Campbell, J. P. (2011). Reconsidering vocational interests for personnel selection: The validity of an interest-based selection test in relation to job knowledge, job performance, and continuance intentions. *Journal of Applied Psychology*, *96*, 13–33.

Van Iddekinge, C. H., Roth, P. L., Raymark, P. H., & Odle-Dusseau, H. N. (2012). The criterion-related validity of integrity tests: An updated meta-analysis. *Journal of Applied Psychology*, *97*, 499–530.

Van Rooy, D. L., Viswesvaran, C., & Pluta, P. (2005). An evaluation of construct validity: What is this thing called emotional intelligence? *Human Performance*, *18*, 445–462.

Vinchur, A., & Bryan, L. L. K. (2012). A history of personnel selection and assessment. In N. Schmitt (Ed.), *The Oxford handbook of personnel assessment and selection* (pp. 9–30). New York: Oxford University Press.

Vinchur, A. J., Schippmann, J. S., Switzer III, F. S., & Roth, P. L. (1998). A meta-analytic review of predictors of job performance for salespeople. *Journal of Applied Psychology*, *83*, 586–597.

Wang, M., Zhan, Y., McCune, E., & Truxillo, D. (2011). Understanding newcomers' adaptability and work-related outcomes: Testing the mediating roles of perceived P-E fit variables. *Personnel Psychology*, *64*, 163–189.

Whetzel, D. L., McDaniel, M. A., & Nguyen, N. T. (2008). Subgroup differences in situational judgment test performance: A meta-analysis. *Human Performance*, *21*, 291–309.

Williamson, L. G., Campion, J. E., Malos, S. B., Roehling, M. V., & Campion, M. A. (1997). Employment interview on trial: Linking interview structure with litigation outcomes. *Journal of Applied Psychology*, *82*, 900–912.

Zickar, M. J., & Lake, C. J. (2011). Practice agenda: Innovative uses of technology-enhanced assessment. In N. T. Tippins & S. Adler (Eds.), *Technology-enhanced assessment of talent* (pp. 394–417). San Francisco, CA: Jossey-Bass.

Zielinski, D. (2014, February). The mobilization of HR tech. *HR Magazine*, *209*, 30–36.

Chapter 7

PERSONNEL SELECTION
Strategic Issues in the Deployment of Selection Systems

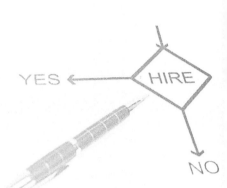

In this chapter we will discuss how to use predictors strategically.

After studying this chapter, you should be able to:
- describe the major strategic issues in the deployment of personnel selection systems
- describe the issues surrounding employee recruitment, including the goals of recruitment for personnel selection
- identify the primary strategies used by organizations in administering predictors to applicants
- describe the different ways of operationalizing test validity according to professional and legal guidelines
- describe the primary legal and ethical issues associated with the use of selection procedures
- describe the ways that predictor data are used, how to choose combinations of predictors, and how to most effectively combine predictor data

Learning goals for this chapter

- differentiate between validity generalization and situational specificity
- describe which selection procedures are preferred by applicants and how to improve applicant reactions
- identify key global issues in selection systems and ·strategies
- describe the current issues and controversies around selection systems and strategies.

Introduction

In Chapter 6, we described the large number of predictors that can be used to make personnel selection decisions. Clearly, there are many options available for organizations when choosing from different types of predictors to hire employees and many tradeoffs among them.

However, we have said relatively little about the strategies that organizations use in implementing these predictors. Understanding these strategic issues is a crucial step to implementing selection systems effectively. They include issues such as attracting the best talent and ensuring that there are enough qualified applicants for each job, ensuring that predictors are valid (job-related) and legally defensible, strategies for administering multiple predictors, and how to combine predictor data to make the best hiring decisions. And finally, the organization should consider how job applicants perceive the selection system and how they are treated throughout the selection process, as this might affect whether applicants accept a job offer and perhaps whether they bring legal challenges. These strategic issues are shown graphically in Figure 7.1.

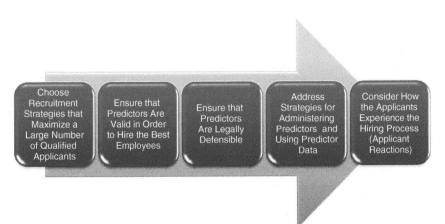

Figure 7.1 Strategic issues in the deployment and use of selection procedures.

For example, say a large retail company is hiring salespeople. They would need to decide which predictors are best for hiring people into that job. Let's say they do a job analysis and determine that personality tests, biodata, and interviews are the best choices. Then they would need to decide when, and in what order, to give the predictors: Do they give all three selection procedures to all applicants? Do they give the selection procedures to applicants in a certain order? Next, after that, they would need to decide how to combine the results from multiple selection procedures: Do they simply average the three procedures together, or are some procedures weighted more heavily than others? And in doing all of this, they need to be sure that they are staying within legal and professional guidelines. I/O psychology, as a profession, has taken the lead on addressing these questions, which is why personnel selection is one of the largest areas of practice among I/O psychologists.

The types of issues we will discuss in this chapter – such as recruitment, technical and legal guidelines to show a test's validity and ensure its legal defensibility, ways of using statistics to ensure good personnel decisions, and how to treat applicants – may appear a bit daunting to a person who has never thought about these issues before. Although understanding the technical details of these issues requires a lot of sophistication – technical knowledge that someone would get from graduate training in I/O psychology – it is certainly possible to understand the basics involved in these personnel selection issues. In this chapter, we will present you with the fundamentals of the technical, statistical, and legal issues involved in the use of predictors for making hiring decisions, providing you with a general understanding of how organizations strategically apply the science of selection to hire the best talent.

Recruitment: An organizational activity focused on increasing the number of job applicants, their quality and fit with the job openings and with the organization's culture, and at the same time meeting the organization's legal and ethical obligations with regard to diversity.

Recruitment

Recruitment is an organizational activity focused on increasing the number of applicants, their quality and fit with the job openings and with the organization's culture, while at the same time meeting the organization's legal and ethical obligations with regard to diversity (Gatewood, Feild, & Barrick, 2011). The importance

Figure 7.2
Strategic issues in the deployment and use of selection procedures: Recruitment.

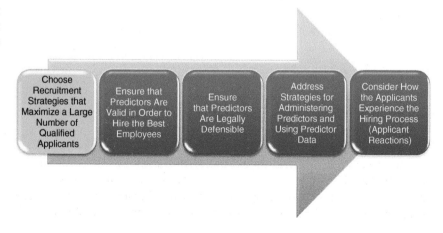

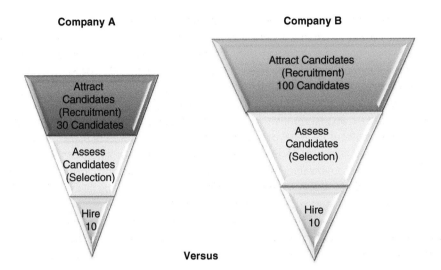

Company A

Company B

Versus

Figure 7.3 The recruitment and selection funnel. Increasing the number of employees recruited allows the organization to be more selective in its hiring decisions. In this case, all other things being equal, which organization is most likely to end up with the 10 best candidates?

of good recruitment for making good hiring decisions cannot be overstated. Thus, companies spend a lot of money and resources on recruitment. For example, it has been estimated that organizations spend approximately $3,300 per hire on recruiting – which comes to $72 billion per year in the US, and triple that world-wide (Bersin, 2013). Given the high costs of recruitment and how important it is for who is hired, it is important to understand each aspect of recruitment as described in our definition above.

First, one goal of recruitment is to increase the number of job applicants for positions. Think of it this way. If you were a manager hiring for a job opening on your team, would you rather get to choose from 2 candidates or 10? Although it might take a little more time to review the 10 candidates, having more candidates to choose from increases your odds of hiring a good candidate. As can be seen in Figure 7.3, increasing the number of candidates recruited into the "selection funnel" allows an organization to be more selective when they go to make hiring decisions. As we will discuss later in this chapter, all things being equal, having more candidates to choose from makes it more worthwhile to go through all of the trouble of putting together a selection system.

Second, it is not good enough to simply have more candidates. What an organization wants is more *qualified* candidates. In other words, 10 candidates who are unqualified or minimally qualified for the job will not help you hire a great, or even good, employee. However, choosing from among 10 highly qualified candidates is an advantageous position to be in, as your odds of getting a good employee are greatly increased. At this point, you may be wondering what is meant by a "highly qualified" candidate. As with so much in I/O psychology, you need to turn to the job analysis, which will state which knowledge, skills, and abilities are needed to perform the job, including what types of training and experience are needed to do the job. The key is to try to reduce the number of unqualified candidates – it is not a good use of time to have to review applications for people who are not qualified and administer selection procedures to them. Moreover, you want to be sure that candidates will fit within the organizational culture. As we will discuss shortly, there is a robust literature on how to be sure to attract candidates who are a good fit for the job and for the organization.

A third goal of recruitment is to increase and maintain workforce diversity. Recruitment is the time to consider the diversity issues surrounding the candidate pool, with the goal of maintaining or increasing the diversity of the organizational members – an important issue both for legal reasons and for reasons of social responsibility. If an organization wants to hire a more diverse workforce, they obviously need to focus on the types of selection procedures they are using, such that adverse impact is minimized. But it is important to consider the flip side as well. If the applicant pool is not diverse, there is no way that the organization can hire a diverse workforce. In other words, to create and maintain diversity among its employees, an organization must start with a diverse pool of job applicants.

Recruitment Methods

There are many ways to recruit employees. These include online advertising via the organization's web page, recruiting through recommendations from current employees, or recruiting via the local newspaper. A recent survey of organizations showed that employers commonly use a wide variety of methods to recruit applicants, such as career websites, employer social networking sites, employee referral programs, and career fairs (The Talent Board, 2014). Each of these methods has its advantages and disadvantages in terms of cost, quality of applicants, the likelihood of attracting applicants from different ethnic groups, and the degree to which the recruitment medium allows the organization to communicate what the job and organization are like. For example, recruiting through current employees is advantageous in terms of getting qualified applicants who know a lot about the organization. On the other hand, an overreliance on recruiting through current employees may cause the organization to attract only applicants who are like the current employees in terms of background, gender, and ethnicity. The point is that

Workplace Application

The Ways of Recruitment

Recruitment has long been considered an important part of any selection system. Companies have known for decades that they needed to do their best to attract the best talent in order to better contend with their competition.

Today recruitment is taken just as seriously as it ever was, although many of the tools have changed. For example, social networking sites such as LinkedIn serve as a useful method for finding the best talent. In fact, many recruiters try to leverage such social networking sites to find "passive" job candidates – talented potential applicants who are not currently looking for work (and who may be happily employed elsewhere). In addition, it is highly recommended that employers keep their websites updated and looking good, because candidates look to employer websites to learn more about a company. Other suggestions include having current employees post job openings on their own social networking accounts and keeping their own LinkedIn profiles up-to-date. Not surprisingly, there is also a "big data" approach to recruitment as well, as some companies are using advanced analytics of millions of online profiles to search for strong job candidates.

In the end, though, much of recruitment is the same as it has ever been: While online recruitment tools are invaluable for casting a wider net, in the end the personal touch is one of most important factors in attracting talent. In other words, at some point, candidates will want to meet an organizational representative and the people they will be working with.

Sources: Campbell, 2014; Cohen, 2013; Hardy, 2014.

no one method is uniquely suitable for attracting applicants to the organization, but that organizations must carefully choose which methods make sense for the particular job and for their recruitment goals.

What Factors Affect Applicant Attraction to the Organization?

There is a good bit of research on what attracts applicants to the organization. Not surprisingly, the main factors that affect applicants' decisions are characteristics of the job and of the organization, behavior of the recruiter, and whether the applicant thinks that they would fit in the organization (Chapman, Uggerslev, Carroll, Piasentin, & Jones, 2005). Moreover, the organization's image among applicants is important, and research has even shown that applicants see different organizations as having different "personalities" (e.g., "innovative", "dominant"; Slaughter, Zickar, Highhouse, & Mohr, 2004). Preserving and maintaining the image of an organization is important. In a study of potential applicants for the Belgian army, Van Hoye and Lievens (2009) found that getting positive information about the organization through word of mouth early in the process was a good predictor of whether applicants decided to actually apply to the organization. In other words, organizations cannot entirely "manage" their image via websites and advertising because word of mouth matters as well. They should also treat applicants with respect (The Talent Board, 2014).

Another issue is whether organizations can try to communicate certain values to attract certain types of applicants. It appears that this kind of communication can be very useful. For example, Gully, Phillips, Castellano, Han, and Kim (2013) found that communicating an organization's values for social and environmental responsibility were related to job-seekers' attraction, perceived fit, and intentions to pursue a job – but only for applicants with a stated desire to make significant impact through their work. Similarly, Phillips, Gully, McCarthy, Castellano, and Kim (2014) found that recruitment messages about travel requirements and an organization's international presence affected applicant attraction and job pursuit intentions – critical issues in today's multinational organizations – but primarily for applicants with higher global openness and with a willingness to travel. And Avery (2003) found that diversity in advertisements did not affect the organization's attractiveness for White students, but it did for Black students if the ads showed supervisor-level diversity.

Today, many large organizations are hiring outside firms to handle the recruitment process for them and which specialize in using the Web to help compete for talent. For example, Apple used one of these firms when it needed to quickly open its retail stores in China (Bersin, 2013). Its flagship store in Shanghai is pictured here.

There are also practical issues about how an employer should use the recruitment choices available to it, especially websites which have such enormous flexibility. One approach is to take advantage of the potential richness of website media. For example, Walker, Feild, Giles, Armenakis, and Bernerth (2009) found that presenting employee testimonials on organization websites did affect applicant attraction, but these testimonials worked best when presented as a video on the website rather than just as written text with a picture of the employee. Taken together, these studies suggest that organizations have a number of options for targeting specific types of job applicants by means of their advertising and recruitment efforts.

In conclusion, employee recruitment is a complex business these days. There are many ways in which to find potential job candidates and to provide information about the organization to potential applicants. The savvy organization will focus on the goals of recruitment – higher numbers of qualified job applicants and increased organizational diversity – and choose the best recruitment methods to achieve these goals.

Validity of Selection Procedures

One of the biggest issues in the use of personnel selection procedures is their validity. We spoke about validity in general terms back in Chapter 2. However, the concept of validity deserves additional attention here because of its importance in the use of personnel selection procedures. This is for three reasons. First, if you do not know that a selection procedure is a valid predictor of job performance, there is little point in using it. Giving a test to applicants uses resources – money and time from the organization and its HR staff, and time from job applicants – so giving a test that is not valid is a poor use of resources. Second, on the positive side, an organization can choose strong predictors that have high validity to enable them to hire the best talent. In today's competitive business environment, using valid predictors to acquire the best talent gives an organization a competitive advantage. Thus, using the selection procedures that are the best predictors of job performance is a critical part of an organization's HR strategy. Third, in the United States, proof of validity is essential for defending tests and other measures in case they are found to have adverse impact

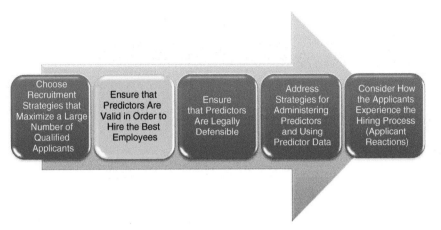

Figure 7.4 Strategic issues in the deployment and use of selection procedures: Ensure validity.

against certain legally protected groups. It is for this reason that validity is not just an academic issue, but guidelines for showing a test's validity are also described in professional standards (SIOP, 2003) and legal documents (e.g., *Uniform Guidelines*) as well, which we use as the basis for much of our discussion below.

In this section we describe each of the primary ways of showing the validity of a selection procedure, which in the *Uniform Guidelines* are described in terms of content validity, construct validity, and criterion-related validity. However, we reiterate the point that we made in Chapter 2, namely, it is usually best to think of "validity" as a single, unitary concept, not three; there are many ways to accumulate evidence that a test is measuring what it is supposed to measure (Landy, 1986). Rather, here we describe validity in the terms typically used in legal contexts. In that light, in Table 7.1 we present a comparison of the most common validation strategies used for legal reasons in selection situations, content validity and criterion-related validity. Note that with all types of validity, the assumption is that a higher test score will be associated with higher performance on the job.

Content Validity

Content validity is the degree to which a selection procedure has been developed to sample the job in terms of the required KSAs (Goldstein, Zedeck, & Schneider, 1993). Rather than showing an empirical relationship between a test and some other measure or outcome, content validity relies on evidence that the test actually does sample the job. How would you do this? As you might expect, it relies heavily on a detailed job analysis and SME opinion (Gatewood et al., 2011). For example, if you wanted to show the content validity of a test for a customer service job, you would do a detailed job analysis to see what critical KSAs it requires and what critical tasks are associated with the KSAs. You could then ask SMEs (current customer service workers and their supervisors) to help you develop items that sample the job, or you might ask them to confirm that the test questions that you have developed are job-related. You could then document their opinions by having the SMEs sign off on the content validity of the items and perhaps rate the test items on their job relatedness. The literature describes a number of possible

Content validity: The degree to which a selection procedure has been developed to sample the job. Content validity relies on evidence (usually job analysis and SME judgments) that the predictor actually does sample the job.

Table 7.1 Comparison of content and criterion-related validation strategies

	Content Validity	Criterion-Related Validity	
What is it?	Development of the selection procedure such that it samples the job.	Demonstration of an empirical relationship between the predictor and a job performance outcome (criterion).	
How is it demonstrated?	Detailed job analysis and documented judgment of job relatedness by SMEs.	Typically by a statistically significant correlation between the predictor and the criterion or by multiple regression to determine the best linear combination of predictors.	
		Predictive Design	**Concurrent Design**
What samples are used? How is it done?	SMEs (see above) and a detailed job analysis. SME judgments should be carefully documented.	Job applicants. Validity is shown by demonstrating the statistical relationship between applicants' predictor scores and their later job performance.	Current employees. Validity is shown by demonstrating the statistical relationship between employees' predictor scores and current job performance.
Timing	N/A	There is a time lag between the predictor and the job performance measure.	There is no time lag between the predictor and the job performance measure.
Issues associated with its use	Particularly useful when criterion-related validity studies cannot be done because, for example, larger samples are not available to do the statistical analyses needed.	Large enough samples must be available to conduct the statistical analyses.	Large enough samples must be available to conduct the statistical analyses. While more convenient, concurrent designs may be limited by, for instance, low motivation on the part of the participants who are current employees rather than actual job applicants.

ways to document the content validity ratings that SMEs provide (e.g., Anderson & Gerbing, 1991; Lawshe, 1975).

There are a few issues to note about content validity. First, people sometimes confuse content validity with **face validity**, which is the degree to which the test seems job-related to a job applicant. Face validity is important: Organizations do want to use selection procedures that seem job-related and fair to applicants, as

Face validity: The degree to which a test appears to be job-related to a job applicant.

we will discuss in the section on "applicant reactions". But content validity is about much more than whether a test looks valid to a job applicant; rather, it involves the judgment of SMEs that the selection procedure is job-related and the thorough documentation of their judgment. Second, because content validity does not involve the demonstration of an empirical relationship between the test and the job, there is some controversy among some I/O psychologists as to its effectiveness (e.g., Guion, 2009; Murphy, 2009). However, it is a legally defined validation method as stipulated by the *Uniform Guidelines* and in the *SIOP Principles*. Third, content validity comes in handy in situations where there are only small samples. In those cases, doing a large empirical study to show validity is impossible, and content validity is the most practical approach.

Construct Validity

We discussed construct validity back in Chapter 2. As a brief refresher, **construct validity** involves showing that a test or measure has an expected pattern of relationships with other measures. Specifically, you might show that a test of conscientiousness is related to other measures of conscientiousness, but that it has a weaker relationship with measures of theoretically unrelated constructs (e.g., a measure of cognitive ability). In the specific case of personnel selection, you would want to first show that the test is in fact a good measure of the intended construct, say, mechanical ability. From there, using a test for personnel selection requires that you demonstrate the link between the construct and the job. How do you do that? You guessed it – through a job analysis. For example, if an organization wanted to use a test of mechanical ability to hire mechanics, they would first be sure that the test actually was measuring mechanical ability – either through their own research or by the research report from the test publisher – and then document through a job analysis that mechanical ability is a construct actually needed to do the job. Note, however, that for technical reasons the use of construct validity as a legal justification for a selection test is more complicated and challenging than other methods, and is thus a less common way to show validity than content or criterion-related validity (Gatewood et al., 2011). For instance, legal guidelines generally indicate that at some point, if possible, the construct validity evidence needs to be followed up with evidence that shows an even more clear relationship between the predictor and job performance. That is usually through criterion-related validity.

Criterion-Related Validity

As we said in Chapter 2, **criterion-related validity** is demonstrated by showing the empirical relationship between a test and some outcome that you care about. In the case of personnel selection, we want to show that the test or predictor actually does have a relationship with job performance. In most cases, this is done through showing that there is a statistically significant correlation between the test and the job performance criterion. This correlation between the predictor and the criterion is referred to as the **validity coefficient**. In addition, as described elsewhere in this chapter, multiple regression can be used to empirically determine the best way to combine predictors, that is, what the relative weights of

Construct validity: Demonstrated by showing that a test has an expected pattern of relationships with other measures and, in the case of selection, that it measures a construct needed for the job as documented through a job analysis.

Criterion-related validity: Demonstrated by showing a statistical relationship between a test and a criterion measure of job performance. This is typically done through correlation or linear regression.

Validity coefficient: The correlation between the test and criterion, demonstrating the magnitude of relationship between the test and job performance.

each predictor should be to result in the best prediction of work performance. As with all validation designs in personnel selection, the process starts with a job analysis to suggest what types of predictors might be most appropriate for the particular job. (There is a detailed discussion of technical issues associated with criterion-related validity in Van Iddekinge & Ployhart, 2008.)

There really are two main ways to do a criterion-related validity study. By that we mean that there are two types of study designs or how you collect the data, and from whom. These two are called predictive validity and concurrent validity.

Predictive Validity

Predictive validity:
A way of showing criterion-related validity where a test is given to a group of applicants and correlated with their later job performance (i.e., after they are hired).

A **predictive validity** study involves giving a test or tests to a group of applicants; in the purest predictive design, you would not use the test to make selection decisions. Then, maybe six months later, you can collect criterion data (i.e., job performance measures; see Chapter 4) from the applicants that you hired. You would show the criterion-related validity by correlating the test scores from the applicants with their later job performance. For example, if you wanted to use a test of extraversion to select sales people, you could give the extraversion test to a group of applicants and then run a statistical correlation between their test scores before they were hired and their later performance (such as sales numbers). If the correlation is statistically significant, you then can feel comfortable that you have a valid predictor of job performance, and you can confidently use the test to make selection decisions in the future.

Concurrent Validity

Concurrent validity:
A way of showing criterion-related validity where a test is given to current employees. Their test scores are then correlated with their current job performance.

The second main way to do a validity study is to use **concurrent validity**. This is where you give a test to current employees – telling them of course that information gathered will be used only for research and that no decisions will be made about them based on the test – and then correlate their test scores with their current job performance. (No waiting for six months!) As in the example above, you might give the extraversion test to current sales people, and then correlate their test scores with their current job performance (e.g., sales). If the correlation is statistically significant, you can feel confident that the test is valid and can be used for selection.

Advantages and Disadvantages of Predictive and Concurrent Validity

What are the advantages and disadvantages of predictive and concurrent validity? Each approach has its uses. Concurrent validity is generally easier. Because it only involves current employees taking a test and then correlating their test scores with their job performance – not administering a test to applicants and waiting to see how they perform on the job – it saves considerable time. Relatedly, some employers are unwilling to have an I/O researcher give a test to applicants and then not use the scores to make decisions.

However, predictive studies have at least two advantages over concurrent designs. First, predictive designs involve *validating the test on the population for which you plan to use it (i.e., applicants)*. Current employees can differ in a number of ways from job applicants: Current employees may have gained some job skills, and they may not be particularly motivated when they take the test, certainly not as much as job applicants would be, as they already have jobs. In these ways, then, job applicants really are different from current employees, and in ways that make them more suitable for test validation research.

The second issue that may cause concurrent validity studies to be less strong than predictive studies is a statistical one called range restriction – where there is reduced variability in test scores – which is shown in Figure 7.5 (Sackett, Putka, & McCloy, 2012). Range restriction occurs because the employee sample used in the concurrent study consists of people who scored high enough on the test to be hired, and those who were performing well enough on the job that they were not terminated. As you can see in Figure 7.5, cutting out the unsuccessful applicants and employees and then doing the validity study only on the restricted sample causes the distribution of scores to be shaped in a way that finding correlation might be difficult. (Instead of an oval distribution of scores, it looks more circular – essentially a low to zero correlation.)

Despite these potential downsides of concurrent validation, it is probably the more commonly used because it is so much more convenient. Furthermore, the potential limitations we have described above do not necessarily affect the results in practice, that is, concurrent validity studies often yield validity results that are as good as those found with predictive validity (Schmitt, Gooding, Noe, & Kirsch, 1984). In short, although researchers should be aware of potential differences between concurrent and predictive studies because of potential differences in the samples (Cascio & Aguinis, 2011), concurrent designs generally are more convenient than predictive designs and yield similar results.

Cross-Validation

No matter which type of criterion-related validity study is used, it is good practice to follow up with a **cross-validation** to be sure of the accuracy found from the validity study. For instance, when using multiple regression, the R^2 value or percentage of variance explained (see Chapter 2) by the predictors can be influenced by chance characteristics of the sample. For that reason, the R^2 value in a second sample will always be a little smaller. This is known as **shrinkage**. Similarly, the regression weights (or "b"s; see discussion of multiple regression in this chapter) will always be somewhat different in the original validation compared to later samples because of small chance differences between the two samples. In any case, what the selection researcher wants to know is if the finding from the original validity study is accurate. They check this by seeing if the original R^2 and regression weights from the original sample are reasonably accurate. (See Gatewood et al., 2011 for a more detailed and technical discussion of cross-validation.) One important note here: The larger the original validation sample used for the study, the more accurate it will be.

How is cross-validation done? There are basically two ways. In empirical cross-validation (see Figure 7.6), one first conducts the criterion-related validity study. Then, using a second sample, the regression weights (see later in this chapter) established in the first sample are tested out to see how accurately they predict the job performance criterion in the second sample. If the weights from the second sample provide similar predicted scores to the first – in other words, there is relatively

Cross-validation:
A process by which the validity established with an initial criterion-related validity study is confirmed with another sample.

Shrinkage: The degree to which the R^2 on a cross-validation sample does not match the R^2 on the original validation sample.

Figure 7.5 Graphic representation of range restriction. Because there is range restriction in the lower graph, the observed correlation between the test score and job performance will be weaker.

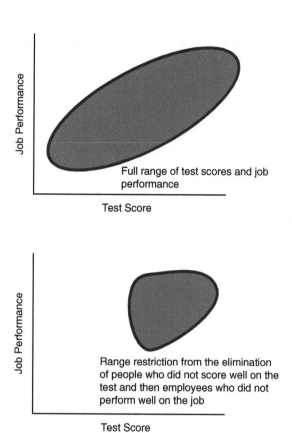

Full range of test scores and job performance

Range restriction from the elimination of people who did not score well on the test and then employees who did not perform well on the job

little shrinkage – that means that the original validities and regression weights are holding up well (Guion, 2011). The second method is statistical cross-validation, and is much more convenient. When calculating a regression equation, most statistical software packages will give you not only an R^2 but also an adjusted R^2. What this means is that the package estimates based on the characteristics of the sample (e.g., its size) how much shrinkage one could expect.

Figure 7.6 Summary of empirical cross-validation.

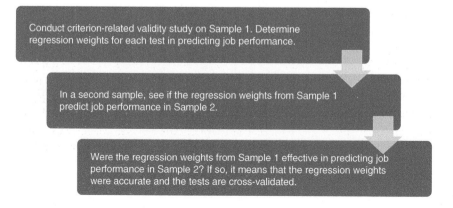

Conduct criterion-related validity study on Sample 1. Determine regression weights for each test in predicting job performance.

In a second sample, see if the regression weights from Sample 1 predict job performance in Sample 2.

Were the regression weights from Sample 1 effective in predicting job performance in Sample 2? If so, it means that the regression weights were accurate and the tests are cross-validated.

Validity Generalization versus Situational Specificity

Now that you know how complex it can be to validate selection tests, you might wonder if there are any shortcuts that an organization might take. One of these is the question of whether an organization has to validate selection procedures, even if these procedures have been validated in other similar organizations. For example, the Main Street Auto Works may want to hire mechanics, and a test vendor tells them that they have a test of mechanical ability that would be just right for them. In fact, the vendor can show that other organizations, which have similar mechanics' jobs to those at Main Street Auto Works, have used the test in the past, and that they found the test had high validity; that is, the tests did a good job of predicting job performance. The question is whether Main Street can now assume that the mechanical ability test is valid for them as well or whether they will need to revalidate the test for their particular group of job applicants.

This dilemma is essentially the heart of the matter around the issue of **validity generalization**, which is the assumption that a test that is valid for one job will be valid for other, similar jobs; as opposed to the **situational specificity hypothesis**, which is the belief that just because a test has been shown to be valid in one setting, you cannot assume that it will be valid in other settings, even if they are similar. What does the science say about these two very different approaches to test validation, and what do the laws say?

The idea of situational specificity dates back many years, but was clearly articulated by Ghiselli (1966), who collected validity studies done over many years. Ghiselli found that test validities for predicting job performance varied considerably from study to study, even if the jobs were fairly similar. For this reason, the idea of situational specificity took hold among I/O psychologists. However, a number of later studies by Schmidt and Hunter (see Schmidt and Hunter, 1981) disconfirmed this conclusion. Instead, they found that the reason that a test might be valid in one situation and not in another was likely due to statistical issues, such as small sample sizes. Today, the assumption among most I/O psychologists is that test validities are likely to generalize across situations (SIOP, 2003), as long as the jobs are similar in terms of the KSAs required for each. This is best shown through a job analysis.

From a legal standpoint, although the science shows that validity generalization exists, the courts and the *Uniform Guidelines* lean toward a situational specificity approach such that tests should be validated for each situation in which they are used (Gatewood et al., 2011). However, even a test that has been shown to be valid for one job cannot always be assumed to be valid for another job that requires different KSAs; in this situation, the test would need to be re-validated or a different test used. Using the mechanical ability test example again, it would make sense for Main Street Auto Works to use the mechanical ability test to select mechanics if a job analysis showed that the mechanics in their company needed to have knowledge and skills similar to the mechanics on whom the test was originally validated. However, if they wanted to use the test to hire customer service representatives, they would need to perform another validation study.

Validity generalization: The assumption that a test that is valid for one job will be valid for other, similar jobs.

Situational specificity hypothesis: The belief that even though a test has been shown to be valid in one setting, one cannot assume that it will be valid in other settings, even if they are similar.

A practical topic related to validity generalization is that of synthetic validity (SIOP, 2003). Although not commonly used (Johnson et al., 2010), synthetic validity is sometimes an option when using tests that have been validated in other contexts. The idea is that even if two jobs are somewhat different, they may share a certain performance dimension in common (e.g., dependability); if so, you might be able to use the information from the one job to show it is valid in another (Lawshe, 1952). For example, let's say that past research has shown that a particular test of conscientiousness predicts the dependability of customer service employees. But you have another job, sales associate, that also requires dependability. Even though the jobs are a bit different, the synthetic validity approach would say that to the extent that the jobs both require dependability, the conscientiousness test can be used for either one.

Legal Issues in Hiring

Throughout both this chapter and Chapter 6, we have referred to legal constraints in the use of selection procedures. We also pointed out in Chapter 1 that the Civil Rights legislation in the US, which originated in the 1960s, was the cause of profound changes in the practice of I/O psychology, particularly personnel selection. In this section, we provide quite a bit more detail regarding legal implications for hiring practices. In fact, in this chapter we do not have a final legal issues section at the end because legal issues are a component of the chapter itself. We point the reader interested in the details of how the US legal system works for selection, including a discussion of specific court cases, to additional sources (e.g., Cascio & Aguinis, 2011; Gatewood et al., 2011; Gutman, Koppes, & Vodanovich, 2010).

Note that much of our discussion in this section focuses on US Civil Rights legislation and case law. This is because of the highly elaborate employment law focused on fair treatment that has developed in the United States, including the development of mechanisms such as the Equal Employment Opportunity Commission

Figure 7.7 Strategic issues in the deployment and use of selection procedures: Ensure legal defensibility.

Table 7.2 Overview of some key US Civil Rights laws related to personnel selection

Civil Rights Law	What It Covers
Title VII of the Civil Rights Act (1964)	Race, color, sex, religion, and national origin
Age Discrimination in Employment Act (1967)	People over 40
The Rehabilitation Act (1973)	Mental and physical disabilities
Immigration Reform and Control Act (1986)	National origin
Americans with Disabilities Act (1990)	Mental and physical disabilities
Civil Rights Act of 1991	Race, color, sex, religion, and national origin. This 1991 Civil Rights Act also outlawed "within group norming" or score adjustment to reduce adverse impact

(EEOC), charged with monitoring and enforcing these laws. However, we point out that many countries around the world have also developed civil rights legislation around employment testing. Although the specifics of these laws vary from country to country, many countries share similar protections for specific groups (e.g., women). Myors et al. (2008) provides a useful comparison of the selection legal environments of 22 countries around the globe. Note that despite the existence of civil rights legislation in many countries, the actual enforcement of these laws varies considerably, with the US having some of the most established channels for enforcement of laws (Dunleavy, Cohen, Aamodt, & Schaeffer, 2008).

Some Background and Definitions

Before getting into our discussion of selection law, it might first be useful to provide some definitions. First is the idea of laws established by the US Congress, such as the 1964 Civil Rights Act. (See Table 7.2 for a list of some essential legislation in the US related to personnel selection.) However, in the US, interpretation of the law is not always clear just from reading the Act that was passed by Congress. From there, the details of how the law is administered – and what it means for job applicants and employers – is developed over the years by means of **case law**. In other words, lawsuits are brought against employers, employers defend themselves from these lawsuits, and the courts issue decisions about who was "right", which then sets a precedent for what other employers should do. It is these laws from the federal courts, including the US Supreme Court, that codify the details of how charges of discrimination are handled, how an organization can defend itself, and how selection systems should be developed. For example, one early court case, Griggs v. Duke Power (1971), was the first to

Case law: Laws as determined by court cases and their associated decisions.

241

In the United States, case law about hiring practices evolves over the years and guides the development and validation of selection procedures. Many of these cases have ultimately been determined by the US Supreme Court.

imply that a job analysis should be done as part of the validation of selection procedures.

Because of the proliferation of so much case law, the US government (specifically, the Equal Employment Opportunity Commission, Department of Labor, Civil Service Commission, and Department of Justice) developed the *Uniform Guidelines on Employee Selection Procedures* (1978; typically referred to as the *Uniform Guidelines*); although they are not technically law, the *Uniform Guidelines* are treated like law by the courts and provide significant guidance to employers about key issues such as how to validate tests. They apply to employers with 15 or more employees. One frequent criticism of the *Uniform Guidelines* is their age: A lot of selection science has emerged since 1978 when the guidelines were last published, as documented in SIOP's standards on testing (*Principles for the Validation and Use of Employee Selection Procedures*; SIOP, 2003). In other words, the *Uniform Guidelines* seem due for an update (McDaniel, Kepes, & Banks, 2011), but at this point in time, they are the standard courts use when dealing with selection cases.

Equal Employment Opportunity Commission (EEOC): The US government agency charged with monitoring employers' activities in relation to providing equal opportunity to all groups, such as through selection procedures and pay.

The **Equal Employment Opportunity Commission** (EEOC) is the US government agency charged with monitoring organizations' activities about providing equal opportunity to all groups, such as through selection procedures and pay. A **protected group** is any subgroup of individuals protected under the law, such as women and people over 40. In this sense, the term "minority" is technically incorrect, as a majority of people of working age in the US fall into some type of protected group. Further, it is important to remember that the law does not only protect one group. For example, laws prohibiting sex discrimination protect both women and men from being discriminated against because of their sex, and race discrimination laws prohibit any selection decision based on race. In addition, according to the *Uniform Guidelines*, the term "selection procedure" is used quite broadly. It could mean tests and other predictors given to external applicants, but it also refers to any procedure used to make any kind of hiring decision. This includes promotion decisions for internal job applicants, or training programs where success in the program leads to hiring or promotion decisions (see Chapter 8).

Protected group: A subgroup of individuals protected under the law, such as women, ethnic minorities, and people over 40.

In addition to the congressional legislation and case law, there is a specific type of law that governs the employment practices of federal contractors. These are known as the Executive Orders (because they were implemented by various US presidents), and an organization that wishes to be a federal contractor must comply with them. Finally, individual states in the US may have extra protections. For example, even though federal age discrimination law applies only to organizations with more than 20 employees, states such as Colorado, Hawaii, Michigan, and Oregon have no minimum size requirement, suggesting that even very small organizations are subject to the law. Therefore, organizations in the US will need to ensure compliance with federal, state, and in some cases city laws.

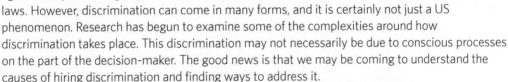

Workplace Application

Hiring Bias in Many Forms and Many Places

In this chapter, much of our focus has been on discrimination against the protected groups identified in US discrimination laws. However, discrimination can come in many forms, and it is certainly not just a US phenomenon. Research has begun to examine some of the complexities around how discrimination takes place. This discrimination may not necessarily be due to conscious processes on the part of the decision-maker. The good news is that we may be coming to understand the causes of hiring discrimination and finding ways to address it.

In a Dutch study, Derous, Ryan, and Serlie (2015) found that recruiters can play a role in making decisions about candidates based on a combination of gender and ethnicity. Using samples of actual recruiters who were non-Arab Dutch, they found that on the basis of submitted résumés, Arab males were rated less hirable than Arab females for certain types of positions. The discrimination seemed to be stronger among recruiters who were higher in ethnic prejudice.

It is important to keep in mind that discrimination may not always be due to conscious processes. In a field study of hiring managers in Sweden, Agerström and Rooth (2011) found that obese job applicants were offered slightly fewer job interviews than normal-weight applicants. What was most interesting, though, was that the discrimination against obese applicants could be mostly explained by the hiring managers' implicit (less conscious) bias against obese people, rather than by any explicit or conscious bias.

There may be some hope in counteracting selection prejudice. Morgan, Walker, Hebl, and King (2013) found some discrimination against pregnant applicants when they went to apply for retail jobs. But they found that pregnancy discrimination could be reduced when the applicant gave information that counteracted the pregnancy stereotype, for example, when the applicant stated that they had a flexible schedule and could work whenever they were needed. This provides some hope that discrimination may not be an insurmountable issue in hiring.

Sources. Agerström & Rooth, 2011; Derous et al., in press; Morgan et al., 2013.

Discrimination: Disparate Treatment versus Adverse Impact

It is important to differentiate between the two different types of discrimination under US law. **Disparate treatment** involves intentional discrimination on the part of an organization or decision-maker. An example would be an overt preference for

Disparate treatment:
Legally, a type of discrimination which involves intentional discrimination on the part of the employer.

males in management jobs, or a preference for younger workers in certain types of jobs. While disparate treatment is illegal, not surprisingly, it can be hard to prove, as it would involve some sort of documentation (e.g., an e-mail) that such a preference was made during the hiring.

More relevant to administering selection procedures, however, is the concept of **adverse impact**. A claim of adverse impact against an employer by a job applicant does not imply intention on the part of the employer. It only requires that a job applicant show that the selection procedure favors one group over another. For example, remember in Chapter 6 where we pointed out that cognitive ability tests tend to have adverse impact against certain ethnic minorities? It is for this reason that many organizations simply do not use these types of tests, because they might lead to a less diverse workforce and lead to the possibility of their being sued. How does an adverse impact lawsuit actually proceed? We describe the three main steps below.

Adverse impact: Legally, a type of discrimination that does not imply intention on the part of the employer, but simply that a test or predictor favors one group over another.

At this point, it is important to note that there are many occasions when an organization may use a practice that has adverse impact, but it goes unchallenged. And there are many times when illegal practices are used, for example, when applicants are asked discriminatory questions because of their sex or ethnicity, but the employer does not get into legal trouble. How does this happen? Many of these legal issues in selection require that some action first be taken by the job applicant, such as reporting a concern to the EEOC. Because many applicants choose not to become involved in such action – or do not know that they can –the employer's practices go unchallenged.

Adverse Impact Case Step 1: Plaintiff Demonstrates Adverse Impact

As a first step to an adverse impact case, a plaintiff (a person bringing a lawsuit) has to establish that a selection procedure used by the organization has adverse impact against the group to which they belong. One classic way to show adverse impact is by means of the **4/5** (or **80 percent**) **rule**. This is a general rule established by the US courts, and it means that the selection ratio for the protected group must be at least 80 percent of that selection ratio (the number of persons hired divided by the number who applied) for the unprotected group. We will go through a simple example.

4/5 or 80 percent rule: A general rule established by the US courts to show adverse impact. It states that the selection ratio for the protected group must be at least 80 percent of that selection ratio for the unprotected group.

We will use a simple example where an organization has 1,000 White men and 100 Black men who apply for job openings. If the organization were to hire 100 of the Whites and 9 of the Blacks, would they be in violation of the 4/5 rule? Let's use the calculations given here:

$$\frac{(9/100)\ \text{Blacks}}{(100/1{,}000)\ \text{Whites}} = .09/.10 = 9/10, \text{ or greater than } 80\%$$

In this case, the employer is not in violation of the 4/5 rule.

Here is a second example. Assume that the organization hires 900 of the 1,000 Whites who apply for a job and 70 of the 100 Blacks who apply for a job, would they be in violation of the 4/5 rule?

$$\frac{(70/100)\ \text{Blacks}}{(900/1{,}000)\ \text{Whites}} = .7/.9 = 78\%, \text{ or less than } 80\%$$

In this case, the employer *is* in violation of the 4/5 rule.

Note that the 4/5 rule is just a simple approach that the US courts have developed to determine whether there is adverse impact. It is important to point out that the 4/5 rule is not based in actual statistical theory, and more sophisticated statistical tests for adverse impact are available (Roth, Bobko, & Switzer, 2006).

Perhaps the best way for employers to minimize the chances of being sued for adverse impact is to choose valid selection procedures which have low adverse impact. It is for that reason that many large employers monitor whether their selection procedures are having adverse impact and when possible choose methods that are less likely to have adverse impact – this allows adverse impact not to become a problem in the first place. But there are a couple of things that an employer cannot do to reduce adverse impact in the US. First, any type of test score adjustment based on a person's ethnicity or gender (often called "within group norming") is not allowed under US law since the 1991 Civil Rights Act. Second, preferential treatment (giving preference in hiring) toward protected groups to increase their rate of hiring is also not allowed under US law (Gatewood et al., 2011). It is for this reason that affirmative action plans in the US should generally take the form of additional recruiting efforts rather than preferential treatment. But in this regard, the US seems to be a bit unusual: Many countries allow or actually encourage preferential treatment of job applicants from some protected groups (Dunleavy et al., 2008).

Adverse Impact Case Step 2: Employer Demonstrates Test Validity

Once a plaintiff has shown that adverse impact exists, the "burden of proof" shifts to the employer, that is, the employer now has to defend themselves or lose the lawsuit. What are the employer's options at this point? One of the most important defenses that the employer can provide is *to show the validity of the selection procedure*. That is, the *Uniform Guidelines* and case law establish the technical requirements for demonstrating that a selection procedure is valid. This is one reason we discussed these ways of showing a test's validity in such detail earlier in this chapter: Test validity is one way for an organization to defend itself against claims of adverse impact. It is for this reason that so many organizations employ industrial psychologists for selection work – not only to ensure that they get the best applicants and to ensure fairness, but also to ensure that their selection procedures are technically valid if they were ever to be challenged in court.

Adverse Impact Case Step 3: Plaintiff Demonstrates Other Predictors Were Available

Finally, if the employer is able to show that their selection procedures are valid, the last recourse on the part of the plaintiff is to show that other, equally valid selection procedures with lower adverse impact were available for the employer to use. This is a fairly high bar for most plaintiffs to reach, and thus most adverse impact cases end if the employer can show that its selection procedures are valid.

Interactive: How an adverse impact case makes its way through the legal system.

"See website for interactive material"

Strategies for Administering Predictors and Using Predictor Data

As we reviewed in Chapter 6, there is a wide range of predictors available to organizations, from cognitive and personality tests, to interviews, SJTs, and bio-data. Obviously, part of the decision in choosing these predictors has to do with their validity, and how convenient they are to use given the size and nature of the samples. However, as we have pointed out, few employers would choose only one of these selection methods; for instance, it is hard to imagine a situation where an employer would choose to give applicants only a personality test without also adding an interview or some other predictor. The question is, how do you strategically determine what combination of predictors to use? How would you administer them to applicants? And what is the best way to combine the results of these predictors and set passing scores to make a selection decision? We discuss each of these issues in this section of the chapter.

Which Predictors Should Be Considered?

As you know, the organization has a number of predictors available that it can use, but the question is which combination makes sense. There are really a few ways to approach this issue. First, consider the KSAs measured by the predictor, and the relevance of these KSAs to the job. We are assuming that you have done some sort of a job analysis at this point (see Chapter 3), and so you know which KSAs you want to measure. For instance, if the job analysis shows that a sales job requires extraversion, integrity (handling money), and prior sales experience handling customers, you might decide to use a personality test, an integrity test, and a structured interview to assess the applicant's experience with customer service.

Figure 7.8 Strategic issues in the deployment and use of selection procedures: Strategies for administering and using predictors.

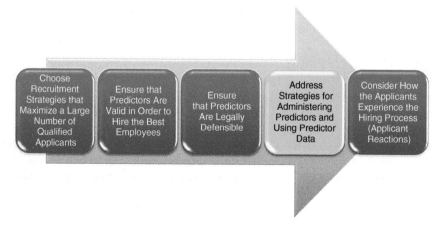

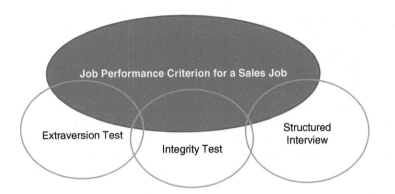

Figure 7.9 Using three different predictors to capture the job performance criterion for a sales job.

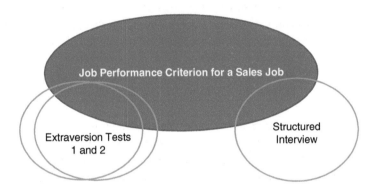

Figure 7.10 Using three different predictors to capture the job performance criterion for a sales job. In this case, two redundant extraversion tests are used instead of an interview, and less unique variance in the job performance criterion is able to be predicted.

But that is just the first step. One important idea to keep in mind is that *you want predictors that measure unique variance in job performance, and that are not redundant with each other*. The concepts of unique variance and low redundancy means that *you generally want predictors that are highly correlated with the criterion of job performance (i.e., valid) but not correlated with each other (are unique – each accounting for something unique and not redundant)*. We show an example in the Venn diagram that follows in describing how three predictors explain the performance of the sales job (see Figure 7.9). As you can see in this figure, the three predictors – a personality test, an integrity test, and an interview – each predict the criterion of sales performance. The three predictors are correlated with the criterion, and not very strongly correlated with each other. (Note that some overlap among predictors is unavoidable.)

Now we turn to the situation shown by the Venn diagram in Figure 7.10. Here the organization has decided to use two tests of extraversion plus a test of integrity, perhaps because they think that extraversion is so important to this sales job. Or, it could be because the organization sees that both tests of extraversion are correlated with the criterion and thus they think that including them is a good thing. But there is a problem with this strategy. Using two tests of extraversion is not very helpful, because the two tests of extraversion are highly correlated with each other; in other words, they are redundant, and they basically explain the same areas of the criterion.

Interactive: Maximizing prediction through combinations of predictors.

"See website for interactive material"

One thing that the reader may be thinking now is, "Wait, even in Figure 7.9 that shows that the three predictors are not correlated with each other, there is still some part of the criterion that is still unexplained by the three predictors." This is true, but it is not atypical. And it is not necessarily a big problem. This is for at least three reasons. First, because both the predictors and the criteria have some error in measurement (they are not perfectly reliable), some variance cannot be explained. Second, work performance is a function not only of the person, but of the context as well, for instance, who their colleagues and supervisor are. For this reason, predictors like tests and interviews cannot entirely predict how a person will behave on the job. Third, this is a good example of why choosing more than one predictor is wise – it can increase the amount of variance in job performance that can be predicted. In any case, even though predictors only account for some portion of job performance, that is, they are not perfect at predicting all of job performance, this is certainly better than random prediction, because over numerous selection decisions, using valid predictors will increase the *odds* that the organization will hire well-qualified applicants.

Another thing that is implied by these Venn diagrams is that adding more and more predictors is not helpful at some point. That is, adding more and more predictors eventually leads to a point of diminishing returns because only so much of the job performance criterion can be accounted for by predictor measures of the person. (Remember we said earlier that part of the job performance criterion is not a function of the person, but of the context?) So most organizations do not use an infinite number of predictors, but must instead choose the best predictors and the best combination of those predictors. These organizations must also decide how to appropriately weight each of the predictors (Guion 2011; Hattrup, 2012), that is, how to decide which tests are worth more than others. We will give you two common-place examples.

Deciding Predictor Weights

First, it may be possible simply to decide the relative weight of each predictor based on the job analysis. The job analysis will give guidance as to how relatively important or critical each KSA is (Hattrup, 2012). For example, if the job analysis showed that interpersonal skills are twice as important as technical knowledge, the predictor of interpersonal skills (e.g., an interview) would be given twice the weight of the technical knowledge measure (e.g., a test). A second approach is to determine the weights of each measure empirically, usually using regression (Hattrup, 2012). (See our discussion of regression in Chapter 2.) The regression equation will show for a particular job what the optimal combination of predictors will be to best fit the data. Finally, the regression equation will show whether adding another predictor is worth it, or is redundant. This means that the organization will need to do a little research in advance of providing weights for the different predictors.

Weighting Predictors Using Regression: An Example

Here we go back to our example of the sales job we described earlier. In this case, the organization is choosing among the following predictors:

- Extraversion Test I
- Extraversion Test II
- Integrity Test
- Interview.

To do their research to decide what the relative weights are for each predictor, the organization has administered the predictors to 300 current employees in a concurrent validity study. They also collect supervisor ratings of performance (the criterion). Then, they calculate the regression equation using a statistical software package, predicting the relationship between these four predictors and job performance. The final regression equation might take this form:

$$Y = bx_{extraversion\ I} + bx_{integrity} + bx_{interview} + a$$

Here, Y is the predicted job performance criterion score, b is the relative weight of each predictor, $x_{extraversion\ I}$ is the score on the Extraversion I, $x_{integrity}$ is the score on the integrity test, and $x_{interview}$ is the score on the interview, and a is the y-intercept or constant. Note that the Extraversion II test is not included in the regression equation because the analysis showed it was redundant and did not account for unique variance.

Now, here is what the regression equation might indicate for the best combination of these predictors for this sales job. It gives us the bs (relative weights) and the y-intercept, so we have this equation:

$$Y = 2x_{extraversion\ I} + 3x_{integrity} + 2x_{interview} + 1.5$$

Notice a few things about this equation. First, the numbers before each of the x values are the bs or the relative weight for each of the predictors as determined by the regression equation to get the best linear combination of each predictor. Second, you will notice that there is no value for Extraversion II; again, that is because in the regression equation, the value of using Extraversion II in predicting job performance is non-significant because it is so highly correlated with Extraversion I and is thus redundant.

Third, and very important, this equation allows us to estimate what a person's job performance might be. Assume that Margot's scores on the three predictors were:

Extraversion Test I = 3
Integrity Test = 2
Interview = 2

Margot's predicted score would be 17.5. Keep in mind that this would only be her *predicted* job performance, or *what it is most likely to be based on these predictors*; her actual job performance might differ from this a bit. (See Chapter 2.)

One important point we would like to make before we leave the topic of combining data from different selection procedures has to do with combining data through mechanistic versus clinical methods. What we have been discussing throughout the section are mechanistic or statistical methods for combining predictor data, such as through regression. The alternative, known as clinical or holistic combination of predictor data, involves the decision-maker simply combining the information in their head. Despite the fact that decision-makers often consider themselves to be capable of effectively combining the predictor data themselves, meta-analytic research has shown that mechanistic methods are consistently more accurate in predicting performance than clinical combinations are (Kuncel, Klieger, Connelly, & Ones, 2013).

Administering Predictors: Sequencing and Setting Cut-Off Scores

Sequencing of Predictors

Another issue is deciding whether to give the predictors all at once or to give them in a sequence. Again, this is based on practical considerations and an organization's selection strategy. The first method, in which all of the predictors are given at the same time, is called the **multiple cut-off approach**. As the name implies, multiple cut-off means that you have set cut-off scores for the procedures. It also means that all of the applicants will take all of the predictors, generally in one day or so. This is a good method if you want to administer the tests and give feedback to applicants quickly; this way, you do not have to worry that some of your applicants – most commonly, the most qualified applicants – will go to another employer. The second method is called the **multiple hurdle approach**, in which the predictors are given in sequence, usually with the more inexpensive selection procedures first (Guion, 2011). Applicants are allowed to proceed to the next "hurdles" only if they pass the first hurdles. This is efficient and economical because the organization can put more expensive selection procedures (e.g., an assessment center) toward the end of the sequence, so that

Multiple cut-off approach: When using a set of predictors to make selection decisions, a system in which applicants must score above a minimum score on each predictor to be considered for hiring.

Multiple hurdle approach: A system in which there is a minimum score on each predictor and predictors are given in sequence. An applicant must pass one predictor before moving on to take the next predictor. Expensive predictors are usually given last (i.e., to the smallest number of applicants) to save money.

The multiple hurdle approach is typically used for public safety jobs such as police officer, where inexpensive predictors like multiple-choice tests can be put first, and expensive hurdles like an individual assessment by a psychiatrist can be put last.

Many well-known organizations use multiple selection procedures in a specific sequence to hire their employees. For example, the procedure at Harrods, an upscale department store in London, includes an initial application, résumé screen, telephone interview, and then a series of live interviews before hiring.

the organization does not have to pay for all applicants to take the expensive selection procedures.

As an example of a situation where it would make sense to use multiple hurdles, let's say an organization has 10 open positions for a customer service job, and they are administering tests of conscientiousness and integrity (recall from Chapter 6 that they are fairly inexpensive) as well as a work sample test (which is more costly). Let's also say they expect to get 100 applicants. That number of applicants is good news in that it means you can be quite selective. But the bad news is that it could be expensive to administer 100 work sample tests. Instead, the organization might decide to administer the conscientiousness and integrity tests first and score them. For those who pass those tests – let's say 30 – the organization can then give them the work sample test. The advantage here is that they can save considerable money by sequencing the cheaper tests first and the expensive test last. The only issue is that they may lose some applicants who do not want to wait until they have scored the first two tests. The good news is that these days, tests can be scored fairly quickly, such that the waiting time for applicants between hurdles can be a matter of a few days or less.

Setting Cut-off Scores

Once you decide how to sequence selection procedures, another strategic decision is whether or not the organization wants to set cut-off scores for each test, such that an applicant has to receive a minimum score on each predictor to be considered for hiring. Or do they want to allow an applicant's high score on one predictor to compensate for their low score on another predictor? This decision can be based on the job analysis, as well as organizational strategies. For example, consider an organization that is using an integrity test and a structured interview to hire sales people. If the organization's strategy was to hire only those sales people who were a low risk in terms of theft, they might decide that even a very high score on the interview would not compensate for a failing score on the integrity test. On

Norm-based cut-off score: A cut-off score based simply on an average score or similar (for example, a score where 70 percent pass) or on the norms of the applicant group. A norm-based cut-off does not necessarily correspond to minimally acceptable job performance.

Criterion-referenced cut-off score: A cut-off score determined to correspond to minimally acceptable job performance.

the other hand, take the example of an organization that is using a conscientiousness test and an SJT to hire customer service representatives. They might decide that a very high score on either of these tests would compensate for a low score on the other.

In addition to deciding whether a high score on one selection procedure can compensate for very low performance on another, there are a few other strategies involved in deciding how to set passing score. One possibility is to use a **norm-based cut-off score**. This would mean the organization would set the cut-off score based simply on an average score or similar (for example, a score where 70 percent pass) based on the norms of the applicant group. The problem with norm-referenced scores is that they say nothing about whether or not the passing score is in any way related to job performance – in this case, it would only say that 70 percent passed. This could mean very different things in a strong group of applicants versus a weak group of applicants.

In contrast, another approach would be a **criterion-referenced cut-off score**. There are two general approaches to setting criterion-referenced cut-off scores. The first approach involves determining which predictor score corresponds to a minimum job performance. This would be determined by using multiple regression; Figure 7.11 shows how a regression line can be used to find out which test score corresponds to a score on the job performance criterion measure. A second approach to setting criterion-referenced cut-offs would be to use SME judgments. A typical method is referred to as the Angoff method (e.g., Guion, 1998; Truxillo, Donahue, & Sulzer, 1996), in which a panel of SMEs judge what predictor score would correspond to minimal competence on the job.

Note that organizations may choose not to set any cut-off score, or simply to set cut-off scores based on their own administrative needs (SIOP, 2003). For example, if there were 50 candidates for 10 job vacancies, the organization might choose to set the cut-off such that 20 candidates pass the test, as that might seem like a reasonable number of people to interview. Finally, some authors caution that the use of a cut-off score can create an unnecessary dichotomy of test scores – those who passed versus those who failed – because the test is actually measuring a continuum (Guion, 1998).

Figure 7.11
Determining a test cut-off score that corresponds to a minimum level of job performance as determined through a regression line.

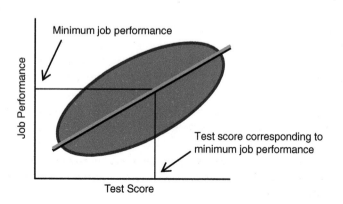

Banding

Related to the topic of cut-off scores is the issue of **banding**, or treating ranges of scores as similar. We provide only a quick conceptual overview of banding here; those interested in a deeper discussion can refer to more technical papers (e.g., Sackett & Wilk, 1994). The concept behind banding is straightforward: Because all selection procedures contain some unreliability and hence some measurement error (see Chapter 2), test scores that are not far apart are essentially equivalent. For example, if Jose had a test score of 93, and Julie had a test score of 92, it is quite possible that they are actually equal because such small test differences may not be meaningful due to measurement error. That is where test score banding comes in: Based on the characteristics of the predictor (typically its reliability), a range of scores can be calculated within which all scores are assumed to be equivalent. In the case above, if the band were calculated to be a range of 5, all scores between 91 and 95 would be considered equivalent, and the differences between Jose and Julie would be considered to be not important; their scores would be equivalent. This is all very logical; but because banding in the US is often used as a way to reduce score differences between different ethnic groups, the arguments surrounding its use often become emotionally and politically charged (Truxillo & Bauer, 1999). And to the extent that they do this, the use of banding can be controversial, not only among organizational decision-makers (e.g., Campion et al., 2001), but among job applicants as well (Truxillo & Bauer, 1999).

Band: A range of predictor scores within which all scores are considered statistically equal. The concept behind banding is that because all selection procedures contain some measurement error, test scores that are not far apart are essentially equivalent.

Accuracy in Prediction

One issue that is implied throughout this chapter is the goal of making accurate selection decisions. Using valid selection procedures should lead to better hiring decisions. As we have seen, there are a number of decisions along the way, including how to sequence the selection procedures and how to combine them in such a way that leads to increased validity. Of course, not all selection decisions will be good: Unless you are using perfectly valid selection procedures (which do not exist), there will always be some hiring errors. It is important to keep this in mind: The use of valid predictors to hire employees will not lead to perfect decisions; however, it will *increase the odds* that you will hire the best talent. As noted earlier, this is because all predictors have some measurement error (they are all unreliable to some degree), and because work performance is a function not only of the person themselves but of the context within which they must work (e.g., their supervisor, coworkers, working conditions).

True positives: Applicants who passed the selection procedure and who turn out to be good performers on the job.

One system for considering how selection decisions are made is to think of decisions as falling into one of four categories or quadrants, as shown in Figure 7.12, which shows a passing score on a test on the x-axis and a point of acceptable performance on the y-axis. The figure shows a situation of moderate validity. In the upper right quadrant are **true positives**, that is, applicants who pass the test and who turn out to be good performers on the job. In the lower left quadrant are **true negatives**, or applicants who did not score high enough on the selection procedure and who would in fact have been poor employees. Together, these good decisions are often referred to as "hits."

True negatives: Applicants who did not pass the selection procedure and who would in fact have been poor employees.

Figure 7.12
Four quadrants of selection decisions under conditions of moderate validity: True positives, true negatives, false positives, and false negatives.

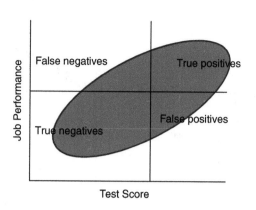

False positives:
Applicants who passed the test but did not turn out to be good employees.

False negatives:
Applicants who failed the selection procedure but who would have been good employees if they had been hired.

In contrast, the employees in the lower right quadrant are **false positives**, or applicants who passed the test but did not turn out to be good employees. On the upper left are **false negatives**, applicants who failed the selection procedure but who would have been good employees. Together, these false positives and false negatives are referred to as "misses".

Notice, however, what happens when we increase the validity of the selection procedure to nearly perfect, or decrease it to 0, as shown in Figure 7.13. In the situation with near perfect validity, the points of the scatterplot hug tightly to the regression line. In essence, there is nothing but true positives and true negatives (hits), and almost no misses at all! In other words, increasing the validity to near 1.00 will allow us to make no errors in hiring. (Note that this is given only as an example of how increased validity improves decisions, and perfect validity is something that cannot really exist in the real world.) On the other hand, in the situation with 0 validity, the quadrants containing the true positives and true negatives are the same size as the quadrants containing the false positives and false negatives. In other words, we are just as likely to make a bad decision as a good decision when there is zero validity.

Now let's turn back to the situation of moderate validity, shown again in Figures 7.14 and 7.15. There are ways that we can adjust the passing score on the predictor to affect the hit rate. First, we can raise the passing score on the test (Figure 7.14), which leads to selecting only people that we know will be good employees on the job. The tradeoff, unfortunately, is that our false negative rate goes up considerably: We would be rejecting a large number of applicants who would be good employees. But some organizations might decide to take this strategy under certain conditions, such as when they must be certain of the job applicant's ability to perform the job such as for highly sensitive positions (e.g., in a nuclear power plant). The other alternative is to lower the passing score on the predictor to a point where you know that you would not be rejecting any applicants with the potential to be good employees. (See Figure 7.15.) The tradeoff here is that you increase the percentage of false positives, or applicants who pass the test but turn out to be poor performers. This strategy may be used by organizations which are in high competition for talent and are willing to hire a few employees who do not work out.

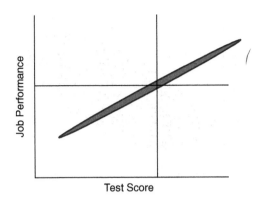

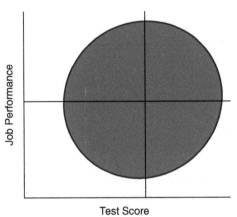

Figure 7.13 Effects of very high validity (top) and very low validity (bottom) on true positives and true negatives (hits) and false positives and false negatives (misses). Note that under conditions of very high validity, the hits are more numerous than the misses. When there is low validity, the numbers of hits and misses are equal.

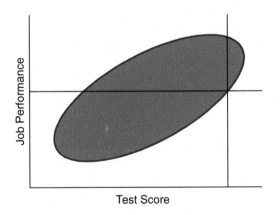

Figure 7.14 Four quadrants of selection decisions under conditions of moderate validity, with a very high passing score on the predictor. Although this creates a large number of people who do not pass but who would have actually been successful on the job (i.e., it leads to more false negatives), it also eliminates all of the false positives. Thus, all employees passing the test would be successful on the job.

In summary, organizational decision-makers should frame the decision to use valid selection procedures as a means to increasing their odds of hiring the best talent. Using more valid selection procedures will increase the chances of making good decisions (hiring the high performers and rejecting poor performers), and using less valid procedures will decrease the chances of good decisions. Further, depending

Figure 7.15 Four quadrants of selection decisions under conditions of moderate validity, with a very low passing score on the predictor. Although this creates a large number of people who may not be successful on the job, it also eliminates all of the false negatives. Thus, all employees that might be successful on the job would be hired. This strategy may be used by organizations which are in high competition for talent and are willing to hire a few employees who do not work out.

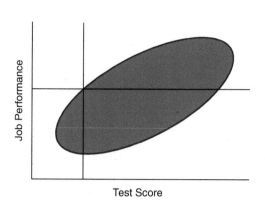

on the strategy of the particular organization, passing scores on predictors can be adjusted up or down depending on the organization's strategy in hiring for a particular type of job.

Interactive: How increased criterion-related validity increases the precision of hiring decisions.

"See website for interactive material"

Predictor Utility

Selection utility: The monetary value of a personnel selection procedure. Utility can be thought of as the return on investment for using a particular selection procedure.

One final strategic issue in administering selection procedures is **selection utility** or the monetary value of a personnel selection procedure. Speaking in US terms, utility is the dollar value of using a particular selection procedure versus not using it, or using a different procedure. In other words, utility analysis is largely a calculation of return on investment (ROI) for using a selection procedure.

Not surprisingly, I/O psychologists have been interested in the study of utility analysis for many years because they have wanted to show to management that there are benefits in using certain selection tests or predictors. One of the first frameworks for utility analysis was the Taylor-Russell tables (Taylor & Russell, 1939) which were developed back before World War II. Since that time, more sophisticated systems for calculating the dollar value of using a particular selection test have been developed (Boudreau, 1983). These models are generally quite complicated and beyond the scope of this book, although we point the interested reader to more in-depth discussions of utility analysis (e.g., Boudreau, 1983; Cascio & Aguinis, 2011).

In any case, one of the challenges with using utility analysis in organizations is that some of the more complex and sophisticated approaches to utility may be difficult for managers and other organizational decision-makers to understand. In fact, one classic study showed that managers may be better able to understand a simple validity coefficient (a correlation between a test and job performance) but may not accept the more complex approaches to utility (Latham & Whyte, 1994). Rather, a recent study of German, Swiss, and Austrian managers showed that utility analysis data should be presented to managers in terms of business analyses that are familiar to them (Winkler, König, & Kleinmann, 2010).

Despite these concerns about the use of specific utility analysis models, the general concept of utility – the value of using a selection procedure – is an important one for I/O psychologists to keep in mind when practicing in the field of selection (Gatewood et al., 2011). Here we discuss three specific issues that can affect the utility or value of a selection procedure – its cost, validity, and the selection ratio.

First, the cost of using a selection procedure can obviously affect how valuable it is to an organization. Consider the following where you have been asked to choose between two integrity tests, both of which have good and approximately equal validity (say around .30). However, the cost of Test A is approximately $1 per applicant, whereas the cost of Test B is approximately $5 per applicant. All other things being equal, Test A will have greater utility because its cost is less. Keep in mind that cost of the test may not be simply what the organization has to pay the test publisher for it. It may also include other costs such as the costs of administering the test. For example, all other things being equal, a test that can be quickly and cheaply scored online will have greater utility than a test that must be scored by teams of trained raters. (Again, all other things such as validity and the dimensions measured by the tests being equal!)

The second factor that can substantially affect the utility of selection procedures is their validity. This makes sense as the better (more accurately) a selection procedure can predict job performance, the more valuable it will be in use. For example, let's say that you are choosing between two mechanical ability tests. One of them has a validity of .30, whereas the other one has a high validity (.50). All other things being equal, the test with a validity of .50 is going to have greater utility – it will maximize correct decisions and minimize false positives and false negatives (see our discussion about how to enhance predictive efficiency).

The third factor, which is an issue that may not be so evident at first, is a factor known as the **selection ratio**. The selection ratio is the number of vacancies available relative to the number of job applicants. It may seem counterintuitive, but a low selection ratio – having a large number of applicants relative to the number of hiring decisions – is a good position to be in and will increase the utility of using the selection procedure. This is because having a large number of qualified applicants relative to the number of vacancies allows the employer to be more selective or "picky" – it increases their chances of hiring the strongest employees. This is why the issue of recruitment, which we discussed earlier in this chapter, is so critical to making good selection decisions. It increases the applicant pool, and thus the value of using a valid selection procedure – which can discriminate between strong and weak candidates – really goes up. These issues around the selection ratio also lead to an interesting phenomenon in very strong economic times when organizations can find few applicants, namely, the value of using a selection procedure goes down when there are relatively few applicants for the number of vacancies. For example, if a company has 10 vacancies, but only 11 job applicants, it may not be worthwhile for them to use elaborate selection procedures, but instead to focus merely on assuring that applicants are minimally qualified and not a safety risk.

In summary, while actually doing a utility analysis can be very complex, some of the basic ideas behind it are good to keep in mind when developing and

Selection ratio: The number of job vacancies relative to the number of job applicants.

administering a selection program. Specifically, it shows how considering the costs of predictors, their validity, and recruitment efforts each can contribute to the value of using selection procedures.

Applicant Reactions: Considering the Job Applicant's Experience

Our focus through much of this chapter has been on the best way for organizations to hire employees – in other words, looking at the selection process from the organization's perspective. Historically, this has been the focus of personnel selection research over the last century. However, over the last 20 years, researchers have come to look at personnel selection procedures through the lens of the job applicant as well. In other words, what do job applicants think about various selection procedures, and what do they think about the companies that use certain procedures? One of the key foci of this research has been whether or not the applicant sees selection procedures as fair (e.g., Bauer et al., 2001; Gilliland, 1993). Other approaches have looked at the treatment of applicants (or "social validity") as a key outcome in itself (Schuler, 1993).

A number of studies have examined what types of selection procedures applicants prefer. These studies have been done in many countries around the world including France (Steiner & Gilliland, 1996), Spain and Portugal (Moscoso & Salgado, 2004), Greece (Nikolaou & Judge, 2007), the Netherlands (Anderson & Witvliet, 2008), Italy (Bertolino & Steiner, 2007), and in Asian countries such as Singapore (Phillips & Gully, 2002) and Vietnam (Hoang, Truxillo, Erdogan, & Bauer, 2012). Meta-analyses of these findings show that no matter what the country, applicants' perceptions of different selection procedures are very similar (Anderson, Salgado, & Hülsheger, 2010; Hausknecht, Day, & Thomas, 2004). Generally, applicants react more positively to methods like work samples and interviews, and they react more negatively to personality tests and integrity tests. (By far, applicants' least preferred

Figure 7.16 Strategic issues in the deployment and use of selection procedures: Address applicant reactions.

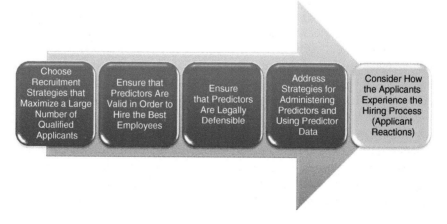

selection method is graphology or handwriting analysis. That's good – we did not even discuss it in Chapter 6 because of its lack of validity for predicting job performance.) Moreover, cultural values appear to play only a minimal role in applicant perceptions (Ryan et al., 2009) – something that is important for multinational companies to keep in mind. These preferences among applicants may be because applicants like procedures that are obviously job-related and give them an opportunity to show what they can do (Schleicher, Venkataramani, Morgeson, & Campion, 2006). Not surprisingly, other research (Ployhart & Ryan, 1998) has found that applicants dislike it when they are treated differently from other applicants.

One of the challenges for employers is that some of the methods applicants like most – such as interviews and work samples – can be the most expensive to administer. This presents a bit of a dilemma for organizations, who would like to keep a positive image among applicants but have to deal with economic realities. One option that appears effective is for employers to explain to applicants why they are using certain selection procedures (e.g., Truxillo, Bauer, Campion, & Paronto, 2002; Truxillo, Bodner, Bertolino, Bauer, & Yonce, 2009). In any case, given that the perceived fairness of procedures may relate to applicants' intentions to bring legal action (Bauer et al., 2001), applicants' perceptions are one more factor for employers to consider. Indeed, a recent study of military applicants suggests that applicants' perceptions about how fairly they were treated during the hiring process can affect whether applicants accept a position that is offered to them (Harold, Holtz, Griepentrog, Brewer, & Marsh, in press). In other words, treating applicants well during selection is an important strategic move in hiring the best talent.

GLOBAL IMPLICATIONS

Throughout both this chapter and Chapter 6, we have noted international and global issues related to the use of personnel selection procedures, including differences in laws related to hiring and applicant perceptions cross-culturally. In addition, with the increases in the numbers of global organizations, it is particularly important to touch on issues associated with personnel selection in different parts of the world and in multinational organizations. Steiner (2012) notes that most reviews of the literature on the validity of selection procedures in different cultures show the validities of many selection procedures (e.g., cognitive ability tests) are consistent across many countries, but that other types of predictors such as biodata items may not be assumed to be equally valid in different cultural settings.

I/O psychologists have, to some degree, identified many of the issues surrounding the use of selection predictors around the world. For example, education differences across nations may affect the range and distribution of scores on tests; differences in skill and education levels in the local economy may affect recruitment strategies; and the diversity of job applicant samples may vary considerably across countries in terms of age and gender (e.g., Steiner, 2012). However, research is still needed as to how to actually implement these systems most effectively (Ryan & Tippins, 2009).

Today's multinational organizations pose some significant challenges for developing personnel selection systems that can be used organization-wide.

As pointed out by Tippins (2010), there are a number of advantages to having integrated selection systems in multinational corporations, that is, a selection system that can be used organization-wide, even across national borders. Having a single, integrated selection system is in many ways more convenient than multiple, separate systems across the company. Moreover, integrated selection systems would allow for comparisons of talent across the entire organization, thus facilitating the more effective use of talent across the organization as a whole. At the same time there are a number of challenges to integrated, multinational selection systems, including having to account for cultural differences in the acceptability of various predictor types in different countries. There is also the considerable expense involved in showing that test questions work the same way and have the same meaning in different cultures. Despite these challenges, there are also a number of recommended best practices in developing multinational selection systems in global corporations (Ryan & Tippins, 2009; Tippins, 2010) including:

- Ensure the jobs with similar titles in different parts of the organization actually share common tasks and KSAs. In other words, jobs with the same job titles may actually involve different responsibilities in different countries and thus may require different types of selection procedures.
- Consider key differences in different parts of the world, such as differences in labor laws and economic conditions which can affect how the predictors are administered.
- Pay close attention to the development of administration and scoring instructions so that the predictors are administered consistently across different countries.

CURRENT ISSUES AND CONTROVERSIES

There are a number of issues regarding recruitment and selection that are appearing on the horizon – or are already here. First, the role of social networking sites for recruitment seems to be establishing itself, even if its use for selection decisions is still problematic (e.g., Roth, Bobko, Van Iddekinge, & Thatcher, in press; see Chapter 6). In addition, given the globalized nature of work today, we see increased interest in how to develop selection systems for global organizations (e.g., Tippins, 2010). Related to the issue of globalization, Ryan and Ployhart (2014) point out that selection research will continue to expand to include other countries. In addition, much of our selection work has examined the relationship between a test score and individual job performance; models that examine outcomes at the group and at the organization level are likely to increase (Ryan & Ployhart, 2014). Finally, there is a call for selection strategies to be more explicitly tied to organizations' broader business strategies and future organizational needs (Hausknecht & Wright, 2012).

WHAT DOES THIS MEAN TO YOU?

As you can see in this chapter, the goal of sophisticated employers is to recruit qualified job applicants, select the best of these, and do it as efficiently and legally as possible. What does this mean for you?

First, when you're searching for a job, be aware of the wide range of channels that organizations use to recruit and attract people. These are the same channels that you as an applicant should be examining so you can learn about the opportunities that fit your skills. It also means that you should be keeping your social media profiles related to work, such as a LinkedIn page, up to date so that your background and skills are apparent to organizations. (This also means that you should be careful what you put on your own social media page!)

Second, selection procedures can often be time-consuming and play out over a period of weeks or months – especially for higher-level and professional jobs. Our point is to be patient – if it's a job you really want, don't worry that the procedure is taking longer than you would like.

Third, be aware of your legal rights as an applicant. Although it may not be worthwhile to pursue legal action against an employer, the way they treat you may be an indicator of how they operate. You may want to consider what it would be like to work for an organization or manager who uses illegal selection practices – and consider looking elsewhere. Relatedly, be aware of your treatment during the selection process, as this may be a signal about the company's culture and the way that it treats people.

Conclusion

As we said at the opening of this chapter, the science of recruiting and hiring the best talent has flourished in I/O psychology, and employers can choose from a range of strategies for recruiting job applicants and using selection data. Like all organizational strategies, those strategies regarding selection should take into account the organization's particular circumstances, including the types of applicants they want and the characteristics of the applicant pool. At the same time, the organization needs to consider the legal environment in which they are operating, how best to deploy the selection procedures, and the applicant's perspective. We foresee continued research in selection, especially as technology changes the way we communicate and work. The challenge for I/O psychology science will be to stay ahead of these trends to address the needs of employers.

YOUR TURN... WHAT DO YOU THINK?

1. Consider the options available to employers for recruiting job applicants. Consider the jobs of sales associate for a large retailer versus engineer for a high-tech maker of computer hardware. What options are best for recruiting to fill these two positions? Explain the reasoning behind your answers.

2. Let's say that you're employed by a mid-sized government agency tasked with enforcing environmental regulations. Most of the employees have master's degrees in biology or chemistry. Your boss has done her homework about recruitment and hiring strategies – she's hired some top-flight I/O consultants to determine the best selection procedures for these jobs. These predictors include a written test of technical skills, a structured interview, and a background check. You expect a high volume of applicants for these

jobs. How would you sequence the administration of these predictors, and why? What are the advantages and disadvantages of your choice?

3. You're working for an Internet sales company specializing in home electronics. It is based in the United States. The company is about to expand into the United Kingdom and Germany. Your boss has asked for your advice on what issues to consider in terms of staffing up the new locations as quickly as possible. What would you tell her?

4. You work for a government organization that is charged with protecting the welfare of young children. The agency hires workers who will need to work closely with families, and often work closely with the children as well. What might be your strategy in setting a cut-off score for a test of integrity? Be sure to discuss the issues of true positives and false positives in your answer.

5. Imagine that you're in charge of the selection procedures in your company – a large retail company – which has used cognitive tests and integrity tests to hire its employees for many years. Your company has done research to show that the tests are excellent predictors of job performance, but you also see that applicants don't like the tests very much – in fact, you recall that you didn't like them much either when you were hired. What are some ways that you might resolve this dilemma? Be specific in terms of how you would balance the company's needs (validity, cost) with applicants' perceptions.

Additional Reading

Cascio, W. F., & Aguinis, H. (2011). *Applied psychology in human resource management* (7th ed.). Upper Saddle River, NJ: Prentice Hall.

Gatewood, R., Feild, H., & Barrick, M. (2011). *Human resource selection*. Mason, OH: Cengage Learning.

Guion, R. M. (2011). *Assessment, measurement, and prediction for personnel decisions*. New York: Routledge.

Gutman, A., Koppes, L. L., & Vodanovich, S. J. (2010). *EEO law and personnel practices* (3rd ed.). New York: Routledge.

McPhail, S. M. (2007). *Alternative validation strategies: Developing new and leveraging existing validity evidence*. San Francisco, CA: John Wiley & Sons.

Outtz, J. L. (Ed.). (2010). *Adverse impact: Implications for organizational staffing and high stakes selection*. New York: Taylor & Francis.

Schmitt, N. (Ed.). (2012). *The Oxford handbook of personnel assessment and selection*. New York: Oxford University Press.

Scott, J. C., & Reynolds, D. H. (2010). *Handbook of workplace assessment*. San Francisco, CA: John Wiley & Sons.

Tippins, N. T., & Adler, S. (2011). *Technology-enhanced assessment of talent*. San Francisco, CA: John Wiley & Sons.

Van Iddekinge, C. H., & Ployhart, R. E. (2008). Developments in the criterion-related validation of selection procedures: A critical review and recommendations for practice. *Personnel Psychology, 61*, 871–925.

CASE STUDY: Security of Assessments Used in Hiring

A perennial issue for people who develop assessments used in selection, whether they are test publishers or employers, is the security of their assessments. This includes not only questions that might be asked on an actual test, but also questions included in a structured interview or assessment center. For example, when one of the authors worked in the public sector developing tests for public safety jobs, tests and other assessments had to be kept in a locked vault (for which only a few people had the combination) so that the questions would not be leaked to job applicants.

The issue of test security has continued to be discussed among I/O psychologists and is affecting organizations today. For instance, with the advent of online testing, the issue of unproctored Internet testing (Tippins, 2009) has been discussed with reference to maintaining the security of a selection test when it is administered on the Internet (see Chapter 6). Very recently, this issue arose regarding the security of selection predictors within a large metropolitan fire department. Specifically, an audit found that there were numerous instances of fire department insiders sharing what was supposed to be secure selection material (such as questions and correct answers) with others who were applying for jobs with the department (Sewell & Pringle, 2015). This case illustrates that the security of test questions used for making hiring decisions is an ongoing concern within large organizations today, and it affects decisions that affect people's lives, such as whether they get a job.

Questions:

1. How do you think that test security issues might affect a test's validity (i.e., the assumption that higher test scores are associated with higher job performance)?
2. Would a security breach of an organization's test materials affect its ability to defend its selection procedures if they faced a legal challenge? If so, how?
3. How might test security breaches affect job applicants and potential applicants? What, if anything, would job applicants do? Consider this in terms of attracting the best applicants during the recruitment process.
4. If you were applying for a job that you really wanted, how would you feel if you learned that some applicants had access to interview questions and the correct answers? Would it affect how you feel about the organization? What, if anything, would you do?

Sources: This case is partially based on information included in Sewell & Pringle, 2015; Tippins, 2009.

References

Agerström, J., & Rooth, D. O. (2011). The role of automatic obesity stereotypes in real hiring discrimination. *Journal of Applied Psychology, 96*, 790–805.

Allen, D. G., Mahto, R. V., & Otondo, R. F. (2007). Web-based recruitment: Effects of information, organizational brand, and attitudes toward a Web site on applicant attraction. *Journal of Applied Psychology, 92*, 1696–1708.

Anderson, J. C., & Gerbing, D. W. (1991). Predicting the performance of measures in a confirmatory factor analysis with a pretest assessment of their substantive validities. *Journal of Applied Psychology, 76*, 732–740.

Anderson, N., Salgado, J. F., & Hülsheger, U. R. (2010). Applicant reactions in selection: Comprehensive meta-analysis into reaction generalization versus situational specificity. *International Journal of Selection and Assessment, 18*, 291–304.

Anderson, N., & Witvliet, C. (2008). Fairness reactions to personnel selection methods: An international comparison between the Netherlands, the United States, France, Spain, Portugal, and Singapore. *International Journal of Selection and Assessment, 16*, 1–13.

Avery, D. R. (2003). Reactions to diversity in recruitment advertising: Are differences black and white? *Journal of Applied Psychology, 88*, 672.

Bauer, T. N., Truxillo, D. M., Sanchez, R. J., Craig, J., Ferrara, P., & Campion, M. A. (2001). Applicant reactions to selection: Development of the Selection Procedural Justice Scale (SPJS). *Personnel Psychology, 54*, 387–419.

Bersin, J. (2013). Corporate recruiting explodes: A new breed of service providers. *Forbes*, May 23. Retrieved March 22, 2014, from http://www.forbes.com/sites/joshbersin/2013/05/23/corporate-recruitment-transformed-new-breed-of-service-providers/.

Bertolino, M., & Steiner, D. D. (2007). Fairness reactions to selection methods: An Italian study. *International Journal of Selection and Assessment, 15*, 197–205.

Boudreau, J. W. (1983). Economic considerations in estimating the utility of human resource productivity improvement programs. *Personnel Psychology, 36*, 551–576.

Campbell, R. (2014). Why I do all my recruiting through LinkedIn. *New York Times*, August 19. Retrieved February 22, 2015, from http://boss.blogs.nytimes.com/2014/08/19/why-i-do-all-of-my-recruiting-through-linkedin/.

Campion, M. A., Outtz, J. L., Zedeck, S., Schmidt, F. L., Kehoe, J. F., Murphy, K. R., & Guion, R. M. (2001). The controversy over score banding in personnel selection: Answers to 10 key questions. *Personnel Psychology, 54*, 149–185.

Cascio, W. F., & Aguinis, H. (2011). *Applied psychology in human resource management* (7th ed.). Upper Saddle River, NJ: Prentice Hall.

Chapman, D. S., Uggerslev, K. L., Carroll, S. A., Piasentin, K. A., & Jones, D. A. (2005). Applicant attraction to organizations and job choice: A meta-analytic review of the correlates of recruiting outcomes. *Journal of Applied Psychology, 90*, 928–944.

Cohen, M. (2013). Online hiring tools are changing recruiting techniques. *New York Times*, May 15. Retrieved February 22, 2015, from http://www.nytimes.com/2013/05/16/business/smallbusiness/online-recruiting-efforts-gain-ground.html?pagewanted=all.

Derous, E., Ryan, A. M., & Serlie, A. W. (2015). Double jeopardy upon résumé screening: When Achmed is less employable than Aisha. *Personnel Psychology., 68*, 615–657.

Dunleavy, E. M., Cohen, D. B., Aamodt, M. G., & Schaeffer, P. (2008). A consideration of international differences in the legal context of selection. *Industrial and Organizational Psychology, 1*, 247–254.

Earnest, D. R., Allen, D. G., & Landis, R. S. (2011). Mechanisms linking realistic job previews with turnover: A meta-analytic path analysis. *Personnel Psychology, 64*, 865–897.

Gatewood, R., Feild, H., & Barrick, M. (2011). *Human resource selection.* Mason, OH: Cengage Learning.

Ghiselli, E. E. (1966). *The validity of occupational aptitude tests.* New York: Wiley.

Gilliland, S. W. (1993). The perceived fairness of selection systems: An organizational justice perspective. *Academy of Management Review, 18*, 694–734.

Goldstein, I. L., Zedeck, S., & Schneider, B. (1993). An exploration of the job analysis-content validity process. In N. Schmitt & W.C. Borman (Eds.), *Personnel selection in organizations* (pp. 3–34). San Francisco: Jossey-Bass.

Griggs v. Duke Power Co. (1971). 401 US 424.

Guion, R. M. (1998). *Assessment, measurement, and prediction for personnel decisions.* Mahwah, NJ: Lawrence Erlbaum Associates.

Guion, R. M. (2009). Was this trip necessary? *Industrial and Organizational Psychology, 2*, 465–468.

Guion, R. M. (2011). *Assessment, measurement, and prediction for personnel decisions.* New York: Routledge.

Gully, S. M., Phillips, J. M., Castellano, W. G., Han, K., & Kim, A. (2013). A mediated moderation model of recruiting socially and environmentally responsible job applicants. *Personnel Psychology, 66*, 935–973.

Gutman, A., Koppes, L. L., & Vodanovich, S. J. (2010). *EEO law and personnel practices* (3rd ed.). New York: Routledge.

Hardy, Q. (2014). Workday to put employees through a big data analysis. *New York Times*, November 5. Retrieved February 22, 2015, from http://bits.blogs.nytimes.com/2014/11/05/workday-to-put-employees-through-a-big-data-analysis/.

Harold, C. M., Holtz, B. C., Griepentrog, B. K., Brewer, L. M., & Marsh, S. M. (in press). Investigating the effects of applicant justice perceptions on job offer acceptance. *Personnel Psychology.* DOI: 10.1111/peps.12101

Hattrup, K. (2012). Using composite predictors in personnel selection. In N. Schmitt (Ed.), *The Oxford handbook of personnel assessment and selection* (pp. 297–319). New York: Oxford University Press.

Hausknecht, J. P, Day, D. V., & Thomas, S. C. (2004). Applicant reactions to selection procedures: An updated model and meta-analysis. *Personnel Psychology, 57*, 639–683.

Hausknecht, J. P., & Wright, P. M. (2012). Organizational strategy and staffing. In N. Schmitt (Ed.), *The Oxford handbook of personnel assessment and selection* (pp. 147–155). New York: Oxford University Press.

Hoang, T. G., Truxillo, D. M., Erdogan, B., & Bauer, T. N. (2012). Cross-cultural examination of applicant reactions to selection methods: United States and Vietnam. *International Journal of Selection and Assessment, 20*, 209–219.

Johnson, J. W., Steel, P., Scherbaum, C. A., Hoffman, C. C., Jeanneret, R. P., & Foster, J. (2010). Validation is like motor oil: Synthetic is better. *Industrial and Organizational Psychology, 3*, 305–328.

Kuncel, N. R., Klieger, D. M., Connelly, B. S., & Ones, D. S. (2013). Mechanical versus clinical data combination in selection and admissions decisions: A meta-analysis. *Journal of Applied Psychology, 98*, 1060–1072.

Landy, F. J. (1986). Stamp collecting versus science: Validation as hypothesis testing. *American Psychologist, 41*, 1183–1192.

Latham, G. P., & Whyte, G. (1994). The futility of utility analysis. *Personnel Psychology, 47*, 31–46.

Lawshe, C. H. (1952). What can industrial psychology do for small business (a symposium) 2. Employee selection. *Personnel Psychology, 5*, 31–34.

Lawshe, C. H. (1975). A quantitative approach to content validity. *Personnel Psychology, 28*, 563–575.

McDaniel, M. A., Kepes, S., & Banks, G. (2011). The *Uniform Guidelines* are a detriment to the field of personnel selection. *Industrial and Organizational Psychology, 4*, 494–515.

Morgan, W. B., Walker, S. S., Hebl, M. M. R., & King, E. B. (2013). A field experiment: Reducing interpersonal discrimination toward pregnant job applicants. *Journal of Applied Psychology, 98*, 799–809.

Moscoso, S., & Salgado, J. S. F. (2004). Fairness reactions to personnel selection techniques in Spain and Portugal. *International Journal of Selection and Assessment, 12*, 187–196.

Murphy, K. R. (2009). Is content-related evidence useful in validating selection tests? *Industrial and Organizational Psychology, 2*, 517–526.

Myors, B. (2008). International perspectives on the legal environment for selection. *Industrial and Organizational Psychology, 1*, 206–246.

Nikolaou, I., & Judge, T. A. (2007). Fairness reactions to personnel selection techniques in Greece: The role of core self-evaluations. *International Journal of Selection and Assessment, 15*, 206–219.

Oostrom, J. K., Bos-Broekema, L., Serlie, A. W., Born, M. P., & Van der Molen, H. T. (2012). A field study of pretest and posttest reactions to a paper-and-pencil and a computerized in-basket exercise. *Human Performance, 25*, 95–113.

Phillips, J. M., & Gully, S. M. (2002). Fairness reactions to personnel selection techniques in Singapore and the United States. *International Journal of Human Resource Management, 13*, 1186–1205.

Phillips, J. M., Gully, S. M., McCarthy, J. E., Castellano, W. G., & Kim, M. S. (2014). Recruiting global travelers: The role of global travel recruitment messages and individual differences in perceived fit, attraction, and job pursuit intentions. *Personnel Psychology, 66*, 153–201.

Ployhart, R. E., & Ryan, A. M. (1998). Applicants' reactions to the fairness of selection procedures: The effects of positive rule violations and time of measurement. *Journal of Applied Psychology, 83*, 3–16.

Roth, P. L., Bobko, P., & Switzer III, F. S. (2006). Modeling the behavior of the 4/5ths rule for determining adverse impact: Reasons for caution. *Journal of Applied Psychology, 91*, 507–522.

Roth, P. L., Bobko, P., Van Iddekinge, C. H., & Thatcher, J. B. (in press). Social media in employee selection-related decisions: A research agenda for uncharted territory. *Journal of Management.* DOI:10.1177/0149206313503018

Ryan, A. M., Boyce, A. S., Ghumman, S., Jundt, D., Schmidt, G., & Gibby, R. (2009). Going global: Cultural values and perceptions of selection procedures. *Applied Psychology, 58*, 520–556.

Ryan, A. M., & Ployhart, R. E. (2014). A century of selection. *Annual Review of Psychology, 65*, 693–717.

Ryan, A. M., & Tippins, N. (2009). *Designing and implementing global selection systems.* Chichester, England: Wiley-Blackwell.

Sackett, P. R., Putka, D. J., & McCloy, R. A. (2012). The concept of validity and the process of validation. In N. Schmitt (Ed.), *The Oxford handbook of personnel assessment and selection* (pp. 91–118). New York: Oxford University Press.

Sackett, P. R., & Wilk, S. L. (1994). Within-group norming and other forms of score adjustment in preemployment testing. *American Psychologist, 49*, 929–954.

Schleicher, D. J., Venkataramani, V., Morgeson, F. P., & Campion, M A. (2006). So you didn't get the job ... *now* what do you think? Examining opportunity-to-perform fairness perceptions. *Personnel Psychology, 59*, 559–590.

Schmidt, F. L., & Hunter, J. E. (1981). Employment testing: Old theories and new research findings. *American Psychologist, 36*, 1128–1137.

Schmitt, N., Gooding, R. Z., Noe, R. A., & Kirsch, M. (1984). Meta analyses of validity studies published between 1964 and 1982 and the investigation of study characteristics. *Personnel Psychology, 37*, 407–422.

Schuler, H. (1993). Social validity of selection situations: A concept and some empirical results. In H. Schuler, J. L. Farr & M. Smith (Eds.), *Personnel selection and assessment: Individual and organizational perspectives* (pp. 11–26). Hillsdale, NJ: Lawrence Erlbaum Associates.

Sewell, A., & Pringle, P. (2015). L.A. County fire officials shared test questions used in hiring, audit finds. *Los Angeles Times.* Retrieved February 22, 2015, from http://www.latimes.com/local/california/la-me-fire-cheating-20150222-story.html.

Shaffer, J. A., & Postlethwaite, B. E. (2012). A matter of context: A meta-analytic investigation of the relative validity of contextualized and no contextualized personality measures. *Personnel Psychology, 65*, 445–493.

Slaughter, J. E., Zickar, M. J., Highhouse, S., & Mohr, D. C. (2004). Personality trait inferences about organizations: Development of a measure and assessment of construct validity. *Journal of Applied Psychology, 89*, 85–103.

Society for Industrial and Organizational Psychology (SIOP). (2003). *Principles for the validation and use of personnel selection procedures* (4th ed.). Bowling Green, OH: Author.

Steiner, D. D. (2012). Personnel selection around the globe. In N. Schmitt (Ed.), *The Oxford handbook of personnel assessment and selection* (pp. 740–767). New York: Oxford University Press.

Steiner, D. D., & Gilliland, S. W. (1996). Fairness reactions to personnel selection techniques in France and the United States. *Journal of Applied Psychology, 81*, 134–141.

Taylor, H. C., & Russell, J. T. (1939). The relationship of validity coefficients to the practical effectiveness of tests in selection: Discussion and tables. *Journal of Applied Psychology, 23*, 565–578.

The Talent Board. (2014). *Candidate experience 2013.* Retrieved March 25, 2014, from http://nam.thecandidateexperienceawards.org/2013-award-winners/.

Tippins, N. T. (2009). Internet alternatives to traditional proctored testing: Where are we now? *Industrial and Organizational Psychology, 2*, 2–10.

Tippins, N. T. (2010). Making global assessments work. *Industrial-Organizational Psychologist, 48*, 59–64.

Truxillo, D. M., & Bauer, T. N. (1999). Applicant reactions to test scores banding in entry-level and promotional contexts. *Journal of Applied Psychology, 84*, 322–339.

Truxillo, D. M., Bauer, T. N., Campion, M. A., & Paronto, M. E. (2002). Selection fairness information and applicant reactions: A longitudinal field study. *Journal of Applied Psychology, 87*, 1020–1031.

Truxillo, D. M., Bodner, T. E., Bertolino, M., Bauer, T. N., & Yonce, C. A. (2009). Effects of explanations on applicant reactions: A meta-analytic review. *International Journal of Selection and Assessment, 17*, 346–361.

Truxillo, D. M., Donahue, L. M., & Sulzer, J. L. (1996). Setting cutoff scores for personnel selection tests: Issues, illustrations, and recommendations. *Human Performance, 9*, 275–295.

Uggerslev, K. L., Fassina, N. E., & Kraichy, D. (2012). Recruiting through the stages: A meta-analytic test of predictors of applicant attraction at different stages of the recruiting process. *Personnel Psychology, 65*, 597–660.

Uniform Guidelines on Employee Selection Procedures. (1978). *Federal Register, 43*, 38290–38315.

Van Hoye, G., & Lievens, F. (2009). Tapping the grapevine: A closer look at word-of-mouth as a recruitment source. *Journal of Applied Psychology, 94*, 341–352.

Van Iddekinge, C. H., & Ployhart, R. E. (2008). Developments in the criterion-related validation of selection procedures: A critical review and recommendations for practice. *Personnel Psychology, 61*, 871–925.

Walker, H. J., Feild, H. S., Giles, W. F., Armenakis, A. A., & Bernerth, J. B. (2009). Displaying employee testimonials on recruitment web sites: Effects of communication media, employee race, and job seeker race on organizational attraction and information credibility. *Journal of Applied Psychology, 94*, 1354–1364.

Winkler, S., König, C. J., & Kleinmann, M. (2010). Single-attribute utility analysis may be futile, but this can't be the end of the story: Causal chain analysis as an alternative. *Personnel Psychology, 63*, 1041–1065.

Chapter 8

TRAINING AND DEVELOPMENT

Organizations spend billions of dollars each year on training and development. In this chapter, you'll learn the steps to diagnosing, developing, implementing, and evaluating such programs.

After studying this chapter, you should be able to:

- describe the steps to a learning needs assessment and the purpose of each step

- describe the key factors – within the individual, within the organization, and that are part of the training – that may improve or impede training effectiveness

- list the major learning principles associated with training in organizations and how these can be used to enhance training effectiveness

- list and describe some of the key training methods and their effectiveness

- explain the central issues in evaluating a training program, including how to measure training outcomes and appropriate training evaluation designs

Learning goals for this chapter

- understand the key issues for maximizing training effectiveness for yourself
- identify key legal and global issues surrounding training and development
- describe the current issues and controversies around training and development.

Workplace Application

United Services Organizations (USO) Launches Training 2.0

The introduction of technology has been transformative for training and development. As a case in point, we share the experiences of the United Services Organizations (USO), a not-for-profit, congressionally chartered, private organization which is tasked with supporting the United States of America's troops and their families globally. Given the size and scope of their organization as well as the global locations of their population of trainees, USO wanted to revamp their training offerings so that their employees and volunteers who support the troops could take training programs at any time, in any time zone, and receive consistent offerings so that everyone received the same great content. They revamped their training program using a new learning management system while offering courses such as a basic training and compliance program, knowledge and practice of ethics, code of conduct, and sexual harassment prevention. Was their transition successful? As reported by Doe and Kegler (2013), within their first 37 days of operation, 1,000 courses were completed. This is impressive given that at the USO these trainings are optional, not required. The USO commissioned a return-on-investment (ROI) analysis and it was determined that they realized a 312 percent ROI within six months.

Introduction

Organizations invest heavily in training in terms of the sheer numbers of dollars spent on it each year. For example, the American Society for Training and Development (ASTD) says that in 2013, US companies spent over $164 billion dollars on training and development activity, with employees spending an average of 33.3 hours in training per year. (Figure 8.1 shows the increasing expenditures on training in the US.) And, in countries where training and development are more in their infancy such as in Brazil, investment in these programs is growing by 6–10 percent per year (Cozzo, 2014). It seems that many of these dollars are a wise investment. An article by Aguinis and Kraiger (2009) illustrates the importance of training and development activities to individuals, teams and work groups, organizations, and even to society as whole. In fact, deciding whether to "buy" skilled workers or to hire employees who will need training is one of the key human resources decisions that organizations must make, and there are tradeoffs with each approach.

Over the last 20 years, I/O psychologists have learned a lot about how to design and deliver training programs to ensure their effectiveness. During that time, the research on training in I/O psychology has expanded significantly – not just in quantity, but in terms of quality and sophistication as well. Most importantly, we now know much more about what kind of training works, when it works, and how to make sure it works most effectively. A recent article by Salas, Tannenbaum, Kraiger, and Smith-Jentsch (2012) summarized this issue by showing a number of

The Stihl Group, a family-owned business based in Germany, designs, produces, and sells power tools used in landscaping. They have more than 40,000 dealers across 160 countries. Fred Whyte, President of Stihl Inc., shared how important this question is for their success, noting, "You can't just place an ad in the paper to find tool and die makers. So to grow our own, we have an extensive apprenticeship program" (Bingham & Galagan, 2014, p. 29).

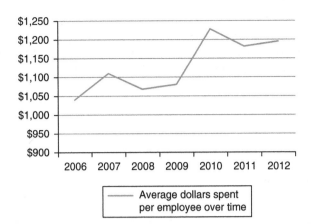

Figure 8.1
Annual average
dollars spent on
employee training.
Source: ASTD
Annual Report.

best practices that can be taken to ensure training quality, such as conducting a training needs assessment before getting started, being sure that the type of training matches the workers, and ensuring that the training translates into changes in job performance.

While examples of good training practice in organizations abound, organizational practices regarding training often do not maximize training effectiveness. For example, we know that doing a training needs assessment adds to training effectiveness by helping define what topics the training should cover and who needs training; however, many organizations fail to do this. In other words, just because research has shown what practices work in organizational training does not mean that organizations are actually following these best practices. Or put differently, how do we know that the money spent on training (remember that it is $164 billion per year in the US as of 2013) is being put to good use?

In this chapter, we will provide an overview of the training process, beginning with the training needs assessment, followed by a discussion of factors within the trainee and in the work context that can help – or hinder – the effectiveness of a training program. We will follow this with a discussion of specific training methods and when to use each of them, and how to evaluate whether or not a training program is working. (See Figure 8.2.) We conclude by discussing current training issues and offering advice for how to take charge of your own training and development.

As we have noted, there is a lot of training going on in organizations, and you almost certainly have been or will be exposed to it in your career. Thus, an overarching goal of this chapter is to make you aware of the ways in which training can be done most effectively to benefit both the organization and the individual as either a trainee, consumer of training, or perhaps as a trainer yourself. Further, given this growth in training in recent years, you may be wondering about what kinds of roles and jobs there are out there for I/O psychologists in the field of training and development. I/O psychologists are deeply involved in the development of training systems – everything from conducting training needs assessments, developing ways to enhance learning through the use of psychological principles, and using robust methods to evaluate training. They also advise organizations on how best to implement their training program to ensure success.

Figure 8.2 The training process within an organization.

| Conduct Training Needs Assessment | Consider Characteristics of the Trainees and the Context | Choose and Administer the Training Method | Conduct Training Evaluation |

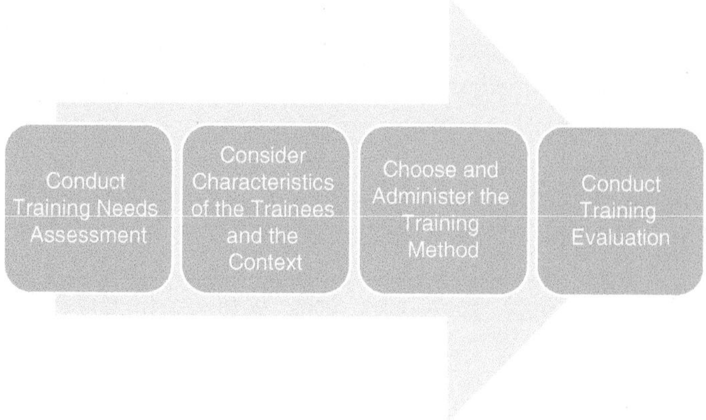

The Training Needs Assessment Process

Training needs assessment: The process by which an organization identifies the key factors in the organization that will support the training program, what needs to be trained, and who needs the training.

As we said in our introduction to this chapter, **training needs assessment** is a "best practice" for starting a training program within an organization (Salas et al., 2012). Training needs assessment is the process by which an organization identifies the key factors in the organization that will support the training program, what needs to be trained, and who needs the training. Here's one way to think about the importance of training needs assessment: It would be hard to start an effective training program in a company if you didn't know the resources you currently had to conduct the training (your budget, for example), which skills need to be trained, which employees need the training the most, and what the employees are currently like in terms of their background and experiences. Unfortunately, however, many organizations conduct training without this kind of consideration. Let's go through each of the steps of the needs assessment.

Organizational Analysis

Organizational analysis: Includes the identification of a broad set of organizational issues that can help or hinder the effectiveness of a training program.

First, the **organizational analysis** includes the identification of a broad set of organizational issues that can help or hinder the effectiveness of a training program, from understanding which group of employees will be trained (will it be salespeople? engineers? teachers?), to how many resources the company will provide towards training. Let's examine the many issues covered in an organizational analysis – including the organization's plans and goals, its available resources, its internal environment, and the external environment (Goldstein & Ford, 2002; Salas et al., 2012).

One of the first things to find out is why the organization wants to start a training program. This includes understanding what the organization's goals are in general, how training will address those goals, and why they are interested specifically in training. It's important that the training is aligned with the organization's strategies and objectives. For example, if the organization prides

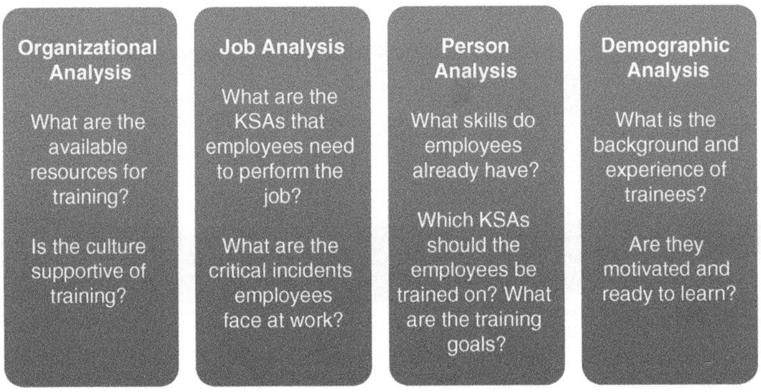

Chapter 8 Training and Development

Organizational Analysis	Job Analysis	Person Analysis	Demographic Analysis
What are the available resources for training? Is the culture supportive of training?	What are the KSAs that employees need to perform the job? What are the critical incidents employees face at work?	What skills do employees already have? Which KSAs should the employees be trained on? What are the training goals?	What is the background and experience of trainees? Are they motivated and ready to learn?

Figure 8.3
Overview of the training needs assessment process.

itself on its customer service, this issue should be addressed by the training program. A second issue is to consider which employees should be the focus of the training (e.g., salesforce? research and development employees?) Third, it is important to know what resources are available for training. For example, what is the available training budget? Who would be the trainers – outside consultants, internal trainers, or simply expert employees who have been trained to be trainers? Another resource issue is what facilities and equipment are available to conduct training, and, if it is a geographically dispersed workforce, what resources are available for travel or perhaps for conducting training online. Fourth, it is important to understand the culture of the organization, such as whether there is support for training and what is being trained. For example, you could put together a fantastic safety training program, but if it does not receive support from supervisors, it may not succeed. This would be a shame, because research shows that highly engaging safety training is related to higher safety knowledge and actual safety behaviors (Burke et al., 2011). Finally, it is important to know about the external business and legal environment within which the organization functions, for instance, understanding what the organization's competition does to train and develop its workforce and any laws that affect the work of the organization and what training employees receive (e.g., safety laws). Moreover, the legal environment is pertinent to training. For example, safety training may be mandated by law for certain jobs and industry, and to the extent that training affects hiring and promotion decisions, training is covered by the *Uniform Guidelines* (see Chapter 7).

Job Analysis

Once the trainer has a good idea of what the organization's goals, plans, resources, and environment are like, the second step of the training needs assessment is one that you are familiar with from previous chapters, the **job analysis** (Goldstein & Ford, 2002). In other words, before embarking on a training program for a group of employees, it would be good to know which tasks employees currently perform on their job, what KSAs they need to be trained on, and what critical incidents employees deal with on the job. As described in Chapter 3, the results of the job analysis would be a list of tasks that employees perform on that job and the KSAs

Job analysis: The process of identifying which tasks employees currently perform on their job and the KSAs needed to do those tasks (see Chapter 3).

needed to perform those tasks. Also, remember that in Chapter 3 we talked about critical incidents. It is especially important for the trainer to understand the critical incidents faced by employees as these can provide good material for training exercises and can be a rich source of information about the work context.

Person Analysis

Person analysis: The process of identifying what current employees can actually do and what KSAs they currently possess.

The third step in the training needs assessment is to perform a **person analysis**, that is, to understand what current employees can actually do and what KSAs they possess (Goldstein & Ford, 2002). Think of it this way: A job analysis might easily identify 20 unique KSAs that employees need to possess to do their jobs effectively, but most employees will already have many of these KSAs. If that's the case, you need to identify the subset of KSAs that some employees actually need to be trained on so that you can make those the focus of your training program. In other words, typically you do not need to train all employees on all aspects of their work. Rather, you can focus only on the KSAs that they are lacking because it would not make sense for the organization to waste time – and resources – on training employees to do things that they can already do.

There are a number of ways to figure out which KSAs employees already have and which they do not. You are already familiar with several of them from previous chapters. These include any ways you can think of that would assess current employee performance and abilities – methods like employee performance ratings, productivity and sales data, customer ratings, and tests. You might also interview supervisors, or even interview or survey employees to see what KSAs they think they need to be trained on.

An example of this type of training needs analysis comes from Google. Individuals within People Operations (their name for the Human Resource function within Google) launched a plan code-named "Project Oxygen." (We discuss Project Oxygen in greater detail in Chapter 10.) Their mission? *To learn how to train individuals to be better bosses.* As reported in a *New York Times* article (Bryant, 2011), they began to analyze all the data at their disposal including performance reviews, nominations for manager awards, feedback surveys, and interviews with bosses. Based on a variety of statistical and qualitative analyses, they determined that effective Google managers engaged in eight key behaviors including: being a good coach; empowering a team while avoiding micromanaging; expressing interest in team member success and well-being; being productive and results-oriented; being a good communicator and listening to team members; helping employees with career development; having a clear vision and strategy for the team; and having key technical skills so that you can advise your team. Based on these findings, they were able to design a state-of-the-art developmental management training course to help managers become more effective.

Developing Training Goals

Training goals: A statement of the purpose of the training and the end state of the trainee in behaviorally specific terms.

Once you've collected the data for these three steps, you're ready to put it all together to establish your **training goals**. The purpose of the training goals is to communicate what trainees are expected to learn *in behaviorally specific terms*.

This is typically done by comparing (1) what the job analysis says that employees *should know and be able to do* versus (2) what the person analysis says that current employees *already know and can do* (Goldstein & Ford, 2002). Put differently, the training goals should focus on the gap between what's needed to do the job and what the current employees can already do.

Why is it important that the training goals be expressed in behavioral terms? Think about a training program for the job of barista. Which would be a more useful training goal in terms of employee and organizational success:

- ability to make espresso drinks

  or

- ability to make different espresso drinks correctly in two minutes using the standard company equipment?

Clearly, the second goal – which is stated in concrete behavioral terms – provides much more information about the job and, therefore, what training is needed to be effective at this job. And this detailed information is important for two different groups of people. First *the trainer* needs to know what the training goals are to be able to develop and provide effective training, to provide feedback to trainees, and to assess whether the training program is successfully meeting its goals. Second, *the trainees* need to have a good understanding of the training goals to be able to learn effectively and understand whether they are on track to master or have mastered the material.

Demographic Analysis

Once you have done the organizational analysis, job analysis, and person analysis, and then established your training goals, you are nearly done with the needs assessment. There are just a few more key bits of information that you should gather, and these can make all the difference to how smoothly the training program goes – and how effective it is in general. This key final step is the **demographic analysis** (Goldstein & Ford, 2002). Specifically, this includes a wide range of issues involved with understanding who the trainees are. For example, what is the education level of the current employees? What is their age? What is their familiarity with technology? Are employees motivated to learn? What personality traits or tendencies do employees have that might affect their learning, such as self-efficacy or conscientiousness? We will discuss these kinds of characteristics later in the chapter, but let's say for now that they are important to take into account so that you develop the right training program for the employees.

Interactive: How to conduct a needs assessment and integrate/interpret the findings.

Demographic analysis: The process of identifying who the trainees are, for example, education, age, and familiarity with technology.

"See website for interactive material"

Figure 8.4
The effects of individual and organizational characteristics on training motivation and training outcomes. *Source*: Based on Goldstein & Ford (2000); Colquitt, LePine, & Noe (2000).

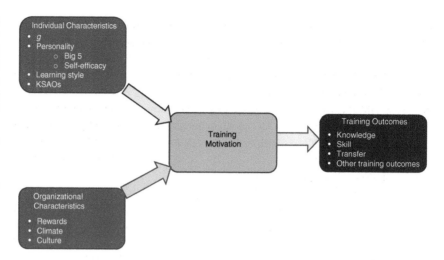

Facilitating Training Effectiveness: The Trainee, Trainer, and Context

Once the training needs assessment is complete, there are a number of factors that can affect whether the training will be effective. Specifically, it is important to consider not only the factors that will enhance trainee learning of important knowledge and skills, but also the likelihood that **transfer of training** will occur, that is, that the training will lead to actual improvements in on-the-job behavior. Research indicates that only a small fraction of knowledge actually transfers back to the job, with some estimates as low as 20 percent (Kazbour & Kazbour, 2013), but steps can be taken to help increase the amount of training that does actually transfer. The best way to think about the ideas in this part of the chapter is like this: Characteristics of the trainee, as well as characteristics of the training and work contexts, all contribute to the effectiveness of a training program. Put differently, these individual and contextual variables together affect training motivation and training outcomes. (See Figure 8.4.)

Transfer of training: The degree to which training leads to improvements in on-the-job behavior.

Individual Differences

There are a number of individual differences that can affect how well a training program works, or that can affect which training program will work for which people. Many of these are individual differences that we have discussed in earlier chapters and that I/O psychologists know affect work behavior of various kinds. In this case, we are interested in those individual differences that affect variables including knowledge and skill acquisition (learning) and transfer back to the workplace.

Why do these individual differences matter to developing good training? There are at least two reasons. First, by understanding differences in how people learn, we can decide what training approaches work best for them. In other words, one type of training may not work well for all learners, and the designer of the training system needs to keep this in mind when selecting their approach to training. Second, a wide variety of learner individual differences within a single group of trainees can pose a significant challenge for a trainer. For example, should the trainer focus his or her materials towards beginners or advanced learners? The following discussion will help the trainer in deciding what individual differences to consider and how to adjust the training program accordingly. As we will see later, certain types of training, such as programmed instruction and learner-centered training techniques (both discussed later in this chapter), can accommodate these kinds of individual differences by allowing people to learn at their own pace, while also directing learners to the training approach that works for them.

Not surprisingly, general cognitive ability or *g* (which we discussed in Chapter 5) is one of the most important determinants of employee learning (e.g., Ree & Earles, 1991). In particular, employees with greater cognitive ability are better able to learn training material, and they are able to learn it more quickly. It is also not surprising that I/O psychologists have spent a lot of time studying the effects of personality on training success. If you recall from Chapter 6, Barrick and Mount's (1991) meta-analysis on Big Five personality and its relationship to work outcomes showed that people who are high in openness to experience, extraversion, and conscientiousness tend to succeed in training programs. Since that time, a number of other studies have looked at the effects of other Big Five dimensions on training. Research has also examined the effects of facets of the Big Five on training, as well as proactive personality. For example, Major, Turner, and Fletcher (2006) found that conscientiousness, openness, extraversion, and proactive personality affected a person's training motivation. However, the relationship between personality and training performance is not always clear. For example, Martocchio and Judge (1997) found that conscientiousness is related to self-efficacy, which is positively related to learning, but that conscientiousness is also related to self-deception, which can be negatively related to learning.

Learning self-efficacy, or a person's belief that they can succeed in training, has been consistently shown to predict how well a person will do in training. Specifically, if a person believes that they can master the training material, it will enhance their training motivation (Colquitt, LePine, & Noe, 2000), and they will be better able to learn it. Related to self-efficacy, locus of control, or a person's belief that their behavior is controlled either by themselves (internal factors) or by outside factors, can also affect training success (Colquitt et al., 2000). For example, a person who thinks that they can largely control their own destiny will probably do better in training than a person who believes that what happens to them is really a function of the situation rather than their own control. Low self-efficacy and external locus of control can best be accommodated by taking training in small steps to allow learners to see that they can succeed. More recently, a related concept known as core self-evaluations (CSE), or what people think about themselves, their ability, and their control, has been shown to affect training as well. Specifically, Stanhope, Pond, and Surface (2013) found that CSE affected training outcomes such as knowledge and skill through its effects on trainee motivation and effort allocation.

One important individual difference that has received much attention in the training literature for the last several years is **goal orientation**, which is *the type of goal*

Learning self-efficacy: A person's belief that they can master the training material.

Goal orientation: The type of goal a person has when learning.

Learning goal orientation: A focus on mastering the training material.

Performance goal orientation: which is focused on doing well on the outcomes, proving their competence to others, and avoiding criticism of their performance.

a person has when learning. Specifically, people who have a **learning goal orientation** will tend to focus on learning training material, while those who are low in learning goal orientation will not. In contrast, some people have a **performance goal orientation**, that is, they will be focused on proving their competence to others, and avoid criticism of their performance. In other words, those with a high learning goal orientation are more interested in learning and acquiring new skills, whereas those with a high performance orientation tend to be more concerned about proving their competence (Payne, Youngcourt, & Beaubien, 2007). Think of the way that different students approach a college class: Some will focus primarily on learning the content regardless of what grade they get, while others will focus on getting a high grade on exams. Note that it is possible for a person to be high on both learning and performance goal orientation, high on only one, or low on both. Not surprisingly, the research has found that people who are focused exclusively on performance (e.g., passing the test) rather than on actual learning do less well in training than those who focus on learning the training content (Payne et al., 2007). However, the research on goal orientation is still emerging (DeShon & Gillespie, 2005), and there is evidence that goal orientation may work in combination with a person's abilities to affect their training performance (Bell & Kozlowski, 2002). Finally, although goal orientation is an individual difference, there is evidence that it may also be dependent on the learning context (DeShon & Gillespie, 2005), and organizations and trainers can change reward systems to get trainees to focus on learning rather than just on their performance.

Another important individual difference that could affect training is an individual's preferred learning style. This refers to how one prefers to acquire new information. For example, if a person likes to acquire information after reading about it, they are probably a visual learner. A person who best enjoys learning by listening to lectures, videos, or conversations is probably an auditory learner. And a kinesthetic learner prefers actually engaging in tasks in an experiential manner. However, just like other individual differences, a primary learning style may be preferred, but trying new approaches to learning can be an effective way to expand one's approach to learning, as research supports the idea that matching learning styles and training modes does not necessarily lead to better retention (Galagan, 2014). Because successful learning is so closely related to student motivation to learn, learning style is a useful way to think about a variety of approaches by trainers.

Meta-cognitive skills: The ability of learners to step back and assess their own learning and mastery of the material.

Finally, another individual difference that can affect learning is **meta-cognitive skills**, which is the ability of learners to step back and assess their own learning. You may not be aware of meta-cognitive skills, but since you are probably reading this book as part of a college class, our bet is that you already use them a lot. Put simply, some people are better able to assess whether they are learning the material, whereas other people are not. In fact, the research suggests that those people who have the lowest skills are the least accurate in assessing their performance. Further, individuals with the lowest skills tend to *overestimate* what they know. In one well-known study, Kruger and Dunning (1999) found that people performing well on a series of tests were more accurate in estimating their scores than those people performing poorly, and that the poorly performing people also overestimated how well they were doing. There is also evidence that even when given feedback, poor performers may discount it, and that high performers may actually be more interested in improving their skills

(Sheldon, Dunning, & Ames, 2014). In the training arena, this suggests that learners who are not gaining the required knowledge and skills may overestimate how well they are doing, and as a result, they may not put in the effort that they should. That is why providing assessments (e.g., short quizzes) and frequent feedback to learners – especially to low performers – may help those with low meta-cognitive skills to see how they are actually doing and adjust their effort towards learning accordingly. Moreover, research has shown that frequent reminders for learners to self-regulate their learning can increase learning (Sitzmann & Ely, 2010). Methods that guide low performers to additional training to improve their performance may also help. The key to doing this effectively is to work to help them maintain their motivation as they are increasing their skills and knowledge via training.

The Organizational Context

At the same time, there are a number of organizational factors that can determine whether a training program is successful and especially whether it leads to transfer of knowledge (Goldstein & Ford, 2002). The first of these is **identical elements**, or the degree to which the training context is similar to the transfer environment. The more similarity there is between the learning environment and the actual work environment, the more likely that training transfer will go smoothly. Another way to think of this is through the concepts of **psychological fidelity** (the degree to which the training elicits the KSAs needed to do the job) and **physical fidelity** (the degree to which the training resembles the physical aspects of the job). Following this approach to training, the equipment used in training should match the equipment used in the work situation as much as possible. For example, take a situation where an organization is training people who repair the machinery on a deep-sea oil drilling platform. If the company were to provide only classroom lectures, making the transfer to the actual work situation could be difficult because the situations are so different. On the other hand, if they were to provide a simulation of the actual conditions on the oil rig, the chances for transfer would be improved. The bottom line is that the degree to which the physical and psychological elements of the training situation and work situation are aligned will affect training transfer. Conversely, the degree to which the training situation and work environment are different can cause the trained knowledge and skills not to transfer to the job, or may even lead to a *decrease* in work performance, because workers are being trained on the wrong KSAs.

Identical elements: The degree to which the training context is similar to the transfer environment.

Psychological fidelity: The degree to which the training elicits the KSAs needed to do the job.

Physical fidelity: The degree to which the training resembles the physical aspects of the job.

Flight simulators, like the Boeing 737-800 one depicted here, are used to train pilots without endangering lives or expensive equipment. They employ identical elements, psychological fidelity, and physical fidelity to enhance transfer.

Transfer through principles: Training employees to understand why they should perform their job in a certain way and the underlying principles behind what they do on the job.

A second way for an organization to enhance transfer is through **transfer through principles**, which refers to training employees to understand why they should perform in a certain way. This means that trainers may want to move beyond simply saying "do this" to saying "do this, and here is why." Take for example a customer service job. One way to train a customer service agent would be simply to say, "If the customer has a problem with a delivery, tell the customer that you will look into it and tell them what is going on." But another way would be to also explain to the customer service agent what the company's policies are and *why* deliveries are handled in a certain way. This second approach would help the customer service agent to know how to handle unique situations not covered in training, and it would thus allow the training to lead to better transfer performance.

Transfer climate: The degree to which the social climate among employees back in the work situation supports training

A third and very different issue that can affect training is the **transfer climate** or the degree to which the social climate among employees back in the work situation supports training and the particular type of training (Tracey, Tannenbaum, & Kavanagh, 1995). Indeed, a recent meta-analysis by Blume, Ford, Baldwin, and Huang (2010) found that a supportive environment enhances training transfer. For instance, learners may have been taught a correct and efficient way to do a task, and they may know it well. But if the supervisor and coworkers do not accept this as the right way to accomplish the work, transfer of the learned skill will not happen. It is not uncommon, for instance, for supervisors or coworkers to tell a newly trained employee, "I know that's what they told you in training, but this is how we do it here." For example, take a situation where newly hired hospital nurses are taught a new way to ensure that patients receive the correct medication. If this method is not accepted by their coworkers back in a particular hospital ward on the job – perhaps because there is already another system in place to monitor patients, and it is well accepted by the nursing staff – the new method taught in the training cannot transfer. This again implies that the transfer situation should be carefully assessed during the needs assessment to identify misalignments between what is trained and actual practice on the job. If such problems are found, the training should either be adapted to fit the actual work practices, or problems with the transfer climate or actual work practices can be addressed.

There are a number of other factors that may lead to increased transfer. For example, Keith and Frese (2008) found in their meta-analysis that error management training – which explicitly treats errors during training as a natural part of learning – can enhance transfer, particularly for novel tasks. Blume et al. (2010) identify the range of factors – cognitive ability, conscientiousness, for example – that can lead to increased transfer of training.

Salas et al. (2012) provide a detailed list of ways that organizations can enhance training transfer after administration of a training program (see Table 8.1). This list provides the organization decision-maker not only with a list of what to do but why, explaining how each action can lead to better transfer for trainees.

Both the Trainee and the Context: Trainee Motivation

Trainee motivation: The degree to which the learner is motivated to gain the KSAs provided in training or to succeed in training.

Another factor that is important for learning is **trainee motivation** (the degree to which the learner is motivated to gain the KSAs provided in training or to succeed in training). Colquitt and his colleagues (2000) conducted a meta-analysis of

Table 8.1 Recommendations for ensuring the training transfer after the training is administered

Remove obstacles to transfer from the work environment and be sure that trainees have a chance to apply what they have learned back on the job.

Provide support to supervisors so they can help employees apply learned skills on the job.

Use real-world debriefs where employees discuss how they have applied what they learned back on the job.

Provide supports to employees like access to databases and resources if they have questions.

Source: Based on Salas et al., 2012.

training motivation to see which antecedent variables lead to training motivation, and whether training motivation affects learning outcomes. They found that training motivation is important, in that it affects training outcomes (such as knowledge and skill acquisition), even beyond the effects of cognitive ability. Interestingly, they also found that motivation was a function of a number of the individual differences we have already discussed – such as pre-training self-efficacy, locus of control, and conscientiousness – as well as the contextual variable of climate. In other words, training motivation is really a function of both the person and the situation that trainees encounter.

A number of theoretical approaches can be used to explain training motivation. We will talk about motivation as a key topic in I/O psychology in Chapter 9, but for now, we will briefly review ways in which we might think about training motivation.

One well-known set of motivation theories is called need theories (Pinder, 2008), such as Maslow's hierarchy of needs. These theories focus on determining the types of needs that different people have. These can include basic needs such as the need for money or the need for satisfaction that comes from doing your job well. Although other theories have supplanted these need theories, need theories do illustrate the important point that training will appeal to different employees for different reasons. For example, some employees may want to be trained so that they can get a promotion, while others will be motivated to learn because it will allow them to do their job better or they might simply enjoy learning new things. The key for the trainer is to understand what it is that motivates individual employees before implementing the training program so that the goals and approach are both in alignment.

Another theory which will be covered in more detail in Chapter 9 is goal-setting theory, which focuses on the fact that people tend to perform best when they are given a specific, difficult goal (Locke & Latham, 2002). In the training situation, this means that learners should be told as specifically as possible what the goals of the training are. Moreover, they should be given feedback about their performance in training so that they are able to adjust their efforts accordingly. For example, they might need to work harder to meet their training goals, or they might be on track in some areas but not others. Without feedback, they may not be able to adjust their effort as needed to meet their goals. One way to remember how to help trainers and learners to effectively utilize goal-setting theory is to remember to keep goals SMART, where the goals are Specific, Measurable, Attainable (Aggressive but Achievable), Relevant, and Timely. (See Figure 8.5.)

Expectancy theory or VIE theory (Vroom, 1964) suggests that people need to believe that their effort will lead to performance and that this performance will lead to an outcome that they want. In the training situation, this means that learners must believe that if they try they will be able to master the material, and that if they master the material it will lead to an outcome that they want (e.g., being able to do their job more effectively). In other words, learners should be supported in their efforts to master material, and they must believe that mastery will lead to an outcome that they desire. One key part of this is that the training should be seen as relevant to the workplace or **meaningful** to learners for them to expend effort towards learning. For example, research suggests that training can become meaningful to employees if they have experienced a dangerous or hazardous situation in the past that the training could have helped them deal with (e.g., Burke et al., 2011; Smith-Jentsch, Jentsch, Payne, & Salas, 1996). Relatedly, reinforcement theory (e.g., Pinder, 2008) makes a similar point: Learners need to believe that their actions (learning efforts) will be reinforced with outcomes that they want such as gaining relevant job knowledge or skills or other rewards such as staying safe.

Meaningfulness: The degree to which the training is seen as relevant to the workplace or to learner.

Workplace Application

Making Safety Training Meaningful to Employees

Safety is often a key training topic for employees in high-risk occupations. While safety training may not be seen as meaningful to some employees, it becomes more meaningful when employees can see a direct connection between the training and staying safe on the job. Research shows that this may especially be the case for employees who have experienced dangerous events in the past that the training could have addressed.

For example, a study of airplane pilots conducted by Smith-Jentsch and colleagues (Smith-Jentsch et al., 1996) showed that pilots improved their training performance when they had experienced a "negative pre-training event" or a dangerous situation. The authors explained that those pilots who had experienced dangers on the job may have perceived the training as more instrumental or meaningful to their safety. Similarly, Burke et al. (2011) found in their meta-analysis of the safety training literature that if trainees had been exposed to hazards in the past, it often enhanced the effectiveness of safety training. In short, understanding and matching employees' backgrounds and viewpoints to training content can be critical in increasing their motivation – and making training programs more effective.

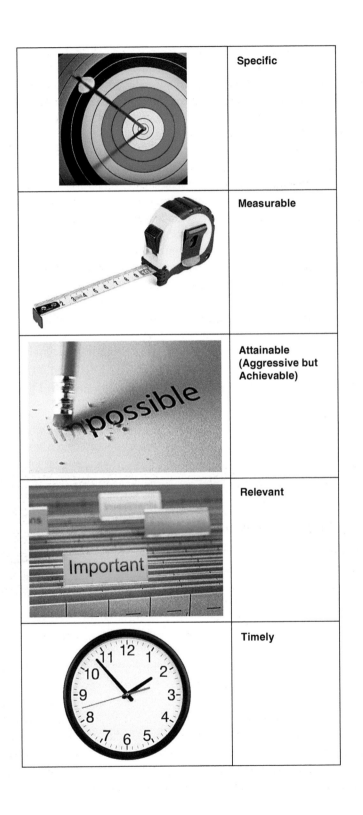

	Specific
	Measurable
	Attainable (Aggressive but Achievable)
	Relevant
	Timely

Figure 8.5 SMART goals in training.

Finally, Bandura's social learning theory (e.g., Bandura, 1965) illustrates the importance of people learning from observing others. In other words, much of human learning is based on our observation of others. This sort of approach is used as the basis of behavioral role modeling training (which we discuss later) which is used in the training of interpersonal skills and the training of supervisors. In summary, training motivation is a key variable which is necessary for learners' success. And while it is a function of individual differences, there is much that the organization can do to support it. This includes building a strong training climate, and also providing support for learners and outcomes that matter to them.

In addition to training motivation, the interaction between the person and situation also creates stress, affecting learning. When individuals are exhausted, they have less attention and mental capacity that they can devote to learning new things. Stress of the training environment influences motivation to learn and exhaustion, which in turn affects learning outcomes (LePine, LePine, & Jackson, 2004). Sometimes, a particular training method is a source of stress, which could result in lower levels of learning. For example in an experiment, Watson and colleagues (2013) examined the effects of monitoring people while they were going through online learning. They found that people who were high in performance goal orientation worried about being evaluated poorly, which resulted in lower levels of learning.

Learning Concepts to Address in Training Design and Delivery

In addition to these individual and situational factors that can affect learning, there are a number of training characteristics that can affect learning as well (Goldstein & Ford, 2002). These are all issues that should be taken into account when designing training programs and delivering them in organizational settings. Some of these issues also arise for pragmatic issues, for example, because of limited organizational resources.

Massed learning: The delivery of training in a condensed session or sessions.

First, **massed learning**, the delivery of training in condensed sessions, can affect learning. In contrast, **spaced learning** involves the delivery of training in small sessions over a longer period of time. For example, a company might bring managers together for an intensive day of training, or it may decide to deliver its training for new supervisors over a period of several weeks. Although spaced learning is generally superior to massed learning for retaining material because it allows learners to organize and integrate what they have learned, there may be practical reasons to use massed learning, such as for its effects on organizational resources. Massed learning also facilitates faster delivery of new skills or knowledge. Therefore, the decision to use massed learning is often made for pragmatic reasons – a trainer or expert is only available for one day, trainees can only be flown to the training location one time, and/or trainees must learn the new material quickly.

Spaced learning: The delivery of training in small sessions over a longer period of time.

Feedback: Providing learners with information about how they are doing leading to their knowledge of results.

Feedback, which refers to providing learners with information about how they are doing, is also essential for learning. We have already discussed briefly how important feedback can be for learners with poor meta-cognitive skills, but all learners need feedback to be able to adjust their learning efforts. Moreover, we have already noted the role of feedback in motivation theories such as goal-setting. Think of it this way: How would it be to take a 14-week college course, with 2 exams and a final, where you never received feedback along the way? It would be challenging

The use of online training – especially via mobile devices – has been steadily increasing each year. It is estimated that in Asia alone, the mobile learning environment will reach $6.8 billion by 2017.

to know how you were doing and whether you were on track towards getting the course grade that you wanted.

Another concept to ensure that trainees are ready to learn is providing them with a **learning schema** (pl. schemata), or a framework for organizing the learning content. Providing a schema to learners can help them to understand how the training content fits together. Research has shown that providing such schemata to learners, such as through an outline or a brief lecture, can help trainees to learn more quickly. Furthermore, research has also shown that as learners become more and more expert on a topic, their schemata become more similar to that of an expert, that is, they organize the information in the same way that an expert would. A highly related concept is that of advanced organizers for learning, or providing learners with the outline and logic of the material prior to training. Consider the way the material for this book is organized – we begin the chapter by providing learning points, which act as both learning goals and as methods for organizing the information. In addition, we organize all of the material in this textbook into a table of contents to help you see how all of the material fits together.

Another factor to consider is **overlearning**. Overlearning is when the trainee practices a behavior so much that it becomes automatic, that is, it requires little attentional capacity or cognitive resources (Kanfer & Ackerman, 1989). Overlearning is especially important when training highly critical skills, behaviors that rarely occur on the job, or those that are used under stressful conditions. If a critical skill does not get practiced very often on the job, overlearning can help ensure that workers know it when it is needed. Similarly, if a behavior is practiced under stressful conditions, overlearning may ensure that workers are still able to perform the behavior when their cognitive resources are depleted by the emergency. Overlearning requires more training time, and hence uses more organizational resource; thus, it is not recommended for learning all kinds of skills. But for these limited types of behaviors, overlearning can be life-saving. For example, teaching emergency procedures to workers at a nuclear power plant to the point of automaticity makes sense – an emergency at a nuclear power plant is very rare and highly stressful for all involved.

Another consideration is whether the training program should fit the average or typical trainee, or whether it should be tailored so that it fits individual trainees. In other words, if you are training a group of new supervisors, you could have a single

Learning schema: A framework for organizing learning content.

Overlearning: A training approach in which the trainee practices a behavior so much that it becomes automatic, that is, it requires little attentional capacity from the learner.

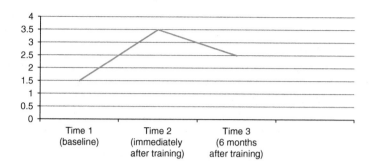

Figure 8.6 Decay of learning over time. Time is shown on the x-axis, and job knowledge is shown on the y-axis.

training program that addresses the needs of most trainees; multiple programs for different groups of trainees (e.g., advanced, average, newbie); or a program that is tailored to each learner's needs. As you might guess, tailoring to individual needs is theoretically the most effective and perhaps the most engaging for trainees because it would not require them to study material they know or to feel overly challenged. On the one hand, the decision on whether to tailor learning is largely a practical matter and driven by organizational resources: Developing and delivering individualized training can be more of a challenge and more costly. On the other hand, the continued development of person-centered learning via computerized and online media is making such adaptation more and more achievable and cost-effective.

Finally, we point out the critical issue of the decay of learning which is the process in which learned knowledge, skills, and behaviors become less accessible to trainees as time passes after training. For example, see the chart in Figure 8.6. As seen in the figure, trainees were able to perform the trained task (dealing with a grouchy client) very well at Time 2 immediately after training – in fact, even better than they were at baseline (Time 1) right before training. However, the ability to perform the behavior has declined at six months later (Time 3). Decay is especially an issue when a learned knowledge or behavior isn't practiced frequently on the job – perhaps in this case, the workers do not have to deal with grouchy customers very often. As we have stated, one way to reduce decay is for trainees to overlearn material. Another way is for organizations to periodically provide "booster" training to employees so they can briefly review training content.

Training Methods

So far we have discussed determining training needs, how individual differences and the context affect training success, training motivation, and learning issues. We have mentioned a few kinds of training in passing, but not directly. At this point you may be wondering, "If this is a training chapter, why aren't they just going over ways to train people?" We decided to explain the factors that affect training success before describing some common training methods so that you could readily identify some of the advantages and disadvantages of some of these training methods by matching them to factors identified in a given needs assessment. Thus, we next describe some of the most common training methods (Goldstein & Ford, 2002).

Keep in mind that while we are presenting some of the most commonly used or frequently discussed training methods, there are many variations on these methods, and they may be adapted as needed to fit learner characteristics and organizational constraints. There are a couple of other things to keep in mind. First, it is important to try to find a balance between learner needs and organizational constraints. For example, learners may do well with an expensive machine simulator, but these may be financially out of reach in an organization. Second, when possible, combining multiple methods of training (e.g., a lecture followed by programmed instruction) will increase learning as it allows the strengths of each method to complement each other and address a range of learner needs.

"Your training will be the next five minutes watching my fingers move at the speed of light."

On-the-Job Training

Perhaps the most common type of training in organizations is **on-the-job training** (OJT), which involves putting the learner right into the job to learn how to do it. Often this involves a coworker showing a learner what to do or letting them watch him or her at work. In theory, there is no better training method than OJT: It has nearly perfect psychological and physical fidelity and thus should lead to perfect transfer. And when done well, OJT is an excellent way to train employees. However, the way that OJT is implemented in many organizations leaves something to be desired. It is commonplace for the "trainer" employee not to be told how to train a new employee – in other words, there is usually no formal "train-the-trainer"

On-the-job training (OJT): Putting the learner into the job to learn how to do it.

Mechanics often learn as apprentices on the job. Here, this apprentice is learning how to fix a car from a master mechanic.

program in place. To make matters worse, this trainer employee must often keep up all of their regular job responsibilities in addition to training the new worker. This is not only very difficult but may cause resentments. In summary, OJT has the potential to be an excellent method as long as the proper resources are invested into making it work. It may also work best where workers are provided with some other sort of training (e.g., lecture) prior to OJT.

Machine Simulators

OJT is a great training method – if done right, there should be perfect transfer to the job because it actually *is* the job. But OJT is not always a good choice. For example, for certain types of jobs where the cost of a mistake is high, or even catastrophic in terms of human lives and property, OJT would be inappropriate. One such example is that of an airline pilot, hardly the type of job where we would want to use strictly OJT (at least if we are the passengers).

Machine simulator: A training environment that reflects the job situation as closely as possible, both psychologically and physically.

A worthy substitute is a **machine simulator**. A machine simulator involves creating a training environment that reflects the job situation as closely as possible. In the case of the airline pilot job, that means creating an entire cockpit that simulates the exact type of plane that a pilot would be flying. Given this, it must be a small room with the ability to tilt and bump to reflect actual flying conditions such as turbulence. As you can imagine, such simulators are costly (upwards of millions of dollars). But using the simulator is not only safer than having pilots initially learn on the job, it also allows learners to experience critical but infrequently occurring situations (Goldstein & Ford, 2002). For instance, wind shear is a dangerous condition that pilots have to know how to deal with when it happens, but it may not happen that often. The simulator can allow the trainer to present various wind shear conditions to trainees to give them practice as to how to react to such situations.

Of course simulations do not have to involve machinery. The key to effective simulations is to create a situation that simulates the actual working conditions as closely as possible. For example, in order to prepare astronauts for their assignment aboard the International Space Station (ISS), the European Space Agency (ESA) had a team of six astronauts live in underground caves in Italy for a week. Astronauts faced working conditions including total isolation from civilization, complete darkness, and physical danger. Participants rated the program very highly due to its close resemblance to actual ISS working conditions (Chow, 2011).

Debriefing: Talking with trainees about what happened in the training program, what could have been done better, and what was learned as a result.

When training is experiential, as in the case of a simulation, **debriefing** becomes very important. Debriefing refers to talking about what happened in the training program, what could have been done better, and what was learned as a result. Debriefing is critical to maximize learning in simulation-based training. By debriefing, individuals and teams turn their experiences into actual learning, draw lessons, and perform better next time (Villado & Arthur, 2013). Debriefs are routinely used as part of Army training exercises and training of surgical teams.

Lecture: The oral presentation of information to trainees, either with or without feedback and discussion.

Lecture

Another frequently used training method is **lecture**. You're probably quite familiar with this approach to learning, but keep in mind that lecture can take a number of forms. At its best, lecture can involve two-way communication for learners

While lecturing has gotten less popular these days than it once was, it can be effective if used to communicate verbal information to a large number of learners or to set up an organizing schema for trainees. It is also best used in relatively small doses, because adult learners process information they hear more slowly than information they read or experience.

to ask questions. But it may also involve strictly one-way communication from the speaker with no chance for questions or feedback from learners. Obviously, the first form of lecture is more effective for learning. The second form of lecture (one-way communication) provides little chance for feedback and is not effective for training on behaviors and skills. Further, it is probably the reason that lecture frequently (and sometimes deservedly) elicits eye-rolling. But many forms of lecture have their uses and can be effective. For instance, lecture is an effective way of disseminating facts or basic knowledge to a large number of learners, and thus it can be a relatively inexpensive and practical method for learning (Goldstein & Ford, 2002). Moreover, lecture can be great when combined with other training methods. Consider, for example, that lecture may be used to communicate a learning schema to a group of learners, and it may be used to give trainees advanced organizers to help them learn the training material more quickly.

Programmed Instruction

Another training method that has been around for quite some time – and one that many of you have probably experienced – is **programmed instruction** (Goldstein & Ford, 2002). The name "programmed" was given to this training not because it is delivered via computer – although often it is. Rather, this method was developed in the 1950s as a program of structured instruction for learners. Programmed instruction involves the presentation of training material in modules. After each module, trainees must take and pass a quiz before being allowed to continue on to the next module. If they do not pass the quiz, they must go back and repeat the module and take the quiz again. Although programmed instruction can be delivered via computer and include written or video content, it was originally presented in terms of a booklet of written content. In addition, what we have described here is known as **linear programmed instruction**, where the learner either continues to the next module or repeats the previous one. By contrast, in **branching programmed instruction**, if the learner gives an incorrect response they may be asked to repeat the module, repeat part of the module, or they may go on to yet another type of "remedial" module. Obviously, branching programmed instruction is more expensive to develop because of its complexity.

Programmed instruction has a number of advantages that align with good training principles. First, it allows learners to go at their own pace. For this reason,

Programmed instruction: Training that involves the presentation of training material in modules. After each module, employees must take and pass a quiz before being allowed to continue on to the next module. In **linear programmed instruction** the learner either continues to the next module, or repeats the previous one if they do not pass the quiz. **Branching programmed instruction** is where the learner may be required to go in various directions if they do not successfully complete a module; for example, they may be asked to repeat the module, repeat part of the module, or they may go on to yet another type of "remedial" module.

An example of programmed instruction you may be familiar with is the Rosetta Stone computer-assisted language learning software in the bright-yellow boxes. The woman pictured above is learning Italian. As she gets answers correct, the program moves on to the next lesson. If she missed a topic, she gets more practice.

programmed instruction addresses a number of the individual differences we described earlier, and in addition takes into account differences in worker abilities and job knowledge. Second, programmed instruction gives feedback to learners. This may be especially useful for learners with poor metacognitive skills who are less able to assess whether they have learned the material. As for drawbacks, the content for programmed instruction can be costly to develop, especially for branching approaches. On the other hand, because this type of modular instruction is now available off-the-shelf for training a number of job skills, an employer doesn't have to develop the materials themselves – thus saving money. In addition, some learners may prefer to interact with an actual trainer rather than a booklet or a computer. On the other hand, when programmed instruction is used in conjunction with an actual trainer, it can significantly free up a trainer's time to address individual learner needs. Finally, while generally effective, programmed instruction is only as good as the training content and the quality of the quizzes used to assess learner performance.

One issue that arises with independent learning approaches such as programmed instruction as well as newer training approaches that may be administered via computer is the idea of learner control in training, that is, providing learners with choices about training features (e.g., degree of feedback, training content). For example, Orvis, Fisher, and Wasserman (2009) found that choice may improve trainee reactions. However, learners may not always make the best choices in training. In other words, methods such as programmed instruction, and other methods that allow the learner some flexibility in choosing their training method, might be best when some sort of guidance is provided for learners as to which methods are best for them (Bell & Kozlowski, 2002). For example, a learner given a number of learning choices may spend their time on activities that don't increase their learning, while ignoring other, more challenging activities that would help them to learn more. As one study found, individuals with greater cognitive ability and pre-training experience may choose more challenging training tasks, which can lead to their doing better in training than others (Hughes et al., 2013). At the same time, as the delivery of training becomes more sophisticated through computer delivery, so-called active training methods, such as those that allow learners to explore and help them to manage their emotions to reduce anxiety, appear to lead to greater training transfer (Bell & Kozlowski, 2008).

Behavior Modeling Training

Behavior modeling training (BMT) is based on Bandura's (1977) social learning theory and is typically used to train behaviorally complex skills such as interpersonal skills. For this reason, it is often used as part of supervisor training. In BMT, learners observe (model) a person performing the desired behavior, such as providing feedback to a low-performing employee. After the model is observed, a learner then role-plays a similar situation and gets feedback from other learners and the trainer. BMT has been around for many years, and the research generally supports it. Taylor, Russ-Eft, and Chan (2005) conducted a meta-analysis on the BMT literature, and it is generally supportive of BMT's effectiveness. BMT seems to affect learning outcomes, and also to a lesser extent, behavior on the job. In addition, the effects on job behavior do not seem to decay very quickly. Another interesting finding is the confirmation of past studies (Baldwin, 1992) showing that presenting learners with both positive and negative models (e.g., both a supervisor doing a good job and a supervisor doing a poor job) seems to help with transfer.

Behavior modeling training: A model is observed, a learner then role-plays a similar situation, and gets feedback from other learners and the trainer.

Diversity Training

The global workforce is growing increasingly diverse, and organizations are seeing the value of diverse teams (e.g., Van Knippenberg & Schippers, 2007). In other words, organizations are already diverse, but the trick is to leverage this diversity to increase organizational functioning (Kalinoski et al., 2013). For these reasons, organizations are seeing value in **diversity training**, focused on the better functioning of diverse groups of employees. However, one of the key questions is whether such training benefits organizations and in what ways. A meta-analytic study by Kalinoski et al. (2013) showed that diversity training increased trainee affective (attitudes; motivation), skill-based (e.g., behaviors), and cognitive outcomes (e.g., knowledge). In addition, the researchers discovered that training utilizing social interaction had greater effects on trainee affect – in other words, they liked it more. Overall, there is accumulating evidence that diversity training does affect a number of outcomes that are important to organizations.

Diversity training: Focused on the better functioning of diverse groups of employees. This includes sensitivity to different groups.

Managerial Training Methods

There are a number of training approaches that are focused specifically on management-level employees. For example, one that you may be familiar with from Chapter 6 is assessment centers. We have already discussed the value of assessment centers for making promotion decisions about managers. Given how expensive and resource-intensive assessment centers are and how important the role of manager is to organizations, why not also use them for training? Well, some organizations do just that. Specifically, no matter whether a manager is promoted or not, they can also be given detailed feedback about how they did and where they might improve. In fact, some organizations focus on purely **developmental assessment centers**, which are not used for making promotion decisions but to give feedback and provide a developmental plan for managers. In addition, there are other types of managerial training, such as **executive coaching**, where a manager works individually with a coach, either at their own or at company expense, on issues and challenges at work. Bono, Purvanova, Towler,

Developmental assessment centers: Assessment centers used to give feedback and provide a developmental plan for managers.

Executive coaching: A manager works individually with a coach, either at their own or at company expense, on issues and challenges at work.

and Peterson (2009) provide a detailed review of the practice of coaching, noting that executive coaches vary in their training (e.g., they may be I/O psychologists, clinical psychologists, or non-psychologists) and in their credentials (such as being certified as coaches or not). Coaches can also provide services anywhere from individual counseling to work-oriented behaviors. Unfortunately, the business of coaching has increased much more rapidly than research on it has, leaving it unclear how much value coaching actually generates for organizations or for employees. Thus, at this point Bono et al. recommend thoroughly considering a coach's education and credentials to match the type of coaching a person or organization feels is needed.

Case study analysis: An in-depth analysis of a particular business case.

Business games and **simulations:** Competition among groups of business teams to improve business decisions.

Role play: Where individuals act out challenging work situations (e.g., a difficult interpersonal situation) in order to enhance their ability in future situations.

Cross-cultural training: Training developed to help increase managers' success in overseas assignments.

A number of other training methods have been used to develop management skills, including **case study analysis** (an in-depth analysis of a particular business case), **business games** and **simulations** (competition among groups of business teams to improve business decisions), and **role plays** (where individuals act out challenging situations in order to enhance their ability in future situations). Another type of managerial training is **cross-cultural training**, or training to help guide managers in overseas assignments. It can include everything from training in cultural awareness and sensitivity, to language training. One study of 15 European managers training for overseas assignments (Lievens, Harris, Van Keer, & Bisqueret, 2003) found that openness to experience predicted cross-cultural performance, whereas cognitive ability was related to acquisition of language skills. STIHL, a German company that makes power tools, uses scenario-based training using an experiential model so that leaders learn to recover after failing. They found that putting leaders in situations where they could fail safely and recover gave them the skills and confidence when they returned to their jobs.

New Employee Onboarding

A survey of HR professionals revealed that onboarding was a major priority, ranging from the need to update their onboarding programs (71 percent) to making major changes in their programs (86 percent). Respondents reported wishing that they had more leadership buy-in and support, greater consistency in their programs, and increased departmental accountability (Gaul, 2013). It is not surprising that onboarding has become such an important organizational issue, as the Bureau of Labor

McDonald's trains its managers and owners from around the world using their state-of-the-art facility located in Oakbrook, IL called "Hamburger University." Since its founding, over 80,000 individuals have been trained there in 28 different languages.

Statistics (2012) reports that the average baby boomer will change jobs over 10 times during their career, and for future generations, the number is predicted to be even higher. Given this, recruitment and selection are critical aspects of the employee life cycle as they help to determine who will become organizational members and who will not. But, as soon as hiring ends, new employee training begins. The first training that most new employees receive is called **onboarding**. It is through this process that employees become familiar with both the task and social demands of their new roles. In addition, it is during this transitional period where newcomers, as they are called, learn about the organization's history, language, politics, people, goals/values, and performance proficiency (Chao, O'Leary-Kelly, Wolf, Klein, & Gardner, 1994). Bauer, Bodner, Erdogan, Truxillo, and Tucker (2007) conducted a meta-analysis of 70 studies of over 12,000 new employees and found that organizations may facilitate new employee hiring by giving clear signals about life within the organization, helping new employees feel welcomed, and having insiders provide them with valuable information. New employees can help themselves by gathering information, seeking feedback, investing in relationships, and showing success early on the job.

As you may have guessed, it is also the process of learning the company's culture. For example, software company Valve, based on Bellevue, Washington, decided to write and share a 57-page "Handbook for New Employees" which includes information such as how not to work too many hours, knowing no one is your boss, that you pick your own projects, and about potential activities you might engage in during the annual tropical company vacation where the entire company and their families take a week off to somewhere warm. After reading things like this, a new employee certainly gets the idea about what type of place Valve isn't.

Of all aspects of onboarding, **new employee orientation** programs (NEO) are the most relevant aspect of new employee training. Almost all organizations conduct some form of NEO. It might last one hour or several months, such as is the case at accounting firms, but this is a key way to help new employees get up and running and ready to contribute to the organization as quickly and painlessly as possible. As Goldstein and Ford (2002) note, orientations typically include goals around:

- communicating information about the job and the organization
- acquiring essential job and safety skills
- typical norms and attitudes that fit into the organization's culture
- understanding how things get done within the organizational structure
- making clear who does what within the organization.

Organizations must also deal with more mundane compliance issues such as completing employment paperwork, getting an employee badge, and setting them up with the basics such as a workstation. However, research shows that while these basic issues are important, doing them in person in a training setting is not effective for helping new employees feel motivated and excited about their new job. In a study of call center employees in India, Cable, Gino, and Staats (2013) found that employees who were brought in and told what a great company they had joined were less likely to perform well and stay with the company than those employees who were encouraged to express their authentic selves. The difference

Onboarding: A process through which employees become familiar with both the task and social demands of their new roles.

New employee orientation programs (NEO): A training process that presents basic information to new employees to help get them up and running and ready to contribute to the organization as quickly as possible.

in the emphasis of the NEO content was subtle but led to big differences in results. When designing a NEO, keep in mind the following key points:

- New employees are nervous about the impression they will make. Make them feel comfortable.
- Paperwork that can be done online or in advance of an employee's first day should be, so that NEO time can focus on important aspects that will help make new employees more effective.
- Making people feel valued motivates them. This is always true, but especially true during new employee onboarding when people feel especially vulnerable.

Evaluating your onboarding program is an important part of continuing to ensure that the program is effectively helping new employees adjust to their new organization. Assess employees' reactions to the program (Level 1), the level of knowledge they have at the end of the onboarding program (Level 2), their behavior (Level 3), and the business outcomes associated with the program (Level 4). Without evaluation, you may miss important opportunities for success. For example, Wakefield and Davis (2013) report that, at Colonial Life & Accident Insurance Company, they realized that new employees who were hired from outside the firm, rather than promoted from within, were reporting challenges in locating and using key organizational resources necessary for success. In other words, employees were not able to effectively gather information due to the way the training materials and resources were set up. They revamped their onboarding program to distribute the training across a longer period of time as well as creating a new e-learning component to their onboarding program. After these changes, the success rate for their managers tripled from the previous rate. In addition, companies such as Kellogg's and Tupperware have created an online onboarding information portal for new employees which allows them to access information at any time, from anywhere.

Online Training

In addition, we point out the explosive growth of online training in organizations in recent years. Online training is particularly attractive to organizations because of its

Regardless of where they are located, employees of Microsoft around the world receive the same New Employee Onboarding (NEO) program (Bauer, 2011).

ease of use: It can be distributed to employees dispersed around the world, and it also allows training to take place at the employee's convenience. But is online training effective? In their meta-analysis, Sitzmann, Kraiger, Stewart, and Wisher (2006) found that it *can* be, depending on how it is done. They found that online training is about the same as classroom training for knowledge. Most importantly, online training was actually more effective than classroom training if trainees were given control of their training and could practice and receive feedback during it.

We anticipate that online training will continue to grow tremendously in the coming years. The trick will be not to simply provide learners with slides of information and "talking head" lectures but to leverage this medium in ways that enrich the learning process. More sophisticated online training can include a number of features that can enhance learning and transfer, with such features as guiding learners through training (e.g., Bell & Kozlowski, 2002) or providing the chance to explore the material in greater depth (Bell & Kozlowski, 2008). An important point to keep in mind is that online training is only a training medium, and not an actual training method, and that its success will largely be driven by whether or not online training follows sound learning principles.

Team Training

Although most of the training methods we have described are applied to individuals, training can be applied to teams as well to help them function together more effectively. Team training methods include cross-training (where team members learn each other's jobs) and coordination and adaptation training among team members. The results can be impressive. One study (Marks, Sabella, Burke, & Zaccaro, 2002) also found that cross-training increased the shared models for team interaction across team members. Salas et al. (2008) found in their meta-analysis that team training can have substantial effects on team performance.

Workplace Application

Mindfulness Training to Reduce Teachers' Stress

Mindfulness, a state of consciousness in which a person allows themselves to notice information non-judgmentally and to be in the present moment, is an issue of growing interest these days, including in the workplace. Although we will touch on mindfulness more in Chapter 12, it is worth noting that researchers are beginning to develop workplace training programs focused on mindfulness to help people to cope with the daily stressors in their lives and to establish a clear mind and healthy body. As one example, Roeser and colleagues (2013) conducted a randomized trial to examine the effects of mindfulness training on job stress and burnout, feelings about home life, and sleep in 113 US and Canadian public school teachers (89 percent female). The training involved 36 hours of group meetings over 8 weeks, and meetings included guided mindfulness and movement practices, group discussions, lectures, poems and stories, and daily home practice. Results showed that teachers who participated in the training reported greater mindfulness, had better attention, and lower levels of stress and burnout than those in the control group, both immediately after the training and four months later. Teachers who received training also reported better moods and greater satisfaction at home, less worry about their jobs when at home, and more and better sleep. These results suggest that mindfulness training is beneficial for the health and well-being of employees, like teachers, who work in attentionally, socially, and emotionally demanding professions.

Evaluating Training Methods

Once the training program is established, it is important to figure out whether or not it has worked. There are really two purposes in doing this. (You may recall our discussion of multiple versus composite criteria back in Chapter 4.) First is to see whether the training needs to be changed to make it more effective. For example, let's say you develop training for a sales job, and your goal is to increase trainees' ability to make sales contacts and to increase their product knowledge. If we found that the training increased ability to make customer contacts, that would be great. However, if it had little effect on product knowledge, that part would not be so great and would suggest that we need to adjust the training in this area. A second major reason to evaluate training is to demonstrate its value and determine whether or not it should be continued. For example, training that is able to make positive, substantial changes to trainee knowledge and behavior is training that is worth the investment.

Unfortunately, in reality organizational training programs are not always evaluated as well as they should be. There are a number of reasons for this. First, some organizations may not feel the need to formally evaluate the training. If everyone said they liked the training, isn't that good enough? We would argue that, no, it is not enough in today's world, where organizational decision-makers are increasingly demanding that the value of programs be demonstrated. Second, some trainers may want to avoid an evaluation of a training program. If you were the person responsible for a $100,000 investment in your company's new training program, maybe it would be more comfortable not to examine its payoff to the company just in case you were to find an answer you didn't like. Third, doing evaluation well can be time-consuming and challenging, and many trainers are themselves not trained in how to do a good evaluation. For example, if poor (unreliable) measures are used to evaluate a training program, what is the more likely outcome? Would it be that a poor training program looks as if it works, or that an excellent program looks as if it did not work? The answer is the latter - a good program might look as if it did not work, meaning that it can be risky to try to evaluate a training program. In short, doing a good job of evaluating a training program is very important, and it is expected of trainers more and more these days, but it is not always easy.

This section of the chapter focuses on how to evaluate training effectiveness. The first part of this section will cover different kinds of measures of training effectiveness, such as tests and performance measures. The second part will focus on how to set up a good study to evaluate a training program. In both cases, we need to consider a balance between strong measures and study designs with organizational realities.

Training Criteria: Measures of Training Effectiveness

There are a number of different measures of training effectiveness that a trainer can use. Trainee opinions (as measured by a survey), tests, and performance samples are just a few ways to measure training effectiveness. In addition, one could look at how well trainees are performing back on the job, or whether the training might actually affect the organization's financial performance. Think back to our discussion of criteria back in Chapter 4. Choosing the criteria to measure has to do with a range of factors including the cost and practicality of the criterion measures, plus, of course, whether the criterion measures are relevant to what the training is supposed to address. In addition, as you should recall from Chapter 4, you need to decide whether to combine criteria into one single composite to address whether the training is generally effective, or whether to keep criteria separate to see which, if any, measures the training is affecting so that training can be adjusted as needed.

Perhaps the most popular framework for considering criterion measures for assessing training effectiveness is that described by Kirkpatrick (Kirkpatrick, 1959; 1998). Specifically, this approach breaks training criteria down into four categories or levels: reactions, learning, behavior, and results. (See Figure 8.7.) First are **reactions**, which is how trainees perceive the training. This includes everything from whether or not they thought the trainer was interesting, to whether the training was useful to their work. Reactions criteria are the most basic level of training criteria and don't really indicate that the training was necessarily effective. At the next level, **learning** criteria are indicators of whether the trainees indicated signs of learning the material. These measures include tests and other assessments given after training to see if the training led to an improvement in knowledge and skills. The third level is **behavior** criteria, which are indicators of whether the training actually led to changes in on-the-job behavior. This would include measures of job performance such as measured by performance ratings or some objective measures of work performance. The final, most difficult level to assess is **results** criteria, or whether the training led to a change in organizational performance such as profitability. Results criteria are by far the most difficult to assess, as many other factors besides training may affect organizational performance, making it hard to show that training had these effects.

Kirkpatrick's model still dominates much of the training literature because it is so intuitively appealing, and it is thus an easy way to explain the measurement of training effectiveness to organizational decision-makers and employees. However, it has been criticized for really being four broad categories of training criteria that largely denote *when* the measures are collected rather than, *qualitatively, what each measure is*. For instance, it has been pointed out that "reactions" can mean anything from whether the trainees enjoyed the training, to whether trainees felt that the training was actually relevant to their work (Alliger, Tannenbaum, Bennett, Traver, &

Reactions: Training criteria focused on how trainees perceive the training.

Learning: Training criteria that are indicators of whether the trainees indicated signs of learning the material in the training sessions.

Behavior: Training criteria which are indicators of whether the training actually led to changes in on-the-job behavior.

Results: Training criteria focused on whether the training led to a change in organizational performance such as profitability.

Figure 8.7
Kirkpatrick's
four levels
of training
criteria.

Level 1: Reactions

This refers to how the trainees perceive the training.

This includes everything from whether or not they thought the trainer was interesting, to whether the training was useful to their work. Reactions criteria are the most basic level of training criteria and don't really indicate that the training was necessarily effective.

Here the questions are:
Did trainees like the training?
Did they think they learned valuable information during their training?

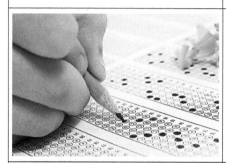

Level 2: Learning

Refers to indicators of whether the trainees indicated signs of learning the material. These measures include tests and other assessments given after training to see if the training led to an improvement in knowledge and skills.

Here the question is:
Do trainees remember what they learned?

Level 3: Behavior

These are indicators of whether the training actually led to changes in on-the-job behavior. This would include measures of job performance such as measured by performance ratings or some objective measures of work performance.

Here the question is:
Are they putting what they learned in training to use on the job?

Level 4: Results

The final, most difficult level to assess is this criterion, or whether the training led to a change in organizational performance such as profitability. Results criteria are by far the most difficult to assess, as many other factors besides training may affect organizational performance, making it hard to show that training had these effects.

Here the question is:
Is the company more effective or profitable based on what employees learned during training?

Shotland, 1997). Without a more precise understanding of which types of training outcomes (e.g., a cognitive skill versus a behavioral skill) are affected by a particular training program, it is difficult to understand which training methods are most useful for particular skills. Defining what the qualitative differences are among different measures of training effectiveness can help us be more precise in understanding the effects of a training intervention.

For that reason, researchers have developed more meaningful categories of training outcomes that can help guide future research and training practice alike. Kraiger, Ford, and Salas' (1993) framework defined training outcomes as falling into the categories of cognitive, skill-based, and affective outcomes. Within each of these categories, the authors provide sub-categories; for example, affective outcomes include changes in attitudes and changes in employee motivation and self-efficacy. Similarly, Alliger et al.'s (1997) framework keeps Kirkpatrick's original four categories but breaks them down with more precision: Reactions includes affective reactions and utility judgments (how useful employees think the training is); learning includes immediate knowledge, knowledge retention, and behavior/skill demonstration; behavior is more explicitly defined as transfer; and results is similar to the results criteria of Kirkpatrick's original model. This more sophisticated break-down of the categories produced some important insights. For example, although researchers consider most reactions criteria to be unimportant, Alliger et al. showed meta-analytically that certain reactions criteria, specifically, trainee perceptions of utility, are related to whether transfer takes place. In other words, trainees may be able to tell you whether or not a training program is effective and whether they can transfer the training to the job. Another finding was that learning outcomes – things that might be assessed by a test – are not necessarily associated with transfer into actual job behaviors. In other words, just because trainees gain knowledge, it doesn't mean that this knowledge is relevant or can actually be applied on the job. While results criteria evidence is not commonly examined, a study by Van Iddekinge and colleagues (Van Iddekinge et al., 2009) indicated that in the 861 units that they assessed in a fast-food organization, the use of the change in the use of training (and selection) was related to customer service and retention, which both help at the organizational level with effectiveness.

In summary, there are different ways to classify measures of training success, and it is important to note that these outcomes are quite different. From the trainer's perspective, it is important to identify which outcomes are of greatest importance (guided by the training needs assessment), gear the training towards those out-comes, and develop sound methods for evaluating those identified outcomes. For example, if one were to develop a diversity training program for an organization, and then evaluate its effectiveness, it would be great if participants liked the training and the trainer. It would also be great if the training affected participants' knowledge of diversity issues in organizations. But if we also found that the participants' attitudes toward diversity were unchanged and that they did not change their job behavior regarding team mates who are different from them, the effectiveness of the diversity training would be called into question. One of the key goals of diversity training is to change attitudes and behavior, and if that is not happening, the training program is of little use.

Designing a Training Evaluation

Once you have settled on the measures of training effectiveness that you will use, it is time to consider what type of evaluation design to use. There are myriad issues to consider, and we point the interested reader to comprehensive discussions of training evaluation designs (e.g., Goldstein & Ford, 2002; Sackett & Mullen, 1993). Think about a training evaluation as though you are conducting a study or experiment in the organization – which you are. We can divide up research designs into (in descending order of rigor) experimental designs, quasi-experimental designs, and pre-experiments, which can be differentiated by the degree to which they use random assignment to conditions and whether they use pretests. These designs vary in the conclusions that can be drawn from them (their rigor), as well as how easy they are to carry out in an actual organizational setting. Also, each type of design controls for different **threats to experimental validity** (see Cook & Campbell, 1979; Cook, Campbell, & Peracchio, 1990), which we review below. Generally, the more rigorous the design, the more threats to experimental validity are controlled, but the more challenging the study will be to implement in an organizational setting.

Threats to experimental validity: Factors which may affect our ability to interpret results of a study such as a training evaluation.

Threats to Experimental Validity

Threats to experimental validity are extraneous factors – issues other than the training itself – that can affect the results of your training evaluation. (Note that these threats to experimental validity are different from the measurement or test validity issues we discussed in Chapter 2 and in the Personnel Selection chapters.) For example, what if you were evaluating the work performance of employees by comparing their work performance before and after training? If performance went up, that would be good. But if during the time of your study, employees got a raise as well, that could be a threat to experimental validity – you don't know whether work performance improved because of the training, or because people were given the raise. Here we consider these various threats to experimental validity.

Threats to Internal Validity

Threats to internal validity are threats that cause us to have concerns about whether the results we got in this particular training evaluation can be called into question. In a classic source on this topic, Cook and Campbell (1979) point out a number of these threats to internal validity. We'll discuss each of these and how they relate to the topic of training:

Threats to internal validity: Factors that can cause us to have concerns with the accuracy of results obtained in this situation.

- **History** is when some event occurs between a pretest and a posttest and at about the same time as the training. An example of a history effect is like the one we gave above, when a pay raise occurs between the pretest and post-test. If that is the case, we can't tell whether the training or the other historical event (the raise) caused the change in employee performance.
- **Maturation** is when the trainees actually mature or change between a pretest and a posttest. This could literally be physical maturation (as is the case with children in a class), but it also applies to workplace training. For example, let's

say that you are evaluating training for new employees who are also working on the job. If their performance improves after training, it could be due to their natural maturation into their work.

- **Testing** is when the pretest affects the results on a posttest. For example, the content of a pretest may cause trainees to understand the key learning goals, and so any improvement you might get on the posttest may only be due to the fact that the pretest was given as well.

- **Instrumentation** is when there is a change in the actual measures from pretest to posttest. This could mean that the evaluator is using different, non-equivalent tests on the pretest and posttest; or it could happen when different supervisors (one more lenient, the other more severe) provide performance ratings on the pretests and the posttests.

- **Statistical regression to the mean** refers to the natural tendency of people with very high scores or very low scores on one occasion to get scores towards the middle of the distribution on the second occasion. Think of it this way: Some of the people with very low or very high scores will get those scores due to random factors (e.g., having a very good or very bad day), and they will tend to get more moderate scores the next time. Statistical regression is an issue for training because often people are chosen for training because they got very low scores (remedial training) or very high scores ("high potentials") on some assessment. We can expect the scores of some people with these extreme scores to regress to the mean.

- **Differential selection of participants** refers to non-random assignment to training or control conditions, and thus any differences found between the two groups could be caused either by the training or some other factor. Let's say you decide to train a group of employees in the San Francisco office, and use the Seattle office as controls. If you find any post-training differences, it is not clear if this was caused by training or was caused by pre-existing differences between the two offices. The key to addressing this issue is having good pretest measures so that you can control (statistically) for any pre-existing differences between the training and control groups when you compare them.

- **Experimental mortality** refers to the issue that sometimes participants will drop out of studies. This could literally be because they died; or more likely in the training situation, that they dropped out of training or left the company. If a number of people drop out of the training, it is hard to know whether or not the training is effective. This could especially be a problem if people who are doing well or poorly in the training drop out at different rates.

- **Compensatory equalization of treatments** occurs when someone outside of the training program decides to do something "special" for those in the control group. For example, what if you have a great training study – two groups of trainees, randomly assigned to training and control conditions, with multiple measures of performance – only to find out that someone in top management decided to give some "perks" to people in the control group who did not get the opportunity to take the training? This would then make it difficult for you to figure out whether the effects were actually caused by the training.

- **Compensatory rivalry between respondents receiving less desirable treatments** refers to a situation where individuals in a control group realize that they are not getting training, and thus decide to compete with the trained group. For example, teacher training accompanied new technology at one elementary school but not the other one across town, you could imagine that if the teachers in the control group found out about it, they might decide to work harder to "show those researchers how good their students are at technology without all those fancy tools." This would cause any differences between the trained and control groups to be minimized – when in fact the training might be quite effective. One way to avoid this threat is to either keep those in the control group blind to the fact that they are part of a control group, or else let them know that they will be able to be trained later.
- **Resentful demoralization of respondents receiving less desirable treatments** occurs when those in the control group resent the fact that they cannot receive the training and actually perform lower as a result. In other words, a control group might perform lower after training, making the trained group look particularly good. Going back to the teacher example, the control group might "give up" when they realize that they don't have access to the latest technology and decide to put in less effort. Again, the best way to avoid this threat is to either keep those in the control group blind to the fact that they are part of a control group, or else let them know that they will be able to be trained later.
- **Diffusion of treatments** occurs when those in a trained group return to the work site and train their coworkers in the control group about their training. In one sense this is great – the control group gets some training from their coworkers. But it is not so good from a training evaluation standpoint, because it might cause the control group to do as well as the trained group. If that happens, it looks as if the training is not causing much change when it might actually be very effective.

Threats to external validity: Threats that cause us to have concerns about whether the results obtained in a particular training evaluation will generalize to other settings.

Threats to External Validity

Threats to external validity are threats that cause us to have concerns about whether the results we got in this particular training evaluation will generalize to other settings. (See Cook and Campbell, 1979, for a description of these threats.) For example, if a training program is tested on one type of worker (e.g., office workers) and is found to be successful, it may not necessarily work with other populations (e.g., construction workers). Here are a couple of major threats that can come up in organizational training situations:

- **Reactive effects of pretesting.** When one is evaluating a training program, you would usually like to do a pretest to get a baseline of workers' current performance. However, if the training is found to cause increase from pretest to posttest, it is possible that the training worked only because the trainees got the pretest and paid greater attention to the material related to it during the training. If you then use the training in other situations where there is no pretest, the training may not work as well.

- **Reactive effects of the experimental setting.** This is what can happen when people in the trained group know that they are part of a study and thus try harder – essentially the Hawthorne effect we discussed in Chapter 1. The concern is that when the training is used outside of a "special" evaluation setting, participants may not do so well.

Training Evaluation (Research) Designs

Like the research designs that we discussed in Chapter 2, training evaluation designs vary in the degree to which they include (1) experimental (trained) and control (untrained) groups, (2) random assignment to conditions, and (3) pretests prior to training to get a baseline of how workers were prior to training. (This third issue is particularly important to consider when participants are not assigned to experimental and control conditions.) The greater the extent to which the design has these three characteristics – experimental and control conditions, random assignment, and pretests – the greater **experimental rigor** the design is said to have, that is, the greater number of threats to validity are controlled for by the design.

Generally, evaluation designs fall into three categories, ranging from the most to least rigorous: true experiments, quasi-experiments, and pre-experiments. We'll talk first about true experiments and pre-experiments, and then talk about quasi-experiments that may be a good, practical compromise in many organizational settings. We point interested readers to classic sources for discussions of research designs in general (e.g., Cook & Campbell, 1979; Cook, Campbell, & Peracchio, 1990), and to discussions of research designs in the evaluation of organizational training (Goldstein & Ford, 2002; Sackett & Mullen, 1993). Also, it's important to note that while we present only six classic examples for discussion, it is possible to have any number of different evaluation designs than these.

Experimental rigor: The degree to which threats to validity can be eliminated as the cause of a study's results. Rigor can be increased by the use of control groups, random assignment, and the use of pretests.

Pre-Experiments

Pre-experimental designs are considered the least rigorous because they control the fewest threats to validity. A classic example is the posttest only, no control group design:

$$X \quad T2$$

where X indicates training and T2 denotes the post-training measure. Because there is no baseline or control group, this design controls for essentially no threats to validity. Basically, this is the design you would use only if you wanted to be sure that trainees possessed the requisite KSAs after the training, but didn't really care if the training caused an improvement in KSAs. As we discuss later, this situation is not all that unusual, so this simple design may be acceptable under certain circumstances – especially once initial effectiveness has been established.

Within the pre-experiments, another level up – and a big improvement in terms of rigor – would be the pretest, posttest, no control group design, which would look like this:

$$T1 \quad X \quad T2$$

In this case, we can actually measure whether there was a change in KSAs from before to after training. The problem, of course, is that this design does not let you know whether the change was due to the training or to some extraneous factor such as history and maturation effects. Still, this design may be acceptable in certain organizational contexts, and is better at ruling out threats to validity than a posttest only or no evaluation at all.

True Experiments

The designs with the highest rigor, true experiments generally have all three characteristics of rigorous designs. One example is the classic pretest, posttest control group design with random assignment. Schematically, the design would be as follows:

T1   X   T2 (R)

T1   T2 (R)

where T1 is the pretest, T2 is the posttest, X designates the training, and (R) indicates random assignment. This design controls for many of the threats to validity, such as history and maturation effects, because not only does it have a baseline, it also allows you to compare the trained group with an equivalent control group that got no training. However, this design does not allow you to control for some of the threats to validity involving testing effects. For that, we focus on the grand and elegant – but often impractical – Solomon 4-group design:

T1   X   T2 (R)

T1   T2 (R)

       X   T2 (R)

              T2 (R)

This design has it all – pretests, control groups, and random assignment – plus it also allows you to see how well the training would work if you did not use the pretest.

So why don't organizations always use true experiments? The problem with these designs is that they may not be practical in many organizational settings, especially with the requirements of random assignment to training and control groups. Take for example the Solomon 4-group design: Creating four separate, randomly assigned groups in an organizational setting, and then tracking who does and does not receive a pretest, can be challenging, if not impossible. It is for this reason that many organizations fall back onto a third family of research designs, the quasi-experiments.

Quasi-Experiments

Luckily there is a third path that the training evaluator can take to get more experimental rigor than the pre-experiments but avoid some of the practical challenges of true experiments. The quasi-experiments (literally meaning "almost experiments") allow the researcher to come up with sufficiently interpretable designs that also are practical in many organizational settings. For example, one classic quasi-experiment is the pretest, posttest control group design with non-random assignment:

T1   X   T2

T1   T2.

This looks like the pretest, posttest control group design that we discussed earlier, except for one thing – there is no random assignment. This might allow you to compare two different, non-equivalent groups in your organization, say the Boston office and the Philadelphia office. The key here is to have the T1 (baseline) measures, which allow you to statistically control for any pre-existing differences between the training and control groups.

What if you do not have the opportunity to use a control group of any kind in your organization? The time series design might just be the one for you.

T1   T2   T3   X   T4   T5   T6.

It looks like a pre-experiment but with additional time points. What's the advantage? This design allows you to see if any kind of maturation effects might be at work. If T1, T2, and T3 are essentially equivalent, and there is a bump in performance between T3 and T4 when the training takes place, it would suggest that maturation effects are probably not affecting your results. In addition, examining T4 through T6 allows you to see how much decay is taking place and whether additional booster training is needed.

So Which Designs Should You Use?

While the trainer is figuring what outcome measures to use to assess the training, he or she should also be considering what type of training evaluation design to use. We've discussed a number of evaluation design options above. What factors determine the best design to use? Sackett and Mullen (1993) weigh practical issues in conducting training evaluations in work organizations.

First, it is important to consider what the purpose of the evaluation is. Second, there should be a practical consideration of what organizational resources are available and how these affect the practicality of certain designs; in fact, certain designs – even the most rigorous designs – might not be suitable for a particular organizational context. In a classic paper, Sackett and Mullen (1993) provide a practical and nuanced discussion of these issues, including whether it might be better to use a relatively "weak", pre-experimental design, depending on the circumstances.

What Is the Purpose of the Evaluation?

Before getting started on an evaluation, you should consider what the purpose of the training is. Is it simply to show that trainees are performing at a satisfactory level? An example would be the training of police officers. While it would be good to know if the training actually affected their job performance, the overriding issue in this situation would be to ensure that the trainees have the requisite KSAs before putting them on the streets with weapons and in positions of authority. For that reason, you may not care so much about whether the training causes changes in the new police recruits, but you would certainly be concerned about whether they are sufficiently qualified to be police officers once the training is complete and they graduate from the police academy. In this case, a simple posttest design, with no pretest or control group, may suffice. On the other hand, if you are examining the effectiveness of a new (and perhaps expensive) training program you've developed for supervisors in your company, you may be asked to show that this training program is actually causing a change in supervisors' knowledge and behavior towards their subordinates; if it is not, you may be asked to eliminate the program, or at least to find out where the flaws are in the training and fix them. In this case, you would probably use some more rigorous design that will allow you to understand if the training or some other extraneous variable caused your effects on the outcome variables.

What Are the Available Organizational Resources? What Are the Constraints?

One consideration in choosing what outcomes to measure and what evaluation design to use is the organizational resources that are available and constraints that limit your choices. Below we provide three scenarios where the use of less rigorous experimental designs might make more sense than a more rigorous design given certain organizational constraints.

Scenario 1: An organization will only allow the trainer to give a pretest and a posttest to people who go through training, and will not make a control group available (posttest only, no control group design). Under these constraints, would it be better not to do any evaluation at all? Certainly not! Especially if certain threats to validity can be eliminated through logical consideration (e.g., history may be confidently eliminated if there was no historical event between the two pretest and the posttest; Sackett & Mullen, 1993), such a design is better than no evaluation at all.

Scenario 2: Suppose an organization was willing to let you conduct a Solomon 4-group design – often considered the "gold standard" in terms of evaluation designs – but there are only 20 participants available. Putting only five people into each condition would not be wise from a statistical point of view – the small sample might keep you from being able to detect whether a good training program is actually effective (see Sackett & Mullen, 1993).

Scenario 3: In another organization, the trainer is told that they will have a sample of 200 employees available. The trainer is also told that she can randomly assign people to experimental (training) and control (no training) conditions. Fantastic! But while this may sound like a great opportunity, it may not be in terms of threats to validity. Trained workers may come back to the worksite and tell their colleagues in the control condition what the training involved (diffusion of the treatment). Or people in the control group may easily find out that they are not being trained and try to improve their performance (compensatory rivalry) or decrease their performance because they haven't been given the training opportunity (resentful demoralization). One solution used in some organizational settings is to randomly assign work groups (rather than individuals) to the trained and untrained groups to decrease diffusion of the treatment. In addition, the use of a quasi-experimental design with non-random assignment but where there is a control group that is not in contact with the trained group may be appropriate.

The point is that while it is generally a good idea to use the most rigorous design available to control for as many threats to validity as possible, there are compelling reasons not to do this given certain organizational constraints. In fact, as shown in the third example, a rigorous design with random assignment may actually introduce additional threats to validity of the research design.

Conclusion

So there you have it – issues to consider in developing an organizational training process from its beginning to end. Of course, actual training programs in organizations are rarely developed and rolled out in such a completely linear, straightforward way.

LEGAL ISSUES

There are a number of legal issues that are involved in training. The first of these relates to the selection issues that we discussed in Chapters 6 and 7. Specifically, to the extent that a training program is used to make hiring or promotion decisions, it is considered a selection procedure, covered by the *Uniform Guidelines* and EEO laws. This means that if a training program is used for selection decisions, the organization needs to monitor whether trainees from protected groups pass the training program at a differential rate than those non-protected groups. For example, if a management training program is used to decide who becomes a manager, and the pass rate for minority trainees is lower compared to white trainees (see the 4/5 rule in Chapter 7), the organization may want to reconsider the use of the training program or be prepared to defend its validity. In addition, organizations need to remember to be fair about who is chosen for training. For example, if men are chosen for training at a higher rate than women, that would be problematic.

In addition, certain training can be important to protecting the organization from legal problems. For example, many organizations provide training on issues such as safety, diversity, and avoiding sexual harassment. These kinds of training programs are important because they protect employees and provide them with a safe and supportive work environment. But in addition, they also decrease the chances of legal liability due to accidents or sexual harassment charges. In fact, not training employees may be a type of negligence on the part of employers, with legal consequences. For example, if an employee harms others in the course of their job-related duties, the organization may be held legally liable for the harm for not adequately training the employee.

GLOBAL IMPLICATIONS

With the growth of multinational corporations (MNCs), international and cross-cultural issues in the area of training have continued to grow. It is for this reason that Aguinis and Kraiger (2009) specifically include a global view of the training function in organizations, with the goal of understanding the importance of training not only to employees and organizations, but to society as well. For example, it is now necessary for managers to be sent for overseas, expatriate assignments and for team members to include people of multiple nationalities – often working remotely. Moreover, as we've already noted, online training now facilitates the use of a single training method over many countries.

Although we are seeing these changes in the workplace – increased mobility of employees across borders and diverse, multi-national teams – far more research is needed to address them. For instance, while we know that cross-cultural training generally works, much more research is needed to understand which types of training are most effective and under which conditions (Littrell, Salas, Hess, Paley, & Riedel, 2006). One of the most pointed questions comes from Salas et al. (2012), who ask which specific competencies are needed for organizations and employees to compete globally. The training research is beginning to tackle these questions which are of keen interest to organizations, workers, and society.

CURRENT ISSUES AND CONTROVERSIES

As you can imagine, given the growth of the training research over the last two decades and enhancements to training technology, there are a number of burning research issues in the field of training. Recent reviews of the training literature (Aguinis & Kraiger, 2009; Salas et al., 2012) discuss a number of these, which we highlight here.

First, as we've discussed, training technology has boomed recently, providing the opportunity for training to take place remotely and also to provide trainees with training choice. While many of these improvements are certainly "cool" and make training more interesting, do they work? It's more than likely that some technological enhancements are more effective for learning than others, and the research needs to uncover which of these improvements (e.g., providing choice to learners) to training delivery actually work, and for which types of employees (e.g., by age group, education, or personality). A second issue is the increasing interest in the "gamification" of training (e.g., Kapp, 2012), that is, motivating learners by making the training process more of a game for them, including awarding them "badges" or various levels of achievement. Despite this increased interest, research on this approach to training in organizations is currently lacking. Third, we know that training leads to significant improvements for individuals. But how does skill acquisition for individual employees (e.g., increased knowledge) actually lead to improvements for the organization (e.g., increased organizational productivity)? Understanding this tie-in between individual training and overall organizational performance could help to develop training systems that have the greatest impact. Fourth, the developing field of neuroscience can say a lot about how individual learning occurs. If so, how can we use neuroscience research on learning to develop better training programs? This seems to be a particularly promising area for future research.

WHAT DOES THIS MEAN TO YOU?

Our approach in this chapter has generally been to consider training from the viewpoint of the organization. However, as you may have been thinking, the material in this chapter is relevant to individuals as well. What are some take-away messages here?

First, you may want to consider what your personal training needs are. What kind of job or career do you want, what knowledge, skills, and abilities are needed, and which of these KSAs do you currently have? What are the gaps that you see in your current KSAs and how will you fill them? As we have already discussed, sometimes it's hard to see what our own training needs are, and so very often those around us, especially a trusted friend, coworker, or supervisor, can help to see where the training needs lie.

Second, how will you fill these gaps? In other words, what types of training – be it class work, outside courses, or experience – will help you to fill these gaps most effectively? And how will you know whether you have successfully acquired the skills that you need?

In any case, keep in mind that you do have some control over your own training and development, and taking charge of them can help you to get where you want to be in your career.

However, the more that training programs can address the issues we've described, the more organizations can benefit from a training program.

As we noted at the outset, the training literature has come a very long way in the last 20 years. We know what the best practices are: do a needs assessment, consider the characteristics of the individual trainees and the training context, and

Table 8.2 Evidence-based practices for training success

- Conduct training needs analysis, including organizational, job, and person analysis.
- Create a supportive learning climate by scheduling training well in advance and working with managers to implement the training.
- Build trainee readiness focusing on trainee motivation, self-efficacy, and learning orientation.
- Use proven training methods.
- Use training technology in ways that fit the learner.
- Encourage transfer of training (e.g., provide a supportive transfer environment).
- Evaluate training.

Source: based on Salas et al., 2012.

choose training methods that fit the training content and the trainee, all the while considering how you will evaluate the training program to demonstrate its value. Salas et al. (2012) provide a list of best practices based on the research that has been conducted to date. (See a summary in Table 8.2.) Now that you have read this chapter, none of these recommendations will seem surprising. The challenge is for organizations to actually follow through with carrying out these best practices. Obviously, not all organizations have the resources to follow all of these recommendations to the letter. But given the large amount of organizational resources spent on training, organizational decision-makers would do well to adopt as many of these as possible.

YOUR TURN...

WHAT
DO
YOU
THiNK?

1. Consider a job that you have now or have had in the past. How would you go about doing a training needs assessment for that job? Consider the organizational resources available. How would you convince managers that they should do a training needs assessment?

2. Consider your own background and experience at the present time and the career plans that you have. What types of training do you need? Given that

the research shows that people may be mostly unaware of their own training needs (e.g., Kruger & Dunning, 1999), how would you find out what your greatest weaknesses are?

3. A friend of yours says that she thinks that lectures are just boring and that she doesn't think that they are any good for learning. What would you tell her about the effectiveness of lectures in organizational training?

4. Why do you think that more organizational leaders are becoming more interested in evaluating training programs? What types of outcomes should top-level managers look at for deciding whether a program is effective?

5. What are some characteristics of the individual and of the organization that can make training more or less effective? What factors affect training transfer?

Additional Reading

Aguinis, H., & Kraiger, K. (2009). Benefits of training and development for individuals and teams, organizations, and society. *Annual Review of Psychology, 60,* 451–474.

Cascio, W. F., & Aguinis, H. (2011). *Applied psychology in human resource management* (7th ed.). Upper Saddle River, NJ: Prentice Hall.

Goldstein, I. L., & Ford, J. K. (2002). *Training in organizations: Needs assessment, development, and evaluation* (4th ed.). Belmont, CA: Wadsworth Cengage Learning.

Kozlowski, S. W., & Salas, E. (Eds.). (2009). *Learning, training, and development in organizations.* New York: Taylor & Francis.

Salas, E., Tannenbaum, S. I., Kraiger, K., & Smith-Jentsch, K. A. (2012). The science of training and development in organizations: What matters in practice. *Psychological Science in the Public Interest, 13,* 74–101.

CASE STUDY: Training to Overcome Unconscious Bias at Google

As we discussed in Chapter 7, discrimination is an issue of concern in many organizations. However, discrimination can occur in subtle ways – ways that the person perpetrating it is not conscious of.

Most of us are familiar with bias that is overt, where the person is conscious of it. This type of discrimination is referred to as explicit bias. Because it is overt it can at least be easier to identify and remedy. In addition, people can try to more easily overcome their own explicit biases because it is part of a conscious process.

However, in recent years social psychologists have also begun to point to the existence of unconscious bias, referred to as implicit bias. The problem with implicit bias is that psychologists believe that *most* people are susceptible to it. In addition, because the individual is unaware of it, by definition he or she won't see that they are doing it and won't try to stop it. [By the way, if you're thinking that you are not susceptible to implicit stereotypes and biases, consider testing that hypothesis by taking the implicit association test which is available here (https://implicit. harvard.edu/implicit/takeatest.html) – you may be surprised by the result.]

One of the challenges within the high-tech industry is its domination by males, with women largely under-represented. For example, at Google, 83 percent of its engineering employees and 79 percent of its managers are men. One of the reasons sometimes cited for these imbalances in the makeup of the high-tech workforce is not high levels of explicit bias so much as implicit bias that may affect the opportunities given to women. Such bias can also make the workplace less inviting and welcoming to women.

Google has already undertaken initiatives to increase diversity in terms of recruitment in hiring. In addition, it has now set out to address this issue of unconscious, implicit bias in its workforce. Laszlo Bock, Google's executive in charge of HR, wondered if some sort of implicit bias might be affecting the gender makeup of their workforce. He noted that Google's social environment was not one that would tolerate overt discrimination. On the other hand, women were under-represented at Google, such that some sort of unconscious beliefs could be at the root of it. Moreover, this lack of gender diversity wasn't only a matter of fairness – it raised concerns at Google in terms of potential losses in creativity, since diverse teams can be more creative.

Thus, Google set out to address the issue of implicit stereotypes through a training course designed by an I/O psychologist at Google, Brian Welle. The 90-minute course was developed to fit the scientific orientation of Google's employees. To date, tens of thousands of Google employees have taken the course. The key points made in the course are that all people are susceptible to unconscious bias and that even small amounts of bias can have profound repercussions for the workplace, but that we can overcome this bias if we can become aware of it. A key component is people feeling comfortable openly identifying and discussing cases of sexism that they see back on the job. The belief is that noticing this subtle sexism in others on the job and talking about it can help employees understand how commonplace unconscious sexism is and thus be able to see it in themselves.

Google is already beginning to see a number of positive outcomes that are attributable to this training. For example, employees now frequently call out their coworkers for making a subtly sexist remark. But the program is still so new at this point that its success is still unknown.

Sources: This case is partially based on information included in Gino, 2014; Manjoo, 2014.

Questions

1. What do you think about the training that Google has developed to overcome unconscious gender bias? If you were developing a training program to overcome unconscious bias, what elements would you include in it? Describe both the content of the training and the training methods that you would use.

2. How do you think the culture of the organization or the industry could affect a training program focused on diversity issues? Provide an example for two different industries or job types.

3. If you were in charge of evaluating Google's training program, how would you measure its success? Consider Kirkpatrick's framework of reactions, learning, behavior, and results.

4. What do you think about the likely transfer of this training? What would you do to ensure effective transfer?

5. Do you think that Google can stop this training at some point, or will it need to continue this training indefinitely? Explain the reasons for your answer.

References

Aguinis, H., & Kraiger, K. (2009). Benefits of training and development for individuals and teams, organizations, and society. *Annual Review of Psychology, 60,* 451–474.

Alliger, G. M., Tannenbaum, S. I., Bennett, W., Traver, H., & Shotland, A. (1997). A meta-analysis of the relations among training criteria. *Personnel Psychology, 50,* 341–358.

American Society for Training & Development. (2013, November). ASTD's 2013 state of the industry report: Workplace learning. *T+D,* 41–45.

Baldwin, T. T. (1992). Effects of alternative modeling strategies on outcomes of interpersonal-skills training. *Journal of Applied Psychology, 77,* 147–154.

Bandura, A. (1965). Influence of models' reinforcement contingencies on the acquisition of imitative responses. *Journal of Personality and Social Psychology, 1,* 589–595.

Bandura, A. (1977). *Social learning theory.* Englewood Cliffs, NJ: Prentice Hall.

Barrick, M. R., & Mount, M. K. (1991). The big five personality dimensions and job performance: A meta-analysis. *Personnel Psychology, 44,* 1–26.

Bauer, T. N. (2011). *Onboarding new employees: Maximizing success.* SHRM Foundation's Effective practice guideline series. Alexandria, VA: Society for Human Resource Management.

Bauer, T. N., Bodner, T., Erdogan, B., Truxillo, D. M., & Tucker, J. S. (2007). Newcomer adjustment during organizational socialization: A meta-analytic review of antecedents, outcomes, and methods. *Journal of Applied Psychology, 92,* 707–721.

Bell, B. S., & Kozlowski, S. W. (2002). Adaptive guidance: Enhancing self-regulation, knowledge, and performance in technology-based training. *Personnel Psychology, 55,* 267–306.

Bell, B. S., & Kozlowski, S. W. (2008). Active learning: Effects of core training design elements on self-regulatory processes, learning, and adaptability. *Journal of Applied Psychology, 93,* 296–316.

Bingham, T., & Galagan, P. (2014). Training powers up at STIHL. *T + D*, January, 28–33.

Blume, B. D., Ford, J. K., Baldwin, T. T., & Huang, J. L. (2010). Transfer of training: A meta-analytic review. *Journal of Management, 36*, 1065–1105.

Bono, J. E., Purvanova, R. K., Towler, A. J., & Peterson, D. B. (2009). A survey of executive coaching practices. *Personnel Psychology, 62*, 361–404.

Bryant, A. (2011). Google's quest to build a better boss. *New York Times*. Retrieved February 20, 2014, from http://www.nytimes.com/2011/03/13/business/13hire.html?pagewanted=all&_r=0.

Bureau of Labor Statistics. (2012). Retrieved January 30, 2014, from http://www.bls.gov/nls/nlsfaqs.htm#anch.

Burke, M. J., Salvador, R. O., Smith-Crowe, K., Chan-Serafin, S., Smith, A., & Sonesh, S. (2011). The dread factor: How hazards and safety training influence learning and performance. *Journal of Applied Psychology, 96*, 46–70.

Cable, D. M., Gino, F., & Staats, B. R. (2013). Breaking them in or eliciting their best? Reframing socialization around newcomers' authentic self-expression. *Administrative Science Quarterly, 58*, 1–36.

Chao, G. T., O'Leary-Kelly, A. M., Wolf, S., Klein, H. J., & Gardner, P. D. (1994). Organizational socialization: Its content and consequences. *Journal of Applied Psychology, 79*, 730–743.

Chow, D. (2011). "Mission" leaves astronauts in the dark – inside a cave. NBCNews.com. Retrieved February 28, 2014, from http://www.nbcnews.com/id/45169003/ns/technology_and_science-space#.UxKvROBqkR1.

Colquitt, J. A., LePine, J. A., & Noe, R. A. (2000). Toward an integrative theory of training motivation: A meta-analytic path analysis of 20 years of research. *Journal of Applied Psychology, 85*, 678–707.

Cook, T. D., & Campbell, D. T. (1979). *Quasi-experimentation: Design and analysis for field setting*. Boston, MA: Houghton Mifflin.

Cook, T. D., Campbell, D. T., & Peracchio, L. (1990). Quasi-experimentation. In M. D. Dunnette & L. M. Hough (Eds.), *Handbook of industrial and organizational psychology* (pp. 491–576). Palo Alto, CA: Consulting Psychologists Press.

Cozzo, I. (2014). Brazilian organizations' investment in training increased last year. *T + D*, February, 16.

DeShon, R. P., & Gillespie, J. Z. (2005). A motivated action theory account of goal orientation. *Journal of Applied Psychology, 90*, 1096–1127.

Doe, K., & Kegler, A. (2013). Training training: An e-learning solution helps a global not-for-profit organization track and bring consistency to its employee and volunteer training. *T + D*, August, 80.

Galagan, P. (2014). Learning styles. *T + D*, January, 22–23.

Gaul, P. (2013). Onboarding has become a major priority in 2013, study finds. *T + D*, December, 17.

Gino, F. (2014, October). Ending gender discrimination requires more than a training program. *Harvard Business Review*. Retrieved January 27, 2015, from https://hbr.org/2014/10/ending-gender-discrimination-requires-more-than-a-training-program/.

Goldstein, I. L., & Ford, J. K. (2002). *Training in organizations: Needs assessment, development, and evaluation* (4th ed.). Belmont, CA: Wadsworth Cengage Learning.

Hayes, J., & Allinson, C. W. (1997). Learning styles and training and development in work settings: Lessons from educational research. *Educational Psychology: An International Journal of Experimental Educational Psychology, 17*, 185-193.

Hughes, M. G., Day, E. A., Wang, X., Schuelke, M. J., Arsenault, M. L., Harkrider, L. N., & Cooper, O. D. (2013). Learner-controlled practice difficulty in the training of a complex task: Cognitive and motivational mechanisms. *Journal of Applied Psychology, 98*, 80-98.

Kalinoski, Zachary T., Steele-Johnson, D., Peyton, E. J., Leas, K. A., Steinke, J., & Bowling, N. A. (2013). A meta-analytic evaluation of diversity training outcomes. *Journal of Organizational Behavior, 34*, 1076-1104.

Kanfer, R., & Ackerman, P. L. (1989). Motivation and cognitive abilities: An integrative/aptitude-treatment interaction approach to skill acquisition. *Journal of Applied Psychology, 74*, 657-690.

Kapp, K. M. (2012). *The gamification of learning and instruction: Game-based methods and strategies for training and education*. San Francisco, CA: John Wiley & Sons.

Kazbour, R., & Kazbour, L. (2013). Strategic techniques to enhance training transfer. *T + D*, October, 92-93.

Keith, N., & Frese, M. (2008). Effectiveness of error management training: A meta-analysis. *Journal of Applied Psychology, 93*, 59-69.

Kirkpatrick, D. L. (1959). Techniques for evaluating training programs. *Journal for the American Society of Training Directors, 13*, 3-9.

Kirkpatrick, D. L. (1998). *Evaluating training programs: The four levels* (2nd ed.). San Francisco, CA: Berrett-Koehler.

Kraiger, K., Ford, J. K., & Salas, E. (1993). Application of cognitive, skill-based, and affective theories of learning outcomes to new methods of training evaluation. *Journal of Applied Psychology, 78*, 311-328.

Kruger, J., & Dunning, D. (1999). Unskilled and unaware of it: How difficulties in recognizing one's own incompetence lead to inflated self-assessments. *Journal of Personality and Social Psychology, 77*, 1121-1134.

LePine, J. A., LePine, M. A., & Jackson, C. L. (2004). Challenge and hindrance stress: Relationships with exhaustion, motivation to learn, and learning performance. *Journal of Applied Psychology, 89*, 883-891.

Lievens, F., Harris, M. M., Van Keer, E., & Bisqueret, C. (2003). Predicting cross-cultural training performance: The validity of personality, cognitive ability, and dimensions measured by an assessment center and a behavior description interview. *Journal of Applied Psychology, 88*, 476-489.

Littrell, L. N., Salas, E., Hess, K. P., Paley, M., & Riedel, S. (2006). Expatriate preparation: A critical analysis of 25 years of cross-cultural training research. *Human Resource Development Review, 5*, 355-388.

Locke, E. A., & Latham, G. P. (2002). Building a practically useful theory of goal setting and task motivation: A 35-year odyssey. *American Psychologist, 57*, 705-717.

Major, D. A., Turner, J. E., & Fletcher, T. D. (2006). Linking proactive personality and the big five to motivation to learn and development activity. *Journal of Applied Psychology, 91*, 927–935.

Manjoo, F. (2014). Exposing hidden bias at Google. *New York Times.* Retrieved January 18, 2015, from http://www.nytimes.com/2014/09/25/technology/exposing-hidden-biases-at-google-to-improve-diversity.html.

Marks, M. A., Sabella, M. J., Burke, C. S., & Zaccaro, S. J. (2002). The impact of cross-training on team effectiveness. *Journal of Applied Psychology, 87*, 3–13.

Martocchio, J. J., & Judge, T. A. (1997). Relationship between conscientiousness and learning in employee training: Mediating influences of self-deception and self-efficacy. *Journal of Applied Psychology, 82*, 764–773.

Orvis, K. A., Fisher, S. L., & Wasserman, M. E. (2009). Power to the people: Using learner control to improve trainee reactions and learning in web-based instructional environments. *Journal of Applied Psychology, 94*, 960–971.

Payne, S. C., Youngcourt, S. S., & Beaubien, J. M. (2007). A meta-analytic examination of the goal orientation nomological net. *Journal of Applied Psychology, 92*, 128–150.

Pinder, C. C. (2008). *Work motivation in organizational behavior.* Upper Saddle River, NJ: Psychology Press.

Porter, C. O., Webb, J. W., & Gogus, C. I. (2010). When goal orientations collide: Effects of learning and performance orientation on team adaptability in response to workload imbalance. *Journal of Applied Psychology, 95*, 935–943.

Ree, M. J., & Earles, J. A. (1991). Predicting training success: Not much more than *g. Personnel Psychology, 44*, 321–332.

Roeser, R. W., Schonert-Reichl, K. A., Jha, A., Cullen, M., Wallace, L., Wilensky, R., ... & Harrison, J. (2013). Mindfulness training and reductions in teacher stress and burnout: Results from two randomized, waitlist-control field trials. *Journal of Educational Psychology, 105*, 787–804.

Sackett, P. R., & Mullen, E. J. (1993). Beyond formal experimental design: Towards an expanded view of the training evaluation process. *Personnel Psychology, 46*, 613–627.

Salas, E., DiazGranados, D., Klein, C., Burke, C. S., Stagl, K. C., Goodwin, G. F., & Halpin, S. M. (2008). Does team training improve team performance? A meta-analysis. *Human Factors, 50*, 903–933.

Salas, E., Tannenbaum, S. I., Kraiger, K., & Smith-Jentsch, K. A. (2012). The science of training and development in organizations: What matters in practice. *Psychological Science in the Public Interest, 13*, 74–101.

Sheldon, O. J., Dunning, D., & Ames, D. R. (2014). Emotionally unskilled, unaware, and uninterested in learning more: Reactions to feedback about deficits in emotional intelligence. *Journal of Applied Psychology, 99*, 125–137.

Sitzmann, T., & Ely, K. (2010). Sometimes you need a reminder: The effects of prompting self-regulation on regulatory processes, learning, and attrition. *Journal of Applied Psychology, 95*, 132–144.

Sitzmann, T., Kraiger, K., Stewart, D., & Wisher, R. (2006). The comparative effectiveness of web-based and classroom instruction: A meta-analysis. *Personnel Psychology, 59*, 623–664.

Smith-Jentsch, K. A., Jentsch, F. G., Payne, S. C., & Salas, E. (1996). Can pretraining experiences explain individual differences in learning? *Journal of Applied Psychology, 81*, 110–116.

Stanhope, D. S., Pond III, S. B., & Surface, E. A. (2013). Core self-evaluations and training effectiveness: Prediction through motivational intervening mechanisms. *Journal of Applied Psychology, 98*, 820–831.

Taylor, P. J., Russ-Eft, D. F., & Chan, D. W. (2005). A meta-analytic review of behavior modeling training. *Journal of Applied Psychology, 90*, 692–709.

Tracey, J. B., Tannenbaum, S. I., & Kavanagh, M. J. (1995). Applying trained skills on the job: The importance of the work environment. *Journal of Applied Psychology, 80*, 239–252.

Van Iddekinge, C. H., Ferris, G. R., Perrewe, P. L., Perryman, A. A., Blass, F. R., & Heetderks, T. D. (2009). Effects of selection and training on unit-level performance over time: A latent growth modeling approach. *Journal of Applied Psychology, 94*, 829–843.

Van Knippenberg, D., & Schippers, M. C. (2007). Work group diversity. *Annual Review of Psychology, 58*, 515–541.

Villado, A. J., & Arthur Jr, W. (2013). The comparative effect of subjective and objective after-action reviews on team performance on a complex task. *Journal of Applied Psychology, 98*, 514–528.

Vroom, V. H. (1964). *Work and motivation*. New York: Wiley.

Wakefield, C., & Davis, J. (2013). Maximizing new manager success. *T + D*, April, 112.

Watson, A. M., Foster Thompson, L., Rudolph, J. V., Whelan, T. J., Behrend, T. S., & Gissel, A. L. (2013). When big brother is watching: Goal orientation shapes reactions to electronic monitoring during online training. *Journal of Applied Psychology, 98*, 642–657.

PART III

ORGANIZATIONAL PSYCHOLOGY

Chapter 9

WORK MOTIVATION

Motivation is a key component of organizational life. It is one of the largest areas of research in I/O psychology, with over 100,000 journal articles and dissertations on the topic in the PsycINFO database for psychology alone. In this chapter, you'll learn about key motivation theories and their applications.

After studying this chapter, you should be able to:

- understand what work motivation is
- describe the needs-based theories of work motivation
- describe the process-based theories of work motivation
- describe the application-based theories of work motivation
- identify key legal and global issues surrounding work motivation
- describe the current issues and controversies around work motivation.

Learning goals for this chapter

Organizations are made up of individuals. Understanding what makes individuals excited about coming to work versus disengaged is a critical part of I/O psychology. For example, have you ever noticed that some individuals are willing to strive for years to reach seemingly impossible goals such as starting their own business, while others are content to pursue much more modest career goals? What separates the employees who come into work early every morning and stay late from those who do not spend a minute more than necessary at the office? What is the difference between these types of people? A big difference is their motivation to direct their energy toward their goals. So, in this chapter, we'll explore what motivates them.

Again, because we are learning about I/O psychology, this book is focused on individuals at work. Therefore, we will keep our discussion primarily on motivation in work settings. Our goal in this chapter is to describe and better understand the evidence-based science in terms of both the theory and practice underlying work motivation.

What Is Motivation?

Work motivation: A set of energetic forces that originate both within as well as beyond an individual to initiate work-related behavior and to determine its form, direction, intensity, and duration.

Work motivation is defined as a set of energetic forces that originate both within as well as beyond an individual to initiate work-related behavior and to determine its form, direction, intensity, and duration (Pinder, 2008). Motivation is of interest to I/O psychologists and others because it pervades all I/O issues, as nearly all behavior is at least partially determined by individual motivation. Motivation is related to many important individual and organizational outcomes, and it is influenced by contexts such as the way jobs are designed or the way individuals are managed. Motivation may be examined in terms of its short-term influence, like making an important deadline at work, or long-term goals, such as career goals in our opening example.

However, it is important to understand the limits of a person's motivation and its effects on behavior. For example, a person might be very motivated to play in the National Basketball Association (NBA), but if he is 5 feet tall, it is challenging to think that any amount of motivation will make this a viable career option. That is because, as depicted in Figure 9.1, performance is a function of motivation, ability, and environment. Thus, if someone is motivated, he or she will *try hard* but may not necessarily reach a specific goal or perform well in a given attempt. In addition to motivation and ability, environment also matters to motivation as well. For example, a highly capable and motivated barista may still perform poorly if the order was

Figure 9.1
Performance is a function of motivation, ability, and environment.

misheard due to noise, or if the espresso maker was broken down, examples of how the environment can negatively influence performance.

As we refer back to our definition of work motivation above, several key aspects of it are salient. First, motivation may originate from within individuals themselves or from the outside world. This is worth discussing further. Work motivation can be thought of as either intrinsic or extrinsic in nature. **Intrinsic motivation** refers to motivation that comes from inside the individual such that they are engaging in behavior because the work is personally rewarding to them. An example of intrinsic motivation would be someone who is not paid well for the work that they do but they do an excellent job anyway: It is not the money that is motivating them but the work or their value system that drives them. For example, social workers are not paid well compared to the cost of obtaining education in this area, but many report that they do the work that they do because they enjoy and value helping others. **Extrinsic motivation** is just the opposite. With this type of motivation, the origin of motivation is from outside the individual. Doing a job one is not excited about because the pay is good would be an example of extrinsic motivation. We'll talk more about the relative importance of intrinsic versus extrinsic motivation later in the chapter.

Intrinsic motivation: Motivation that comes from inside the individual such that they are engaging in behavior because it is personally rewarding to them

Extrinsic motivation: Motivation originating from outside the individual.

Theories of Work Motivation

Work motivation theories are plentiful. In fact, when it comes to what both managers and academics care about, motivation is often at the top of the list. Over the years, I/O scholars have proposed and tested dozens of motivation theories. In this chapter, we will be covering several key theories under three headings. These include needs-based theories, process-based theories, and application-based theories of work motivation.

Needs-Based Theories of Work Motivation

As we mentioned previously, several work motivation theories exist. In this section, we review the main needs-based theories that have emerged in I/O psychology. Needs-based theories focus on which individual needs must be fulfilled in order for an employee to be properly motivated. The major theories include Maslow's hierarchy of needs, ERG theory, two-factor theory, and acquired needs theory.

Workplace Application

Meeting Needs at the Container Store

The Container Store has an innovative recruitment method that helps them meet their hiring needs while tapping into the interest and needs of their customers. In essence, they encourage their sales associates to look for

opportunities to turn customers into employees. First, they offer employee referrals of $500 for full-time employees who make it to the 90-day mark and $200 for part-time employees. This is a successful form of recruitment for them as referrals make up 40 percent of the company's hiring. A big perk for customers who love to shop at the Container Store is the fact that if they become an employee, they can get a 40 percent discount off their own purchases. This is a creative application that displays an understanding of what may motivate the customer to want to become an employee (Raphael, 2003).

Hierarchy of Needs

Hierarchy of needs: Abraham Maslow's 1943 theory that our actions are motivated by our quest to fulfill five basic human needs.

Physiological needs: The first need in the hierarchy of needs theory, including water, food, and air.

Security needs: The second need in the hierarchy of needs theory, including safe housing, steady employment, and healthcare.

Researchers have been thinking about motivation for a long time. In 1943, Abraham Maslow, a psychologist then working at Brooklyn College in New York, introduced a theory that our actions are motivated by our quest to fulfill five basic human needs in his classic paper and book *Motivation and Personality*. Maslow proposed a hierarchy where you must fulfill the lower level (basic) needs before moving up to the higher order needs which he called *fulfillment progression*. For example, he argued that people first must meet their basic needs, such as things needed to survive, before moving on to their higher level needs. The pyramid depicted in Figure 9.2 is a summary of how he arranged the order of needs such that a person would need to satisfy the basic **physiological needs** at the base of the pyramid, such as water, food, and air, before moving up to **security needs** such as safe housing, steady employment, or healthcare benefits. **Social needs** include such things as friendships, feeling accepted at work, and romantic attachments. Relatedly, Baumeister and Leary (1995) have developed belongingness theory to describe what they see as the need humans have to affiliate with one another. **Esteem needs** include feeling social recognition, feeling one has done a good job,

Figure 9.2
Maslow's hierarchy of needs is often depicted as a pyramid.

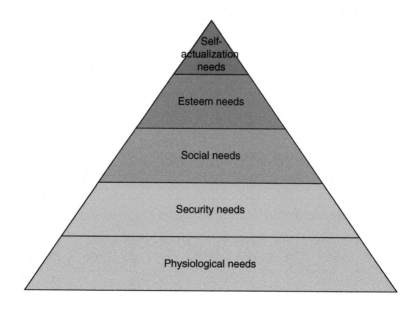

and accomplishment. Finally, **self-actualization needs** include the goal of being self-aware and focusing on personal growth, which can include doing meaningful work. The rise in social entrepreneurship seems in line with the self-actualization level in Maslow's hierarchy as it allows individuals to combine their work with social causes they feel are important. Subsequent work by Ryan and Deci (2000) similarly proposed that universal human needs exist and that fulfilling them is likely to be motivating to individuals.

As we mentioned, according to the hierarchy of needs theory, individuals must focus on the lower-level needs before "moving up" the hierarchy to the higher-order needs. However, initial research did not support this aspect of the theory for many years. For example, Hall (1968) found no strong evidence for Maslow's hierarchy in a sample of AT&T employees over five years. He did find that as managers moved up in their organization to higher levels, their need for safety decreased, while their needs for affiliation, achievement and esteem, and self-actualization increased. Wahba and Bridwell (1976) reviewed all the literature to that date on Maslow's hierarchy and concluded that there was some support, but not much. That was the general consensus until research by Tay and Diener (2011) found, using global data gathered by the Gallup organization across 123 countries, that "the emergent ordering of need fulfillment for psychological needs were fairly consistent across country conditions" (p. 354) and that their "analysis indicates support for this approach [Maslow's theory], in that there was a tendency, but not a strong one, to fulfill the needs in a specific order" (p. 361). At a minimum, Maslow's theory can be a helpful heuristic for thinking about what individuals need, and that different people may focus on different needs and outcomes at work. And anyone who has taken a psychology class probably remembers this theory because it makes intuitive sense. Thus, it can be a powerful and useful heuristic to help us all remember that the fulfillment or lack of fulfillment of people's needs does indeed motivate attitudes and behaviors.

ERG Theory

Following Maslow's hierarchy of needs, Clayton Alderfer developed **ERG theory**, which posits that individuals have three core needs: existence, relatedness, and growth. **Existence needs** include Maslow's first two levels of physiological and security needs. **Relatedness needs** subsume Maslow's levels of social needs. **Growth needs** refer to inner esteem and self-actualization. Thus, Alderfer theorized that there were only three levels of needs to consider rather than five. He further argued that ERG needs may all be operating at the same time and that individuals who are frustrated by one need or level of that need may go back and focus on a lower-level need. He termed this the *frustration-regression principle*, which states that if a need is not met, a person may focus on other, lower-level needs to compensate for this. In other words, a person might focus on growth and then relatedness rather than working his or her way up the hierarchy as is proposed in Maslow's theory.

Alderfer (1969) tested his hypothesis using data gathered from 110 bank employees. We note that by today's research standards, his was not a strong research design. However, his initial work did show more support for his theory than for Maslow's. And again, later work by Tay and Diener (2011) would generally

Social needs: The third need in the hierarchy of needs theory, including friendships and romantic attachments.

Esteem needs: The fourth need in the hierarchy of needs theory, including social recognition and accomplishment.

Self-actualization needs: The fifth need in the hierarchy of needs theory, including self-awareness and personal growth.

ERG theory: Posits that individuals have three core needs: existence, relatedness, and growth.

Existence needs: The needs in ERG theory that include Maslow's first two levels of physiological and safety needs.

Relatedness needs: The needs in ERG theory that include Maslow's levels of social needs.

Growth needs: Needs that satisfy an individual's desire to develop as a person.

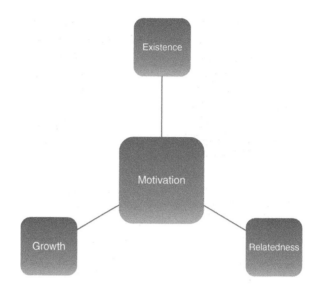

Figure 9.3 ERG theory consists of three needs rather than five.

"See website for interactive material"

support the idea of frustration-regression rather than a strict ordering of the hierarchy as well. They found that there is a tendency to go through Maslow's hierarchy of needs in order but argued that the most important aspect relating to happiness and well-being is to live a balanced life that shifts between the different aspects of ERG.

Two-Factor Theory

Two-factor theory:
Frederick Herzberg's theory (also known as the motivator-hygiene theory) of job satisfaction, which differentiated between hygiene and motivator factors.

Hygiene factors:
Two-factor theory elements which do not motivate but may serve to lower motivation if not met.

Motivator factors:
Two-factor theory elements which motivate employees if they are present.

Frederick Herzberg is another American psychologist who made major contributions to our understanding of human motivation. His **two-factor theory** (also known as the motivator-hygiene theory) is actually a theory of job satisfaction. He argued that **hygiene factors** (such as pay) are those which do not motivate when they are present, but may serve to lower motivation if they are not met; high levels of hygiene factors do not motivate. Conversely, **motivator factors** (such as opportunity for advancement) are those which do motivate if they are present. At the time, this was revolutionary thinking because it proposed that dissatisfaction (low motivation) and satisfaction (high motivation) are not on one continuum, but rather are on different ones, and that different factors lead to satisfaction and dissatisfaction (see Figure 9.4).

An example of a hygiene factor at work involves trash. We bet that you would not jump up and down and say, "I love my job" when you come into your office or cubicle in the morning and find that your trash can has been emptied. Imagine, however, that you come in and it has not been emptied and this goes on for weeks! All of a sudden, this thing that does not serve to make you feel more positive about work becomes a major distractor and dissatisfier that gets in the way of your being able to focus on anything else at work. That's a hygiene factor. As a completely different example, imagine that you are recognized at work for your excellent performance. This is not something you expect to hear every day at work since most days are routine, but it sure is nice to hear it occasionally. This serves as a motivator.

Hygiene Factors	Motivators

- Work policies and rules
- Supervision and relationships at work
- Working conditions
- Salary
- Job security

- Achievement
- Recognition
- Interesting work
- Responsibility
- Advancement opportunities

Figure 9.4 The two-factor theory of motivation posits that the absence of hygiene factors leads to dissatisfaction at work and that motivators lead to satisfaction.

It should be kept in mind, however, that what motivates someone is not universal. For example, in collectivist countries such as China, Japan, or Panama, singling out an individual for special recognition can actually serve to embarrass them rather than motivate them, as their self-image tends to be defined as "we" rather than "I" as noted by Hofstede (2001). In these cases, recognizing the group or team can be an important way to recognize achievement while avoiding concerns related to focusing on just one individual.

While intuitively appealing, the two-factor theory has not found overwhelming support (e.g., Salancik & Pfeffer, 1977; Wigdor, 1967). Critics argue that the research underlying the theory is weak and that the limited support that has been found may be due to priming and to the particular samples on which the original studies were conducted. So, most of the research done on this theory is decades old, and many have discounted the theory based on this perception of out-datedness. However, it makes sense that there are some things that serve to boost your motivation and others that can just plain make you mad when they go wrong, like when the Internet connection in your house goes down, but the same factors don't relate to being more motivated.

Acquired Needs Theory

David McClelland posited that human motivation is determined by the needs of that person and that each person has a different constellation of three needs. **Need for achievement** (N-Ach) is related to wanting to excel and succeed. **Need for power** (N-Pow) refers to wanting to influence others and make an impact. As you might imagine, he posited that this was a key motivator for leadership and politics. And **need for affiliation** (N-Affil) refers to wanting to have friendships, to feel accepted, and to engage with others. Each individual has a dominant need, and that most dominant need is thought to motivate that individual more than the other needs.

Acquired needs theory: States that human motivation is determined by the needs of that person and that each person has a different constellation of three needs (achievement, power, and affiliation).

Need for achievement: The need in acquired needs theory to excel and succeed.

Need for power: The need in acquired needs theory to influence others and make an impact.

Need for affiliation: The need in acquired needs theory to have friendships, feel accepted, and to engage with others.

Thematic Apperception Test (TAT): Projective employee assessment test based on acquired needs theory that elicits and assesses reactions to images such as drawings or photographs in order to reveal a person's motivations.

In the workplace, job applicant or employee needs are sometimes assessed using the **Thematic Apperception Test** (TAT). The TAT is a projective test based on Acquired Needs theory that elicits and assesses reactions to images such as drawings or photographs. Individuals are asked to view images and to tell as dramatic a story as they can for each image including factors such as what led up to the image shown, what is happening at that moment, what the figures in the image are feeling, and the ultimate outcome of the story. The idea is that by using the TAT (which can be subjective), a person's motivations will be revealed. For example, if the story you created has elements consistent with high need for achievement such as setting goals, stories of success or failure, or being celebrated for creative ideas or solutions, this would indicate high need for achievement. If your story contains themes such as influencing others or leading a team, high need for power is indicated. Finally, if your story contains themes of friendship, love, or being with others, this indicates a high need for affiliation. However, the use of the TAT is not very common in selection practice.

Of all the needs theories we have covered in this section, Acquired Needs theory has consistently received the most research support. For example, research has shown that those with high need for achievement enjoy success and are likely to set goals that are challenging but realistic. These individuals also desire a great deal of feedback so they can see how they are doing relative to their goals and they persist toward their goals long after others would have given up (Campbell, 1982). They tend to be attracted to organizations where rewards are based on merit rather than on seniority. Research shows that these individuals do particularly well in sales or as entrepreneurs, as well as being scientists and engineers (Harrell & Stahl, 1981; Trevis & Certo, 2005; Turban & Keon, 1993). This is probably due to the high level of feedback inherent in these jobs and the opportunity to generate new goals regularly. Those with high need for power walk a fine line. When their goals are directed toward simply getting what they want, these individuals can be damaging to an organization as well as to their own relationships (Spreier, 2006). However, when they focus their attention toward change for the greater good, they can be quite effective. And, those with a high need for affiliation can find a good fit in jobs where they interact with others who need them, such as social work or teaching. As a manager, a high need for affiliation may serve as a challenge to effectiveness as the desire to be liked and avoid conflict can make the job unpleasant and difficult for these individuals (Harrell, 1984).

Self-Determination Theory

Earlier in this chapter we covered the concepts of intrinsic and extrinsic motivation. While these distinctions are made as we think about motivation, most of the time our motivation comes from some combination of intrinsic and extrinsic motivation (Deci & Ryan, 1985). In particular, Deci and Ryan (1985) framed motivation on a continuum of fully extrinsic to fully intrinsic motivation in their self-determination theory, which is summarized in Figure 9.5. It illustrates the importance of intrinsic motivation to sustained motivation at work.

In support of the importance of intrinsic motivation, Grant (2008a) found that firefighters who reported high prosocial (helping) motivation and intrinsic

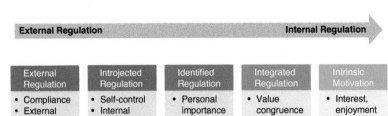

Figure 9.5 The motivation regulation spectrum.

motivation were more likely to work overtime a month later. Similarly, he found that paid call center fundraisers raised more money when they had high prosocial and intrinsic motivation. This relationship was mediated by the number of calls made. In other words, those who were more intrinsically motivated made more calls and were more effective on those calls in terms of generating donations from those they called.

Other important aspects of our definition of motivation include the goal at which motivation is directed, its intensity, and its duration. For example, you might be motivated to do well on an upcoming exam or to help stop world hunger. Both goals will be affected by your motivation level, but one is inwardly directed as it only involves your own effort while the other is outwardly directed as it affects others and would probably require the effort of many. In addition, a lot of effort across a short period of time is all that is needed to achieve a solid test score. However, given the complexities and scope of world hunger, even a lifetime of effort may not be enough. Recently, additional research has shown the relative importance of intrinsic and extrinsic motivation. A meta-analysis of 183 studies found that both intrinsic and extrinsic motivation matter for performance (Cerasoli, Nicklin, & Ford, 2014).

Self-Assessment: Rate Your Motivation

For each item below, please note why do you, or would you, put effort into your current job using the following scale: 1 = not at all; 2 = very little; 3 = a little; 4 = moderately; 5 = strongly; 6 = very strongly; 7 = completely.

1. Because I have fun doing my job.
2. Because what I do in my work is exciting.
3. Because the work I do is interesting.
4. Because I personally consider it important to put effort into this job.
5. Because putting effort into this job aligns with my personal values.
6. Because putting effort into this job has personal significance for me.
7. Because I have to prove to myself that I can.
8. Because it makes me feel proud of myself.
9. Because otherwise I will feel ashamed of myself.
10. Because otherwise I will feel bad about myself.
11. Because others will reward me financially only if I put enough effort into my job (e.g., employer, supervisor ...).

12. Because others will offer me greater job security if I put enough effort into my job (e.g., employer, supervisor ...).
13. Because I risk losing my job if I don't put enough effort into it.
14. To get others' approval (e.g., supervisor, colleagues, family, clients ...).
15. Because others will respect me more (e.g., supervisor, colleagues, family, clients ...).
16. To avoid being criticized by others (e.g., supervisor, colleagues, family, clients ...).

Scoring:

Step 1: Add your scores for items 1–3. This is your score on *intrinsic motivation*.

A score of 3–9 indicates that you are low on intrinsic motivation. A score of 10–15 indicates that you are somewhat intrinsically motivated. A score of 16–21 indicates that you are highly intrinsically motivated.

Step 2: Add your scores for items 4–6. This is your score on *values regulated motivation*.

A score of 3–9 indicates that you are low on values motivation. A score of 10–15 indicates that you are somewhat values motivated. A score of 16–21 indicates that you are highly values motivated.

Step 3: Add your scores for items 7–10. This is your score on *guilt regulated motivation*.

A score of 4–10 indicates that you are low on guilt motivation. A score of 11–19 indicates that you are somewhat guilt motivated. A score of 20–28 indicates that you are highly guilt motivated.

Step 4: Add your scores for items 11–13. This is your score on *extrinsic reward motivation*.

A score of 3–9 indicates that you are low on extrinsic reward motivation. A score of 10–15 indicates that you are somewhat extrinsically reward motivated. A score of 16–21 indicates that you are highly extrinsically reward motivated.

Step 5: Add your scores for items 14–16. This is your score on *social motivation*.

A score of 3–9 indicates that you are low on social motivation. A score of 10–15 indicates that you are somewhat socially motivated. A score of 16–21 indicates that you are highly socially motivated.

Source: Adapted from Gagné et al. (2015). Used by permission of Routledge.

Summary of Needs-Based Theories

Needs-based theories of motivation have the potential to help individuals to understand their own motivations and for managers to begin to identify what different employees need to be motivated at work. Needs-based theories define motivated behavior as needs satisfaction. In other words, individuals have needs, and they are motivated to try to satisfy these needs. If a manager can identify what an employee needs, the manager can understand what motivates the employee. As a result, needs-based theories help identify what individuals are striving for at a given point.

We covered five specific theories in this section including Maslow's hierarchy of needs, which is represented by a pyramid of basic human needs (physiological, security, social, esteem, and self-actualization). ERG theory consists of a more streamlined approach to needs and includes existence needs, relatedness needs, and growth needs. The two-factor theory differentiates between aspects of work which are likely to lead to satisfaction (motivators) versus those that are likely to lead to dissatisfaction (hygiene factors). Acquired need theory examines which of three needs (e.g., need for achievement) dominates an individual's behavior. Finally, self-determination theory with its focus on intrinsic and extrinsic motivation was described.

One issue with needs-based theories is that they consider relatively stable elements within the individual – needs – that are motivating, rather than more dynamic processes. As the field of psychology evolved, newer, process-based theories of motivation emerged. We will cover these next.

Process-Based Theories

Process-based work motivation theories differ from needs-based theories in that these theories focus on how motivation arises and what factors cause motivation to exist. These theories have a cognitive component to them. As you'll recall from Chapter 6, cognitive abilities are related to a person's ability to "perceive, process, evaluate, compare, create, understand, manipulate, or generally think about information and ideas" (Guion, 1998, p. 124). Motivation can be seen as either a cognitive choice or, as you'll see in the next section, a cognitive appraisal and self-regulation process. These include the equity, justice, and expectancy theories of motivation. All of these are process-based theories of work motivation.

Equity Theory

John Stacey Adams' (1963) **equity theory** refers to the comparison that individuals make to determine if what they are receiving is fair compared to the amount they are giving. This comparison is depicted by the following formula (see Figure 9.6). Inputs are things that the person brings to and contributes to the situation, such as education, experience, and effort. Outcomes are things that the person gets from the organization, such as recognition, pay, or promotions. A key component to this theory is that it is the *comparison* of the ratio that matters most to understanding someone's feelings of equity rather than the absolute amount they have put in or received. If an individual perceives that he or she is contributing an enormous amount to a company but receiving little in return, he or she will probably feel unfairly treated. On the other hand, an employee who feels he or she contributes little and receives little in return may perceive a high sense of equity fairness in the organization. A key part of this is the referent other comparison person: This could be a coworker, a person from a different organization, or a combination of people in the employee's mind. It's not just what you give and what you get from work, but how well this ratio fits with other people. Using the same example, if a person puts in little effort but gets paid little, that's one thing; but if their coworker puts in little effort and gets paid a lot, that causes feelings of inequity. Where does motivation come into this? Because inequity is an unpleasant state, the lack of equity will initiate behavior in the focal person: For example, they might ask for a raise, quit their job, put in less effort, or change their referent comparison person to help get the ratio into balance.

Equity theory: The comparison that individuals make to determine if what they are receiving is fair compared to the amount they are giving.

Figure 9.6 Equity theory calculations consist of comparing the ratio of one's own inputs and outcome to a referent other's inputs and outputs. When the ratio is in balance, employees are theorized to be comfortable, particularly if they are high in equity sensitivity.

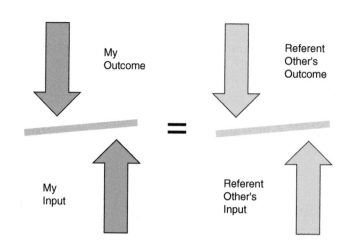

Figure 9.7 Entitleds prefer receiving a higher ratio of outcome to inputs compared to others as depicted in the first equation, while benevolents have a higher tolerance for receiving a lower ratio as depicted in the second equation.

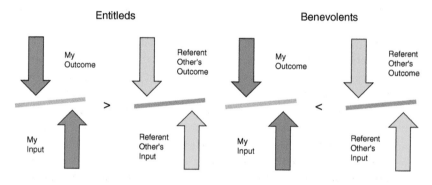

Benevolents: Those who are comfortable giving more inputs than the outcomes they receive.

Equity sensitives: Those with an orientation to prefer an equal ratio of inputs and outcomes.

Entitleds: Those with an orientation to prefer receiving more in outcomes than they input.

But, of course, the original theory has evolved since its inception. For example, it is hard to imagine that all employees have exactly the same ideas about equity and what is the ideal ratio. In fact, based on this idea, motivation scholars have studied just this question of equity sensitivity. Equity sensitivity refers to how much an individual prefers to receive an outcome relative to his or her inputs in comparison to a relevant other. In other words, it represents an individual's orientation toward exchange relationships (Sauley & Bedeian, 2000). Based on work by King, Miles, and Day (1993) as well as King and Hinson (1994), individuals may be classified as either **benevolents**, if they have a greater tolerance for, and are comfortable with, giving more inputs than the outcomes they receive; **equity sensitives**, if they prefer an equal ratio of inputs and outcomes; or as **entitleds**, who prefer to receive more in outcomes than they put in as inputs.

Self-Assessment: Rate Your Equity Preference

Here you may take the equity preference survey in order to see where you stand when it comes to equity evaluations.

Please read each of the statements which follow and indicate how much you agree with each one of them using the following scale, from 1 = strongly disagree to 5 = strongly agree.

1. I prefer to do as little as possible at work while getting as much as I can from my employer.
2. I am most satisfied at work when I have to do as little as possible.
3. When I am at my job, I think of ways to get out of work.
4. If I could get away with it, I would try to work just a little bit slower than the boss expects.
5. It is really satisfying to me when I can get something for nothing at work.
6. It is the smart employee who gets as much as he/she can while giving as little as possible in return.
7. Employees who are more concerned about what they can get from their employer rather than what they can give to their employer are the wise ones.
8. If I had to work hard all day at my job, I would probably quit.

9. When I have completed my task for the day, I help out other employees who have yet to complete their tasks.
10. Even if I received low wages and poor benefits from my employer, I would still try to do my best at my job.
11. I feel obligated to do more than I am paid to do at work.
12. At work, my greatest concern is whether or not I am doing the best job I can.
13. A job which requires me to be busy during the day is better than a job which allows me a lot of loafing.
14. At work, I feel uneasy when there is little work for me to do.
15. I would become very dissatisfied with my job if I had little or no work to do.
16. All other things being equal, it is better to have a job with a lot of duties and responsibilities than one with few duties and responsibilities.

Scoring:

Step 1: Sum your responses to items 9–16 and place your total here _____.
Step 2: Reverse score your responses to items 1–8 using the following key:
    For each question, if you put 1, write down 5.
    If you put 2, write down 4.
    If you put 3, write down 3.
    If you put 4, write down 2.
    If you put 5, write down 1.
Step 3: Sum your reverse scored numbers for items 1–8 and place your total here _____.
Step 4: Add the numbers from step 1 and step 3. *Scores range between 16 and 80.*
Step 5: Where does your score put you? Scores between 16–39 indicate an **entitlement** orientation. Scores between 40–56 indicate **equity sensitivity**. Scores between 57–80 indicate **benevolence**.

Source: Items and scoring adapted from Sauley & Bedeian (2000). Used by permission of Sage Publications.

Organizational Justice Theory

Justice: How fair an employee believes the employer is to its employees.

Organizational justice theory grew out of equity theory. (We mentioned organizational justice theory briefly back in Chapter 2.) While equity theory primarily focused on the fairness of outcomes, justice theory expands the focus to include the fairness of process and interpersonal treatment as well. Research shows that perceptions of **justice** (defined as the idea that an action or decision is fair and just) are powerful predictors in understanding how much motivation and trust an individual will have (Colquitt, Scott, & LePine, 2007). An employee's sense of organizational justice reflects how fair he or she believes the employer is to employees. Studies have consistently shown that justice perceptions relate to three aspects of fairness, including procedural justice, interpersonal justice, and distributive justice. **Distributive justice** refers to perceptions of fairness regarding the actual outcomes of a decision or action; with its focus on outcomes, distributive justice is similar to equity theory. **Procedural justice** refers to the fairness of policies and guidelines used to make decisions. For example, you might not get the promotion you wanted, but you would feel better about it if you felt that a fair process was used. Finally, **interpersonal justice** refers to the way in which one is treated by others within the organization. For example, you would feel better about your not getting a promotion if you were treated with respect during the promotion process.

Distributive justice: Perceptions of fairness regarding the actual outcomes of a decision or action.

Procedural justice: Perceptions of the fairness of the policies and guidelines used to make decisions.

Interpersonal justice: Perception of fairness related to the way in which one is treated by others within the organization.

Justice perceptions are important antecedents to individual and organizational outcomes such as organizational commitment, perceived organizational support, and the quality of one's relationship with one's supervisor. It is highly related to motivation because it can affect task performance, helping behaviors, and counterproductive work behaviors (Colquitt et al., 2013; Rupp, Shao, Jones, & Liao, 2014). Additional research by Johnson, Lanaj, and Barnes (2014) shows that while justice is generally seen as a desirable thing, procedural justice may come at a cost to individuals who may suffer from energy depletion when enacting procedural justice over time from "fighting the good fight," while those engaging in interpersonal justice behaviors see their energy replenished from social relationships which are enhanced. And, research consistently shows that individuals feel injustice much more strongly than justice. Thus, much like hygiene factors, organizational justice has relatively less ability to motivate but a strong ability to lead to a lack of motivation in cases of violation.

Expectancy Theory

Expectancy theory: Theory made up of three core components: expectancy, instrumentality, and valence. Expectancy (E) represents the extent to which individuals believe that their efforts will lead to their desired performance; Instrumentality (I) reflects whether individuals expect their performance to lead to an outcome or reward; and valence (V) defines the value that a person places on that reward.

Expectancy theory (VIE theory), originally developed by Victor Vroom (1964), explains what motivates people to behave one way instead of another, focusing on their goals and where they put their efforts. There are three core components to expectancy theory: expectancy, instrumentality, and valence. These are tied into a person's beliefs about the degree to which effort leads to performance, and that performance will lead to a desired outcome (see Figure 9.8). *Expectancy* (E) represents the extent to which individuals believe that their efforts will lead to their desired performance. For example, if Jorge believes his effort is likely to lead to higher performance, he is said to have high expectancy. Expectancy can be influenced by how capable a person believes he is at performing this particular behavior, how difficult it is, and how much control he believes he has over the results. *Instrumentality* (I) reflects the degree to which individuals expect their performance to lead to an outcome or reward, which may be external, such as a bonus, or internal, such as the satisfaction experienced from doing a task well. For example, if Janice believes that higher performance will result in a reward she should be more motivated. In order to have high instrumentality, the employee must be able to trust in the connection between effort and outcomes, such as through a formal company policy outlining the terms of the required behavior and its rewards, or a supervisor who consistently rewards good performance. Instrumentality may also be impacted by the level of performance required to result in the desired outcome: if employees are promoted on a strict system of seniority, then there is no need for an employee to attempt to work hard to receive a promotion, and her instrumentality will consequently be low. Finally, *valence* (V) defines the value that a person places on that reward. Using the previous example, if Janice wants a bonus, she should be motivated but if the bonus is small, say a $5 gift card, it probably won't do much to motivate her and might even lead to feelings of injustice. It is important to keep in mind that variables such as a person's values, needs, and goals influence how valuable, and thus motivating, rewards are to that individual. Different people will have a high valence for different types of rewards. Extrinsically motivated employees may highly value a promotion or paid time off, while a more intrinsically motivated employee may place the most value on an opportunity to choose his or her next assignment or be entrusted with a more meaningful task.

Together, expectancy, instrumentality and valence are used to calculate *motivational force,* which is V × I × E. Note that because this is a multiplicative formula, if any one of the key components of V, I, or E goes to 0, motivation will fall. The underlying assumption in expectancy theory is that individuals choose to behave in the way that produces the most motivational force. Another concept inherent to expectancy theory is that it is based on an individual's *belief* in V, I, and E, not necessarily the reality of the situation. Using this theory, to determine if someone is motivated, one would ask the following three questions: Do you believe that effort is likely to lead to performance (expectancy)? Do you believe that performance is likely to lead to outcomes (instrumentality)? Do you value these likely outcomes (valence)?

In a meta-analysis of 77 studies of expectancy theory, Van Eerde and Thierry (1996) concluded that while the components of VIE do predict work-related criteria, it is not clear that the model works as predicted, in that a simple multiplicative relationship for V, I, and E may not work, but that it is more of an additive relationship. However, they recommend additional research to examine this further. At the heart of the debate around the efficacy of the VIE model is differences in how the expectancies are calculated. For example, should they be multiplied or added? Research in the areas of training motivation (Mathieu, Tannenbaum, & Salas, 1992) and test-taking motivation (e.g., Sanchez, Truxillo, & Bauer, 2000) have consistently found that at least some aspects of the VIE model affect motivation in those arenas.

Managers tell us that they find this theory useful because it helps them to explicitly diagnose why a given employee might not be motivated, for example, by

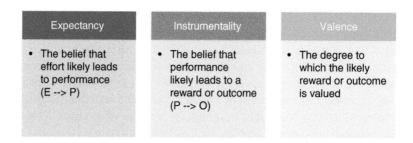

Figure 9.8
Expectancy
theory consists of
three important
components:
Expectancy,
Instrumentality
and Valence

asking three simple questions, starting with: *Has this employee done this job effectively in the past?* If not, it may be an issue of the employee not having enough resources, such as good training, rather than motivation. *Does an employee's good performance lead to good outcomes in this organization?* If not, the reward system may need to be redesigned to make the job more motivating. *Does this employee appear to value the reward for a job well done?* If not, this is an opportunity to reconsider what employees do find valuable. Perhaps it's additional time off or being recognized by upper management or a bonus. Asking each of these questions and considering the associated answers can be a valuable tool for those hoping to disentangle the motivation puzzle.

Summary of Process-Based Theories

Motivation impacts cognitive assessments of where to direct your effort, how intensely you work, and how long you work. As noted above, process-based theories of motivation focus on the mental processes of employees to understand their motivation and for managers to identify what they can do to help their employees be motivated at work. We covered three specific theories in this section including equity theory, which posits that employees are demotivated when the ratio of their inputs to outcomes, compared to a key other person, are not in the ratio that they prefer. Organizational justice theory takes equity theory one step further to consider not only the outcomes (distributive justice) but also the procedures used and interpersonal treatment received. Finally, expectancy theory (VIE) argues that employees are motivated when they see a clear link between their effort and their performance (Expectancy), a link between their performance and outcomes (Instrumentality), and when they value the outcomes (Valence). Because I/O psychology focuses on the realm of work, it makes sense that I/O motivation theorists wanted to build upon needs-based and process-based theories of motivation to develop specific applications of motivation at work. We will cover these next.

Application-Based Theories of Work Motivation

Up until this point we have examined theories of motivation that are needs-based as well as process-based in nature. While the next category draws upon both of these types of motivation, what they have in common is their applied nature. Thus, these are termed application-based theories of work motivation. These include goal-setting theory, the job characteristics model, and performance reinforcement and incentives.

Goal-Setting Theory

There are few theories in I/O which have been studied more or garnered more support than goal-setting theory. In fact, even back in 2003, Mitchell and Daniels wrote that goal-setting was "quite easily the single most dominant theory in the field" (p. 231). When it comes to goal-setting, it is important to make sure they are **SMART goals**. (We mention SMART goals briefly in Chapter 8.) This acronym may help you remember the five key components of effective goal-setting theory. To be effective, goals should be Specific, Measurable, Attainable (Aggressive but Achievable), Relevant, and Time-Bound. Let's take each of these in turn. First, we have all heard, or said, "It's okay, just do your best." However, it turns out that this is some of the *worst* advice we can give someone if we are interested in increasing their performance. The reason for this is that for many goals this advice is simply too general to be useful. Similarly, if a goal is not measurable, how will you know when you reach it? Research also shows that if a goal is challenging, it is great for motivation; however, it must also be achievable and relevant because an impossible goal is likely to lead to giving up in the face of failure whereas a challenging goal can push someone beyond what they felt was possible (Latham & Budworth, 2004; Lee, Locke, & Phan, 1997). Finally, to be effective, goals should have a time frame associated with them so you know what you are aiming for and how long you have to get there.

Let's work through an example to bring this all together. Say James wanted to score well on the GRE exam to help him get into a great graduate school. If his friends and family all encourage him to do his best, how will he ever know if he achieved his goal? Instead, imagine if he had done some research and determined that in order to get into the school of his choice, he would need to score at least at the 90th percentile on verbal reasoning and 85th percentile on quantitative reasoning. Now James has something to work toward! He has a specific goal, it is also measureable, so he

SMART goals:
Acronym for the five key components of effective goal-setting theory. Goals should be Specific, Measurable, Attainable (Aggressive but Achievable), Relevant, and Time-Bound.

To get the most out of goal-setting, be sure to focus on SMART goals.

will know if he made it or not, and it may be achievable with enough time and effort. Hopefully it is attainable, as he's already in college and has been doing very well in his classes and had high scores on his SAT exams, and it is timely, as he knows when he will have to take the GRE test and whether or not he has time to retake it if necessary. Now, that's a SMART goal!

Other effects of goal-setting include a necessary narrowing of attention: goals cause individuals to focus on these at the expense of other tasks. This may have a positive or negative impact on performance, depending on the appropriateness of the goal. Goals may also be motivational in one of several ways: they may encourage individuals to use their existing knowledge or to seek out the new knowledge necessary to reach their goals. Goals that are established as learning goals rather than pure performance goals may help individuals succeed on long-term, difficult goals, and framing goals positively as challenges rather than threats also has been shown to produce higher performance (Locke & Latham, 2006). Examples include such real-world examples as faster typing, truck drivers increasing their loads to be more efficient, and even loggers cutting trees more quickly (Latham, 2012).

Goal commitment, or the determination of an individual to reach his or her goal, has been an integral part of goal-setting theory since its early development, with the understanding that if no commitment were present, the goal's power to motivate would be absent. In other words, in the scenario above, if it turned out that James really did not want to go to a top graduate school, his commitment and thus James' GRE exam preparation performance would probably flag. However, despite its potential importance, goal commitment remained largely understudied for decades (Klein, Wesson, Hollenbeck, & Alge, 1999). In the end, studies on goal-setting and goal commitment have shown that the highest performance results from both high goal commitment and high difficulty goals. Other factors that have been shown to have a positive relationship with goal commitment include expectancy, goal attractiveness, and motivational force (Klein et al., 1999).

There is little debate regarding goal-setting as an effective tool that influences behavior by directing attention to a target and increasing persistence (Locke & Latham, 2002). However, there is evidence that using goals inappropriately such as increasing goal targets as soon as the last one is reached such that "good" performance becomes increasingly more challenging over time can lead to a multitude of negative outcomes, including increased stress and unethical behavior. For instance, Soman and Cheema (2004) found that not meeting goals leads to declines in future behavior in both the instances of personal savings and meeting deadlines. Further, Welsh and Ordóñez (2014) argued that striving too much toward goals can lead a person to depletion. That is, people eventually get tired and this might, over time, diminish a person's ability to regulate their own resources. With these depleted resources, it is more challenging to make ethical choices in the face of ethical dilemmas: The overuse of challenging goals led to higher instances of unethical behavior. Thus, it is important to think of goal-setting as a tool which should not be used blindly but, rather, in the context of the larger organizational environment and mental and physical health of employees.

Both employees and managers should consider the aspects of SMART goals as well as goal commitment as a way to help meet important outcomes at work.

Goal commitment: The determination of an individual to reach his or her goal.

Managers should keep in mind that challenging goals that are assigned to employees without employee input and acceptance are likely to be unsuccessful. However, including goal-setting as part of an employee's review process and developmental plan is likely to lead to positive outcomes. Goal-setting also indicates that giving feedback about goal progress and removing obstacles to achieving goals are important things managers can do to help employees stay motivated and be effective.

Self-Regulation, Self-Efficacy, and Goal Orientation

At this juncture, it is important to mention other related motivational concepts, self-regulation, self-efficacy, and goal orientation. Noted psychologist Albert Bandura developed a social cognitive theory of **self-regulation**, which is akin to aspects of expectancy theory as well as to goal-setting theory. His theory states that three factors – *self-observation* (how much attention we pay to our own behavior), *self-evaluation* (how much attention we pay to feedback), and *self-reactions* (the internal processes we use in response to self-evaluation) – are important for understanding motivation and sustained effort. **Self-efficacy** (which we mention in Chapter 8 as an important antecedent of learning success) refers to expectations which are similar to expectancy in expectancy theory in that self-efficacy relates to one's belief in one's own abilities. As an outgrowth of Bandura's work, psychologists have also developed the concept of different goal orientations (also mentioned in Chapter 8 in relation to training success), which include a learning goal orientation, or how much one is motivated by opportunities to develop and learn, versus a performance goal orientation, which refers to wanting to do well as the primary motivation. A learning goal orientation can lead to higher performance if an individual has high ability (recall the equation at the start of this chapter which states that performance is a function of motivation, ability, and environment). Sitzmann and Ely (2011) conducted a meta-analysis of this research domain and found that across the hundreds of studies they examined, goal level, persistence, effort, and self-efficacy had the strongest effects on learning, accounting for 17 percent of the variance in learning even after controlling for prior knowledge and cognitive ability (g).

Self-regulation: The capacity to control one's impulses.

Self-efficacy: A person's belief that they can succeed.

Job Characteristics Theory

The next theory we will discuss is the **job characteristics theory** by Hackman and Oldham (1975, 1980), which is helpful in both understanding jobs and changing or redesigning them to make them more meaningful and thus motivating to employees (Parker, 2014). The model posits that to understand work motivation, one must examine key contextual features of both the job and the individual. They proposed five core job dimensions, or characteristics (skill variety, task identity, task significance, autonomy, and feedback from the job), which lead to three critical psychological states (meaningfulness, responsibility, and knowledge of results), which lead to work outcomes such as motivation, performance, or job satisfaction.

Skill variety refers to the degree of variety in job tasks and differing abilities the job requires, with jobs that require greater skill variety being more meaningful to the employee. The job of professor at a university is high in skill variety because

Job characteristics theory: Proposes five core job characteristics: skill variety, task identity, task significance, autonomy, and feedback.

Skill variety: The degree of different job tasks and differing abilities the job requires.

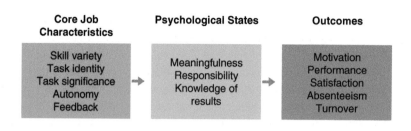

Figure 9.9 Key tenets of the job characteristics model.

Core Job Characteristics	Psychological States	Outcomes
Skill variety Task identity Task significance Autonomy Feedback	Meaningfulness Responsibility Knowledge of results	Motivation Performance Satisfaction Absenteeism Turnover

Figure 9.10 The formula for the Motivating Potential Score (MPS).

$$MPS = \frac{Skill\ variety + Task\ identity + Task\ significance}{3} \times Autonomy \times Job\ Feedback$$

Task identity: How well an employee is able to associate his or her assigned task with the job's ultimate outcome.

Task significance: How strongly employees perceive their job to impact others' lives, whether it is others in the company or externally.

Autonomy: The extent to which employees have the freedom to dictate their own approach to their job tasks and decisions.

Feedback: Receiving direct information regarding how effective one's performance is.

professors must navigate the teaching, research, and service aspects of their jobs. **Task identity** refers to how well an employee is able to associate his or her assigned task with the job's ultimate outcome. Generally, employees who are able to participate in multiple parts of a process and not just a single assigned part have higher motivation. A profession that is characterized by high task identity includes artists such as painters or sculptors. **Task significance** refers to how strongly employees perceive their job to impact others' lives, whether it is others in the company or externally. Examples of professions that have high task significance include those in the medical professions or social workers. **Autonomy** refers to the extent to which employees have the freedom to dictate their own approach to their job tasks, and how much the results of their job will be dependent upon their own efforts rather than factors outside their control. A job high on autonomy is that of freelance writer. **Feedback** refers to how well employees can receive direct information regarding how effective their job performance is. Someone who works in customer service might get a lot of feedback. While the feedback might not all be positive, the job would allow them to know how they are performing.

According to the theory, these five job characteristics combine to create a single *motivating potential score* (MPS) of a particular job. As you can see from the formula in Figure 9.10, the most important two factors are autonomy and job feedback. This is because their influence has more "mathematical weight" than skill variety, task identity, and task significance, which are divided by three.

One question is whether all employees will want an enriched job or not. To address this question, Hackman and Oldham proposed that growth needs strength (GNS), or how much an individual wants or needs higher-level needs, such as recognition or self-actualization, would vary. It has been argued that individuals who are high in GNS would be more strongly motivated by the motivating potential of a job. However, this is the most controversial aspect of the model. While Fried and Ferris (1987) found research that GNS changed the relationship between the job characteristics and job performance, overall, GNS has not seen a great deal of research support.

However, research has generally been supportive of the model overall. For example, in a meta-analysis of almost 200 studies, Fried and Ferris (1987) found that job characteristics related both to attitudes such as satisfaction as well as to behaviors such as performance and withdrawal. In addition, they found that the psychological states mediated these relationships. Grant (2008b) found that those working at a call center as fundraisers who received a simple task significance intervention of sharing specific stories regarding the positive benefits of the dollars raised increased their performance in terms of donations generated. He also found that task significance increased the job dedication and helping behavior of lifeguards.

In addition, as research has evolved, additional factors have been studied, and researchers have suggested the addition of other job characteristics (Humphrey, Nahrgang, & Morgeson, 2007; Morgeson & Humphrey, 2008). These additional job characteristics include job complexity, social characteristics such as social support and interdependence of tasks, as well as work context characteristics such as the ergonomics of the job and working conditions. In their meta-analysis of 256 studies of job design, Humphrey et al. (2007) found that the 14 work characteristics they examined explained, on average, 14 percent of the variance in the attitudinal and behavioral outcomes they studied. For example, job characteristics explained 25 percent of the variance in subjective performance ratings and 34 percent of the variance in workers' job satisfaction. In other words, job characteristics appeared to be important not only to workers' job satisfaction but to their performance as well.

Job Redesign

In addition to the overall job characteristics model, some core ideas around the concept of job redesign include job rotation, job enlargement, and job enrichment. We will discuss each of these in turn, starting with rotation. **Job rotation** refers to the policy of employees performing one of several assigned job tasks, with responsibility for performing a certain set of job tasks rotating on a set schedule, such as monthly. It can be seen as a type of on-the-job training (see Chapter 8). It can be considered an alternative to a company's focus on producing highly specialized employees (Cosgel & Miceli, 1998). **Job enlargement** refers to expanding an employee's duties and responsibilities to beyond those that he or she was previously performing. This method increases the amount of variety in the tasks performed, and may reduce monotony, but it does not increase the "depth" and responsibility of the tasks performed. In contrast, **job enrichment** refers to increasing the motivational potential of a job such as by increasing the level of authority and control the person has over the job. The core dimensions of job enrichment theory include the five core job characteristics discussed in the Job Characteristics Model (Umstot, Bell, & Mitchell, 1976). Taking these factors into consideration when designing or redesigning jobs can be helpful.

Reinforcement and Incentives

Reinforcement Theory

As you have seen in the present chapter, motivation is part of the performance equation. When it comes to reinforcement theory you may already be familiar with its basic premise that behavior that is reinforced tends to be repeated, while behaviors that are punished or ignored tend to be extinguished or curbed. In other words, *behaviors are dependent upon what happens as a result of them.* Reinforcement theory grew out of the behaviorist school of thought. A pioneer in behaviorism was B. F. Skinner,

Job rotation: The policy of employees performing one of several assigned job tasks, with responsibility for performing a certain set of job tasks rotating on a set schedule, such as monthly.

Job enlargement: Expanding an employee's duties and responsibilities to beyond those that he or she was previously performing.

Job enrichment: Increasing the motivational potential of a job such as by increasing the level of authority and control the person has over the job.

"You all deserve a personal pat on the back."

Operant conditioning:
Learning in which behavior is influenced by its antecedents and consequences (such as rewards and punishments).

Reinforcers: Anything that has an effect on the behavior preceding it, and either makes the behavior more likely or less likely to happen in the future.

Positive reinforcement: The introduction of something positive after a desired behavior.

Negative reinforcement: The removal of something unpleasant after a desired behavior.

Punishment: The introduction of an unpleasant consequence after an undesired behavior.

Extinction: The removal of a positive consequence which results in decreases in the behavior.

an American psychologist who contributed a great deal to the field of experimental psychology. In fact, a 2002 survey of psychologists published in the *Review of General Psychology* identified him as one of the most influential psychologists of the twentieth century. In terms of I/O psychology, he is best known for his research on **operant conditioning**, which is defined as learning in which behavior is influenced by its antecedents and consequences (such as rewards and punishments).

Under this theory, there are four types of **reinforcers** (Skinner, 1938). A reinforcer can be anything that has an effect on the behavior preceding it, and either makes the behavior more likely or less likely to happen in the future. You are probably well aware of reinforcers in your everyday life, but let's review them specifically. First is **positive reinforcement**, the introduction of something positive after a desired behavior. For example, if your classmate thanks you for doing such a great job on your first draft of your group project, she has just engaged in positive reinforcement. At work, positive reinforcement may come in many different forms. For example, in a recent World at Work (2013) survey, it was found that the top five recognition awards included certificates or plaques, cash, gift certificates, company logo merchandise, and food. Next is **negative reinforcement**, the removal of something unpleasant after a desired behavior. If you're late getting the first draft to the group and your classmates keep calling, texting, and e-mailing to see when it will be done and they stop as soon as you send them the draft, this is a form of negative reinforcement. In this example, the negative reinforcer was the cessation of the nagging being done by the group. Similarly, **punishment** is the introduction of an unpleasant consequence after an undesired behavior. For example, if you turn in your group paper a day late and your professor mentions she is going to lower your grade by one letter for being late, this is a form of punishment. Finally, **extinction**, the removal of a positive consequence which results in decreases in the desired behavior, occurs when something that used to be positively reinforced is stopped. For example, let's say that a coworker is making inappropriate jokes at work. When coworkers laugh, this behavior is unintentionally rewarded. However, if they stop laughing, the inappropriate behavior will likely stop as well leading to extinction of the undesired behavior.

Of course, each of these types of reinforcement can be appropriately or inappropriately used to help individuals learn what is expected of them – either on purpose or inadvertently. For example, positive reinforcement can be effective, but if you've ever

	Positive	Negative
Introduce something	*Positive reinforcement* Example: Manager praises an employee for a job well done.	*Punishment* Example: Manager gives an employee fewer hours due to poor performance.
Remove something	*Extinction* Example: Manager ignores an employee's great performance.	*Negative reinforcement* Example: Manager stops nagging an employee once their report is submitted.

Figure 9.11
Summarizing types of reinforcement.

encountered someone who thanks you for every little thing that you do, after a while, you start not to pay much attention to them. In other words, the positive reinforcement starts to wear off because it is being overused. Similarly, if you always reward someone for doing something at work and then suddenly stop, they are likely to stop as well. Punishment should be used sparingly if at all, since punishment generally just works when there is someone who can administer the punishment; once the punishment stops, the undesired behavior often resumes. And there are keys to punishment's effectiveness. So, if you choose to go this route in response to an undesired behavior, please keep the following in mind. First, punishment should always be paired with the act. Being timely is important because if a long period of time passes between the behavior and the punishments, they are less effective. Second, be sure you are being consistent. As we saw earlier in this chapter for justice theory, being consistent is a key component of fairness. Thus, if you decide to punish an employee for a behavior, be sure to do this with all employees who engage in this behavior in order to be fair. Finally, make sure you use this technique infrequently. As will be covered in more depth in Chapter 10, abusive supervision refers to nonphysical forms of hostility by managers toward their employees (Tepper, 2007). A manager who regularly uses punishment as a way to motivate others can be seen as an abusive manager. It is easy to underestimate how much power you have as a manager and how your actions affect others. We recommend positive reinforcement as an alternative. For example, "catching" someone doing the right things and praising them is much more effective than punishment, which may work in the short run but may damage the relationship in the long run. We next turn our attention toward the schedules of reinforcement.

It is important to understand the rest of the theory, which relates to the questions of how and when to introduce them. **Reinforcement schedules** refer to how and when reinforcers are applied. Schedules can be broken into two categories including **continuous reinforcement** (applying a consequence after a behavior occurs on a predictable cycle) or **variable reinforcement** (applying a consequence only some of the times that a behavior occurs). Thus, there are four types of reinforcement schedules. For continuous schedules, they might be **fixed ratio** (where reinforcement is applied after a specific *number* of behaviors are observed) or **fixed interval** (where reinforcement is applied after a specific *period of time* has passed). For variable

Reinforcement schedules: How and when reinforcers are applied.

Continuous reinforcement: Applying a consequence after a behavior occurs on a predictable cycle.

Variable reinforcement: Applying a consequence only some of the time that a behavior occurs.

Fixed ratio schedule: Continuous reinforcement schedule where reinforcement is applied after a specific number of behaviors are observed.

Fixed interval schedule: Continuous reinforcement schedule where reinforcement is applied after a specific period of time has passed.

Figure 9.12 Examples of different reinforcement schedules.

Below are some examples of reinforcement schedules.

A **continuous schedule** means that you reward or punish a behavior EVERY time it occurs.

Sales organizations sometimes ring a bell every time a sale is made. If you work at one of these organizations, that sound can be very motivating.

A **fixed ratio** means that you reward a behavior the *n*th time it occurs.

When you receive a free cup of coffee after purchasing 10 of them, you are enjoying the benefits of the fixed ratio schedule.

A **fixed interval schedule** means that you reward a behavior after a set period of time.

Receiving a weekly paycheck is a classic example of a fixed interval schedule in the workplace.

A **variable ratio schedule** means that you reward for behaviors after a random number of responses unknown to the person.

Gambling casinos figured out a long time ago that random rewards for behaviors such as feeding quarters into a slot machine are powerful for maintaining such behaviors.

Variable interval schedule: Reinforcing behaviors on a random interval schedule.

Variable ratio schedule: Reinforcing behaviors after a random number of behaviors are observed.

schedules it is the same except the number and period of time are varied. When it comes to learning new skills, continuous reinforcement helps us learn to acquire new skills quickly. However, once you stop reinforcing the behavior, it tends to extinguish, or stop, the behavior. When it comes to learning skills that are less likely to extinguish, variable reinforcement has been shown to lead to the most persistent behavior. We illustrate examples of these reinforcement schedules in Figure 9.12.

Behaviorism is not embraced by everyone. Critics of behaviorism argue that it can be too simplistic, that is, that work in the twenty-first century is so complex that such a simple theory cannot fully capture what happens at work. For example, as summarized in his book *Drive: The surprising truth about what drives us*, Daniel Pink (2009) argues that rewards work well to motivate for simple tasks but may actually interfere with more complex, creative tasks which many knowledge workers engage in each day. His TED Talk (http://www.ted.com/talks/dan_pink_on_motivation) has been viewed millions of times since he gave it in 2009, as has his animated talk (http://www.youtube.com/watch?v=u6XAPnuFjJc) on YouTube. Since we can never be certain what others are unable or unwilling to tell us, behaviorism may be too dependent on publicly observable stimuli and behaviors, at the expense of internal processes that are nevertheless vital to having a complete understanding of motivation (Moore, 2013). Another criticism is that it is manipulative to view human behavior this way (Kohn, 1999). However, considering some principles of behaviorism can be useful for organizations. Organizations often inadvertently reward bad behavior and wonder why it continues. For example, if people who check in with their boss frequently always receive tough assignments from the boss, the word will get around, and workers may decide never to check in with their boss to avoid the tough assignments. In short, organizations should be sure that their reward systems provide reinforcement for the behaviors they want employees to perform and don't reward poor behaviors.

Compensation

Although it is not a theory *per se*, we would be remiss if we did not include a discussion of **compensation**. Interestingly, money doesn't seem to be the only reason we go to work. When eight workers from a ConAgra meatpacking plant in Nebraska won $365 million in the Powerball lottery, three of them immediately elected to stop working. But, as reported in *Forbes* magazine, several reported straight back to work at their graveyard shifts. Another example of this is when a survey asked, "What motivates you at work?," 29 percent of employees said that it was doing something meaningful, 25 percent said money, and 17 percent indicated that recognition motivated them (Lavinsky, 2010). This indicates that while many of us work for a paycheck, there are other important motivational aspects to working that are unrelated to actual pay. However, it is still important to recognize that compensation systems and incentives are part of the equation of understanding motivation at work. Asking employees what they would like is a great way to make sure you are meeting their expectations. Unfortunately, this seems relatively rare, as a survey found that only 11 percent of respondents indicated that their company involved employees in the design of reward programs.

Compensation: The total amount of both monetary and non-monetary pay provided to an employee by an employer.

Workplace Application

Incentives Keep Things Heated Up at Nucor Steel

Nucor Steel focuses on aligning company goals with employee goals. Nucor is made up of over 20,000 employees whose stated goal is to "take care of our customers." Employees are rewarded through generous pay and bonuses based on the company's annual performance for contributing to the company by being safe, producing high-quality steel, keeping costs low, being productive, and remaining profitable. In fact, production incentive bonuses can more than double an employee's take-home pay. Would these incentives be motivating to you? Why or why not?

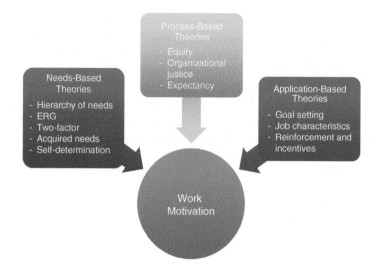

Figure 9.13
Summary of
theories of work
motivation.

Summary of Application-Based Theories

Application-based theories of motivation focus directly on ways to help make employees more motivated at work. We covered three specific theories in this section including goal-setting and the use of SMART goals to help focus and energize employees toward specific work goals. Job characteristics have been found to be important aspects to understanding motivation at work, as the way that a job is designed is important to many outcomes including motivation. Finally, reinforcement and incentives are important factors when considering motivation at work. We covered how different schedules of reinforcement influence behavior as well as how compensation relates to motivation. We next cover legal issues followed by global implications.

LEGAL ISSUES

The way in which we compensate individuals for the work that they do is an important legal consideration. One area where this has shown up lately is in terms of statistics on pay differences based on gender, with women getting the short end of the stick. We discussed this issue in terms of comparable worth back in Chapter 3. In Chapters 6 and 7, we described the importance of understanding how to avoid and detect discrimination in the recruitment and selection process based on protected classes such as women; the same holds for compensation. In the United States, women are paid (on average) 77 cents for every dollar paid to men.

In the United States, there are laws designed to prevent sex discrimination in pay. In other words, two people who have similar qualifications, similar performance, and are performing similar jobs should be paid similarly. The Equal Pay Act came into existence in 1963 when President Kennedy signed it into law. It amended the Fair Labor Standards Act and stated that an employer may not pay an employee less than another employee of the opposite gender if they engage in the same work and have the same qualifications and performance level. Furthermore, the Civil Rights Act of 1964 prohibits discrimination in employment conditions, including pay and advancement, based on sex. The 2009 Lilly Ledbetter Fair Pay Act is a US federal statute that has important implications for deterring and rectifying pay discrimination. The Act amends the Civil Rights Act of 1964 in important ways. In the case that led to this Act, Ledbetter v. Goodyear Tire & Rubber Co., Ms. Ledbetter was originally awarded $3.3 million by a jury for compensatory and punitive damages because of the blatant sex discrimination in pay during her 20 years working for the company. However, based on the fact that the 180-day period to file such claims had passed, since the discrimination was decades long, higher courts reversed the verdict. Such a ruling could create an incentive for employers to keep such situations secret to make it past the 180-day limit. However, the Fair Pay Act states that every discriminatory paycheck resets the 180-day limit to file. This creates an incentive for organizations to proactively avoid and correct any discrimination that may exist, thus protecting pay fairness.

GLOBAL IMPLICATIONS

Motivation exists in all cultures, but as we have previously mentioned, the factors that generate motivation may vary across cultures. For example, among Japanese workers, the concept of lifetime employment has traditionally been a major motivator that does not generally exist among North American employees these days, with an emphasis on internal promotion and job security above all else driving these employees' decisions at work (Brislin, MacNab, Worthley, Kabigting, & Zukis, 2005). However, the general Japanese employee mindset may be shifting to personal employability as a motivator, which comes with an increased emphasis on learning marketable skills if changing jobs becomes necessary.

Further, studying motivation levels among other cultures can produce surprising results. In a study of need satisfaction and motivation in Bulgarian employees, though the results of the Bulgarians and Americans were generally comparable, researchers found that Bulgarian employees reported higher satisfaction of their need for autonomy (which is a driver of motivation) than the American sample group did, as well as less job pressure, despite poorer working conditions (Deci et al., 2001). In addition, some of the stereotypes of what motivates people in different cultures may not be accurate, and in fact, the assumptions made by managers may not be correct. In a study by

In a meta-analytic study of 190,000 employees working in 32 different countries, Shao, Rupp, Skarlicki, and Jones (2013) found that justice effects are strongest among nations characterized by individualism, a nurturing orientation, uncertainty avoidance, and a low power distance where there is relatively little power difference between employees and supervisors.

DeVoe and Iyengar (2004) on managers in companies in North America, Asia, and Latin America, even employees' own managers were not always correct in understanding employees' motivations. While employees from all three regions tended to report being more intrinsically motivated than extrinsically motivated, North American managers typically perceived their employees as being more extrinsically motivated, while Asian managers tended to perceive equal levels of motivation between intrinsic and extrinsic factors (DeVoe & Iyengar, 2004). Only Latin American managers tended to perceive the same intrinsic motivation that most of their employees reported. In short, managers are not always accurate in assessing what motivates employees, and the aspects of work motivation that are emphasized by employees can vary significantly across cultures. This should be taken into consideration in today's multinational organization: It is not "one size fits all."

CURRENT ISSUES AND CONTROVERSIES

As we noted at the start of this chapter, motivation is a popular topic. Given this, new avenues of research are evolving all the time. One of these has to do with the role of time in motivation. Judge, Simon, Hurst, and Kelley (2014) note that historically psychologists have ignored how individual motivation varies over time. Instead researchers have tended to compare individuals. Lately, however, research has begun to examine the daily variations in motivation as well as the role of the external environment on motivation. For example, Judge et al. (2014) found that over 10 days, individuals did have variation in their motivation due both to their own personalities as well as due to experiences in the workplace. They found that intrinsic motivation positively predicted how agreeable and conscientious someone was the next day. Lee, Gino, and Staats (2014) studied the role of weather (sunny versus rainy) on productivity and they found that "bad" weather days were related to higher productivity, perhaps because

The CEO of Zynga, a company which develops games for social media websites such as *FarmVille*, *CityVille*, and *Words with Friends*, earned $57.8 million in 2013 in total compensation including stock options. This made him one of the highest-paid CEOs for that year (de Aenlle, 2014).

employees were less distracted. This was consistent across countries (Japan and the US) and in the field and the lab. In addition, time in terms of a person's lifespan has been hypothesized to affect work motivation (Kanfer & Ackerman, 2004), with different types of work motivation taking precedence at different life stages. There has been some empirical support for this proposition: One meta-analysis found that although younger workers are more extrinsically motivated, older workers may focus more on intrinsic motives (Kooij, de Lange, Jansen, Kanfer, & Dikkers, 2011).

A current controversy deals with CEO pay, and whether the current compensation levels of upper management at large firms are appropriate. This has been a contentious issue for decades. Part of the Dodd-Frank Act requires publicly traded organizations to disclose to the US Securities and Exchange Commission the ratio of the compensation of its CEO to the median compensation of its employees. There is no doubt that a typical CEO's compensation has been increasing at a rate much faster than the average worker's. For example, in 1991, the average CEO of a large company was compensated at a rate approximately 140 times greater than that of the average worker. By 2003, the gap had widened to 500 times greater (Bebchuk & Fried, 2006).

Regardless of the validity of the arguments on each side of the debate, for our purposes, we are interested in the impact that executive compensation has on employee motivation and CEO motivation. There have been attempts to move CEO compensation to be more clearly aligned with firm performance, so that when the company does well, so does the CEO. This led Larry Ellison, Oracle's CEO, to earn $96.2 million in 2013, making him the highest-paid CEO of that year. However, based on the tenets of equity theory it is not always clear how employees are affected by such wide gaps in pay. To the degree that employees feel that the CEO is doing a good job and is contributing a great deal in terms of inputs – and bringing them along in terms of pay and other benefits – these higher outcomes for CEOs will be deemed warranted. However, at some point, it is hard to imagine that anyone is able to put in 500 times more than an entry-level employee who works full-time.

WHAT DOES THIS MEAN TO YOU?

This chapter shows that motivation matters and is influenced by a great number of factors - some within an individual's control and some outside of their control. But what does this mean for you as an employee or manager of other employees?

First, focus on how you can set goals most effectively. Start with small goals and then work your way up to larger and longer-term goals. Perhaps you are interested in getting a job in a particular industry or organization. What are the factors that will influence you on this goal? By breaking up a large goal into smaller pieces, you can more easily tackle them one at a time until you are there. This will also improve your motivation in terms of expectancy because you will be better able to have some your efforts lead to successful performance.

Second, you may be asked to manage others. Even if you are an individual contributor now, over time you may be tapped to step up and lead other employees. The information in this chapter can be very helpful in your success in such a position. For example, we know that research shows that listening to, focusing on, and helping to meet your employees' needs will increase the chances of them being motivated and willing to put in effort toward their and your goals at work.

Third, understanding intrinsic motivation is important. A major takeaway from research in this area is that when individuals enjoy what they do and find intrinsic motivation in it, it is much more powerful and long-lasting than when they are motivated by extrinsic rewards such as pay only. For example, if an employee is only working at your firm because they are paid well, there is very little incentive for them to stay if another firm is willing to pay them more. We know that turnover is a major problem as it costs time, money, and lost opportunities every time someone leaves. If you can help individuals find more meaning in their work, this is a win-win for you and them. This is also an application of the job characteristics model which shows that meaning matters.

Conclusion

Motivation is an important part of I/O psychology that pervades other areas such as selection, training, performance appraisal, and leadership. In this chapter, we provided an overview of some of the key foundational and more modern motivation theories and discussed the work-related issues that individuals, groups, and organizations need to take into consideration to understand and manage motivation. The systems that are most motivating are perceived as fair and useful, fit the company strategy, and are practical. When it comes to motivation, one of the key things to consider is unintended consequences. While a new program or incentive plan might be put into place with the hopes of leading to higher levels of motivation, given the complexities of both today's workplace and the complex science of human motivation, such programs may lead to unwanted outcomes unless they are carefully considered and revisited.

YOUR TURN...

1. How much are you personally motivated by intrinsic versus extrinsic factors? Is this stable across all situations? If not, what does it depend upon? Have you seen a difference in your own or others' performance depending upon which type of motivation seems the most salient?

2. Consider the job of lifeguard. If you were designing a program to help motivate lifeguards, what would you do? Describe how you would approach this task.

3. Imagine you have been asked to redesign the job of teacher in K-12 schools to make it more attractive to new college graduates as a profession and to help them be more effective. What would you do? Which theories would you draw upon? Which of the job characteristics model factors might matter the most for this profession?

4. Think of a time when you have been highly motivated or highly unmotivated. With this example in mind, do you have any new insights into why this was after reading about motivation theory and research in this chapter? Please describe and share any insights or questions you related to the example you generated, using the theories and concepts from the chapter to explain your answer.

Additional Reading

Kanfer, R., Chen, G., & Pritchard, R. D. (2012). *Work motivation: Past, present, and future.* SIOP Organizational Frontiers series. New York: Routledge.

Latham, G. P. (2012). *Work motivation: History, theory, research and practice.* Thousand Oaks, CA: Sage.

Maslow, A. H. (1954). *Motivation and personality.* New York: Harper.

Pink, D. H. (2011). *Drive: The surprising truth about what motivates us.* New York: Riverhead Books.

Vroom, V. (1994). *Work and motivation.* New York: Jossey-Bass.

CASE STUDY: Wegmans Is a Motivating Place to Work

Depending upon which part of the world you live in, you may not have ever heard of Wegmans. However, since *Fortune* magazine created its list of the *Best Companies to Work For*, Wegmans has consistently appeared on the ranking, and the most recent list is no exception. It seems that the grocery store continues to garner awards such as receiving the Food Network's award for the nation's top supermarket, Best Companies for Working Mothers, the Dale Carnegie Leadership Award, and more. Wegmans is a thriving grocery store chain based in Rochester, New York, that has grown to 84 stores across Maryland, New Jersey, New York, Pennsylvania, and Virginia in the United States. Wegmans is also a family-run business. Daniel (Danny) Wegman, the organization's CEO, is the grandson of the company's cofounder. Daniel's daughter Colleen Wegman is currently the President of the company.

When it first appeared back in the 1980s, the *Fortune* magazine ranking came as a surprise to many in the grocery industry, as Wegmans, like other grocery stores in the food industry, is characterized by low profit margins, low-paying, often tedious jobs, and demanding customer interactions. However, there are many reasons that Wegmans has such loyal, motivated workers and a turnover rate of only 3.6 percent for their nearly 44,000 employees (compared to the industry average, which is closer to 100 percent). They utilize job sharing and a compressed workweek and also offer telecommuting for some employees. Ultimately, Wegmans created an environment that shows employees that they matter. The company motto, "Employees first. Customers second," is based on the belief that when employees feel cared for, they will in turn show concern for the customers they serve. In response to the 2008 ranking as the third-best company in the United States to work for, CEO Danny Wegman said, "Every one of our employees and customers should stand up and take a bow, because together they make Wegmans a special place."

Wegmans has also consistently brought innovations to a fairly traditional industry. For example, Wegmans was an early technology adopter and launched a website for its stores back in 1996, which was well before this was the norm, with specifics on health and recipes and other helpful information for its customers. Many have called the experience at Wegmans "Food Theater." To help ensure quality and remain on the cutting edge for the huge growth of sales of organic foods in the United States, which soared to $32 billion in 2013, Wegmans supermarkets started its own 50-acre organic research farm. Its goal is to develop best practices in terms of health and efficiency and to share those practices with the hundreds of farmers that supply their stores with fresh fruits and vegetables.

Wegmans is demonstrating that being both socially and environmentally responsible can increase employee motivation, loyalty, growth, and profits, creating a win-win situation for the organization, important stakeholders such as employees and customers, and the communities where they are located.

Questions

1. What lessons can other companies in the grocery industry, or other "lean margin" industries, learn from the Wegmans experience in terms of motivating its workers?

2. Is innovation an important part of continued employee and customer satisfaction?

3. As an organization, what values and qualities do you think Wegmans looks for in an employee? How might this relate to employee motivation?

4. Was it surprising to learn that despite the fact that many of the jobs at Wegmans are tedious and low-paying, Wegmans still enjoys a low turnover rate? Explain why using at least two theories of motivation.

Sources: Partially based on information contained in Bauer & Erdogan, 2009, modified and reproduced under the Creative Commons License (CCL); Ezzedeen, Hyde, & Laurin, 2006; Fortune, 2013; Martin, n.d.

References

Adams, J. S. (1963). Towards an understanding of inequity. *Journal of Abnormal and Social Psychology, 67,* 422–436.

Alderfer, C. P. (1969). An empirical test of a new theory of human needs. *Organizational Behavior and Human Performance, 4,* 142–175.

Bandura, A. (1998). Personal and collective efficacy in human adaptation and change. In J. G. Adair, D. Belanger, & K. L. Dion (Eds.), *Advances in psychological science: Personal, social and cultural aspects* (pp. 51–71). Hove, England: Psychological Press.

Bauer, T. N., & Erdogan, B. (2009). *Organizational behavior* (1st ed.). Washington, DC: Flat World Knowledge.

Baumeister, R. F., & Leary, M. R. (1995). The need to belong: Desire for interpersonal attachments as a fundamental human motivation. *Psychological Bulletin, 117,* 497–529.

Bebchuk, L. A., & Fried, J. M. (2006). Pay without performance: Overview of the issues. *Academy of Management Perspectives, 20,* 5–24.

Brickman, P., Coates, D., & Janoff-Bulman, R. (1978). Lottery winners and accident victims: Is happiness relative? *Journal of Personality and Social Psychology, 36,* 917–927.

Brislin, R. W., MacNab, B., Worthley, R., Kabigting, F., & Zukis, B. (2005). Evolving perceptions of Japanese workplace motivation: An employee–manager comparison. *International Journal of Cross Cultural Management, 5,* 87–104.

Campbell, D. J. (1982). Determinants of choice of goal difficulty level: A review of situational and personality influences. *Journal of Occupational Psychology, 55,* 79–95.

Cerasoli, C. P., Nicklin, J. M., & Ford, M. T. (2014). Intrinsic motivation and extrinsic incentives jointly predict performance: A 40-year meta-analysis. *Psychological Bulletin, 140,* 980–1008.

Colquitt, J. A., Scott, B. A., & LePine, J. A. (2007). Trust, trustworthiness, and trust propensity: A meta-analytic test of their unique relationships with risk taking and job performance. *Journal of Applied Psychology, 92,* 909–927.

Colquitt, J. A., Scott, B. A., Rodell, J. B., Long, D. M., Zapata, C. P., Conlon, D. E., & Wesson, M. J. (2013). Justice at the millennium, a decade later: A meta-analytic test of social exchange and affect-based perspectives. *Journal of Applied Psychology, 98,* 199–236.

Cosgel, M. M., & Miceli, T. J. (1998). On job rotation. *Economics Working Papers* 199802. Storrs, CT: University of Connecticut.

de Aenlle, C. (2014). More scrutiny, still spectacular: C.E.O. pay still huge, as boards show independence. *New York Times,* June 7. Retrieved February 27, 2015, from http://www.nytimes.com/2014/06/08/business/average-total-pay-for-most-highly-paid-executives.html?_r=0.

Deci, E. L., & Ryan, R. M. (1985). *Intrinsic motivation and self-determination in human behavior.* New York: Plenum Press.

Deci, E. L., & Ryan, R. M. (2000). The "what" and "why" of goal pursuits: Human needs and the self-determination of behavior. *Psychological Inquiry, 11,* 227–268.

Deci, E. L., Ryan, R. M., Gagné, M., Leone, D. R., Usunov, J., & Kornazheva, B. P. (2001). Need satisfaction, motivation, and well-being in the work organizations of a former eastern bloc country: A cross-cultural study of self-determination. *Personality and Social Psychology Bulletin, 27,* 930–942.

DeVoe, S. E., & Iyengar, S. S. (2004). Managers' theories of subordinates: A cross-cultural examination of manager perceptions of motivation and appraisal of performance. *Organizational Behavior and Human Decision Processes, 93,* 47–61

Dishman, L. (2012). One easy way to motivate your staff. *FastCompany.* Retrieved February 27, 2015 from http://www.fastcompany.com/1835978/one-easy-way-motivate-your-staff.

Ezzedeen, S. R., Hyde, C. M., & Laurin, K. R. (2006). Is strategic human resource management socially responsible? The case of Wegmans Food Markets, Inc. *Employee Responsibility and Rights Journal, 18,* 295–307.

Fortune. (2013). 100 best companies to work for. Retrieved February 27, 2015, from http://archive.fortune.com/magazines/fortune/best-companies/2013/snapshots/5.html.

Fried, Y., & Ferris, G. R. (1987). The validity of the job characteristics model: A review and meta-analysis. *Personnel Psychology, 40,* 287–322.

Gagné, M., Forest, J., Vansteenkiste, M., Crevier-Braud, L., van den Broeck, A., Aspeli, A. K., ..., & Westbye, C. (2015). The multidimensional work motivation scale: Validation evidence in seven languages and nine countries. *European Journal of Work and Organizational Psychology, 24,* 178–196.

Gardner, J., & Oswald, A. J. (2007). Money and mental wellbeing: A longitudinal study of medium-sized lottery wins. *Journal of Health Economics, 26,* 49–60.

Grant, A. M. (2008a). Does intrinsic motivation fuel the prosocial fire? Motivational synergy in predicting persistence, performance, and productivity. *Journal of Applied Psychology, 93,* 48–58.

Grant, A. M. (2008b). The significance of task significance: Job performance effects, relational mechanisms, and boundary conditions. *Journal of Applied Psychology, 93,* 108–124.

Guion, R. M. (1998). *Assessment, measurement, and prediction for personnel decisions.* Mahwah, NJ: Lawrence Erlbaum Associates.

Hackman, J. R., & Oldham, G. R. (1975). Development of the job diagnostic survey. *Journal of Applied Psychology, 60,* 159–170.

Hackman, J. R., & Oldham, G. R. (1980). *Work redesign.* Reading, MA: Addison-Wesley.

Hall, D. T. (1968). An examination of Maslow's need hierarchy in an organizational setting. *Organizational Behavior and Human Performance, 3,* 12–35.

Harrell, A. M. (1984). McClelland's trichotomy of needs theory and the job satisfaction and work performance of CPA firm professionals. *Accounting, Organizations and Society, 9,* 241–252.

Harrell, A. M., & Stahl, M. J. (1981). A behavioral decision theory approach for measuring McClelland's trichotomy of needs. *Journal of Applied Psychology, 66,* 242–247.

Hofstede, G. (2001). *Culture's consequences: Comparing values, behaviors, institutions and organizations across nations.* Thousand Oaks, CA: Sage Publications.

Humphrey, S. E., Nahrgang, J. D., & Morgeson, F. P. (2007). Integrating motivational, social, and contextual work design features: A meta-analytic summary and theoretical extension of the work design literature. *Journal of Applied Psychology, 92,* 1332–1356.

Johnson, R. E., Lanaj, K., & Barnes, C. M. (2014). The good and bad of being fair: Effects of procedural and interpersonal justice behaviors on regulatory resources. *Journal of Applied Psychology, 99,* 635–650.

Judge, T. A., Simon, L. S., Hurst, C., & Kelley, K. (2014). What I experienced yesterday is who I am today: Relationship of work motivations and behaviors to within-individual variation in the five-factor model of personality. *Journal of Applied Psychology, 99,* 199–221.

Kanfer, R., & Ackerman, P. L. (2004). Aging, adult development, and work motivation. *Academy of Management Review, 29,* 440–458.

King, W. C., & Hinson, T. D. (1994). The influence of sex and equity sensitivity on relationship preferences, assessment of opponent, and outcomes in a negotiation experiment. *Journal of Management, 20,* 605–624.

King, W. C., Miles, E. W., & Day, D. D. (1993). A test and refinement of the equity sensitivity construct. *Journal of Organizational Behavior, 14,* 301–317.

Klein, H. J., Wesson, M. J., Hollenbeck, J. R., & Alge, B. J. (1999). Goal commitment and the goal-setting process: Conceptual clarification and empirical synthesis. *Journal of Applied Psychology, 84,* 885–896.

Kohn, A. (1999). *Punished by rewards: The trouble with gold stars, incentive plans, A's, praise, and other bribes.* Boston, MA: Houghton Mifflin Harcourt.

Kooij, D. T. A. M., de Lange, A. H., Jansen, P. G. W., Kanfer, R., & Dikkers, J. S. E. (2011). Age and work-related motives: Results of a meta-analysis. *Journal of Organizational Behavior, 32*, 197-225.

Latham, G. P., & Budworth, M. (2004). The study of employee motivation in the 20th century. In L. Koppes (Ed.), *The science and practice of industrial organizational psychology: The first hundred years* (pp. 353-381). Mahwah, NJ: Lawrence Erlbaum Associates.

Lavinsky, D. (2010). The employee-motivation checklist. *FastCompany*. Retrieved March 6, 2015, from http://www.fastcompany.com/3002877/employee-motivation-checklist.

Lee, J. J., Gino, F., & Staats, B. R. (2014). Rainmakers: Why bad weather means good productivity. *Journal of Applied Psychology, 99*, 504-513.

Lee, T. W., Locke, E. A., & Phan, S. H. (1997). Explaining the assigned goal-incentive interaction: The role of self-efficacy and personal goals. *Journal of Management, 23*, 541-559.

Locke, E. A., & Latham, G. P. (2002). Building a practically useful theory of goal setting and task motivation: A 35-year odyssey. *American Psychologist, 57*, 705-717.

Locke, E. A., & Latham, G. P. (2006). New directions in goal-setting theory. *Current Directions in Psychological Science, 15*, 265-268.

Martin, M. J. (n.d.). Data on employee turnover in the grocery industry. *Huston Chronicle*. Retrieved February 27, 2015, from http://smallbusiness.chron.com/data-employee-turnover-grocery-industry-18817.html.

Mathieu, J. E., Tannenbaum, S. I., & Salas, E. (1992). Influences of individual and situational characteristics on measures of training effectiveness. *Academy of Management Journal, 35*, 828-847.

Mitchell, T. R., & Daniels, D. (2003). Observations and commentary on recent research in work motivation. *Motivation and Work Behavior, 7*, 225-254.

Moore, J. (2013). Sketch: Three views of behaviorism. *Psychological Record, 63*, 681-691.

Morgeson, F. P., & Humphrey, E. E. (2008). Job and team design: Toward a more integrative conceptualization of work design. In J. Martocchio (Ed.), *Research in personnel and human resources management, Vol. 27* (pp. 39-92). Bingley, England: Emerald Group.

Parker, S. K. (2014). Beyond motivation: Job and work design for development, health, ambidexterity, and more. *Annual Review of Psychology, 65*, 661-691.

Pinder, C. C. (2008). *Work motivation*. New York: Psychology Press.

Raphael, T. (2003). Recruiting "retail consultants" at the Container Store. *Workforce*. Retrieved February 27, 2015, from http://www.workforce.com/articles/recruiting-retail-consultants-at-the-container-store.

Rupp, D. E., Shao, R., Jones, K. S., & Liao, H. (2014). The utility of a multifoci approach to the study of organizational justice: A meta-analytic investigation into the consideration of normative rules, moral accountability, bandwidth-fidelity, and social exchange. *Organizational Behavior and Human Decision Processes, 123*, 159-185.

Ryan, R. M., & Deci, E. L. (2000). Self-determination theory and the facilitation of intrinsic motivation, social development, and well-being. *American Psychologist, 55*, 68-78.

Salancik, G. R., & Pfeffer, J. (1977). An examination of need-satisfaction models of job attitudes. *Administrative Science Quarterly, 22*, 427–456.

Sanchez, R. J., Truxillo, D. M., & Bauer, T. N. (2000). Development and examination of an expectancy-based measure of test-taking motivation. *Journal of Applied Psychology, 85*, 739–750.

Sauley, K. S., & Bedeian, A. G. (2000). Equity sensitivity: Construction of a measure and examination of its psychometric properties. *Journal of Management, 26*, 885–910.

Shao, R., Rupp, D. E., Skarlicki, D. P., & Jones, K. S. (2013). Employee justice across cultures: A meta-analytic review. *Journal of Management, 39*, 263–301.

Sitzmann, T., & Ely, K. (2011). A meta-analysis of self-regulated learning in work-related training and educational attainment: What we know and where we need to go. *Psychological Bulletin, 137*, 421–442.

Soman, D., & Cheema, A. (2004). When goals are counterproductive: The effects of violation of a behavioral goal on subsequent performance. *Journal of Consumer Research, 31*, 52–62.

Spreier, S. W. (2006, June). Leadership run amok. *Harvard Business Review, 84*, 72–82.

Tay, L., & Diener, E. (2011). Needs and subjective well-being around the world. *Journal of Personality and Social Psychology, 101*, 254–365.

Tepper, B. J. (2007). Abusive supervision in work organizations: Review, synthesis, and research agenda. *Journal of Management, 33*, 261–289.

Trevis, C. S., & Certo, S. C. (2005). Spotlight on entrepreneurship. *Business Horizons, 48*, 271–274.

Turban, D. B., & Keon, T. L. (1993). Organizational attractiveness: An interactionist perspective. *Journal of Applied Psychology, 78*, 184–193.

Umstot, D. D., Bell, C. H., & Mitchell, T. R. (1976). Effects of job enrichment and task goals on satisfaction and productivity: Implications for job design. *Journal of Applied Psychology, 61*, 379–394.

Van Eerde, W., & Thierry, H. (1996). Vroom's expectancy models and work-related criteria: A meta-analysis. *Journal of Applied Psychology, 81*, 575–586.

Vroom, V. (1994). *Work and motivation*. New York: Jossey-Bass.

Wahba, M. A., & Bidwell, L. G. (1976). Maslow reconsidered: A review of research on the need hierarchy theory. *Organizational Behavior and Human Performance, 15*, 212–240.

Welsh, D. T., & Ordóñez, L. D. (2014). The dark side of consecutive high performance goals: Linking goal setting, depletion, and unethical behavior. *Organizational Behavior and Human Decision Processes, 123*, 79–89.

Wigdor, L. A. (1967). Herzberg's dual-factor theory of job satisfaction and motivation: A review of the evidence and a criticism. *Personnel Psychology, 20*, 369–389.

World at Work. (2013). *Trends in employee recognition*. Retrieved February 27, 2015, from http://www.worldatwork.org/waw/adimLink?id=72689.

Wrzesniewski, A., & Schwartz, B. (2014). The secret of effective motivation. *New York Times*. Retrieved February 27, 2015, from http://www.nytimes.com/2014/07/06/opinion/sunday/the-secret-of-effective-motivation.html?_r=0.

Chapter 10

LEADERSHIP AT WORK

Leaders provide direction and mobilize effort toward a common goal. Leaders have a powerful influence over individual effectiveness and attitudes, as well as group and organizational outcomes. This chapter will outline theories and approaches to understanding leadership.

After studying this chapter, you should be able to:

- define leadership and explain why it matters to organizations
- list the characteristics that are related to leadership effectiveness
- outline the behaviors that are associated with effective leadership
- describe the situational perspective to explaining leadership
- contrast contemporary leadership approaches and theories with earlier approaches
- identify key legal and global issues surrounding leadership
- describe the current issues and controversies around leadership.

Learning goals for this chapter

Introduction

In politics, for-profit and not-for-profit business, as well as in military and religious organizations, some people emerge as leaders, and some are chosen as leaders. Leaders organize other people's effort around a common goal, energize and motivate people, and influence them to behave in ways they might not otherwise behave. Unlike many topics of this book that came about in the twentieth century, leadership as a topic has been around since antiquity. Consider these quotations:

"He who has never learned to obey cannot be a good commander." – Aristotle

"A leader is best when people barely know he exists, when his work is done, his aim fulfilled, they will say: we did it ourselves." – Lao Tzu

"A ruler should be slow to punish and swift to reward." – Ovid

"A leader is a dealer in hope." – Napoleon Bonaparte

"The first method for estimating the intelligence of a ruler is to look at the men he has around him." – Niccolò Machiavelli.

Probably much of the wisdom contained within these quotations is still valid to this day (even though we no longer assume that a leader has to be a man!). While a lot has been written about this topic, the systematic study of leadership dates back to early in the twentieth century.

In this chapter, we will review the evolution of leadership theories over time. The history of leadership approaches has witnessed the development of a large number of theories that answer specific questions about leadership – who is the best leader, and how he or she should behave. Each theory provides one more piece of information and adds to our understanding of these questions: Who is a leader? What does a leader do? What should they do? What is the difference between effective and ineffective leaders? Are leaders born, or are they developed? And of course, what is the role of an I/O psychologist in developing leadership capabilities?

What Is Leadership?

Leadership has many definitions. Jago (1982) defines leadership as the use of non-coercive means to ensure that group tasks are accomplished. In other words, leadership is the process of influencing others to act in particular ways, but this influence involves ensuring cooperation rather than forcing others to do something. Smircich and Morgan (1982) define leadership as the process in which one person attempts to define and succeeds in defining the reality of others. This definition emphasizes that leadership is a process, and it underlines that leaders not only influence other people's actions, but also their perceptions and how they view their environment.

> **Leadership:** The process of influencing the way others act, their perceptions, and how they view their environment through cooperation.

Where Does the Power to Lead Come From?

The act of leading is intertwined with power and influence. It is hard to imagine a powerless leader being an effective one. Because of this, it makes sense to focus

Figure 10.1
French and Raven's bases of power.

Type of Power	Basis of Power	Example
Coercive Power	The ability to use force to gain compliance from another.	A supervisor threatening to fire an employee if they do not comply with his or her wishes.
Expert Power	The ability to use one's unique and respected knowledge to influence another.	A professor is an expert in the classroom.
Information Power	The ability to use one's unique knowledge.	A support employee who is the only person who understands how to fix the network has a great deal of information power.
Legitimate Power	An elected, selected, or appointed position of authority.	A supervisor asking an employee to create a new ad campaign by the end of the week.
Referent Power	Possessing positive affect and liking.	A well-liked colleague asking coworkers to support his ideas for a new product.
Reward Power	The use of the right to offer desired incentives.	A peer nominating a colleague for a merit award.

Coercive power: The ability to use force to gain compliance from another.

Expert power: The ability to use one's unique and respected knowledge to influence another.

Information power: The ability to use one's unique knowledge.

Legitimate power: Power that comes from being elected, selected, or appointed to a position of authority.

Referent power: Power that comes from possessing positive affect and liking.

Reward power: Power that is the use of the right to offer desired incentives.

Power: The ability to influence or control the behavior of others.

on what exactly power is and which types of power a leader may have at his or her disposal to influence others. **Power** is the capacity to influence or control the behavior of others. Two social psychologists, French and Raven (1959), pioneered work in the area of power and have continued to work to evolve the theory (Raven, 1992). They conducted a series of studies and determined that there are six main sources of power. These include coercive, expert, information, legitimate, referent, and reward power. These bases of power are defined in Figure 10.1, which also includes examples of each of these types of power. In general, these bases of power have been supported by subsequent research (e.g., Elias, 2008; Hinkin & Schriesheim, 1989). Some of these come from formal positions within an organization such as being a supervisor and having legitimate, reward, and coercive power. However, other types of power can be possessed by anyone within an organization. For example, referent power resides within the person and among the individuals who feel liking and admiration for the person. Leadership involves the ability to influence others through bases of power that are not coercive (Rost, 1993).

Outcomes of Leadership

Leadership emergence: Whether someone is perceived as a leader within the work group.

In leadership studies, there are usually two types of criterion variables or outcomes of interest: leadership emergence and leadership effectiveness. These two outcomes are quite different. **Leadership emergence** refers to whether someone is perceived as a leader within the work group. Studies of leadership emergence aim to identify characteristics that make someone seem "leader-like." In studies examining leadership emergence, usually small, leaderless groups are asked to engage in a group discussion or perform a task, and following the completion of the task each person would be asked who they perceived to be the leader in the group (Hogan, Curphy, & Hogan, 1994). In contrast, **leadership effectiveness** refers to what the leader actually accomplishes. There are multiple metrics capturing leadership effectiveness such as supervisor or subordinate ratings of effectiveness: subordinate satisfaction with the leader, or group or unit productivity may be used to measure leadership effectiveness. Research shows that emergence and effectiveness are related to each other. People who emerge as leaders are more likely to be promoted to higher level positions, and later be rated as effective (Foti & Hauenstein, 2007).

> **Leadership effectiveness:** What the leader actually accomplishes.

Do leaders really make a difference in organizations? In fact, there are those who question this very assumption. For example, the notion of "Romance of Leadership" (Meindl, Ehrlich, & Dukerich, 1985) is the idea that too much of a group's or an organization's performance or effectiveness is attributed to the influence of leaders. There are those who believe that as a society – or even as a species – we are enamored with the idea of leaders making a difference, even though it may not be true. At the same time, there is plenty of anecdotal and empirical evidence suggesting that leaders do matter. Research shows that leaders exert significant influence over organizational performance (Thomas, 1988). In Chapter 14, we will explore in more detail the influence leaders have on organizational structure and culture. For the employees in question, leadership matters a great deal. In Chapter 11, we will discuss the important role leaders have in shaping job attitudes and effectiveness of employees, and in Chapter 12 we will discuss the role that leaders play in affecting employee health and safety. In fact, a common saying that has research support behind it is that people don't leave jobs or companies, but they leave managers. And, in Chapter 13 on teams, team leadership is a key factor related to team effectiveness. In other words, a manager's leadership ability greatly matters for happiness, performance, well-being, and retention of the workforce.

Who Are Leaders? The Trait Approach to Leadership

Prior to the twentieth century, historians such as Scottish writer Thomas Carlyle popularized the notion that leaders are "great men." Leadership was thought to be within the purview of a small number of people, usually men, who were different from the general population. It was assumed also that leaders were born, not made. When it came to leadership, you either "had it" or you didn't.

A direct extension of this idea dominated early twentieth-century leadership studies. The question of what the characteristics of effective leaders were loomed large. Studies explored many personal factors including gender, age, intelligence, height, and personality in relation to leadership emergence and effectiveness. This approach, referred to as the **trait approach to leadership**, had the goal of identifying a limited number of traits that would predict leadership emergence and effectiveness. A seemingly endless list of traits was studied. However, this approach to the study of leadership ran out of steam following an influential review by Stogdill (1948)

> **Trait approach to leadership:** The approach of identifying a limited number of traits that would predict leadership emergence and effectiveness.

pointing out inconsistent findings and suggesting that leadership is something that goes beyond possessing particular traits.

Interestingly, the trait approach made a comeback more recently following the development and popularization of the five-factor approach to personality (see Chapter 6). Part of the problem with early trait studies was that there was no comprehensive framework for studying personality. The development of the five-factor framework allowed scholars to make sense of earlier findings and to conduct new studies with more comprehensive and reliable instruments. Another critique of earlier reviews was that they did not have the benefit of meta-analytic techniques (Lord, De Vader, & Alliger, 1986). With the development of these advanced statistical techniques, it became possible to systematically examine patterns of relationships across different studies. These subsequent analyses suggested that traits such as personality and intelligence had non-trivial relations with both leadership emergence and effectiveness. Next we provide a summary of what we know about the relationship between traits and leadership.

Personality and Leadership

Judge, Bono, Ilies, and Gerhardt (2002) conducted a meta-analysis of earlier personality studies, classifying them under the framework of the five-factor model. The results suggested that there were traits that mattered for both leadership emergence and effectiveness. Extraversion was by far the strongest correlate of leadership ($r = .31$) followed by conscientiousness ($r = .28$). As a reminder, extraverts are socially dominant, assertive, and outgoing, whereas conscientious people are typically organized, reliable, and punctual. This meta-analysis also yielded some findings about the effects of the situation on leadership. For example, these two traits mattered the most for leadership emergence in student groups, probably because someone who is talkative and sociable and has good organizing skills can quickly earn the status of leadership among students. For leadership effectiveness in actual organizations, however, extraversion and openness mattered most. Finally, there were some differences between business versus government/military settings, with openness to new experiences mattering relatively less, and emotional stability (which includes self-confidence) mattering more in government and military settings.

Personality and leadership may have an even stronger relationship than has been identified so far. This is because studies typically measure leader personality from the leader's own perspective, which may not always be accurate. Colbert, Judge, Choi, and Wang (2012) showed that the relationship might be even stronger if self-reports of personality are supplemented with observer ratings.

There is also emerging evidence that when trying to understand the effects of leader traits, we should not forget about the followers. Grant, Gino, and Hofmann (2011) showed that extraverted leaders were most successful when followers demonstrated low levels of proactive behaviors such as suggesting new ideas. In teams where followers displayed high levels of proactivity, extraversion acted as a disadvantage for group effectiveness. This was because extraverted leaders, probably due to their desire to be dominant, were less receptive to ideas coming from their teams, whereas introverted leaders were better at harnessing the proactivity of the team.

Even though there seems to be an extraversion advantage to leadership, the advantage is not so large as to be insurmountable. There are plenty of introverted CEOs, perhaps most notably the person who revolutionized how many people relate to each other: the founder and CEO of Facebook, Mark Zuckerberg, pictured here.

Intelligence and Leadership

Are smart leaders more effective, and are smart people more likely to be perceived as leaders? This has been an interesting area of study. As you might recall from Chapter 6, general mental abilities are important for job performance, and are one of the most important predictors of effectiveness at work. Would the same relationship hold for leadership? There are two reasons to expect that they would. First, we all have **implicit leadership theories** (ILTs) in our minds. ILTs are prototypes of what we consider a leader's traits that we as individuals have in our minds. If you were to make a list of what makes someone a leader, what would your list include? Those characteristics (such as being kind, tall, decisive, or fair) constitute your ILTs. When a particular leader has characteristics that fit with our prototype of an ideal leader (that is, the traits that make up our own ILT), we tend to react more favorably to them. It turns out that intelligence is a consistent part of ILTs across most followers. Lord, Foti, and De Vader (1984) showed that out of 59 such traits examined (including honesty and charisma), intelligence was the only consistent characteristic individuals identified as something all leaders should possess. Second, intelligent leaders can make sense of greater amounts of information, can make better decisions, and may be more effective in leading their teams to success.

Judge, Colbert, and Ilies (2004) conducted a meta-analysis and found that individuals who were *perceived* as intelligent were more likely to be thought of as leaders. When actual intelligence scores (assessed via tests such as Wonderlic, as seen in Chapter 6) were used, the results were bigger than zero, but not as strong. For example, leader effectiveness and measured intelligence were correlated at .25. In other words, intelligence matters for leadership emergence and effectiveness, but intelligence as perceived by followers seems more important than intelligence test scores. Interestingly, leader intelligence mattered most when the leader was using a directive style rather than a participative style. This is probably not surprising, as directive leaders need to rely primarily on their own intelligence to solve problems, whereas participative leaders can mobilize the cognitive resources available to the entire team.

Implicit leadership theories: The prototypes of leaders we have in our minds.

Gender and Leadership

Another important issue with societal implications is whether gender is related to leadership emergence or effectiveness. When it comes to women in leadership, a

Glass ceiling:
A discriminatory barrier
that prevents women
from advancing to senior
management.

glass ceiling (or a discriminatory barrier that prevents women from advancing to senior management) is thought to exist. In fact, it is noteworthy that while women are 42 percent of all full-time employees in the USA (Bureau of Labor Statistics, 2013), they are only 5.3 percent of all Fortune 1000 CEOs (Catalyst, 2014).

In the past, the "ideal leader" was defined as someone who is stereotypically male: assertive, dominant, and confident. This is known as the "think manager–think male" syndrome (Schein, Mueller, Lituchy, & Liu, 1996). Over time, with the changing nature of jobs, the necessity to operate within teams, and the increasingly less hierarchical nature of organizations, a different prototype has been emerging. Research has shown that the prototype of effective leadership has become increasingly feminine over time, with traits including being collaborative, sensitive, and open (Koenig, Eagly, Mitchell, & Ristikari, 2011). This new prototype is referred to as "think manager–think female" and has led scholars to speculate that there may be a feminine advantage to leadership (e.g., Vecchio, 2002). Others are finding evidence that effective leadership is neither feminine nor masculine, but instead is androgynous, or a blend of stereotypically masculine and feminine traits (Kark, Waismel-Manor, & Shamir, 2012).

When it comes to whether male or female leaders are regarded as more effective by others, and in particular by their managers, meta-analytic results suggest that the magnitude of difference is small and largely determined by the situation (Paustian-Underdahl, Walker, & Woehr, 2014). Specifically, in male-dominated organizations (such as the military), male leaders have a slight advantage, whereas in female-dominated organizations (such as social services), the slight advantage belongs to female leaders. Across all settings, women were seen as somewhat more effective both in top management and middle management positions. One explanation for this difference in perceptions of leaders in higher management positions could be the "extra competence" argument, which is the presumption that there are so many barriers to women's advancement that those who make it to the top must have extra skills.

Finally, there is some evidence that once individuals become leaders, male and female leaders may adopt slightly different styles. Consistent with the stereotype that women may be more interpersonally oriented, one meta-analysis showed that women had a greater tendency to behave more democratically whereas male leaders were somewhat more likely to adopt an authoritarian style (Eagly & Johnson, 1990). A subsequent meta-analysis showed that female leaders were less likely to adopt passive and ineffective styles of leadership and more likely to engage in visionary and charismatic styles (Eagly, Johannesen-Schmidt, & van Engen, 2003).

It seems that any gender differences in leadership are small, and where differences exist, they are in a direction that would put women at an advantage. So, what explains the underrepresentation of women in higher-level positions, if not leadership ability? There are literally hundreds of studies on this issue, and the answer is complex. First, the perception that women have more responsibilities at home is a factor. Research shows that managers perceive female employees as experiencing greater conflict between their jobs and families, and therefore rated them as less promotable (Hoobler, Wayne, & Lemmon, 2009). This finding was beyond the actual family responsibilities of women and women's own perceptions of work–family

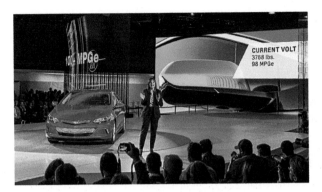

The notion of a glass cliff suggests that it often takes a crisis to bring women to leadership positions. This phenomenon seems to be frequently observed among female CEOs of Fortune 500 companies, and examples include Mary Barra's appointment to the leadership of the struggling GM (pictured), Marissa Mayer's appointment to the CEO position of Yahoo, and the National Football League's appointment of Dawn Hudson to be chief marketing officer amid image problems due to harassment and abuse scandals.

conflict, suggesting that the societal perception that women have their attention divided between work and home (even when this may not be true) puts women at a disadvantage. Second, when women are successful in a traditionally male-typed job, they tend to be liked less and are derogated more, suggesting that success comes at a cost, and performance may not always translate to promotions (Heilman, Wallen, Fuchs, & Tamkins, 2004). Finally, even in their promotions, women may be facing a **glass cliff**. This refers to the notion that women are overrepresented in top leadership positions that are risky and fragile, such as taking on the CEO role of a company about to go bankrupt (Ryan & Haslam, 2007). A series of studies showed that ideal managers for poorly performing companies were thought to be female. Women were also thought to be more suitable to take the heat during times of organizational failure and crises (Ryan, Haslam, Hersby, & Bongiorno, 2011). Outsider women were more likely to be brought to leadership positions following poor corporate performance, and when they failed, were more likely to be replaced with insider white male leaders (Cook & Glass, 2013). Taken together, these researchers' findings indicate that more progress is needed when it comes to understanding that both men and women can be effective (or ineffective) leaders, and that the perceptions surrounding gender and leadership do not always match reality.

Glass cliff: Refers to the notion that women are overrepresented in top leadership positions that are risky and fragile, such as taking on the CEO role of a company about to go bankrupt.

Race and Leadership

As of this writing, only six of the Fortune 500 companies are led by a African-American CEO (1.2 percent of the total). Furthermore, of these 500 companies, 9 (1.8 percent) have Asian, and 10 (2 percent) have Latino CEOs (DiversityInc, 2015). Is this underrepresentation of minorities in the highest levels of organizations due to a lack of qualified and interested candidates? Or are there systematic barriers that hold back qualified individuals from rising to these positions?

Research to date examining any leadership style differences based on race revealed few, if any, systematic differences based on race (Ospina & Foldy, 2009). Instead, much of the academic literature points out systematic patterns of differences in how minority versus Caucasian leaders are perceived and evaluated. This literature typically involves experiments where subjects (who are often undergraduate or graduate students, but also may be drawn from the industry) are presented with identical information regarding the actions, behaviors, or qualifications of a leader, with the race of the leader manipulated across conditions. After reading the vignette, subjects report their perceptions about the leadership qualities of the person described. Note that these studies do not require respondents to report on their biases. Instead, unconsciously, individuals may make snap judgments about someone else based on whether the person fits with their unconsciously held leadership prototypes (or ILTs) and stereotypes while incorrectly assuming that they are making an objective, data-driven decision. (See Chapter 8 for a discussion of these unconscious or "implicit" stereotypes.)

As a case in point, Rosette, Leonardelli, and Phillips (2008) showed that "being White" appears to be part of leadership prototypes. Again, note that this is an unconsciously held bias that emerges in people's choices rather than something they admit to the researchers. In a series of experiments, they showed that when the person in the vignette was described as an employee (rather than a manager), respondents inferred the race of the person from information provided about the organization's racial composition. If the organization was described as 50 percent (as opposed to 20 percent) White, the employee in the vignette was assumed to be White. However, when the person in the vignette was referred to as a manager, then the organization's racial composition became less relevant, and more subjects made the assumption that the person in question would be White. Studies also suggest that perceived effectiveness of a leader seems to depend on race, even in the face of identical performance information. Sy and colleagues (2010) conducted an experiment where subjects gave higher leadership ratings to the person described when they thought they were rating a Caucasian, as opposed to an Asian leader. Interestingly, among those reading about an Asian leader, leadership capabilities were rated higher if the leader was described as an engineering leader as opposed to a sales leader, suggesting that stereotypes about occupations and leader-occupation fit may also be in play, similar to what research has shown for women in leadership.

Intersectionality: How different aspects of a person's identity combine in different ways to shape their reality.

Finally, there is some research on **intersectionality** (Sanchez-Hucles & Davis, 2010). Intersectionality refers to how different aspects of a person's identity combine in different ways to shape their reality. For example, an African-American female leader's experiences will likely be different from those of a Caucasian female or an African-American male leader. The available research in this area suggests that this may be a situation of "double jeopardy." Rosette and Livingston (2012) showed that when reading a scenario of a successful company and its leader, leadership ratings were higher if the leader was described as a Caucasian male (as opposed to Caucasian female, African-American male, or African-American female). When the company was described as failing, then the leader who was rated as the least effective was the African-American female.

One limitation of these studies is that they involve experiments where the leader is only described on paper. At the same time, it is unnerving that even when presented with identical information, the results favor Caucasian and male leaders. This tendency is also not necessarily restricted to "paper people" (those described in résumés only). Park and Westphal (2013) surveyed CEOs and journalists, asking them to comment on low firm performance (disappointing earning disclosures) of their competitors. Caucasian CEOs commenting on the poor performance of competitor firms were more likely to blame the poorly performing company's CEO (rather than external circumstances) when the CEO in question was a minority. Further, this tendency to blame the minority CEO was stronger when the journalist was Caucasian. In summary, the available evidence indicates that race plays a role in how organizational actors react to others and evaluate each other, resulting in systematic biases favoring some groups while excluding others. Organizations need to take meaningful action to create a merit-based organization that provides opportunities to assume leadership roles and thrive in these roles regardless of their race.

What Do Leaders Do? The Behavioral Approach

Prior to the 1940s, most studies of leadership focused on traits. Discouraged due to the inability to arrive at a fixed set of traits that would characterize effective leaders across all situations, scholars turned their attention to a different question. What do leaders *do*? This **behavioral approach to leadership** sought to answer this question by identifying the *behaviors* that distinguished effective leaders from ineffective leaders.

At about the same time (the 1950s), researchers at the University of Michigan and Ohio State University, independently of each other, conducted studies on this topic, and arrived at very similar answers. Specifically, the Ohio State University group identified two types of behaviors that effective leaders demonstrate. **Initiating structure** refers to task-oriented behaviors leaders display, such as clarifying roles, ensuring that employees perform up to standards, and communicating standards of performance. **Consideration** refers to relational behaviors leaders engage in, including looking out for the well-being of members, being approachable, and being a good listener. The University of Michigan researchers also confirmed the existence of these two dimensions.

The identification of these two leader behaviors moved the field away from thinking about leadership as innate traits. Therefore, this approach was a major contribution to the social scientific study of leadership. At the same time, this approach met with a key problem: The researchers' assumption was that these two types of behaviors would predict leadership effectiveness under all situations. However, this assumption was not confirmed by the subsequent research (Korman, 1966). The failure to identify consistent relationships with outcomes of interest resulted in disillusionment with the behavioral approach at the time (House & Aditya, 1997). As a result, starting from the 1960s, behavioral approaches slowly gave way to theories that account for the role of situation. Instead of specifying what behaviors leaders should *always* do, later theories started specifying what behaviors would be effective *in specific situations*. It is perhaps fair to say that as it stands today, leadership is mostly behavior-focused, and there are several contemporary theories we will discuss later in this section exploring what effective leaders do. At the same time, contemporary theories usually adopt a **contingency approach to leadership**, and aim to specify the situational factors affecting when different behaviors and styles are more appropriate and result in the greatest leader effectiveness.

So, what happened to the concepts of consideration and initiating structure in leadership research? Even though interest in these two categories of leadership behaviors waned over time, more recent meta-analyses looking at all the behavioral

Behavioral approach to leadership: The leadership approach that attempted to identify the behaviors that distinguished between effective and ineffective leaders.

Initiating structure: Task-oriented behaviors leaders display, such as clarifying roles, ensuring that employees perform up to standards, and communicating standards of performance.

Consideration: Relational behaviors leaders engage in, including looking out for the well-being of members, being approachable, and being a good listener.

Contingency approach to leadership: Theories that specify the situational factors affecting when different leadership behaviors and styles are more appropriate.

leadership studies conducted over the past several decades showed that these two types of leader behavior actually do a pretty good job predicting leadership outcomes and therefore should not be dismissed as mere historical artifacts. For example, initiating structure behavior of leaders was meta-analytically correlated with follower motivation at .40, and with leadership effectiveness at .39. Consideration was correlated with satisfaction with the leader at .78 and with leader effectiveness at .52 (Judge, Piccolo, & Ilies, 2004). Further, DeRue, Nahrgang, Wellman, and Humphrey (2011) included these behaviors along with other leadership traits and behaviors identified in the twenty-first century to examine their relative importance. Their meta-analytic results indicated that initiating structure is actually the most important leadership predictor of group performance, and its effect is equivalent to a style termed transformational leadership (which is discussed later in this chapter). Consideration is the biggest predictor of follower satisfaction with the leader, surpassing the role of all other traits and behaviors. In other words, consideration and initiating structure behaviors are important pieces of the puzzle of leadership.

Traits or Behaviors: What Matters More?

More recently, researchers have begun to re-examine the relative value of traits and behaviors in understanding leader effectiveness and emergence. DeRue and colleagues (2011) compared the relative importance of different traits, and also looked to see whether traits or behaviors mattered more for leadership. It is probably not a surprise that leader behaviors are vastly more important than leader traits. For example, the effects of leader traits on follower job satisfaction are minimal (just 2 percent), but leader behaviors account for more than 50 percent of the variation in follower job satisfaction. Similarly, traits explain 6 percent of satisfaction with leader, whereas behaviors explain 70 percent. In other words, what leaders do seems to be much more important than who they are. At the same time, these researchers found some evidence that the two approaches can be integrated such that leader traits are related to leader effectiveness *through* their influence over leader behaviors. Leader personality affects the propensity of leaders to display task- and relationship-oriented behaviors, which shapes follower attitudes and team performance. There is emerging evidence that the effects of intelligence

Workplace Application

Project Oxygen Explores Ingredients of Effective Leadership at Google

In 2009, Google set out to answer one question that was critical to the future of the company. Do leaders matter? Conventional wisdom says that they do, but Googlers usually are skeptical about such wisdom, and they wanted to understand what matters for leadership at Google. In a project code named Project Oxygen, the People Operations team, which included I/O psychologists, examined data from performance appraisals and feedback surveys, trying to understand what makes someone an effective leader. Ordered by importance, here is their list:

1. Being a good coach: Conducting one-on-one meetings to offer feedback and develop employees.
2. Empowering the team: Not micromanaging, giving the team room to operate independently.
3. Care about employees: Make employees feel that you care about them.
4. Be results-oriented: Make sure that work gets done.
5. Effective communications: Listen, and be ready to engage in dialogue
6. Help employees develop in their careers.
7. Have a vision for the team and communicate it to the team.
8. Have technical skills to provide advice to the team.

You probably realize that the list includes a lot of behaviors discussed in this chapter, including #3 and #4, roughly equating consideration and initiating structure. It is also interesting that even in a technically oriented company such as Google, having the technical skills was at the bottom of the list, suggesting that how leaders interact and communicate with their employees matters much more (Aquino, 2011).

and personality on leadership effectiveness is actually through behaviors adopted by leaders (e.g., Cavazotte, Moreno, & Hickmann, 2012).

Contingency Approaches to Leadership

Following the seemingly disappointing results of the trait and behavioral approaches, the 1960s and 70s witnessed the development of theories that explicitly incorporated the role of situational factors into their predictions. Known as contingency theories, these theories attempted to match the leadership behaviors with a particular configuration of situational factors. We review three such theories in this section.

Fiedler's Contingency Model of Leadership

Fiedler's (1964) contingency model predicted that leadership effectiveness would depend on the match between the behavior of the leader and the characteristics of the situation. He contended that leaders would have a predominant leadership behavior that comes to them naturally: They are either task-oriented or relationship-oriented. Unlike the Ohio State studies, Fiedler thought of these as more permanent styles, and that leaders would have one or the other style, but not necessarily both. A leader's style would be identified by putting the leader through a questionnaire labeled **Least Preferred Coworker Scale** (LPC), which gauged the leader's reaction to a difficult person they have worked with in the past. Here's how it works. Think of a person that you've had great difficulty working with. This person is your least preferred coworker. Answer the following questions about that person: How pleasant is this person? How friendly? How sincere, loyal, and interesting? If you are describing your least preferred coworker in positive terms (and therefore your LPC score is high), you are a relationship-oriented leader. This is because you can distinguish your ability to work with someone from your ability to relate to that person. If your answers are negative (and your LPC score is low),

Least Preferred Coworker Scale (LPC): A questionnaire a leader would be put through to identify whether the leader is task- or relationship-oriented.

Figure 10.2 A
summary of
Fiedler's (1964)
contingency
model of
leadership.

Situation Favorability to the Leader			
	Unfavorable	**Moderately Favorable**	**Favorable**
Leader–follower relations	Poor	Any other combination	Great
Task structure	Unstructured task		Highly structured
Leader position power	Weak		Strong
Appropriate leadership style	**Task-oriented (low LPC leader)**	**Relationship-oriented (high LPC leader)**	**Task-oriented (low LPC leader)**

you are a task-oriented leader. This is because to you, not being able to work with someone is the same as not liking that person.

In addition to focusing on two types of behaviors of leaders, the theory describes three characteristics of the context in which the leader operates. These are leader–follower relations, structure of the task, and position power of the leader. When the leader is trusted and liked by followers, when the task is highly structured so that everyone knows what is expected of them, and when the leader has a lot of organizational power and authority, then the situation is thought to be highly favorable. In contrast, if the leader is disliked and not trusted, when the task is vague and unclear, and the leader is relatively low in his/her organizational power, then the situation is unfavorable to the leader. Fiedler predicted that when the situation is highly favorable or highly unfavorable, task-oriented leadership would work best, whereas when the situation was moderate in how favorable it is, relationship-oriented leadership would work best.

Fiedler's theory is one of the most systematic and structured theories of leadership. While Fiedler's own review of laboratory and field studies testing the predictions of the theory were supportive of the theory (e.g., Fiedler, 1971), other scholars using meta-analytic techniques noted weak empirical support (Peters, Hartke, & Pohlmann, 1985). Further, the theory assumes that the leader cannot change his or her style, and that the situation should instead be changed – something that is difficult to do in most organizations. Thus, the theory later fell out of favor, but it is important for being the first theory to formulate the key role of fitting the leader to the situation.

Directive leadership:
Clarifying role
expectations and
coordinating work.

Supportive leadership:
Providing a friendly
and communicative
atmosphere.

Participative leadership:
Consulting with
employees and involving
them in decision-making.

Achievement-oriented leadership: Setting goals
for subordinates and
motivating them to meet
challenging goals.

Path-Goal Theory of Leadership

House and Mitchell (1974) proposed that leaders may display one of four styles. These are **directive leadership**, or clarifying role expectations and coordinating work (akin to initiating structure), **supportive leadership**, or providing a friendly and communicative atmosphere (equivalent to consideration behaviors we discussed earlier), **participative leadership**, which involves consulting with employees and involving them in decision-making, and **achievement-oriented leadership**, involving setting goals for subordinates and motivating them to meet challenging goals. Depending on the characteristics of the person, the task, and the work group, some of these styles will be expected and motivational, whereas

Situation	Appropriate Style	Inappropriate Style
Ambiguous task, where employees have low preference for independence	Directive	
Ambiguous task, where employees have high preference for independence	Participative	
Employees feel that they are highly capable		Directive
Tasks are clear but dissatisfying	Supportive	Directive
The issue at hand is highly relevant to employees	Participative	
Employees are highly independent	Achievement-oriented	
Employees are achievement-oriented	Achievement-oriented	

Figure 10.3
Summary predictions of path-goal theory (based on information from House, 1996).

others will be useless at best, and frustrating at worst. Path-goal theory viewed effective leadership as an interaction between the leader's style and the context. But unlike Fiedler's model, this model assumed that leaders may display different styles at different times.

The path-goal theory is so named because it proposes that the leader's job is to identify the road blocks in the way of subordinates that prevents them from reaching their goals (House, 1971), and that it is the leader's job to ensure that goal accomplishment is rewarding for the individual in question. The theory is closely linked to the expectancy theory of motivation (Chapter 9), and using the theory's language, it regards the leader's job as increasing the expectancy, instrumentality, and valence for the followers. The theory's specific formulations are summarized in Figure 10.3.

Path-goal theory has received a lot of research attention, and its predictions have received some support (e.g., Wofford & Liska, 1993). Even though recent years have not seen much work on this theory, the basic idea behind it is still observable in all contemporary leadership theories: The leader's function may change in different situations and leaders may have to take different roles in different contexts. Whether they are more useful to their teams as a commander, cheerleader, facilitator, or coach will depend on the subordinates, the tasks, and the work group characteristics. The best style will be the one that delivers what employees need.

Vroom's Normative Model of Leadership

Leaders make decisions. A key issue when it comes to decision-making is who should be involved in the actual making of the decision. Should the leader make

Jane Park, the founder and CEO of Seattle-based nail polish and beauty products company Julep, feels that everyone says they are collaborative, but this is not necessarily true: "It is not collaborative if you listen, but then go off and do your own thing. You have to be willing to sit there and hear input and be willing to let the person impact the final decision. That takes strength, but it also takes vulnerability to be open to the fact that maybe what you had in mind is not perfect, or that there was one element you didn't think about, or that there's a way to make it better. You have to be open to that possibility ..." (Bryant, 2014).

Decide: The situation where the leader makes a decision alone, with no input from the group.

Consult individually: The situation where the leader goes to group members individually to get their input, but then the decision is made solely by the leader.

Consult group: The situation where the leader shares the problem with the entire group, invites them to give their opinions, followed by the leader making the decision alone.

Facilitate: The situation where the leader solves the problem with the group, acting like a facilitator but not dictating the answer, enabling and helping the group to arrive at the solution.

Delegate: When the leader completely delegates the problem to the group, and plays no direct role in the actual solving of the problem, beyond answering questions or being there when needed.

the decision alone, with little to no information sought from team members? Should the leader check in with the members, but then make the decision alone? Should the leader present the problem to the group and let them decide?

Originally developed by Vroom and Yetton (1973) and later revised by Vroom (2000), the normative model helps answer these questions. The model is presented in the form of a decision aid, and asks the leader to answer a series of questions regarding the context in which the decision-making will take place. The assumption of the model is that as the leader is in a situation where subordinates have the information the leader needs, or implementing the decision requires the leader to convince employees, then a more participative approach will work better. In contrast, if employee interests are not aligned with organizational interests or the leader has more information than employees, a more authoritarian style will become more appropriate.

According to the normative model, the leader may display one of five different styles: **decide** (making the decision alone), **consult individually** (the leader goes to members individually for input, but makes the decision alone), **consult group** (the leader shares the problem with the group, invites them to give opinions, then makes the decision alone), **facilitate** (the leader jointly solves the problem with the group), **delegate** (the leader plays no direct role beyond answering questions or being there when needed). The situation is diagnosed by answering the seven questions at the top of the decision tree in order. Let's work on an example. Imagine that you are redesigning the office space. You are faced with a number of choices ranging from type of furniture to whether you need offices or open spaces. How should you decide? Note that the answers we give are just examples, and your different answers would take you to a different style.

Decision significance: High. Once the job is done, you will have to live with the choice for the next 5-10 years.

Importance of commitment: High. If they don't like it, they will work from home or the local coffee shop. You want them to like the new office.

Leader expertise: Low. You are not an expert in office design.

Likelihood of commitment: Low. If you were to make the decision by yourself, how likely is it that the team will go along with it? You suspect that given the individual needs of team members and high need for autonomy, they would be frustrated.

TIME-DRIVEN MODEL

Copyright © Victor Vroom 2003

Instructions: The matrix operates like a funnel. You start at the left with a specific decision problem in mind. The column headings denote situational factors which may or may not be present in that problem. You progress by selecting High or Low (H or L) for each relevant situational factor. Proceed down from the funnel, judging only those situational factors for which a judgment is called for, until you reach the recommended process.

Decision Significance	Importance of Commitment	Leader Expertise	Likelihood of Commitment	Goal Alignment	Group Expertise	Team Competence	
H	H	H	H	-	-	-	Decide
H	H	H	L	H	H	H	Facilitate
H	H	H	L	H	H	L	Consult (Group)
H	H	H	L	H	L	-	Consult (Group)
H	H	H	L	L	-	-	Consult (Group)
H	H	L	H	H	H	H	Delegate
H	H	L	H	H	H	L	Consult (Individually)
H	H	L	H	H	L	-	Consult (Individually)
H	H	L	H	L	-	-	Consult (Individually)
H	H	L	L	H	H	H	Facilitate
H	H	L	L	H	H	L	Consult (Group)
H	H	L	L	H	L	-	Consult (Group)
H	H	L	L	L	-	-	Consult (Group)
H	L	H	-	-	-	-	Decide
H	L	L	-	H	H	H	Facilitate
H	L	L	-	H	H	L	Consult (Individually)
H	L	L	-	H	L	-	Consult (Individually)
H	L	L	-	L	-	-	Consult (Individually)
L	H	-	H	-	-	-	Decide
L	H	-	L	-	-	H	Delegate
L	H	-	L	-	-	L	Facilitate
L	L	-	-	-	-	-	Decide

(Left side vertical label: PROBLEM STATEMENT)

Figure 10.4
Vroom's (2000) normative model of leadership.

Goal alignment (between employee and company goals): Low. You feel that the employees are more interested in the look and feel of the office whereas the company is mostly concerned about the budget.

Group expertise: High. The team knows how they can be best productive and which office design would help with that.

Team competence: High. Can your team work together to solve the problems? How competent are they? You have trust in the abilities of your team.

If you apply these answers to the decision tree, answering the first five questions in this way leads you to the answer *consult group*. Answering any of the questions in a different way would have led you to a different answer, and a different style.

Research has shown that decisions using the style depicted by the model are more effective than the ones made using different styles (Field, 1982; Vroom & Jago, 2007). This theory of leadership is valid and potentially useful, albeit somewhat complicated to actually apply. A unique aspect of this model is its prescriptive nature, that is, it tells the leader what style he or she should use. Perhaps no other leadership theory is as explicit in its prescriptions as this one is.

Contemporary Approaches to Leadership

The contingency approaches to leadership have made important contributions to the study and understanding of leadership. Now we turn our attention to contemporary theories of leadership, or more recent additions to the study of leadership. As you will see, each contemporary theory provides a framework for what leaders do and the different styles they might display. The original formulations of contemporary theories are typically not as rigid and formulaic as contingency theories. Instead, contemporary theories usually start by describing a particular leadership style, and subsequent researchers test this style to identify the conditions under which that particular style becomes more or less effective. In this section, we discuss more current theories of leadership, focusing on transformational leadership theory, leader–member exchange theory, authentic leadership, and servant leadership.

Transformational Leadership Theory

Perhaps the most frequently studied theory of leadership in the twenty-first century distinguishes between transformational and transactional leaders (Burns, 1978). **Transformational leadership** is characterized by four distinct behaviors: idealized influence (also known as charisma), inspirational motivation, intellectual stimulation, and individualized consideration. In contrast, **transactional leaders** are those who demonstrate contingent reward, active management by exception, passive management by exception, and laissez-faire leadership styles. Simply put, transactional leaders motivate employees by rewards and punishments and by providing support when needed. In contrast, transformational leaders transform employee values so that employees become loyal to the organization and see their own well-being and the organization's well-being as fully intertwined. An important distinction is that transformational leaders are viewed as charismatic. **Charisma** is defined as rare personal qualities of leaders that create high levels of devotion and enthusiasm on the part of followers (Burns, 1978). Transformational leaders shape employee self-concept and self-confidence, and they allow employees to act in ways that are consistent with their values, resulting in devotion to the leader and to the cause the leader is supporting (Shamir, House, & Arthur, 1993). Detailed definition of the behaviors displayed by transformational and transactional leaders may be found in Figure 10.5.

Meta-analytic evidence suggests that transformational leadership behaviors are positively related to work unit effectiveness (Lowe, Kroeck, & Sivasubramaniam, 1996). Research conducted in a bank has shown that when leaders were trained to display transformational leadership, employee commitment to the organization increased, and branch performance improved (Barling, Weber, & Kelloway, 1996). Transformational leaders shape employee performance because employees trust these leaders more and see their values as more aligned with the leader's values (Jung & Avolio, 2000).

A recent meta-analysis concluded that for a broad range of outcomes such as follower motivation, employee satisfaction with the leader, and follower performance, transformational leadership was the most positive predictor, but one transactional leader behavior, contingent rewards, also had almost as positive relations with these outcomes. In contrast, laissez-faire leadership behaviors were negatively

Transformational leadership: Leadership that is characterized by four distinct behaviors: idealized influence (also known as charisma), inspirational motivation, intellectual stimulation, and individualized consideration.

Transactional leaders: Leaders who demonstrate contingent reward, active management by exception, passive management by exception, and laissez-faire leadership styles.

Charisma: Rare personal qualities of leaders that creates high levels of devotion and enthusiasm on the part of followers.

Transformational leaders	Idealized influence (charisma)	Leader acts as a role model, showing conviction, emphasize the importance of purpose.
	Inspirational motivation	Articulating an appealing vision, creating excitement around the vision.
	Intellectual stimulation	Questioning old assumptions, encouraging expression of new ideas.
	Individualized consideration	Treating followers as individuals, providing support, caring about their personal development.
Transactional leaders	Contingent reward	Providing rewards and punishments based on performance, providing assistance along the way.
	Active management by exception	Leader proactively monitors performance and intervenes if there is a threat that something will go wrong.
	Passive management by exception	Leader intervenes after things go wrong.
	Laissez-faire	Leader is largely absent even when needed, avoids managing the team, does not express views to guide the team.

Figure 10.5
Transformational and transactional leader behaviors (Bass, 1991).

"See website for interactive material"

correlated with leadership effectiveness. These results suggest that even though there is overall support that transformational behaviors are helpful to groups, the relationship between transactional behaviors and effectiveness depends on the dimension of transactional leadership under consideration (Judge & Piccolo, 2004). Transformational leadership and contingent reward behaviors help teams as well: In a study on light infantry platoons, both leadership styles were related to unit performance because members of these teams were more confident in the team's abilities to conquer challenges, and were more cohesive (Bass, Avolio, Jung, & Berson, 2003).

Workplace Application

Charismatic Leader Elon Musk

An important factor separating transformational and transactional leaders is that transformational leaders are viewed as charismatic. What do charismatic people do? A lot of people think of charisma as something that is inborn – you have it or you don't. Leadership scholars disagree. In fact, charismatic leaders do very specific things, and these can be learned and emulated. Conger and Kanungo (1998) specified three things charismatic leaders do. Let's analyze the charisma of a business leader using this framework. Elon Musk is the CEO of Tesla Motors, the maker of the first fully electric sports car.

1. **They have an appealing vision that challenges the status quo.** Musk's vision for Tesla challenges the status quo. He is interested in manufacturing fully electric cars and not hybrids. He wants to build cars that drive and park themselves.

He is selling the cars only directly from the company, eliminating the need for dealerships and transforming how cars are sold.

2. **They communicate the vision in an inspirational manner.** Musk is a passionate advocate for the need to switch to electric cars. He is quoted as saying, "We're running the most dangerous experiment in history right now, which is to see how much carbon dioxide the atmosphere can handle before there is an environmental catastrophe."

3. **They execute the vision in unconventional ways where they serve as role models and engage in self-sacrifice.** At a critical juncture, he invested the majority of his personal wealth in Tesla and took on the leadership of the company. In 2014, he made the surprising decision to release all Tesla patents to others who are interested in using its technology.

Leader–Member Exchange (LMX) Theory

LMX theory is a novel contribution to the leadership literature because the theory's premise is that leaders lead through the unique and dyadic relationships they build with each of their employees (Bauer & Erdogan, 2015). "The secret" of leadership resides not in who the leader is or what they do, but in the relationships they build with employees (Dansereau, Graen, & Haga, 1975). In fact, you may have noticed that leaders typically have different types of relationships with different employees. With some, the relationship is based on trust, mutual liking, and professional respect. In these **high-quality LMX relationships**, the leader and the employee feel a certain degree of mutual obligation to support each other and not let each other down. In **low-quality LMX relationships**, the relationship is based on lower levels of liking, loyalty, and respect. The employee feels that the main obligation he/she has to the leader is to perform the tasks in the job description, and there is no special loyalty or desire to support the manager. Perhaps the biggest distinction between high- and low-quality exchanges is the degree of trust. LMX researchers have shown that LMX development is a process of trust development (Bauer & Green, 1996). The early days of the relationship are a trial period where the employee shows how reliable and competent they are. The manager delegates tasks to the employee, and continues to delegate if the employee performs well. The result is a situation where the manager thinks of the employee as someone they can trust.

Should employees care about the type of relationship they have with their manager? It turns out having a high LMX relationship benefits the employee directly, as summarized in Figure 10.6. High LMX members enjoy their jobs more (Gerstner & Day, 1997). These employees are given higher autonomy (Liden, Wayne, & Sparrowe, 2000) and enjoy a more supportive work environment. They receive higher performance ratings, even when their objective performance does not warrant it (Duarte, Goodson, & Klich, 1993). High LMX employees also enjoy faster salary progress (Wayne, Liden, Kraimer, & Graf, 1999) and are more influential at work (Sparrowe & Liden, 2005). The experiences of high LMX employees are decidedly more positive and more pleasant compared to those who have a poorer quality relationship with their manager.

High-quality LMX relationships: The relation between the leader and employee is characterized by high levels of trust, mutual liking, professional respect, and mutual felt obligation not to let each other down.

Low-quality LMX relationships: The relationship between the leader and employee is characterized by lower levels of liking, loyalty, and respect.

In return for these benefits, high LMX members provide advantages to organizations. Research has shown that these employees are more committed and attached to the organization, and are somewhat less likely to leave the company (Dulebohn, Bommer, Liden, Brouer, & Ferris, 2012). They also are more likely to go "above and beyond," performing behaviors that benefit others even if it is not part of their job. For example, if the manager is looking for urgent help over the weekend, these employees are more likely to come through.

Of course, a high-quality relationship with one's manager may not be equally desirable for employees. Researchers have shown that, indeed, sometimes the relationship makes little difference to employees. A study in the pharmaceutical industry has shown that high-quality exchanges matter much more to introverted newcomers to an organization (Bauer, Erdogan, Liden, & Wayne, 2006). This is because extraverts may receive a lot of the support and information they need through other interactions they have. Further, having a high-quality exchange with the manager becomes more important as the manager gains more power within the organization (Erdogan & Enders, 2007).

How does a high-quality exchange develop? First of all, early on, perceived similarity (Liden, Wayne, & Stilwell, 1993) and personality traits (agreeableness and extraversion) are important influences, whereas later on, the employee's contributions become more important (Nahrgang, Morgeson, & Ilies, 2009). Leader behaviors matter too: Whether they engage in contingent reward behaviors (a type of transactional leadership we discussed above), how fair they are, and the frequency of transformational leadership behaviors seem to matter (Dulebohn et al., 2012). Employee actions are important as well: By being reliable, high-performing, and competent, it is possible to increase the possibility of developing a high-quality exchange. Finally, employees may engage in impression management behaviors. Engaging in self-promoting behaviors (such as bringing one's effort to the attention of the manager) and ingratiation (such as doing favors or complimenting the manager to appear more likeable) help build a better quality relationship. In other words, leaders are human too ... and therefore they are susceptible to employee efforts to be likeable, appear trustworthy, and reliable.

Should leaders strive to have high-quality relations with all of the employees they manage? Is it a problem if the manager has some higher quality and some lower quality exchanges within the same group? These questions are not fully answered, but there are some informative studies. First, employees seem to enjoy even more benefits if they feel that they have a "better" relationship with their manager compared to other employees (Hu & Liden, 2013; Vidyarthi, Liden, Anand, Erdogan, & Ghosh, 2010). At the same time, having both high- and low-quality relations within the same team was problematic for the team – with increased team conflict as a possible result (Hooper & Martin, 2008). When there are both high- and low-quality exchanges within the group, fairness becomes very important, and in the absence of a justice climate, employees experience detachment (Erdogan & Bauer, 2010). Finally, even though high-quality relations with managers are beneficial in general, there is one notable downside: When the manager leaves, employees who are close to them are likely to follow suit (Ballinger, Lehman, & Schoorman, 2010).

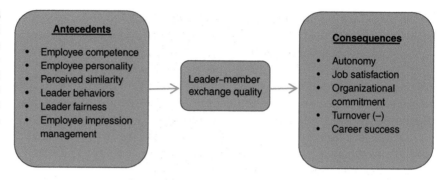

Figure 10.6
Antecedents and
consequences
of LMX qual-
ity (based on
information
from Erdogan &
Bauer, 2014).

It is possible to conclude that in principle, having a high-quality relationship with one's employees is desirable, but it may not always be possible (and may have unintended side effects), so managers are advised to invest time in developing an effective relationship with their employees, and if this is not possible, ensure that a climate of fairness permeates the group, to avoid perceptions of favoritism and political behaviors.

Authentic Leadership

Authentic leadership:
Leadership theory
describes authentic
leaders as those
who "remain true to
themselves." These
leaders display self
awareness, honesty, and
sincerity.

Authentic leadership is a leadership theory that has gained much traction in academic and practitioner circles. This theory emerged at a time when corporate ethics scandals such as Enron's collapse in 2001 dominated the news. As a result, this theory places great emphasis on the values and ethics of leaders. Specifically, authentic leaders are those who "remain true to themselves." These leaders are first and foremost self-aware: They are aware of their own values, strengths, and limitations, and can admit to themselves when they were wrong. They also display honesty and sincerity in their interactions with others: They do not hide their weaknesses, and they are not afraid to display vulnerabilities. They do not engage in "ego-defensive" behaviors. They do not pretend to be someone they are not, and they have a strong sense of what is right and what is wrong (Walumbwa, Avolio, Gardner, Wernsing, & Peterson, 2008).

Authentic leaders provide a number of benefits to employees, including higher chances of satisfying the needs of their employees, and thereby improving employee performance (Leroy, Anseel, Gardner, & Sels, in press). Authentic leaders end up developing a higher-quality relationship (LMX) with their employees (Wang, Sui, Luthans, Wang, & Wu, 2014), contributing to employee performance. Finally, authentic leaders help employees become more resilient in the face of difficulties, become more optimistic, more hopeful about the future, and to feel more confident, which translates into more desirable behaviors from followers such as higher creativity (Rego, Sousa, Marques, & Pina e Cunha, 2012).

Authentic leadership theory is not without its critics. Recently, some aspects of the theory were challenged as paradoxes. One of these is that organizational life may be necessarily inauthentic – we monitor our behaviors, consider the impact on the group, and manage our impressions. Therefore, authenticity may be an unreachable, and even an undesirable ideal (Algera & Lips-Wiersma, 2012). Second, being true to

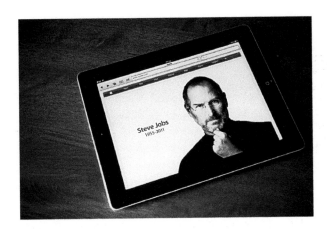

Authentic leaders do not imitate someone else's style. Instead, they are in touch with who they are, and find their own style. Nowhere is this more evident than at Apple Inc., where the visionary CEO Steve Jobs' unique style was an important part of Apple's success narrative. Tim Cook, Apple's current CEO, is clearly not trying to imitate the iconic Jobs. Unlike Jobs, he is demonstrating a more democratic, socially responsible, consensus-building style. One former employee describes the difference as: "Steve was a wartime CEO, while Tim is a peacetime CEO" (Wakabayashi, 2014).

oneself does not necessarily imply being ethical. The theory seems to suggest that once leaders are true to themselves, more moral actions will follow, but this would only be true if the leader truly has a strong moral compass, which may not exist in all leaders (Sparrowe, 2005). Others argue that authentic leadership skills are a challenge to teach. This is because authentic leadership is thought to develop as a result of one's critical life events and career history. There are important events in everyone's life that change the way they decide to live their lives, and it is unclear how this leadership style can be developed and improved through interventions (Cooper, Scandura, & Schriesheim, 2005). Despite these concerns, the theory provides a unique approach to the study and practice of leadership.

Servant Leadership

In contrast to the idea of a leader who takes followers to a destination by inspiring and supporting them, **servant leaders** are those who lead by serving their followers and helping them reach their full potential. Servant leaders are sensitive to the needs and desires of their followers and to those of other organizational stakeholders (Graham, 1991). These leaders care about their employees, build and cultivate long-term relationships with them, and support their career development, but this interest in followers does not necessarily come from a desire to reach organizational goals. Instead, these leaders see follower growth, happiness, and well-being as an end in and of itself (rather than a means to an end) (Liden, Wayne, Zhao, & Henderson, 2008). Servant leaders can subordinate their self-interests to those of their employees (Greenleaf, 1977). The characteristics of servant leadership are shown in Figure 10.7.

Servant leaders: Those who lead by serving their followers and helping them reach their full potential.

Research has shown that servant leadership is related to organizational commitment, job performance, and even the degree to which employees are good citizens of the broader community (e.g., community volunteering) (Liden et al., 2008). At the team level, servant leadership has been associated with team confidence, performance, and citizenship behaviors (Hu & Liden, 2011). Servant leaders help build employee confidence and increase perceptions of fairness as well (Walumbwa, Hartnell, & Oke, 2010). CEO-level servant leadership behaviors have been shown to be related to firm performance (Peterson, Galvin, & Lange, 2012).

Figure 10.7
Characteristics of
servant leaders (van
Dierendonck, 2011).

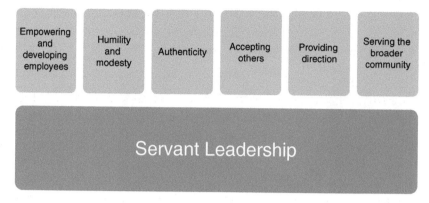

Abusive Supervision

In addition to studies and theories examining how leaders can help their followers, groups, and organizations to succeed, there is a stream of literature examining how they can do harm. A case in point is the study of abusive supervision. **Abusive supervision** refers to the sustained display of hostile and demeaning behaviors, excluding physical contact (Tepper, 2000). Examples of abusive behaviors managers may display include ridiculing employees, reminding them of personal failures and mistakes, being rude to employees, and invading their privacy.

Not surprisingly, employees reporting to abusive supervisors are more likely to quit their jobs, and when for some reason they are unwilling or unable to move, they experience lower levels of job satisfaction, organizational commitment, a sense that work interferes with their family lives, and stress (Tepper, 2000). These employees experience a lower sense of organizational fairness (Zellars, Tepper, & Duffy, 2002). Of course, employees are not necessarily passive recipients of such behaviors, and they often retaliate in a way that will hurt the supervisor or the organization (Mitchell & Ambrose, 2007). Further, abusive behaviors supervisors engage in seem to spread to other people: When employees are abused by their supervisors, they are more likely to undermine their partners or spouses when they get home, suggesting that when people are mistreated, they are more likely to mistreat others (Hoobler & Brass, 2006). Further, supervisors' own abusive behaviors toward employees may stem from how they are treated by their own superiors. For example, when supervisors feel that the organization treats them unfairly, they are more likely to act in abusive ways toward their employees (Tepper, Duffy, Henle, & Lambert, 2006), suggesting that when it comes to disrespectful treatment, there may be a "trickle-down effect." Needless to say, elimination of such behaviors from organizations will go a long way in improving the health, well-being, and ultimate effectiveness of organizational members.

How Do We Cultivate Good Leadership? Leadership Development

An important question that has kept both scholars and leaders busy over the years has been whether leadership is inborn or learned. There is some evidence that genes play a role. Studies on twins have shown that around 30 percent of the variation in whether someone occupies a managerial role can be attributed to heredity

(Arvey, Rotundo, Johnson, Zhang, & McGue, 2006). Similarly, 58 percent of the variation in self-rated transformational leadership and 47 percent of the variation in self-rated transactional leadership can be attributed to genes (Johnson, Vernon, Harris, & Jang, 2004). Although this shows that genes do affect leadership, it also leaves plenty of room to develop a person's leadership abilities.

The ability to lead others requires the development of leadership skills – the ability to motivate, influence, and collaborate with others. Not everyone who is promoted to a management position will be ready to lead others, and often managers simply rely on their formal position to get things done, even though having leadership skills would have made them effective. In particular, larger organizations with bigger training budgets utilize a variety of methods to teach employees and managers leadership skills.

Leadership development is a huge part of organizational training budgets. Consider this: in 2014, US businesses spent over $70 billion on employee training and development, 35 percent of which was spent on management and leadership development (Bersin, 2014). Leadership development is different from management training where managers are taught how to plan, organize, coordinate, and control the work of the group. Instead, it focuses on ensuring that managers have leadership skills (Fulmer, 1997). In this section, we will review some of the common methods that are used for this purpose (Day, 2001).

360 Feedback, Coaching, and Mentoring

As we saw in Chapter 5, feedback is an important tool in leadership development, because employees often are not good observers of how their actions and behaviors affect others. By feeding information from subordinates, colleagues, and higher-level managers back to the focal manager, organizations can create self-awareness. However, simply providing feedback is not sufficient. The focal person would need to be motivated to change, and would have to figure out how to change. This is where coaching comes into play. Coaching, as we discussed in Chapter 8, is a one-on-one, goal-based method of personal change. The coach meets with the person to help them discover the answers to the problems and challenges they encounter. The organization may also utilize mentoring as a way to teach people the norms of the workplace and to provide assistance with problems and challenges.

Developmental Assignments

An essential part of developing leadership capabilities is to take on developmental assignments. Many major organizations see this as the most important part of leadership development. Organizations such as Nike, GE, and Coca-Cola prepare people for future leadership roles by carefully crafting developmental assignments which may involve serving in an overseas assignment, managing a different team, or serving in a role that stretches different "muscles". Through carefully planned assignments, managers are placed in positions where they acquire skills and knowledge that they will need in a higher-level managerial role.

Experience, by itself, is unlikely to lead to self-awareness. Instead, if it is coupled with reflection, it leads to new insights. An experimental study involved having participants take part in a developmental experience where their leadership behaviors were assessed. Then, those in the experimental condition took part in an after-action review, and (with the help of a trained facilitator) reflected on their challenges, how they

Kenneth Chenault, CEO and chairman of American Express since 2001, views his early career experiences as critical forces for his later leadership style. Working as a management consultant early on helped him gain experience in a variety of industries and quickly assess the situation to solve problems. Managing a part of American Express that sells merchandise via mail helped him learn how to run all aspects of business including sales, customer service, and operations, as well as learn how to turn around a low-performing unit (Collis, 2014).

behaved, and how they could have behaved differently. Compared to the control condition, these employees improved their leadership behaviors in the next assignment (DeRue, Nahrgang, Hollenbeck, & Workman, 2012), suggesting that combining developmental experiences with feedback and coaching will yield greater improvements.

Formal Leadership Training

Off-the-job training in a classroom or online setting is usually part of systematic efforts to develop leadership, with over 80 percent of companies utilizing classroom training as part of leadership development (Day, 2001). However, its importance pales in comparison to feedback, coaching, mentoring, and learning by doing. The Center for Creative Leadership proposed the 70-20-10 model of leadership development: 70 percent of the development occurs on the job and through novel and challenging assignments, 20 percent occurs through coaching and mentoring, whereas only 10 percent happens via classroom training (Rabin, 2014). This is because, as we noted in Chapter 8, what is learned in a classroom setting may not immediately transfer to the actual work environment. Despite difficulties in training transfer, classroom training is an important part of leadership development programs.

Workplace Application

Leadership Development at P&G

Each year, *Chief Executive* magazine ranks organizations that do a great job in developing leadership talent. In 2014, P&G was at the top of this list. The company was also consistently in the top five of a similar list compiled by the Hay group since 2005. What exactly does P&G do that sets it apart from others?

P&G Headquarters in Cincinnati, Ohio.

First, P&G emphasizes developing leaders from within. By relying on inside talent when it is time to fill managerial positions, the company ensures that there is a steady supply of willing and able managers with leadership capabilities. This gives managers the motivation to stay in the company and develop their skills. Another motivator is that managers are assessed based on how good they are in developing their followers. Managers who ignore their subordinates and do not work hard to develop, motivate, and listen to them are penalized in their own evaluations.

Second, the company engages in a number of different methods of leadership development. The company has mentoring programs where high-level executives are paired with lower-level managers. They use both developmental assignments and classroom training purposefully. Managers are assigned to positions not only to prove themselves but also to acquire the skills they will need in future roles. The company also uses classroom training by sending future leaders to training programs held in the Center for Creative Leadership in North Carolina and the US Military Academy in West Point.

Sources: Filipkowski & Donlon 2014; Hay Group 2013.

LEGAL ISSUES

Organizations often find themselves in trouble with the law when they engage in actions that society deems to be unethical. Having a discriminatory employment culture, having an unsafe and hazardous workplace environment, producing goods and services that harm customers, bystanders, or the environment could all be among the reasons why corporations were found to have acted illegally and had to pay the price.

Having an organizational culture (Chapter 14) that emphasizes ethical behavior can cut down on misbehavior of organizations. Research shows that whether an organization develops a culture that emphasizes doing the right thing even when it is costly comes down to whether leaders, starting with the CEO, consider the ethical consequences of their actions. Leaders with a moral compass set the tone when it comes to ethical dilemmas. Employees take their ethical cues from their leaders. For example, in 1982, James Burke, then CEO of Johnson & Johnson, faced a crisis: seven people died after taking Tylenol that was laced with cyanide (it was later discovered that the capsules were tampered with). He made the decision to issue a nationwide recall, and spent over $100 million to develop tamper-proof packages and re-release the drug two months later. By putting safety first, acting promptly and with candor, he not only saved the reputation of the company, but also helped create a culture of "doing the right thing" (Moore, 2012). When leaders behave ethically, employees speak up and challenge management more (Walumbwa & Schaubroeck, 2009), protecting organizations from wrongdoing.

Can the manager's leadership style have legal implications? One style we covered in this chapter, abusive supervision, may be illegal under some circumstances. Yelling and screaming at employees, acting like a bully, and terrorizing employees are definitely bad and unethical management practices, but when they target the sex, race, age, or another protected characteristic of the employee, they may also constitute illegal treatment. If the abuse is laced with discriminatory comments directed at the person's protected characteristics, it constitutes illegal harassment. Title VII of the Civil Rights Act, Age Discrimination Act (ADEA), and Americans with Disabilities Act all regard harassment as a violation of the law. To be unlawful, the conduct of the manager does not need to cause economic harm. Insults, put-downs, and other demeaning behavior based on sex, race, religion, age (over 40), color, disability status, and national origin that is persistent and would be offensive to a reasonable person are deemed to be illegal. Furthermore, offensive remarks about someone's sex (such as making derogatory remarks about women in general) as well as unwelcome sexual advances constitute sexual harassment, which is also unlawful under Title VII of the Civil Rights Act. Note also that such acts are illegal regardless of the sex of the victim and harasser. Organizations have a legal obligation to protect their employees from illegal harassment, and if sued, they can only defend themselves by showing that when the harassment was brought to their attention, they promptly tried to correct the behavior and did not retaliate against the victim. Therefore, organizations are advised to create channels so that employees can bring their concerns to upper management without fearing retaliation or negative consequences.

GLOBAL IMPLICATIONS

The Global Leadership and Organizational Behavior Effectiveness (GLOBE) project is a collaboration of over 170 scholars in 62 countries, collecting and analyzing data from over 17,000 managers. The project involved first identifying culture dimensions that distinguished countries. Then, the scholars examined the relationship between culture and dominant leadership styles. The project also identified the culturally endorsed leadership styles in different regions of the world (House, Javidan, Hanges, & Dorfman, 2002).

The GLOBE study provided important insights. It seems that some leadership prototypes vary across cultures and others remain the same. Analyzing results from over 15,000 middle managers from 60 countries, the GLOBE researchers reported that characteristics associated with transformational leadership such as having foresight, being trustworthy, dynamic, and being a confidence builder were universally endorsed. Other characteristics such as being a risk-taker, being self-effacing, self-sacrificing, and being compassionate were contingent on culture. There were also leader attributes that were universally undesirable, including being a loner, being

In low power distance cultures such as the Netherlands, Sweden, or Denmark, a manager biking to work is a familiar sight. This is unlikely to happen in more power distant cultures, where managers are expected to show their power. In a high power distance culture, driving a modest car, let alone riding a bike, will be seen as not fitting the status the manager should have.

irritable, and being dictatorial (Den Hartog, House, Hanges, Ruiz-Quintanilla, & Dorfman, 1999; Javidan, Dorfman, Sully de Luque, & House, 2006).

The degree of power distance is a likely explanation for some cultural differences in leadership. Cultures with high power distance such as Asian and Middle Eastern cultures view the unequal distribution of power to be relatively more acceptable. In these cultures, leaders' authoritarian behaviors are more common, whereas low power distance cultures (such as Scandinavian cultures) emphasize egalitarian norms. In high power distance cultures, leaders are expected to be powerful, so modesty or being self-effacing may not be regarded as important characteristics to have for leaders.

In addition to culture, scholars looked for other explanations for the endorsement of different leadership styles. Van de Vliert (2006) used GLOBE data to show that in countries with harsh climates and poor economies, authoritarian styles were more likely to be endorsed. The argument is that the leadership style that emerges as appropriate in a given geography is not due to chance. Poor countries in difficult geographies may have historically benefited from authoritarian (as opposed to democratic and participative) styles for survival. The historical roots of a dominant leadership style suggests that societal change will be slow, and companies operating in multiple geographies will need to train managers to vary their style depending on where they operate.

How about effectiveness of leadership styles around the world? The GLOBE study recently started to tackle this question. In a study of over 1,000 CEOs and their direct reports in 24 countries, results showed that when CEO leadership style was aligned with the society's expectations of effective leaders, the CEOs were more effective. Further, some leader behaviors such as transformational leadership were universally effective, whereas the effectiveness of others such as participative leadership depended on the cultural context (Dorfman, Javidan, Hanges, Dastmalchian, & House, 2012).

CURRENT ISSUES AND CONTROVERSIES

We have reviewed a large number of leadership theories and discussed many attributes that seem to be related to leadership emergence and effectiveness. Are these attributes truly different from each other? Many scholars argue that the leadership literature suffers from "construct proliferation," which means that we have many theories, frameworks, and labels that essentially may be measuring the same thing. In fact, when all these behaviors and attributes are analyzed together, many lose their predictive validity. This is because the leader behaviors are highly correlated with each other. Imagine that you are given a lengthy questionnaire and are asked to rate your manager with respect to transformational, transactional, authentic, and servant leadership, as well as LMX quality. Chances are, your answers will not be so different, because if you like and trust your manager, you are likely to see your manager in a positive manner, so you will give positive responses to positively worded questions and negative responses to descriptions of socially undesirable behaviors. Therefore, a current challenge in leadership research today is to integrate the leadership theories. Leadership scholars also argue that the bar for a new theory of leadership should now be higher, and those proposing new theories should demonstrate the novelty of what they are proposing (DeRue et al., 2011).

Another current issue is the changing nature of work and leadership. Much of the body of literature on leadership comes from organizations with traditional structures: Managers and employees interact regularly, work in the same location, and employees report to one manager. However, the workplace of the twenty-first century is shaping up to be somewhat different: Increasingly, employees are performing their jobs at home or at a location away from their managers. Oftentimes the manager and the employee may interact only through technology. The unity of command principle, or the idea that each employee reports to one manager only (Chapter 14), is often violated. Does effective leadership in these settings look similar to what we discussed in this chapter? If not, what is different? It will be important to adapt and test contemporary theories in these newer, nontraditional structures before we assume that leaders of yesterday will be similar to leaders of tomorrow. For example, Vidyarthi, Erdogan, Anand, Liden, and Chaudhry (2014) investigated what happens to leadership when employees report to two managers – not a rare situation today. In their study of IT consultants, they showed that when the treatment employees receive from the two leaders diverged (meaning, they have a high-quality relationship with one, but not with the other), employees experience more negative job attitudes and turnover. This is because employees may be comparing their relations with different managers, and if they are very different from each other, the employees feel the loss of what they are missing more keenly. While such studies provide an interesting start, we still don't know what style is more effective and what traits would affect outcomes when leaders are working in tandem and managing the same group.

WHAT DOES THIS MEAN TO YOU?

The theories and concepts described in this chapter can be helpful in improving your effectiveness as a leader or supervisor. For example, you need to demonstrate behaviors that keep the team focused on the task and make sure that things get done and tasks are completed. At the same time, you need to provide support and engage in relational behaviors. As a leader, it is also important to understand the role of the context, such as the nature of the task or the personalities, knowledge, and abilities of your team members. What behaviors do they need the most to be successful? Reading the situation accurately should help you select the type of behaviors that would be most effective. Employees performing stressful yet simple tasks need your support, not direction. Employees performing vague tasks would appreciate clear direction.

There are also actions you can take as a follower. Out of the theories we described, one leadership theory regards leadership as a mutual influence process, and you could use its findings to help increase your effectiveness in your profession. The LMX theory suggests that the relationship you cultivate with your manager is perhaps the most important work-related relationship you will have. Therefore, you may want to be proactive in how you establish this relationship. Your competence and reliability will matter. At the same time, putting in effort to build the relationship will also be helpful. For example, we know that perceived similarity is related to the development of a high-quality relationship. The good news is that every individual is similar to another individual in some ways. You may be different in gender, race, or political affiliations, but in what areas are you alike? Maybe you are both parents. Maybe you both studied in the same city. Maybe you both dislike cilantro in your food. Focusing on similarities rather than differences may put you on the path to a high-quality exchange. Further, employee impression management behaviors make a difference in good relationships. By complimenting your manager's positive actions, recognizing and thanking them for their supportive acts, and volunteering to do things for them at work, you have a lot of opportunities to develop a high-quality exchange. Remember that you have as much power as your manager in the development of this relationship.

Finally, our discussion about leadership development should give you some clues as to how to go about developing your leadership capabilities further. Only 10 percent of your leadership abilities develop as a result of classroom training. You could read books on leadership (and there is a wide selection out there) and participate in online programs, watch TED Talks (http://www.ted.com/talks), and develop these skills independently (see Additional Reading section for ideas). At the same time, you need opportunities to put these skills into practice. You could consider volunteering for assignments giving you opportunities to coordinate and manage other people's work. You could even do this as part of your community service. Finally, seeking feedback about your skills from a senior person you trust and respect may help you hone these skills even further.

Conclusion

Leadership is the ability to get things done by influencing others. It seems that leaders share certain personality traits, but more importantly, effective leaders demonstrate particular behaviors and avoid demonstrating others. These behaviors include paying attention to the task and giving people direction, and supporting employees at a personal level. Leaders may provide the vision and transform the values of the group, or they may motivate by ensuring that high performance is rewarded and employee needs are met. Leadership also involves having honesty and integrity, and being true to oneself, and at times having the ability to put followers first. What seems most important is that effective leadership emerges within the context of a specific group of employees, organizational structure, and culture, and different behaviors may be more effective depending on the context. Effective leaders will be the ones who can read the situation, and modify their behavior depending on the needs of the situation; so developing the flexibility to demonstrate the particular behaviors required by the context is essential.

YOUR TURN...

1. At a university, college professors are sometimes asked to teach night classes. There is often great demand for those courses, given that many students work. Full-time faculty interest in teaching these courses vary – some may prefer teaching evenings and do other things during the day, and others who are "morning people" or with family obligations may prefer to avoid them. Universities may staff those courses with adjunct faculty (who prefer to teach at night as they hold full-time jobs in the industry during the day). Imagine that a group of students from one major complain to the dean that they are having difficulty signing up for evening classes because there are not enough course offerings. The dean is considering e-mailing all faculty, announcing to them that they are now required to teach one evening section a year to be fair to all faculty.

a. What decision style would this be according to Vroom and Yetton's model?

b. What would be the potential consequences of this decision? Would this decision be fair?

c. According to Vroom and Yetton's model, what should the dean do?

2. Think about a leader you are familiar with, preferably a leader you worked with. Which leadership theory would describe his/her style? Do you feel that this style fits the conditions under which you worked? Which style would have been more appropriate?

3. If you were tasked with writing a blog post titled "Seven rules for leadership" what would be the rules that you would discuss?

4. If you were interviewing someone applying for a leadership position, what questions would you ask or which method would you use as part of the hiring process to assess the person's leadership potential?

5. Do effective leaders do anything other than what was discussed in this chapter? In your opinion, what are the behaviors, traits, or attributes effective leaders have that were not discussed?

Additional Reading

Cain, S. (2012). *Quiet: The power of introverts in a world that can't stop talking.* New York: Broadway Paperbacks.

Covey, S. R. (2013). *Seven habits of highly effective people.* New York: Simon & Schuster.

Gardner, H. (2011). *Leading minds: An anatomy of leadership.* New York: Basic Books.

Goleman, D., Boyatzis, R., & McKee, A. (2013). *Primal leadership: Unleashing the power of emotional intelligence.* Boston, MA: Harvard Business Review Press.

House, R. J., Hanges, P. J., Javidan, M., Dorfman, P. W., & Gupta, V. (2004). *Culture, leadership, and organizations: The GLOBE study of 62 societies.* Thousand Oaks, CA: Sage.

Kouzes, J., & Posner, B. (2012). *The leadership challenge: How to make extraordinary things happen in organizations.* San Francisco, CA: Jossey Bass.

TED Talks. https://www.ted.com/topics/leadership. Some examples of short talks relating to leadership including Simon Sinek's *Why good leaders make you feel safe*, Rosalinde Torres' *What it takes to be a great leader*, and Sheryl Sandberg's *Why we have too few women leaders*.

CASE STUDY: Jeff Bezos at the Helm of Amazon

Amazon.com is without a doubt one of the most successful companies in the world, and the success story of the Internet era. Founded in Jeff Bezos' garage in Seattle in 1994, the company quickly became the largest bookseller in the world, and then became one of the largest online marketplaces in the world, and then became the manufacturer of Kindle e-book readers and a provider of cloud computing businesses. It is a $75 billion-a-year business, still being managed by its founder. Building something from the ground up is practically the definition of leadership effectiveness, so Bezos is clearly an effective leader. But who is he, and how does he lead the company he built?

Bezos is only 50 years old as of this writing. One of his formative influences was his stepfather, a Cuban immigrant who put himself through college by sheer determination and grit, and then rose through the ranks at Exxon as a petroleum engineer. Bezos himself studied engineering in Princeton, but at the height of the dot.com era left his high-paying job at a hedge fund company at the age of 30 to start Amazon. If you are curious about his personal life, there is not much information about it out there, perhaps because he is famously reluctant to talk about himself. Instead, he prefers to talk about the new products and developments in his business. So we have to look at his business to understand who he is and how he leads.

Amazon's mission statement is "to be Earth's most customer-centric company, where customers can find and discover anything they might want to buy online, and endeavors to offer its customers the lowest possible prices." He lives by these values. He is known to be very frugal. He has a modest salary (around $80,000) and does not get bonuses (but owns 20 percent of the company, so there is no question that he is wealthy). His philosophy is to spend money on things that make a difference in the customer experience, but nothing else. Amazon employees make industry-average salaries. They get restricted stock, but they vest toward the end of a four year period, so newcomers who stay one or two years get little to nothing. In the 1990s, Bezos avoided giving employees bus passes with the argument that he did not want employees to run out the door to catch the bus. There is no free or subsidized food (but vending machines accept credit cards). Newcomers are given a backpack and a few pieces of equipment when hired, and when leaving the company they are asked to return everything, including the backpack.

Bezos' leadership can be summarized as putting customers first. He has access to amazing amounts of data, and can see how .1 second delay in the loading of a webpage affects customer activity on the page. So at Amazon, decisions are made based on data. At the same time, anecdotal evidence carries a lot of weight as well. One of the scarier things for Amazon leaders is to receive a forwarded e-mail about a customer complaint, with an added question mark. This is a call to action and everyone is expected to drop everything else and fix the problem: What happened? What went wrong? Bezos expects a quick answer and a solution to any customer e-mail he receives. In fact, he has a public e-mail address (jeff@amazon.com) and he reads and takes action on these messages himself. A famous anecdote about his customer focus is that he always leaves a chair empty at meetings, and tells attendees that they should consider that chair to be occupied by the most important person in the room: the customer.

The idea to put customers first often means that short-term shareholder value is not his concern. He makes decisions to improve the customer experience and create customer loyalty. Therefore his interest is in long-term growth, and he is very open about this fact. Early on, a book publisher asked him why he allowed negative reviews on the website, stating "don't you make money when you sell things?" His answer was that they don't make money when they sell things, but when they help customers make purchasing decisions.

Bezos is a demanding boss and working with him is not easy. Similar to other high-tech leaders with abrasive personalities, he reportedly has a mean streak. He has a temper that shows itself when confronted with what he considers incompetence. Some quotes collected from his subordinates include "Are you lazy, or just incompetent?"; "Why are you wasting my life?"; and "This document was clearly written by the B team. Can someone get me the A team document? I don't want to waste my time with the B team document." Those who work with him think that he lacks empathy and treats employees as expendable resources. At the same time, he is viewed as an intelligent person who tends to be right. Even those on the other side of his temper often grudgingly report that he was right. The culture he created is highly confrontational: He does not believe in the value of group cohesion and expects everyone to challenge each other for the sake of the best idea. Managers who supervise more than 50 employees are expected to rate employees on a curve and terminate the least-effective employees. Many employees say that working with him is uncomfortable, but that it is exciting, intense, and full of learning opportunities. Not to mention, full of surprises: When Bezos personally acquired the major newspaper *Washington Post* in 2013 for $250 million, he attracted worldwide attention. What is his grand plan for this ailing major newspaper that has been struggling to adapt to the digital age? Only time will tell.

Questions

1. Using each of the leadership theories discussed in this chapter, describe Jeff Bezos' leadership style. Which behaviors does he demonstrate? Which leadership theory explains his actions and influence the best?

2. Which aspects of Bezos' leadership do you feel are responsible for the success of Amazon.com? Which aspects are potentially detrimental to the success of the company?

3. Which aspects of Bezos' leadership style would you want to emulate?

4. Would you have wanted to work with a leader such as Bezos? Would you have been effective when working with such a leader?

5. Do you think this leadership style is important and useful in all kinds of businesses across industries? Which industries and companies would find Bezos' style ineffective or at least less effective?

Sources: This case is partially based on information contained in Hansen, Ibarra, & Peyer (2013); Inside Amazon's culture of metrics (2012); Maurer (2012); Murphy, Lyons, & Adamo (2011); Rieder (2013); Stone (2013); Wingfield & Streitfeld (2013).

References

Algera, P. M., & Lips-Wiersma, M. (2012). Radical authentic leadership: Co-creating the conditions under which all members of the organization can be authentic. *Leadership Quarterly, 23,* 118–131.

Aquino, J. (2011). 8 traits of stellar managers, defined by Googlers. *Business Insider,* March 15. Retrieved October 2, 2014, from http://www.businessinsider.com/8-traits-of-stellar-managers-defined-by-googlers-2011-3?op=1&IR=T.

Arvey, R. D., Rotundo, M., Johnson, W., Zhang, Z., & McGue, M. (2006). The determinants of leadership role occupancy: Genetic and personality factors. *Leadership Quarterly, 17,* 1–20.

Ballinger, G. A., Lehman, D. W., & Schoorman, F. D. (2010). Leader–member exchange and turnover before and after succession events. *Organizational Behavior and Human Decision Processes, 113,* 25–36.

Barling, J., Weber, T., & Kelloway, E. K. (1996). Effects of transformational leadership training on attitudinal and financial outcomes: A field experiment. *Journal of Applied Psychology, 81,* 827–832.

Bass, B. M. (1991). From transactional to transformational leadership: Learning to share the vision. *Organizational Dynamics, 18,* 19–31.

Bass, B. M., Avolio, B. J., Jung, D. I., & Berson, Y. (2003). Predicting unit performance by assessing transformational and transactional leadership. *Journal of Applied Psychology, 88,* 207–218.

Bauer, T. N., & Erdogan, B. (2015). *The Oxford handbook of leader–member exchange.* New York: Oxford University Press.

Bauer, T. N., Erdogan, B., Liden, R. C., & Wayne, S. J. (2006). A longitudinal study of the moderating role of extraversion: Leader–member exchange, performance, and turnover during new executive development. *Journal of Applied Psychology, 91,* 298–310.

Bauer, T. N., & Green, S. G. (1996). Development of leader–member exchange: A longitudinal test. *Academy of Management Journal, 39,* 1538–1567.

Bersin, J. (2014). Spending on corporate training soars: Employee capabilities now a priority. Forbes.com, February 4, 2014. Retrieved October 10, 2014, from http://www.forbes.com/sites/joshbersin/2014/02/04/the-recovery-arrives-corporate-training-spend-skyrockets/.

Bryant, A. (2014). To succeed, fly like a bumblebee. *New York Times,* September 7, Business News: p. 2(L).

Bureau of Labor Statistics. (2013). *Labor force statistics from the current population survey.* Retrieved September 30, 2014, from http://www.bls.gov/cps/cpsaat08.htm.

Burns, J. M. (1978). *Leadership.* New York: Harper & Row.

Catalyst. (2014). *Women CEOs of Fortune 1000.* Catalyst, September 19. Retrieved September 30, 2014, from http://www.catalyst.org/knowledge/women-ceos-fortune-1000.

Cavazotte, F., Moreno, V., & Hickmann, M. (2012). Effects of leader intelligence, personality and emotional intelligence on transformational leadership and managerial performance. *Leadership Quarterly, 23,* 443–455.

Colbert, A. E., Judge, T. A., Choi, D., & Wang, G. (2012). Assessing the trait theory of leadership using self and observer ratings of personality: The mediating role of contributions to group success. *Leadership Quarterly, 23*, 670–685.

Collis, C. (2014, March). The service ethic. *Business Strategy Review, 25*(1), 30–32.

Conger, J. A., & Kanungo, R. N. (1998). *Charismatic leadership in organizations.* Thousand Oaks, CA: Sage.

Cook, A., & Glass, C. (2013). Above the glass ceiling: When are women and racial/ethnic minorities promoted to CEO? *Strategic Management Journal, 35*, 1080–1089.

Cooper, C. D., Scandura, T. A., & Schriesheim, C. A. (2005). Looking forward but learning from our past: Potential challenges to developing authentic leadership theory and authentic leaders. *Leadership Quarterly, 16*, 475–493.

Dansereau, F. Jr., Graen, G., & Haga, W. J. (1975). A vertical dyad linkage approach to leadership within formal organizations: A longitudinal investigation of the role making process. *Organizational Behavior and Human Performance, 13*, 46–78.

Day, D. V. (2001). Leadership development: A review in context. *Leadership Quarterly, 11*, 581–613.

Den Hartog, D. N., House, R. J., Hanges, P. J., Ruiz-Quintanilla, S. A., & Dorfman, P. W. (1999). Culture specific and cross-culturally generalizable implicit leadership theories: Are attributes of charismatic/transformational leadership universally endorsed? *Leadership Quarterly, 10*, 219–256.

DeRue, D. S., Nahrgang, J. D., Hollenbeck, J. R., & Workman, K. (2012). A quasi-experimental study of after-event reviews and leadership development. *Journal of Applied Psychology, 97*, 997–1015.

DeRue, D. S., Nahrgang, J. D., Wellman, N. E. D., & Humphrey, S. E. (2011). Trait and behavioral theories of leadership: An integration and meta-analytic test of their relative validity. *Personnel Psychology, 64*, 7–52.

DiversityInc. (2015). Where's the diversity in Fortune 500 CEOs? *Diversity*, July 28–August 3. Retrieved January 20, 2015, from http://www.diversityinc.com/diversity-facts/wheres-the-diversity-in-fortune-500-ceos/.

Dorfman, P., Javidan, M., Hanges, P., Dastmalchian, A., & House, R. (2012). GLOBE: A twenty year journey into the intriguing world of culture and leadership. *Journal of World Business, 47*, 504–518.

Duarte, N. T., Goodson, J. R., & Klich, N. R. (1993). How do I like thee? Let me appraise the ways. *Journal of Organizational Behavior, 14*, 239–249.

Dulebohn, J. H., Bommer, W. H., Liden, R. C., Brouer, R. L., & Ferris, G. R. (2012). A meta-analysis of antecedents and consequences of leader–member exchange: Integrating the past with an eye toward the future. *Journal of Management, 38*, 1715–1759.

Eagly, A. H., Johannesen-Schmidt, M. C., & Van Engen, M. L. (2003). Transformational, transactional, and laissez-faire leadership styles: A meta-analysis comparing women and men. *Psychological Bulletin, 129*, 569–591.

Eagly, A. H., & Johnson, B. T. (1990). Gender and leadership style: A meta-analysis. *Psychological Bulletin, 108*, 233–256.

Elias, S. (2008). Fifty years of influence in the workplace: The evolution of the French and Raven power taxonomy. *Journal of Management History, 14*, 267–283.

Erdogan, B., & Bauer, T. N. (2010). Differentiated leader–member exchanges: The buffering role of justice climate. *Journal of Applied Psychology, 95,* 1104–1120.

Erdogan, B., & Bauer, T. N. (2014). Leader–member exchange (LMX) theory: The relational approach to leadership. In D. Day (Ed.), *The Oxford handbook of leadership and organization.* (pp. 407–433). New York: Oxford University Press.

Erdogan, B., & Enders, J. (2007). Support from the top: Supervisors' perceived organizational support as a moderator of leader–member exchange to satisfaction and performance relationships. *Journal of Applied Psychology, 92,* 321–330.

Fiedler, F. (1964). A contingency model of leadership effectiveness. *Advances in Experimental Social Psychology, 1,* 149–190.

Fiedler, F. E. (1971). Validation and extension of the contingency model of leadership effectiveness: A review of empirical findings. *Psychological Bulletin, 76,* 128–148.

Field, R. G. (1982). A test of the Vroom-Yetton normative model of leadership. *Journal of Applied Psychology, 67,* 523–532.

Filipkowski, J., & Donlon, J. P. (2014). 2014 best companies for leaders. *Chief Executive,* January 14. Retrieved October 10, 2014, from http://chiefexecutive. net/2014-best-companies-for-leaders.

Foti, R. J., & Hauenstein, N. (2007). Pattern and variable approaches in leadership emergence and effectiveness. *Journal of Applied Psychology, 92,* 347–355.

French, J. R. P., & Raven, B. (1959). The bases of social power. In D. Cartwright (Ed). *Studies in social power* (pp. 150–167). Oxford, England: University of Michigan Press.

Fulmer, R. M. (1997). The evolving paradigm of leadership development. *Organizational Dynamics, 25,* 59–72.

Gerstner, C. R., & Day, D. V. (1997). Meta-analytic review of leader–member exchange theory: Correlates and construct issues. *Journal of Applied Psychology, 82,* 827–844.

Graham, J. W. (1991). Servant-leadership in organizations: Inspirational and moral. *Leadership Quarterly, 2,* 105–119.

Grant, A. M., Gino, F., & Hofmann, D. A. (2011). Reversing the extraverted leadership advantage: The role of employee proactivity. *Academy of Management Journal, 54,* 528–550.

Greenleaf, R. K. (1977). *Servant leadership, Vol. 7.* New York: Paulist Press.

Hansen, M. T., Ibarra, H., & Peyer, U. (2013, January–February). The best-performing CEOs in the world. *Harvard Business Review,* 81–95.

Hay Group. (2013). *2013 global top 20.* Retrieved October 10, 2014, from http:// www.haygroup.com/bestcompaniesforleadership/research-and-findings/ global-top-20.aspx.

Heilman, M. E., Wallen, A. S., Fuchs, D., & Tamkins, M. M. (2004). Penalties for success: Reactions to women who succeed at male tasks. *Journal of Applied Psychology, 89,* 416–427.

Hinkin, T. R., & Schriesheim, C. A. (1989). Development and application of new scales to measure the French and Raven (1959) bases of social power. *Journal of Applied Psychology, 74,* 561–567.

Hogan, R., Curphy, G. J., & Hogan, J. (1994). What we know about leadership: Effectiveness and personality. *American Psychologist, 49*, 493–504.

Hoobler, J. M., & Brass, D. J. (2006). Abusive supervision and family undermining as displaced aggression. *Journal of Applied Psychology, 91*, 1125–1133.

Hoobler, J. M., Wayne, S. J., & Lemmon, G. (2009). Bosses' perceptions of family–work conflict and women's promotability: Glass ceiling effects. *Academy of Management Journal, 52*, 939–957.

Hooper, D. T., & Martin, R. (2008). Beyond personal leader–member exchange (LMX) quality: The effects of perceived LMX variability on employee reactions. *Leadership Quarterly, 19*, 20–30.

House, R. J. (1971). A path-goal theory of leader effectiveness. *Administrative Science Quarterly, 16*, 321–339.

House, R. J. (1996). Path-goal theory of leadership: Lessons, legacy, and a reformulated theory. *Leadership Quarterly, 7*, 323–352.

House, R. J., & Aditya, R. N. (1997). The social scientific study of leadership: Quo vadis? *Journal of Management, 23*, 409–473.

House, R., Javidan, M., Hanges, P., & Dorfman, P. (2002). Understanding cultures and implicit leadership theories across the globe: An introduction to project GLOBE. *Journal of World Business, 37*, 3–10.

House, R. J., & Mitchell, R. R. (1974). Path-goal theory of leadership. *Journal of Contemporary Business, 3*, 81–97.

Hu, J., & Liden, R. C. (2011). Antecedents of team potency and team effectiveness: An examination of goal and process clarity and servant leadership. *Journal of Applied Psychology, 96*, 851–862.

Hu, J., & Liden, R. C. (2013). Relative leader–member exchange within team contexts: How and when social comparison impacts individual effectiveness. *Personnel Psychology, 66*, 127–172.

Inside Amazon's culture of metrics. (2012, June). *Executive Leadership, 27*, 1–2.

Jago, A. G. (1982). Leadership: Perspectives in theory and research. *Management Science, 28*, 315–336.

Javidan, M., Dorfman, P. W., Sully de Luque, M., & House, R. J. (2006, February). In the eye of the beholder: Cross cultural lessons in leadership from project GLOBE. *Academy of Management Perspectives, 20*, 67–90.

Javidan, M., House, R. J., Dorfman, P. W., Hanges, P. J., & Sully de Luque, M. (2006). Conceptualizing and measuring cultures and their consequences: A comparative review of GLOBE's and Hofstede's approaches. *Journal of International Business Studies, 37*, 897–914.

Johnson, A. M., Vernon, P. A., Harris, J. A., & Jang, K. L. (2004). A behavior genetic investigation of the relationship between leadership and personality. *Twin Research, 7*, 27–32.

Judge, T. A., Bono, J. E., Ilies, R., & Gerhardt, M. W. (2002). Personality and leadership: A qualitative and quantitative review. *Journal of Applied Psychology, 87*, 765–780.

Judge, T. A., Colbert, A. E., & Ilies, R. (2004). Intelligence and leadership: A quantitative review and test of theoretical propositions. *Journal of Applied Psychology, 89*, 542–552.

Judge, T. A., & Piccolo, R. F. (2004). Transformational and transactional leadership: A meta-analytic test of their relative validity. *Journal of Applied Psychology, 89,* 755-768.

Judge, T. A., Piccolo, R. F., & Ilies, R. (2004). The forgotten ones? The validity of consideration and initiating structure in leadership research. *Journal of Applied Psychology, 89,* 36.

Jung, D. I., & Avolio, B. J. (2000). Opening the black box: An experimental investigation of the mediating effects of trust and value congruence on transformational and transactional leadership. *Journal of Organizational Behavior, 21,* 949-964.

Kark, R., Waismel-Manor, R., & Shamir, B. (2012). Does valuing androgyny and femininity lead to a female advantage? The relationship between gender-role, transformational leadership and identification. *Leadership Quarterly, 23,* 620-640.

Koenig, A. M., Eagly, A. H., Mitchell, A. A., & Ristikari, T. (2011). Are leader stereotypes masculine? A meta-analysis of three research paradigms. *Psychological Bulletin, 137,* 616-642.

Korman, A. K. (1966). "Consideration," "Initiating Structure," and organizational criteria: A review. *Personnel Psychology, 19,* 349-361.

Leroy, H., Anseel, F., Gardner, W. L., & Sels, L. (in press). Authentic leadership, authentic followership, basic need satisfaction, and work role performance: A cross-level study. *Journal of Management.*

Liden, R. C., Wayne, S. J., & Sparrowe, R. T. (2000). An examination of the mediating role of psychological empowerment on the relations between the job, interpersonal relationships, and work outcomes. *Journal of Applied Psychology, 85,* 407-416.

Liden, R. C., Wayne, S. J., & Stilwell, D. (1993). A longitudinal study on the early development of leader–member exchanges. *Journal of Applied Psychology, 78,* 662-674.

Liden, R. C., Wayne, S. J., Zhao, H., & Henderson, D. (2008). Servant leadership: Development of a multidimensional measure and multi-level assessment. *Leadership Quarterly, 19,* 161-177.

Lord, R. G., De Vader, C. L., & Alliger, G. M. (1986). A meta-analysis of the relation between personality traits and leadership perceptions: An application of validity generalization procedures. *Journal of Applied Psychology, 71,* 402-410.

Lord, R. G., Foti, R. J., & De Vader, C. L. (1984). A test of leadership categorization theory: Internal structure, information processing, and leadership perceptions. *Organizational Behavior and Human Performance, 34,* 343-378.

Lowe, K. B., Kroeck, K. G., & Sivasubramaniam, N. (1996). Effectiveness correlates of transformational and transactional leadership: A meta-analytic review of the MLQ literature. *Leadership Quarterly, 7,* 385-425.

Maurer, R. (2012, July). The power of the empty chair. *Journal for Quality & Participation,* 10-11.

Meindl, J. R., Ehrlich, S. B., & Dukerich, J. M. (1985). The romance of leadership. *Administrative Science Quarterly, 30,* 78-102.

Mitchell, M. S., & Ambrose, M. L. (2007). Abusive supervision and workplace deviance and the moderating effects of negative reciprocity beliefs. *Journal of Applied Psychology, 92,* 1159–1168.

Moore, T. (2012). The fight to save Tylenol. *Fortune,* October 7. Retrieved October 14, 2014, from http://fortune.com/2012/10/07/the-fight-to-save-tylenol-fortune-1982/.

Murphy, R., Lyons, C., & Adamo, M. (2011). The 2011 businessperson of the year. *Fortune International, 164,* December 12.

Nahrgang, J. D., Morgeson, F. P., & Ilies, R. (2009). The development of leader–member exchanges: Exploring how personality and performance influence leader and member relationships over time. *Organizational Behavior and Human Decision Processes, 108,* 256–266.

Ospina, S., & Foldy, E. G. (2009). A critical review of race and ethnicity in the leadership literature: Surfacing context, power and the collective dimensions of leadership. *Leadership Quarterly, 20,* 876–896.

Park, S. H., & Westphal, J. D. (2013). Social discrimination in the corporate elite: How status affects the propensity for minority CEOs to receive blame for low firm performance. *Administrative Science Quarterly, 58,* 542–586.

Paustian-Underdahl, S. C., Walker, L. S., & Woehr, D. J. (2014). Gender and perceptions of leadership effectiveness: A meta-analysis of contextual moderators. *Journal of Applied Psychology, 99,* 1129–1145.

Peters, L. H., Hartke, D. D., & Pohlmann, J. T. (1985). Fiedler's contingency theory of leadership: An application of the meta-analysis procedures of Schmidt and Hunter. *Psychological Bulletin, 97,* 274–285.

Peterson, S. J., Galvin, B. M., & Lange, D. (2012). CEO servant leadership: Exploring executive characteristics and firm performance. *Personnel Psychology, 65,* 565–596.

Rabin, R. (2014). *Blended learning for leadership: The CCL approach.* Center for Creative Leadership White Paper. Retrieved October 13, 2014, from http://www.ccl.org/Leadership/pdf/research/BlendedLearningLeadership.pdf.

Raven, B. H. (1992). A power/interaction model of interpersonal influence: French and Raven thirty years later. *Journal of Social Behavior and Personality, 7,* 217–244.

Rego, A., Sousa, F., Marques, C., & Pina e Cunha, M. (2012). Optimism predicting employees' creativity: The mediating role of positive affect and the positivity ratio. *European Journal of Work and Organizational Psychology, 21,* 244–270.

Rieder, R. (2013). What's Jeff Bezos' plan for the "Post"? *USA Today,* September 3.

Rosette, A. S., Leonardelli, G. J., & Phillips, K. W. (2008). The White standard: Racial bias in leader categorization. *Journal of Applied Psychology, 93,* 758–777.

Rosette, A. S., & Livingston, R. W. (2012). Failure is not an option for black women: Effects of organizational performance on leaders with single versus dual-subordinate identities. *Journal of Experimental Social Psychology, 48,* 1162–1167.

Rost, J. C. (1993). *Leadership for the twenty-first century.* Westport, CT: Praeger Publishing.

Ryan, M. K., & Haslam, S. A. (2007). The glass cliff: Exploring the dynamics surrounding the appointment of women to precarious leadership positions. *Academy of Management Review, 32,* 549–572.

Ryan, M. K., Haslam, S. A., Hersby, M. D., & Bongiorno, R. (2011). Think crisis–think female: The glass cliff and contextual variation in the think manager–think male stereotype. *Journal of Applied Psychology, 96,* 470–484.

Sanchez-Hucles, J. V., & Davis, D. D. (2010). Women and women of color in leadership: Complexity, identity, and intersectionality. *American Psychologist, 65,* 171–181.

Schein, V. E., Mueller, R., Lituchy, T., & Liu, J. (1996). Think manager–think male: A global phenomenon? *Journal of Organizational Behavior, 17,* 33–41.

Shamir, B., House, R. J., & Arthur, M. B. (1993). The motivational effects of charismatic leadership: A self-concept based theory. *Organization Science, 4,* 577–594.

Smircich, L., & Morgan, G. (1982). Leadership: The management of meaning. *Journal of Applied Behavioral Science, 18,* 257–273.

Sparrowe, R. T. (2005). Authentic leadership and the narrative self. *Leadership Quarterly, 16,* 419–439.

Sparrowe, R. T., & Liden, R. C. (2005). Two routes to influence: Integrating leader–member exchange and social network perspectives. *Administrative Science Quarterly, 50,* 505–535.

Stogdill, R. M. (1948). Personal factors associated with leadership: A survey of the literature. *Journal of Psychology, 25,* 35–71.

Stone, B. (2013). The secrets of Bezos. *Bloomberg Businessweek, 4350,* October 14.

Sy, T., Shore, L. M., Strauss, J., Shore, T. H., Tram, S., Whiteley, P., & Ikeda-Muromachi, K. (2010). Leadership perceptions as a function of race-occupation fit: The case of Asian Americans. *Journal of Applied Psychology, 95,* 902–919.

Tepper, B. J. (2000). Consequences of abusive supervision. *Academy of Management Journal, 43,* 178–190.

Tepper, B. J., Duffy, M. K., Henle, C. A., & Lambert, L. S. (2006). Procedural injustice, victim precipitation, and abusive supervision. *Personnel Psychology, 59,* 101–123.

Thomas, A. B. (1988). Does leadership make a difference to organizational performance? *Administrative Science Quarterly, 33,* 388–400.

Van de Vliert, E. (2006). Autocratic leadership around the globe: Do climate and wealth drive leadership culture? *Journal of Cross-Cultural Psychology, 37,* 42–59.

Van Dierendonck, D. (2011). Servant leadership: A review and synthesis. *Journal of Management, 37,* 1228–1261.

Vecchio, R. P. (2002). Leadership and gender advantage. *Leadership Quarterly, 13,* 643–671.

Vidyarthi, P. R., Erdogan, B., Anand, S., Liden, R. C., & Chaudhry, A. (2014). One member, two leaders: Extending leader–member exchange theory to a dual leadership context. *Journal of Applied Psychology, 99,* 468–483.

Vidyarthi, P. R., Liden, R. C., Anand, S., Erdogan, B., & Ghosh, S. (2010). Where do I stand? Examining the effects of leader–member exchange social comparison on employee work behaviors. *Journal of Applied Psychology, 95,* 849–861.

Vroom, V. H. (2000). Leadership and the decision-making process. *Organizational Dynamics, 28,* 82–94.

Vroom, V. H., & Jago, A. G. (2007). The role of the situation in leadership. *American Psychologist, 62,* 17–24.

Vroom, V. H. & Yetton, P. W. (1973). *Leadership and decision-making.* Pittsburgh, PA: University of Pittsburgh Press.

Wakabayashi, D. (2014). Tim Cook's vision for "his" Apple begins to emerge; CEO pushes executives to be more collaborative, broaden its legendary laser focus. *Wall Street Journal,* July 7.

Walumbwa, F. O., Avolio, B. J., Gardner, W. L., Wernsing, T. S., & Peterson, S. J. (2008). Authentic leadership: Development and validation of a theory-based measure. *Journal of Management, 34,* 89–126.

Walumbwa, F. O., Hartnell, C. A., & Oke, A. (2010). Servant leadership, procedural justice climate, service climate, employee attitudes, and organizational citizenship behavior: A cross-level investigation. *Journal of Applied Psychology, 95,* 517–529.

Walumbwa, F. O., & Schaubroeck, J. (2009). Leader personality traits and employee voice behavior: Mediating roles of ethical leadership and work group psychological safety. *Journal of Applied Psychology, 94,* 1275–1286.

Wang, H., Sui, Y., Luthans, F., Wang, D., & Wu, Y. (2014). Impact of authentic leadership on performance: Role of followers' positive psychological capital and relational processes. *Journal of Organizational Behavior, 35,* 5–21.

Wayne, S. J., Liden, R. C., Kraimer, M. L., & Graf, I. K. (1999). The role of human capital, motivation and supervisor sponsorship in predicting career success. *Journal of Organizational Behavior, 20,* 577–595.

Wingfield, N., & Streitfeld, D. (2013). A mogul gets a landmark in the capital. *New York Times,* August 6.

Wofford, J. C., & Liska, L. Z. (1993). Path-goal theories of leadership: A meta-analysis. *Journal of Management, 19,* 857–876.

Zellars, K. L., Tepper, B. J., & Duffy, M. K. (2002). Abusive supervision and subordinates' organizational citizenship behavior. *Journal of Applied Psychology, 87,* 1068–1076.

Chapter 11

JOB ATTITUDES AND EMOTIONS AT WORK

A sense of satisfaction with one's job and the experience of positive emotions are both associated with positive outcomes at work. In this chapter, we discuss job attitudes and emotions in relation to workplace behavior.

After studying this chapter, you should be able to:

- explain why work attitudes are important to organizations
- contrast job satisfaction and organizational commitment
- explain the antecedents and consequences of job attitudes
- identify the role of emotions in workplace behaviors
- identify key legal and global issues surrounding job attitudes and emotions at work
- describe the current issues and controversies around job attitudes and emotions at work.

Learning goals for this chapter

Introduction

How people feel about their jobs is a topic of much investigation and interest in I/O psychology. As of this writing, a search in the PsycINFO database, which is a collection of scientific articles in psychology and related disciplines, reveals over 33,000 articles, book chapters, and dissertations on the topic of just one type of job attitude, job satisfaction. You may also have come across the topic of job attitudes in the popular press. For example, a study by the Society for Human Resources Management in 2012 shows that 81 percent of US workers reported being at least somewhat satisfied with their jobs. In short, happiness at work is often measured, talked about, and thought to be relevant to workplace behavior.

Employee feelings about their jobs can have important consequences. In fact, **job attitudes**, or feelings and beliefs about one's job, organization, supervisor, or another aspect of the workplace, tend to be related to behaviors and outcomes that organizations care about. At the same time, some of what the systematic, empirical research has shown about job attitudes may surprise you. In this chapter, we discuss job attitudes that are most relevant to workplace behaviors and examine how work attitudes develop. I/O psychologists are often interested in the measurement of job attitudes, and therefore we will also discuss different ways in which job attitudes can be measured in organizations and tracked to enhance organizational health. Finally, we will cover the experience of emotions in the workplace on a day-to-day basis and review findings relating to the expression and suppression of emotions in the workplace.

> **Job attitudes:** Feelings and beliefs about one's job, organization, supervisor, or another aspect of the workplace.

Why Do Job Attitudes Matter?

Job attitudes are related to behaviors. But why? The reason may become clearer if we look more closely at a job attitude. As shown in Figure 11.1, job attitudes are thought to have three parts including cognitive (our beliefs), affective (our emotions), and behavioral (our intentions to behave in a particular way) components (Rosenberg & Hovland, 1960). For example, you may have a positive attitude toward your manager. You may believe that she is rational and fair (cognitive), feel a sense of liking and loyalty to her (affective), and may intend to continue to work with her and work extra hard to help her (behavioral).

Individuals prefer their attitudes and behaviors to be aligned. Otherwise, we experience a sense of **cognitive dissonance**, which refers to the discomfort we experience when our attitudes and behaviors are not aligned (Festinger, 1962). For example, if you feel very strongly about caring for the environment, you would likely try to avoid using plastic bags. If, for some reason, you find yourself having to use plastic bags at a store, you would probably rationalize your use of plastic bags (I usually bring my own bags, so just once in a while is OK), push the inconsistent behavior to the back of your mind, change your attitudes (maybe I am not so green after all?), or change your behavior (return the plastic bag). Having behaviors that conflict with your attitudes is uncomfortable and poses a threat to one's self-image (Steele, Spencer, & Lynch, 1993). Similarly, when employees have negative attitudes toward their manager, doing favors for the manager will be stressful because it results in a misalignment between attitudes and

> **Cognitive dissonance:** Discomfort experienced when attitudes and behaviors are not aligned.

Figure 11.1
Components of
job attitudes.

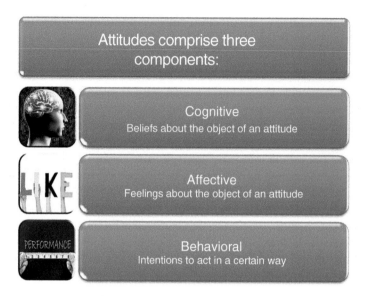

Attitudes comprise three
components:

Cognitive
Beliefs about the object of an attitude

Affective
Feelings about the object of an attitude

Behavioral
Intentions to act in a certain way

behaviors. We usually try to avoid situations like this, and when it is unavoidable, we may justify it to ourselves ("He is really not so bad ..." or "If I help him, he may get a promotion, and I may end up with a different boss ...").

Even though individuals will try to behave in ways that are consistent with their attitudes, this may not always be possible. Someone who is happy at work may still leave their job for reasons such as a desire to try something new, the need to move to another town for family reasons, or because they are offered a salary that they cannot pass up. An employee who is happy at work may be less likely to actively search for a job, but given how complicated human motives are, the correlation between what we feel and how we act isn't always high. In other words, people may behave in ways that are not consistent with their attitudes because there are other factors – such as people in the work environment or in their personal lives – that affect their behavior.

Also, attitudes are related to behaviors if the target of the attitude and behavior are consistent (Ajzen & Fishbein, 1977). For example, satisfaction with one's manager may strongly predict one's behaviors toward the manager, such as volunteering to help the manager with a work issue, but it would be a weaker predictor of doing a personal favor for a coworker. Conversely, satisfaction with social activities at work may predict whether you go to the company picnic next year, but it probably would not mean that you would work harder or help out your boss more. Therefore, when trying to understand the attitude to behavior relationship, we should not have the unrealistic expectation that loving one aspect of one's job would translate into all kinds of positive behaviors.

Theory of planned behavior: A theory that describes the conditions under which attitudes would relate to behaviors. According to the theory, behavior is a function of intentions, norms, and control.

Finally, as presented in Figure 11.2, the **theory of planned behavior** by Ajzen (1991) describes when attitudes do and do not relate to behaviors by describing factors that limit the effects of attitudes on behavior. Specifically, behavior is a direct consequence of *intentions*. Let's take a specific behavior as an example: quitting your job. Before you quit your job, you would develop an intention to quit your job. Where would this come from? Your *attitudes* toward your job and company are certainly important reasons, but there are two other influences: norms and control. *Norms* would indicate whether it is appropriate to others to display this behavior. Would others approve or disapprove this behavior? For example, if you have a lot of credit card and student loan debt and you are the sole income earner in your family, you may feel that given your family needs, it would not be appropriate to quit your job now. Or, if you feel a strong attachment to your colleagues at work, you might decide that leaving now in the middle of a project would not be appropriate, so you may delay your action so as not to inconvenience your colleagues. Finally, *control* refers to factors that would make it easier or more difficult to perform this behavior. For example, you might feel that due to a recession and high unemployment rate, even if you wanted to quit, it would be challenging to find a new job, so you may feel that you are unable to quit now. Alternatively, if you feel that your skills are highly marketable and you can find a new job easily, you would feel greater control. As you can see, attitudes matter to understanding behavior, but the attitude and behavior link is indirect and contingent on many factors in the situation.

In sum, there is a connection between attitudes and behaviors. It is stressful when our attitudes and behaviors are not aligned. At the same time, although attitudes are related to some behaviors some of the time, they are not the only causal influences over why we behave the way we do in organizational settings. Still, knowing that people would prefer to align their attitudes and behaviors, it is easy to see that job attitudes have the potential to relate to behaviors organizations care about, such as job performance, the tendency to help others, speak up, or quit one's job. Given their important implications for workplace behaviors, we should get a sense of what attitudes matter the most at work. In the next several sections, we will discuss major job attitudes, how to measure them, their causes, and consequences.

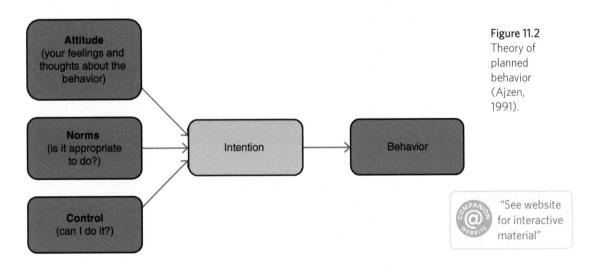

Figure 11.2
Theory of planned behavior (Ajzen, 1991).

"See website for interactive material"

Key Job Attitudes: Job Satisfaction and Organizational Commitment

Job satisfaction: A pleasurable or positive emotional state resulting from the appraisal of one's job or job experiences.

In this chapter, we will primarily focus on two key job attitudes that have been the subject of thousands of studies. **Job satisfaction** is defined as "a pleasurable or positive emotional state resulting from the appraisal of one's job or job experiences" (Locke, 1976). Put differently, it is a sense of contentment with one's job. **Organizational commitment** refers to the degree to which the employee identifies with and feels involved in the organization (Mowday, Steers, & Porter, 1979). In other words, it is the overall attachment felt toward the organization. Theoretically, these are thought to be two distinct job attitudes. In other words, it is possible for a person to love their job and dislike their company and vice versa. However, in reality these two attitudes have a great deal of overlap. For example, a meta-analysis showed that organizational commitment and overall job satisfaction are highly correlated at .69 (Mathieu & Zajac, 1990). Therefore, because job satisfaction and organizational commitment are so highly correlated, we will treat our discussion of their causes and consequences together in this chapter.

Organizational commitment: The degree to which the employee identifies with and feels involved in the organization.

Job satisfaction and organizational commitment are not the only job attitudes of interest. A recent addition to the literature is **work engagement**, a job attitude consisting of being dedicated to and absorbed with work, and bringing a sense of excitement and passion to work (Schaufeli, Bakker, & Salanova, 2006). Research has shown that work engagement is distinct from job satisfaction and organizational commitment (with meta-analytic correlations of .52 and .59 respectively; Christian, Garza, & Slaughter, 2011), and that this job attitude adds unique value to understanding behaviors at work. Our focus in this chapter will be on the more commonly studied attitudes of job satisfaction and organizational commitment, but note that this relatively new addition to the job attitudes literature is quickly gaining in popularity, with over 25 million employees worldwide having taken part in the Gallup engagement survey, a 12-item questionnaire administered by Gallup (Gallup, 2015).

Work engagement: A job attitude consisting of being dedicated to and absorbed with work, and bringing a sense of excitement and passion to work.

Workplace Application

Tracking Job Attitudes at Work

Organizations systematically track the attitudes of their employees in two basic ways. First, periodic employee opinion surveys are a staple of leading organizations. Organizations such as Campbell Soup Company, 3M, Zappos, Google, and REI conduct attitude surveys regularly, and turn the results into actions to improve job attitudes. In addition to "home-grown" measures developed by individual organizations and scientifically validated measures developed by academics, consulting companies such as Valtera, Gallup, Towers-Watson, Kenexa, and the Hay Group have their own proprietary measures of employee engagement and job attitudes and may be hired to survey and analyze employee opinions.

Second, organizations find out about factors causing employee unhappiness through **exit interviews**, or interviews conducted with departing employees. By having one last conversation with departing employees, companies may find out about systemic issues that could lead to the loss of additional talent. Of course, the employee may not be inclined to share their parting thoughts for fear of damaging relationships, but by showing genuine interest in what the employee has to say, the organization can learn valuable information.

Exit interview: An interview conducted with departing employees to explore why the employee is leaving.

Measurement of Job Attitudes

Measures of Job Satisfaction

There are two different approaches to measurement of job satisfaction. **Global measures of satisfaction** present respondents with a series of Likert-type (where the answer format ranges such as between 1 = strongly disagree to 5 = strongly agree) statements pertaining to their overall job satisfaction. A sample item would be: "How much do you agree with the following statement: All in all, I am satisfied with my job." This is likely the most straightforward way to assess job satisfaction. Respondents are allowed to evaluate what matters to them about their job, and report their *overall* sense of contentment. **Facet-based measures of satisfaction** ask respondents a series of questions about different aspects of their jobs, such as pay, promotion opportunities, the work itself, and quality of supervision. Then, the responses to different dimensions are averaged to arrive at the overall score of satisfaction. For example, the Job Descriptive Index (JDI), a copyrighted measure, includes five facets of satisfaction: pay, promotions, supervision, coworkers, and work itself (Smith, Kendall, & Hulin, 1969). The Minnesota Satisfaction Questionnaire (MSQ; Weiss, Dawis, England, & Lofquist, 1967) is also a copyrighted measure and consists of a long form of 100 items, or a short form of 20 items. The long form of the scale can capture 20 facets of job satisfaction, including ability utilization, recognition, security, and working conditions. The 20-item short form of the scale is typically used to measure **intrinsic job satisfaction** (or the satisfaction with the work itself and opportunities to use one's skills) and **extrinsic job satisfaction** (or satisfaction with pay, promotion, or other material benefits of the job). Figure 11.3. shows some sample items from different job satisfaction scales.

Which method of measuring job satisfaction is preferable? First, keep in mind that global job satisfaction is only modestly correlated with the average of facet satisfaction (Aldag & Brief, 1978). In other words, using a facet measure and averaging the scores for different dimensions will not necessarily give you the overall satisfaction employees have with their jobs. Why would this be?

Remember that different individuals may weigh facets differently in terms of their importance. For example, you may be satisfied with your supervisor, coworkers, promotion opportunities, and the nature of the work itself, but be quite unhappy with your pay. Thus, the average of facet satisfaction will be high. However, if all you care about in your work is your pay, your overall satisfaction level measured through a

Global measures of satisfaction: A series of Likert-type (where the answer format ranges such as between 1 = strongly disagree to 5 = strongly agree) statements pertaining to overall job satisfaction.

Facet-based measures of satisfaction: A series of questions about different aspects of one's job, such as pay, promotion opportunities, the work itself, and quality of supervision. The responses to different dimensions are averaged to arrive at the overall score of satisfaction.

Intrinsic job satisfaction: Satisfaction with the work itself and opportunities to use one's skills.

Extrinsic job satisfaction: Satisfaction with pay, promotion, or other material benefits of the job.

Sample items from Minnesota Satisfaction Questionnaire

Item	Not Satisfied	Somewhat Satisfied	Satisfied	Very Satisfied	Extremely Satisfied
	1	2	3	4	5
The way my boss handles his/her workers.					
The working conditions.					
The pay and the amount of work I do.					
The freedom to use my own judgment.					
The feeling of accomplishment I get from the job.					
The chance to do different things from time to time.					

Sample Items from Job Descriptive Index (JDI)

	Yes (describes my job)	No (does not describe my job)	? (you cannot decide)
People on your present job			
Stimulating			
Likeable			
Smart			
Work on present job			
Fascinating			
Respected			
Dull			
Pay			
Fair			
Comfortable			
Underpaid			
Opportunities for promotion			
Promotion on ability			
Very limited			
Regular promotions			
Supervision			
Supportive			
Tactful			
Knows job well			

global scale will be low. In other words, simply averaging the facets will miss the fact that employees assign different weights to different aspects of their jobs, and that a person's happiness or unhappiness may be driven through a single aspect of the job.

Which scale is more appropriate to use in an organizational setting will depend on what we are trying to accomplish. Overall measures of job satisfaction are simple, straightforward, and can measure satisfaction easily, asking only a few questions. In fact, research has shown that even single-item, overall measures of job satisfaction can be acceptable measures, with correlations of over .60 with longer measures of satisfaction (Wanous, Reichers, & Hudy, 1997). One frequently used single-item, overall satisfaction measure is the Faces scale (Kunin, 1955), which simply consists of faces with different levels of smiles and frowns. This method is particularly useful for samples with limited reading ability, although it has the downside of making it impossible to calculate inter-item reliability. In a questionnaire, having several questions about the same topic allows researchers to have more reliable measurement.

Circle the face that represents your feelings about the job in general.

Figure 11.4 An example of using faces to measure job satisfaction.

Regardless of their length, overall measures of satisfaction can be tracked through time to give an organization an overall sense of how satisfied employees are with their jobs and patterns in satisfaction over time.

The downside of global measures is that they do not allow organizations to identify which aspects of their jobs employees are most happy or unhappy with. Is it the pay, supervision, or the work itself that employees find most problematic? Therefore, facet-level measures give the organization a better sense of what the areas of improvements are. If time and space allows, asking employees to report their facet satisfaction as well as using a short global satisfaction scale will be helpful in achieving both objectives. This way, you can get a sense of the over-all levels of happiness, as well as examine which factors are the most important influences over job satisfaction.

Measures of Organizational Commitment

Organizational commitment can also be measured using previously validated and scientifically sound scales. (See Figure 11.5 for examples.) A well-known measure of a uni-dimensional measure of organizational commitment is the Organizational Commitment Questionnaire (OCQ). In addition to those who view commitment as an overall feeling of attachment to the organization, there are those that think of it as multi-dimensional (Meyer & Allen, 1991). According to this view, commitment consists of three components (Figure 11.6). **Affective commitment** is commitment to the organization because of a sincere emotional attachment. **Continuance commitment** is being committed to the organization due to a lack of other job alternatives or a feeling that one would lose a lot with a job change. Finally, **normative commitment** is being committed due to a sense of obligation to the organization and because of a sense that it is the right thing to do. For example, if you are someone who is very passionate about helping people and if you are working for a humanitarian organization where you are treated well and have a chance to make a difference, you may develop a sense of affective commitment. If you have been working for an organization for the past decade and now feel that even if you don't like the company much, it would be very hard to give up your seniority and find comparable alternatives, any sense of attachment you feel is likely to be continuance commitment. Finally, if your company paid for your college tuition and accommodated you for a long time when you were taking care of a sick family member but you feel that you are currently underutilized, the feelings of attachment you feel to the company may be normative commitment. As you may guess, affective commitment is more important in shaping employee behaviors such as on-the-job behaviors and turnover, so this is the commitment type we will focus on in this chapter.

Affective commitment: Commitment to the organization because of a sincere emotional attachment.

Continuance commitment: Being committed to the organization due to a lack of other job alternatives or a feeling that one would lose a lot with a job change.

Normative commitment: Being committed due to a sense of obligation to the organization and because of a sense that it is the right thing to do.

Figure 11.5
Measurement
of organizational
commitment.
Sources: Allen &
Meyer (1990);
Mowday et al.
(1979).

Sample items from Organizational Commitment Questionnaire (OCQ)					
Item	Strongly Disagree	Disagree	Neither Agree nor Disagree	Agree	Strongly Agree
	1	2	3	4	5

I find that my values and the organization's values are very similar.
I am extremely glad that I chose this organization to work for over others I was considering at the time I joined.
Deciding to work for this organization was a definite mistake on my part. (Reverse Coded Item)
I could just as well be working for a different organization as long as the type of work was similar. (Reverse Coded Item)

Sample items from Multidimensional Commitment Scale					
Item	Strongly Disagree	Disagree	Neither Agree nor Disagree	Agree	Strongly Agree
	1	2	3	4	5

Affective Commitment Scale
I really feel as if this organization's problems are my own.
This organization has a great deal of meaning for me.
Continuance Commitment Scale
It would be very hard for me to leave my organization right now, even if I wanted to.
Too much in my life would be disrupted if I decided to leave my organization now.
Normative Commitment Scale
If I got another offer for a better job elsewhere, I would not feel it was right to leave my organization.
One of the major reasons I continue to work in this organization is that I believe loyalty is important and therefore feel a sense of moral obligation to remain.

Figure 11.6
Three types of
organizational
commitment.

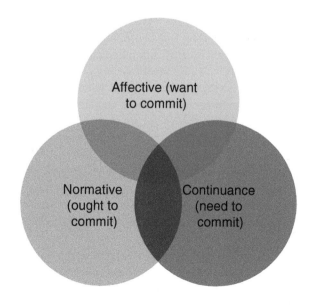

Antecedents of Job Attitudes

Studies exploring how job attitudes shape and develop have concluded that personal and situational factors matter to the development of particular job attitudes. Of course, aspects of the work environment such as job characteristics or a manager's behaviors matter. At the same time, to some extent satisfaction is also an individual difference (e.g., an inherited trait), and the employees themselves can have a role in shaping their own level of satisfaction and commitment as well: some people seem to be happier with their jobs wherever they go, and others may be better at creating and selecting the work environment they will thrive in. In this section, we discuss factors that are associated with job attitudes at work. A summary of causes and consequences of job attitudes can be seen in Figure 11.7.

Job Characteristics

As we have discussed in detail in Chapter 9, job characteristics are important for employee motivation and job attitudes. In fact, meta-analytic evidence suggests that job characteristics are a significant influence over job satisfaction. Loher, Noe, Moeller, and Fitzgerald (1985) showed that there was a consistent relationship between job characteristics, the opportunity to use a variety of skills at work, the ability to complete identifiable pieces of output, doing meaningful and significant work, having autonomy and receiving feedback about how well one is doing, and job satisfaction. Among these job characteristics, autonomy was the most powerful correlate of job satisfaction, suggesting that a sense of self-determination is particularly important for happiness in the workplace. Job characteristics mattered more to those employees who displayed a high need for growth. In other words, to those of us who are interested in personal growth, learning, and self-actualization, having a job with a high motivating potential (see Chapter 9) mattered more, whereas to those who view their jobs just as a paycheck, job characteristics seem to matter much less. Importantly, though, to a lot of people, their job is more than their paycheck. In a 2014 Gallup study of over 1,000 adults in the USA, 55 percent reported that their job is an important piece of their personal identity, or how they see themselves. This percentage is much higher for college graduates, with 70 percent reporting that they get their sense of identity from their jobs (Riffkin,

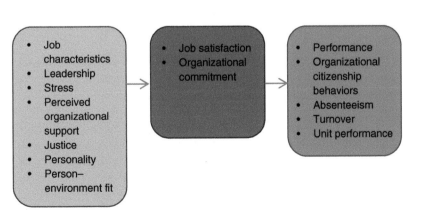

Figure 11.7
Summary figure of antecedents and consequences of job attitudes.

"See website for interactive material"

Twitter, the San Francisco-based social networking firm, has been ranked number one in Culture and Values, and number two in the list of Best Places to Work in 2014 by Glassdoor, a website where employees can rate their present or past companies. Current and former employees praise Twitter for the opportunity to work with others who care about their work, the collaborative environment, amount of support provided to employees, and generous perks.

2014). This means that enriching jobs by paying attention to job characteristics may result in happier, more committed workers.

Leadership

It is commonly said that people make the place. Not surprisingly, leaders are among those people who make a workplace what it is. (See Chapter 10.) The actions, decisions and indecision, the way they treat employees, and the way they communicate with their direct reports end up playing a powerful role in shaping job attitudes. Many of the other factors that we think are related to satisfaction end up being traced back to leadership. For example, autonomy matters for job satisfaction, and the more your manager trusts you, the more autonomy you will have. As a result, many job features are not easily separated from leadership style of the manager. As we discussed in Chapter 10, the quality of the relationship employees have with their manager matters greatly for the ultimate satisfaction they experience (Gerstner & Day, 1997). Further, the negative style of a manager may be a big cause of unhappiness. For example, Mathieu, Neumann, Hare, and Babiak (2014) showed that having manipulative, insensitive, unreliable, and aggressive leaders resulted in distress, which added to a sense of unhappiness at work. It is also important to remember that not all managers are equal in their influence to shape job attitudes. For example, research shows that when managers are perceived by employees to embody the organization they work for – because they are powerful, are at a high hierarchical level, and are regarded as a representative of the organization – they have more opportunities to shape employee job attitudes (Eisenberger et al., 2010).

Stress

Mindfulness: A state of nonjudgmental attentiveness and awareness of the moment, without thinking and worrying about the past or the future.

One reason for unhappiness at work and low levels of organizational commitment can be the level of stress experienced. When employees feel emotionally drained and exhausted (for example, due to long hours, poor leadership, or daily hassles), they experience unhappiness and detachment from the organization (e.g., Mathieu & Zajac, 1990). Therefore, as we will see in greater detail in Chapter 12, interventions that reduce the level of stress or increase coping ability of employees will be helpful for increasing job satisfaction. For example, Hülsheger, Alberts, Feinholdt, and Lang (2013) recently showed that organizational interventions focused on **mindfulness**, or a state of nonjudgmental attentiveness and awareness of the moment (see "Workplace Application: Mindfulness Training," Chapter 8), without thinking and worrying about the past or the future, could be helpful for employees. Employees who were more mindful, and who were taught to be mindful, experienced lower levels of emotional exhaustion, which increased their job satisfaction.

An important stressor in today's organizations is work–life conflict (which we will discuss in greater detail in Chapter 12). When the demands of work make it difficult to meet the demands of the employee's home and personal life, employees experience lower levels of attachment to the organization. Therefore, family-supportive work practices could be a very important tool to increase the loyalty of employees to the organization (Wayne, Casper, Matthews, & Allen, 2013). This is not only because the employee feels less stress and experiences a more positive mood, but also because their partner at home ends up developing higher commitment to the employee's organization (as in: "My partner is working in such a supportive company ... They have flexible hours, which make it possible for us to have a healthy and balanced home life. I hope he will work for this company for a long time").

Finally, another contemporary stressor that erodes job satisfaction and organizational commitment is job insecurity. Organizational mergers, acquisitions, layoffs, and downsizing often result in a situation where employees worry about being let go. The sense that they might lose their jobs in the foreseeable future has been shown to be negatively related to both job satisfaction and organizational commitment (Sverke, Hellgren, & Näswall, 2002). In other words, organizations may increase employee happiness and attachment by avoiding or minimizing the likelihood of layoffs and managing them fairly when they become unavoidable.

Perceived Organizational Support

Whom do you feel loyal to? Chances are it is a reciprocal process. In other words, you are loyal to those who are loyal to you. Similarly, research shows that employees are more likely to feel a sense of attachment to organizations that in turn care about their employees. **Perceived organizational support** is the perception that the organization is committed to and cares about its employees. When employees feel that the organization cares about their well-being and does not see them only as a way to increase production, they in turn feel a sense of attachment to the organization (Eisenberger, Huntington, Hutchison, & Sowa, 1986). How would employees know whether the company cares about their well-being? There are many signals that occur throughout the workday, and there are even signals that occur before a person is hired. For example, one of the authors of this text recalls receiving an invitation to interview for a junior auditor position at one of the big four audit firms when she was a graduating senior in college in Turkey. The interview was going to take place on the day of her college graduation ceremony and the recruiter firmly refused to move the date, signaling the level of respect and support new employees could expect from the company (needless to say, she attended her graduation). Similarly, employees of an organization make sense of their daily interactions and experiences. What happens to an employee when they make an honest mistake? What happens to them when they feel sick and cannot come to work for a few days? Is the company considerate toward employees' personal lives, or are employees expected to forgo their family and friends and dedicate

Perceived organizational support: The perception that the organization is committed to and cares about its employees.

The SAS Institute, a leader in business analytics, has over 10,000 employees worldwide, and a voluntary turnover rate of around 2–3 percent in an industry with an average turnover of 22 percent. This is largely due to its dedication to its employees. Unlimited sick time, free healthcare center, and subsidized childcare are only some of the benefits available to its employees. In fact, Google modeled many of its famous perks and benefits on those offered at SAS. http://archive.fortune.com/magazines/fortune/best-companies/2012/snapshots/3.html

their lives to the company? The daily treatment of the employee by organizational decision-makers such as managers and HR department are influential in shaping these feelings, which in turn result in organizational commitment.

Organizational Justice

Interactional justice: Fairness of the interpersonal treatment received from one's manager.

We discussed organizational justice or the fair treatment of employees back in Chapters 2 and 9. One of the most important predictors of job attitudes is perceived fairness within the organization. In particular, **interactional justice**, or the fairness of the interpersonal treatment received from one's manager, is an important predictor. In addition, **distributive justice**, or perceived fairness of rewards received from the organization, and **procedural justice**, or perceived fairness of the processes used to make important decisions within the organization, are correlates of organizational commitment (Meyer, Stanley, Herscovitch, & Topolnytsky, 2002). When individuals are treated unfairly, it is hard for them to love what they do or feel a sense of attachment to the company.

Distributive justice: Perceived fairness of rewards received from the organization.

Personality

Procedural justice: Perceived fairness of the processes used to make important decisions within the organization.

Finally, there is some evidence that happiness is in the eye of the beholder. Some people seem to be attached to their jobs regardless of what job they hold, because of their personality. First, the personality variables of **positive affectivity** (a tendency to experience positive emotions such as feeling energetic, enthusiastic, and happy) and **negative affectivity** (a tendency to experience negative emotions such as anger, sadness, and guilt) have correlations of .49 and −.33 with job satisfaction according to meta-analytic evidence (Connolly & Viswesvaran, 2000), suggesting that the degree to which a person habitually experiences more positive or more negative moods has a role in the level of satisfaction he or she finds at work. Second, core self-evaluations (which we discussed in Chapter 7 in terms of selection), consisting of self-esteem, self-efficacy, internal locus of control, and emotional stability, show meta-analytic correlations with job satisfaction ranging between .24 and .45 (Judge & Bono, 2001). Why would this be? Individuals who have a positive opinion of themselves, feel in control of their own destiny, and feel a sense of confidence about their abilities may be more likely to be persistent in their job search and do not settle for a job that will not make them happy; and once they are working, they may be more active in removing barriers to their happiness

Positive affectivity: A tendency to experience positive emotions such as feeling energetic, enthusiastic, and happy.

Negative affectivity: A tendency to experience negative emotions such as anger, sadness, and guilt.

at work. Further, people high in core self-evaluations may end up performing better at work, which may result in a better relationship with their manager, greater
access to organizational resources, and better treatment by the organization,
which should further increase their happiness at work.

Person–Environment Fit

Finally, the fit between the person and the organizational context also matters for
job attitudes, and particularly organizational commitment. Scholars have identified
at least two types of ways that people can fit in at work. First, **person–organization
fit** is the similarity between a person's own values and values held by the organization. In contrast, **person–job fit** is the degree to which the person's skills, abilities,
and knowledge are aligned with job requirements so that the person is not over-
or under-qualified. Both of these types of fit seem to matter to job attitudes. For
example, a meta-analysis showed that person–organization fit is correlated with
organizational commitment at .28 (Verquer, Beehr, & Wagner, 2003). Also, each
of these types of fit uniquely relate to job satisfaction (Lauver & Kristof-Brown,
2001). A person who will be happy in a start-up may feel very unhappy in a large
government organization.

Person–organization fit: Similarity between a person's own values and values held by the organization.

Person–job fit: Degree to which the person's skills, abilities, and knowledge are aligned with job requirements so that the person is not over- or under-qualified.

How about Pay?

By this point, you may be asking yourselves: How about pay? A lot of people
assume that pay must explain a big part of why employees would feel happiness
at work. In fact, when asked directly about what matters to them about their jobs,
employees often bring up their pay, as evidenced by a survey by the Society for
Human Resource Management where respondents named pay the number-one
driver of their job satisfaction (Schramm, 2014). However, academic research
does *not* support this assumption. A meta-analysis based on 115 studies has
shown that pay level had a very weak ($r =.15$) positive correlation with job satisfaction (Judge, Piccolo, Podsakoff, Shaw, & Rich, 2010). In other words, the absolute level of pay matters relatively little to job satisfaction. This probably makes
sense – a pre-school teacher making less than $50,000 a year may be much hap-
pier than a lawyer who makes more than $150,000, or vice versa for a number of
non-pay-related reasons. The same study has shown that pay satisfaction (rather
than monetary level of pay) and job satisfaction are more strongly correlated, but
the relationship is still modest ($r = .23$).

These results suggest that pay may be something we take for granted on a daily
basis – as long as our basic needs are met. Of course it matters a great deal for those
who are working but still trying to make ends meet. Unfortunately, despite holding
jobs, 10.4 million people in the US lived below the official poverty line in 2011. In fact,
13 percent of all service workers were classified as working poor (Bureau of Labor
Statistics, 2011). Our discussion should not be taken to mean that money does not
matter for job attitudes; in fact, for those experiencing financial stress, it matters
a great deal. For people who are not experiencing financial stress, though, it may
be important when choosing a job, but it is not something that strongly influences
our opinions while at work. Pay, especially set up as commissions and incentives,
may motivate short-term behavior, but it seems that it has a more modest role for

job satisfaction. While pay satisfaction does little for job satisfaction, other factors like pay dissatisfaction, financial stress, and pay unfairness may be bigger negative influences over our job attitudes.

Workplace Application

Which Organizations Are the Happiest Places to Work?

Job seekers are interested in finding companies where they will be happy. Companies have a motivation to show that they can satisfy their employees so that they can attract better qualified employees. Finding information about working conditions within organizations is challenging unless you know people within a company. There are a few places that rank organizations with respect to different criteria, which may be a place to start. Magazines such as *Forbes* and *Fortune* have lists of the happiest workplaces in the US. *Fortune* has an annual "best places to work" list. The rankings are based on the results of a survey as well as a culture audit where the company reports the types of benefits, hiring practices, training, and diversity programs. The company needs to actively apply to participate in the rankings. There are also more specialized lists, such as the "best places for working moms" by the *Working Mother* magazine, "best start-ups to work" by *Business Insider*, or "the top companies for diversity" put together by *DiversityInc.* Again, these lists depend on the company's own initiative to take part in the surveys and provide the information requested by list compilers. Another downside of these lists (other than being completely unscientific) is that they tend to focus on companies in the USA, so they are less helpful as reflections of conditions in other countries. Finally, Glassdoor.com is a website where employees from all around the world can submit information about a company they worked for. The company verifies e-mail addresses of respondents and asks users to share the pros and cons of working for an organization, and whether they approve of the CEO. These websites, although they may contain a certain level of bias, may be useful tools for both job seekers and company management to get a sense of what employees value, what they are frustrated with, and areas for improvement.

Consequences of Job Attitudes

Performance

Are happy workers productive workers? This seemingly common-sense assertion has been tested and debated extensively in the past several decades. The current thinking seems to be that yes, job satisfaction and performance are correlated, with a meta-analysis calculating a correlation of .30 between the two (Judge, Thoresen, Bono, & Patton, 2001). The same study also suggests that in complex jobs there is a stronger relationship. As job complexity goes up, the role of a person's motivation and abilities to influence the job will also go up, which would explain why satisfaction would make more of a difference for an engineer compared to an assembly line worker. As for commitment, the relationship is positive but small, with a correlation of .13 between organizational commitment and performance measures in a meta-analysis (Mathieu & Zajac, 1990).

While job satisfaction and performance are correlated, the correlation may have been lower than you expected. A correlation of .30 means that even though it is a positive relationship, there are many employees who will perform well despite being unhappy with their jobs, and there will be plenty of workers who perform poorly despite being satisfied with their jobs. To understand the connection between attitudes and performance, it is also important to examine how much discretion a person has in influencing the quality of their work. A person working at a fast-food restaurant like McDonald's or In-N-Out Burger probably has few opportunities to produce a uniquely delicious hamburger or an extremely poor-tasting one, because the organization has systems in place to minimize variations in the taste of the burgers. When employees are doing highly standardized work, even unhappy workers would show acceptable levels of performance and happy workers may not be able to outperform their peers. Further, employees who are unhappy at work but do not see other immediate alternatives will have to maintain an acceptable level of performance in order to hold on to their jobs, which should weaken the relationship between happiness and performance.

At the same time, organizations benefit when employees do things beyond their job descriptions. These behaviors that are not part of an employee's job description but still contribute to the effectiveness of the organization are termed **organizational citizenship behaviors** (closely related to the idea of contextual performance discussed in Chapter 4). Helping a new employee learn their job, doing one's job with a positive attitude and without complaint, and organizing social activities so that employees build camaraderie are among citizenship behaviors employees engage in, and these behaviors are more likely to be demonstrated by employees who are happier at work and are committed to their companies (Bateman & Organ, 1983; Meyer et al., 2002). One potential reason for this is that happier employees tend to be in a more positive mood, which makes them more likely to engage in behaviors that will benefit others.

> **Organizational citizenship behaviors:** Behaviors that are not part of an employee's job description but still contribute to the effectiveness of the organization.

While we typically consider job performance a consequence of job attitudes, it has also been recognized that the relationship might in fact be reciprocal and that high performers may end up being more satisfied with their jobs. This could occur through many different mechanisms. For example, high performers tend to feel more successful, boosting their self-esteem and also resulting in recognition, respect, and organizational rewards. These employees may feel that they are making good progress toward their career goals. Finally, feeling successful may result in overall positive emotions, all of which could boost job-related attitudes (Judge et al., 2001). In other words, performance may be the cause of job satisfaction as well as a consequence.

Absenteeism

Unplanned absences from work are costly for organizations. According to a report by Circadian (2005), a Massachusetts-based performance and safety solutions

One way many organizations are combating both poor employee attitudes and absenteeism is through flexible work schedules. By allowing workers to pick their hours and work from home when desired, organizations enable workers to manage work–life conflict more effectively, and become more committed to their companies, in turn reducing absenteeism.

business, unscheduled absenteeism costs US businesses $3,500 per hourly worker per year, and that at any given time, about 1 in 10 workers is absent even though they should be at work. Of course, part of absenteeism is involuntary and due to uncontrollable factors such as illness or the need to care for a sick family member. However, part of absenteeism can be traced back to work attitudes: When employees are unhappy and feel detached from the organization, they may feel justified in missing work and take a "mental day off." Research shows that organizational commitment is negatively related to voluntary absenteeism (Somers, 1995).

Turnover

Turnover intentions:
An employee's reported desire to leave the company.

Are unhappy workers less likely to stay with the organization? Job satisfaction and organizational commitment are both significantly correlated with **turnover intentions** (or reported desire to leave the company) and actual turnover, but the relationships with actual turnover are more modest (Griffeth, Hom, & Gaertner, 2000; Mathieu & Zajac, 1990). This is probably not very surprising, because not everyone who intends to leave ends up leaving, and some people may leave on short notice, without reporting high intentions to leave. Unhappiness may trigger job-search behavior, but then the individual will assess the likelihood of finding a better job, and the costs of leaving (such as leaving behind seniority, supportive colleagues, a short commute, etc.). In other words, a lot of other things need to happen before unhappy workers actually leave (Mobley, 1977). Instead, employees may quit without actually leaving. In other words, they may start withholding effort, be absent more often (Smith, 1977), and detach from work psychologically (Burris, Detert, & Chiaburu, 2008) without actually changing jobs. (Think back to Chapter 9 and our discussion of equity theory.)

Research has shown that organizational commitment may be a better predictor of turnover compared to job satisfaction (Porter, Steers, Mowday, & Boulian, 1974). Why would this be? If you are unhappy with your work but like the company, you may be more willing to try to change your job within the same organization and think of leaving as a last resort. You could find a different position within the same company, move to a different team, or try to modify some undesirable aspects of the job. This would explain why commitment may be more important in understanding employee stay/quit decisions as opposed to job satisfaction.

Recently, researchers started realizing that it is not necessarily the overall level of job satisfaction that predicts what the person will do in the future, but *changes* in levels of job satisfaction. When job conditions change for the worse and job satisfaction declines, there tend to be increases in intentions to leave the organization. This is because changing job conditions signal to employees what the future will bring and affects their expectations of future happiness (Chen, Ployhart, Thomas, Anderson, & Bliese, 2011). In other words, anything that would result in significant changes to the job satisfaction levels of employees (such as changes in job descriptions, leadership, or working conditions) are worth monitoring and managing very closely, given their potential influences on the flight risk of employees.

Counterproductive Work Behaviors

In addition to performing their jobs, helping others, showing up to work, and staying as members of the organization, organizations also expect employees to avoid displaying behaviors that would harm the company. **Counterproductive work behaviors** may be defined as behaviors that are contrary to an organization's legitimate interests (Sackett, 2002). Examples of these behaviors include theft, misuse of information such as revealing confidential information, unsafe behaviors in the form of ignoring safety protocols, alcohol and drug use at work, and misuse of time and organizational equipment. Research shows that there is a relationship between employee satisfaction, commitment, and the frequency with which they display these behaviors (Dalal, 2005).

Counterproductive work behaviors: Behaviors that are contrary to an organization's legitimate interests such as theft, misuse of information, unsafe behaviors in the form of ignoring safety protocols, alcohol and drug use at work, and misuse of time and organizational equipment.

Unit Performance

Given that job attitudes are related to job performance, higher citizenship, lower counterproductive behaviors, and lower turnover, it should also have implications for the financial performance of the business unit and overall company. Research supports this prediction. For example, Chi and Gursoy (2009) showed that in a sample of 250 hotels, employee satisfaction had indirect effects on financial performance (profitability, return on investment, and net profit) through its effects on customer satisfaction. Similarly, Harter, Schmidt, and Hayes (2002) showed that business-unit level satisfaction and engagement had significant correlations with unit performance indicated by profitability, productivity, customer satisfaction, turnover, and accidents. It seems that by caring for employee happiness, companies benefit by improving their bottom-line performance.

Newcomers: An Early Opportunity to Influence Job Attitudes

So far, we have discussed the importance of job attitudes, and factors that contribute to happiness and attachment of employees at work. Our coverage of the antecedents of job attitudes should have given you a sense of what organizations can do in order to have happier and more committed workers: provide interesting, challenging, and meaningful work. Provide trustworthy, supportive leadership. Be fair in your treatment of employees. Support employees. Help them manage their stress well, and ensure that stress levels at work are manageable. Ensure high

Figure 11.8 Employee reactions to unhappiness at work.
The Exit, Voice, Loyalty, and Neglect model (Farrell, 1983) explains how employees respond to unhappiness at work. The model suggests that in addition to reducing performance (neglect) and quitting their jobs (exit), employees may choose inaction and wait for things to get better (loyalty), or talk to superiors, take action and speak up to make things better (voice). The model reiterates that the relation between employee behaviors and job attitudes is not simple and straightforward, and instead situational.

levels of person–job fit given that personality makes a difference. All these are useful methods, but there is also a special, one-time opportunity to influence job attitudes: when employees are new to the company.

The first few weeks on the job is an important time in the career of the employee within that company, and unfortunately there are no "do-overs." It is natural for a newcomer to feel a sense of uncertainty and anxiety in the first weeks. *Am I going to fit in? Will I be able to perform my job well? Did I make the right choice accepting this offer?* In their first few weeks, employees are actively seeking information, trying to understand their jobs and the company culture, and attributing a lot of meaning to individual events. (See our discussion of onboarding and new employee socialization in Chapter 8.) For example, if they feel lonely in the first few weeks, it would be easy for them to think that the company is not very supportive of people, even if this may not be true and they simply started work at a very busy time. Our own research shows that companies that follow a structured approach to bringing employees on board ensures that newcomers experience greater attachment to the company and satisfaction, which in turn relates to higher retention of newcomers (Bauer, Bodner, Erdogan, Truxillo, & Tucker, 2007).

Workplace Application

Newcomer Onboarding at L'Oréal

L'Oréal Paris is a company that takes a very structured approach to bringing newcomers on board. Newcomers go through a six-part integration program (named L'Oréal FIT, or Follow-up and Integration Track), consisting of an orientation, mentoring and job shadowing, and meeting key insiders (Crush, 2014). Taking such a structured approach to new employee onboarding prevents employees from feeling lonely in their first weeks, gets them connected to organizational insiders early on, and signals that the company cares about and values its employees.

Emotions at Work

Job attitudes and behaviors are intimately connected with our emotions. Job attitudes develop as a result of positive or negative experiences over an extended period of time, and they have the potential to affect our behavior into the future. At the same time, our momentary feelings, thoughts, and reactions to positive and negative events in our environment also have the potential to affect workplace behavior. **Emotion** can be defined as the momentary feelings and thoughts that arise in response to specific events in the environment. They are different from moods in that moods have less clear causes and are longer in duration. Regardless, emotions matter for both attitudes and behaviors. In fact, affective events theory (AET; Weiss & Cropanzano, 1996) suggests that day-to-day emotions are important to understand job attitudes and behaviors. For example, when an employee frequently experiences positive emotions such as happiness and excitement for accomplishing things, being recognized, and being treated well, over time, such positive emotions at work will translate into more positive job attitudes. Further, emotions cause "affect-driven behavior." If you are feeling happy, you are more likely to engage in spontaneous actions that will benefit others, such as helping someone else, attending an optional meeting, or doing a spontaneous favor to someone else. Because of the connection between emotions, job attitudes, and behaviors, we devote this section to emotions at work.

Emotion: Momentary feelings and thoughts that arise in response to specific events in the environment.

Felt Emotions and Their Consequences

Psychologist Paul Ekman, named one of the 100 most influential people in the world by *Time* magazine, is famous for his work on emotions and facial expressions and the Fox TV crime series *Lie to Me* is based on him and his work. Ekman (1992) proposed that there are six basic categories of emotions, which have universal signals that do not vary by culture: anger, happiness, disgust, fear, sadness, and surprise. We certainly experience all of these emotions from time to time. From the perspective of a working adult, it may be more useful to think of positive emotions such as excitement, positive affect, happiness, and joy, and negative emotions such as anxiety, sadness, and anger. Emotions arise as a result of what is going on in our daily environment. For example, organizational change is a time when employees experience a lot of negative emotions due to worries about their working conditions, reduced status, and how they are treated and will be treated by the organization (Kiefer, 2005). Similarly, job insecurity is a working condition that results in negative emotions such as anxiety and anger (Reisel, Probst, Chia, Maloles, & König, 2010). When someone does us a favor or when things go our way, we are more likely to experience positive emotions, and when we are treated rudely, when we encounter hassles, we are likely to experience negative emotions.

Do our momentary feelings matter, in the greater scheme of things? According to **broaden and build theory**, they do. This theory suggests that when we experience positive emotions, we build personal resources because we switch to a more flexible, exploratory way of thinking that encourages experimentation. In other words,

Broaden and build theory: The theory that suggests when we experience positive emotions, we build personal resources because we switch to a more flexible, exploratory way of thinking that encourages experimentation.

Paul Ekman's work focuses on *micro expressions*, which are very brief facial expresses. These are *really* quick – lasting only a fraction of a second. According to Ekman, "They occur when a person either deliberately or unconsciously conceals a feeling."

positive emotions stimulate creativity and novel thought. This is in direct opposition to negative emotions, which stimulate narrow-mindedness and a fight or flight response (Fredrickson, 1998). As a result, positive emotions, particularly as they accumulate over time, stimulate well-being, creativity, and resilience. In fact, there is evidence to suggest that the experience of positive emotions leads to higher levels of employee engagement (Ouweneel, Le Blanc, Schaufeli, & van Wijhe, 2012). Further, positive emotions increase our resilience, optimism, hope for the future, and feelings of efficacy, which results in higher levels of satisfaction with work, lower levels of stress, and lower levels of intentions to leave (Siu, Cheung, & Lui, 2015). In other words, it is possible to think of positive emotions as helping us build resources for the future. In contrast, experiencing negative emotions at work over extended periods of time erodes trust in the organization and increases the desire to leave (Kiefer, 2005). In short, the emotions we experience matter a lot for our job attitudes as well as behaviors at work.

To make matters more complicated, emotions spread within the work group because individuals express their emotions through verbal and nonverbal mechanisms. This is called **emotional contagion**. When you are happy, you are cheerful, you smile more, you do spontaneous favors to others, and probably are nicer to others. Then, others around you experience a mood shift. Of course, the opposite could also occur – when you have someone who is unhappy, sad, or angry in your department, others may start feeling the same way (Barsade, 2002). So one consequence of feeling positive or negative emotions is the possibility that others start to feel the same way.

Finally, one other impact of emotions on behavior is that they influence our perceptions. For example, a series of experiments have shown that when angry, individuals were more likely to perceive neutral objects as guns (Baumann & DeSteno, 2010). Our auditory perception is also affected by our emotions. A study manipulated individual emotions by having subjects listen to sad or happy music. Those who listened to sad music were more likely to hear "morning" as "mourning" or "pane" as "pain" (Halberstadt, Niedenthal, & Kushner, 1995). So if you feel that when

Emotional contagion: Emotions being spread within the work group, since individuals express their emotions through verbal and nonverbal mechanisms.

It is common for organizations to conduct annual attitude surveys, but emotions and moods can be early indicators of job attitudes. An employee who experiences negative emotions frequently at work will eventually experience low job attitudes. How to detect these early warning signals? Some companies started implementing "pulse" surveys, capturing snapshots of how employees are feeling at work. Sears, in a project named "MoodRing," captures how employees are feeling at the end of their shift. They found that at stores where employees report being "unstoppable" rather than "so so" or "exhausted," sales and customer satisfaction are higher (Silverman, 2014).

you are down, the whole world is out to get you, this may simply be your emotions guiding your perception and reactions.

Display of Emotions and Emotional Labor

When you are happy, do you always look happy? Or conversely, if you are smiling and acting upbeat, does this mean that you are really feeling happy? In fact, except for very young children, it is expected that emotions that are expressed are regulated and monitored. For example, anyone working in customer service, especially in the US, will be expected to demonstrate "service with a smile." In fact, companies such as Southwest Airlines pride themselves on selecting employees with a positive attitude. There are of course jobs in which negative emotions are expected to be displayed. For example, a collection agent may be expected to display negative emotions such as anger at the customers who do not pay their bills. A funeral home director will be expected to show a reserved, somber, and compassionate demeanor. A poker player's earnings depend on monitoring emotions so that they remain neutral and avoid signaling the quality of their hands to other players. In other words, different jobs and different companies may have norms around what emotions are appropriate to display.

For a customer service job, greeting customers with a smile may even be part of the performance evaluation of the employee. In addition to hiring employees with a positive attitude, companies may teach their expectations for proper emotional expression starting from the early days of employment, and through mentoring and modeling.

The requirement to show a particular emotion and monitor the use of emotions is referred to as **emotional display rules**. Such display rules seem to work for companies: When employees display positive emotions, customers seem to be more satisfied with service quality (Pugh, 2001). At the same time, customer service employees may sometimes choose to be not very friendly with customers in order to provide better service. As an example, when the line is long and the store is busy, employees may be less friendly in order to ensure that customers do not initiate a lengthy conversation with the clerk, which would hold the line, and anger the customers waiting in line (Sutton & Rafaeli, 1988). In other words, providing

Emotional display rules: The requirements to show a particular emotion and monitor the use of emotions.

If you visit Portland, Oregon, a trip to Voodoo Doughnuts is a must, even if you do not like doughnuts. It is among the top 10 things to do in Portland according to *Time* magazine, and the shop is known for unique flavors such as the bacon maple bar or Fruit Loop-topped doughnuts. With tourists flocking to their Oregon or Colorado locations, the challenge for Voodoo employees is not to "voo" the customers, but to get them quickly out the door. The company does not rely on repeat business. So, employees are allowed to be abrupt with customers. Service with a smile makes customers linger in the shop, which holds up the line (Cottell, 2014).

high-quality customer service oftentimes depends on employees displaying the right emotions that fit the situation.

If you have ever performed a customer service job where you had to monitor your emotions, you should be familiar with how difficult and exhausting it can be. In fact, having to display emotions you do not feel is hard work, and it is referred to as **emotional labor** in the literature. Emotional labor can be highly stressful and can lead to burnout. At the same time, individuals have different ways in which they deal with emotional display rules in the workplace. If you think of emotional labor as "acting," as if you were acting on a stage, there are two alternative types of acting you can engage in: surface acting and deep acting. **Surface acting** refers to changing the expression of emotions without changing the emotions themselves. Feeling frustrated with a customer but still managing to smile and make small talk with him is an example of surface acting. In this type of emotional labor, the employee would continue to feel the negative emotions, but acts in a way that disguises the emotion by displaying fake emotions. In **deep acting**, instead of only changing how one acts, the person makes an effort to change the underlying emotion. In other words, instead of smiling while feeling upset, the employee would try to re-evaluate and rethink the encounter, try to feel empathy with the customer and see things from his point of view, and as a result change the emotion in addition to how one expresses the emotion. Research shows that surface acting is related to experienced stress and fatigue (Beal, Trougakos, Weiss, & Dalal, 2013).

Emotional labor: Having to display emotions you do not feel.

Surface acting: Changing the expression of emotions without changing the emotions themselves.

Deep acting: Instead of only changing how one acts, the person makes an effort to change the underlying emotion.

In fact, surface actors can manage the outward expressions of their emotions on a day-to-day basis, but they tend to find it difficult; they devalue themselves, and experience negative emotions more (Beal, Trougakos, Weiss, & Green, 2006). Further, deep acting is received better by customers, probably because it seems more genuine (Grandey, 2003).

Individual Differences: Emotional Intelligence

Finally, individuals seem to differ in their ability to monitor and manage their emotions. **Emotional intelligence** is a personality trait that captures individual differences in appraising, identifying, and managing one's emotions. (We discussed the issues and controversies around the use of emotional intelligence in personnel selection in Chapter 6.) Psychologist Daniel Goleman (2004) outlines five characteristics of emotionally intelligent persons: self-awareness (ability to identify their own emotions at a given time), self-regulation (controlling how they experience and express their emotions), social skills (the ability to manage one's interpersonal relationships), empathy (the ability to understand other people's emotions), and motivation (the ability to motivate themselves). Research shows that emotional intelligence is related to outcomes companies care about: emotionally intelligent people seem to have higher levels of job satisfaction and job performance (Sy, Tram, & O'Hara, 2006). A meta-analysis suggests that emotional intelligence explains variance in job performance beyond personality and cognitive abilities, but this relationship seems to be stronger when emotional intelligence is measured using self-reported or peer-reported measures as opposed to using tests of emotional intelligence (O'Boyle, Humphrey, Pollack, Hawver, & Story, 2011).

Emotional intelligence: A personality trait that captures individual differences in appraising, identifying, and managing one's emotions.

However, as mentioned in Chapter 6, there is some question about how much emotional intelligence predicts job performance over other measures such as personality and cognitive ability (Christiansen, Janovics, & Siers, 2010). There is also some debate regarding whether emotional intelligence is anything new. In fact, the way it is described in the popular press tends to be so broad as to make this concept a mishmash of other personality traits, resulting in an elusive scientific definition and blurring of the boundary between this concept and other well-studied personality traits (Mayer, Salovey, & Caruso, 2008).

LEGAL ISSUES

Employee job attitudes may have legal implications. Of course, having a boring and unchallenging job is not against the law. However, employees who are unhappy with their jobs and the organization, particularly if they feel that they are unfairly treated, are more likely to sue their companies. Even if the ultimate judgment is in favor of the company, the lawsuit is likely to cost the company time, money, negative public relations, and mental anguish for all people involved. Therefore, one of the side effects of treating employees well is the likelihood of reducing chances of a lawsuit (Bies & Tyler, 1993).

Unhappy workers are also more likely to join a union in the workplace (Tremblay & Roussel, 2001). Employees' rights to unionize are protected under the law. Specifically, the National Labor Relations Act gives employees the right to join and participate in a union without fear of punishment or retaliation by the organization. Therefore, if management finds out about employee activities that support unionization, they should be aware that such employee actions are protected under the law, and the organization cannot promise employees pay raises or better conditions if they vote to keep the union out. Further, taking any disciplinary action against employees who are supporting the union activities, or shutting down a branch or plant in order to avoid unionizing, is considered to be illegal. Employees are allowed to discuss unionization efforts outside of work hours and outside the workplace. There are also activities labor unions are not allowed to engage in, such as threatening other employees that their jobs would be lost without the union (National Labor Relations Board, 2014). In short, both employees and management need to be cognizant of the laws governing rights and obligations that are a part of the unionization process.

GLOBAL IMPLICATIONS

Job attitudes are meaningful concepts around the world (Gelfand, Erez, & Aycan, 2007). However, research suggests that factors resulting in happier, more committed workers seem to be somewhat different depending on the cultural context. The reason for these differences could be national culture: what makes employees happy in an individualistic, present-oriented, and egalitarian society is likely to be different from what would make them happy in a collectivistic, long-term-oriented, and power-distant culture. Further, countries are not only culturally but also economically different. Therefore, employees in developed countries may be looking for jobs that challenge them, give them meaning, or fit with their values, whereas employees working in developing countries may be happy when they have a job that is relatively secure.

For example, consider the issue of fitting in with the company culture or with the job. Meta-analytic evidence suggests that even though these concepts matter to employees around the world, they are more important in North America and to a lesser extent in Europe, and least important in East Asia. Instead, employees in East Asian cultures were more attentive to fitting in with their supervisor and with their group, probably due to the different levels of collectivism (Oh et al., 2014).

Similarly, the relationship between work–life conflict and job satisfaction varied across cultures in a study of 20 countries. Specifically, work–family conflict was negatively related to job satisfaction in countries in the Anglo cluster including Australia, Canada, and the USA, whereas there was no relationship in the more collectivistic Eastern Europe cluster including Bulgaria, Romania, and Ukraine (Spector et al., 2007).

How job attitudes translate into behaviors at work also varies by culture: Research has shown that employees in individualistic cultures were more inclined to engage in withdrawal behaviors such as intending to quit in individualistic cultures (Gelfand et al., 2007). Similarly, for individualists, normative commitment (or the idea that you should be committed to the organization) was a less important influence over turnover intentions compared to what was found for employees who had collectivistic values (Wasti, 2003). In other words, what makes people happy and what happy people do may be slightly different depending on the cultural context.

In addition to differences in job attitudes, the display of emotions is contingent on culture. In a study of 33 different countries, researchers have shown that individualistic cultures emphasize more expressiveness of emotions in general, and particularly expect more positive emotions to be expressed (Matsumoto et al., 2008). This might explain behaviors such as service with a smile or smiling and making small talk with strangers in elevators or on the street in North America, which may be alien concepts in Asian cultures. In fact, many Asian cultures place emphasis on controlling all emotions, with those displaying emotional behavior regarded as childish. This would mean that simply observing facial expressions will not be very helpful in trying to figure out what the other person feels in a collectivistic culture, where the norm is to not show any emotions, or politely smile. In fact, in parts of Asia, people may smile when they are embarrassed, so even something as simple as a smile may have different meanings when interacting with others in a different culture.

Are they smiling under the masks? Working in Disneyland, or the "happiest place on earth," brings with it requirements about which emotions are appropriate to display at work. Of course, local culture needs to be taken into account when setting emotional display rules. Disneyland found that the rule of smiling at customers within 60 seconds of entering into the theme park did not go so well in Disneyland Paris, because of different local norms regarding emotional displays (Matusitz, 2010).

CURRENT ISSUES AND CONTROVERSIES

As the nature of work evolves to include more knowledge work, the definition of citizenship behaviors and the types and forms of citizenship behaviors employees may engage in may need to be modified. For example, in a study conducted at Google, Dekas, Bauer, Welle, Kurkoski, and Sullivan (2013) found that in addition to helping others at work, participating in health and well-being activities to improve one's health and support coworkers' health and well being, and celebrating coworkers' life events emerged as some new types of citizenship behaviors. (They also practice what they preach: When Professor Bauer was at Google for a summer as a Visiting Scholar, her colleagues brought in cupcakes for her birthday with the Portland State University logo on them for everyone to share!) In other words, as the nature of work evolves, behaviors that are expected of workers may evolve as well, and the science will need to keep up with these changes.

A topic that is not currently controversial but perhaps should be relates to the value of positive emotions and costs of negative emotions in the workplace. With the rising importance of positive psychology, and accumulated research evidence suggesting the benefits of happiness and positive emotions, we may be losing sight of the fact that negative emotions may also add value. For example, Forgas and East (2008) conducted experiments that showed that positive moods make us more likely to believe in other people's claims, which may make us more gullible and less likely to detect deception. Gruber, Mauss, and Tamir (2011) caution that happiness may have a dark side: How we pursue happiness may be inappropriate, and experiencing and displaying emotions that do not fit with what is regarded as appropriate in the context may induce penalties. In short, while we know that positive emotions have benefits, similar benefits may also exist for negative emotions, depending on the context.

WHAT DOES THIS MEAN TO YOU?

This chapter outlines the factors that affect job attitudes, and in turn the effects that job attitudes can have on other variables. A review of these factors should indicate that your degree of happiness at work is largely in your own hands. Even for factors that appear to be purely under the control of the organization, there are things you can do to find yourself in situations where job satisfaction is more likely.

Consider job characteristics. It is true that it is ultimately within the organization's power to assign you tasks that are challenging, meaningful, and give you autonomy. At the same time, it probably helps to know that these are the factors that have the likelihood for a happier work life. So when on the job market, paying attention to current and future job characteristics and not sacrificing these in favor of a little more money would make sense. A place where you can find meaning and freedom is valuable and will likely lead to a more sustainable career. In short, when deciding whether or not to take a job, think deeply about it in terms of the various factors involved beyond money.

There are things you can do to improve your relation with your manager, which could be the key to getting access to many of the things in this list, such as autonomy, interesting and challenging work, and lower levels of stress. Investing time in your relationship with the manager starting from your first day at work (in an authentic way) and being someone the manager can rely on can have long-lasting effects.

Stress is such an important reason for unhappiness (and we'll talk more about stress in Chapter 12), therefore being proactive in stress management will be important – this might involve talking to your managers and negotiating your hours, clarifying job expectations, or ensuring that you are employable by constantly updating your skills. It may involve taking care of your body and mind by eating healthily, exercising, and engaging in effective time management habits. It may even involve knowing when to quit so that your work does not damage your mental and physical well-being and your relationships.

Conclusion

Job attitudes are important because they are an important explanation for why people behave the way they do at work. Two key job attitudes, job satisfaction and organizational commitment, are oftentimes measured and managed in organizations. Organizations can improve job attitudes through a number of means, including enriching jobs, ensuring that employees are supported, and offering them a chance to do jobs that are aligned with their interests. A person's own personality is also an explanation for job attitudes. Interestingly, the level of pay or satisfaction with pay is not very important as an explanation for job attitudes, but fairness of pay and treatment by the organization matter a great deal. In addition to job attitudes, employee emotions influence behavior at work, and the gap between experienced and displayed emotions may make a job stressful and erode satisfaction level.

YOUR TURN...

WHAT DO YOU THiNK?

1. The HR manager of a company recently found out that the employees of the company are leaving comments on a popular careers website, badmouthing the company. The manager feels that this information is inaccurate, and he wants to correct the information on the board or contact the managers of the board to take down the information. He also thinks he knows who these employees might be, so he is considering whether to confront them to correct their perceptions and ask them to take down their comments. What would you advise this manager to do?

2. The HR manager of a company says that job satisfaction surveys are useless and instead companies should measure employee engagement. What would be your response to this statement?

3. What are some things organizations can do during a recession to ensure that job attitudes do not suffer?

4. Based on what you learned in this chapter, if you were tasked to design an employee attitude survey to be implemented in your organization annually, what would it look like? What would you measure? What would be some things that you would do to ensure that the response rate is high and the responses are useful?

5. As today's world of work relies more on technology and the number of employees engaged in virtual work is increasing, how do you think factors shaping job attitudes, and the role of job attitudes in relation to job performance, citizenship, and turnover, is changing?

Additional Readings

Goleman, D. (1997). *Emotional intelligence: Why it can matter more than IQ.* New York: Bantam Books.

Grant, A. (2013). *Give and take: Why helping others drives our success.* New York: Penguin Books.

Hochschild, A. R. (2012). *The managed heart: Commercialization of human feeling.* Berkeley, CA: University of California Press.

Hsieh, T. (2010). *Delivering happiness: A path to profits, passion, and purpose.* New York: Business Plus.

Macey, W. H., Schneider, B., Barbera, K. M., & Young, S. A. (2009). *Employee engagement: Tools for analysis, practice, and competitive advantage*. Malden, MA: Blackwell Publishing.

Spector, P. (1997). *Job satisfaction: Application, assessment, causes, and consequences*. Thousand Oaks, CA: Sage.

CASE STUDY: Putting Employees First at Costco

Happy workers make better workers. Whether or not this is always true, this mantra has been around for some years, and today seems to be most familiar in high-tech firms, consulting firms, or firms that rely on highly qualified and educated workers. In the retail industry, where profit margins are slim, competition is fierce, and businesses fear going out of business due to online competition, it is too easy for employees to be short-changed in terms of happiness. There are exceptions, though. One of them is the Issaquah, Washington-based Costco.

Costco is the third largest retailer in the US, following Walmart and Kroger. Its business model is slightly different from a typical retailer: It is a membership-based retailer, so only those who pay the $55 annual membership fee can shop there. The company sells well-known brands that are deeply discounted. To deliver on its low price promise, Costco's business model is based on thrift: The company does not have a PR person. It does not have a nicely furnished boardroom or a CEO office. The warehouses where merchandise is stored are built with efficiency and cost in mind, not looks. But the one area where the company does not act frugally is the employees.

The average wage for a Costco employee is $21 an hour. Compare this with the federal minimum wage of $7.25. This is 40 percent higher than what its closest competitor, Sam's Club, pays. Plus, all employees who work more than 20 hours a week receive benefits. To put things into perspective, a 2014 survey revealed that Costco employee satisfaction with their compensation is second only to that of Google employees. Further, the company promises more than a paycheck to employees. With few exceptions, promotions are from within. This means that the CEO, top managers, and warehouse managers all started in the front lines, at the check-out counter or pushing carts. The company offers chances of advancement and pay for the schooling of employees. The company empowers and values employees: Some things are routinized, but for the rest, employees are expected to use their judgment.

What are the benefits to the company? The company does not find it hard to attract job seekers. For example, when they opened a new store in 2005, before the recession, they received over 5,000 applications for 160 openings. Turnover is extremely low as well: It is 5.5 percent in an industry (retail) that is known for its high turnover. They have customer satisfaction ratings close to that of Nordstrom (a clothing retailer known for its service quality). And their sales per square foot is 70 percent higher than their closest competitor's. Unlike most retailers, which treat their employees as a cost to be minimized, Costco seems to put employees on an even footing with the value placed on customers. In fact, the CEO Craig Jelinek notes "If you treat customers with respect, and treat employees with respect, good things are going to happen to you." In return, Jelinek has been rated by employees as the sixth most highly rated CEO of large companies in 2014 on Glassdoor.com.

Questions

1. Why aren't businesses such as Costco more common? What prevents some organizations from treating employees well and putting employees first?

2. Some analysts comparing other retailers and Costco claim that because Costco has half the number of employees as Walmart per square foot, its stores are only in richer neighborhoods, and people buy in bulk, its model is not possible to replicate in other retailers. Do you agree? Why or why not?

3. If an organization that behaved differently in the past decides to truly put employees first, how do you think such a change can be brought about? What would be the steps that are necessary to go through? What would be the roadblocks?

4. In this chapter, we noted that pay is not a strong influence on employee satisfaction. However, Costco pays employees quite well, and it is one of the distinguishing factors compared to other retailers. Do you think this is contradictory information? What part of Costco's employee happiness is due to pay?

Sources: This case is partially based on information included in Cohn, 2014; Fisher, 2013; O'Donnell & McElhaney, 2014; Stone, 2013; Ton, 2012.

References

Ajzen, I. (1991). The theory of planned behavior. *Organizational Behavior and Human Decision Processes, 50,* 179–211.

Ajzen, I., & Fishbein, M. (1977). Attitude–behavior relations: A theoretical analysis and review of empirical research. *Psychological Bulletin, 84,* 888–918.

Aldag, R. J., & Brief, A. P. (1978). Supervisory style and police role stress. *Journal of Police Science and Administration, 6,* 362–367.

Allen, N. J., & Meyer, J. P. (1990). The measurement and antecedents of affective, continuance and normative commitment to the organization. *Journal of Occupational Psychology, 63,* 1–18.

Barsade, S. G. (2002). The ripple effect: Emotional contagion and its influence on group behavior. *Administrative Science Quarterly, 47,* 644–675.

Bateman, T. S., & Organ, D. W. (1983). Job satisfaction and the good soldier: The relationship between affect and employee "citizenship". *Academy of Management Journal, 26,* 587–595.

Bauer, T. N., Bodner, T., Erdogan, B., Truxillo, D. M., & Tucker, J. S. (2007). Newcomer adjustment during organizational socialization: A meta-analytic review of antecedents, outcomes, and methods. *Journal of Applied Psychology, 92,* 707–721.

Baumann, J., & DeSteno, D. (2010). Emotion guided threat detection: Expecting guns where there are none. *Journal of Personality and Social Psychology, 99,* 595–610.

Beal, D. J., Trougakos, J. P., Weiss, H. M., & Dalal, R. S. (2013). Affect spin and the emotion regulation process at work. *Journal of Applied Psychology, 98*, 593–605.

Beal, D. J., Trougakos, J. P., Weiss, H. M., & Green, S. G. (2006). Episodic processes in emotional labor: Perceptions of affective delivery and regulation strategies. *Journal of Applied Psychology, 91*, 1053–1065.

Bies, R. J., & Tyler, T. R. (1993). The "litigation mentality" in organizations: A test of alternative psychological explanations. *Organization Science, 4*, 352–366.

Bureau of Labor Statistics. (2011). *A profile of the working poor, 2011.* Retrieved September 24, 2014, from http://www.bls.gov/cps/cpswp2011.pdf.

Burris, E. R., Detert, J. R., & Chiaburu, D. S. (2008). Quitting before leaving: The mediating effects of psychological attachment and detachment on voice. *Journal of Applied Psychology, 93*, 912–922.

Chen, G., Ployhart, R. E., Thomas, H. C., Anderson, N., & Bliese, P. D. (2011). The power of momentum: A new model of dynamic relationships between job satisfaction change and turnover intentions. *Academy of Management Journal, 54*, 159–181.

Chi, C. G., & Gursoy, D. (2009). Employee satisfaction, customer satisfaction, and financial performance: An empirical examination. *International Journal of Hospitality Management, 28*, 245–253.

Christian, M. S., Garza, A. S., & Slaughter, J. E. (2011). Work engagement: A quantitative review and test of its relations with task and contextual performance. *Personnel Psychology, 64*, 89–136.

Christiansen, N. D., Janovics, J. E., & Siers, B. P. (2010). Emotional intelligence in selection contexts: Measurement method, criterion-related validity, and vulnerability to response distortion. *International Journal of Selection and Assessment, 18*, 87–101.

Circadian. (2005). *Absenteeism: The bottom-line killer.* Retrieved September 3, 2014, from http://www.workforceinstitute.org/wp-content/themes/revolution/docs/Absenteeism-Bottom-Line.pdf.

Cohn, E. (2014). Costco employees happier with pay than many in Silicon Valley. *Huffington Post*, May 23. Retrieved September 5, 2014, from http://www.huffingtonpost.com/2014/05/23/costco-pay-benefits-glassdoor_n_5375193.html.

Connolly, J. J., & Viswesvaran, C. (2000). The role of affectivity in job satisfaction: A meta-analysis. *Personality and Individual Differences, 29*, 265–281.

Cottell, P. (2014). The hole story: 3 months behind the counter at Voodoo Doughnut. *Willamette Week*, January 15. Retrieved September 27, 2014, from http://www.wweek.com/portland/article-21767-the_hole_story.html.

Crush, P. (2014, August). How to stop your new joiners quitting. *People Management*, 40–41.

Dalal, R. S. (2005). A meta-analysis of the relationship between organizational citizenship behavior and counterproductive work behavior. *Journal of Applied Psychology, 90*, 1241–1255.

Dekas, K. H., Bauer, T. N., Welle, B., Kurkoski, J., & Sullivan, S. (2013). Organizational citizenship behavior, version 2.0: A review and qualitative investigation of OCBs for knowledge workers at Google and beyond. *Academy of Management Perspectives, 27*, 219–237.

Eisenberger, R., Huntington, R. H., Hutchison, S., & Sowa, D. (1986). Perceived organizational support. *Journal of Applied Psychology*, *71*, 500-507.

Eisenberger, R., Karagonlar, G., Stinglhamber, F., Neves, P., Becker, T. E., Gonzalez-Morales, M. G., & Steiger-Mueller, M. (2010). Leader–member exchange and affective organizational commitment: The contribution of supervisor's organizational embodiment. *Journal of Applied Psychology*, *95*, 1085-1103.

Ekman, P. (1992). An argument for basic emotions. *Cognition & Emotion*, *6*(3-4), 169-200.

Farrell, D. (1983). Exit, voice, loyalty, and neglect as responses to job dissatisfaction: A multidimensional scaling study. *Academy of Management Journal*, *26*, 596-607.

Festinger, L. (1962). *A theory of cognitive dissonance*. Stanford, CA: Stanford University Press.

Fisher, A. (2013). A blueprint for creating better jobs – and bigger profits. Fortune. com, December 13. Retrieved 27 May, 2015, from http://fortune.com/2013/12/12/a-blueprint-for-creating-better-jobs-and-bigger-profits/.

Forgas, J. P., & East, R. (2008). On being happy and gullible: Mood effects on skepticism and the detection of deception. *Journal of Experimental Social Psychology*, *44*, 1362-1367.

Fredrickson, B. L. (1998). What good are positive emotions? *Review of General Psychology*, *2*, 300-319.

Fredrickson, B. L. (2001). The role of positive emotions in positive psychology: The broaden-and-build theory of positive emotions. *American Psychologist*, *56*, 218-226.

Gallup. (2015). *Gallup Q12 employee engagement survey*. Retrieved January 26, 2015, from https://q12.gallup.com/Public/en-us/Features.

Garvin, D. A. (2013, December). How Google sold its engineers on management. *Harvard Business Review*, *91*, 74-82.

Gelfand, M. J., Erez, M., & Aycan, Z. (2007). Cross-cultural organizational behavior. *Annual Review of Psychology*, *58*, 479-514.

Gerstner, C. R., & Day, D. V. (1997). Meta-analytic review of leader–member exchange theory: Correlates and construct issues. *Journal of Applied Psychology*, *82*, 827-844.

Goleman, D. (2004, January). What makes a leader? *Harvard Business Review*. Retrieved January 27, 2015, from https://hbr.org/2004/01/what-makes-a-leader.

Grandey, A. A. (2003). When "the show must go on": Surface acting and deep acting as determinants of emotional exhaustion and peer-rated service delivery. *Academy of Management Journal*, *46*, 86-96.

Griffeth, R. W., Hom, P. W., & Gaertner, S. (2000). A meta-analysis of antecedents and correlates of employee turnover: Update, moderator tests, and research implications for the next millennium. *Journal of Management*, *26*, 463-488.

Gruber, J., Mauss, I. B., & Tamir, M. (2011). A dark side of happiness? How, when, and why happiness is not always good. *Perspectives on Psychological Science*, *6*, 222-233.

Halberstadt, J. B., Niedenthal, P. M., & Kushner, J. (1995). Resolution of lexical ambiguity by emotional state. *Psychological Science, 6*, 278–282.

Harter, J. K., Schmidt, F. L., & Hayes, T. L. (2002). Business-unit-level relationship between employee satisfaction, employee engagement, and business outcomes: A meta-analysis. *Journal of Applied Psychology, 87*, 268–279.

Hülsheger, U. R., Alberts, H. J., Feinholdt, A., & Lang, J. W. (2013). Benefits of mindfulness at work: The role of mindfulness in emotion regulation, emotional exhaustion, and job satisfaction. *Journal of Applied Psychology, 98*, 310–325.

Judge, T. A., & Bono, J. E. (2001). Relationship of core self-evaluations traits – self-esteem, generalized self-efficacy, locus of control, and emotional stability – with job satisfaction and job performance: A meta-analysis. *Journal of Applied Psychology, 86*, 80–92.

Judge, T. A., Piccolo, R. F., Podsakoff, N. P., Shaw, J. C., & Rich, B. L. (2010). The relationship between pay and job satisfaction: A meta-analysis of the literature. *Journal of Vocational Behavior, 77*, 157–167.

Judge, T. A., Thoresen, C. J., Bono, J. E., & Patton, G. K. (2001). The job satisfaction–job performance relationship: A qualitative and quantitative review. *Psychological Bulletin, 127*, 376–407.

Kiefer, T. (2005). Feeling bad: Antecedents and consequences of negative emotions in ongoing change. *Journal of Organizational Behavior, 26*, 875–897.

Kunin, T. (1955). The construction of a new type of attitude measure. *Personnel Psychology, 8*, 65–77.

Lauver, K. J., & Kristof-Brown, A. (2001). Distinguishing between employees' perceptions of person–job and person–organization fit. *Journal of Vocational Behavior, 59*, 454–470.

Locke, E. A. (1976). The nature and causes of job satisfaction. In M. D. Dunnette (Ed.), *Handbook of industrial and organizational psychology* (pp. 1297–1349). Chicago, IL: Rand McNally.

Loher, B. T., Noe, R. A., Moeller, N. L., & Fitzgerald, M. P. (1985). A meta-analysis of the relation of job characteristics to job satisfaction. *Journal of Applied Psychology, 70*, 280–289.

Mathieu, C., Neumann, C. S., Hare, R. D., & Babiak, P. (2014). A dark side of leadership: Corporate psychopathy and its influence on employee well-being and job satisfaction. *Personality and Individual Differences, 59*, 83–88.

Mathieu, J. E., & Zajac, D. M. (1990). A review and meta-analysis of the antecedents, correlates, and consequences of organizational commitment. *Psychological Bulletin, 108*, 171–194.

Matsumoto, D., Yoo, S. H., Nakagawa, S. et al. (2008). Culture, emotion regulation, and adjustment. *Journal of Personality and Social Psychology, 94*, 925–937.

Matusitz, J. (2010). Disneyland Paris: A case analysis demonstrating how glocalization works. *Journal of Strategic Marketing, 18*, 223–237.

Mayer, J. D., Salovey, P., & Caruso, D. R. (2008). Emotional intelligence: New ability or eclectic traits? *American Psychologist, 63*, 503–517.

Meyer, J. P., & Allen, N. J. (1991). A three-component conceptualization of organizational commitment. *Human Resource Management Review, 1*, 61–89.

Meyer, J. P., Stanley, D. J., Herscovitch, L., & Topolnytsky, L. (2002). Affective, continuance, and normative commitment to the organization: A meta-analysis of antecedents, correlates, and consequences. *Journal of Vocational Behavior, 61,* 20-52.

Mobley, W. H. (1977). Intermediate linkages in the relationship between job satisfaction and employee turnover. *Journal of Applied Psychology, 62,* 237-240.

Mowday, R. T., Steers, R. M., & Porter, L. W. (1979). The measurement of organizational commitment. *Journal of Vocational Behavior, 14,* 224-247.

National Labor Relations Board. (2014). *Employer/union rights and obligations.* Retrieved September 24, 2014, from http://www.nlrb.gov/rights-we-protect/employerunion-rights-and-obligations.

O'Boyle, E. H., Humphrey, R. H., Pollack, J. M., Hawver, T. H., & Story, P. A. (2011). The relation between emotional intelligence and job performance: A meta-analysis. *Journal of Organizational Behavior, 32,* 788-818.

O'Donnell, J., & McElhaney, A. (2014). Costco's model may explain its pay. *USA Today,* January 30.

Oh, I. S., Guay, R. P., Kim, K., Harold, C. M., Lee, J. H., Heo, C. G., & Shin, K. H. (2014). Fit happens globally: A meta-analytic comparison of the relationships of person–environment fit dimensions with work attitudes and performance across East Asia, Europe, and North America. *Personnel Psychology, 67,* 99-152.

Ouweneel, E., Le Blanc, P. M., Schaufeli, W. B., & van Wijhe, C. I. (2012). Good morning, good day: A diary study on positive emotions, hope, and work engagement. *Human Relations, 65,* 1129-1154.

Porter, L. W., Steers, R. M., Mowday, R. T., & Boulian, P. V. (1974). Organizational commitment, job satisfaction, and turnover among psychiatric technicians. *Journal of Applied Psychology, 59,* 603-609.

Pugh, S. D. (2001). Service with a smile: Emotional contagion in the service encounter. *Academy of Management Journal, 44,* 1018-1027.

Reisel, W. D., Probst, T. M., Chia, S. L., Maloles, C. M., & König, C. J. (2010). The effects of job insecurity on job satisfaction, organizational citizenship behavior, deviant behavior, and negative emotions of employees. *International Studies of Management and Organization, 40,* 74-91.

Riffkin, R. (2014). In U.S., 55% of workers get sense of identity from their job. *Gallup Poll Briefing,* August 22.

Rosenberg, M. J., & Hovland, C. I. (1960). Cognitive, affective and behavioral components of attitudes. In M. J. Rosenberg and C. I. Hovland (Eds.), *Attitude organization and change: An analysis of consistency among attitude components.* New Haven, CT: Yale University Press.

Sackett, P. R. (2002). The structure of counterproductive work behaviors: Dimensionality and relationships with facets of job performance. *International Journal of Selection and Assessment, 10,* 5-11.

Saks, A. M., & Gruman, J. A. (2014). What do we really know about employee engagement? *Human Resource Development Quarterly, 25,* 155-182.

Schaufeli, W. B., & Bakker, A. B., & Salanova, M. (2006). The measurement of work engagement with a short questionnaire: A cross-national study. *Educational and Psychological Measurement, 66,* 701-716.

Schramm, J. (2014, August). Pay disparity may breed discontent. *HR Magazine*, 49–50.

Silverman, R. E. (2014). Careers: Are you happy in your job? Bosses push weekly surveys. *Wall Street Journal*, B1, December 3.

Siu, O. L., Cheung, F., & Lui, S. (2015). Linking positive emotions to work well-being and turnover intention among Hong Kong police officers: The role of psychological capital. *Journal of Happiness Studies, 16*, 367–380.

Smith, F. J. (1977). Work attitudes as predictors of attendance on a specific day. *Journal of Applied Psychology, 62*, 16–19.

Smith, P. C., Kendall, L. M., & Hulin, C. L. (1969). *The measurement of satisfaction in work and retirement*. Skokie, IL: Rand McNally.

Society for Industrial and Organizational Psychology (SIOP). (2012). *2012 employee job satisfaction and engagement: How employees are dealing with uncertainty*. Executive Summary. Retrieved September 5, 2014, from http://www.shrm.org/Research/SurveyFindings/Articles/Documents/SHRM-Employee-Job-Satisfaction-Engagement-Executive-Summary.pdf.

Somers, M. J. (1995). Organizational commitment, turnover and absenteeism: An examination of direct and interaction effects. *Journal of Organizational Behavior, 16*, 49–58.

Spector, P. E., Allen, T. D., Poelmans, S., Lapierre, L. M., Cooper, C. L., O'Driscoll, M., & Widerszal-Bazyl, M. (2007). Cross-national differences in relationships of work demands, job satisfaction and turnover intentions with work–family conflict. *Personnel Psychology, 60*, 805–835.

Steele, C. M., Spencer, S. J., & Lynch, M. (1993). Self-image resilience and dissonance: The role of affirmational resources. *Journal of Personality and Social Psychology, 64*, 885–896.

Stone, B. (2013). How cheap is Craig Jelinek? *Bloomberg Businessweek*, June 10, 4333.

Sutton, R. I., & Rafaeli, A. (1988). Untangling the relationship between displayed emotions and organizational sales: The case of convenience stores. *Academy of Management Journal, 31*, 461–487.

Sverke, M., Hellgren, J., & Näswall, K. (2002). No security: A meta-analysis and review of job insecurity and its consequences. *Journal of Occupational Health Psychology, 7*, 242–264.

Sy, T., Tram, S., & O'Hara, L. A. (2006). Relation of employee and manager emotional intelligence to job satisfaction and performance. *Journal of Vocational Behavior, 68*, 461–473.

Ton, Z. (2012, January/February). Why "good jobs" are good 4 retailers. *Harvard Business Review, 90*.

Tremblay, M., & Roussel, P. (2001). Modeling the role of organizational justice: Effects on satisfaction and unionization propensity of Canadian managers. *International Journal of Human Resource Management, 12*, 717–737.

Verquer, M. L., Beehr, T. A., & Wagner, S. H. (2003). A meta-analysis of relations between person–organization fit and work attitudes. *Journal of Vocational Behavior, 63*, 473–489.

Wanous, J. P., Reichers, A. E., & Hudy, M. J. (1997). Overall job satisfaction: How good are single-item measures? *Journal of Applied Psychology, 82*, 247–252.

Wasti, S. A. (2003). Organizational commitment, turnover intentions and the influence of cultural values. *Journal of Occupational and Organizational Psychology, 76*, 303–321.

Wayne, J. H., Casper, W. J., Matthews, R. A., & Allen, T. D. (2013). Family-supportive organization perceptions and organizational commitment: The mediating role of work-family conflict and enrichment and partner attitudes. *Journal of Applied Psychology, 98*, 606–622.

Weiss, H. M., & Cropanzano, R. (1996). Affective events theory: A theoretical discussion of the structure, causes and consequences of affective experiences at work. *Research in Organizational Behavior, 18*, 1–74.

Weiss, D. J., Dawis, R. V., England, G. W., & Lofquist, L. H. (1967). *Manual for the Minnesota Satisfaction Questionnaire.* Minneapolis, MN: University of Minnesota Industrial Relations Center.

Chapter 12

STRESS AND OCCUPATIONAL HEALTH PSYCHOLOGY

Occupational health psychology (OHP) encompasses important topics such as workplace well-being, stress management, and safety. OHP is its own area of psychology, with journals and societies devoted to it within the US and around the world. It is also related to many areas of psychology (e.g., clinical) as well as to I/O psychology given its focus on individuals at work.

After studying this chapter, you should be able to:

- understand what occupational health psychology is
- describe the stress and strain process
- understand ways to avoid and manage stress
- describe features of workplace wellness
- describe features of safety at work
- identify key legal and global issues surrounding occupational health psychology
- describe the current issues and controversies in occupational health psychology.

Learning goals for this chapter

Introduction

Occupational health psychology (OHP) is a relatively new discipline within psychology and is primarily concerned with the health and safety of workers. This includes both their psychological and physical health and safety. Job stress is estimated to cost US organizations over $300 billion per year in the form of absenteeism, turnover, reduced productivity, as well as high costs of medical bills (Rosch, 2001). In the UK, it is estimated that 105 million days are lost to stress each year, costing billions of dollars each year (Stress Management Society, 2014). When it comes to safety, estimates are equally serious, with approximately 2.8 million cases of occupational injury and 154,800 cases of occupational illness in private industry reported in 2012 in the United States alone (Bureau of Labor Statistics, 2013). These numbers indicate a growing challenge for organizations and workers alike. Being able to identify, avoid, and manage workplace stressors and safety challenges in order to enhance employee well-being is not an easy task, but it is an important one.

Thus, OHP is also an important part of I/O psychology, and no introductory textbook on the topic would be complete without this chapter because of the focus in I/O psychology on individuals at work. Research on these OHP topics has emerged from disparate areas such as health psychology, industrial engineering, and public health, but given our focus on I/O psychology in this book, we will especially focus on the work in this area from I/O psychology. Our goal in this chapter is to describe OHP so that you can better understand its key areas, including the stress and strain process and how to manage it, as well as the safety of employees. Let's start by understanding the concept of stress.

Stress

You've probably heard or said it yourself. The phrase, "I'm so stressed out" has become commonplace in our everyday language. However, while it is prevalent, most people don't think too much about stress and stress management as a process that is unfolding around us all the time. In this chapter, we hope to open your eyes to the process of stress, specific models of stress, as well as its antecedents, consequences, and stress management techniques. In doing so, it is our hope that your evidence-based knowledge of stress will increase and you may learn new techniques for managing your own stress levels.

Stress is defined by psychologists as the body's reaction to a change that requires a physical, mental, or emotional adjustment or response. That change is referred to as a **stressor**, which is anything that induces stress. Stress is so costly because it is so pervasive. When the Gallup organization asked working adults about their stress levels in 2012, 41 percent reported that they had felt stressed the day before (Hamblin, 2013). The American Psychological Association (2009) found that 65 percent of employees reported that work is a significant source of stress.

Stress: The body's reaction to a change that requires a physical, mental, or emotional adjustment or response.

Stressor: Events, contexts, or demands which cause a stress reaction by elevating levels of adrenaline and other responses.

While many people look forward to getting married as a joyous occasion, research (and reality TV) shows that it can be a very stressful period in people's lives. This is an example of even a happy event being stressful. In fact, there's even a name for such events. **Eustress** refers to "good stress."

Eustress: "Good" stress, caused by a positive response to a desired stressor, such as a wedding or a new job.

To make things worse, 35 percent of Americans report that their stress level has increased in the last year. Thus, it is clear that stress is not going away any time soon and is a part of every working adult's life.

However, not all people respond to stress in the same ways. For instance, some people become stressed at the slightest challenges, while others remain calm in the face of extreme situations. Thus, in addition to discussing sources of job stress, we will also cover individual differences in the experience of stress later on in this chapter.

The Stress Process

To help us understand stress, we will focus on three important models of stress. We will start with one of the earliest attempts to understand stress, referred to as General Adaption Syndrome (GAS). Following this, the Conservation of Resources (COR) model has gained popularity, then the Transactional Model of Stress and Coping. Finally, we will cover more recent approaches to understand stress such as the Job Demands–Resources model and challenge and hindrance stressors. Each of these models offers important insights into understanding the stress process. This is the first step in identifying workplace sources of stress and ways to cope with and lessen stress.

General Adaptation Syndrome

Hans Selye (1907-82), a European-born medical doctor, conducted thousands of studies resulting in 1,700 research articles during his time at the University of Montreal, Canada. He was also the founder of the International Institute of Stress. Selye was interested in understanding the relationship between stress and the body's immunological responses to stress. While this relationship is commonly accepted today, he was one of the first to posit and study such a connection. The model he developed around this idea was termed **General Adaption Syndrome** (GAS), which predicts that when confronted with a threat, an individual's body responds instinctively via the "fight or flight" response. This response boils down to one simple question: "Can I handle this or should I flee?" Each person may be able to tolerate a different level of stress, but eventually, we all have a point when our resistance weakens and negative health outcomes begin.

General Adaption Syndrome (GAS): The three-stage stress response model developed by Hans Selye.

From an evolutionary perspective, this automatic response made sense as the choice to flee or battle a predator might be the difference between survival or extinction. However, these days, the need to increase one's heart rate, and adrenaline and cortisol levels (all of which are physiological responses to stress) doesn't always serve us well when we are getting ready for a major presentation or meeting a new group of people, as a shaky voice or sweaty palms don't instill confidence in those around us. Because the body's response to perceived threats is the same for a wild animal attack or an important test, it's easy to see how we are a society of stressed-out individuals.

Alarm stage: The first stage in the GAS model when an outside stressor is detected, and the body responds by preparing the body by increasing cortisol and adrenaline levels.

Resistance stage: The second stage of the GAS model, when the body continues to release cortisol and begins the process of tapping stores of sugars and eventually fats in order to meet the ongoing demands of the stressor.

Exhaustion stage: The third stage of the GAS model, when the body has effectively run out of fats and sugars to draw upon, and the long-term release of cortisol has taken its toll, leaving the individual in a weakened state.

The GAS model describes stress as affecting individuals in three steps. The first step is the **alarm stage**. In the alarm stage, an outside stressor is detected, and the body responds by preparing itself by increasing cortisol and adrenaline levels. If an effective response to this stressor is given, the person is able to relax and the body returns to its resting state. However, if the body is not able to effectively resolve things in the alarm stage, the next step is the **resistance stage**. Once the resistance stage kicks in, the body continues to release cortisol and begins the process of tapping stores of sugars and eventually fats in order to meet the ongoing demands of the stressors. This helps to increase the energy available to deal with the ongoing stressors. But as you might imagine, this is not an effective long-term strategy. The body begins to adapt to the resistance phase and eventually it gives out. Thus, if the individual experiencing stress is not able to successfully resist the stressors he or she is experiencing, the third stage sets in: exhaustion. During the **exhaustion stage**, because the body has been working so hard for so long, it has effectively run out of fats and sugars to draw upon, and the long-term release of cortisol has taken its toll on the body, leaving the individual in a weakened state. In this situation, maladaptive behaviors such as consuming energy drinks, too much caffeine, drugs, alcohol, and junk food may be more tempting because of the quick boost of energy that comes from the rush of such calories or chemicals being released into the body. However, this can create a vicious cycle where the body is running on short-term solutions to long-term needs.

Stress is linked to negative effects on the cardiovascular, renal, and pulmonary systems (Szabo, Tache, & Somogyi, 2012). And research shows that the neurological changes caused by stress as described by the GAS framework, particularly in the case of chronic stress, are correlated with a multitude of negative health outcomes, including immunosuppression, certain chronic diseases, and a variety of mental health disorders, such as melancholic depression and anorexia nervosa (Tsigos & Chrousos, 2002). However, as you might imagine, while the GAS model has been an important one for understanding the stress process, it is not the only one. We discuss the transactional model of stress and coping next.

Transactional Model of Stress and Coping

Have you ever noticed that one person can work on a single project and be very stressed at school while others might be working on four projects but show no signs of stress? How does that work? Work by Lazarus and colleagues (Lazarus, 1966; Lazarus & Folkman, 1984) altered the view of stress beyond Selye's GAS framework to understand this observation better. They posited that stress does not originate from the event itself but rather from one's interpretation of the event,

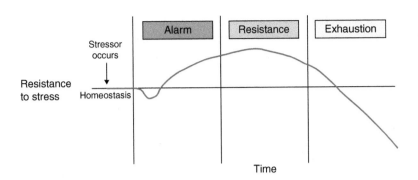

Selye's General
Adaptation
Syndrome
consists of three
phases: alarm,
resistance, and
exhaustion.

or appraisal of what the event means and whether it is a threat, along with an evaluation of what resources the individual has with which to react to the event (Lazarus, 1999). The act of coping follows appraisal and represents the individual's emotional response to his or her perception of the event's meaning. According to this model, individuals display differing coping strategies due to appraising various events differently. A key aspect of the transactional model is that stress, and coping with stress, is a process. To understand stress, stressors, and coping, one also needs to understand cognitive, affective, as well as coping factors.

Though the transactional model's conceptualization of stress and coping as an interrelated process has certainly moved the research forward, the model has its detractors. In particular, it has been criticized for being of little applied use, as well as for researchers' inability to find solid evidence pointing to what determines how well a person will cope (Dewe & Trenberth, 2004). Lazarus (2000) provides guidance for addressing these issues by emphasizing the importance of future research that uses large sample sizes, longitudinal designs, and daily contextual data points in order to capture the true processes of cognition and behavior that people undergo in their daily lives. Though research continues, many scientists seem to believe that despite the value found in the theoretical foundation of the transactional model, its methodological and measurement shortcomings have not yet been fully overcome. We discuss the Conservation of Resources model next.

Conservation of Resources Model

While the GAS model of stress is helpful for understanding the biological responses to stress, the research on workplace stressors and **strain** (the response to stress) has evolved. As noted before, the stress responses and stages described by Selye are useful in a general sense for understanding how our bodies respond to stress. However, as more and more individuals work in cubicles and experience stress at work, it makes sense to specifically examine stressors, especially those that are related to the workplace. Stevan Hobfoll, a professor of behavioral sciences, proposed the **Conservation of Resources** (COR) model (1989) of stress as a set of resources that individuals seek to acquire and maintain in order to accommodate, withstand, or overcome potential threats. These resources include objects such as a home or clothing, conditions such as one's living arrangements or financial security, personal characteristics such as self-esteem or feelings of autonomy, and energies such as time or knowledge. He then generated a list of 74 specific

Strain: A response to stress.

Conservation of Resources (COR) model: A model of stress as a set of resources that individuals seek to acquire and maintain in order to accommodate, withstand, or overcome potential threats.

443

resources within these categories which, he writes, are "a comprehensive set that appears to have validity in many Western contexts" (2001, p. 341). Thus, stress is proposed to occur when there is a loss of resources or a threat of loss of resources which serve to deplete one's resources (Hobfoll, 1989).

Research support for the COR model has been varied. For example, Grandey and Cropanzano (1999) found when studying a sample of university professors that family and work role stressors were related to both job and family distress, which in turn were related to employee turnover intentions, life distress, and poor physical health. However, they did not find that self-esteem moderated these relationships as posited by Hobfoll. Some have criticized the COR model as being so broad and general that it includes nearly everything. This issue is argued to undermine its usefulness because it is difficult to think of something that might not fit the definition of a stressor (Ganster & Perrewé, 2010; Ganster & Rosen, 2013).

Job Demands–Resources Model

Job demands–resources (JDR) theory: A model of job stress that states that strain results from mismatches between job demands and the resources available to the employee; all jobs have demands which require resources to be expended, and stress is caused when the demands of a job outweigh the resources available to the employee.

The **Job Demands-Resources (JDR) model** grew out of earlier work by Karasek, who developed the job demands–control model (Karasek, 1979), and who had established that job control is a major factor in understanding employee stress. The JDR model expanded the major focus on job control by placing it within the larger context of resources that may serve to buffer or reduce the effects of the demands of one's job (Demerouti, Bakker, Nachreiner, & Schaufeli, 2001). The JDR model argues that strain results from mismatches between job demands and the resources available to the employee. The model makes it explicit that all jobs have demands which require resources to be expended. Thus, stress is caused when the demands of a job outweigh the resources available to the employee. For example, let's consider two employees, Greg and Max, who are both under a tight deadline to complete a complex, difficult project. For both employees, the tight deadline would be a major job demand leading them to experience job strain. However, while Greg's boss is available as a resource to answer Greg's questions, Max's boss is out of town and not answering e-mail. You can see that under the JDR model, Max's experienced strain would be greater than Greg's, since Greg has an additional resource (his boss's advice) to deal with the deadline.

Research on the JDR model has been largely supportive of it. One study of over 800 Finnish teachers found the teachers' stress levels depended upon the job resources available to teachers and their ability to weather the significant stress associated with disruptive student behavior (Bakker, Hakanen, Demerouti, & Xanthopoulou, 2007). Another study examining the impact of job crafting (when employees perform their jobs in a way that works best for them) on job resources found that job crafting was positively linked to employees' increased job resources and resulted in positive outcomes such as increased work engagement and job satisfaction, as well as decreased burnout (Tims, Bakker, & Derks, 2013).

Challenge and Hindrance Stressors

Hindrance stressors: "Bad" stressors, job demands that are negatively linked to work engagement.

Before we conclude our discussion of theories of stress, we wanted to turn to the idea of challenge and hindrance stressors. **Hindrance stressors** are the "bad ones" and are defined as job demands that are negatively linked to work engagement

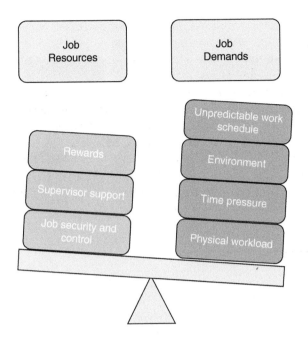

Figure 12.2 The job demands-resources model highlights the importance of balancing job resources with job demands.

"See website for interactive material"

(Crawford, LePine, & Rich, 2010). Examples include job constraints, hassles, lack of resources, or organizational politics. **Challenge stressors**, on the other hand, are the "good" kind of stressors which are posited to be developmental and are positively related to engagement. Examples of these include role demands, time urgency, and one's workload. One study of learning linked challenge stressors to increased learning performance, while hindrance stressors were linked to decreased performance (LePine, LePine, & Jackson, 2004).

Challenge stressors: "Good" stressors, job demands that are developmental and positively related to engagement.

Research summarized in meta-analyses has established that while hindrance stressors have traditionally been more frequently studied, challenge stressors are able to account for job outcomes beyond what hindrance stressors can explain (Podsakoff, LePine, & LePine, 2007). Further, while both types of stressors are related to strain and burnout, not surprisingly hindrance stressors have a bigger influence on such negative outcomes (Podsakoff et al., 2007).

Antecedents of Stress

Up to this point we have covered four different models of stress which have included some examples of stressful situations. Stressors are events, contexts, or demands which cause a stress reaction, thus causing people to experience increased strain. When it comes to stressors, it is important to keep in mind that they are cumulative. That is, the more stressors a person has, and over a greater length of time, the more likely that negative outcomes of stress will manifest. For example, one stressor might not be a big deal, and maybe even 10 small stressors

Figure 12.3
Antecedents of stress.

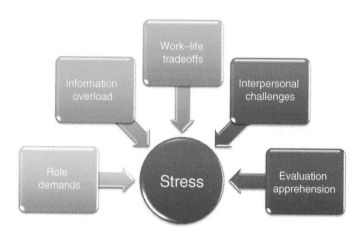

would be something you can handle. But sometimes that one last little thing is too much for you to handle. Again, this is because stressors are cumulative, and a person's resistance to stressors breaks down over time.

Role Demands

At work we all have a variety of roles we are expected to fulfill. In other words, we are hired to do certain things. As you might imagine, the expectations placed upon us at work can be stressful. Researchers have spent a great deal of time and effort identifying such demands. For example, **role ambiguity** is defined as a lack of clarity regarding one's work roles. Role ambiguity can happen when the organization does not give the employee enough information about what is expected from them. **Role conflict** is defined as having multiple contradictory demands at work. In this situation, it is unclear how to complete tasks and fulfill roles because doing one task to one person's specifications may mean disappointing someone else. For example, imagine a new supervisor, Betina, who started her job at a large sales organization just two months ago. She is still learning the ropes of being an employee there. Betina is told by her boss, the regional director, to increase sales this quarter by having the salesforce work as many hours as possible. However, Betina knows she also has a mandate from the Chief Operating Officer not to offer any overtime to employees and to try to save on personnel costs this quarter by having them work minimal hours. Betina would experience role conflict, because she has two expectations placed upon her, and they directly contradict each other.

Research shows that role demand stressors significantly impact many aspects of employees' lives, both at work and at home. A meta-analysis of 42 studies found that role ambiguity was negatively correlated with job satisfaction, which in turn predicted organizational citizenship behavior, while role conflict was also negatively associated with both job satisfaction and organizational citizenship behavior (Eatough, Chang, Miloslavic, & Johnson, 2011). Another meta-analysis examining the relationship between occupational stressors and physiological symptoms found that role conflict had a significant association with five of the eight physical symptoms studied, including back pain, gastrointestinal problems, and sleep

Role ambiguity: A lack of clarity regarding one's work roles.

Role conflict: Having multiple contradictory demands at work.

disturbances, while role ambiguity had a significant correlation with fatigue (Nixon, Mazzola, Bauer, Krueger, & Spector, 2011).

Because different jobs have different role demands, they differ in terms of how stressful they are overall. A list of the most stressful jobs in America has been created by CareerCast.com. We have summarized the results of the top 10 most stressful jobs below. As you can see, putting your life on the line in the course of duty is not the only way to get on the list, but it appears to be an important component.

The Top 10 Most Stressful Jobs in America

Some jobs are just more inherently stressful based on the different demands they place on individuals such as heavy travel, competitiveness, physical demands, and hazards. CareerCast.com ranks jobs on more than 100 criteria to determine the top 10 most stressful jobs in America and the median salary for each job. In 2013, the list was heavily populated with jobs that include putting your life on the line as part of going to work (Adams, 2013).

Here they are, along with their associated average annual salaries:

1. enlisted military personnel ($46,000)
2. military general ($196,000)
3. firefighter ($42,000)
4. commercial airline pilot ($92,000)
5. public relations executive ($58,000)
6. senior corporate executive ($101,000)
7. photojournalist ($29,000)
8. newspaper reporter ($36,000)
9. taxi driver ($22,000)
10. police officer ($55,000).

What do you think of the accuracy of this list?
What do many of these jobs have in common?
Can you think of any jobs that you feel are more stressful?

Information Overload

As a nation, we are overloaded: Never before have people received more information in so many ways. This includes both personal and professional information. Does this scenario sound familiar? Ken wants to go see a movie with David at 7 p.m. He calls David's house and doesn't get an answer. He tries David's cell phone but no one picks up. He tries texting him. That doesn't work so he gets on Facebook and sends him a message. Finally, just in case David is working on the computer, he sends him an e-mail. When Ken can't get in touch with David within 10 minutes, he becomes very frustrated with him for being so unresponsive. But hold on a minute! David never told Ken he wanted to go to the movies that night. It seems that Ken's being unfair to David, but it is now part of our culture to be available all the time.

All of this "being available" is leading to **information overload**, which is defined as the exposure to too much information or data. We all know that "unplugging"

Information overload: Exposure to too much information or data.

from information is not as easy as it seems. In fact, a poll of 5,000 people across 8 countries by Qualcomm and *Time* magazine found that 68 percent of those surveyed sleep with their smart phone within reach, and that 59 percent of those aged 18–29 said that one hour was the longest they could go without looking at their mobile devices (Gibbs, 2012). A poll by Right Management found that over 50 percent of those queried shared that they had been sent work e-mails from their bosses after hours, including evenings, weekends, or while on vacation (Gibson, 2014).

Beyond being annoying, our inability to unplug from so much information actually interferes with effective performance at work because multitasking and fragmented attention is related to decreases in focus, efficiency, and mental acuity (König, Bühner, & Mürling, 2005). In fact, this overload has been perceived as such a big problem that in Germany and other parts of Europe, formal steps are being taken to help employees unplug without suffering undesired consequences. For example, both Volkswagen and Deutsche Telekom have made strides toward eliminating e-mailing their employees during the evenings. Similarly, the German Labor Ministry is trying to lead by example by telling their own managers that they should stop contacting employees outside of working hours. In France, similar policies have been put into place to discourage e-mails after 6 p.m. Companies such as Intel and e-Verifile are also encouraging the sending of fewer e-mails during the workweek as well. Both have tried "No E-mail Friday" where employees are encouraged to pick up the phone or walk over to see colleagues rather than send e-mails. Anecdotal evidence indicates that employees like the change of pace, although this varies – some employees would rather be able to work remotely and even on weekends as this helps them balance their work and family lives.

Workplace Application

Daimler Eliminates Vacation E-mail Overload

Daimler Group, a German-based automotive company, known for designing and manufacturing Mercedes-Benz cars and Daimler big rig trucks and buses, has come up with a radical solution to post-vacation e-mail overload. While you can set your e-mail to send a vacation reply alerting senders that you are on vacation, the e-mails normally still get through, meaning that you return to an inbox stuffed with e-mails all needing your attention, making you wonder if that vacation was worth it. So, instead of just sending out e-mail replies, when you send a German Daimler employee a message while he or she is away, your reply informs you that your message has been deleted and that if it is important, you may contact another person who is identified as covering for the vacationing employee or resend it upon the employee's return from their vacation. Oliver Wihofszki, Daimler's spokesperson, told *Time* magazine that it works well for them so that vacationing employees "can come back to work with a fresh spirit" (Gibson, 2014). The program is optional, but knowing that it is an option is a powerful signal that a vacation should be a worry-free time away from the distractions of work. It also addressed the fact that 26 percent of individuals surveyed report that they feel guilty not promptly replying to work-related messages. While Daimler operates in the United States as well, it is not offering this program to its employees there ... yet.

Work–Life Tradeoffs

There are only so many hours in the day and only so much energy available to do everything we want and need to do. In fact, there are exactly 168 hours in a week. How to spend one's time is an inherent work–life tradeoff because the more time and energy spent, both physically and mentally, the less time we have for the rest of the things we may want to do in our life. Given that 25 percent of Americans work more than 40 hours each week with the average hours worked being 46, and 7 percent report working 60 hours or more (US Census Bureau, 2012), there are only 122 or fewer hours available each week to get all our basic functions like eating, sleeping, and taking trips to the bathroom as well as doing errands, house-work, and enjoying leisure pursuits. If we sleep the recommended 8 hours per day, really only 76 hours remain. As a caregiver to others such as children, aging parents, and other dependents, there is even less time available for oneself. Thus, one of the most commonly studied work–life tradeoffs is **work–family conflict** (sometimes referred to as work–life conflict), which is when demands from work and nonwork domains are negatively affecting one another.

Work–family conflict: When demands from work and nonwork domains negatively affect one another.

Life Changes

As you have probably experienced yourself, stress can result from both positive and negative changes in your life. Remember that stressors are cumulative. Applying this concept, researchers Holmes and Rahe (1967) found that those individuals who reported more life changing events over the course of one year were more likely to experience negative health outcomes. The Holmes-Rahe scale assigns different point values to different life events that range from the common, such as taking a vacation, to more serious life events, such as the death of a spouse. By adding up a person's "stress units" across 43 life events, the person is given a score which relates to their likelihood of experiencing poor health. Let's see how you score.

Self-Assessment

Please circle each event that you have experienced in the past 12 months and then add up all the events which you circled to calculate your final score.

	Life Event	Associated "Stress" Units
1.	Death of a spouse	100 points
2.	Divorce	73 points
3.	Marital separation	65 points
4.	Jail term	63 points
5.	Death of close family member	63 points
6.	Personal injury or illness	53 points
7.	Marriage	50 points
8.	Fired at work	47 points

	Life Event	Associated "Stress" Units
9.	Marital reconciliation	45 points
10.	Retirement	45 points
11.	Change in health of family member	44 points
12.	Pregnancy	40 points
13.	Sex difficulties	39 points
14.	Gain of new family member	39 points
15.	Business readjustment	39 points
16.	Change in financial state	38 points
17.	Death of close family friend	37 points
18.	Change to different line of work	36 points
19.	Change in number of arguments with spouse	35 points
20.	Large mortgage	31 points
21.	Foreclosure of mortgage or loan	30 points
22.	Change in responsibilities of work	29 points
23.	Son or daughter leaving home	29 points
24.	Trouble with in-laws	29 points
25.	Outstanding personal achievement	28 points
26.	Spouse beginning or ending work	26 points
27.	Beginning or ending school	26 points
28.	Change in living conditions	25 points
29.	Revision of personal habits	24 points
30.	Trouble with boss	23 points
31.	Change in work hours or conditions	20 points
32.	Change in residence	20 points
33.	Change in schools	20 points
34.	Change in recreation	19 points
35.	Change in church activities	19 points
36.	Change in social activities	18 points
37.	Small mortgage or loan	17 points
38.	Change in sleeping habits	16 points
39.	Change in the number of family get-togethers	15 points
40.	Change in eating habits	15 points
41.	Vacation	13 points
42.	Christmas or other major holiday	12 points
43.	Minor violations of the law	11 points

Scoring

- If you scored fewer than 150 points on the scale, you have a 30 percent chance of developing a stress-related illness in the near future.
- If you scored between 150–299 points on the scale, you have a 50 percent chance of developing a stress-related illness in the near future.
- If you scored 300 or more points on the scale, you have an 80 percent chance of developing a stress-related illness in the near future.

Source: Adapted from Holmes & Rahe (1967). Used by permission from Elsevier.

Research shows that work–family conflict is related to many important outcomes such as decreased work and life satisfaction (Kossek & Ozeki, 1998), decreased self-assessed and general work performance (Gilboa, Shirom, Fried, & Cooper, 2008), and increased feelings of negative emotions such as guilt and hostility (Judge, Ilies, & Scott, 2006). Risk factors for experiencing work-to-family conflict (in which work affects family) and family-to-work conflict (in which family responsibilities affect work) include neuroticism and negative affect, while an internal locus of control, optimism, higher self-efficacy, and a positive affect have been linked with lower levels of work-family conflict (Allen et al., 2012). Job factors that may influence work–family conflict include a greater commute time, bringing work home, and being contacted about work at home (Voydanoff, 2005). A study of working parents found that those with greater **mindfulness** (see "Workplace Application: Mindfulness Training," Chapter 8), a state of consciousness which allows noticing but not evaluating or ruminating about information, had better work–family balance, slept better, and had more vitality overall (Allen & Kibruz, 2012).

Mindfulness: A state of consciousness which allows noticing but not evaluating or ruminating about information.

How Supportive Is Your Boss?

Complete the following scale to find out.

Factor	Item/Factor
Emotional support	1. My supervisor is willing to listen to my problems in juggling work and nonwork life.
	2. My supervisor takes the time to learn about my personal needs.
	3. My supervisor makes me feel comfortable talking to him or her about my conflicts between work and nonwork.
	4. My supervisor and I can talk effectively to solve conflict between work and nonwork issues.
Instrumental support	5. I can depend on my supervisor to help me with scheduling conflicts if I need it.

Factor	Item/Factor
	6. I can rely on my supervisor to make sure my work responsibilities are handled when I have unanticipated nonwork demand.
	7. My supervisor works effectively with workers to creatively solve conflicts between work and nonwork.
Role model	8. My supervisor is a good role model for work and nonwork balance.
	9. My supervisor demonstrates effective behaviors in how to juggle work and nonwork balance.
	10. My supervisor demonstrates how a person can jointly be successful on and off the job.
Creative work–family management	11. My supervisor thinks about how the work in my department can be organized to jointly benefit employees and the company.
	12. My supervisor asks for suggestions to make it easier for employees to balance work and nonwork demands.
	13. My supervisor is creative in reallocating job duties to help my department work better as a team.
	14. My supervisor is able to manage the department as a whole team to enable everyone's needs to be met.

Rated on a scale from 1 (strongly disagree) to 5 (strongly agree).

Source: Hammer, Kossek, Yragui, & Bodner, 2009. Used by permission from Sage Publications.

Work–life conflict as a type of stressor has been on the rise as Americans are working longer than ever before, as more women are working outside of the household, and as more working men take on family responsibilities. In addition, as we saw in the information overload section previously, technology has made it harder than ever to disconnect from work and family demands no matter where we are or what we are trying to focus on doing. To help combat some of these challenges, the European Union prohibits employees from working more than 48 hours per week, and some countries such as Germany and France allow even fewer hours to be worked each week.

Workplace Application

Life Balance ... Research Finds There Is More Than One Way to Make It Work

Research by Ellen Kossek and Brenda Lautsch (2008) identified three strategies that individuals employ as they attempt to balance work and personal life demands. *Segmenters* prefer to work in specific blocks of time where they can have clear demarcations between work and personal life demands. These individuals are not likely to make appointments to meet the roofer for their house during work hours if they can help it. *Integrators* like to blur the lines between work and life demands all day long. You will find these individuals in meetings and then on the phone with their child's school, then off to another meeting, and then volunteering at their children's schools at various times during the day. *Volleyers* have periods of high segmentation and then high integration depending on the demands of their job. For example, accountants who have high intensity and lower intensity time demands during the year might employ the volleyer strategy.

Interpersonal Challenges

You may have heard the statement, "People don't quit their jobs; they quit their managers." It is true that interpersonal stress stemming from conflicts with managers is commonplace (Skakon, Nielsen, Borg, & Guzman, 2010). If you think about the role of a manager, it is their job to set up schedules, assign work, and generally set the work climate. A reasonable, fair, supportive manager can make any job a joy. However, a moody, unpredictable, capricious manager who seems to think only of him or herself can make a great job unbearable. Of course, some forms of interpersonal stressors are mild, such as simply not liking a manager or coworkers. But other forms of interpersonal stressors can be quite serious, such as an abusive supervisor (as we covered in Chapter 10) or workplace bullying. In addition to managers, coworkers as well as customers can be sources of stress. In fact, research has shown that a climate of mistreatment, which is an organizational climate that supports bullying and aggression, can lead to increased strain and more negative job attitudes (Yang, Caughlin, Gazica, Truxillo, & Spector, 2014).

Evaluation Apprehension

Sometimes what makes us feel stressed involves us "putting ourselves out there" because when we do, we will be evaluated. **Evaluation apprehension** refers to concerns about being evaluated or judged by others. Research shows that being evaluated can be helpful in creating arousal and motivating us to expend a great deal of effort (Kerr & Tindale, 2004). For example, imagine you are preparing for the presentation of your life. Based on your performance over the summer, you have been selected as one of the top five interns in the nation. As part of this honor, you are asked to give a presentation to the company's top executive team. You will be flown to the corporate headquarters and given 30 minutes to present and answer questions. This is a huge honor! But, it's also a potentially stressful situation because you want to do well. In fact, speaking before a group is often mentioned on lists of top fears. This makes sense as standing in front of a group and presenting is truly a situation where you will be evaluated.

Evaluation apprehension also has ramifications beyond its impact on an individual employee. Intellectual capital is an important resource for companies, yet high levels of evaluation apprehension have been shown to reduce employees' willingness to share knowledge in the workplace (Bordia, Irmer, & Abusah, 2006). Cultural

Evaluation apprehension: People's concerns about being evaluated or judged by others.

norms also play a role in evaluation apprehension. For example, Asian-Americans and Chinese have been shown to report more favorable self-evaluations when their evaluation apprehension is low (such as when they feel their self-evaluations are not monitored), while European Americans show no differing evaluation apprehension when completing self-evaluations in public versus private contexts (Kim, Chiu, Peng, Cai, & Tov, 2010). Of course, these findings are based on averages, so it is important to keep in mind that individuals within a given country vary on this as well as other dimensions.

Tips for Overcoming Fear of Making Presentations

1. *Practice, practice, practice.* This may seem obvious, but the more you practice your talk in the same manner you will give it, the more your body will have a chance to relax and develop "muscle memory" of delivering a calm and confident presentation.
2. *Learn to relax your body.* One key way to calm your fear of presenting is to learn breathing exercises. Slow your breathing down until you are breathing in for five to six seconds and then breathing out for five to six seconds. This will calm your fight or flight response.
3. *Bite the side of your tongue.* If you experience your mouth getting dry when you are presenting or preparing to present, try biting down on the side of your tongue gently but firmly. This will cause your body to produce extra saliva and help relieve the dryness.
4. *Join Toastmasters.* One great way to get practice is to join a support group such as Toastmasters, which is there to offer support and practice to speakers of all levels.
5. *Fake it 'til you make it.* The old adage is true. If you act confidently, you will be perceived as more confident. By going for it, others will respect your effort and hear your message.

Consequences of Stress

Up to this point, we have alluded to several potential consequences of stress over time. We have learned that stress is expensive to organizations and disruptive to the well-being of individuals. But, what exactly are the outcomes of stress in terms of what happens to employees? In this section, we will review three major categories of outcomes including physiological, psychological, and behavioral consequences of stress at work.

Physiological Consequences of Job Stress

As we saw in our earlier discussion of the stress process, stress leads to many physiological changes in the body. That is why much of the research on stress has traditionally been conducted by medical doctors, as they have a great deal of experience with understanding and measuring such changes. Their work identified key changes in the body based on short- and long-term stress including increased heart rate, rapid and shallow breathing patterns, slowed metabolism, physical aches and pains, headaches, skin problems, and greater risk of heart attacks.

If you are thinking that none of those outcomes sounds very good, you are correct. Research has made it clear that stress (particularly, the increased cortisol levels caused by stress) is related to a higher incidence of illness and disease, including cardiovascular disease, cognitive impairment, and Type II diabetes (Lundberg, 2005). Other studies have linked job stress to asthma, stomach ulcers, and alcohol and tobacco misuse (Peltzer, Shisana, Zuma, Van Wyk, & Zungu-Dirwayi, 2009), and another linked job stress to insomnia (Yeh, Lin, Lin, & Wan, 2010).

Psychological Consequences of Job Stress

While the physical consequences of stress are problematic, the psychological effects of long-term stress can be equally damaging. **Depression**, a condition where a person feels sad and hopeless, and **anxiety**, a fear or nervousness about what might happen, are highly correlated conditions and both are serious concerns. In addition, the prevalence of depression and anxiety seems to be growing, as 19 percent of those in the millennial generation have been diagnosed with depression (APA, 2013). And both are psychological outcomes of experienced stress, with long-term stress leading to changes in the brain's chemistry.

Rumination refers to the inability to stop thinking of past events and to continually think about them. Research shows that those individuals who ruminate about problems such as being evaluated have greater difficulty learning new tasks (Watson et al., 2013). And ruminating at night about past events such as negative customer interactions can affect one's mood the next day – and not for the better (Wang et al., 2013). While rumination can lead to higher stress levels, it is also something that is more likely to come up when one is already stressed out.

In addition, other psychological outcomes of stress include frustration and **burnout**, which refers to long-term exhaustion and diminished interest in work. Burnout is a condition where someone who was previously engaged in their work becomes unable to cope with their job demands due to experiencing low levels of energy and feelings of job dissatisfaction. Individuals with high aspirations who are driven to get things done are more likely to experience burnout. One study of Chinese teachers found that employees' proactivity and sense of self-efficacy had a negative correlation with burnout, which in turn was linked to negative mental health outcomes (Tang, Au, Schwarzer, & Schmitz, 2001).

Behavioral Consequences of Stress

Outcomes of stress and burnout include several dysfunctional behaviors such as decreased performance, increased withdrawal, expressions of anger and even violence, and abusing drugs and/or alcohol. After learning about how negative stress can be, you might be thinking that stress is always a "bad" thing. However, it is really a matter of degree. Research shows that when it comes to performance and work-induced stress, much like Goldilocks' porridge, our level of stress should be "just right": not too much and not too little. That is because if one's stress level is very low, one might not care enough to expend the effort necessary to perform well. At the same time, too much stress can lead a person into the stress

Depression: A condition in which a person continually feels sad and hopeless.

Anxiety: A fear or nervousness about what might happen in the future.

Rumination: The inability to stop continually thinking about past events.

Burnout: Long-term exhaustion and diminished interest in work.

Figure 12.4 The
stress-performance
relationship.

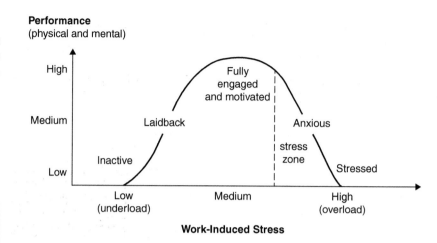

Performance
(physical and mental)

High — Fully engaged and motivated

Medium — Laidback — Anxious

stress zone

Inactive — Stressed

Low

Low (underload) — Medium — High (overload)

Work-Induced Stress

"See website
for interactive
material"

zone where their performance is impaired. Thus, as indicated by Figure 12.4, just enough stress to fully engage a person is the amount we are seeking for optimal performance.

Another behavioral outcome of stress is withdrawal from the organization. This might take the form of lack of engagement at work, tardiness, absenteeism, or even leaving the organization (Podsakoff et al., 2007). For example, in a survey of over 2,000 adults by MetLife Employee Benefits, 20 percent reported that they had taken time off of work due to stress (Crawford, 2014). Turnover is extremely costly to organizations, ranging from a low of 13 percent for jobs under $30,000 a year to upwards of over 200 percent to replace executives (Lucas, 2012).

Even worse than employees who do not withdraw due to stress are those employees who remain and create problems within the organization. For example, stress can lead employees toward anger, moodiness, and even violence. Another potential behavioral outcome of stress is the abuse of drugs and alcohol. For example, research shows that approximately 23 percent of the American workforce drank enough to be hung over the next day (Frone, 2006), and employees are twice as likely to be absent from work after consuming alcohol the previous day (McFarlin & Fals-Stewart, 2002). And research by Liu, Wang, Zhan, and Shi (2009) conducted in China found that following a stressful day, individuals were more likely to increase the amount of alcohol they drank that night, and each additional stressor increased their desire to drink more, leading to even greater consumption of alcohol.

Workplace Application

Microsoft Seeks to Find the 'Sweet Spot' for Keeping Employees Engaged but Not Stressed

	DEMAND	
	Low	**High**
CONTROL **Low**	Passive Job: 10% of employees	High Strain Job: 18% of employees
High	Low Strain Job: 11% of employees	Active Job: 60% of employees

Employees at Fortune 500 high-tech companies often have demanding jobs. It is simply the nature of the competitive market that employees in some tech companies find themselves in a situation where standing still means falling behind. This is certainly the case for Microsoft employees. However, Microsoft's HR research and analytics team had an idea. While they couldn't change the level of demands made on employees at a fundamental level, they could vary how much control employees had over how, when, and where their work was done. Drawing from Karasek's (1979) job demand–control model, their hypothesis was that having more control would lead to lower levels of exhaustion and higher levels of engagement. So, they embarked on a study to see if their hypothesis was correct. They asked employees how demanding their jobs were and then categorized employees into those with either low- or high-demand ones. They next asked employees how much control they had over their work. Survey questions like "I have a lot of freedom to decide how I do my work" and "My job allows me to make a lot of decisions on my own" were used to categorize individuals into either low- or high-control jobs.

So, what did they find? They found that those individuals who had high demand and low levels of control were indeed reporting high levels of strain. And they found that most employees were in active jobs which they reported as demanding but engaging. The high level of control did seem to make a big difference. This is helpful to know for several reasons. First, the fact that most employees are engaged but not exhausted is good news. That frees up resources to really examine how to help those employees reporting high levels of strain. And, the findings indicate that training managers and employees in how to build greater personal control over how, when, and where to do their work when possible can make a big difference. The results are also summarized in the accompanying figure.

Case information and figure used with permission of Microsoft Corporation.

Individual Differences

When it comes to experiencing stress, as we've noted throughout this chapter, no two people react to the same set of stressors in the same way. People differ in terms of their knowledge, skills, abilities, and personalities. So for example, while one person might be stressed to be asked to do a job analysis of 10 jobs within two months, another person with a great deal of experience conducting job analyses would most likely find this a routine, non-stressful assignment. One of the most frequently studied aspects of individual differences and stress is personality. And of the personality variables considered, none has received more attention than the distinction between **Type A personality** and **Type B personality**.

These personality types are measured by the Jenkins Activity Scale (Jenkins, Rosenman, & Zyzanski, 1974) where Type As are characterized as those who display high levels of impatience, do things quickly, are highly involved in their jobs, and are highly competitive. These individuals are prone to experiencing stress. Conversely, Type B individuals are characterized by a weaker sense of time urgency, being less devoted to their work, and being less competitive than Type A individuals. Early research found that Type A individuals were at a higher risk for negative health outcomes such as heart attacks (Friedman & Rosenman, 1959). However, more recent research has found different results, with Type As being less susceptible to heart problems. This may be that in today's era of online medical advice and access to healthcare, Type A individuals may be more likely to seek out medical advice than Type B individuals. However, this explanation is just a hypothesis. More recent studies have focused on the relationship between coronary heart disease and a different personality type, termed Type D, which represents people with a negative outlook and social inhibitions. Several studies have found a significant relationship between Type Ds and negative cardiovascular outcomes (Bunker et al., 2003; Denollet, Vaes, & Brutsaert, 2000).

After reading this, you might expect that Type A individuals are more successful than Type B individuals. However, research has not identified such a difference. This may be the case for several reasons. For instance, people are complex, and categorizing them into only two groups is a fairly crude metric. In addition, how one behaves is, at least partially, influenced by the situation, so that different types might be better suited for certain jobs. For instance, a Type B individual is less status conscious and less competitive, which may produce better results in teamwork-oriented or collaborative jobs, while Type A personalities might outperform in fast-paced or demanding jobs. It might also be that a Type A may be perceived as overbearing and, therefore, less effective in some circumstances.

Have you ever known someone who worked all the time and just couldn't seem to stop working? **Workaholism** is defined as a condition where individuals work excessively and compulsively. In addition, they might not even enjoy the work they do. They just feel guilty and like they have not worked enough when they stop. As you might imagine, workaholism is related to several negative outcomes such as negative physical and mental health (Kanai, Wakabayashi, & Fling, 1996; Taris, Schaufeli, & Verhoeven, 2005) and higher work–family conflict (Bakker, Demerouti, & Burke, 2009). But, it is also related to positive outcomes such as higher work satisfaction (Ng, Eby, Sorenson, & Feldman, 2005). Clark, Michel, Zhdanova, Pui,

Type A personality: Individuals who display high levels of impatience, do things quickly, are highly involved in their jobs, and are highly competitive.

Type B personality: Individuals who display a weaker sense of time urgency, less devotion to their work, and less competitiveness than Type A individuals.

Workaholism: A condition where individuals work excessively and compulsively and feel guilty as if they have not worked enough when they stop.

Why do some individuals experience a situation as stressful while others are able to relax in the face of the same situation? One answer has to do with their personalities. Research shows that the profile of an individual less prone to experiencing stress is someone who has a Type B personality, has high positive affect and self-efficacy, and low negative affect and neuroticism (Jamal, 1990; Ong, Bergeman, Bisconti, & Wallace, 2006).

and Baltes (in press) conducted a meta-analysis to help understand the correlates of workaholism and found that achievement-oriented personality characteristics like Type A personality and perfectionism were related to workaholism but that other factors such as conscientiousness, self-esteem, gender, and marital status were not.

Beyond Type A and B personalities and workaholism, research has uncovered other personality variables that affect stress as well. For example, in a meta-analysis of dispositional variables and work-family conflict, Allen et al. (2012) found that what they characterized as negative trait-based variables such as negative affect and neuroticism made individuals more vulnerable to experiencing work–family conflict. Conversely, positive affect and self-efficacy helped to buffer individuals from experiencing it.

Individual Approaches to Stress Management

We have seen in the previous sections how damaging unchecked stress can be. In 2013, an American Psychological Association survey found that 84 percent of participants reported stress equal to or greater than the year before, but only 35 percent thought they were managing their stress levels well. Although much of the responsibility for reducing work stress falls onto factors controlled by employers, it also makes sense that individuals consider personal steps to control and manage their own stress levels. When it comes to individual stress management, there are many ways you can do this. We will focus on five topics: diet, exercise, sleep, time management, and social support.

Diet

Author Tom Rath summarizes three key ingredients for health and stress management. His book, entitled *Eat Move Sleep*, summarizes the importance of these three behaviors when it comes to avoiding the problems associated with stress. For example, in a study of over 80,000 individuals, the amount of fruits and vegetables consumed was related to their overall happiness levels. One easy way to determine which fruits and vegetables are the best for us is to focus on their color. The darker and more colorful they are, the better they tend to be for us (Rath, 2013).

What we eat affects us also in our energy levels and our ability to manage stress. Have you ever noticed that after eating a candy bar you get energized but this is followed by a sleepy, low-energy feeling 30 minutes later? That's because the sugar in a candy bar is received by the body as fuel – but only for a short time. Insulin is produced by the body to process the sugar, and when too much insulin is released, blood sugar drops below normal, which is why we often feel lousy after that candy bar. However, it is not just candy bars that boost insulin levels. White rice increases Type II diabetes by 16 percent but brown rice does not because it contains more fiber and does not spike sugar levels (Sun et al., 2010). As you might imagine, this is also why wholegrain bread is a healthier alternative to white bread.

Exercise

Moving more is good for you. This is no surprise. There are really three types of exercise (and we'll add a fourth one below) that work together for stress management in different ways. Aerobic exercise is low enough in intensity that you can sustain it for several minutes. Endurance training, or aerobic exercise, increases blood flow and strengthens our heart muscles, which are both helpful in managing stress. Sustained aerobic exercise can also lead the body to produce endorphins, leading to a euphoric feeling and boost of energy sometimes referred to as a "runner's high" (Boecker et al., 2008). Strength training, or anaerobic exercise, on the other hand, is intense and triggers the formation of lactic acid, which helps to build muscles over time. These exercises are short in duration – under two minutes. Flexibility is another key component of a properly working body, and this is achieved by the third type of exercise – those exercises which serve to elongate muscles and tendons. The goal of flexibility training is to build and maintain an appropriate range of motion (Pollock et al., 1998).

The American Heart Association notes that walking just 30 minutes every day can have dramatic health benefits, including reducing the risk of coronary heart disease, improving blood pressure and blood sugar levels, and enhancing mental well-being (American Heart Association, 2015). While all of these sound like good outcomes, the other side effect is that when your body is healthier and your mind is more at ease, you are better able to cope with the stressors that come your way on a daily basis. However, finding the time (and energy) to exercise every day can be a challenge – especially for those of us who work sitting at the computer all day long. One new idea in building more movement into a desk job is the "walking desk" where you walk 1.5 to 2 miles per hour while working. The pace is slow enough that it is not overly strenuous. Research shows that those who use this type of desk lose weight (around 8 pounds per year) (Koepp et al., 2013) and perform their work better over time (Ben-Ner, Hamann, Koepp, Manohar, & Levine, 2014). The walking desk can be an expensive device or simply a table that fits over a treadmill, but it does take some time to get used to it. Participants in the study above took around three months before their performance gains kicked in as they were learning to read, write, and navigate a keyboard and mouse while walking in this new position.

Endurance	Strength	Flexibility	Breathing

• Walking • Jogging • Swimming • Biking • Climbing • Basketballl • Dancing	• Lifting weights • Using resistance band • Leg and arm lifts • Pilates	• Stretching • Yoga • Pilates	• Yoga • Pilates • Equal breathing (in for 4 seconds, out for 4 seconds) • Deep breathing (take a deep breath through the nose until the diaphragm (not the chest) inflates – repeat 6 to 10 times)

Figure 12.5
Examples of different types of exercises.

Sleep

According to the Centers for Disease Control (CDC), school-aged children need at least 10 hours each night and adults need at least 7 to 8 hours of sleep per night. However, Americans don't get enough sleep (Institute of Medicine, 2006). This is a problem as sleep is essential for replenishing depleted cognitive and physical resources. There are many reasons why we don't get enough sleep, including work. For example, extended shifts, travel that takes us across time zones, work–life demands, or ruminating about problems at work can all wreak havoc on our body's ability to get a good night's sleep. Sleep deprivation is related to many negative outcomes such as performance decrements, impaired cognitive functioning, and less innovative thinking (Barnes, 2012). Furthermore, sleep debt tends to accumulate (Rupp et al., 2010). Four consecutive nights of five hours of sleep has been found to affect functioning as much as a blood alcohol level of .06 percent does, which is above the legal limit in many states (Elmenhorst et al., 2009). Ways to get more sleep include working with your body's own circadian rhythms and going to sleep and waking at similar times each day, limiting caffeine in the afternoon and evening, exercising during the day, and avoiding screens in the hours before bed as the light-wave lengths produced by computers and other portable devices can fight the body's natural release of melatonin, a hormone which helps regulate sleep (Porges, 2012).

Time Management

One of the major stressors in today's work environment is time urgency, with frequent deadlines and heavy workloads. Therefore, a key factor in managing stress is to have effective time management strategies. This is important because research shows that those with better time management have lower stress levels. For example, one study that trained employees with a time management seminar resulted in less reported worry and avoidance behavior, in addition to an increased ability to manage their time (Van Eerde, 2003). Another time management training intervention resulted in employees reporting increased perceived control of their time, as well as decreased stress (Häfner & Stock, 2010). One successful time management intervention that resulted in less increased stress in the experimental group, compared to the control group, used task prioritizing, goal-setting techniques (setting proximal, challenging, and specific goals and monitoring goal achievement), mental simulations of the tasks the participants desired to perform the next day, and structuring the next work day by deciding where and when they wanted to work (Häfner, Stock, Pinneker, & Ströhle, 2014).

Social Support

The song lyrics "I get by with a little help from my friends" by the band The Beatles is apt when it comes to stress management. Research finds that social support is one of the key factors related to those who are able to cope with demands placed on them and those who are not. There are several levels of social support. For example, a close friend or family member might provide a valuable source of emotional support during a difficult personal experience, while a helpful manager might provide informational support, such as constructive feedback on job performance. A coworker or subordinate might provide instrumental support by helping an employee perform a task.

While social support has an impact on all aspects of one's life, what is most relevant for our purposes is how it impacts workers' lives. The research shows many positive effects of employees having a strong social support system. One study in China showed that social support moderated the relationship between stressors and job performance (Siu, Lu, & Spector, 2013). Another study of American MBA graduates showed that social support moderated the relationship between job insecurity and job satisfaction, proactive job search behavior, and life satisfaction (Lim, 1996).

Organizational Approaches to Stress Reduction and Stress Management

There are countless ways that organizations can help reduce and manage employee stress. These can involve everything from small changes to larger, more comprehensive interventions, such as those used to support military personnel (e.g., Lester, McBride, Bliese, & Adler, 2011). We will cover four of these here, including creating healthy work environments, providing flexible work arrangements, providing ample recovery experiences, and offering employee support programs.

Healthy Work Environments

As we saw from Chapter 9 on motivation, how one designs a job can make a big difference. Creating jobs which have clear expectations and which provide employees with a great deal of autonomy can be helpful ways for organizations to lower employee stress levels. This can be challenging, as there are inherent tradeoffs. For example, Grandey and Diamond (2010) note that while jobs where employees interact with customers can be positively related to a sense of personal accomplishment as well as higher job satisfaction, they can also be related to negative outcomes such as anger and burnout. However, the ability to create jobs which are fulfilling and organizational climates and cultures which are supportive and empowering has the potential to lead to strong dividends when it comes to reducing the stress placed on individual employees.

Job crafting refers to employees' proactive attempts at changing the cognitive, task, and/or relational boundaries of their jobs to shape their roles and relationships at work (Wrzesniewski & Dutton, 2001). The concept of job crafting celebrates the idea that employees are not always passive recipients of job assignments, but often take actions to shape their roles to fit with their personality, interests, and capabilities. Organizations which allow, and even encourage, employees to engage in job crafting can help employees manage their stress by focusing on what they are good at and creating meaningful work.

As we also saw in Chapter 9, fairness matters to employees. When organizations and group works are characterized by fair decisions and employee treatment free of abuse and workplace bullying, employee stress is lowered. Not only is being the victim of bullying stressful, new research across 41 hospital units and involving 357 nurses shows that simply being a witness to such negative behaviors can traumatize bystanders (Houshmand, O'Reilly, Robinson, & Wolff, 2012). Creating healthy environments includes both the climate of the organization and work groups within it and the physical characteristics of the work location.

We know that getting enough sleep is a key to successful recovery. We also know that what happens during the day at work matters to other aspects of our lives. But, it may not be apparent how much our physical work environment affects our sleep patterns. For example, research published in the *Journal of Clinical Sleep Medicine* finds that employees who have a window in their workspace get 46 more minutes of sleep per night than those in windowless workspaces, and exposure to natural light during the day was related to individuals exercising more often (Boubekri, Cheung, Reid, Wang, & Zee, 2014). And nurses who were exposed to natural light communicated more effectively with their colleagues and laughed more, while sleepiness and "bad" moods decreased (Zadeh, Shepley, Williams, & Eun Chung, in press).

The popularity of **open offices**, where employees work together with no walls and/or minimal cubicles between them, is on the rise. However, research on the negative outcomes such an environment has on stress levels indicates that they are not healthy environments and lead to higher levels of stress and lower satisfaction due to less privacy and more chaotic work environments (Konnikova, 2014). For example, the negative impact of noise, even low-level noise, is compelling. Researchers created an experiment where 40 female clerical workers were exposed to low levels of noise for three hours. Another comparable group were left in quiet environments for the same period of time. After this, all participants were given a puzzle which was impossible to solve. Those who had been exposed to the noisier environments gave up after only a few attempts while those who had enjoyed the quieter environment persisted longer (Evans & Johnson, 2000). This line of research is relevant to the recent adoption of open office designs by many organizations: While proponents of the open office argue that such designs promote communication and idea flow, research has found that while more information

Job crafting: Employees' proactive attempts at changing the cognitive, task, and/or relational boundaries of their jobs to shape their roles and relationships at work.

Open offices: Office setting in which employees work together with no walls or cubicles between them.

is shared, it tends to be more superficial in nature in an open office environment. And as one senior art director said about such arrangements, "Headphones have replaced cubicles. I wear them to let people know I'm busy. Or that I don't like them" (Van Hoven, 2014).

Flexible Work Arrangements

Telecommuting: Working a portion of time away from one's conventional workplace.

When it comes to managing work and life demands, flexible work arrangements can be invaluable. **Telecommuting**, defined as working a portion of time away from the conventional workplace, has become a popular work arrangement with 30 percent of all employees working remotely at least one day per week (Tugend, 2014) and 54 percent of employers offering this benefit (SHRM, 2014). A recent survey of those who telecommute found that 74 percent say it helps with work–life balance, and 10 percent report that they would take lower pay to maintain such flexibility (Wright, 2014). Further, 65 percent of employers who allow workers this flexibility report happier employees and lower absenteeism. On the other hand, although telecommuting has many benefits, it can cause workers to be "out of the loop" about what is going on at work.

Hoteling: A flexible work arrangement where employees are provided flexible, unassigned office space as needed.

Beyond working remotely, organizations are also offering flexible work arrangements such as **hoteling**, where employees are provided flexible, unassigned office space as needed, a practice that has been increasing. It allows those who work from home to have a location to work when they come in without having underutilized space while they are away. This works better for some industries than for others. For example, accounting and consulting companies have been quick to embrace this as employees are often at client sites for long periods of time. Booz Allen Hamilton employs such an arrangement for many of its employees.

Having a flexible and predictable schedule is also important for balancing work and life spheres. Jannette Navarro is a 22-year old barista who works at Starbucks. When the *New York Times* ran an article (Kantor, 2014) about how the unpredictable nature of her schedule made her life "into a chronic crisis over the clock," it didn't take long for Starbucks to respond. Within 24 hours they had revised their policies to end irregular schedules and instituted at least one week's advance notice of schedules for 130,000 of its baristas.

Marissa Mayer was one of the original employees at Google: In fact, she was employee number 20. She is known for having a strong design sense and is widely credited with establishing Google's look and feel. At one point, she was personally responsible for approving every "Doodle" that appeared on the search giant's homepage, and she was involved in highly visible and successful projects such as Google Maps, News, Street View, and Gmail. She became CEO of Yahoo! in 2012. One of her early decisions generated a great deal of controversy as it goes against the trend of 54 percent of organizations offering telecommuting: she got rid of it. Although her ban on telecommuting only directly affected 200 of Yahoo's 12,000 employees, her decision

to ban telecommuting sent shockwaves throughout the industry. She felt that everyone be together would help coordination, communication, and creative ideas emerging. Ms. Mayer made it clear that she was not necessarily against the practice but that, "It's not right for us, right now." Specifically, "We need to be one Yahoo, and that starts with physically being together," read the memo from Jackie Reses, Yahoo's director of human resources. Best Buy instituted a similar policy shortly after this.

Sources: Marissa Mayer biography. Retrieved February 11, 2015, from http://www.biography.com/people/ marissa-mayer-20902689; Swisher, 2013; Tkaczyk, 2013.

Recovery Opportunities

When it comes to stress, research shows a clear connection between recovery opportunities and stress management. This is because detachment and recovery are vital for helping to cope with the stressors one encounters in day-to-day interactions and to avoid exhaustion. Employees able to "unwind" from job stress when not working are healthier and have higher well-being than those who do not (Sonnentag & Fritz, 2007). For example, Makikangas et al. (2014) studied 256 Finnish employees and found that successful recovery was a key facet to high energy levels at work.

While it is ultimately up to individuals to take advantage of recovery opportunities, organizations play a vital role in terms of both short- and long-term recovery being possible. For example, a common long-term vehicle for recovery is a vacation from work. In addition, paid sabbaticals are a perk which is highly attractive to employees. But, research also shows that detaching for weekends, evenings, or even micro-breaks is helpful for combating stress.

Employee Resource Programs

Employee assistance programs (EAPs) are a confidential counseling benefit offered by employers to help employees maintain well-being and deal with any problems which may distract them from their work. Such confidential programs include free referrals and short-term help with workplace conflict and productivity issues, stressful life events, financial challenges, alcohol or chemical dependencies, or other counseling. They are offered by 74 percent of all companies surveyed by SHRM (2014). Another type of employee resource program are workplace wellness programs (WWP). WWPs are designed to help employees make healthy choices. They often include such programs as reimbursement for gym memberships, smoking cessation programs, weight loss programs, and either rewards or penalties for specific behaviors such as filling out health risk assessments. In the United States, the Affordable Care Act created new incentives and built on past wellness programs. In addition, SHRM reports that when done correctly, wellness programs can lead to high return on investments (Cyboran & Paralkar, 2013).

Employee assistance programs (EAPs):
A confidential counseling benefit offered by employers to help employees maintain well-being and deal with any problems.

Figure 12.6
Different types
of recovery
opportunities.

Sabbaticals

Paid sabbaticals, a period of leave granted away from work, are good for employees and employers who can afford it. While these are commonplace for academics who are normally eligible every 5 to 8 years, according to SHRM, only 5% of U.S. companies offer this attractive perk, but 25% of employers on *Fortune's* 100 *Best Companies to Work For* offer them.

Employees often engage in charity work and/or travel during their sabbaticals which tends to show them a different perspective than the constant grind of working. Companies such as IBM, American Express, Intel, and REI find that employees return recharged and more full of purpose.

Vacations

When people go on vacations they tend to come back to work rejuvenated and refreshed. While in Sweden laws require that all employees have five weeks of paid vacation each year, American workers don't use all their vacation time, letting some 557 million unused days go each year. In fact, the U.S. is the only developed nation that does not require employers to provide paid vacation time, with 25% of workers not receiving paid vacations or holidays. However, those who take vacations are less likely to have heart attacks or suffer from depression. The policy of having a national vacation time works for some countries. For example, in Europe, many workers take the month of August off for vacations. Because everyone is gone, there is less pressure (or use) in working during this time. Some companies, such as Netflix and Jive Software, have progressive vacation policies that allow employees to take off as much time as they need. Software company Evernote takes vacations so seriously that they pay employees up to $1,000 to take their vacation days.

Personal days

Personal days are an employee benefit where paid or unpaid days of leave from work taken at the employee's discretion for reasons not related to illness or vacation.

These have become standard in many organizations in the U.S. and they help employees deal with unexpected as well as planned work-life challenges.

Evenings

After work we get a chance to recharge each day. Activities that are effective at reducing stress and well-being include low-effort activities such as reading as well as active blocks of time such as engaging in exercise. Socializing with others is also associated with positive outcomes. What is not helpful is checking email or watching TV for the last hour before going to sleep. And sleep is one of the most important aspects of recovery as that is when our minds and bodies literally enter "repair mode."

Naps

Rather than having employees fall asleep at their desks, many companies such as Ben & Jerry's, Zappos, Nike, British Airways, and Time Warner have created comfortable nap rooms for employees to recover. Companies such as Procter & Gamble and AOL have even purchased special chairs for such a purpose called "Energy Pods." Given that 43% of Americans don't get enough sleep at night, naps make sense as long as they are not too long-longer than 20 minutes may interfere with evening sleep-and not taken too late in the day.

Micro breaks

These are non-structured breaks taken throughout the day to help employees stay energized. Some of the activities during these breaks are effective at helping refresh us such as restroom breaks, learning something new, or building positive relationships. However, research shows that getting coffee, sugary snacks, or smoking cigarettes hurts our stress management in the long run. Organizations which provide free food and snacks all day long to employees include Google who found that simple changes such as putting sugary drinks below eye level, offering smaller plates in addition to regular sized ones, and putting sugary snacks in opaque containers so they were less visible notably reduced consumption.

Workplace Application

Intel Invests in Employees via Health for Life Centers

Intel has invested in onsite medical centers, called *Health for Life Centers*, for employees and their families at its Arizona, New Mexico, and Oregon locations. The centers are run by  Take Care Health Systems, part of Walgreens Health and Wellness division. As Peter Hotz, VP for this division, stated, "Intel is on the forefront of an employer trend to provide innovative pharmacy, health, and wellness benefits at the workplace by moving from an occupational health program to a more comprehensive array of health services for employees." As this statement indicates, Intel is not alone in making such investments. Many other Fortune 500 companies including General Electric, Citibank, and Disney also offer onsite medical facilities for their employees, and Walgreens operates nearly 400 worksite health centers in the United States.

Sources: Hillsboro Argus, 2011; BusinessWire, 2011.

Workplace Safety

Another key area of Occupational Health Psychology is employee safety. In the US, over 4,400 workers were killed at work in 2013 (Bureau of Labor Statistics, 2013). This doesn't include any number of unreported non-fatal accidents and injuries. Obviously, working in a safe environment is important to workers, and all organizations should be concerned about worker safety. But there are also practical reasons that organizations should be concerned about safety: Employee accidents and injuries can lead to bad publicity, government fines, and increased insurance rates. Although accidents are often the result of factors in the physical environment, they are also a function of the psychological characteristics of the work environment and the worker. In this section, we will discuss different measures of workplace safety, and what the research shows are some of the causes of employee accidents and injuries.

Measuring Workplace Safety

Like other measures of performance (see Chapter 4), safety behavior can be broken down into objective and subjective measures. One of the most common objective measures of workplace safety is the number of accidents. For instance, if a particular work group in an organization is found to have a high number of accidents and injuries, it suggests that there could be problems with the work environment, the manager, or the workers in that group. Other objective measures of safety performance include the workers' compensation claims made in an organization and the size of insurance payouts as a result of injuries.

However, as we mentioned in Chapter 4, objective measures of performance are not perfect, and the same holds true of safety measures. Perhaps the biggest problem with these objective measures of safety is their **low base rate**, that is, the fact that accidents do not happen very often and thus are hard to predict statistically. In other words, actual accidents may be fairly infrequent in organizations, so if a company has only one or two accidents in a year, it may be that these were just chance occurrences. That's not to say that these objective measures of safety performance are not important, or that employers (and the government) do not care about them, just that some actual accidents may happen due to unforeseen factors out of the control of the company or the employee.

Perhaps the best way to think of this issue – this "criterion problem" (see Chapter 4) with measures of safety performance – is to consider that all unsafe behaviors, practices, and situations do not necessarily lead to accidents and injuries. However, it is important to keep in mind that factors like unsafe behaviors on the part of managers and employees, unsafe work practices, and unsafe situations *will increase the odds* of an actual workplace accident or injury. In other words, safety-related behaviors are the antecedents of workplace accidents and injuries, and thus, measuring safety behaviors is important in organizations – perhaps just as important as measuring actual accidents and injuries.

You may be wondering just what we mean by safety behaviors. Recall that in Chapter 4 we discussed two of the key components of work performance, core

Low base rate: Incidents that do not happen very often on the job and thus are hard to predict statistically. For example, actual accidents may be fairly infrequent in organizations.

task performance and contextual performance. Safety researchers (e.g., Griffin & Neal, 2000) have used this general framework to define safety performance as well, using the terms **safety compliance** and **safety participation**. Safety compliance behavior has to do with performing core safety behaviors such as following the safety rules and using safety equipment. Safety participation behavior has to do with supporting coworkers and safety norms within the organization. Thus, framing safety behaviors as a twofold phenomenon – performing safety behaviors yourself and helping your coworkers to stay safe – recognizes the fact that safe behaviors affect not only the employee himself or herself, but coworkers as well.

The Antecedents of Safety Behavior

Given the importance of safety to organizations as well as to individuals, it's not surprising that a good bit of attention has been focused on understanding which factors affect workplace safety so that accidents and injuries can be avoided. At this point it is important to acknowledge that a good part of what causes workplace safety is the actual physical work environment – things like the physical design of the workplace. The physical work environment is important to psychologists who study safety, but it is primarily the realm of professionals like safety engineers and ergonomists. But over the last 30 years, we've learned that a number of psychological factors can also affect workplace safety, and many employers have learned the importance of these psychological factors in reducing accidents and injuries. These psychological factors include those in the social environment of the organization, as well as individual difference factors within the individual.

Psychological Environment

There are many psychological factors in the workplace that can affect workplace safety, but perhaps the one that has received the most research attention and support is **safety climate**. Safety climate is the shared understanding that workers have about the priority of safety in the organization (Christian, Bradley, Wallace, & Burke, 2009; Zohar & Luria, 2005). For example, if managers tell workers that doing work quickly is more important than safety, whether verbally or by the rewards they give, the organization is likely to develop a poor safety climate. In fact, one meta-analysis (Christian et al., 2009) found that safety climate is the strongest predictor of workplace accidents, and another found that it had a consistent effect on safety participation and compliance (Clarke, 2006).

Given the importance of the supervisor to communicating and modeling safe behaviors to support the safety climate, it's not surprising that people have looked at safety through the lens of leadership as well. Remember that we discussed the importance of leadership in Chapter 10. Research has also found that leaders can be essential to safety climate (e.g., Kelloway, Mullen, & Francis, 2006), because of their importance in communicating safety information to employees and allowing for open communication with employees regarding safety issues and questions (e.g., Zohar & Polachek, 2014). Thus, because of their importance to workplace safety, training supervisors to be good leaders with regards to safety and providing them with feedback about their communication with employees can be

Safety compliance behavior: Core safety behaviors such as following the safety rules and using safety equipment. It is parallel conceptually to task performance.

Safety participation behavior: Worker behaviors like supporting coworkers and safety norms within the organization. Conceptually it is parallel to contextual performance.

Safety climate: The shared understanding that workers have about the priority of safety in the organization.

This photo depicts the aftermath of the Metro-North passenger train which derailed on December 1, 2013, in the Bronx on its way to New York City, killing 4 passengers and injuring more than 70. In its March 2014 report, the Federal Railroad Administration cited the safety culture as a primary culprit in the accident. Specifically, the report points to a culture that over-emphasized on-time performance over safety. As other signs of a poor safety culture, the report cited safety briefings that tended to be poorly attended and a lack of time allotted to making repairs to tracks (Flegenheimer, 2014).

Figure 12.7 A model of the antecedents of workplace safety, from Christian et al. (2009), *Journal of Applied Psychology.* Copyright American Psychological Association.

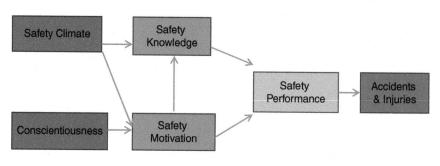

useful in improving safety (Mullen & Kelloway, 2009; Zohar & Polachek, 2014). For example, how would it feel to have a boss who encourages you to bring up safety issues when you see them, as opposed to a boss who discourages you from discussing safety issues that you notice on the job?

Psychological Factors within the Individual

Safety motivation: An employee's desire to behave safely at work and the valence or degree to which they want to behave safely.

There are also a number of individual-level factors and factors within the individual employee that can affect workplace safety as well. For instance, research has shown that **safety motivation**, or an employee's desire to behave safely at work and the valence or degree to which they want to behave safely (Christian et al., 2009; Neal & Griffin, 2006) can affect safety behavior. Not surprisingly, safety motivation is affected by whether there is a strong safety climate. Additional individual antecedents of safety found through meta-analysis include worker conscientiousness and safety knowledge (Christian et al., 2009). Christian et al.'s meta-analysis provides a good model for understanding and summarizing the antecedents of workplace safety. Their model is summarized in Figure 12.7.

In summary, while some of the causes of safety problems at work can be attributed to employees (and are therefore a selection issue), a good bit of responsibility for safety falls on the organization. In addition to creating a physically safe environment, managers can also set the tone for the degree to which safety is given priority – the safety climate. In addition, workers should be trained about workplace safety, and supervisors can also be trained to be effective leaders that support a safe workplace.

LEGAL ISSUES

Not only are recovery opportunities such as physical breaks from work recommended to help employees manage their stress levels, they are also the law. For example, Lily Prince, a 51-year-old employee working at Electrolux's (a Swedish company) factory in Minnesota sued her employer for not allowing her to take regular bathroom breaks. Similarly, Walmart and Sam's Club were found guilty of denying regular bathroom breaks for employees – and not just a few of them. The judge determined that 1.5 million shortened or missed breaks occurred between 1998 and 2004 (Stapleton, 2014).

The Occupational Safety and Health Administration, or OSHA, is a US Department of Labor agency that was designed to protect employees by overseeing working conditions and enforcing minimum safety standards in the workplace. Inspections are conducted without advanced notice to the employer, and employees are also able to report violations by their own employer, and are legally protected from retaliation, such as firing or disciplining the whistle-blowing employee.

A 2010 study of Pennsylvania OSHA violations showed that OSHA penalties did lead to reduced workplace injuries, though there was not always a direct link between the specific violation and the resulting types of injuries reduced (Haviland, Burns, Gray, Ruder, & Mendeloff, 2010). The researchers postulated that the effect was perhaps due to the company increasing its overall safety efforts as a result of the penalty (Haviland et al., 2010).

Privacy, drug use and abuse (both prescription drugs and illegal substances), and alcohol abuse laws are important to consider when it comes to support from organizations. For example, employee assistance programs (EAPs as discussed earlier in this chapter) can be a valuable tool to employees struggling with drug and alcohol addictions, yet their utilization rate at many companies is low. Studies have shown that several factors, including supervisor attitudes, social support, confidentiality, and perceived helpfulness of the program, drive employees' decisions in whether to use these services (Zarkin, Bray, Karuntzos, & Demiralp, 2001). To increase employee participation, many companies have EAP confidentiality policies that keep employee information completely private from employers, and substance abuse counselors or services that are federally assisted (as most are) are required by law to protect employee confidentiality unless the employee gives written consent to share that information (Electronic Code of Federal Regulations, 2014).

GLOBAL IMPLICATIONS

We know that downsizing, unemployment, and job insecurity can cause stress. Downsizing around the globe has become commonplace. For instance, in the United States, over 6.5 million jobs were eliminated during the aftermath of the 2008 recession. However, the issue of job loss and unemployment is truly a global problem. Downsizing, which is related to higher levels of stress, is surprisingly common for countries such as Japan, China, South Korea, and Taiwan, where lifetime employment was so recently the norm. In 2014, unemployment rates for many European countries for people under 25 were high. For example, youth unemployment is at 40 percent in Italy, 56 percent in Spain, and 65 percent in Greece. In these countries, not only is it difficult for younger people to find work, but also to find a permanent work contract. However, in examining perceptions of job insecurity across 24 countries, researchers (Debus, Probst, Konig, & Kleinmann, 2012) found that perceptions of job insecurity are buffered by a country's social safety net (e.g., training opportunities for the unemployed; unemployment benefits).

In today's labor market it is tough to find job security. However, those organizations that are able to avoid layoffs can see huge success. For example, no employee has ever been laid off at Wegmans Food Markets, SAS, the Container Store, or Lincoln Electric. These are all in very different industries, but they all can boast that they have never laid off a single employee, and each of these organizations has remained competitive in tough economic times.

Bloomberg (2013) conducted a survey of stress around the globe and found that while stress levels are rising worldwide, many of the top 10 countries reporting the highest stress levels were also dealing with core livability issues such as high homicide rates, low GDP per capita, large income inequity, and high unemployment rates. The United States ranked 54th in terms of stress of the 74 countries surveyed.

The top 10 countries in terms of high stress are:

1. Nigeria
2. South Africa
3. El Salvador
4. Mongolia
5. Guatemala
6. Colombia
7. Pakistan
8. Jamaica
9. Macedonia
10. Bolivia.

The impact of stress and well-being on older employees is of particular importance in the work setting, as industrialized countries around the world face an aging workforce (Finkelstein, Truxillo, Kanfer, & Fraccaroli, 2015). People are aging more slowly and are living longer. In some countries with lower birth rates (e.g., Japan), there may be relatively few workers to support retirees in the coming decades. With longer lives, retirement systems become unsustainable because they will have to pay out retirement benefits for a longer period, and thus many countries have increased the retirement age. In addition, individuals are choosing to work longer because they can't afford to retire or are pursuing second careers. The result is that the average age of the workforce is becoming higher, and people of different ages are working side by side. This challenge of age diversity at work will be a growing issue in the twenty-first century in many countries, with serious social and economic impact. Thus, researchers across countries are examining how organizations can use HR systems to support people who are working into their later years (Kooij, Jansen, Dikkers, & De Lange, 2010; Truxillo, Cadiz, & Rineer, 2014). Further, stress, particularly chronic stress, is associated with worse health outcomes in older adults compared to younger adults, including higher blood pressure (Uchino, Holt-Lunstad, Bloor, & Campo, 2005).

CURRENT ISSUES AND CONTROVERSIES

Because of the many advances in psychological science as well as economic and workplace changes, there are a number of research areas on employee stress that are currently unfolding. First, stress researchers are now beginning to consider physiological pathways in explaining workplace behavior and attitudes. For example, Yang, Bauer, Johnson, Groer, and Salomon (2014) used a stress model to explain how interactional unfairness (unfair treatment) can lead to workplace deviance. Specifically, the researchers found that unfair treatment led to increased levels of cortisol (a hormone associated with stress), which in turn led to deviant behavior. We expect to see the continued use of physiological and neurological measures to understand and prevent workplace stress.

Second, OHP researchers have begun to point out that much of the I/O psychology and OHP literature focuses on middle-class and professional workers. This is unfortunate because many of today's employees are low-income workers who may face a very different set of stressors, such as difficult work schedules and job insecurity (Sinclair, Probst, Hammer, & Schaffer, 2013). As such, much is needed to expand our understanding of this under-studied group, who may be highly stressed, as well as ways to better support them.

Third, there has been an increased recognition that worker stress, health, safety, and well-being are conceptualized separately, while in reality they may be also intertwined in organizations: For example, an organization with a culture that supports and promotes worker health will likely care about worker safety as well. For this reason, the National Institutes of Occupational Safety and

Health have recently focused on the concept of Total Worker Health™ (http://www.cdc.gov/niosh/twh/totalhealth.html), with an emphasis not only on health promotion but worker safety and psychological well-being. Although there have been relatively few published studies of interventions that take a Total Worker Health™ focus (Anger et al., 2015), this approach provides a fresh pathway for thinking about ways to promote both health and safety at work and prevent accidents and injuries.

WHAT DOES THIS MEAN TO YOU?

This chapter discusses some very serious outcomes of stress, some of which are caused by factors outside of the employee's control. What can one employee do to protect himself or herself from the effects of stress levels that can get overwhelming at times?

First, find out what resources are available to you as an employee. Does your company offer an employee assistance program, an option to telecommute a certain number of times per month, or any other employee health and wellness program that you may not be using? Take advantage of all the benefits that you qualify for and that will help reduce your stress. They will not only help you; they will likely help your employer as well, by making you a more productive and happier employee.

Next, schedule some of the stress reduction factors we discussed in this chapter into your life. Stress has very real (and often very negative) impacts on health, and you should be counteracting these effects to the extent that you can. Schedule time for exercise into your day, even if your only free time is during your lunch break – a 30-minute walk is all you need to keep your mind and body healthy. We discussed healthier food choices that you can substitute for your usual snacks. In addition, other stress reduction techniques can also be fitted into even the busiest of workdays, since it can be as brief as a few breaths, but it will help you relax your mind and refocus.

Third, learn to pay attention to your stress levels. Everyone handles different stressors differently, so don't compare your own ability to manage stress to anyone else's. Learn what causes you the greatest amount of stress, and see if there is a feasible way to remove or reduce that stressor. A supportive manager may be able to help you find solutions to work-related stressors that benefit both you and your employer.

To an extent, stress is a reality that everyone must live with, but with a little effort, stress levels can often be reduced to a manageable level that will allow you to work productively while also fully enjoying your nonwork life.

Conclusion

Stress is a major aspect of employees' lives and affects both on-the-job measures such as job performance and work absenteeism and employees' physical and mental health. In this chapter, we reviewed some of the major frameworks that detail the stress response, the personal and job factors that can contribute to increased stress (including the impact of personality types), and some common outcomes of stress. Fortunately, there are many ways to combat stress, and we next discussed personal health measures, such as diet and exercise that can help the body manage stress, as well as measures that organizations can take to reduce stress in their employees, including flexible work arrangements and employee assistance programs. We also described the rich literature on workplace safety and key psychological factors that can reduce accidents and injuries. Finally, we discussed stress from a broader perspective, including the legal environment, the ramifications of job stress globally, including job insecurity and workplace aging, and current issues such as the total worker health concept.

YOUR TURN... WHAT DO YOU THiNK?

1. How much do you think that feeling stressed at work is an employee's choice? Please explain your answer.

2. Consider the job of firefighter. How do you think these individuals combat their own fight or flight response? What things did we cover in this chapter that might be helpful for a new firefighter to manage his or her stress better? What can an employer do to help manage firefighter stress?

3. Imagine you have been asked to design a customer service job that is effective and engaging but relatively low in terms of stressors. Is this possible? Where would you begin to try to figure this out? What factors would you focus on?

4. Think of a time when you have been highly stressed. What did you do to manage your stress? After reading this chapter, do you think you'd manage your own stress differently or in the same way? Why or why not?

5. Many supervisors are under pressure to keep production up, while at the same time to maintain a safe work environment. What are some ways that they can manage this balance between meeting goals and taking care of employees? What is the role of top management?

Additional Reading

Beus, J. M., Payne, S. C., Bergman, M. E., & Arthur Jr., W. (2010). *Safety climate and injuries: An examination of theoretical and empirical relationships. Journal of Applied Psychology, 95,* 713–727.

Cooper, C. L., Quick, J. C., & Schabracq, M. J. (Eds.). (2010). *International handbook of work and health psychology* (3rd ed.). Chichester, England: Wiley-Blackwell.

Hobfoll, S. E. (1989). Conservation of resources: A new attempt at conceptualizing stress. *American Psychologist, 44,* 513–524.

Moran, M. M. (2014). *The OSHA answer book for general industry* (12th ed.). (n.p.): Moran Associates.

Quick, J. C., & Tetrick, L. E. (Eds.). (2010). *Handbook of occupational health psychology* (2nd ed.). Washington, DC: American Psychological Association.

CASE STUDY: Training Supervisors to be Supportive

When it comes to employee stress reduction, some of it is an individual employee's responsibility, but much of it could be the organization's responsibility. Clearly, after reading this chapter, you can see that the employment context plays a role both in causing stress and in reducing it. However, it is also apparent after reading this chapter that reducing employee stress can help not only the employee and the organization, but also can impact the coworkers around that employee.

Research shows that supervisors can have an enormous influence on employee stress reduction and increased work–life balance. This makes sense as the supervisor helps to structure the work, is responsible for deadlines associated with the job, and is an often-cited reason for employee stress and turnover.

One work–family linkages researcher is Leslie Hammer, our colleague at Portland State University, who studies these issues with the support of large, federally funded grants. She is also the associate director for the Oregon Healthy Workforce Center, based at Oregon Health and Science University and the Director of the Center for Work-Family Stress, Safety, and Health, which was originally funded by the National Institute for Child Health and Human Development and the National Institute for Occupational Safety and Health. As one of six funded centers across the United States, it is part of the national Work, Family, and Health Network through 2014.

More recently, Professor Hammer was awarded a major grant from the Department of Defense to study ways to increase supervisor support and enhance employment retention for military veterans reintegrating into the workforce. This includes ways in which organizations can help reduce work and family stress and improve positive spillover among employees by training supervisors how to provide support to their employees who have family responsibilities. Research shows that supervisor support – including emotional support, instrumental support, role modeling, and creative work–family management – can help improve employee well-being, improve job satisfaction, decrease turnover intentions, and lead to improved reports of health.

Questions

1. What lessons can supervisors and organizations learn from this line of applied research?

2. Do you think that stress management and prevention is more of the employee's responsibility or the organization's responsibility? Why?

3. In addition to helping manage work and family responsibilities, can you think of other ways that supervisors and coworkers can be supportive toward employees?

4. How effective do you think this type of training is long term? Please explain your answer.

Sources: This case is partially based on information included in Leslie Hammer, Worker Wellness. Retrieved February 12, 2015, from http://www.pdx.edu/profile/leslie-hammer; Hammer et al. (2009).

References

Adams, S. (2013). The most stressful jobs of 2013. *Forbes*, January 3. Retrieved February 12, 2015, from http://www.forbes.com/sites/susanadams/2013/01/03/the-most-stressful-jobs-of-2013/.

Allen, T. D., Johnson, R. C., Saboe, K. N., Cho, E., Dumani, S., & Evans, S. (2012). Dispositional variables and work–family conflict: A meta-analysis. *Journal of Vocational Behavior, 80*, 17–26.

Allen, T. D., & Kiburz, K. M. (2012). Trait mindfulness and work–family balance among working parents: The mediating effects of vitality and sleep quality. *Journal of Vocational Behavior, 80*, 372–379.

American Heart Association. (2015). *American Heart Association recommendations for physical activity in adults.* Retrieved February 11, 2015, from http://www.heart.org/HEARTORG/GettingHealthy/PhysicalActivity/FitnessBasics/American-Heart-Association-Recommendations-for-Physical-Activity-in-Adults_UCM_307976_Article.jsp.

American Psychological Association. (2009). *Stress in America 2009.* Retrieved 27 May, 2015, from https://www.apa.org/news/press/releases/stress/2009/stress-exec-summary.pdf.

American Psychological Association. (2013). *Stress in America.* Retrieved September 3, 2014, from http://www.apa.org/news/press/releases/stress/2012/full-report.pdf.

Anger, W. K., Elliot, D. L., Bodner, T., Olson, R., Rohlman, D. S., Truxillo, D. M., Kuehl, K. S., Hammer, L. B., & Montgomery, D. (2015). Empirical research in total worker health interventions. *Journal of Occupational Health Psychology, 20*, 226–247

Bakker, A. B., Demerouti, E., & Burke, R. (2009). Workaholism and relationship quality: A spillover-crossover perspective. *Journal of Occupational Health Psychology, 14*, 23–33.

Bakker, A. B., Hakanen, J. J., Demerouti, E., & Xanthopoulou, D. (2007). Job resources boost work engagement, particularly when job demands are high. *Journal of Educational Psychology, 99*, 274.

Barnes, C. M. (2012). Working in our sleep: Sleep and self-regulation in organizations. *Organizational Psychology Review, 2*, 234–257.

Ben-Ner, A., Hamann, D. J., Koepp, G., Manohar, C. U., & Levine, J. (2014). *Treadmill workstations: The effects of walking while working on physical activity and work performance.* PLOS. Retrieved September 8, 2014, from http://www.plosone.org/article/info%3Adoi%2F10.1371%2Fjournal.pone.0088620.

Bloomberg. (2013). *Most stressed-out: Countries.* Retrieved January 25, 2015, from http://www.bloomberg.com/visual-data/best-and-worst//most-stressed-out-countries.

Boecker, H., Sprenger, T., Spilker, M. E., Henriksen, G., Koppenhoefer, M., Wagner, K. J., ... Tolle, T. R. (2008). The runner's high: Opioidergic mechanisms in the human brain. *Cerebral Cortex, 18*, 2523–2531.

Bordia, P., Irmer, B. E., & Abusah, D. (2006). Differences in sharing knowledge interpersonally and via databases: The role of evaluation apprehension and perceived benefits. *European Journal of Work and Organizational Psychology, 15*, 262–280.

Boubekri, M., Cheung, I. N., Reid, K. J., Wang, C. H., & Zee, P. C. (2013). Impact of windows and daylight exposure on overall health and sleep quality of office workers: A case-control pilot study. *Journal of Clinical Sleep Medicine, 10*, 603–611.

Bunker, S. J., Colquhoun, D. M., Esler, M. D., Hickie, I. B., Hunt, D., Jelinek, V. M., ... Tonkin, A. M. (2003). "Stress" and coronary heart disease: Psychosocial risk factors. *The Medical Journal of Australia, 178*, 272–276.

Bureau of Labor Statistics. (2013). *Occupational injuries and illnesses: industry data* [Data file]. Retrieved September 6, 2014, from http://www.bls.gov/iif/data.htm.

Bureau of Labor Statistics. (2014). *Number of fatal work injuries, 1992–2013.* Retrieved February 2, 2015, from http://www.bls.gov/iif/oshwc/cfoi/cfch0012.pdf.

BusinessWire. (2011). Walgreens Take Care Health Systems and Intel expand healthcare relationship. Retrieved February 11, 2015, from http://www.businesswire.com/news/home/20110106005500/en/Walgreens-Care-Health-Systems-Intel-Expand-Health#.VN0Wa7DF9WI.

Christian, M. S., Bradley, J. C., Wallace, J. C., & Burke, M. J. (2009). Workplace safety: A meta-analysis of the roles of person and situation factors. *Journal of Applied Psychology, 94*, 1103–1127.

Clark, M. A., Michel, J. E., Zhdanova, L., Pui, S. Y., & Baltes, B. B. (in press). All work and no pay? A meta-analytic examination of the correlates and outcomes of workaholism. *Journal of Management.*

Clarke, S. (2006). The relationship between safety climate and safety performance: A meta-analytic review. *Journal of Occupational Health Psychology, 11*, 315–327.

Crawford, E. R., LePine, J. A., & Rich, B. L. (2010). Linking job demands and resources to employee engagement and burnout: A theoretical extension and meta-analytic test. *Journal of Applied Psychology, 95,* 834–848.

Crawford, R. (2014). 20% take time off work due to stress. Insuresphere.com, April 11. Retrieved September 4, 2014, from http://insuresphere.com/20-take-time-off-work-due-to-stress/.

Cyboran, S. F., & Paralkar, S. (2013). *Wellness program ROI depends on design and implementation.* Alexandria, VA: Society for Human Resource Management. Retrieved September 5, 2014, from http://www.shrm.org/hrdisciplines/benefits/articles/pages/wellness-roi-design.aspx.

Debus, M. E., Probst, T. M., König, C. J., & Kleinmann, M. (2012). Catch me if I fall! Enacted uncertainty avoidance and the social safety net as country-level moderators in the job insecurity–job attitudes link. *Journal of Applied Psychology, 97,* 690–698.

Demerouti, E., Bakker, A. B., Nachreiner, F., & Schaufeli, W. B. (2001). The job demands-resources model of burnout. *Journal of Applied Psychology, 86,* 499–512.

Denollet, J., Vaes, J., & Brutsaert, D. L. (2000). Inadequate response to treatment in coronary heart disease adverse effects of Type D personality and younger age on 5-year prognosis and quality of life. *Circulation, 102,* 630–635.

Dewe, P., & Trenberth, L. (2004). Work stress and coping: Drawing together research and practice. *British Journal of Guidance & Counselling, 32,* 143–156.

Eatough, E. M., Chang, C. H., Miloslavic, S. A., & Johnson, R. E. (2011). Relationships of role stressors with organizational citizenship behavior: A meta-analysis. *Journal of Applied Psychology, 96,* 619–632.

Electronic Code of Federal Regulations. (2014). *Title 42: Public Health.* Retrieved September 6, 2014, from http://www.ecfr.gov/cgi-bin/text-idx?rgn=div5;node=42%3A1.0.1.1.2.

Elmenhorst, D., Elmenhorst, E.-M., Luks, N., Maass, H., Mueller, E.-W., Vejvoda, M., Wenzel, J., & Samel, A. (2009). Performance impairment during four days of partial sleep deprivation compared with the acute effects of alcohol and hypoxia. *Sleep Medicine, 10,* 189–197.

Evans, G. W., & Johnson, D. (2000). Stress and open-office noise. *Journal of Applied Psychology, 85,* 779–783.

Finkelstein, L. M., Truxillo, D. M., Fraccaroli, F., & Kanfer, R. (2015). Facing the challenges of a multi-age workforce: A use-inspired approach. In L. Finkelstein, D. Truxillo, F. Fraccaroli, & R. Kanfer (Eds.), *Facing the challenges of a multi-age workforce: A use-inspired approach.* SIOP Organizational frontiers series. New York, NY: Routledge.

Flegenheimer, M. (2014, March). Report finds punctuality trumps safety at Metro North. *New York Times.* Retrieved September 28, 2014, from http://www.nytimes.com/2014/03/14/nyregion/safety-is-lacking-at-metro-north-us-review-finds-after-a-fatal-crash.html.

Friedman, M., & Rosenman, R. H. (1959). Association of specific overt behavior pattern with blood and cardiovascular findings: Blood cholesterol level, blood clotting time, incidence of arcus senilis, and clinical coronary artery disease. *Journal of the American Medical Association, 169,* 1286–1296.

Frone, M. R. (2006). Prevalence and distribution of alcohol use and impairment in the workplace: A U.S. national survey. *Journal of Studies on Alcohol, 76,* 147–156.

Ganster, D. C., & Perrewé, P. L. (2010). Theories of occupational stress. In J. C. Quick & L. E. Tetrick (Eds.), *Handbook of occupational health psychology* (2nd ed.) (pp. 37–53). Washington, DC: American Psychological Association.

Ganster, D.C., & Rosen, C.R. (2013). Work stress and employee health: A multidisciplinary review. *Journal of Management, 39,* 1085–112

Gibbs, N. (2012). Your life is fully mobile: We walk, talk and sleep with our phones. But are we more- or less-connected? *Time.* Retrieved September 8, 2014, from http://techland.time.com/2012/08/16/your-life-is-fully-mobile/.

Gibson, M. (2014). Here's a radical way to eliminate vacation email overload. *Time.* Retrieved February 12, 2015, from http://time.com/3116424/daimler-vacation-email-out-of-office/.

Gilboa, S., Shirom, A., Fried, Y., & Cooper, C. (2008). A meta-analysis of work demand stressors and job performance: Examining main and moderating effects. *Personnel Psychology, 61,* 227–271.

Grandey, A. A., & Cropanzano, R. (1999). The conservation of resources model applied to work–family conflict and strain. *Journal of Vocational Behavior, 54,* 350–370.

Grandey, A. A., & Diamond, J. A. (2010). Interactions with the public: Bridging job design and emotional labor perspectives. *Journal of Organizational Behavior, 31,* 338–350.

Griffin, M. A., & Neal, A. (2000). Perceptions of safety at work: A framework for linking safety climate to safety performance, knowledge, and motivation. *Journal of Occupational Health Psychology, 5,* 347–358.

Häfner, A., & Stock, A. (2010). Time management training and perceived control of time at work. *Journal of Psychology, 144,* 429–447.

Häfner, A., Stock, A., Pinneker, L., & Ströhle, S. (2014). Stress prevention through a time management training intervention: An experimental study. *Educational Psychology, 34,* 403–416.

Hamblin, J. (2013). The most stressful places to live. *The Atlantic,* April 23. Retrieved 27 May, 2015, from http://www.theatlantic.com/health/archive/2013/04/the-most-stressful-places-to-live/275223/.

Hammer, L. B., Kossek, E. E., Yragui, N. L., & Bodner, T. E. (2009). Development and validation of a multidimensional measure of family supportive supervisor behaviors (FSSB). *Journal of Management, 35,* 837–856.

Haviland, A., Burns, R., Gray, W., Ruder, T., & Mendeloff, J. (2010). What kinds of injuries do OSHA inspections prevent? *Journal of Safety Research, 41,* 339–345.

Hillsboro Argus. (2011). Intel to open on-site medical center at Jones Farm campus. January 4, 2011. Retrieved February 11, 2015, from http://www.oregonlive.com/argus/index.ssf/2011/01/intel_to_open_on-site_medical.html.

Hobfoll, S. E. (1989). Conservation of resources: A new attempt at conceptualizing stress. *American Psychologist, 44,* 513–524.

Hobfoll, S. E. (2001). The influence of culture, community, and the nested-self in the stress process: Advancing conservation of resources theory. *Applied Psychology, 50,* 337–421.

Hobfoll, S. E. (2010). Conservation of resources theory: Its implications for stress, health, and resilience. In S. Folkman (Ed.), *The Oxford handbook of stress, health, and coping* (pp. 127–147). New York: Oxford University Press.

Holmes, T. H., & Rahe, R. H. (1967). The social readjustment rating scale. *Journal of Psychosomatic Research, 11,* 213–218.

Houshmand, M., O'Reilly, J., Robinson, S., & Wolff, A. (2012). Escaping bullying: The simultaneous impact of individual and unit-level bullying on turnover intentions. *Human Relations, 65,* 901–918.

Institute of Medicine. (2006). *Sleep disorders and sleep deprivation: An unmet public health problem.* Washington, DC: The National Academies Press.

Jamal, M. (1990). Relationship of job stress and Type-A behavior to employees' job satisfaction, organizational commitment, psychosomatic health problems, and turnover motivation. *Human Relations, 43,* 727–738.

Jenkins, C. D., Rosenman, R. H., & Zyzanski, S. J. (1974). Prediction of clinical coronary heart disease by a test for the coronary-prone behavior pattern. *New England Journal of Medicine, 290,* 1271–1275.

Judge, T. A., Ilies, R., & Scott, B. A. (2006). Work–family conflict and emotions: Effects at work and at home. *Personnel Psychology, 59,* 779–814.

Kanai, A., Wakabayashi, M., & Fling, S. (1996). Workaholism among employees in Japanese corporations: An examination based on the Japanese version of the Workaholism Scales. *Japanese Psychological Research, 38*(4), 192–203.

Kantor, J. (2014). Working anything but 9 to 5. *New York Times,* August 13, 2014. Retrieved February 5, 2015, from http://www.nytimes.com/interactive/2014/08/13/us/starbucks-workers-scheduling-hours.html.

Karasek, R. A. (1979). Job demands, job decision latitude, and mental strain: Implications for job redesign. *Administrative Science Quarterly, 24,* 285–308.

Kelloway, E. K., Mullen, J., & Francis, L. (2006). Divergent effects of transformational and passive leadership on employee safety. *Journal of Occupational Health Psychology, 11,* 76–86.

Kerr, N. L., & Tindale, R. S. (2004). Group performance and decision making. *Annual Review of Psychology, 55,* 623–655.

Kim, Y. H., Chiu, C. Y., Peng, S., Cai, H., & Tov, W. (2010). Explaining East–West differences in the likelihood of making favorable self-evaluations: The role of evaluation apprehension and directness of expression. *Journal of Cross-Cultural Psychology, 41,* 62–75.

Koepp, G. A., Manohar, C. U., McCrady-Spitzer, S. K., Ben-Ner, A., Hamann, D. J., Runge, C. F., & Levine, J. A. (2013). Treadmill desks: A 1-year prospective trial. *Obesity, 4,* 705–711.

König, C. J., Bühner, M., & Mürling, G. (2005). Working memory, fluid intelligence, and attention are predictors of multitasking performance, but polychronicity and extraversion are not. *Human Performance, 18,* 243–266.

Konnikova, M. (2014). The open-office trap. *New Yorker,* January 7. Retrieved September 1, 2015, from http://www.newyorker.com/business/currency/the-open-office-trap.

Kooij, D. T. A. M., Jansen, P. G. W., Dikkers, J. S. E., & de Lange, A. H. (2010). The influence of age on the associations between HR practices and both affective commitment and job satisfaction: A meta-analysis. *Journal of Organizational Behavior, 31,* 1111–1136.

Kossek, E. E., & Lautsch, B. A. (2008). *CEO of me: Creating a life that works in the flexible job age.* Philadelphia, PA: Wharton School Publishing.

Kossek, E. E., & Ozeki, C. (1998). Work-family conflict, policies, and the job–life satisfaction relationship: A review and directions for organizational behavior–human resources research. *Journal of Applied Psychology, 83,* 139–149.

Lazarus, R. S. (1966). *Psychological stress and the coping process.* New York: McGraw-Hill.

Lazarus, R. S. (1999). *Stress and emotion: A new synthesis.* New York: Springer.

Lazarus, R. S. (2000). Toward better research on stress and coping. *American Psychologist, 55,* 665–673.

Lazarus, R. S., & Folkman, S. (1984). *Stress, appraisal and coping.* New York: Springer.

LePine, J. A., LePine, M. A., & Jackson, C. L. (2004). Challenge and hindrance stress: Relationships with exhaustion, motivation to learn, and learning performance. *Journal of Applied Psychology, 89,* 883–891.

Lester, P. B., McBride, S., Bliese, P. D., & Adler, A. B. (2011). Bringing science to bear: An empirical assessment of the Comprehensive Soldier Fitness program. *American Psychologist, 66,* 77.

Lim, V. K. (1996). Job insecurity and its outcomes: Moderating effects of work-based and nonwork-based social support. *Human Relations, 49,* 171–194.

Liu, S., Wang, M., Zhan, Y., & Shi, J. (2009). Daily work stress and alcohol use: Testing the cross-level moderation effects of neuroticism and job involvement. *Personnel Psychology, 62,* 575–597.

Lucas, S. (2012). How much does it cost companies to lose employees? *Moneywatch.* Retrieved February 2, 2015, from http://www.cbsnews.com/news/how-much-does-it-cost-companies-to-lose-employees/.

Lundberg, U. (2005). Stress hormones in health and illness: The roles of work and gender. *Psychoneuroendocrinology, 30,* 1017–1021.

Mäkikangas, A., Kinnunen, S., Rantanen, J., Mauno, S., Tolvanen, A., & Bakker, A. B. (2014). Association between vigor and exhaustion during the workweek: A person-centered approach to daily assessments. *Anxiety, Stress, & Coping, 27,* 555–575.

McFarlin, S. K., & Fals-Stewart, W. (2002). Workplace absenteeism and alcohol use: A sequential analysis. *Psychology of Addictive Behaviors, 16,* 17–21.

Mullen, J. E., & Kelloway, E. K. (2009). Safety leadership: A longitudinal study of the effects of transformational leadership on safety outcomes. *Journal of Occupational and Organizational Psychology, 82,* 253–272.

Neal, A., & Griffin, M. A. (2006). A study of the lagged relationships among safety climate, safety motivation, safety behavior, and accidents at the individual and group levels. *Journal of Applied Psychology, 91,* 946–953.

Ng, T. W., Eby, L. T., Sorensen, K. L., & Feldman, D. C. (2005). Predictors of objective and subjective career success: A meta-analysis. *Personnel Psychology, 58,* 367–408.

Nixon, A. E., Mazzola, J. J., Bauer, J., Krueger, J. R., & Spector, P. E. (2011). Can work make you sick? A meta-analysis of the relationships between job stressors and physical symptoms. *Work & Stress*, *25*, 1–22.

Ong, A. D., Bergeman, C. S., Bisconti, T. L., & Wallace, K. A. (2006). Psychological resilience, positive emotions, and successful adaptation to stress in later life. *Journal of Personality and Social Psychology*, *91*, 730–749.

Peltzer, K., Shisana, O., Zuma, K., Van Wyk, B., & Zungu-Dirwayi, N. (2009). Job stress, job satisfaction and stress-related illnesses among South African educators. *Stress and Health*, *25*, 247–257.

Podsakoff, N. P., LePine, J. A., & LePine, M. A. (2007). Differential challenge stressor-hindrance stressor relationships with job attitudes, turnover intentions, turnover, and withdrawal behavior: A meta-analysis. *Journal of Applied Psychology*, *92*, 438–454.

Pollock, M. L., Gaesser, G. A., Butcher, J. D., Després, J. P., Dishman, R. K., Franklin, B. A., & Garber, C. E. (1998). ACSM position stand: The recommended quantity and quality of exercise for developing and maintaining cardiorespiratory and muscular fitness, and flexibility in healthy adults. *Medicine & Science in Sports & Exercise*, *30*, 975–991.

Porges, S. (2012). Fighting back against the health menace of LCD screens. *Forbes*, October 8. Retrieved February 11, 2015, from http://www.forbes.com/sites/sethporges/2012/10/08/fighting-back-against-the-health-menace-of-lcd-screens/.

Rath, T. (2013). *Eat move sleep: How small choices lead to big changes*. Jackson, TN: Missionday.

Rosch, P. J. (2001). The quandary of job stress compensation. *Health and Stress*, *3*, 1–4.

Rupp, T. L., Wesensten, N. J., & Balkin, T. J. (2010). Sleep history affects task acquisition during subsequent sleep restriction and recovery. *Journal of Sleep Research*, *19*(2), 289–297.

Sinclair, R. R., & Probst, T., Hammer, L. B., & Schaffer, M. M. (2013). Low income families and occupational health: Implications of economic stress for work–family conflict research and practice. In A.-S. G. Antoniou & C. L. Cooper (Eds.), *The psychology of the recession on the workplace* (pp. 308–323). Northampton, MA: Edward Elgar.

Siu, O. L., Lu, C. Q., & Spector, P. E. (2013). Direct and indirect relationship between social stressors and job performance in Greater China: The role of strain and social support. *European Journal of Work and Organizational Psychology*, *22*, 520–531.

Skakon, J., Nielsen, K., Borg, V., & Guzman, J. (2010). Are leaders' well-being, behaviors and style associated with the affective well-being of their employees? A systematic review of three decades of research. *Work & Stress*, *24*, 107–139.

Society for Human Resource Management. (2014). *2014 employee benefits: An overview of employee benefits offerings in the U.S.* Retrieved February 2, 2015, from http://www.shrm.org/Research/SurveyFindings/Documents/14-0301%20 Benefits_Report_TEXT_FNL.pdf.

Sonnentag, S., & Fritz, C. (2007). The Recovery Experience Questionnaire: Development and validation of a measure for assessing recuperation and unwinding from work. *Journal of Occupational Health Psychology, 12,* 204-221.

Stapleton, M. (2014). Minnesota: Worker denied restroom break sues Electrolux. Retrieved February 2, 2015, from http://www.wsws.org/en/articles/2014/ 03/17/minn-m17.html.

Stress Management Society. (2014). *Practical help to ease stress in the workplace.* Retrieved February 2, 2015, from http://www.stress.org.uk/Stress-at-work. aspx.

Sun, Q., Spiegelman, D., van Dam, R. M., Holmes, M. D., Malik, V. S., Willet, W. C., & Hu, F. B. (2010). White rice, brown rice, and risk of type 2 diabetes in US men and women. *JAMA Internal Medicine, 170,* 961-969.

Swisher, K. (2013). "Physically together": Here's the internal Yahoo no-work-from-home memo for remote workers and maybe more. *All ThingsD,* February 22. Retrieved February 11, 2015, from http://allthingsd.com/20130222/ physically-together-heres-the-internal-yahoo-no-work-from-home-memo-which-extends-beyond-remote-workers/

Szabo, S., Tache, Y., & Somogyi, A. (2012). The legacy of Hans Selye and the origins of stress research: A retrospective 75 years after his landmark brief "letter" to the editor of Nature. *Stress, 15,* 472-478.

Tang, C. S. K., Au, W. T., Schwarzer, R., & Schmitz, G. (2001). Mental health outcomes of job stress among Chinese teachers: Role of stress resource factors and burnout. *Journal of Organizational Behavior, 22,* 887-901.

Taris, T. W., Schaufeli, W. B., & Verhoeven, L. C. (2005). Workaholism in the Netherlands: Measurement and implications for job strain and work–nonwork conflict. *Applied Psychology, 54,* 37-60.

Tims, M., Bakker, A. B., & Derks, D. (2013). The impact of job crafting on job demands, job resources, and well-being. *Journal of Occupational Health Psychology, 18,* 230-240.

Tkaczyk, C. (2013). Marissa Mayer breaks her silence on Yahoo's telecommuting policy. *Fortune,* April 19. Retrieved February 11, 2015, from http://fortune.com/2013/04/19/marissa-mayer-breaks-her-silence-on-yahoos-telecommuting-policy/.

Truxillo, D. M., Cadiz, D. M., & Rineer, J. R. (2014). The aging workforce: Implications for human resource management research and practice. In S. Jackson (Ed.), *Business and management.* Oxford handbooks online. DOI: 10.1093/oxfor dhb/9780199935406.013.004

Tsigos, C., & Chrousos, G. P. (2002). Hypothalamic–pituitary–adrenal axis, neuroendocrine factors and stress. *Journal of Psychosomatic Research, 53,* 865-871.

Tugend, A. (2014). It's unclearly defined, but telecommuting is fast on the rise. *New York Times,* March 7. Retrieved February 2, 2015, from http://www. nytimes.com/2014/03/08/your-money/when-working-in-your-pajamas-is-more-productive.html?_r=2.

US Census Bureau. (2012). *Labor force statistics from the current population*. Retrieved February 2, 2015, from http://www.bls.gov/cps/cpsaat19.htm.

Uchino, B. N., Holt-Lunstad, J., Bloor, L. E., & Campo, R. A. (2005). Aging and cardiovascular reactivity to stress: Longitudinal evidence for changes in stress reactivity. *Psychology and Aging, 20,* 134.

van Eerde, W. (2003). Procrastination at work and time management training. *Journal of Psychology, 137,* 421–434.

Van Hoven, M. (2014). RIP cubicles: Why agencies are gaga over open-office plans. Digiday.com, January 31. Retrieved September 1, 2015, from http://digiday.com/agencies/open-office-space-pros-cons/.

Voydanoff, P. (2005). Consequences of boundary-spanning demands and resources for work-to-family conflict and perceived stress. *Journal of Occupational Health Psychology, 10,* 491–503.

Wang, M., Liu, S., Liao, H., Gong, Y., Kammeyer-Mueller, J., & Shi, J. (2013). Can't get it out of my mind: Employee rumination after customer mistreatment and negative mood in the next morning. *Journal of Applied Psychology, 98,* 989–1004.

Watson, A. M., Foster Thompson, L., Rudolph, J. V., Whelan, T. J., Behrend, T. S., & Gissel, A. L. (2013). When big brother is watching: Goal orientation shapes reactions to electronic monitoring during online training. *Journal of Applied Psychology, 98,* 642–657.

Wrzesniewski, A., & Dutton, J. E. (2001). Crafting a job: Revisioning employees as active crafters of their work. *Academy of Management Review, 26,* 179–201.

Wright, A. D. (2014). 10% would take less pay to telecommute, study says. SHRM Online, June 13. Retrieved February 2, 2015, from http://www.shrm.org/hrdisciplines/technology/articles/pages/less-pay-to-telework.aspx.

Yang, L. Q., Bauer, J., Johnson, R. E., Groer, M. W., & Salomon, K. (2014). Physiological mechanisms that underlie the effects of interactional unfairness on deviant behavior: The role of cortisol activity. *Journal of Applied Psychology, 99,* 310–321.

Yang, L. Q., Caughlin, D. E., Gazica, M. W., Truxillo, D. M., & Spector, P. E. (2014). Workplace mistreatment climate and potential employee and organizational outcomes: A meta-analytic review from the target's perspective. *Journal of Occupational Health Psychology, 19,* 315–335.

Yeh, Y. C., Lin, B. Y. J., Lin, W. H., & Wan, T. T. (2010). Job stress: Its relationship to hospital pharmacists' insomnia and work outcomes. *International Journal of Behavioral Medicine, 17,* 143–153.

Zadeh, R. S., Shepley, M. M., Williams, G., & Eun Chung, S. S. (in press). The impact of windows and daylight on caregivers' physiological, psychological, and behavioral health and on medication errors. Retrieved February 2, 2015, from https://www.herdjournal.com/article/impact-windows-and-daylight-acute-care-nurses-physiological-psychological-and-behavioral-hea.

Zarkin, G. A., Bray, J. W., Karuntzos, G. T., & Demiralp, B. (2001). The effect of an enhanced employee assistance program (EAP) intervention on EAP utilization. *Journal of Studies on Alcohol and Drugs, 62,* 351–358.

Zohar, D., & Luria, G. (2005). A multilevel model of safety climate: Cross-level relationships between organization and group-level climates. *Journal of Applied Psychology, 90,* 616–628.

Zohar, D., & Polachek, T. (2014). Discourse-based intervention for modifying supervisory communication as leverage for safety climate and performance improvement: A randomized field study. *Journal of Applied Psychology, 99,* 113–124.

Chapter 13

TEAMS AT WORK

The Blue Angels flight team is composed of team members from the US Navy and Marine Corps who have applied and been selected for the team. The ability to successfully maneuver multiple planes while going at top speeds in a precision formation comes from thousands of hours of practice and top teamwork skills by all 16 team members in the air and on the ground. As a result of their remarkable teamwork, they are able to draw crowds and delight over 11 million fans on the ground each year. In this chapter you will learn about teamwork.

After studying this chapter, you should be able to:

- understand what teams are and what they are not
- describe the team development process
- understand ways to maximize process gains and minimize process losses
- describe features of effective teams
- describe team decision-making
- identify key legal and global issues surrounding work teams
- describe the current issues and controversies around work teams.

Learning goals for this chapter

Introduction

Landing on the moon. Delivering packages from New York to Copenhagen, Brazil, and Japan on the same day. Mobilizing the Red Cross to provide humanitarian aid in the face of a disaster. None of these things can be accomplished alone. They are simply too big and too complex for a single person to execute. This is one of the reasons that teams are an important component of what gets done day to day around the world. Not surprisingly, then, teams are also, in large part, how work is organized and gets done within organizations. Because of this, I/O psychologists need to understand teams in the workplace.

You probably already have some experience working in a team. At a minimum, as a student in college you have probably worked in a student team, or even many teams, to complete an assignment. You may have had a positive experience where everyone was respectful and responsible and produced great outcomes such as an effective team project or presentation that was well received. Or it may have been something that you simply tried to "survive" because it wasn't going well. When it comes to teams and teamwork, one's experience is a function of a number of key components we will cover in this chapter.

While groups and teams have always been around in the daily lives of humans, it wasn't until more recently that organizations and organizational researchers began to systematically study teams and understand what can be done to make them more effective. Over the past several decades, workplace design has been increasingly focused on team efforts and performance rather than individual, as organizational processes become more complex and thus reliant on the efforts of multiple employees to accomplish the organization's objectives (Kozlowski & Ilgen, 2006). The latest research on the functioning of teams considers teams to be dynamic entities within a larger organizational framework, which adapt to an evolving organizational context, including changing work demands and the addition and subtraction of team members (Kozlowski & Ilgen, 2006). Research into work teams, and especially the pursuit of increasing team performance, has resulted in the development of 130 models of how teams work, most of which address the relationships between the inputs, processes, and outputs of the team (Salas, Cooke, & Rosen, 2008). Though extensive organizational research into teams is a relatively recent development, both organizations and researchers have quickly recognized the team as an organizational structure that can address the demands of a changing workforce and leverage the efforts of individuals to drastically improve the organization's effectiveness and performance.

Luckily for I/O psychology, while research on teams has only really taken off in recent years, the explosive growth in research on teams and teamwork means we know more than ever before about issues such as how teams form and develop, factors associated with team effectiveness, key roles within teams, as well as different types of teams. I/O psychologists are often tasked with helping to design work which often includes teams (see Chapter 9 on motivation). In addition, we know more about group decision-making than ever before as well, which is helpful because much of the work done by those within organizations, including I/O psychologists, includes identifying problems and critically assessing options for different courses of action. Thus, our goal in this chapter is to describe and better understand the key aspects of teamwork. We start by understanding what work groups and teams are and how they are each defined.

When you think about how work gets done these days, it is hard to imagine that organizations did not begin to consistently and intentionally implement teams until the 1980s. Today, teams of one sort or another almost exclusively run top brands and organizations such as those depicted.

Group Dynamics

Types of Groups

A **group** is defined as a collection of individuals who interact with each other such that one person's actions have an impact on the others (Bauer & Erdogan, 2016). Groups may differ in terms of how formal or informal they are. **Formal groups** consist of deliberate and systematic groupings of people in an organization. **Informal groups** consist of natural and spontaneous groupings of people. With that in mind, we can think of several examples of each type of group. For example, a formal group might exist because your instructor has asked your class to form groups of five in order to complete a course assignment. Given that it is a deliberate and systematic group, this is a formal group. However, perhaps a small group of students from the class discover that they all enjoy the same kind of music. An informal group might form as they make plans to see a particular band that is coming to town. In an organizational setting, a **work team** is defined as "interdependent collections of individuals who share responsibility for specific outcomes for their organizations" (Sundstrom, DeMeuse, & Futrell, 1990, p. 120). Even though there are theoretical differences between groups and teams (for example, groups are more general collections of individuals, while teams are more specific forms of groups), in this chapter, we are not going to make a large distinction between these concepts. There are some differences, but for our purposes, we will be using the terms interchangeably.

Group: A collection of individuals who interact and where one person's actions have an impact on the others.

Formal group: Deliberate and systematic groupings of people in an organization.

Informal group: Natural and spontaneous groupings of people.

Work team: Interdependent collections of individuals who share responsibility for specific outcomes for their organizations.

The Life Cycle of a Group

Over your lifetime, it is likely that you will be involved in many groups. Some of your current group memberships may be maintained for your entire life, such as

Figure 13.1 The stages of group development as envisioned by Tuckman (1965) are depicted here.

Forming: The first stage of the group process, where work group members come together for the first time. Interactions include sharing general information about one another.

Storming: The second stage of the group forming process and the most tumultuous stage, as group members work to understand their task and question how things will get done.

Norming: The third stage of the group forming process, when the group develops norms and roles.

Performing: The fourth stage of the group forming process, where groups spend a majority of their time completing their tasks with competence and addressing any dissent constructively.

Adjourning: The last stage of the group forming process, when group members move on to new tasks and the group disbands.

being a member of your family. However, other groups, especially those at work or at school, form and disband over time. This process was studied and described by Bruce Tuckman, who developed the Tuckman's Five Stages model of group development (Tuckman, 1965; Tuckman & Jensen, 1977).

This model consists of a series of stages, the first of which is **forming** (Bonebright, 2010). In this stage, work group members come together for the first time. Interactions include sharing general information about one another, and interactions tend to remain relatively superficial. It is here that group members begin to understand the task and discuss initial norms. The second stage is called the **storming** stage. This is the most tumultuous stage of group development. As group members work to understand their task and question how things will get done, conflicts may arise. In addition, group members may be testing one another to see who will emerge as the more powerful group members and which roles members will take on as a result of this stage. Interactions may include resistance and emotional and task conflict. The third stage is **norming**. In this stage, the group has worked through their storming phase enough to begin to develop norms around how the group operates and which roles exist. In terms of interactions, group members are probably now more likely to express their personal opinions. **Performing** is the fourth stage. Typically groups spend the greater part of their time in this stage, completing their tasks with competence and addressing any dissent constructively. Finally, the last stage is **adjourning**. In this stage, group members move on to new tasks and the group disbands. This is a good opportunity to reflect on what went well and what the team members might do differently in the future. The idea behind this model is that it describes the life cycle of groups and it became a widely adopted paradigm for understanding them.

Connie Gersick, a former faculty member at UCLA, is well known for her study in the 1980s of team development. As we've seen, Tuckman's model was the accepted understanding of how groups developed. But, as often happens, such findings do not always remain unquestioned. Gersick's study included a sample of eight teams which were meeting multiple times to accomplish a variety of goals across a range of group life cycles (between a week and six

Punctuated Equilibrium Model

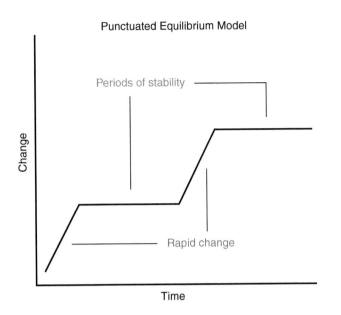

Figure 13.2 The Punctuated Equilibrium Model of Teamwork describes periods, or phases, of team activity including both periods of stability and rapid change over time.

Interactive: The Punctuated Equilibrium Model.

"See website for interactive material"

months). She sat in on their meetings and observed their interactions. As alluded to above, what she found was surprising to her in view of what she had learned about group development models such as Tuckman's. While some of the groups did progress through the stages suggested by such models, other groups did not (Gersick, 1988). Those groups that behaved in unexpected ways progressed through what she termed a pattern of **punctuated equilibrium**. What she observed was that at around the halfway point between when the groups started their work and their upcoming deadlines, they began to change course in their approach to their work. Gersick's work built upon the findings by researchers who argued that it is iterative cycles that teams go through rather than straightforward, linear steps or stages (e.g., Poole, 1983). This point of view has been supported by subsequent research (e.g., Chang, Bordia, & Duck, 2003; Okhuysen & Waller, 2002). More recent scholars in the area of teams research define two time periods – the transition (or planning) phase and the action phase – and propose that teams cycle back and forth between these two phases to accomplish their work (Marks, Mathieu, & Zaccaro, 2001; Morgeson, DeRue, & Karam, 2010). If Gersick had not used observational methods, it is not clear that this finding would have emerged. Thus, one thing that this indicates, beyond the finding that teams do not work in a purely linear way toward their goals, is how important it is to use multiple research methods– an issue you'll recall from Chapter 2.

In our experience, some student teams happily move right into the performance stage without much attention to the forming, storming, or norming stages. When that happens, the teams are at greater risk of having to go back to the storming stage late in the process if process or content issues arise. At that point, resolving group dynamic issues is more challenging as time pressures are often stronger and deadlines loom large.

Punctuated equilibrium: How groups change course in their approach to their work over time and teams go through iterative cycles rather than linear steps.

Types of Teams

Cross-trained teams: Teams where members are trained to perform multiple roles beyond their own.

Action and performing teams: Teams that deal with emergencies and crises, such as surgical teams and bomb squads.

Advisory teams: Teams that include task forces (teams with one-time objectives) and quality control groups that make suggestions to improve a product.

Management teams: Teams that include the top leaders within organizations, usually consisting of the highest executive and his or her direct subordinates.

Production teams: Teams that make or process things, such as computer chip manufacturers.

Cross-trained teams are those where team members are trained to perform multiple roles beyond their own. This can be helpful to avoid becoming overly dependent on one particular person. For example, imagine you are working in a team to complete a project for an important class. If roles have been divided, what would happen if one person suddenly became ill and could not perform his or her duties? Of course, in a short-term project team, it makes less sense to have everyone learn how to perform all the tasks. However, if you were a product development team expected to work together for years, that investment in cross-training might make a great deal of sense for when someone leaves the organization.

There are a variety of other typologies that can be used to categorize teams including Sundstrom, McIntyre, Halfhill, and Richards' (2000) six-factor typology, which includes action and performing teams, advisory teams, management teams, production teams, project teams, and service teams. **Action and performing teams** deal with emergencies and crises. Surgical teams and bomb squads are examples of action and performing teams. **Advisory teams** include task forces (teams with one-time objectives) and quality control groups that make suggestions to improve a product. **Management teams** include the top leaders within organizations, usually consisting of the highest executive and his or her direct subordinates. **Production teams** make or process things. Examples include computer chip manufacturers or those working in an oil refinery. **Project teams** deal with ideas and are often cross-functional, that is, they include people from different functional areas in the organization such as Marketing and Manufacturing. Knowledge workers and those in Research and Development are often put into project teams. Finally, **service teams** work to ensure high-quality outcomes over repeated situations. Examples include flight attendants and customer support representatives.

Figure 13.3 Action, Management, Production, and Service teams are just four of many groups and teams you may interact with each day.

| Action and Performing Teams | Management Teams | Production Teams | Service Teams |

When it comes to the pit crews who support drivers such as on the Ferrari F1Team shown here, effectiveness is measured in fractions of seconds.

Factors Related to Team Effectiveness

The increased reliance on teams within organizations has created an even greater need to understand how to design, organize, and maintain teams in a way that increases their chances of success. This section of the chapter will focus on just that, starting with what team effectiveness is and moving into the key factors that influence it.

Team effectiveness refers to two facets of teams: their performance and their viability (Sundstrom et al., 1990). According to Nielsen (2007), **team performance** refers to successful delivery of an output to customers inside or outside the organization, while **team viability** refers to the ability and desire of group members to continue to work with one another. Both are important aspects of evaluating team effectiveness, but they focus on different aspects of it: Performance is "getting the job done well", while viability relates to the possible longevity of the work group or team.

Scholars have often studied groups following the input-process-output model (Ilgen, 2005). Figure 13.4 summarizes the factors we will cover in this chapter. To help us understand what makes teams effective, we will focus on three important categories of groups, including *group composition* (input), *group processes* (process), and *group affect* (emotion), which are all related to *team effectiveness* (output).

Group Composition

One of the most important factors relating to team effectiveness is group composition. While there are many different approaches to understanding team composition (Mathieu, Tannenbaum, Donsbach, & Alliger, 2013), we will cover four of the most salient ones here, including group size, group tenure, group personality, and group diversity.

Project teams: Teams that deal with ideas. Often cross-functional. Knowledge workers and those in Research and Development are often put into project teams.

Service teams: Teams that work to ensure high-quality outcomes over repeated situations, such as flight attendants and customer support representatives.

Team effectiveness: A measure of two facets of teams: their performance and their viability.

Team performance: Successful delivery of an output to customers inside or outside the organization.

Team viability: The ability and desire of group members to continue to work with one another.

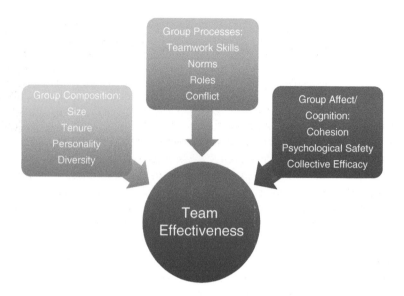

Figure 13.4 Factors relating to team effectiveness.

Group size: How many members belong to the group.

Social loafing: The tendency for group members to put forth less effort when they are participating in a joint activity than they would if they were acting individually.

Group Size

One of the commonly examined features of group composition is **group size**, or how many members belong to the group. You might be wondering if larger groups are more productive than smaller ones. On the one hand, we can imagine that larger groups have a performance advantage given the old adage, "Many hands make light work." On the other hand, as groups grow in size, it becomes more challenging to coordinate and motivate team members toward common goals. **Social loafing** is defined as the tendency for group members to put forth less effort when they are participating in a joint activity than they would if they were acting individually. It is the result of deindividuation within a group setting leading to decreased individual effort, whether consciously or unconsciously (Liden, Wayne, Jaworski, & Bennett, 2004). It is well established that individuals in larger groups expend less effort (Latane, Williams, & Harkins, 1979), take less responsibility (Wicker & Mehler, 1971), and have lower performance than those in smaller groups (Liden et al., 2004). Liden et al. (2004) studied 23 work groups consisting of 168 employees. Interestingly, they found that perceptions of coworker social loafing were associated with reduced social loafing rather than an increase. Schippers (2014) studied 209 student teams working on a complex task above the skill levels of the 644 individuals on the teams. She found that social loafing was not an issue when the team members had high levels of conscientiousness. Further, when teams had members with high levels of both conscientiousness and agreeableness, performance showed no decrement. In another study, Mueller (2012) set out to examine this relationship across 26 teams of 212 knowledge workers. She found that as size of groups increased, members had lower feelings of support or relational connection. This loss was associated with lowered individual performance even after controlling for extrinsic motivation and coordination losses associated with the individual and the team.

Overall gains in team performance do increase as group size increases, but there is a point of diminishing returns (Stewart, 2006). In other words, adding more

Workplace Application

Pret A Manger Tasks Teams with Selection

Pret A Manger (which means "ready to eat" in French) is a sandwich shop which started in the UK and has since been expanding across Europe and the United States. What makes this sandwich shop relevant for this chapter is their extreme emphasis on teamwork. Employees are rewarded based on how their team performs overall. Though this strategy is not overly unusual since many companies use team rewards to help foster teamwork, what makes Pret A Manger truly unique is their approach to hiring. Those job applicants who the manager thinks might be good employees are invited to work a six-hour shift at an actual store. At the end of the shift, the individual is paid for his or her time no matter what. However, whether or not they are hired is based on what the team thinks of the worker: Established employees vote on whether to keep the applicant on as a new employee or not. This peer-driven selection approach to teamwork is unique.

team members might make the team's performance higher, but the gains diminish as more and more members are added. Interestingly, while research consistently shows that teams do suffer from process loss (the difference between the input of effort and output quantity), individuals and organizations do not often take this factor into account when creating deadlines, which can result in falling behind in the schedule (Staats, Milkman, & Fox, 2012).

Group Tenure

Group tenure is a measure of how long members have belonged to a certain group. For teams, group tenure is a complicated factor to understand as new members often come, go, return, and are replaced. What is clear is that these different levels of group tenure have implications for team effectiveness. For example, Lewis, Belliveau, Herndon, and Keller (2007) found that groups with high "churn" – where group members joined and exited frequently – were related to lower effectiveness. Similarly, Chen (2005) studied 65 project teams and found that new group member initial performance as well as improvement in performance was related to team overall performance. Gruenfeld, Martorana, and Fan (2000) found that groups were more prolific idea generators when members left to join another group and then returned, compared to before they left or when they were simply gone. In addition, Summers, Humphrey, and Ferris (2012) found that whether or not member changes are good or bad for the group depends upon the relative abilities of the people who stay versus those who leave.

Group tenure: A measure of how long members have belonged to a certain group.

Group Personality

We will discuss personality in terms of the "Big Five" personality factors we covered in Chapter 5. The study of personality traits within a team is often divided into the traits' elevation and variability, with elevation being the mean personality score within a group, and variability being the variance from the group's mean personality score (how big the differences are in personality among group members). So which types of personalities are related to team effectiveness?

For extraversion, both negative and positive correlations with team effectiveness have been proposed. On the one hand, extraversion is expected to produce team members with positive attitudes toward the work required and high performance expectations; on the other, extraverts tend to be dominant, resulting in conflict if other extraverts are present, and they may be more interested in social interaction than in performing the task at hand. A meta-analysis by Peeters, Van Tuijl, Rutte, and Reymen (2006) found no significant correlation to team performance in either direction for either variability or elevation of extroverted traits.

It is interesting to note that research has consistently found that team member agreeableness is one of the strongest personality predictors of how well teams perform as a group, but it is one of the weakest at predicting individual performance (Bell, 2007). Bradley, Baur, Bandford, and Postlethwaite (2013) set out to understand this. They examined 107 projects teams and found that agreeableness affected team performance by making communication more effective and cohesion higher. Interestingly, they found that these results only held in face-to-face groups and went away in virtual team settings. Peeters et al. (2006) found similar results: a team's consistent levels of agreeableness were positively associated with its performance, while variability in agreeableness was negatively associated with team performance.

What about the other Big Five traits? Conscientiousness, which is the most consistent Big Five trait predictor of individual performance (see Chapter 6), is positively correlated to team performance only when the similarity in conscientiousness among group members is high (Barrick, Stewart, Neubert, & Mount, 1998; Peeters et al., 2006). Elevation of emotional stability scores has so far not been found to predict team performance. This may be because the factors used in past studies were too broadly defined to apply to emotional stability in the context of team performance (Peeters et al., 2006). Finally, neither elevation nor variability in openness to experience has been linked to team performance (Peeters et al., 2006). However, due to small sample sizes, further studies are also needed on this trait to validate these findings.

The relationship between team personality and performance can become complicated to understand. Yet, when researchers have examined more nuanced questions such as, "When does conflict lead to higher team performance?", interesting findings have emerged. For example, Bradley, Klotz, Postlethwaite, and Brown (2013) studied 117 student teams to see how personality and team conflict related to performance. They found that task conflict had a *positive* effect when members were higher on openness and/or emotional stability versus the *negative* effects for teams with lower levels of these traits. In other words, conflict wasn't good or bad for teams. Rather, how they dealt with it – openly and calmly versus secretly and volatility – was what mattered most.

Group Diversity

We know that team diversity can set the stage for team success. We also know that group diversity can present challenges for team effectiveness (Chatman & Flynn, 2001). Diversity can include demographics such as gender, race, or age. In addition, diverse experiences, abilities, cultures, and physical characteristics may also be factors on which people differ. Recent research has even begun to examine how differences in how individuals perceive time influence teams and their effectiveness (Mohammed & Nadkarni, 2014). When differences lead to lowered cohesion and/or unhealthy communication patterns, groups face lowered team effectiveness (Jackson et al., 2003).

Another concern is when subgroups form and fracture the level of cohesion in a group. These are referred to as group faultlines. **Faultlines** are defined as "hypothetical dividing lines that may split a group into subgroups based on one or more attributes" (Lau & Murnighan, 1998). Such faultlines are problematic to the degree to which they trigger members to form in-groups and outgroups based on shared diversity characteristics. A study which examined group dynamics across student groups working together across 10 countries found that geographic differences were related to higher conflict and lowered trust (Polzer, Crisp, Jarvenpaa, & Kim 2006). Further, the faultlines were strongest when a team consisted of two equally sized subgroups from the same country and when those subgroups were more similar to one another. The implications of these findings are intriguing. It may be that it is not diversity *per se* that creates challenges for groups, but multiple subgroups that are not necessarily working toward a common goal or working with a common set of norms. Carton and Cummings (2013) set out to resolve the issue of whether subgroups created by faultlines were helpful or not by studying 326 teams. They found that it depended on the type of subgroups that formed. The most effective teams had subgroups based on knowledge, and those teams that suffered the most had subgroups based on identity.

Despite introducing challenges, there are also many potential benefits to diverse groups. For example, diverse groups have additional information available to them, a greater variety of experiences, and the ability to approach problems in a greater number of ways. Unfortunately, it is not always clear when diversity is helpful to group performance or a hindrance. Additional research has identified some of the conditions which are helpful for drawing out the benefits of group diversity. For example, Chatman, Polzer, Barsade, and Neale (1998) studied diverse groups and found that those in MBA teams which emphasized commonalities in terms of goals and interests among team members rather than focusing on differences were more effective. In related research, Polzer, Milton, and Swann (2002) found that members who were able to express their differences to the group were more effective than groups where members sought to suppress their differences. This indicates that being authentic to oneself and sharing in the forming stage may be an effective way to put differences "on the table" so that they do not become sources of process loss for the group but rather can be owned by the group as characteristics which may make them stronger. Finally, other research has suggested that differences such as gender, ethnicity, and age are "surface level traits" that over time may not affect group processes as people get to know each other at a deeper level; rather, deep-level traits

Faultlines: Social dividing lines that may split a group into subgroups based on one or more attributes.

(e.g., skills) are more important to group functioning (Harrison, Price, & Bell, 1998; Harrison, Price, Gavin, & Florey, 2002).

Another type of diversity relates to cross-functional teams comprising "a group of people representing a variety of departments, disciplines, or functions, whose combined effort is required to achieve the team's purpose" (Wang & He, 2008, p. 753). The findings regarding the effectiveness of cross-functional teams is mixed (Ehrhardt, Miller, Freeman, & Hom, 2014). There is evidence that tasks related to innovation or creativity are the most effective use of cross-functional teams (Bell, Villado, Lukasik, Belau, & Briggs, 2010), and some studies have shown positive effects such as better team creativity, faster decision-making, and higher team effectiveness (Hsieh, 2010). However, other studies have illustrated that these findings are not universal. In particular, team members with a strong functional identity who are also in the minority of the team may decrease team performance, perhaps because of feeling discouraged as a result of being in the minority or not contributing to group efforts out of self-interest (Randel & Jaussi, 2003). Any organization implementing a group diversity initiative should be careful not to make the assumption that diversity will improve team performance under all circumstances.

Group Processes

Group process: How the group approaches its work; can help or hinder the team's effectiveness.

As noted above, another important factor for team effectiveness is **group process**, which is defined as how the group approaches the process of doing its work (as opposed to the work itself). Group process can be something which helps or hinders the team's effectiveness. We will cover four important processes here: teamwork skills, norms, roles, and conflict.

Workplace Application

Agile's Scrum Method for Software Development Teams

If you design software, you have probably heard of the *Agile Methodology*. It was a direct response to previous project management approaches. In 2001, the pioneers of Agile (all 17 of them) met at a ski resort in Utah and issued their "Agile Manifesto," which is the foundation of methods in use at well-known companies today such as GE, IBM, and Valve Software, with over 66 percent of software developers using Scrum or Scrum variants. Scrum is a methodology for efficiently planning and implementing team projects. Unlike other software project management frameworks, with Agile tasks are not defined up-front or driven by management; rather, they evolve as the team members with the relevant expertise encounter problems and identify hurdles to overcome. The Scrum process is divided into "sprints", which are one- to four-week-long stages of the process that begin with team members defining their desired outcomes for the stage in a planning meeting, completing the necessary tasks to achieve the outcome, and concluding the "sprint" with a review meeting. Brief, ongoing meetings take place daily to synchronize team members, review what they accomplished yesterday, identify any problems, and discuss members' tasks for the day. The Scrum process utilizes two leadership positions: the ScrumMaster, a "coach" who keeps the team focused on its tasks, but does not provide direct task assignments; and the Project Owner, who defines the vision of the team's end result and directs the team toward completing that goal.

Sources: http://scrummethodology.com/ and http://www.mountaingoatsoftware.com/agile/scrum.

Teamwork Skills

Stevens and Campion (1994) developed a teamwork survey which tested individuals in terms of their knowledge of basic teamwork skills. This employment test was designed to be a valid predictor of an individual's teamwork skills (see Chapters 6 and 7), especially compared to interviews, where a prospective employee might describe himself or herself as an excellent team player even if he or she is not. They found that those individuals who scored higher on the test were more effective within their own teams at a later point in time and were rated higher on peer and supervisor evaluations. Later work in a variety of contexts has consistently supported the idea that teamwork knowledge, skills, and abilities among team members are related to better team performance (e.g., Hirschfeld, Jordan, Feild, Giles, & Armenakis, 2006; Morgeson, Reider, & Campion, 2005; Mumford, Van Iddekinge, Morgeson, & Campion, 2008).

Other effective methods to determine an individual's teamwork skills include structured interviews specifically designed to assess social skills and group exercises designed to measure social and leadership skills (Stevens & Campion, 1994). Morgeson et al. (2005) found that social skills are correlated with teamwork knowledge, perhaps because there is an unknown mental ability connecting the two variables, because those with high teamwork knowledge gained from past experiences have also improved their social skills, or those with greater knowledge also articulate these skills more effectively. More research is needed to determine the exact mechanism underlying this connection.

Other teamwork skills include knowledge regarding team processes such as effective meeting behaviors. Meetings are costly in terms of time and energy. However, not having meetings introduces problems of ineffective coordination and misunderstandings. Thus, it makes sense to understand key factors in helping teams use meetings more effectively. According to Rogelberg, Shanock, and Scott (2012), best practices for meetings include:

- providing agendas before meetings
- starting meetings on time
- running meetings effectively
- coming to meetings having prepared for them
- using meeting time strategically to address critical issues
- covering relevant issues

- creating an environment where people feel comfortable voicing concerns in meetings
- listening carefully and actively during meetings
- not allowing any one person to dominate the meeting.

Stand-up meetings: Short meetings held standing up to help teams coordinate and share information regularly and efficiently.

Some organizations have even found that having short meetings standing up (aptly termed **stand-up meetings**) helps teams to coordinate and share information regularly and efficiently. In an experiment of 56 teams by Bluedorn, Turban, and Love (1999), individuals were assigned to groups using standing or sitting meetings. Those in the standing meetings condition were done making decisions sooner (it took 34 percent less time) with no difference in the quality of the decisions between the two groups. In addition, in an experiment with 54 groups, researchers Knight and Baer (2014) found that teams that interacted more while standing were better at elaborating on information and had better performance than groups with members who sat during the meetings.

Workplace Application

Silent Meeting Time at Amazon.com

Jeff Bezos, CEO of online mega-retailer Amazon. com, starts meetings off with several minutes of quiet communal reading time. This is not a stress reduction strategy, although it might help calm everyone down a bit. Rather, all meetings of senior executives at Amazon begin with participants quietly reading relevant information and memos on their meeting topic at the same time before the discussion begins.

Why does Bezos do this? In his interview with *Fortune*, he noted that the act of reading at the same time guarantees that everyone is giving the material his or her undivided attention. In the age of information overload and multi-tasking, pre-meeting preparation doesn't always happen, and yet key decisions are made at such meetings. With the approach that Bezos and his team use, everyone is on the same page – *literally*. Further, knowing that everyone will be reading your memo in front of you makes the authors much more thoughtful and clear than they might otherwise be while composing them.

Group Norms

Norms: The understood rules about how group members should behave. Help members understand what is expected of them and others.

Norms are defined as the understood rules about how group members should behave. Such group norms at work were first noticed in the Hawthorne studies back in the 1920s (see Chapter 1). They help members to understand what is expected of them as well as creating consensus regarding what is expected of others. As you might imagine, norms can be helpful to group functioning over time. In fact, learning the norms of a group one is just joining is one of the major tasks (Bauer, Bodner, Erdogan, Truxillo, & Tucker, 2007; Moreland & Levine, 1982).

There are many norms that we adhere to every day that we don't think about much. For example, which way do you face while going up in an elevator? Without even thinking about it, it's a good bet that you face the doors. But, why is this the case? Did anyone ever tell you to? Does it save time? The answer to these questions is probably "no." However, if you are up for trying a small social experiment, the next time you walk onto an elevator with other individuals on it, remain standing facing the back of the elevator rather than the doors. In our experience, you will receive very strong social signals that this is not the norm.

One important aspect of norms is closely related to how the team thinks. In our day-to-day nomenclature we refer to this as "being on the same page." Research on **team mental models** (TMM), defined as the degree to which individual conceptualizations are shared across the team, shows that when teams are higher on TMM, they are more effective. For example, a team could have a shared understanding of the steps needed to complete a project. When examining factors related to the emergence of TMM, Fisher, Bell, Dierdorff, and Belohlav (2012) found that when trust was high and racial diversity existed, TMM was still high.

Team Mental Models (TMM): The degree to which individual conceptualizations are shared across the team.

When it comes to norms, one important norm relates to how much effort team members are expected to expend toward group goals and how the team evaluates and reinforces such expectations. One important consideration for teams to keep in mind is that the larger the group gets, the less each member puts forth effort (or social loafing, as we discussed earlier in this chapter). Communication in large groups also gets more cumbersome and complex, simply because there are more people involved.

Roles

When it comes to teams at work, it is impossible to ignore the influence of the different types of work that teams are asked to do. Thus, there are the task roles of the team as well as the internal roles which individual members perform. McGrath (1984) identified four main types of tasks teams are asked to do, including generating tasks, choosing tasks, negotiating tasks, and executing tasks, which vary in terms of how much coordination and cognitive resources they demand of the team. More recently, Mumford, Campion, and Morgeson (2006) created a team role typology which defines 10 key roles that exist in groups. (See Figure 13.5.) In this typology, five roles are focused on tasks: the contractor, creator, contributor, completer, and critic. Social roles include the calibrator, communicator, and cooperator. Finally, the boundary-spanning roles are consul and coordinator. Subsequent research by Mumford et al. (2008) found that teams with members who score higher in terms of understanding the importance of roles had higher overall role performance (which comprised both task and social role performance dimensions).

Research shows that task assignments that are highly specific ("do this") type tasks are helpful for teams focused on overcoming cultural differences. However, when it comes to creative tasks, having low task specificity is better so that people can have the freedom to be creative, and can even be more important for overcoming

Figure 13.5 The 10 roles of the team role typology as defined by Mumford et al. (2006).

cultural differences within the team (Nouri et al., 2013). Thus, it seems clear that different types of tasks influence the factors important for effective team functioning.

One additional key role that deserves special attention is that of **team leadership**. In their review, Morgeson et al. (2010) summarized the research on leadership in teams up until that point. They concluded that a more comprehensive examination of the roles that leaders play is important for understanding and maximizing team effectiveness. They determined that the types of team leadership vary on two dimensions. Leadership can be *internal* (embedded in the team) or *external* (working outside the team). In addition, leadership may be either *formal* (a person who holds the official title of "team leader") or *informal* (a person who is looked at by group members as a leader, even if they are not formally recognized as one by the organization). For example, emergent leadership comes from within the team (it is internal) and is informal (it is not an "assigned" role) versus a project manager which is within the team (also internal) but is formal because this is a role recognized by everyone as being assigned to this person. In Figure 13.6, we summarize examples of these different types of team leadership roles.

Hauschildt and Konradt (2012) conducted two laboratory studies of teams and self-leadership, that is, intentionally influencing your own thinking, feeling, and/or behaviors to achieve goals (Bryant & Kazan, 2012). They found that self-leadership was positively related to both individual and team performance and that self-leadership was related to better adaptivity and proactivity in teams. Williams, Parker, and Turner (2010) studied teams working in a British chemical processing plant. They found that the most proactive teams (that is, teams that were engaged in planning and looking ahead to remove obstacles and make things happen) were more likely to have strong self-management and team leaders who were seen as transformational. Chen, Farh, Campbell-Bush, Wu, and Wu (2013) studied Chinese firms and found that transformational leadership was related to team innovation performance because it helped to increase individual motivational states. Gajendran and Joshi (2012) found that effective leader–member exchange (LMX) relationships and frequent communication were related to better team functioning in globally distributed teams. When it comes to directive versus empowering leadership, the

Team leadership: How leadership impacts team effectiveness. Varies on two dimensions: internal (embedded in the team) or external (working outside the team). Can also be either formal (a person who holds the title of "team leader") or informal (a person who is looked at by others as a leader).

Formality of Leadership

		Formal	Informal
Internal to the Team		Team Leader	Shared
		Project Manager	Emergent
External to the Team		Sponsor	Mentor
		Coach	Champion
		Team Advisor	Executive
			Coordinator

(row label on left axis: **Locus of Leadership**)

Figure 13.6 Types of leadership roles in teams (Morgeson, DeRue, & Kram, 2010).

findings are interesting and in line with group formation research. It seems that teams with directive leaders perform well initially compared to those teams led by empowering leaders. However, as time goes on, teams led by empowering leaders tend to perform at a higher level (Lorinkova, Pearsall, & Sims, 2013). The authors noted that this is due to better team learning, coordination, and mental model development.

Conflict

Talk to anyone with much teamwork experience and he or she will probably be able to tell you that conflict among team members is a potential problem. Conflicts may be interpersonal between two individual team members or between coalitions with a team. There may also be conflict between teams within an organization. Conflicts might be over fundamental issues such as what needs to get done or about how to get things done. Some conflict around what to do and how to do it can be a normal and healthy part of team development (as noted by the *storming phase* of group development discussed earlier in this chapter). Some conflict is a sign that team members care about the group's process and outcomes and are engaging with their work. However, when conflict becomes personal in nature (rather than about the task or process) or when there is simply too much conflict to move forward into the norming and performing stages, performance suffers. Thus, Figure 13.7 depicts the classic relationship between conflict and performance as an inverted U where either too much or too little creates a situation where performance suffers (Jehn, 1994).

For years, researchers and textbook authors reported that this finding of an inverted U holds for task conflict and team creativity (Farh, Lee, & Farh, 2010). However, subsequent meta-analyses have found that task conflict is not related to better performance (De Dreu & Weingart, 2003; de Wit, Greer, & Jehn, 2012). De Wit et al. did find that team performance was negatively related to both relationship and process conflict. Thus, rather than encourage task conflict, Ilgen et al. (2005) recommend that teams do well under conditions where rich, unemotional debate is done in a context of trust (Simons & Peterson, 2000), where team members

Figure 13.7
Original hypothes-
ized curvilinear
relationship
between con-
flict and team
performance.

feel comfortable expressing doubts and changing their minds (Lovelace, Shapiro, & Weingart, 2001), and do not strive for premature consensus or compromise (Kim, Choi, & Kim, 1999; Montoya-Weiss, Massey, & Song, 2001). In essence, this points to the importance of psychological safety for team members when there is a conflict. One recent meta-analysis of 28,000 team members and over 6,000 teams found that task conflict can be helpful in certain instances such as when quality of decision-making was examined (O'Neill, Allen, & Hastings, 2013). Thus, it seems that the relationship between conflict and team performance is a nuanced and complex one, but that it is important to keep in mind that too much conflict is a problem for teams.

So, what can be done to help reduce conflict within groups? Research shows that face-to-face *developmental* feedback from a person that a team member considers a peer can reduce conflict and that such feedback is most effective when delivered about halfway through a team's task (Druskat & Wolff, 1999). De Cremer and van Knippenberg (2002) found that these results were also true when leaders, rather than peers, gave the feedback. Other options include introducing large goals that the group is inspired by as well as a common enemy to work against such as a major competitor.

Group Affect and Cognition

Group Cohesion

Cohesion: The degree to which the group wishes to stay together in the future.

Cohesion is defined as the degree to which the group wishes to stay together in the future. Members of cohesive groups are characterized by a collective iden-tity, a shared sense of purpose, and satisfaction with the way the group operates (Carron & Brawley, 2000). Cohesion is one of the most heavily researched areas of teams (Mathieu, Maynard, Rapp, & Gilson, 2008). This research shows that cohesion tends to be higher when group members are similar to one another (O'Reilly, Caldwell, & Barnett, 1989), have a smaller number of members (Carron & Spink, 1995), have a history of success (Zaccaro & McCoy, 1988), and the group is perceived as exclusive (i.e., hard to get into) (Gerard & Matthewson, 1966). On the negative side, cohesion can also be associated with groupthink (which we will discuss later in the chapter), which is a negative outcome, but studies have shown that in certain work environments designed to benefit creative employees completing difficult tasks, there is a positive correlation between group cohesion and group performance (Chang, Jia, Takeuchi, & Cai, 2014). Stewart, Courtright, and Barrick (2012) found that both normative group cohesion (the social sense of belonging and commitment) and peer-based rational control (having aligned economic interests with team members) enhanced team performance.

A meta-analysis of the relationship between team cohesion and performance in groups conducted by Beal, Cohen, Burke, and McLendon (2003) found that the relationship was strongest when performance was measured as a behavior rather than as an outcome of the group's behavior, and when efficiency measures (e.g., group output over a specific period of time, supervisor ratings of efficiency) were employed rather than effectiveness measures (e.g., ratings or counts of total group output, quality of group decisions). Similarly, in their meta-analysis, Gully, Devine and Whitney (1995) describe the need for studies of group cohesion that use group-level measures in their operational definitions. Many studies they reviewed used individual-level measures to capture group cohesion: This is a problem because cohesion is a group-level concept (the shared belief among group members), not an individual-level one. These examples also illustrate that how we choose to measure variables in organizational research can have a profound effect on the results we find. Again, this is consistent with what we discussed in Chapter 2 on research methods in relation to the measurement of variables.

Further, group cohesion has an interesting relationship with group effectiveness. Overall the correlation is .32 (Gully et al., 1995). By definition, if a group is high on cohesion, group members are attracted to one another and wish to remain on the team. On the other hand, the relationship between group cohesion and team performance is not as clear cut. In their meta-analysis Gully et al. found that the relationship between cohesion and performance, while generally positive, was moderated by factors such as task interdependence among group members. A recent study by De Jong, Curşeu, and Leenders (2014) reiterated this view of the importance of task interdependence in their study of 73 intact work teams in a variety of settings such as city governments, banks, charities, police stations, and retail organizations. Specifically, De Jong et al. found that it actually was possible to neutralize the negative effects of having problematic relationships on the team, factors that we normally associate with low cohesion and thus weaker team effectiveness. Instead, what mattered to team effectiveness was the level of task-interdependence and how well team members understood one another. Their study sheds light on understanding why some teams thrive with lower cohesion while others shut down and perform poorly.

Psychological Safety

Psychological safety is defined as perceptions of the negative or positive consequences of taking interpersonal risks in the workplace (Edmondson, 1999). A core tenet of psychological safety is that the safer individuals feel, the more

Psychological safety:
Perception of negative or positive consequences of taking interpersonal risks in the workplace.

	Weak Performance Norms	Strong Performance Norms
Low Group Cohesion	*Consistently Related to Poor Performance*	*Mixed Findings for Performance*
High Group Cohesion	*Consistently Related to Poor Performance*	*Consistently Related to High Performance*

they will be willing to share their ideas and act in a communal way. Research has established that psychological safety is related to information and knowledge sharing (Collins & Smith, 2006) as well as to engaging in voice behaviors (i.e., speaking up; Liang, Farh, & Farh, 2012). Another common finding is that high levels of psychological safety are related to a team's motivation and ability to learn and perform (Edmondson & Lei, 2014). So, as you might imagine, it is very important to have a psychologically safe climate if teams are expected to work through conflict and work with one another toward important goals. We will cover the concept of "groupthink" later in this chapter. But, as a preview, psychological safety and having individual team members willing to speak out against ideas is an effective way to decrease the process loss and other negative consequences associated with groupthink.

Team Efficacy

Team efficacy: The extent to which a group believes that it can perform its tasks well.

Team efficacy refers to a team's belief that it can perform its tasks well (Bandura, 1997). Research shows that team efficacy is related to team effectiveness across a number of situations. For example, Gibson (1999) studied nursing teams and found that team efficacy was related to the performance of nurses. Similarly, Prussia and Kinicki (1996) found that team efficacy was related to collective goals as well as team performance. And, as summarized in a meta-analysis by Gully, Incalcaterra, Joshi, and Beaubien (2002), overall, there is a significant relationship between team efficacy and team performance (correlation of .41), and it is even stronger in situations where the team's tasks are more interdependent. Thus, efforts toward building up a team's confidence can have profound effects on their performance.

Decision-Making in Groups and Teams

As we discussed earlier in this chapter, one of the key types of team tasks are those associated with decision-making and idea generation. Heterogeneous groups (those with different types of members) might arguably be better at such tasks given that they possess among their members a greater variety of information, perspectives, and knowledge (Van Knippenberg, De Dreu, & Homan, 2004). However, it is not the case that such groups always outperform their more homogeneous counterparts. This poses the question, "Why?" One potential answer relates to the many factors we reviewed earlier in this chapter. The team's composition, skills, process, and affect all matter as well.

The Decision-Making Process

One of the most established team decision-making process models is the rational decision-making model. It comprises six steps. The first step is to identify the problem or opportunity at hand. Using precise language and identifying root causes are best (e.g., "team members are frequently given tasks at the last minute by upper management, forcing some members to come late to our meetings" is better than "meetings always start late"). The second step involves developing several potential solutions or courses of action. It is important to generate several solutions to the core problems. Research shows that generating alternatives in the second step can be one of the most challenging of the steps (Nutt, 1984). In the third step, the team evaluates all expected positive and negative outcomes of the problem. This is important because one solution (such as "postpone all assignments from upper management") might technically solve the problem, but likely at too high a cost. The objective is to find the solution where the difference between positive and negative outcomes is lowest. Fourth, the team should come to a decision on the appropriate solution after considering a thorough list of possibilities, followed by the fifth step of implementing the decision. This entire framework, while critical to making rational decisions, is ultimately meaningless if the team does not follow through on its decision. Finally, evaluating the impact of the decision is vital for reviewing how effective the team's decision was, as well as providing feedback on where the decision-making process could be improved in the future.

When it comes to the rational decision-making process, all of these steps matter, but the reflection or debrief (discussion after the process is over) aspect of the process can be especially important for groups to be effective. Research shows that teams that debrief are more effective than those teams that do not. And a recent meta-analysis by Tannenbaum and Cerasoli (2013) found that debriefs resulted in a team performance differential of 20 percent on average – in other words, debriefs are important. This finding was also supported in an intervention study by Eddy, Tannenbaum, and Mathieu (2013).

Brainstorming

Group **brainstorming** has long been seen as an effective way to generate ideas (Osborn, 1953). The brainstorming process includes trying to generate as many ideas as possible, not judging or evaluating the ideas during this process, encouraging creative or outrageous ideas even if they do not seem feasible (because these outrageous ideas may lead to good ones), and "piggybacking" on others' ideas to improve upon them. It can also be a key aspect of the second step in the decision-making process (developing alternative solutions to the problem). However, group brainstorming as the optimal way to generate the most and best

Brainstorming: Trying to generate as many ideas as possible, to not judge or evaluate the ideas during the brainstorming session, to encourage creative ideas even if they do not seem feasible, and to "piggyback" on others' ideas to improve upon them.

Figure 13.9 The steps in the decision-making process.

ideas has come under greater scrutiny as more recent research has brought this assumption into question. Kohn and Smith (2011) asked 160 students to form 40 groups of 4. Half the groups did traditional brainstorming while the other half were asked to use instant messaging, where they could see the ideas of the other three individuals but did not know whose ideas they were. They found that the individuals using this instant messaging approach to brainstorm generated 44 percent more ideas than the face-to-face group participants. Thus, it may be that the best way to engage in brainstorming is to encourage group members first to brainstorm by themselves and to write down their ideas when things are quieter, and then to bring people together as a group and ask them to share the ideas that they came up with. A recommendation more directly tied to the study described above would be to use technology to increase the number of ideas the group produces by blending real-time brainstorming with technology to decrease the social pressures of face-to-face meetings. Considering ways to reduce social apprehension (being nervous about sharing your ideas in front of others) or process loss in teams is especially important when you have communication challenges or barriers such as shy team members, differences in group members' status, or culturally diverse teams that do not share a common language (Jackson, Joshi, & Erhardt, 2003).

"Today's theme is 'Getting Beyond Group Think'."

Groupthink: A tendency to desire group harmony and avoid critical debate during decision-making.

Groupthink

Have you ever been in a group situation where you didn't actually agree with the group but you didn't speak up to say so? If this has happened to you, you may have been a victim of groupthink. **Groupthink** refers to a desire for group harmony that results in the avoidance of critical debate during decision-making. Groupthink has been linked to a number of negative group outcomes such as a sense of collective efficacy too early in the process and suppressing productive conflict, resulting in overconfidence and a lack of sufficient time spent on the decision-making process (Goncalo, Polman, & Maslach, 2010).

Type I: Overestimations of the group	Type II: Closed-mindedness	Type III: Pressures toward uniformity

• Illusions of invulnerability of the group • Unquestioned belief in the morality of the group and its decisions	• Rationalizing or discounting warnings that might challenge the group's assumptions • Negatively stereotyping those who are opposed to the group	• Self-censorship of ideas that deviate from the *apparent* group consensus • Illusions of unanimity among group members • Direct pressure to conform placed on members who question the group • Mindguards (people who serve as self-appointed members) who shield the group (and especially the group's leader) from dissenting information

Figure 13.10 The eight symptoms of groupthink may be grouped into three types proposed by Janis (1972).

Groupthink was first described in 1972 by Irving Janis, a psychology professor at Yale University, as having eight "symptoms" which can help to diagnose whether the group has a groupthink problem. These are summarized in Figure 13.10. In essence, the idea is that when a group values harmony or perceives that debate will slow the group down, members may come to believe things which encourage conformity and discourage healthy group discussion and debate. For instance, if the group is overestimating its probabilities for success and feels that it is doing important and moral work, they may become careless and take shortcuts when it comes to group decision-making. Similarly, another symptom of groupthink is a tendency of the group to become hostile to outside critics. This can also happen within the team, when there are pressures toward conformity such as self-censorship, as when a member doesn't speak up and voice his or her concerns. Hostility towards criticism can also arise from direct pressure exerted by members if a person does attempt to speak up. Phrases like "Everyone who disagrees with us is an idiot" or "We don't need to discuss this; we're all obviously on the same page" may indicate that the group is suffering from groupthink.

Much of Janis' original work focused on case analyses of decisions rooted in famous historical events, such as US decisions surrounding Pearl Harbor, the escalation of the Korean War, and the decision by the Kennedy administration to invade Cuba at the Bay of Pigs (Janis, 1972). Based on these case analyses, Janis (1972, 1982) posited that group cohesion – something considered to be a good thing in moderation – was one of the most important antecedents of groupthink behavior. In addition, he felt that other antecedents such as structural faults, the lack of impartial leadership, overly similar group members (leading to little diversity of opinion), as well as the situational context such as external threats and moral dilemmas, could lead to groupthink.

Case studies have been generally supportive of the theory of groupthink (e.g., Moorhead, Ference, & Neck, 1991). However, laboratory research has been limited and has not necessarily supported all aspects of Janis' original conceptualization of the theory. For instance, laboratory tests of the relationship between group cohesion

Figure 13.11 Tips for avoiding groupthink.

Discuss the symptoms of groupthink and how to avoid them.

Assign a rotating "devil's advocate" within the group to challenge the group's decisions

Invite experts not part of the core decision-making group to react to ideas.

Encourage a culture of difference where different ideas are valued.

Debate the ethical implications of the decisions and potential solutions being considered.

and groupthink symptoms have received limited support (Aldag & Fuller, 1993; Esser, 1998; Turner & Pratkanis, 1998). However, they also found that more cohesive groups made poorer decisions when groupthink conditions existed. Following his detailed review of 25 years of groupthink research, Esser wrote, "I conclude that groupthink research has had and continues to have considerable heuristic value" (p. 116). We agree. While the exact theory of groupthink may not be fully descriptive of group decision-making in all instances, it can be good for teams to become aware of groupthink as a potential problem in a group and avoid the potential pitfalls associated with it. Figure 13.11 includes several suggestions for how to avoid groupthink, such as by making group members aware of groupthink as a problem and encouraging debate within the team.

 "See website for interactive material"

Interactive: Avoiding groupthink.

LEGAL ISSUES

In this chapter we have seen how important team cohesion is. This creates potential diversity problems, however, given that people tend to be attracted to those individuals who are most like them. It is important to make sure that the attraction-selection-attrition (ASA) effect (discussed in Chapter 14; Schneider, 1987; 1995) does not lead to homogenous teams for both performance reasons as outlined in this chapter as well as for legal reasons. As you'll recall from Chapter 7 which included legal issues related to employment, one cannot discriminate against those in protected classes. If such discrimination does take place, organizations may find themselves in a tough place in terms of how to protect themselves legally.

Improved teamwork may also help organizations avoid costly lawsuits by increasing safety and reducing mistakes. For example, a key reason for malpractice lawsuits and preventable errors in the healthcare industry is communication breakdowns within the team. At one point, the airline industry in the USA experienced similar problems, with 80 percent of all fatalities traced back to poor communication and teamwork. One of the major responses of the commercial airline industry to this crisis was to have teams go through teamwork training, which resulted in dramatic improvements in the safety of the industry. In other words, by improving communication and teamwork, organizations can keep their employees and customers safe, which would also have the side effect of staying on the right side of the law (Harden, 2014).

Diversity can become a legal issue if things get out of hand and result in discrimination or a hostile work environment. Team faultlines are a team diversity issue that should be addressed if they are causing conflict or discrimination within the group. Faultlines between team members of different locations and genders have been linked to increased conflict and decreased quality of decisions made (Chiu & Staples, 2013). Chiu and Staples (2013) found that using task elaboration techniques for team members to share ideas relevant to the task and therefore increase communication quickly decreased the negative effects of faultlines on the team. There is also some evidence that transformational leaders can overcome existing faultlines and direct teams toward higher productivity despite their divisions (Kunze & Bruch, 2010).

GLOBAL IMPLICATIONS

One of the new realities of teams is that they are not always physically located in the same place. While it was rare in the past to have teams with members from multiple locations, now it is often the norm in large organizations (Hoch & Kozlowski, 2014). The advent of increasingly sophisticated communication technologies means that working around the globe is now feasible. Given this growing reality, researchers have begun to examine factors related to virtual teams.

Advantages of virtual teams include the ability to gather experts from anywhere to work on challenging problems. Avoiding the expense of flying to a central location, such experts can now be gathered virtually, saving a great deal of time and money. Some organizations have used virtual teams located around the globe to work on projects 24 hours a day, as it is always "work time" in one part of the world. For example, imagine that you are working on a team comprising four individuals working from Vancouver, Canada, Paris, France, Bangalore, India, and Melbourne, Australia. Given the time differences, when you wake up and go to work at 9 a.m. in Vancouver, you can pick up on the work of your colleague in Paris, where it is now 6 p.m. and he is heading home. Your colleague in Bangalore is getting ready for bed at 10:30 p.m. And your colleague in Melbourne is fast asleep as it's 4 a.m. there. Thus, you have the opportunity to "pick up" where your Parisian team mate left off. Similarly, when you are done at 6 p.m., your team mate in Bangalore will be ready to go at 7:30 a.m. However, as you can see by this example, coordinating across these time zones and finding a common time to discuss the project can be extremely challenging. In fact, it can be so challenging that websites exist which aid in planning team meetings across time zones.

Other potential disadvantages of virtual teams have been well documented. For example, research has found that virtual team members sometimes report lower scores on group affect factors such as team cohesion, work satisfaction, trust, and commitment to team goals (Hoch & Kozlowski, 2014). Hoch and Kozlowski studied 565 team members and team leaders who worked in global manufacturing research and development departments. This sample was useful for examining factors related to "how virtual" teams were: Some teams were primarily face to face, with some virtuality, and others were primarily virtual. They found that leadership was related to team effectiveness regardless of how virtual the teams were.

Research has demonstrated that at the individual level, multicultural experiences (exposure to foreign cultures) can be helpful for individuals in terms of helping people be more effective by promoting expansive thinking, generating new perspectives and approaches to problems, and fostering a capacity to view issues from multiple perspectives (Leung, Maddux, Galinsky, & Chiu, 2008). In an additional argument in favor of getting as much experience with as many cultures as possible to be effective in teams, research shows that when it comes to creativity, members' multicultural experience matters. Tadmor, Satterstrom, Jang, and Polzer (2012) studied culturally diverse teams engaged in dyadic brainstorming sessions. They found that, even after controlling for individual levels of creativity, multicultural experience was related to high fluency (the number of ideas), flexibility (the number of different types of ideas), and novelty of creative ideas (how unique the ideas were from previous ideas). When both dyad partners had higher multicultural experience, the teams performed best. This is heartening, and we believe that this is true from our own experiences. Collectively, the authors of this textbook have lived in many different countries including France, Italy, Turkey, the United Kingdom, and the United States. We have published research with multicultural author teams from several countries across five continents. In addition, we have traveled to 27 countries (and counting). Being exposed to different cultures and ways of doing work around the world has enriched our work and helped us to see I/O psychology from a variety of perspectives.

Various studies of cultural diversity in teams have found differing correlations with team performance, including both positive and negative outcomes. Van Knippenberg et al. (2004) developed a model which posited that cultural diversity improves team performance to the extent that information elaboration – the sharing and discussion of task-related information – exceeds the intergroup biases and closed-minded thinking that cultural diversity may engender. In this model, the motivational effort that team members put into actually *utilizing* the greater information provided by a culturally diverse team is important to experiencing benefits from cultural diversity.

CURRENT ISSUES AND CONTROVERSIES

Top management teams (TMTs) are those that hold the highest positions in corporations. Unfortunately, it's been noted that there is often not much diversity on boards of directors. According to the Catalyst Census of Fortune 500 (2013), women held only 17 percent of corporate board seats, and only 15 percent of executive officer positions were held by women. Women of color were poorly represented on board seats, holding a mere 3 percent. These percentages have remained relatively unchanged in the last several years. What makes this so surprising is the fact that research has consistently shown that having women in such positions is related to higher financial performance (Catalyst, 2007). In particular, Dezsö and Ross (2012) studied the top management of S&P 1500 companies from 1992 to 2006 and found that companies that had at least one woman in top management generated 1 percent more in economic value (roughly $40 million) and also had superior accounting performance.

Another current issue already discussed in this chapter is virtual teams, which are becoming more and more prevalent in work settings. Watkins (2013) provides 10 tips for working effectively via technology:

1. Get the team together physically as it is forming.
2. Clarify tasks and processes.
3. Establish the norms of communication.
4. Use the best communication technologies for the team.
5. Build a work rhythm within the team.
6. Develop and use a shared language.
7. Create a "virtual water cooler".
8. Clarify and track commitments.
9. Foster shared leadership.
10. Don't forget to connect one on one at least some of the time.

Finally, another current issue relates to the ways that teams coordinate. For example, to share information, teams will often call meetings or send e-mails. Both of these mechanisms may work, but they come at a price. Research shows that teams with better meetings, including more integration of topics and an action orientation, reported being more satisfied with their meetings and also had higher productivity (Kauffeld & Lehmann-Willenbrock, 2012). The modern-day reality of e-mail overload has been well established, with employees around the world collectively receiving nearly 109 billion e-mails each day (The Radicati Group, Inc., 2013). E-mail filters, technology that helps people sort through all of the e-mails they receive, abound. As we saw in Chapter 12, stress due to information overload is a big issue. Understanding how to manage meetings and e-mails is an important part of time management and lessening the pressures of the coordination costs associated with teamwork.

WHAT DOES THIS MEAN TO YOU?

You are very likely the member of at least one team, and you will likely be part of many more over the course of your life. This chapter may have given you some ideas to improve your team's performance, or even just to improve your experience of being on a team. For example, given that the punctuated equilibrium model of team development indicates that setting earlier deadlines will help teams complete this cycle more quickly, doing so can be helpful in breaking large deadlines into smaller ones. While it's not a guarantee that you'll make the final deadline, it can't hurt to get things done early in your teams!

Diversity also matters to teams. At some point in your life, you are likely to be a member of a group that is in the minority within a team and feel that your voice is not given equal weight. If this happens, keeping in mind some of the key findings related to diversity in teams may be useful. Similarly, if you are in the majority, keeping these in mind and reminding others of the importance of diversity can help your team perform well and value everyone on your team.

If you feel your team meetings or team processes are not as productive as they could be, you may want to discuss your thoughts with the team and propose one or more of the solutions we discussed in this chapter, such as techniques to avoid groupthink or how to make rational decisions.

Conclusion

Work teams are becoming an increasingly important area of study in I/O psychology as tasks become more complex and organizations place greater emphasis on employees working together in groups. In this chapter, we discussed how teams form and develop over time and the factors that contribute to team effectiveness, including group composition, size, personality, and diversity. We learned how team members can be effective members of a group via their teamwork knowledge, and how companies can lead effective problem-solving and decision-making processes by brainstorming and avoiding groupthink. We discussed how diversity impacts teams, from virtual and global teams structures to underrepresentation of minority groups, and how diversity may create faultlines and how we can constructively and fairly address the need for diversity in organizational teams.

YOUR TURN...

1. Think about what groups or teams you are part of now. How effective is your group or team? What could you do to boost your team's performance?

2. Using the information in this chapter, how would you form an effective team at your school or organization to provide input to faculty members on course content and course offerings? For example, what size would it be? What personality traits would you want in your members? What types of diversity would you want it to have to be most effective?

3. If the punctuated equilibrium model of group development is true, how might you use it to help your team on a class project to be most effective? Explain your rationale.

4. Do you think organizations (both work and schools) use teams too much, too little, or just about the right amount? Please explain your answer. What are the advantages and disadvantages?

5. What are the key issues related to team decision-making? If you were designing an "ideal" decision-making team to run your university, what steps would you take to ensure they did a good job? Please provide specific details on issues such as team size and makeup.

Additional Reading

Forsyth, D. (2009). *Group dynamics*. Belmont, CA: Cengage Learning.

Hackman, J. R. (2002). *Leading teams: Setting the stage for great performances.* Boston, MA: Harvard Business Press.

Levi, D. (2013). *Group dynamics for teams*. Thousand Oaks, CA: SAGE Publications.

Salas, E., Goodwin, G. F., & Burke, C. S. (2008). *Team effectiveness in complex organizations: Cross-disciplinary perspectives and approaches.* New York: Routledge.

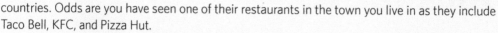

CASE STUDY: Teamwork Is Business as Usual at **Yum! Brands**

Yum! Brands Inc. is headquartered in Louisville, Kentucky but has restaurants throughout the world, including the one pictured above located in Shanghai, China. In fact, Yum! is one of the world's largest food companies, with more than 40,000 restaurants in more than 125 countries. Odds are you have seen one of their restaurants in the town you live in as they include Taco Bell, KFC, and Pizza Hut.

The company is ranked #216 on the Fortune 500 list, with more than $13 billion worth of sales. Originally Yum! was part of PepsiCo, but in 1997 it was made into its own company (called a spin-off), and since then its stock has returned 16.5 percent annually (compared to the S&P 500's 3.9 percent during the same time). In China, Yum! is the largest restaurant company – they open 700 restaurants per year. In order to fuel that tremendous growth, Yum! has created its own educational center called Whampoa Academy, where in 2013, nearly 25,000 team members received over 652,000 hours of learning. But if you think that's a lot of people, consider that Yum! Brands employs 1.5 million associates globally.

Ann Byerlein, Chief People Officer for Yum!, notes, "Our recognition culture is what sets us apart from our competition. We motivate and inspire each other to bring our best to work every day so that not only do we have great happy team members, but we have very satisfied customers." David Novak, CEO of Yum! Brands, has been described as a successful CEO, but he's also known for something else. Colvin (2013) wrote in a profile of him and his approach to results, "Novak ... may be the business world's ultimate team builder."

So, what does Novak do? He gives employees a floppy rubber chicken when he thinks they do a good job. **Really**. When Novak took over KFC, it was not doing well. He was able to turn that trend around and he credits teamwork for that change, saying, "I changed out a couple of people, and that made a difference, but the biggest thing is I got the existing team working at a much higher level together." And, "I think the reason we got there is that we took recognition and had more fun with it than most people." Enter the floppy chicken. Novak believes in giving recognition right away, so if he attends a meeting and someone does a great job, he'll go to office, get a chicken, write a special message on it, and then present it to the person. This idea was so successful that around the world, Yum! team members give away items with limited financial value but which are a lot of fun and mean a great deal to the people who give and receive them.

Of course, there is more to it than just rubber chickens. Novak asks employees to take training sessions where they learn about teamwork. The first step, however, is that they are asked to reflect upon themselves first. They rate themselves on all sorts of characteristics such as truthfulness, reliability, openness, and even self-centeredness. They think about how they treat others on their team and how they would like to be treated. It is only in the last stage of the team training sessions that recognition is introduced, including how and why to give it.

Novak teaches others how to do a great job with team building (both in person and via his book). He recommends that other leaders looking to see success follow three simple steps. First, put people first. Hire great people who are capable of doing the job. Second, constantly recognize achievers. And third, be self-aware and constantly grow.

Questions

1. Why do you think Novak has been so successful?

2. Do you think you would like the kind of environment described in this case? Explain why or why not.

3. What do you think about Novak's assumption that to build a strong team, you need to start with understanding yourself?

4. What other things are important for teamwork that were not discussed in this case?

Sources: This case is partially based on information contained in Colvin, 2013; Kruse, 2014; Novak, 2012; Yum! Brands website. Retrieved November 1, 2014, from http://www.yum.com/company/.

References

Aldag, R. J., & Fuller, S. R. (1993). Beyond fiasco: A reappraisal of the groupthink phenomenon and a new model of group decision processes. *Psychological Bulletin, 113*, 533–552.

Bandura, A. (1997). *Self-efficacy: The exercise of control.* New York: W. H. Freeman.

Barrick, M. R., Stewart, G. L., Neubert, M. J., & Mount, M. K. (1998). Relating member ability and personality to work-team processes and team effectiveness. *Journal of Applied Psychology, 83*, 43–51.

Bauer, T. N., & Erdogan, B. (2016). *Organizational behavior.* Washington DC: Flat World Knowledge.

Bauer, T. N., Bodner, T., Erdogan, B., Truxillo, D. M., & Tucker, J. S. (2007). Newcomer adjustment during organizational socialization: A meta-analytic review of antecedents, outcomes, and methods. *Journal of Applied Psychology, 92*, 707–721.

Beal, D. J., Cohen, R. R., Burke, M. J., & McLendon, C. L. (2003). Cohesion and performance in groups: A meta-analytic clarification of construct relations. *Journal of Applied Psychology, 88*, 989–1004.

Bell, S. T. (2007). Deep-level composition variables as predictors of team performance: A meta-analysis. *Journal of Applied Psychology, 92*, 595–615.

Bell, S. T., Villado, A. J., Lukasik, M. A., Belau, L., & Briggs, A. L. (2010). Getting specific about demographic diversity variable and team performance relationships: A meta-analysis. *Journal of Management, 37*, 709–743.

Bluedorn, A. C., Turban, D. B., & Love, M. S. (1999). The effects of stand-up and sit-down meeting formats on meeting outcomes. *Journal of Applied Psychology, 84*, 277–285.

Bonebright, D. A. (2010). 40 years of storming: A historical review of Tuckman's model of small group development. *Human Resource Development International, 13*, 111–120.

Bradley, B. H., Baur, J. E., Banford, C. G., & Postlethwaite, B. E. (2013). Team players and collective performance: How agreeableness affects team performance over time. *Small Group Research, 44*, 680–711.

Bradley, B. H., Klotz, A. C., Postlethwaite, B. E., & Brown, K. G. (2013). Ready to rumble: How team personality composition and task conflict interact to improve performance. *Journal of Applied Psychology, 98*, 385–392.

Bryant, A., & Kazan, A. L. (2012). *Self-leadership: How to become a more successful, efficient, and effective leader from the inside out.* New York: McGraw Hill.

Carron, A.V., & Brawley, L.R. (2000). Cohesion: Conceptual and measurement issues. *Small Group Research, 31*, 89–106.

Carron A. V., & Spink, K.S. (1995). The group-size cohesion relationship in minimal groups. *Small Group Research, 26*, 86–105.

Carton, A. M., & Cummings, J. N. (2013). The impact of subgroup type and subgroup configurational properties on work team performance. *Journal of Applied Psychology, 98*, 732–758.

Catalyst. (2007). The bottom line: Corporate performance and women's representation on boards. October 15, 2007. Retrieved November 7, 2014, from http://www.catalyst.org/knowledge/bottom-line-corporate-performance-and-womens-representation-boards.

Catalyst. (2013). Catalyst 2013 census of Fortune 500: Still no progress after years of no progress. December 10, 2013. Retrieved November 7, 2014, from http://www.catalyst.org/media/catalyst-2013-census-fortune-500-still-no-progress-after-years-no-progress.

Chang, A., Bordia, P., & Duck, J. (2003). Punctuated equilibrium and linear progression: Toward a new understanding of group development. *Academy of Management Journal, 46*, 106–117.

Chang, S., Jia, L., Takeuchi, R., & Cai, Y. (2014). Do high-commitment work systems affect creativity? A multilevel combinational approach to employee creativity. *Journal of Applied Psychology, 99*, 665–680.

Chatman, J. A., & Flynn, F. J. (2001). The influence of demographic heterogeneity on the emergence and consequences of cooperative norms in work teams. *Academy of Management Journal, 44*, 956–974.

Chatman, J. A., Polzer, J. T., Barsade, S. G., & Neale, M. A. (1998). Being different yet feeling similar: The influence of demographic composition and organizational culture on work processes and outcomes. *Administrative Science Quarterly, 43*, 749–780.

Chen, G. (2005). Newcomer adaptation in teams: Multilevel antecedents and outcomes. *Academy of Management Journal, 48*, 101–116.

Chen, G., Farh, J. L., Campbell-Bush, E. M., Wu, Z., & Wu, X. (2013). Teams as innovative systems: Multilevel motivational antecedents of innovation in R&D teams. *Journal of Applied Psychology, 98*, 1018–1027.

Chiu, Y. T., & Staples, D. S. (2013). Reducing faultlines in geographically dispersed teams: Self-disclosure and task elaboration. *Small Group Research, 44*, 498–531.

Collins, C. J., & Smith, K. G. (2006). Knowledge exchange and combination: The role of human resource practices in the performance of high-technology firms. *Academy of Management Journal, 49*, 544–560.

Colvin, G. (2013). Great job! Or how Yum! Brands uses recognition to build teams and get results. *Fortune*, August 12, 62–66.

De Cremer, D., & Van Knippenberg, D. (2002). How do leaders promote cooperation? The effects of charisma and procedural fairness. *Journal of Applied Psychology, 87*, 858–866.

de Dreu, C. K. W., & Weingart, L. R. (2003). Task versus relationship conflict, team performance and team member satisfaction: A meta-analysis. *Journal of Applied Psychology, 88*, 741–749.

de Jong, J. P., Curșeu, P. L., & Leenders, R. T. A. (2014). When do bad apples not spoil the barrel? Negative relationships in teams, team performance, and buffering mechanisms. *Journal of Applied Psychology, 99*, 514–522.

de Wit, F. R. C., Greer, L. L., & Jehn, K. A. (2012). The paradox of intragroup conflict: A meta-analysis. *Journal of Applied Psychology, 97*, 360–390.

Dezsö, C. L., & Ross, D. G. (2012). Does female representation in top management improve firm performance? A panel data investigation. *Strategic Management Journal, 33*, 1072–1089.

Druskat, V. U., & Wolff, S. B. (1999). Effects and timing of developmental peer appraisals in self-managing work groups. *Journal of Applied Psychology, 84*, 58–74.

Eddy, E. R., Tannenbaum, S. I., & Mathieu, J. E. (2013). Helping teams to help themselves: Comparing two team-led debriefing methods. *Personnel Psychology, 66*, 975–1008.

Edmondson, A. (1999). Psychological safety and learning behavior in work teams. *Administrative Science Quarterly, 44*, 350–383.

Edmondson, A. C., & Lei, Z. (2014). Psychological safety: The history, renaissance, and future of an interpersonal construct. *Annual Review of Organizational Psychology and Organizational Behavior, 1*, 23–43.

Ehrhardt, K., Miller, J. S., Freeman, S. J., & Hom, P. W. (2014). Examining project commitment in cross-functional teams: Antecedents and relationship with team performance. *Journal of Business and Psychology, 29*, 443–461.

Esser, J. K. (1998). Alive and well after 25 years: A review of groupthink research. *Organizational Behavior and Human Decision Processes, 73*, 116–141.

Farh, J. L., Lee, C., & Farh, C. I. (2010). Task conflict and team creativity: A question of how much and when. *Journal of Applied Psychology, 95*, 1173–1180.

Fisher, D. M., Bell, S. T., Dierdorff, E., & Belohlav, J. (2012). Facet personality and surface-level diversity as team mental model antecedents: Implications for implicit coordination. *Journal of Applied Psychology, 97*, 825–841.

Gajendran, R. S., & Joshi, A. (2012). Innovation in globally distributed teams: The role of LMX, communication frequency, and member influence on team decisions. *Journal of Applied Psychology, 97*, 1252.

Gerard, H. B., & Mathewson, G. C. (1966). The effect of severity of initiation on liking for a group: A replication. *Journal of Experimental Social Psychology, 2*, 278–287.

Gersick, C. J. G. (1988). Time and transition in work teams: Toward a new model of group development. *Academy of Management Journal, 31*, 9–41.

Gibson, C. B. (1999). Do they do what they believe they can? Group efficacy and group effectiveness across tasks and cultures. *Academy of Management Journal, 42*, 138–152.

Goncalo, J. A., Polman, E., & Maslach, C. (2010). Can confidence come too soon? Collective efficacy, conflict and group performance over time. *Organizational Behavior and Human Decision Processes, 113*, 13–24.

Google. (2014, January). *Diversity*. Retrieved October 30, 2014, from http://www.google.com/diversity.

Gruenfeld, D. H., Martorana, P. V., & Fan, E. T. (2000). What do groups learn from their worldliest members? *Organizational Behavior and Human Decisions Processes, 82*, 45–59.

Gully, S. M., Devine, D. J., & Whitney, D. J. (1995). A meta-analysis of cohesion and performance effects of level of analysis and task interdependence. *Small Group Research, 26*, 497–520.

Gully, S. M., Incalcaterra, K. A., Joshi, A., & Beaubien, J. M. (2002). A meta-analysis of team-efficacy, potency, and performance: Interdependence and level of analysis as moderators of observed relationships. *Journal of Applied Psychology, 87*, 819.

Harden, S. W. (2014). Surgeons and teamwork. *AAOS* Now, March 2011. Retrieved September 1, 2015, from http://www.aaos.org/news/aaosnow/mar11/managing3.asp.

Harrison, D. A., Price, K. H., & Bell, M. P. (1998). Beyond relational demography: Time and the effects of surface- and deep-level diversity on work group cohesion. *Academy of Management Journal, 41*, 96–107.

Harrison D. A., Price K. H., Gavin J. H., & Florey A. T. (2002). Time, teams, and task performance: Changing effects of surface- and deep-level diversity on group functioning. *Academy of Management Journal, 45*, 1029–45.

Hauschildt, K., & Konradt, U. (2012). The effect of self-leadership on work role performance in teams. *Leadership, 8*, 145–168.

Hirschfeld, R. R., Jordan, M. H., Feild, H.S., Giles, W. F., & Armenakis, A. A. (2006). Becoming team players: Team members' mastery of teamwork knowledge as a predictor of team task proficiency and observed teamwork effectiveness. *Journal of Applied Psychology, 91*, 467–474.

Hoch, J. E., & Kozlowski, S. W. (2014). Leading virtual teams: Hierarchical leadership, structural supports, and shared team leadership. *Journal of Applied Psychology, 99*, 390–403.

Hsieh, P. J. (2010). Cross-functional team selection concerning members' cooperative effects and capabilities overlap. *Systems Research and Behavioral Science, 27*, 301–318.

Ilgen, D. R., Hollenbeck, J. R., Johnson, M., & Jundt, D. (2005). Teams in organizations: From input-process-output models to IMOI models. *Annual Review of Psychology, 56*, 517–543.

Jackson, S. E., Joshi, A., & Erhardt, N. L. (2003). Recent research on team and organizational diversity: SWOT analysis and implications. *Journal of Management, 29*, 801–830.

Janis, I. L. (1972). *Victims of groupthink: A psychological study of foreign-policy decisions and fiascoes*. Oxford, England: Houghton Mifflin.

Janis, I. L. (1982). *Groupthink: Psychological studies of policy decisions and fiascoes*. Boston, MA: Cengage Learning.

Jehn, K. A. (1994). Enhancing effectiveness: An investigation of advantages and disadvantages of value-based intragroup conflict. *International Journal of Conflict Management, 5*, 223–238.

Kauffeld, S., & Lehmann-Willenbrock, N. (2012). Meetings matter: Effects of team meetings on team and organizational success. *Small Group Research, 43*, 130–158.

Kim, S. H., Choi, S. H., & Kim, J. K. (1999). An interactive procedure for multiple attribute group decision making with incomplete information: Range-based approach. *European Journal of Operational Research, 118*(1), 139–152.

Knight, A. P., & Baer, M. (2014). Get up, stand up: The effects of a non-sedentary workspace on information elaboration and group performance. *Social Psychological and Personality Science, 5*, 910–917.

Kohn, N. W., & Smith, S. M. (2011). Collaborative fixation: Effects of others' ideas on brainstorming. *Applied Cognitive Psychology, 25*, 359–371.

Kozlowski, S. W., & Ilgen, D. R. (2006). Enhancing the effectiveness of work groups and teams. *Psychological Science in the Public Interest, 7*, 77–124.

Krishnan, H. A., & Park, D. (2005). A few good women – on top management teams. *Journal of Business Research, 58*, 1712–1720.

Kruse, K. (2014). Leadership secrets from Yum! Brands CEO David Novak. *Forbes*, June 25. Retrieved November 1, 2014, from http://www.forbes.com/sites/kevinkruse/2014/06/25/david-novack-leadership-advice/;

Kunze, F., & Bruch, H. (2010). Age-based faultlines and perceived productive energy: The moderation of transformational leadership. *Small Group Research, 41*, 593–620.

Latane, B., Williams, K., & Harkins, S. (1979). Many hands make light work: The causes and consequences of social loafing. *Journal of Personality and Social Psychology, 37*, 822–832.

Lau, D. C., & Murnighan, J. K. (1998). Demographic diversity and faultlines: The compositional dynamics of organizational groups. *Academy of Management Review, 23*, 325–340.

Leung, A. K. Y., Maddux, W. W., Galinsky, A. D., & Chiu, C. Y. (2008). Multicultural experience enhances creativity: The when and how. *American Psychologist, 63*, 169–181.

Lewis, K., Belliveau, M., Herndon, B., & Keller, J. (2007). Group cognition, membership change, and performance: Investigating the benefits and detriments of collective knowledge. *Organizational Behavior and Human Decisions Processes, 103*, 159–178.

Liang, J., Farh, C. I., & Farh, J. L. (2012). Psychological antecedents of promotive and prohibitive voice: A two-wave examination. *Academy of Management Journal, 55*, 71–92.

Liden, R. C., Wayne, S. J., Jaworski, R. A., & Bennett, N. (2004). Social loafing: A field investigation. *Journal of Management, 30*, 285–304.

Lorinkova, N. M., Pearsall, M. J., & Sims, H. P. (2013). Examining the differential longitudinal performance of directive versus empowering leadership in teams. *Academy of Management Journal, 56*, 573–596.

Lovelace, K., Shapiro, D. L., & Weingart, L. R. (2001). Maximizing cross-functional new product teams' innovativeness and constraint adherence: A conflict communications perspective. *Academy of Management Journal, 44*, 779–793.

Marks, M. A., Mathieu, J. E., & Zaccaro, S. J. (2001). A temporally based framework and taxonomy of team processes. *Academy of Management Review, 26*, 356–376.

Mathieu, J., Maynard, M. T., Rapp, T., & Gilson, L. (2008). Team effectiveness 1997–2007: A review of recent advancements and a glimpse into the future. *Journal of Management, 34*, 410–476.

Mathieu, J. E., Tannenbaum, S. I., Donsbach, J. S., & Alliger, G. M. (2013). A review and integration of team composition models moving toward a dynamic and temporal framework. *Journal of Management, 40,* 130-160.

Mohammed, S., & Nadkarni, S. (2014). Are we all on the same temporal page? The moderating effects of temporal team cognition on the polychronicity diversity-team performance relationship. *Journal of Applied Psychology, 99,* 404-422.

Montoya-Weiss, M. M., Massey, A. P., & Song, M. (2001). Getting it together: Temporal coordination and conflict management in global virtual teams. *Academy of Management Journal, 44,* 1251-1262.

Moorhead, G., Ference, R., & Neck, C. P. (1991). Group decision fiascoes continue: Space shuttle Challenger and a revised groupthink framework. *Human Relations, 44,* 539-550.

Moreland, R. L., & Levine, J. M. (1982). Socialization in small groups: Temporal changes in individual-group relations. *Advances in Experimental Social Psychology, 15,* 137-192.

Morgeson, F. P., DeRue, D. S., & Karam, E. P. (2010). Leadership in teams: A functional approach to understanding leadership structures and processes. *Journal of Management, 36,* 5-39.

Morgeson, F. P., Reider, M. H., & Campion, M. A. (2005). Selecting individuals in team settings: The importance of social skills, personality characteristics, and teamwork knowledge. *Personnel Psychology, 58,* 583-611.

Mueller, J. S. (2012). Why individuals in larger teams perform worse. *Organizational Behavior and Human Decision Processes, 117,* 111-124.

Mullen, B., & Copper, C. (1994). The relation between group cohesion and performance: An integration. *Psychological Bulletin, 115,* 210-227.

Mumford, T. V., Campion, M. A., & Morgeson, F. P. (2006). Situational judgment in work teams: A team role typology. In J. A. Weekley & R. E. Ployhart (Eds.), *Situational judgment tests: Theory, measurement, and application* (pp. 319-343). Mahwah, NJ: Lawrence Erlbaum Associates.

Mumford, T. V., Van Iddekinge, C. H., Morgeson, F. P., & Campion, M. A. (2008). The team role test: Development and validation of a team role knowledge situational judgment test. *Journal of Applied Psychology, 93,* 250-267.

Nielsen, T. M. (2007). The evolving nature of work teams: Changing to meet the requirements of the future. In C. Wankel (Ed.), *21st century management: A reference handbook* (pp. 3-14). Thousand Oaks, CA: Sage.

Nouri, R., Erez, M., Rockstuhl, T., Ang, S., Leshem-Calif, L., & Rafaeli, A. (2013). Taking the bite out of culture: The impact of task structure and task type on overcoming impediments to cross-cultural team performance. *Journal of Organizational Behavior, 34,* 739-763.

Novak, D. (2012). *Taking people with you: The only way to make big things happen.* New York: Penguin.

Nutt, P. C. (1984). Types of organizational decision processes. *Administrative Science Quarterly, 29,* 414-450.

Okhuysen, G. A., & Waller, M. J. (2002). Focusing on midpoint transitions: An analysis of boundary conditions. *Academy of Management Journal, 45,* 1056-1065.

O'Neill, T. A., Allen, N. J., & Hastings, S. E. (2013). Examining the "pros" and "cons" of team conflict: A team-level meta-analysis of task, relationship, and process conflict. *Human Performance, 26,* 236–260.

O'Reilly III, C. A., Caldwell, D. F., & Barnett, W. P. (1989). Work group demography, social integration, and turnover. *Administrative Science Quarterly, 34,* 21–37.

Osborn, A. F. (1953). *Applied imagination.* Oxford, England: Scribner's.

Peeters, M. A., Van Tuijl, H. F., Rutte, C. G., & Reymen, I. M. (2006). Personality and team performance: A meta-analysis. *European Journal of Personality, 20,* 377–396.

Pieterse, A. N., Van Knippenberg, D., & Van Dierendonck, D. (2013). Cultural diversity and team performance: The role of team member goal orientation. *Academy of Management Journal, 56,* 782–804.

Polzer, J. T., Crisp, C. B., Jarvenpaa, S. L., & Kim, J. W. (2006). Extending the faultline model to geographically dispersed teams: How collocated subgroups can impair group functioning. *Academy of Management Journal, 49,* 679–692.

Polzer, J. T., Milton, L. P., & Swann, W. B. (2002). Capitalizing on diversity: Interpersonal congruence in small work groups. *Administrative Science Quarterly, 47,* 296–324.

Poole, M. S. (1983). Decision development in small groups II: A study of multiple sequences of decision making. *Communication Monographs, 48,* 1–24.

Prussia, G. E., & Kinicki, A. J. (1996). A motivational investigation of group effectiveness using social-cognitive theory. *Journal of Applied Psychology, 81,* 187–198.

The Radicati Group, Inc. (2013, April). *Email statistics report, 2013–2017.* Retrieved November 7, 2014, from http://www.radicati.com/wp/wp-content/uploads/2013/04/Email-Statistics-Report-2013-2017-Executive-Summary.pdf.

Randel, A. E., & Jaussi, K. S. (2003). Functional background identity, diversity, and individual performance in cross-functional teams. *Academy of Management Journal, 46,* 763–774.

Rogelberg, S. G., Rhoades Shanock, L., & Scott, C. W. (2012). Wasted time and money in meetings: Increasing return on investment. *Small Group Research, 43,* 236–245.

Salas, E., Cooke, N. J., & Rosen, M. A. (2008). On teams, teamwork, and team performance: Discoveries and developments. *Human Factors: The Journal of the Human Factors and Ergonomics Society, 50,* 540–547.

Schippers, M. A. (2014). Social loafing tendencies and team performance: The compensating effect of agreeableness and conscientiousness. *Academy of Management Learning & Education, 13,* 62–81.

Schneider, B. (1987). The people make the place. *Personnel Psychology, 40,* 437–453.

Schneider, B., Goldstein, H. W., & Smith, D. B. (1995). The ASA framework: An update. *Personnel Psychology, 48,* 747–773.

Simons, T. L., & Peterson, R. S. (2000). Task conflict and relationship conflict in top management teams: The pivotal role of intragroup trust. *Journal of Applied Psychology, 85,* 102–111.

Staats, B. R., Milkman, K. L., & Fox, C. R. (2012). The team scaling fallacy: Underestimating the declining efficiency of larger teams. *Organizational Behavior and Human Decision Processes, 118,* 132–142.

Stevens, M. J., & Campion, M. A. (1994). The knowledge, skill, and ability require-ments for teamwork: Implications for human resource management. *Journal of Management, 20,* 503–530.

Stewart, G. L. (2006). A meta-analytic review of relationships between team design features and team performance. *Journal of Management, 32,* 29–55.

Stewart, G. L., Courtright, S. H., & Barrick, M. R. (2012). Peer-based control in self-managing teams: Linking rational and normative influence with individual and group performance. *Journal of Applied Psychology, 97,* 435–447.

Summers, J. K., Humphrey, S. E., & Ferris, G. R. (2012). Team member change, flux in coordination, and performance: Effects of strategic core roles, information transfer, and cognitive ability. *Academy of Management Journal, 55,* 314–338.

Sundstrom, E., De Meuse, K. P., & Futrell, D. (1990). Work teams: Applications and effectiveness. *American Psychologist, 45,* 120–133.

Sundstrom, E., McIntyre, M., Halfhill, T., & Richards, H. (2000). Work groups: From the Hawthorne studies to work teams of the 1990s and beyond. *Group Dynamics: Theory, Research, and Practice, 4,* 44.

Tadmor, C. T., Satterstrom, P., Jang, S., & Polzer, J. T. (2012). Beyond individual creativity: The superadditive benefits of multicultural experience for collective creativity in culturally diverse teams. *Journal of Cross-Cultural Psychology, 43,* 384–392.

Tannenbaum, S. I., & Cerasoli, C. P. (2013). Do team and individual debriefs enhance performance? A meta-analysis. *Human Factors: The Journal of the Human Factors and Ergonomics Society, 55,* 231–245.

Tuckman, B. W. (1965). Developmental sequence in small groups. *Psychological Bulletin, 63,* 384–399.

Tuckman, B. W., & Jensen, M.-A. C. (1977). Stages of small group development revisited. *Group and Organizational Studies, 2,* 419–427.

Turner, M. E., & Pratkanis, A. R. (1998). Twenty-five years of groupthink theory and research: Lessons from the evaluation of a theory. *Organizational Behavior and Human Decision Processes, 73,* 105–115.

Van Knippenberg, D., de Dreu, C. K. W., & Homan, A. C. (2004). Work group diversity and group performance: An integrative model and research agenda. *Journal of Applied Psychology, 89,* 1008–1022.

Wang, S., & He, Y. (2008). Compensating nondedicated cross-functional teams. *Organization Science, 19,* 753–765.

Watkins, M. (2013, June). Making virtual teams work: Ten basic principles. *Harvard Business Review.* Retrieved January 27, 2015, from https://hbr.org/2013/06/making-virtual-teams-work-ten/.

Wicker, A. W., & Mehler, A. (1971). Assimilation of new members in a large and small church. *Journal of Applied Psychology, 55,* 151–156.

Williams, H. M., Parker, S. K., & Turner, N. (2010). Proactively performing teams: The role of work design, transformational leadership, and team compos-ition. *Journal of Occupational and Organizational Psychology, 83,* 301–324.

Zaccaro, S. J., & McCoy, M. C. (1988). The effects of task and interpersonal cohe-siveness on performance of a disjunctive group task. *Journal of Applied Social Psychology, 18,* 837–851.

Chapter 14

ORGANIZATIONAL STRUCTURE, CULTURE, AND CHANGE

Organizational structure defines how work is formally distributed and divided within an organization. In this chapter you will learn about organizational structure and culture as important factors in employee and organizational effectiveness and well-being.

After studying this chapter, you should be able to:

- explain different approaches to organizational design
- identify the main components of an organization's structure and their impact on employees
- list the dimensions of an organization's culture
- explain the origins of organizational culture and how it evolves in an organization
- describe the functions of organizational culture for an organization
- evaluate the effectiveness of a particular organizational change effort

Learning goals for this chapter

- identify key legal and global issues surrounding structure, culture, and change
- describe the current issues and controversies around structure, culture, and change.

Introduction

As you will recall from Chapter 3 on job analysis and Chapter 9 on motivation, organizations create a structure for individual jobs in order to get things done efficiently and effectively. How work is designed at the individual level influences employee motivation, performance, and well-being. In addition to work design and distribution of labor within a work group, how the organization itself is structured and how it structures work groups and teams (see Chapter 13) make a difference in the day-to-day lives of employees and the effectiveness of the organization. How should the organization design its departments? How much of an emphasis will there be on managing people by rules versus by unwritten norms? How many layers will there be in the organizational hierarchy? Will employees on the front lines have the power to make important decisions, or will they have to check with their supervisors first?

The answers to these questions reflect the mentality of organizational founders, the current management of the organization, the type of work that it does, the types of people it employs, and the particular environment in which the organization must operate. Once a particular structure is in place, it will affect employees' actions, their ability to get things done, and their health and well-being. Organizational structure is also a powerful influence over a company's values. Even though values and norms within an organization are often unwritten, they shape and affect employee behaviors and attitudes at work.

Sometimes, an organization will have a structure, technology, or values that do not serve it well. The survival of the organization may rely on its ability to change to develop a more suitable structure and a set of values. Planning, implementing, and monitoring change is a place where I/O psychologists can add value to organizations. Effective management of change will require an understanding of why organizations have particular structures and cultures, as well as an understanding of how to enact constructive change in organizations. In this chapter, we will give you only a brief introduction to the topics of organizational structure, organizational culture, and change and how they affect employee attitudes and behavior. Remember that each of these is a huge topic in and of itself. For example, change management is a specialization within I/O psychology that is referred to as Organization Development (OD). If you are interested, we encourage you to pursue independent reading in this area to learn more.

Organization Theory and Design

Organization design refers to structures of accountability and responsibility, HR practices, and business process that exist in an organization and that the organization uses to implement its strategy (Greenwood & Miller, 2010). An organization's structure, systems, and processes are tools that exist to enable the organization to enact its strategy. Organizations exist because they have goals that cannot be achieved by a single person. In order to reach their goals (whether the goal is to provide disaster relief to an affected area or to bring long-term value to shareholders), they need to orchestrate the efforts of individuals. This is where organizational design comes in. How should people and work be organized in order to make it more likely that the organization is going to achieve its goals?

Organization design: The structures of accountability and responsibility, HR practices, and business processes existing in an organization that the organization uses to implement its strategy.

Historical Perspectives on the Design of Organizations

In order to understand how organizations are designed and should be designed, we need to understand some of the history of organization theory (which refers to the study of organizational design). Specifically, over the past few decades, different perspectives have guided the answer to the question of how to design organizations.

Classical organization theory was the dominant view at the start of the twentieth century. Major personalities in this movement included Frederick Taylor (a figure you may recall from Chapter 1), Henri Fayol, and Max Weber. The common philosophy prevalent at the time was that there was one best way to structure work and design organizations, and it was the job of managers to make organizations more efficient. Frederick Taylor, author of *Principles of Scientific Management* (1911), contended that the manager's job was to monitor and collaborate with employees to ensure that work would be done in the expected manner, and it was the duty of employees to perform their jobs using the methods and procedures designed by the organization. Henri Fayol was a French mining engineer. He proposed that the manager's job was to plan, organize, command, coordinate, and control employees. He also came up with 14 principles that should guide every organization, including discipline (everyone should respect the rules of the organization), unity of command (every employee should report to only one manager), and centralization (managers retain the ultimate authority in decision-making) (Fayol, 1930). Max Weber, the German sociologist who published his original writings in German in the 1920s, described the ideal organizational form as a bureaucracy (Weber, 1947). While today the term "bureaucracy" has very negative connotations – an overemphasis on rules, forms, and paperwork – Weber originally saw it as highly rational and an improvement over the loosely designed organizations of the time. This ideal bureaucratic organization would emphasize rule-based decision-making and obeying and following the hierarchy. Taken together, these classical organizational theories emphasized the importance of efficiency as the goal of organizational design, and utilized hierarchy, structure, and written processes to achieve this goal.

Classical organization theory: An approach to organizational design that emphasizes the importance of efficiency as the goal and utilizes hierarchy, structure, and written processes to achieve this goal.

The **Human Relations movement**, typically traced back to the Hawthorne studies of the 1920s (see Chapter 1), also influenced how people thought about the

Human Relations movement: An approach to organization design in which it was assumed that workers were able to self-manage effectively, and that they would flourish if allowed to do so.

System 4 design: An organizational design consisting of goal-setting, decision-making, leadership, and reward systems that would maximize trust between employees and management, and facilitate two-way communication.

design of work and organizations. With the realization of the importance of social norms, employee motivation, and job satisfaction as influences over productivity, organizational design gained a more humanistic outlook. Now the objective was not solely to maximize efficiency, and human beings were no longer relegated to the role of a cog in a machine, or a passive recipient of their roles. Rather, workers were assumed to be able to self-manage effectively, and it was believed that they would flourish if allowed to do so. For example, Rensis Likert (1967) recommended all organizations adopt a design termed **System 4 design**, consisting of goal-setting, decision-making, leadership, and reward systems that would maximize trust between employees and management, and facilitate two-way communication. However, in its way this approach was just as naïve as classical organization theory: Human Relations approaches assumed that there was "one best way" to organize work (i.e., let people self-manage) and did not take into account that some workers may not be good at self-management.

Situational paradigm: An approach to organizational design where the key factor is understanding the context in which the organization operates, and configuring an organizational structure that meets the needs of the organization.

Nowadays, a **situational paradigm** can be said to be in effect. In other words, contemporary researchers who study organizations came to the conclusion that there may be no one best way of organizing. Instead, the effectiveness of a particular design seems to depend on the context: the environment the organization operates in, the size of the organization, and the type of technology and strategy the organization utilizes. The key factor is understanding the context in which the organization operates, and configuring an organizational structure that meets the needs of the organization. The main point to remember is that there may be more than one way to achieve an organization's goals and that there may be multiple alternative approaches to designing an organization, all of them resulting in desired outcomes. For example, organizations may choose varying degrees of centralized control or employee empowerment depending on the organizational environment and the kind of work they do.

It is also important to note that organizational decision-makers are not always rational actors who know which structure will work in a given context. Therefore, it is not unusual for organizations to have the "wrong" structure for their goals. For example, research has shown that when the environment is turbulent and uncertain, having a lot of rules, regulations, and centralized authority is not the most effective way of organizing. Ironically, when the environment is turbulent and uncertain, this is exactly what organizations tend to do, to introduce more rules and hierarchy (Bourgeois, McAllister, & Mitchell, 1978). *Why?* Uncertainty is stressful to decision-makers, and oftentimes they try to reduce uncertainty by creating rules and structure. In other words, organizations are not often designed in a rational manner by decision-makers who have perfect information about the consequences of their actions. Instead, they are designed by imperfect human beings whose emotions, self-interests, and perceptual biases affect how they react to the environment.

Dimensions of Organizational Structure

Organizational structure: Choices the organization makes regarding who does what, who reports to whom, how employees are grouped together, and how groups relate to each other.

Organizational structure refers to the choices the organization makes regarding who does what, who reports to whom, how employees are grouped together, and how groups relate to each other. It determines how information flows in the organization, how authority is distributed, and how responsibilities are assigned. We

Too many rules sometimes result in employees trying to break the rules to get their work done, ultimately defeating the purpose of the rules. For example, frequent requests to change passwords may actually reduce safety of information when employees follow the rule, but not the spirit of the rule, such as writing their password on a Post-it note.

will review four important aspects of an organization's structure: degree of formalization, level of centralization, type of departmentalization, and width of span of control.

Formalization

Organizations that are highly formalized have a lot of rules and procedures and low tolerance for deviations from rules. In fact, decision-making in these organizations tends not to be on a case-by-case basis, and instead the organization tries to predict situations and problems that will be encountered by employees and present codified responses to them. In other words, these organizations supplant personal discretion with rules and procedures. Organizations that take this too far and do not allow deviations from rules will end up becoming overly bureaucratic, preventing innovation and change. At the same time, formalization of organizational procedures may actually create freedom for teams at lower levels, because formalization creates structures and reduces uncertainty, which frees up individuals and teams to work within these boundaries (Hempel, Zhang, & Han, 2012). For example, a group of maintenance workers tasked with taking care of a company's buildings might be more successful operating with lots of rules and codes: This could actually free them up from having to decide what to fix and how to fix it, because the rules would spell that out for them. Rather, they could focus on actually getting their work done efficiently. In highly formalized organizations, you may expect to find thick operational manuals and employee handbooks, specific job descriptions, and an emphasis on written communication.

Formalization: The degree to which the organization is characterized by rules and procedures and the extent to which deviations from rules are tolerated.

Centralization

In organizations that are highly centralized, decision-making authority is concentrated in the hands of a small number of decision-makers at higher levels. Power resides in those at high levels, and there is little involvement of lower-level employees in strategic decision-making. In contrast, in organizations that are relatively decentralized, decisions are made by individuals at all levels, and by people who are closer to the problem being experienced. In centralized organizations, lower-level employees are not expected to proactively notice problems or produce

Centralization: The degree to which the decision-making authority is concentrated in the hands of a small number of decision-makers at higher levels.

McDonalds sells the standardization of its burgers. Every burger should taste exactly the same, wherever you eat it. So, the company relies heavily on the formalization and centralization of its operations. The 300+ page operations manual contains specific guidance regarding how to prepare burgers including how long the buns should be toasted for (17 seconds), and the amount of sanitizer to use when cleaning the shake machine (1 packet for every 2.5 gallons of water) (Kruger, 2004).

solutions to them. Further, the organization does not expect low-level employees to make decisions and therefore key information that would facilitate such decision-making is not necessarily shared with lower-level employees. Therefore, these organizations may be slow to notice opportunities and threats that exist in their environments (Fredrickson, 1986). Using the same example of the maintenance employees, if they are told that it is their job to fix only the things management tells them to fix and not notice problems that might arise, it could be disastrous. An employee who was told to paint the wall of a storage room might notice that the wall is failing due to a slow water leak, but would say nothing about it, since it is not his job to notice the problems, only to do what he is told. In contrast, in relatively decentralized organizations, employees experience greater levels of autonomy, which contributes to their sense of fairness of the organization, and serves as a motivator (Schminke, Ambrose, & Cropanzano, 2000). In these situations, employees are trusted to communicate with their supervisors.

Departmentalization

Functional departments: Departments that combine employees working in the same function (such as marketing, manufacturing, and accounting) within the same department.

How work is organized around departments will make a difference as well. Historically, organizations created departments based on functional areas. **Functional departments** will combine employees working in the same function (such as marketing, manufacturing, and accounting) within the same department. This is also the typical form of organizing in smaller organizations. This form of organizing provides specific advantages. First, these departments tend to be more efficient as there is no duplication of effort. All marketing expertise is collected within the same department, and employees can learn from others working in their own functional area. At the same time, these structures are slower to respond to the needs of a particular customer. For example, sales employees will need to be familiar with and pay equal attention to each product line the company offers, without focusing their energy on any product category. As a result, these structures may be slower to respond to the unique needs of their customers or specific products.

Departmentalization by customer: Different departments are used for different customer categories.

A survey of US businesses indicates that functional departmentalization is no longer the norm, and businesses organizing around products or customer groups will soon exceed 50 percent (Day, 2006). Organizations that use **departmentalization**

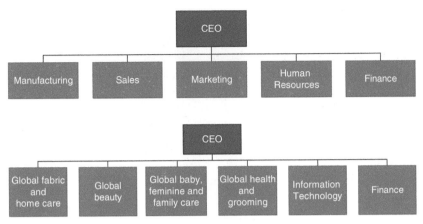

Figure 14.1 Sample organizational chart departmentalized by function.

Figure 14.2 Partial organizational chart of Procter & Gamble. This structure is a hybrid of departmentalization by product and function. Drawn based on information retrieved February 11, 2015, from http://www.pg.com/en_US/company/purpose_people/executive_team/index.shtml.

by customer have different departments for different customer categories. For example, there may be different departments for high-tech customers and for retail customers. Similarly, organizations that use **departmentalization by product** have a separate department for each product category. Finally, organizations that use **departmentalization by geography** have separate departments for separate regions of the country or world. You can find examples for different styles of departmentalization in Figures 14.1–14.4.

Companies that use departmentalization by product, customer, or geography place marketing, sales, and operations expertise under each department, thereby allowing quicker response to the needs of the market. At the same time, there will be duplication of effort, and departments may start competing for resources and with each other. Typically, even when they organize by customer or product category, the organization will choose to retain some functional areas such as human resources management, information technology, or finance as separate departments.

Departmentalization by product: Separate departments are used for each product category.

Departmentalization by geography: Separate departments are used for separate regions of the country or world.

Span of Control

Span of control refers to the number of employees that report to a single manager. As span of control increases, the ability of a manager to carefully review the work done by each employee, supervise and monitor them closely, and answer questions frequently will diminish, because each additional employee will tax the limited resources of managers. As a result, when employees need to be closely supervised, the span of control will be narrow (or there will be few people reporting to a single manager) as opposed to wide. Of course, when the span of control is narrow, the leadership style of the manager plays an important role in how employees work and react to their environment (Gümüşlüoğlu, Karakitapoğlu-Aygün, & Hirst, 2013). There is no consensus on how wide span of control should be, but in Roman times, 10 was believed to be the ideal, whereas Napoleon believed 5 to be the appropriate number, and management theorist Henri Fayol advocated for a

Span of control: Number of employees that report to a single manager.

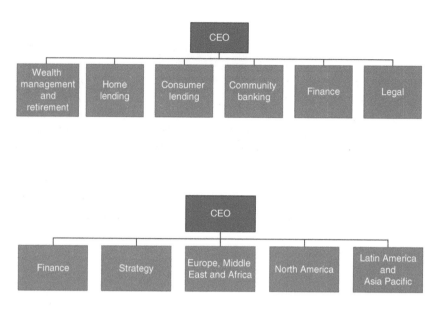

Figure 14.3 Partial organizational chart of Wells Fargo bank. This structure is a hybrid of departmentalization by customer and function. Drawn based on information retrieved February 11, 2015, from https://www.wellsfargo. com/about/corporate/ executive_officers/.

Figure 14.4 Partial organizational chart of Budget Rental Cars. This structure is a hybrid of departmentalization by function and geography. Drawn based on information retrieved February 11, 2015, from http://www.budget. com/budgetWeb/ html/en/aboutus/com- panyinfo/execbios/ index.html.

span between 5 and 15. When work is standardized, is relatively straightforward, routine, and not too complex, a wider span of control can be effective (Topp & Desjardins, 2011). Ultimately, the appropriate number of workers who report to each supervisor will likely depend on the maturity and competence of employees and complexity of the job at hand. Research in a chemical company has shown that increases in span of control correlated with increased levels of unsafe behaviors and accidents (Hechanova-Alampay & Beehr, 2001). Therefore, particularly if the job is safety sensitive, the size of the span of control needs to be decided carefully.

Types of Organizational Structures

You may have realized that the four dimensions of organizational structure – formalization, centralization, departmentalization, and span of control – are not really independent of each other and instead they tend to go together. Specifically, some organizations tend to be highly formalized, centralized, have narrow spans of control and tall hierarchies, and typically are organized around functional departments. In contrast, others tend to be more informal, decentralized, have wide spans of control and flat hierarchies, and are departmentalized by customer, product, or geography. You can think of these two different categories as prototypes of organizational structures. In the literature, these are referred to as mechanistic and organic structures, respectively.

Organic structures: Structures of organizations which tend to be more informal, decentralized, have wide spans of control and flat hierarchies, and are departmentalized by customer, product, or geography.

Organic structures are built for flexibility and adaptability. These organizations sacrifice efficiency and predictability in favor of quick action. As a result, organic structures are relatively more common in entrepreneurial organizations, even when they are large in size. Examples may be found among companies operating in quickly changing industries and in companies competing based on the quality of their products and services, such as Apple, 3M, and Google. In contrast, **mechanistic**

structures emphasize governance with rules and regulations. Their strength lies in the predictability of their operations. They are much more orderly than the organic structures and therefore they have an advantage in producing goods and services at minimal cost and being efficient. Examples include companies that emphasize low prices such as McDonalds and Walmart, and companies operating in government as well as highly regulated and safety-sensitive industries such as pharmaceuticals and healthcare. Employees tend to be given greater leeway in organic structures, and therefore perceive greater levels of empowerment (Dust, Resick, & Mawritz, 2014). Further, employees perceive greater levels of fairness and display organizational citizenship behaviors more frequently in organic structures (Ambrose, Schminke, & Mayer, 2013), suggesting that organic structures may be more supportive of positive relationships between management and employees, as well as better relations among employees.

Still, it is important to remember that organic structures are not necessarily *the* ideal structure. The structure should be a good fit for the industry, the change of pace, the organizational environment, and the strategy of the organization. Companies with a mechanistic structure will struggle if their industry requires innovation and quick action, as in the example of IBM in the 1980s, whereas other companies may struggle to fit the regulations or safety requirements of their industries as a result of an insufficient number of procedures or decentralized decision-making.

Further, we should caution you against assuming that organizations are purely mechanistic or organic. It is safer to assume that mechanistic and organic structures are two ends of a spectrum and that in reality organizations will be placed somewhere between the two extremes. Even among organizations within the same heavily regulated industry such as the pharmaceutical industry, there will be some that are more agile, more flexible, less centralized, and less formalized than others.

Mechanistic structures: Structures of organizations which tend to be highly formalized, centralized, have narrow spans of control and tall hierarchies, and typically are organized around functional departments.

Contemporary Organizational Structures

Today's organizations are experimenting with alternative ways of organizing in order to increase their flexibility, and achieving a balance between pursuing market opportunities quickly while maintaining stability. We will review three relatively new types of structures in this section.

Matrix Structure

The **matrix structure** combines a functional structure with a project-based one. Each employee reports to a functional manager and a project manager. Thus, matrix structures typically involve dual reporting relationships with each employee reporting to two managers (see Figure 14.5). This structure first originated in the aerospace industry, and it has been adopted by organizations in healthcare, technology, and banking among others (Duncan, 1979). The primary advantage of a matrix structure is its ability to respond to the needs of a specific product or market. Employees can be pulled from different areas of expertise to serve the needs of a product or customer. As a result, this structure facilitates collaboration and communication across functions (Lee, Kozlenkova, & Palmatier, 2014). It has advantages over permanently creating departments for different products or customers, because at the conclusion of the project the employees

Matrix structure: The structure that combines a functional structure with a project-based one.

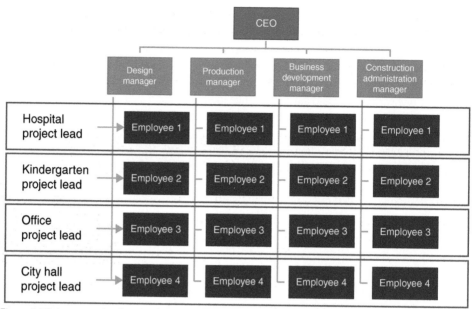

Figure 14.5 An example of a matrix structure in an architecture firm, with each employee having one functional supervisor (e.g., design, production) and one focused on particular projects (e.g., hospital, kindergarten).

"See website for interactive material"

can be assigned to different projects. But there are many interpersonal challenges to working in a matrix structure. A common one is serving two bosses. Project managers and department managers will need to coordinate their expectations so that the employee can function without experiencing role conflict, confusion, and stress. It has been proposed that matrix structures may increase competition among employees and create ambiguity in one's role, necessitating employees to have social skills to overcome these problems (Sy & Côté, 2004).

Lattice Structure

Lattice structure:
Structure that is characterized by person-to-person communication, and absence of assigned authority.

Lattice structure does not have a typical, top-down, traditional hierarchy. Instead, organizations with this structure are characterized by person-to-person communication, and absence of assigned authority. This structure is radically unique and different, such that there are no assigned managers. Each employee is expected to initiate or join a project of their own choosing. What makes someone a leader is their ability to persuade others to join their projects, and not necessarily their designation as a "manager". Each person will need to get to know others in this organization, communicate effectively with them, and secure buy-in for their ideas (Manz, Shipper, & Stewart, 2009). Perhaps the biggest company that uses this structure is W. L. Gore, the maker of products such as Gore-tex fabrics, Elixir guitar strings, and implantable medical devices. How can this structure work in a company with over 10,000 workers? British anthropologist Robin Dunbar (1993) proposed that the maximum size of a human collective where every person knows every other person and can maintain relationships with them is 150, which has come to be known as "Dunbar's number." Knowingly or unknowingly, W. L. Gore is following this principle, because in order to facilitate the direct and face-to-face communication required in this structure, the company limits the size of its facilities to 150 to 200 employees, and opens up a new site when the plant or the office grows past this number (Deutschman, 2004). Of course, this structure is best used under specific circumstances where innovation is highly desired.

Workplace Application

Eliminating the Hierarchy (and the Boss) at Valve

There are hundreds of companies in the video game industry. Industry experts and publications report that out of all these companies, the best place for a game developer to work is Valve. The company is the maker of award-winning game *Half-Life* and the internet-based game distribution and networking platform Steam.

In their Seattle-based office, Valve has over 300 employees but no managers. Instead, employees work on a project of their own choosing, join teams, leave teams, and commit to projects based on their buy-in. Employees are involved in all functions typically performed by HR departments, including hiring, termination, and determination of pay raises. The company believes that if a project does not have employees to work on it, it is probably not worth doing. Of course such a system relies heavily on having highly skilled and highly self-reliant workers, so the company puts a lot of emphasis into these characteristics in its hiring process. For example, the company made a job offer (unsuccessfully) to Markus Persson, the founder of Mojang (and creator of the very popular game *Minecraft*), which was acquired by Microsoft in 2014 for $2.5 billion.

Efficiency is sacrificed and sometimes employees who are a bad fit for this structure may remain longer than they would in a more typical hierarchy with closer supervision. Still, employees like it, the company is successful, and the lattice model is just one way in which companies are experimenting with eliminating hierarchy to have more flexibility and agility.

Sources: Makuch, 2013; Ovide & Rusli, 2014; Suddath, 2012.

Virtual Organizations

When organizations need skills, expertise, or technology that resides within a different company, they often engage in a merger or acquisition. However, when companies merge, they do so permanently. This means that the operations, processes, and the culture of the business would need to be streamlined, which is a major endeavor. Instead of a permanent merger, a company may choose to collaborate with a different organization by establishing a virtual organization. This is a company outside of a company that exists for a specific purpose and to take advantage of a market opportunity. An example of this is the creation of Glad Press'n Seal, a product that is used to seal and wrap food products. When Procter and Gamble came up with the idea for a new way of wrapping food, realizing that

Virtual organization: A company outside of a company that exists for a specific purpose and to take advantage of a market opportunity.

Virtual organizations are not limited to the private industry. In 2011, NASA and the Department of Defense joined forces to create the virtual organization National Institute for Rocket Propulsion Systems (NIRPS) to preserve and advance the propulsion capabilities of the USA for current and future needs.

they did not have the market presence in this segment, they approached Clorox, the maker of Glad plastic wraps, for a collaboration. The resulting joint venture is successful, and the companies continue to collaborate in this company, while their parent companies retain their independence and continue to compete in other markets (Anand & Daft, 2007).

Virtual organizations have many advantages, including increased flexibility and the ability to take advantage of a market opportunity or focus on a particular goal. However, they also come with their unique set of challenges. Because this is an organization jointly established by other organizations, a major challenge is to establish a new organizational identity for the employees of the virtual organization and have them see themselves as employees of the new organization, with allegiances to this new organization as opposed to the old ones. A clear description of their goals is also important. Otherwise, at least initially, members of a virtual organization will experience a great deal of uncertainty (Heneman & Greenberger, 2002).

As you have seen, organizations may be structured in different ways. It is possible for very different types of structures to be successful – organizational structures are simply tools; they are ways of organizing the work that needs to be performed within an organization in order to help the organization reach its objectives. For different products, services, and markets, different structures may be appropriate. At the same time, you may have realized that structure affects employee attitudes and behaviors. For example, employees seem to react better to structures that communicate valuing employee judgment. Therefore, decentralized, flat structures may have greater potential to make employees more satisfied with their work and potentially more creative. Also, the fit between the structure and the job incumbent matters a great deal: for example, the lattice structure in Valve Corporation may be a great fit for an employee who is excited about building cool video games and someone who has self-discipline and initiative. However, for an employee who is extrinsically motivated and who expects a lot of guidance and direction from others, this structure will be a poor fit.

Organizational structure matters to individual and organizational productivity because it shows people who reports to whom, how work gets done, and how communication flows. It is an important influence over behavior, but not the only one. Organizations also have unwritten norms and values that are powerful influences over employee actions. Now we turn our attention to organizational culture as a source of motivation, guidance, and coordination.

Organizational Culture and Climate

In addition to structures, organizations have cultures in place. You might think of culture as an organization's personality. Specifically, **organizational culture** is defined as shared, "taken-for-granted" assumptions that members of an organization have and which affect the way they act, think, and perceive their environment (Schein, 1996). Organizational culture is an important influence over employee behavior, and it may even be thought of as an informal control mechanism over individuals at work. For example, Nordstrom is a retailer that is known for its customer service culture. Employees learn from day one that they need to go "above and beyond" when it comes to meeting customer needs. Tales of customer service heroics abound. One author describes a shopping experience where she tries nine pairs of shoes with the help of a sales associate, but learns that the store does not have the color/size combination she wants. Just when she is about to leave, another sales associate steps up, finding the shoes at a Macy's (a rival store), and has them shipped to the customer. The customer later overhears an interaction between the two associates, where the second associate is frustrated with the first one for not trying hard enough, and for "letting us down" (Chatman & Cha, 2003). In other words, peers hold each other accountable for performing behaviors that are aligned with the organizational culture.

> **Organizational culture:** Shared, "taken-for-granted" assumptions that members of an organization have and which affect the way they act, think, and perceive their environment.

If you have work experience, you are probably familiar with how culture influences behavior. Do you start your day chitchatting with your coworkers and giving them a breakdown of your weekend, or do you get your computer powered up and get straight to work? Do you receive e-mails after hours? If you do, are you expected to reply immediately, or can it wait until the morning? Do you dress to impress, or are your weekend jeans and a T-shirt your uniform? The answers to each of these questions signal what type of a culture that company has. Note that the answers to many of these questions will not be written anywhere (with the possible exception of a dress code). But not following the norms will probably be informally discouraged (something we learned from the Hawthorne studies in Chapter 1). If the company culture puts work before family life, then you will be expected to drop everything and answer your e-mail late at night, or face consequences (such as coworkers asking you if you were sick). If you dress more formally than everyone else around you, colleagues may jokingly ask if you have a job interview somewhere else. In other words, culture will act as an informal control mechanism that gives behavior direction, and members of the organization hold each other accountable to follow the norms.

Culture or Climate: Is There a Difference?

In addition to organizational culture, you may come across the term **organizational climate** in the literature. Organizational climate is a term closely related to organizational culture, and is also used to describe an organization in aggregate. Organizational climate refers to the shared perceptions about a work unit's policies, practices, and what behaviors are rewarded and expected (Schneider, Ehrhart, & Macey, 2013). Originally, organizational climate and culture referred to very different phenomena. Organizational culture was the unobservable values

> **Organizational climate:** Shared perceptions about a work unit's policies, practices, and what behaviors are rewarded and expected.

and assumptions shared by employees, and climate referred to more temporary and observable behavioral tendencies. Researchers thought that due to the unobservable nature of culture, it could only be investigated through direct observation and experience by researchers, who would spend about a year observing and living in an organization, acting like a cultural anthropologist. In contrast, organizational climate was thought to be more suitable to study through surveys, and organizational climate typologies would allow researchers and practitioners to measure the level and strength of climate. Nowadays though, no such distinction seems to exist, and there are scholars who believe that the similarities between culture and climate outweigh any theoretical differences (Denison, 1996; Glick, 1985). There are two exceptions, though. First, when referring to the shared values, behavioral patterns, and assumptions of a work unit or team (rather than the entire organization), you are more likely to come across the term group "climate". Second, **psychological climate** refers to an individual person's perception of the behavioral patterns of an entity (such as a group or organization). Psychological climate is different from organizational culture or climate, because psychological climate is simply one person's perception of the climate, whereas the organizational or team climate usually involves some measure of consensus among members of the unit regarding the values, norms, and behavioral patterns that exist.

Finally, the study of climate tends to be more focused on a single dimension as opposed to culture. Whereas culture studies tend to use a typology of organizational culture and explore multiple dimensions, climate researchers nowadays typically focus on a single dimension, such as safety climate, customer service climate, empowerment climate, ethics climate, diversity climate, and justice climate. (For example, we discussed the importance of safety climate in Chapter 12.) Due to its more permanent nature and pervasiveness throughout the organization, we will keep our focus on culture rather than climate in the rest of this chapter.

Dimensions of Culture

What types of cultures are there? There are several typologies of cultures, similar to the dimensions of personality we covered in Chapter 6 such as the five-factor model. Thinking in terms of culture dimensions may make it easier to visualize and recognize them and see if they meet an organization's needs. A well-known framework is Quinn and Rohrbaugh's (1983) Competing Values Framework. According to this framework, organizations may be characterized by four different types of cultures, as illustrated in Figure 14.6.

The **adhocracy culture** is one that puts innovation first. This culture values entrepreneurial action and encourages risk-taking. Instead of punishing failures, this culture celebrates attempts to try something new. Google, 3M, and Facebook are organizations that seem to display this culture type. **Market culture** values being successful in the market. Therefore, the ultimate goal is more along the lines of market share and outperforming competition. Achievement and competition are key values in these cultures. Examples might include Apple, Salesforce.com, and Netflix. **Clan culture** values employee satisfaction and commitment, and therefore there is a great emphasis on fairness, employee empowerment, and putting employees first. Examples include Costco and SAS Institute. Finally, **hierarchy culture** emphasizes

Psychological climate: An individual person's perception of the behavioral patterns of an entity.

Adhocracy culture: Culture that puts innovation first.

Market culture: Culture that values being successful.

Clan culture: Culture that values employee satisfaction and commitment and therefore has a great emphasis on fairness, employee empowerment, and putting employees first.

Hierarchy culture: Culture that emphasizes efficiency and timeliness.

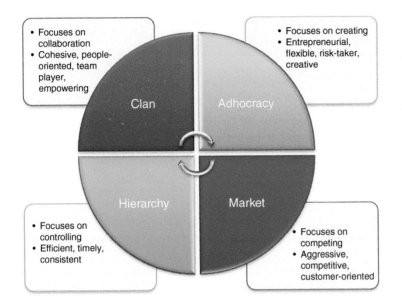

Figure 14.6
Culture dimensions based on Competing Values Framework (Quinn & Rohrbaugh, 1983).

efficiency and timeliness. These cultures will have greater emphasis on trying to make things predictable by instituting a lot of procedures and rules and then following them. Examples include Boeing and Walmart.

The Competing Values Framework proposes that these dimensions are independent of each other, and therefore an organization that displays values of one dimension will not display the values of other dimensions. However, empirical research does not support this. Instead, there is significant overlap across dimensions (Hartnell, Ou, & Kinicki, 2011). This is probably not surprising. For example, Google is known as an innovative company and therefore is a great example of an adhocracy, but it also is competitive and cares about outperforming its competition, and it also puts employees first, so it also displays market and clan culture characteristics as well.

It is also noteworthy to remember that an organization may have more than one culture. In fact, subcultures are a frequent occurrence within organizations, with different departments and teams having different cultures. For example, in a software company, the overall organizational culture may be highly innovative and entrepreneurial. The sales department may embrace these values, but may also be highly aggressive and competitive. Further, organizations may sometimes have **counter-cultures**. These are identifiable units within the organization that embrace values and assumptions that directly contradict the overall organization's values (Martin & Siehl, 1983). Even though they conflict with the broader organization's culture, the organization may tolerate these cultures because they are needed, powerful, or effective.

Countercultures: Identifiable units within the organization that embrace values and assumptions that directly contradict the overall organization's values.

Acquisition Creates Counterculture

Ben & Jerry's is a premium ice-cream maker that is known for its social activism as much as its unique flavors of treats. When this ice-cream maker with a social conscience was acquired by the British–Dutch giant multinational consumer goods company Unilever in 2001, critics assumed that this would be the end of their unique, creative, and environmentally sensitive ways. The predictions did not turn into reality, and Unilever managed to preserve the uniqueness of Ben & Jerry's, giving them room to operate and keep their culture intact, while at the same time making some unpopular changes to keep the company profitable. The result is that Ben & Jerry's culture survives as a counterculture within Unilever. This leads to interesting situations such as Unilever joining other companies suing the state of Vermont in the USA for its laws on mandatory labeling of Genetically Modified Organism (GMO) ingredients in food products while their company, Ben & Jerry's, was acting as a leading supporter and champion of the law. At the same time, observers attribute the increasing social responsibility of Unilever to the influence of Ben & Jerry's (Buss, 2014; Caligiuri, 2012), suggesting that countercultures may sometimes lead to changes in the broader culture within which they reside.

Why Does Culture Matter?

Culture Matters for Organizational Performance

It has been proposed that culture is a source of competitive advantage for organizations because strong and healthy cultures are valuable, rare, and difficult to imitate (Barney, 1986). Meta-analytic evidence supports this view (Hartnell et al., 2011). Specifically, market and adhocracy cultures tend to be highly innovative. Market cultures also have a higher quality of products and services, higher profits, and higher growth. In other words, the type of culture an organization has will have some bearing on the actual performance of the organization, even though correlations with objective figures such as profits are modest. Studies also have shown that hierarchical cultures tend to imitate their competitors, whereas adhocracies tend to try to be pioneers in their industries (Naranjo-Valencia, Jiménez-Jiménez, & Sanz-Valle, 2011). In other words, culture is a remote but still important influence over the ability of an organization to compete in the marketplace.

Culture Matters for Employee Attitudes and Behaviors

Are there cultures where employees are happier? The meta-analysis by Hartnell et al. (2011) showed that clan culture had the strongest correlation with job satisfaction and organizational commitment, suggesting that when the organization puts people first and emphasizes collaboration and teamwork, employees tend to be happier and more committed. This is probably not a surprise to you. How about the other culture dimensions, though? Do you think employees at Apple, Xerox, or Boeing are happy at work and are committed to their companies?

Research has shown that what matters seems to be the fit between the person's values and the organizational culture's values, or **person–organization fit**. The same organizational culture may be very attractive to some people whereas it falls short of meeting the needs of others. If you are someone who prefers receiving clear direction from managers and you have a preference for working alone, a company that emphasizes employee empowerment and teamwork such as Nike may not be a great fit. A study by O'Reilly, Chatman, and Caldwell (1991) showed the importance of fitting in with the culture for newcomers. In their first few days at work, new employees joining accounting firms provided rankings of their own values using a 50-item instrument called Organizational Culture Profile. Managers in each of the firms used the same instrument to provide rankings of their organization's values. Using these two pieces of information, researchers created a culture fit score for each newcomer in their first week at work. Employees who had higher fit early on actually had higher job satisfaction and organizational commitment scores a year later. Further, these employees were more likely to still be employed in the same company two years later, attesting to the value of fitting in with the company culture for job attitudes and retention of employees.

Person–organization fit: The fit between the person's values and the organizational culture's values.

Culture Signals What Matters

Culture serves as a signal with respect to what behavior is appropriate and which behaviors would be expected from organizational members. This may even shape how and based on what factors relationships are developed. In a study conducted in educational settings by one of the authors of this book (Erdogan, Liden, & Kraimer, 2006), the relationship between principals and teachers was shaped by culture such that in aggressive cultures, the relationship quality was a function of how rewards within the school were distributed, whereas in cultures that emphasized respect for people, the relationship quality was a function of whether the employee was treated with dignity and respect.

How Can We Measure a Company's Culture?

To understand what type of culture a company has, getting the viewpoint of insiders certainly helps. However, what an organization's members say about their culture may not necessarily reflect the reality. For example, a manager may honestly say that the company cares about its people, but employees at lower levels may feel that this is not so. In other words, organizational agents may report opinions that do not reflect the broader organization. Or, the answers they give may try to put a positive spin on the culture and reflect the reality they wish to live in, rather than the one that actually exists. Surveying organizational members using an established culture survey such as the Organizational Culture Inventory by Human Synergistics International (2012), the Denison Organizational Culture Survey by Denison Consulting (2014), or the Organizational Culture Assessment Instrument (based on the Competing

Cultural artifacts are challenging to interpret because they may have multiple meanings. Does the beach ball signify a culture with a relaxed, fun, friendly atmosphere? Or is this a workplace where there is little accountability and employees avoid doing any serious work when the manager is not around? What is the more relevant artifact here: the ball, or the dress code?

Values Framework) by OCAI online (2014) are some methods to capture employee opinions on the subject.

Organizational culture can also be detected through direct observation. It may help to know that culture resides at three levels, ordered from the most to least visible (Schein, 1990). The most visible elements are referred to as **artifacts**. These could be anything you can directly observe, such as a dress code, office design, building architecture, employee handbooks, rules and regulations, and even stories told about organizational history. For example, imagine that you are looking at an employee handbook that is 300 pages long. Without peeking inside, what can you tell about this organization? Probably that they are inflexible, consistent, and stable. These would be the **values** of the organization, which refer to standards of behavior or principles about what is important. Values in turn reflect fundamental **assumptions**, or "taken-for-granted" beliefs about human nature. In the case of the 300-page handbook, the assumptions might be: "employees need to be told down to the greatest detail how to act," and "without rules, you have chaos."

Artifacts: The most visible elements of the culture.

Values: Standards of behavior or principles about what is important.

Assumptions: "Taken-for-granted" beliefs about human nature

Figure 14.7 Levels of organizational culture, with assumptions least visible, and artifacts the most directly observable.

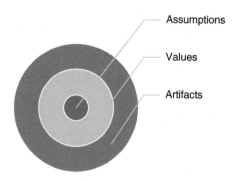

Assumptions

Values

Artifacts

Culture Creation

Founder's Values

Founders shape the culture of an organization beginning from its early days. Entrepreneurs tend to have assumptions about how the world works, what motivates people, and how business should be structured. The choices they make, the first employees they hire, the manner in which they make decisions, and what behaviors they reward and punish result in embedding their own values into the organization's culture (Schein, 1983). A founder's influence may remain visible even decades after an organization is first established, provided that the company is successful. This is because survival and success of the organization will reinforce the belief that the founder's values are the right ones to have.

History

Organizational culture is a part of an organization's history. Researchers have proposed that culture develops as the organization copes with its environment (Schein, 1983). From their early days, organizations compete in the marketplace, and their efforts either help them succeed or fail. Whatever elements of their culture are regarded as having helped them survive are the culture values they eventually retain and pass on to future generations.

Attraction	Selection	Attrition

Employees are attracted to organizations that share their values	Companies are more likely to select people who share their values	People who do not fit in tend to leave. Those who fit the company are more likely to stay

Figure 14.8
Attraction-selection-attrition (ASA) process.

Attraction-Selection-Attrition (ASA)

Organizations have a particular culture because culture protects and sustains itself. One way this happens is a process known as ASA (Schneider, Goldstein, & Smith, 1995), which is outlined in Figure 14.8.

"See website for interactive material"

Interactive: Attraction-selection-attrition in action.

For example, imagine a company like IDEO. This is a very innovative design company that encourages taking risks and being creative. So if you are someone who is very creative and a risk-taker, you are more likely to want to work there. This is the Attraction component of the ASA framework. Further, innovative people who don't hold back their ideas will find it easier to be hired into the company, because the interview process actually involves a brainstorming session to see you in action. This is the Selection component of the ASA framework. Finally, let's imagine that even though you are not very innovative, outspoken, or open-minded, you impressed the hiring managers enough to be hired. Your tenure there likely will be of short duration, because you will realize that you don't fit in. You will be different from your coworkers, will not behave in the organizationally expected ways, and will either voluntarily leave or be encouraged to leave. This is the attrition part of the ASA model.

As you can see, as a result of this process, culture ends up protecting and preserving itself, because people who don't fit in won't want to work there, will not be hired, or will leave even when hired, leaving behind like-minded individuals who buy into the culture's most important values.

Newcomer Onboarding

Organizations pass their cultures on to new employees. As we have seen in Chapter 11, once new employees are hired, they learn about how work is done, and the fundamental assumptions, values, and behavioral practices of the organization. In other words, starting from their early days, new employees not only are taught how to perform their jobs, but also start learning about their organization's culture. Through orientation programs, the assignment of a formal mentor or the development of a mentoring relationship with a senior colleague, or direct experiences within the organization, newcomers learn about the corporate culture. As a result, newcomer onboarding is a way in which the existing culture of the organization is perpetuated.

Leadership Style

A major influence over organizational culture is the leadership style of managers. Managers set the tone in the organization as a result of their day-to-day actions. The behaviors they encourage, model, and punish end up determining the nature of the culture the organization and a particular department have. In fact, research has shown that leaders influence organizational performance indirectly, through the culture they help develop in the organization (Ogbonna & Harris, 2000). In a study of over 1,000 managers in the Australian private sector, Sarros, Cooper, and Santora (2008) showed that when managers articulated a strong vision, provided individual support to employees, and communicated high performance, it helped shape the organizational culture and aided the development of a climate supporting innovativeness.

Reward Systems

The reward system in place helps shape the culture. If a company rewards short-term results over long-term performance, then employees will learn that this is the way to behave. In other words, employees will notice which employees are rewarded, recognized, and promoted for their behaviors. Are they the people with the highest integrity? Are they the people with the highest sales record? Are they the people who help coworkers? Are they the people who praise their boss the most? The organization's formal reward system will shape the culture by telling people what really matters, but the informal reward system – what managers actually do and what they encourage other people do – will send a clear message as well.

Organizational Change

In order to survive, organizations often find themselves in need of change. Change may take the form of a new structure, new technology, or new strategy. Even more

Influences over culture	Explanation	Example
Founder values	Founders infuse their own assumptions about how work should be organized, what motivates people, and the purpose of business, shaping the culture.	Zappos is an online shoe and clothing retailer with core values based around employee happiness and excellent customer service. The culture is traced back to founder and CEO Tony Hsieh's fundamental beliefs and early management practices to build and preserve this particular culture.
History	Whichever values provide a survival advantage to the organization are retained and passed on to future generations.	Costco views its clan culture a big part of its success. So, the company retains and preserves these people-oriented values that put employees first.
ASA framework	Culture protects itself through Attraction-Selection-Attrition.	If you are innovative and creative, you are more likely to be attracted to IDEO, more likely to be selected as an employee, and stay there for a long time, resulting in IDEO maintaining a culture of innovation.
New employee onboarding	The process of bringing new employees on board includes not only teaching employees how to perform their jobs, but also the company culture.	New Apple employees don't know their job until they are actually hired. On their first day, they are given an iMac, but no tech support. (It is expected that employees are smart enough to figure it out themselves.) The head of security comes to tell them that they will be fired if they leak information about a new product. Thus, the company passes on the culture of secrecy and fending for oneself (Yarow, 2012) from the first day on the job.
Leadership style	Managers and supervisors influence organizational culture through the behaviors they encourage, discourage, and role model.	Maurice Hilleman (1919–2005) was one of the most important microbiologists of our time, having developed more than 40 vaccines while heading the Virus and Cell Biology department at Merck pharmaceuticals. His leadership style of working 7 days a week, not tolerating poor performance in himself or others, and protecting his employees from layoffs and upper management interference created a culture of high performance orientation as well as fierce loyalty to the leader (Offit, 2007).
Reward systems	Rewards tell people what really matters in that organization, reinforcing a particular type of culture.	Regardless of how much a company talks about work–life balance, if the people who are rewarded, promoted, and recognized are those people who forgo vacations or weekends and work very long hours, then the culture will not be a clan culture.

Figure 14.9

Summary of factors affecting the development and preservation of organizational culture.

challenging is the need to change an organization's culture. Inability to change when needed is a surefire sign of doom for organizations, and having a history of success is not a guarantee that the same organizational structures and strategies will assure future success. Iconic brands that have been around for years such as Quiznos subs, RadioShack, and Sbarro have filed for bankruptcy protection, and many others are struggling. At the same time, others such as Apple, IBM, and Yahoo managed to find ways to adapt to challenges and changes in their environment and made dramatic turnarounds. How can organizations change? What are the ingredients of successful change? And can I/O psychologists play a role in facilitating change?

In the news media, organizational change is often portrayed as revolutionary (as opposed to incremental) and as directly attributable to the actions of specific individuals, most notably a new CEO, or a few heroic individuals. These accounts of change often discuss the bright idea instituted by the change agent, which would be just the right formula to provide adaptation to the environment and avert a crisis. In contrast, the I/O psychology literature, by systematically

Meineke Discount Muffler Shops made 90 percent of its revenue from changing automobile mufflers in its early days. In the 1990s, when car makers started making mufflers that would last a lifetime, this could have been the end of Meineke's business. Instead, the manufacturer rebranded itself as Meineke Car Care centers, providing full service auto repair and maintenance. This change required a major culture shift at Meineke – now they needed to build a long-term relationship with customers, requiring changing how the stores looked, how the sales people acted, and ultimately changing their entire organizational culture (Daley, 2014).

examining the phenomenon of change, has generated a large body of literature describing the ingredients of successful change. What this literature suggests is that the success of a change effort is ultimately the result of how change recipients – those employees who are affected by the change – receive it. (Bartunek, Rousseau, Rudolph, & DePalma, 2006). Changing an organization's culture, structure, or technology is not as simple as figuring out what the right culture, structure, or technology looks like. Instead, successful change requires a clear understanding of how and why employees resist change, and how to design the change effort in a manner that accounts for this resistance. Given the importance of the human element in successful planning and implementation of change, I/O psychology has a lot to contribute to organizational change management.

Organization Development (OD):
A field of study that applies behavioral science principles to enact change.

In fact, a subfield of study I/O psychologists can pursue is **Organization Development** (OD). OD refers to behavioral science-based theories, techniques, and systems that can help in the planning of organizational change by changing individuals' on-the-job-behavior (Porras & Robertson, 1992). The fact that understanding the human side of organizational change is a profession with its own accumulated body of knowledge should tell you the importance of understanding and managing employee resistance to change.

Figure 14.10
Summary of OD interventions.

Human process approaches	Technostructural approaches	Strategic change approaches
☐ Team building	☐ Job enrichment	☐ Changing structure
☐ Survey feedback	☐ Re-engineering	☐ Changing organizational culture
☐ Appreciative inquiry	☐ Total Quality Management	☐ Changing strategy

Human process approaches: OD interventions that have the goal of changing human processes and increasing employee satisfaction to increase individual and organizational functioning.

OD Interventions

OD is the field that applies behavioral science principles to enact change. In order to achieve this goal, the field of OD has identified a number of interventions, or methods of change. We will review three classes of OD interventions here (Cummings & Worley, 2014), as summarized in Figure 14.10.

Human process approaches are interventions with the objective of changing human processes and increasing employee satisfaction to increase individual and organizational functioning. These interventions assume that organizational effectiveness stems from individual fulfillment. Under this class of interventions, a notable one is **team building**. This intervention involves clarifying the goals and objectives of the group and the roles and responsibilities of team members, explaining and redesigning how work actually gets done, and improving the quality of relations among members in order to increase the level of cohesiveness (McLean, 2006). This may involve restructuring team member tasks so that they are better aligned, and an examination of member roles within the team to ensure that they complement each other. Team building may be accomplished through a careful examination of roles in the team and by exercises that can illustrate team members' strengths and weaknesses and where they may need further development. **Survey feedback** refers to the systematic gathering of information from employees to identify potential problem areas, stimulating conversation around these particular areas, and establishing motivation to change. A key part of many survey feedback efforts is compiling the survey results for each team within the organization and feeding them back to the team to help the team identify how to improve their processes. Finally, **appreciative inquiry** is a different and relatively new approach to OD. Unlike other OD interventions that focus on identifying problem areas, challenges, and an attempt to "fix" the organization, appreciative inquiry involves identifying the unique strengths and best aspects of the organization, followed by generating ideas about how to build on them (Head & Sorensen, 2006).

Technostructural approaches involve changes in the technology or structure of the organization to increase its effectiveness. This category may involve **job enrichment** or changing the content of jobs and redesigning them to increase their motivating potential (Chapter 9). Job enrichment involves increasing the variety of tasks performed and giving employees more control over the tasks being performed. **Re-engineering** involves re-envisioning the organization's structure to increase coordination and efficiency. Re-engineering involves a radical redesign of how work is done such as eliminating unnecessary functions and instead of incrementally changing and improving processes, recommends starting over. As a result, this is a type of change effort that would attract a high level of resistance. Finally, **Total Quality Management** involves an emphasis on continuous and incremental improvement in the quality of work done and processes employed to accomplish tasks. Unlike re-engineering, its incremental nature and continuous questioning of the status quo with an eye toward improvements is a better fit for employees' natural tendency to resist change.

Strategic change involves a large-scale change effort, targeting the strategy, organizational design, or organizational culture of an organization. These interventions have the purpose of achieving greater alignment between the organization's culture, structure, and strategy and its environment, with the aim of increasing organizational effectiveness. Strategic change is a very large-scale change effort, usually implemented with the initiative of the top levels of an organization. In particular, organizational culture change, because it involves the unwritten, core values of an organization and how it does business, is a major effort that would necessitate concerted action.

Team building: Intervention for clarifying goals and objectives of the group and roles and responsibilities of team members, explaining and redesigning how work actually gets done, and improving the quality of relations among members in order to increase the level of cohesiveness.

Survey feedback: Systematic gathering of information from employees to identify potential problem areas, stimulating conversation around these particular areas, and establishing motivation to change.

Appreciative inquiry: OD intervention that, instead of focusing on problem areas and attempting to "fix" the organization, identifies the unique strengths and best aspects of the organization and generates ideas about how to build on them.

Technostructural approaches: OD intervention that involves changes in the technology or structure of the organization to increase its effectiveness.

Job enrichment: Changing the content of jobs to increase their motivating potential.

Re-engineering: Re-envisioning the organization's structure to increase coordination and efficiency.

Campbell Soup is an iconic brand in the USA, but as the prepared-food industry is struggling with a shift in public opinion towards healthier eating, the company has had to find ways to survive. Denise Morrison, when she became CEO in 2011, realized that the company needed to stop playing it safe, and instead be bolder and take more risks. Such a change seems simple on paper, but it requires a shift in how people behave on a daily basis, taking ownership at work instead of waiting to be told what to do, going outside their comfort zone and speaking up, and setting more ambitious goals. To achieve this, what leaders do matters a great deal. Leaders need to set the direction, serve as role models, and applaud those demonstrating the correct behaviors (Morrison, 2014).

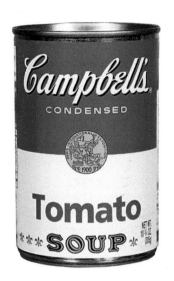

Total Quality Management: Technostructural approach that involves an emphasis on continuous and incremental improvement in the quality of work done and processes employed to accomplish tasks.

Strategic change: Large-scale change effort, targeting the strategy, organizational design, or organizational culture of an organization.

Why Do Change Recipients Resist Change?

Successful implementation of change often requires an understanding of how to overcome employees' resistance to it. As a result, it helps to understand why individuals resist change efforts. Such understanding can help in the planning and implementation phases of change. Resistance to change has three components, similar to the three components of job attitudes we covered in Chapter 11 (Piderit, 2000). The cognitive component refers to thoughts and beliefs about change (e.g., "the proposed change is poorly planned; it will make us less efficient"). The affective component includes feelings and emotions generated by change (e.g., "I hate the new method! I am so disappointed that this is what they came up with after all this work"). Finally, the behavioral component deals with behavioral reactions to change (e.g., Refusing to use the new method, talking negatively about it to colleagues). There are many reasons for why people resist change, which are detailed next.

Habits

We are all creatures of our habits. Habits simplify our lives, and allow us to function on "auto-pilot" during most of our day. When we take on a task that requires focus, our brain switches gears, and we move into an active thinking mode (Louis & Sutton, 1991). You probably are familiar with the feeling of driving for 20 minutes and all of a sudden realizing that you have reached your destination, but do not actually remember anything about the journey … Change forces active thinking, such as when you are driving carefully, and realizing that your regular route is under construction and now you need to find an alternate path. You now need to think about what you are doing, and figure out the best way to get where you are going. Often you feel frustrated, worried, and stressed when you have to start thinking about something that did not require thinking in the past. In addition, until new habits develop, you will continue to try to perform in the old way. If your permanent route is under construction for a long time, you will probably take the wrong turn for several days, until you remember to take the right route. Our habits

"What if we don't change at all ...
and something magical just happens?"

explain why even the simplest change such as a minor upgrade to your favorite computer program can be angst-inducing. When some frequently used buttons or icons move, this means extra effort and thinking exerted into a task that should have been automatic. This probably explains how simple system upgrades may result in vast number of users flocking to discussion boards to share their frustrations. In short, then, people resist change in their work environments because it means they will need to let go of some automatic thinking and put more cognitive effort into tasks that were once routine.

Personality

You may also realize that some people are more open to change than others. A comprehensive review of the literature shows that individuals who have a high internal locus of control, high levels of self-efficacy, and high positive affectivity are less resistant to change (Oreg, Vakola, & Armenakis, 2011). In other words, those who feel in control of their lives, feel confident in their skills, and have a positive outlook toward life in general are more welcoming of change, possibly because they believe that they can cope with it more effectively.

Trust in the Organization and Management

In addition to people who are more open to change in general, those who are more committed to the company, who trust management and the organization, and who feel that the organization supports them are less likely to resist change (Oreg et al., 2011). If there is a culture of trust, and a sense that the organization has employees' interests at heart, then any change effort is interpreted and reacted to within that context. In contrast, when trust in management is low, it is easy to feel that the change could result in loss of employment, or loss of one's status and work conditions within the organization, and such negative anticipatory feelings could result in resistance. The same review of the literature identifies some contradictory findings here as well: organizational commitment could result in higher or lower resistance to change. On the one hand, if people are committed to the organization, they tend to be more open to change that benefits the organization. On the other hand, depending on what exactly is changing, there may be more resistance because the factors causing their initially high levels of commitment may be at risk. For example, people who are highly committed to the organization because they admire and respect the management of the company may have low resistance to changes in technology, but very high resistance to change in management.

Personal Impact of Change

Change does not affect everyone to the same degree, and not all change results in losses as opposed to gains. When change results in higher job insecurity, loss of status and power, loss of income, or increase in work hours, we would expect to see greater resistance. In contrast, when change increases employee autonomy, increases the meaningfulness of one's work, allows employees greater balance between personal and professional lives, or increases the power and status of the individual, we would expect less resistance (Oreg et al., 2011). Status loss is a particularly important change that is damaging to high-status people (Marr & Thau, 2014). If the change means the person will do a less important job, will lose special expertise, or will become less important within a work group, there will be greater reasons to resist.

Features of Change Implementation

In addition to "what" the change involves, "how" it is implemented will have effects on change resistance. First, perceived fairness of the change will matter. If the change is perceived as unfair (such as redistributing territories in a sales department with more negative effects on some sales associates than others), there will be more negative reactions. Second, how the change was communicated, whether individuals were treated with dignity and respect, and whether they received a clear and constructive explanation will have effects on the level of resistance. At the same time, sometimes the amount of communication may increase resistance by making employees aware of more things to resist! Finally, employee involvement and participation in the change process seems to be related to lower levels of resistance. Employee involvement results in change that actually meets employee needs, makes employees aware of why particular tradeoffs were made, and increases felt control over one's own destiny, all having effects on the level of resistance to change (Oreg et al., 2011).

Change Models

Through the years a number of models have developed that describe how change takes place in organizations. In addition, these models can help prescribe the best way for change to take place in organizations.

Lewin's Three-Stage Model of Change Implementation

A well-known and simple model of change implementation that perhaps forms the basis of all other change models comes from Lewin (1951). According to

Unfreeze	Change	Refreeze
• Prepare employees for upcoming change • Motivate employees for change and show its value • Communicate the plan	• Implement the actual change • Provide support during the change	• Reinforce new behaviors • Prevent reverting back to former behaviors

Figure 14.11
Lewin's
three-stage model
of change.

this model, planned change may be viewed as a three-step process: unfreezing, change, and refreezing. The change process starts with **unfreezing**, which is the stage in which those involved need to understand the necessity for change, and be motivated to change. This stage is where assumptions are questioned and the people involved become aware of the consequences of not changing. In other words, individuals should be given a compelling reason for change, and feel a sense of urgency to change. This could take the form of discussing the financial situation relative to competitors, or the change in technology and how it is changing the business model. During unfreezing, it is also important to prepare individuals for the upcoming changes by answering any questions, providing the necessary training and involving those to be affected by the change in the actual design of the change process. Communication is key in the unfreezing phase. Employees should know what will happen, when, why, and how they will be affected. The second phase, **change**, is the actual implementation stage. The new technology, structure, or strategy is implemented in this stage, and success of the change will often rely on removing roadblocks, providing support, help, and mentoring during this stage. Finally, **refreezing** is the final stage, where the new ways of working or organizing are made permanent. This is important because in the absence of refreezing, individuals may revert back to old habits. In this stage, change is embraced as the new way to do things, with reinforcement given to those who display the correct behaviors, and interventions for those who have not yet made the change. This simple model is helpful because it points out that the organization needs to take certain steps both before and after the actual change itself, and without sufficient planning and post-change action, change may be short-lived. However, despite the fact that this model's strength may lie in its simplicity, by the same token it may not be detailed enough to represent the realities of change in organizations. For that reason, more detailed change models have also been developed.

Unfreezing: The stage of the change process in which those involved need to understand the necessity for change, and be motivated to change.

Change: The second stage of the change process that is the actual implementation stage.

Refreezing: The final stage of the change process, where the new ways of working or organizing are made permanent.

Workplace Application

Changing the Leadership to Change Siemens

Siemens was able to leverage a corporate bribing scandal that ultimately cost the company $1.6 billion in legal fines to its advantage. The German electronics conglomerate is an iconic brand with a history of innovation. Such companies often find themselves stuck in history, because employees and management are less likely to feel the need to change. The crisis ended

up being the impetus to hire Peter Löscher, the company's first outsider CEO since its founding in 1847. The new CEO was able to execute changes that would reduce the level of bureaucracy, make the company more nimble, and increase customer orientation. The change also necessitated forming a coalition and removing top managers blocking the execution of changes. The new vision of the company included focus on sustainability, infrastructure, and innovation. The new CEO took bold action to enact the vision and remove obstacles. For example, one barrier on the road to success was the lack of diversity. By making a statement to the newspaper the *Financial Times* that "Siemens was too white, too male, and too German," Löscher underlined the roadblocks and created public accountability to solve the problem, appointing women to the board for the first time (Löscher, 2012).

While the crisis was averted and the company was able to transform its culture into a more ethical, more nimble one, Löscher was ousted from the company in 2013 for failing to meet earnings targets. The new CEO is continuing to revamp the structure by removing layers and empowering lower-level managers to increase the competitiveness of the business (Boston, 2013).

Kotter's Eight-Step Model of Change

John Kotter, a professor of leadership at Harvard University, proposed an eight-step change model that has received widespread acceptance. This model (Kotter, 1995) suggests that following these steps would minimize resistance and prevent change effort from failing. You can apply this model to any type of major organizational change, including organizational culture and organizational structure change. The steps of this model are presented in Figure 14.12.

1. *Establish a sense of urgency.* Successful change effort usually comes from a sense that not changing will cause problems or failure for the organization. Often, people resist change unless there is a strong reason. Having a compelling reason to change (such as impending financial difficulties) would result in more immediate action. In fact, a crisis may be an excellent way to justify change and it could be a good opportunity to enact change that would be resisted at other times.

2. *Form a coalition.* Change agents who initiate the change are more likely to succeed if they can build a coalition consisting of those who are enthusiastic about change. There is power in numbers. Having a powerful coalition consisting of high-level individuals and opinion leaders will result in greater chances of success.

3. *Create a vision.* What is the ultimate goal of change? If a vision is communicated along with the change, employees are more likely to have buy-in, because structural, technological, or procedural changes will be perceived as more meaningful and necessary. This will also provide the inspiration or motivation for employees to adopt the new ways of doing things.

4. *Communicate the vision.* Having a vision is not enough unless it is communicated. Often, change effort is clearly tied to a vision, but the vision is not

Figure 14.12
Kotter's eight-step model of planned change.

1. Establish a sense of urgency	2. Form a coalition	3. Create a vision	4. Communicate the vision

5. Remove obstacles	6. Create small wins	7. Don't quit prematurely	8. Anchor changes in corporate culture

communicated in a compelling manner to all parties involved, resulting in a lack of excitement or energy.

5. *Remove obstacles.* In any change effort, there will be obstacles preventing success, and identifying and removing those will be important to the success of change effort. This could involve the removal of stubborn employees who sabotage the change efforts for political reasons, or ensuring that employees are prepared and ready for the new ways of performing.

6. *Create small wins.* Success breeds success when it comes to change. In contrast, suspicions that the new ways of performing will simply be a waste of time and therefore will be abandoned will result in some employees deciding to take a "wait and see" approach with respect to change. In other words, instead of starting to follow policy, these employees may decide to wait until it goes away. If the organization can communicate the immediate benefits of the change (such as implementing the change on a pilot basis in one department, ensuring that it is successful, and communicating the results with excitement to other departments) this would reduce employee motivation to resist. Therefore, testing the change on a small scale, seeing if it works, and publicizing success and using it as leverage in motivating change in a different part of the organization will be helpful.

7. *Don't quit prematurely.* Declaring victory too early in the process may result in waning excitement. Instead, once early success is achieved, reinforcing it by making even more changes along the same lines to implement the vision and reinvigorating the change by constantly bringing in additional change agents to continue to support the change effort is advisable.

8. *Anchor change in corporate culture.* Finally, change needs to be institutionalized in order to remain permanent. If change becomes identified as one person's personal initiative, it becomes dependent on that one person, and possibly rejected by others. Long-lasting change can instead be achieved by making it a key part of the organization's culture, or ensuring that it is thought of as "this is how we do things around here."

LEGAL ISSUES

The way an organization is structured may result in more legal liability for the organization, or may increase the chances of facing lawsuits involving employees. In highly centralized, hierarchical organizations where power is concentrated at high levels of the organization, the power dynamics among employees and managers will be uneven. As a result, the organization will need to take additional steps to protect the rights of employees and ensure that discrimination or harassment is not occurring; even if they do occur, organizations should take steps to ensure that employees feel comfortable bringing them to the attention of HR departments. As the formal power of employees declines, and as they are physically and psychologically removed from higher levels, employees may find it difficult to report these behaviors, which would contribute to an environment where employees do not feel psychologically safe, and increase the potential legal liability of the organization.

In addition to the existing structure of the organization, organizational restructuring is a time of critical change with legal implications. During restructuring, employees may be transferred, demoted, or laid off. If such changes are disproportionately affecting one legally protected group more than the other, the organization may face legal problems. For example, imagine that an organization is reducing the number of employees within a department by laying off poorly performing employees. However, it turns out that the "poor performers" are all women who are over 50 years old. While this information does not necessarily mean that the organization is intentionally taking an illegal action, if the decision is legally challenged, the organization would need to demonstrate that the decision was based on a sound and objective performance appraisal system (as discussed in Chapter 5).

When an organization finds itself in legal trouble due to discriminatory, unethical, or unsafe behavior, its culture is often implicated. Given that culture consists of an organization's norms and behavioral patterns, not having a culture that emphasizes safety, ethical behavior, and fair treatment of employees is a key reason for the occurrence of unacceptable behaviors. For example, when GM found itself in a crisis as a result of covering up defects in its cars, it was traced back to a culture of cover-up and secrecy that values face-saving and financial savings over the safety of customers (Scudder, 2014). In 2010, an explosion at a BP drill rig in the Gulf of Mexico resulted in the deaths of 11 workers and resulted in the largest ever accidental marine oil spill. The resulting investigation implicated the absence of a safety culture at BP. In other words, simply instituting rules or procedures will not be sufficient to tackle these problems, but changes in the informal culture are necessary as well. The way the company does business and the fundamental assumptions behind how managers and employees think will need to change to increase the health, safety, and well-being of workers as well as preventing such damaging and costly disasters, as we saw in Chapter 12.

Not having a safety culture is potentially damaging to companies, the environment, and society in general. Therefore, a culture emphasizing the right values can be an organization's biggest asset. This picture depicts the 2013 oil spill in the Koh Samet region of Thailand by the regional oil company PTT Global Chemical. The regional tourist industry was severely affected by the spill, leading to a 1-billion-baht lawsuit against the oil company (Bangkok Post, 2014).

GLOBAL IMPLICATIONS

National culture affects an organization's structure, culture, and the overall process of change. An organization's structure is often a reflection of the national culture. Culture will affect how high-level decision-makers interpret their environment (as an opportunity versus as a risk), and their subsequent actions in how they structure their organizations (Schneider & De Meyer, 1991). Further, the effectiveness of a particular structure will depend on the national culture. For example, research conducted in over 200 manufacturing plants in nine countries showed that the relationship between organic structures and continuous learning and improvement depended on whether the national culture endorsed participative management. Thus, in power distant cultures, such organic structures will be harder to implement, and may not yield the results they would in a more egalitarian culture (Huang, Rode, & Schroeder, 2011). When the structure fits the national culture, employees tend to be happier and less stressed as well. In a study conducted in Greece, research has shown that the hierarchical, formalized, and highly centralized structure was a better fit with the high uncertainty avoidance and high power distance values of Greek managers, resulting in lower stress and higher performance among managers working in these structures (Joiner, 2001).

National culture and organizational culture are related, but they are not the same thing (Schneider et al., 2013). In fact, only a small portion of the variation in organizational culture seems to come from national culture (Gerhart, 2009). Still, the fundamental assumptions of the national culture such as egalitarianism, being entrepreneurial and risk-taking, and collectivism are often reflected within the organizational cultures.

Finally, national culture has implications for the methods of change utilized, their ability to successfully enact change, and the level of resistance that may be expected. Some scholars contended that OD as a field is culturally bound. For example, OD as a field has assumptions such as belief in the inherently good nature of human beings, valuing diversity, being willing to take risks, and valuing collaboration (Jaeger, 1986). Such values are not necessarily universal, which may serve as a barrier against the OD intervention implementations. The type of intervention in question may also be easier or harder to transfer across borders. For example, the implementation of self-managing teams will depend on individual values as they relate to self-management as well as teamwork, the level of power distance, and cultural values of collectivism (Kirkman & Shapiro, 1997). In other words, change interventions will need to account for the cultural resistance to change in general, as well as the fit between the content of change with the national culture.

CURRENT ISSUES AND CONTROVERSIES

In the area of organizational design, organizations are experimenting with new structures such as virtual organizations, lattice organization, or the matrix. Some of these forms, particularly the lattice, remain controversial. Even though reading about these structures may lead one to believe that the lattice structure is replacing the traditional hierarchy (Benko, 2010), we do not have systematic evidence that such structures are better, that they result in better corporate performance and individual well-being, or that they are here to stay. In any case, the next decade is likely to see more experimenting with organizational design. Some organizations are trying having multiple bosses at the highest level of the organization, such as Whole Foods and Chipotle being run by co-CEOs. Organizations trying different methods of organizing and being risk-taking are likely to be advantageous in the near future, but we should not yet jump to the conclusion that a strong organizational hierarchy is obsolete.

The idea that organizations often hire those who will fit into their culture is probably noncontroversial. Do you see the downside of this approach, though? Hiring for fit perpetuates a culture, but it will not necessarily be helpful for changing the culture. Culture fit tends to be less straightforward to assess compared to assessing fit with the job, and may be affected by outward appearance and job-irrelevant characteristics. If a small, entrepreneurial company where the average age is 27 and 80 percent of employees are male refuses to hire a 50-year-old female job applicant coming from a hierarchical and formal organization, the company may claim that the decision is based on culture fit, but this may simply be a code word for "you are too different from us." In other words, the idea to hire based on culture fit, along with advantages such as higher retention (e.g., O'Reilly et al., 1991), may have downsides such as reduced innovativeness and diversity.

Finally, a recent study sheds some doubt on the traditional approaches to newcomer onboarding. Typically, new employees are welcomed into the organization through orientations communicating corporate culture and emphasizing the greatness and the unique qualities of the organization the newcomers have just joined. As we briefly mentioned in Chapter 8, in a field experiment conducted in Wipro, the IT consulting and outsourcing company based in India, Cable, Gino, and Staats (2013) showed that an alternative onboarding approach that encourages new call center employees to express themselves and bring their authentic selves to work resulted in greater retention and greater customer service quality six months after hiring. This novel finding suggests that instead of taking the approach of "breaking in" the newcomers and assimilating them into the culture, an organization may be better off showing excitement for what the newcomers are bringing, which may result in better, longer-term results for newcomers and organizations.

WHAT DOES THIS MEAN TO YOU?

This chapter discussed macro (organization-wide) influences that may have effects on an employee's happiness, well-being, and productivity. Thus, you should realize that the structure of the business you are joining will affect your work life. In a mechanistic structure, your job and career will be more predictable, but you will have less autonomy and fewer opportunities to change and impact the way things are done. In an organic structure, you will be able to display your personality and skills more, and there will be fewer controls over your behavior, so there will be greater opportunities for risk-taking, entrepreneurial behavior, and personal success and failure. Knowing who you are, what you want, and what type of a workplace structure is a better fit for you would be helpful. In fact, many prestigious and well-known companies, due to their sheer size, tend to be closer to the mechanistic end of the spectrum rather than organic. Understanding that while the size of the organization brings resources and external prestige, there will likely be costs in the degree of empowerment and upward influence you might have would be useful in plotting your future.

The culture of the company you are joining matters a great deal as well. The degree of alignment between your values and those of the company you join will have an important influence over your satisfaction, commitment, and desire to stay within the organization. There are many places you can exercise and develop your skills and pursue your passions, and the culture of the organization you join may have more to do with your future happiness, well-being, and effectiveness compared to the prestige of the brand or the size of the paycheck. In addition, keep in mind that you should consider not only the culture of the company as a whole but also the specific work group you will be joining.

Finally, change is a fact of life in organizations, and your effectiveness in your job will often rely on your ability to change things in your department and influence your colleagues to change their ways. To understand how to enact change successfully, an understanding of why people resist change and how to plan change to execute it more effectively would be helpful. Even when you are a manager and have a degree of formal power, change is more than simply announcing that there is now a new rule. Instead, anticipating potential resistance and planning for it will help you be more successful in this endeavor.

Conclusion

Employee behavior in the workplace is coordinated through organizational structure and culture. How the work is organized, the reporting relationships that exist, the degree to which the decision-making power is designated to reside in upper management, and the size of the span of control are among the important influences over how work gets done and employee reactions to their jobs. The unwritten norms and behavioral patterns also exert a powerful influence over employee behavior and attitudes at work. In addition, organizations are not static and oftentimes change their structures, cultures, technology, or the way things are done. The planning and execution of change will rely on understanding and proactively managing employee reactions to the change effort. I/O psychology as a field has amassed a large body of knowledge that could be useful to organizational change agents.

YOUR TURN...

WHAT DO YOU THiNK?

1. Do you have any experience with a failed change effort? In an organizational or college setting, can you recall an instance where the organization changed something, which resulted in user resistance? What was the reason for the resistance? Did people resist the change for good reasons or not? What could the organization have done differently to get different results?

2. Under what conditions do you think newcomers can change an organization's culture or the way things are done?

3. Imagine that you are a high-level employee in a company where there is a "culture of incivility." People are rude to each other, there are instances of bullying, and the result is high levels of stress and turnover among employees. How could you try to change this culture? Develop a step-by-step plan.

4. Out of the cultures discussed in this chapter, which ones do you feel are a good match for you? Why?

5. When you go on a job interview, what are the things you might observe or investigate that would reveal to you the type of organizational culture they would have?

Additional Reading

Cameron, K. S., & Quinn, R. E. (2011). *Diagnosing and changing organizational culture: Based on the competing values framework.* San Francisco, CA: Jossey-Bass.

Cummings, T. G., & Worley, C. G. (2013). *Organization development and change.* Stamford, CT: Cengage Learning.

Denison, D. R. (1990). *Corporate culture and organizational effectiveness.* Wiley series on organizational assessment and change. Oxford, England: John Wiley & Sons.

Kotter, J. P. (2012). *Leading change.* Cambridge, MA: Harvard University Press.

McKay, P. F., Avery, D. R., Tonidandel, S., Morris, M. A., Hernandez, M., & Hebl, M. R. (2007). Racial differences in employee retention: Are diversity climate perceptions the key? *Personnel Psychology, 60,* 35–62.

Schein, E. H (2010). *Organizational culture and leadership.* San Francisco, CA: Jossey-Bass.

CASE STUDY: The Story of a Corporate Turnaround at Nissan

One of the most dramatic organizational change stories of the past two decades is the turnaround of Japanese carmaker Nissan. What makes the story so intriguing is the ability of Nissan to enact change in an industry plagued with problems, in a cultural context that typically resists change, by a then-new CEO who did not even speak Japanese.

At the end of the 1990s Nissan was a troubled carmaker. It had not recorded a profit for the past eight years, and its market share had been declining. When Renault acquired over 40 percent of Nissan shares in 1999, Carlos Ghosn was charged with turning around Nissan, subsequently assuming the CEO position. The company had many serious problems at the time: Its costs were very high because it had long-lasting relationships with suppliers. Because of the Japanese government's tendency to bail out companies, no one in the company really worried about the future of the business: There was little individual accountability, or a sense of what each person contributed to the business. They did not even know which models were making a profit and which were not, and a later analysis showed only 4 out of 43 models were profitable. As Mr. Ghosn saw it, the problem was not a training or a technology problem, but one of culture. The effects of Japanese culture were evident: There was an emphasis on lifetime employment and rewards based on seniority. The business had too much capacity, but layoffs were culturally taboo. There was a sense of risk aversion and evading personal accountability permeating the organization. Face-saving was important, and no one wanted to criticize the business. Despite all the problems, there was a sense of complacency: "The house was on fire, and they were just sitting around," Ghosn said in an interview in 2000.

Even though his work was cut out for him, Mr. Ghosn was an inspired choice and was up to the challenge. Being an outsider and a foreigner would allow him to tackle some of the decisions an insider may not have dared to take on. At the same time, he was someone who could leverage the strengths of the Nissan and Japanese cultures. Born in Brazil, and having lived in Lebanon, been educated in France, and been immersed in the automobile industry all his professional life, the new CEO spoke four languages (but not Japanese) and was a humble, inspiring, and respectful person. In a few years, he tackled the changes that needed to be made within the company, including shutting down several plants, instituting individual performance targets, tying pay and bonuses to company performance, and ensuring that design was not placed at an inferior position compared to engineering.

Perhaps what made him a success in enacting these difficult decisions and changes is not what he did, but how. Unlike many corporate takeovers where the acquirer sends out a team to take over the management and execute the new business plan, at Nissan change came from within, with Ghosn as the facilitator. He instituted cross-functional and cross-company teams as the primary agents of change. These teams brought together employees and managers from diverse areas who had no experience interacting and working with each other. These committees met frequently, reported to upper management, and had broad participation. As a result, there was a wide base of employees who were fully engaged in the planning process for the change. He also ensured that he communicated fully with these teams, sharing all information, not making any information off limits.

By ensuring that employees had voice in the change effort, Ghosn was able to mobilize the collectivism, performance orientation, and sense of pride in the company. Throughout the process, he showed that he was not an outsider trying to squeeze profits out of Nissan for Renault, but a believer in Nissan trying to restore this Japanese icon to its former glory. He was visible in the company, talking to factory workers every day, participating in committee meetings, listening more than talking, encouraging dissent and risk-taking.

Carlos Ghosn currently serves as the CEO of both Nissan and Renault, as well as serving as the CEO of Renault-Nissan Alliance. His success as a transnational leader won him awards and helped brand him a national hero in Japan (with a superhero comic book series describing his life), and the Nissan turnaround is likely to be studied and analyzed as a model of change for future generations.

Questions

1. What did Nissan corporate culture look like prior to 2000? How did it look afterwards? Use the concepts from the chapter in your description.

2. What had created the old culture in place at Nissan?

3. How does Nissan's transformation fit with the models of change covered in this chapter?

4. What challenges and threats do you see for Nissan's corporate culture for the future?

Sources: This case is partially based on information included in Fulford, 2000; Ghosn, 2002; Gill, 2012; Risaburo, 2014; Taylor, 2005.

References

Ambrose, M. L., Schminke, M., & Mayer, D. M. (2013). Trickle-down effects of supervisor perceptions of interactional justice: A moderated mediation approach. *Journal of Applied Psychology, 98*, 678–689.

Anand, N., & Daft, R. L. (2007). What is the right organization design? In G. Robinson Hickman (Ed.), *Leading organizations: Perspectives for a new era* (pp. 307–322). Thousand Oaks, CA: Sage.

Bangkok Post. (2014, July 29). PTTGC sued for B1bn over oil spill. Retrieved February 12, 2015, from http://www.bangkokpost.com/news/local/422994/koh-samet-businesses-seek-redress-for-rayong-oil-spill.

Barney, J. B. (1986). Organizational culture: Can it be a source of sustained competitive advantage? *Academy of Management Review, 11*, 656–665.

Bartunek, J. M., Rousseau, D. M., Rudolph, J. W., & DePalma, J. A. (2006). On the receiving end: Sensemaking, emotion, and assessments of an organizational change initiated by others. *Journal of Applied Behavioral Science, 42*, 182–206.

Benko, C. (2010, November). How the corporate ladder became the corporate lattice. *Harvard Business Review*. Retrieved September 21, 2014, from http://blogs.hbr.org/2010/11/how-the-corporate-ladder-becam/.

Boston, W. (2013). Siemens revamps corporate structure. *Wall Street Journal*, October 17. Retrieved September 19, 2014, from http://online.wsj.com/news/articles/SB10001424052702304410204579141330057795494.

Bourgeois, L. J., McAllister, D. W., & Mitchell, T. R. (1978). The effects of different organizational environments upon decisions about organizational structure. *Academy of Management Journal, 21*, 508–514.

Buss, D. (2014). In Vermont, Unilever fights – and Ben & Jerry's funds – anti GMO activism. Brandchannel.com, June 16. Retrieved September 16, 2014, from http://www.brandchannel.com/home/post/140616-Unilever-Ben-Jerrys-GMO.aspx.

Cable, D. M., Gino, F., & Staats, B. R. (2013). Breaking them in or eliciting their best? Reframing socialization around newcomers' authentic self-expression. *Administrative Science Quarterly, 58*, 1–36.

Caligiuri, P. (2012). When Unilever bought Ben & Jerry's: A story of CEO adaptability. *Fast Company*, August 12. Retrieved September 16, 2014, from http://www.fastcompany.com/3000398/when-unilever-bought-ben-jerrys-story-ceo-adaptability.

Chatman, J. A., & Cha, S. E. (2003). Leading by leveraging culture. *California Management Review, 45,* 20–34.

Cummings, T., & Worley, C. (2014). *Organization development and change.* Stamford, CT: Cengage Learning.

Daley, J. (2014, September). Turn, turn, turn. *Entrepreneur,* 97–101.

Day, G. S. (2006). Aligning the organization with the market. *MIT Sloan Management Review, 48,* 41–49.

Denison Consulting. (2014). *Culture and leadership diagnostics: The Denison organizational culture survey.* Retrieved October 28, 2014, from http://www.denison-consulting.com/diagnostics/organizational-culture.

Denison, D. R. (1996). What is the difference between organizational culture and organizational climate? A native's point of view on a decade of paradigm war. *Academy of Management Review, 21,* 619–654.

Deutschman, A. (2004, December). The fabric of creativity. *Fast Company,* 54–60.

Dunbar, R. I. (1993). Coevolution of neocortical size, group size and language in humans. *Behavioral and Brain Sciences, 16,* 681–694.

Duncan, R. (1979). What is the right organization structure? Decision tree analysis provides the answer. *Organizational Dynamics, 7,* 59–80.

Dust, S. B., Resick, C. J., & Mawritz, M. B. (2014). Transformational leadership, psychological empowerment, and the moderating role of mechanistic–organic contexts. *Journal of Organizational Behavior, 35,* 413–433.

Erdogan, B., Liden, R. C., & Kraimer, M. L. (2006). Justice and leader–member exchange: The moderating role of organizational culture. *Academy of Management Journal, 49,* 395–406.

Fayol, H. (1930). *General and industrial management.* London: Pitman and Sons.

Fredrickson, J. W. (1986). The strategic decision process and organizational structure. *Academy of Management Review, 11,* 280–297.

Fulford, B. (2000). Renaissance at Nissan. *Forbes,* October 2, 80–84.

Gerhart, B. (2009). Does national culture constrain organization culture and human resource strategy? The role of individual level mechanisms and implications for employee selection. *Research in Personnel and Human Resources Management, 28,* 1–48.

Ghosn, C. (2002, January). Saving the business without losing the company. *Harvard Business Review, 80,* 37–45.

Gill, C. (2012). The role of leadership in successful international mergers and acquisitions: Why Renault-Nissan succeeded and DaimlerChrysler-Mitsubishi failed. *Human Resource Management, 51,* 433–456.

Glick, W. H. (1985). Conceptualizing and measuring organizational and psychological climate: Pitfalls in multilevel research. *Academy of Management Review, 10,* 601–616.

Greenwood, R., & Miller, D. (2010). Tackling design anew: Getting back to the heart of organizational theory. *Academy of Management Perspectives, 24,* 78–88.

Gümüşlüoğlu, L., Karakitapoğlu-Aygün, Z., & Hirst, G. (2013). Transformational leadership and R&D workers' multiple commitments: Do justice and span of control matter? *Journal of Business Research, 66,* 2269–2278.

Hartnell, C. A., Ou, A. Y., & Kinicki, A. (2011). Organizational culture and organizational effectiveness: A meta-analytic investigation of the competing values framework's theoretical suppositions. *Journal of Applied Psychology, 96,* 677–694.

Head, T. C., & Sorensen, P. F. (2006). *Global organization development: Managing unprecedented change.* Greenwich, CT: Information Age Publishing.

Hechanova-Alampay, R., & Beehr, T. A. (2001). Empowerment, span of control, and safety performance in work teams after workforce reduction. *Journal of Occupational Health Psychology, 6,* 275–282.

Hempel, P. S., Zhang, Z. X., & Han, Y. (2012). Team empowerment and the organizational context decentralization and the contrasting effects of formalization. *Journal of Management, 38,* 475–501.

Heneman, R. L., & Greenberger, D. B. (2002). *Human resource management in virtual organizations.* Greenwich, CT: Information Age Publishing.

Huang, X., Rode, J. C., & Schroeder, R. G. (2011). Organizational structure and continuous improvement and learning: Moderating effects of cultural endorsement of participative leadership. *Journal of International Business Studies, 42,* 1103–1120.

Human Synergistics International. (2012). *Organizational culture inventory.* Retrieved February 11, 2015, from http://www.humansynergistics.com/Products/OrganizationDevelopment/OrganizationalCultureInventory.

Jaeger, A. M. (1986). Organization development and national culture: Where's the fit? *Academy of Management Review, 11,* 178–190.

Joiner, T. A. (2001). The influence of national culture and organizational culture alignment on job stress and performance: Evidence from Greece. *Journal of Managerial Psychology, 16,* 229–242.

Kirkman, B. L., & Shapiro, D. L. (1997). The impact of cultural values on employee resistance to teams: Toward a model of globalized self-managing work team effectiveness. *Academy of Management Review, 22,* 730–757.

Kotter, J. P. (1995, March–April). Leading change: Why transformation efforts fail. *Harvard Business Review, 73,* 59–67.

Kruger, D. (2004). You want data with that? *Forbes,* March 29, 58–59.

Lee, J. Y., Kozlenkova, I. V., & Palmatier, R. W. (2014). Structural marketing: Using organizational structure to achieve marketing objectives. *Journal of the Academy of Marketing Science, 43,* 1–27.

Lewin, K. (1951). Intention, will and need. In D. Rapaport (Ed.), *Organization and pathology of thought* (pp. 95–153). New York: Columbia University Press.

Likert, R. (1967). *The human organization: Its management and values.* New York: McGraw Hill.

Louis, M. R., & Sutton, R. I. (1991). Switching cognitive gears: From habits of mind to active thinking. *Human Relations, 44,* 55–76.

Löscher, P. (2012, November). The CEO of Siemens on using a scandal to drive change. *Harvard Business Review, 90,* 39–42.

Makuch, E. (2013). Why Minecraft creator turned down job at Valve. Gamespot.com, December 10. Retrieved February 11, 2015, from http://www.gamespot.com/articles/why-minecraft-creator-turned-down-job-at-valve/1100-6416641/.

Manz, C. C., Shipper, F., & Stewart, G. L. (2009). Everyone a team leader: Shared influence at WL Gore & Associates. *Organizational Dynamics, 38,* 239–244.

Marr, J., & Thau, S. (2014). Falling from great (and not so great) heights: How initial status position influences performance after status loss. *Academy of Management Journal, 57*, 223–248.

Martin, J., & Siehl, C. (1983). Organizational culture and counterculture: An uneasy symbiosis. *Organizational Dynamics, 12*, 52–64.

McLean, G. N. (2006). National human resource development: A focused study in transitioning societies in the developing world. *Advances in Developing Human Resources, 8*, 3–11.

Morrison, D. M. (2014, September). The main ingredient of change. *Harvard Business Review.* Retrieved 27 May, 2015, from https://hbr.org/2014/09/the-main-ingredient-of-change.

Naranjo-Valencia, J. C., Jiménez-Jiménez, D., & Sanz-Valle, R. (2011). Innovation or imitation? The role of organizational culture. *Management Decision, 49*, 55–72.

OCAI online. (2014). *About the Organizational Culture Assessment Instrument (OCAI).* Retrieved February 11, 2015, from http://www.ocai-online.com/about-the-Organizational-Culture-Assessment-Instrument-OCAI.

O'Reilly, C. A., Chatman, J., & Caldwell, D. F. (1991). People and organizational culture: A profile comparison approach to assessing person-organization fit. *Academy of Management Journal, 34*, 487–516.

Offit, P. A. (2007). *Vaccinated: One man's quest to defeat the world's deadliest diseases.* New York: HarperCollins.

Ogbonna, E., & Harris, L. C. (2000). Leadership style, organizational culture and performance: Empirical evidence from UK companies. *International Journal of Human Resource Management, 11*, 766–788.

Oreg, S., Vakola, M., & Armenakis, A. (2011). Change recipients' reactions to organizational change: A 60-year review of quantitative studies. *Journal of Applied Behavioral Science, 47*, 461–524.

Ovide, S., & Rusli, E. M. (2014). Microsoft gets "Minecraft" – not founders. *Wall Street Journal*, September 15.

Piderit, S. K. (2000). Rethinking resistance and recognizing ambivalence: A multi-dimensional view of attitudes toward an organizational change. *Academy of Management Review, 25*, 783–794.

Porras, J. I., & Robertson, P. J. (1992). Organizational development: Theory, practice, and research. In M. D. Dunnette & L. M. Hough (Eds.), *Handbook of industrial and organizational psychology, Vol. 3* (pp. 719–822). Palo Alto, CA: Consulting Psychologists Press.

Quinn, R. E., & Rohrbaugh, J. (1983). A spatial model of effectiveness criteria: Towards a competing values approach to organizational analysis. *Management Science, 29*, 363–377.

Risaburo, N. (2014). From globalization to a new corporate culture. *OECD Observer*, No. 298, Q1.

Sarros, J. C., Cooper, B. K., & Santora, J. C. (2008). Building a climate for innovation through transformational leadership and organizational culture. *Journal of Leadership & Organizational Studies, 15*, 145–158.

Schein, E. H. (1983). The role of the founder in creating organizational culture. *Organizational Dynamics, 12*, 13–28.

Schein, E. H. (1990). Organizational culture. *American Psychologist, 45*, 109–119.

Schein, E. H. (1996). Culture: The missing concept in organization studies. *Administrative Science Quarterly, 41*, 229–240.

Schminke, M., Ambrose, M. L., & Cropanzano, R. S. (2000). The effect of organizational structure on perceptions of procedural fairness. *Journal of Applied Psychology, 85*, 294–304.

Schneider, B., Ehrhart, M. G., & Macey, W. H. (2013). Organizational climate and culture. *Annual Review of Psychology, 64*, 361–388.

Schneider, B., Goldstein, H. W., & Smith, D. B. (1995). The ASA framework: An update. *Personnel Psychology, 48*, 747–773.

Schneider, S. C., & De Meyer, A. (1991). Interpreting and responding to strategic issues: The impact of national culture. *Strategic Management Journal, 12*, 307–320.

Scudder, V. (2014). How a culture of secrecy plagued GM. *Public Relations Strategist, 20*(2), 18–20.

Suddath, C. (2012). Why there are no bosses at Valve. *Bloomberg Businessweek*, April 27.

Sy, T., & Côté, S. (2004). Emotional intelligence: A key ability to succeed in the matrix organization. *Journal of Management Development, 23*, 437–455.

Taylor, A. (2005). Advice from a fellow outsider. *Fortune*, April 4, 104.

Taylor, F. W. (1914). *The principles of scientific management.* New York: Harper & Brothers Publishers.

Topp, K., & Desjardins, J. H. (2011). Span of control: Designing for organizational effectiveness. In J. A. Wolf, H. Hanson, & M. J. Moir (Eds.), *Organization development in health care* (pp. 211–230). Greenwich, CT: Information Age Publishing.

Weber, M. (1947). *The theory of social and economic organization.* New York: The Free Press.

Yarow, J. (2012). What it's like on day one as an Apple employee. *Business Insider*, January 26. Retrieved February 11, 2015, from http://www.businessinsider.com/what-its-like-on-day-one-as-an-apple-employee-2012-1.

IMAGES AND CREDIT LINES

Chapter 1

Top: mertcan/Shutterstock.com. 3
Middle left: Vitchanan
Photography/Shutterstock.com, 3
Middle right: michaeljung/Shutterstock.com, 3
Bottom left: wavebreakmedia/Shutterstock.com, 3
Bottom right: Luiz Rocha/Shutterstock.com, 3

Figure 1.1:
Pressmaster/Shutterstock.com, 5

Figure 1.3:
gui jun peng/Shutterstock.com, 13
Dabarti CGI/Shutterstock.com, 13
Brandon Bourdages/Shutterstock.com, 13
Everett Historical/Shutterstock.com, 13
Dragon Images/Shutterstock.com, 13

Dusit/Shutterstock.com, 15
Hugo Munsterberg: Wikicommons, 17
James McKeen Cattell: Wikicommons, 18
Frederick Taylor: Wikicommons, 19
Lillian Gilbreth: Wikicommons/Rutgers
University Archive, 20
Maksim Kabakou/Shutterstock.com, 22
Robyn Mackenzie/Shutterstock.com, 23
kbuconi/Shutterstock.com, 23
Maksim Shmeljov/Shutterstock.com, 24
marekuliasz/Shutterstock.com, 24

Figure 1.6:
Marcin Balcerzak/Shutterstock.com, 25
Konstantin Chagin/Shutterstock.com, 25
Rawpixel/Shutterstock.com, 25
Chris Warham/Shutterstock.com, 25
Zerbor/Shutterstock.com, 25
ChristianChan/Shutterstock.com, 25
Snezana Ignjatovic/Shutterstock.com, 25
Andrew Zarivny/Shutterstock.com, 26
Lakeview Images/Shutterstock.com, 27

Nikiforov Volodymyr/Shutterstock.com, 28
Ivelin Radkov/Shutterstock.com, 29

Chapter 2

Stuart Miles/Shutterstock.com, 34
Ivelin Radkov/Shutterstock.com, 38
Feng Yu/Shutterstock.com, 45
zimmytws/Shutterstock.com, 45

Figure 2.4:
marekuliasz/Shutterstock.com, 48
igor.stevanovic/Shutterstock.com, 48
Sarawut Aiemsinsuk/Shutterstock.com, 48
asharkyu/Shutterstock.com, 48

Sinseeho/Shutterstock.com, 53
zimmytws/Shutterstock.com, 63
Kbuconi/Shutterstock.com, 64

Marekuliasz/Shutterstock.com, 65
Nikiforov Volodymyr/Shutterstock.com, 66
Ivelin Radkov/Shutterstock.com, 67
Monkey Business Images/Shutterstock.com, 69

Chapter 3

kpatyhka/Shutterstock.com, 75
Top left: Monkey Business
Images/Shutterstock.com, 77
Top right: Andresr/Shutterstock.com, 77
Bottom left: EDHAR/Shutterstock.com, 77
Bottom right: Monika
Wisniewska/Shutterstock.com, 77

Figure 3.4:
auremar/Shutterstock.com, 85

Chapter 4

Chapter 5

Chapter 6

Chapter 7

Chapter 8

Chapter 9

Chapter 10

Chapter 11

Chapter 12

Chapter 13

Chapter 14

NAME INDEX

ORGANIZATIONS INDEX

Page numbers in *italics* are figures; with 't' are tables.

SUBJECT INDEX

Page numbers in *italics* are figures; with "t" are tables.